Handbook of International Trade

Blackwell Handbooks in Economics

Handbook of International Macroeconomics
Edited by Frederick van der Ploeg

Handbook of Environmental Economics
Edited by Daniel W. Bromley

Handbook of Applied Econometrics: Vol. I: Macroeconomics
Edited by M. Hashem Pesaran and Michael R. Wickens

Handbook of Applied Econometrics: Vol. II: Microeconomics
Edited by M. Hashem Pesaran and Peter Schmidt

Handbook of International Trade
Edited by E. Kwan Choi and James Harrigan

Handbook of
International Trade

Edited by

E. Kwan Choi and
James Harrigan

Blackwell
Publishing

© 2003 by Blackwell Publishing Ltd
except for editorial material and organization © 2003 by E. Kwan Choi and
James Harrigan

350 Main Street, Malden, MA 02148-5018, USA
9600 Garsington Road, Oxford, OX4 2DQ, UK
550 Swanston Street, Carlton, Victoria 3053, Australia

First published 2003 by Blackwell Publishing Ltd

3   2007

Library of Congress Cataloging-in-Publication Data

Handbook of international trade / edited by E. Kwan Choi and
James Harrigan.
p.   cm. – (Blackwell handbooks in economics)
Includes bibliographical references and index.
ISBN 978-0-631-21161-7 (hbk : alk. paper)
1. International trade.   I. Choi, Eun Kwan, 1946–
II. Harrigan, James.   III. Series.
HF1379.H364   2003
382–dc21   2002155271

A catalogue record for this title is available from the British Library.

Set in 10/12 Times
by SNP Best-set Typesetter Ltd., Hong Kong
Printed and bound in the United Kingdom
by TJ International Ltd, Padstow, Cornwall

For further information on
Blackwell Publishing, visit our website:
http://www.blackwellpublishing.com

Contents

Part II: Trade Policy

Part III: Investment

Part IV: New Trade Theory

Figures

Tables

Contributors

Bruce A. Blonigen is the Knight Professor of Social Science in the Economics Department at the University of Oregon. He is also an Associate Editor for the *Journal of International Economics* and a Research Associate with the National Bureau of Economic Research.

E. Kwan Choi has been a Professor of Economics at Iowa State University since 1985. He is currently the editor of the *Review of International Economics* and *Review of Development Economics*. He has published articles in *Quarterly Journal of Economics* and *Journal of Political Economy*, and edited *Economic Growth and International Trade* and *Globalization and the Labor Markets* (Blackwell Publishing).

Jai-Young Choi is Professor of Economics at Lamar University (Beaumont, Texas). His primary research interests are in the analyses of international economic problems and policies. His articles have appeared in such journals as *Economica*, *Oxford Economic Papers*, *Canadian Journal of Economics*, *Southern Economic Journal*, *International Economic Journal*, and *Journal of Economics*.

Donald R. Davis is Professor of Economics at Columbia University and a Research Associate of the National Bureau of Economic Research. Previously he was an Assistant and Associate Professor of Economics at Harvard University. His research interests include the theory and empirics of international trade, economic geography, and the impact of trade on inequality in the global economy.

Robert C. Feenstra is Professor of Economics at the University of California, Davis. He is a former editor of the *Journal of International Economics*, and currently an associate editor of that journal, along with the *American Economic Review* and the *Review of Economics and Statistics*. Feenstra also heads the International Trade and Investment research program at the National Bureau of Economic Research. Most recently, Feenstra is author of the graduate textbook *Advanced International Trade: Theory and Evidence* (forthcoming).

Kishore Gawande is Associate Professor of Economics at the University of New Mexico. His research interests include empirical political economy, empirical trade policy, and trade and environment. He has published numerous articles in such journals as *Review of International Economics*, *Southern Economic Review*, and *Canadian Journal of Economics*.

Gordon H. Hanson is Professor of Economics in the Graduate School of International Relations and Pacific Studies at the University of California, San Diego. He is currently a Research Associate in the National Bureau of Economic Research and on the Board of Editors for the *American Economic Review* and the *Journal of International Economics*.

James Harrigan is a Senior Economist in the International Research Department of the Federal Reserve Bank of New York. He has also taught at the University of Pittsburgh and Columbia University, and is a member of the National Bureau of Economic Research. He is a former co-editor of the *Journal of International Economics*.

Ronald W. Jones is Professor and Department Chair of Economics at the University of Rochester. He has spent most of his career doing international trade theory at the university. He has thoroughly investigated multiple aspects of simple competitive general equilibrium models of trade, including the specific-factors model.

Pravin Krishna is Professor of Economics at Brown University. A recent Visiting Professor of Economics at Princeton University, he is also a Faculty Research Fellow with the National Bureau of Economic Research. He is a co-author of *Trade Blocs: Alternate Analyses of Preferential Trade Arrangements* (with Jagdish Bhagwati and Arvind Panagariya, 1999).

Robert E. Lipsey is a Research Associate and Director of the New York Office of the National Bureau of Economic Research and Professor Emeritus of Economics at Queens College and the Graduate Center of the City University of New York. At various times in the past he was Director of International and Financial Studies and Vice President of the NBER, and a Lecturer in Economics at Columbia University.

James R. Markusen is Professor of Economics at the University of Colorado, Boulder, specializing in the theory of international trade, and direct foreign investment. He is associate editor of the *Journal of International Economics* and is widely published in the top economic journals.

Keith E. Maskus is Professor of Economics at the University of Colorado, Boulder, and is also a Research Fellow at the Institute for International Economics. In 2001–2002 he was a Lead Economist in the Development Research Group at the World Bank. He was associate editor of *Review of International Economics* and is now the editor of *The World Economy: the Americas*.

Henry G. Overman is a Lecturer in Economic Geography at the London School of Economics. He is also affiliated with the CEPR and the CEP's globalization programme. His research focuses on applied location theory and policy. He has published work on Economic Geography in a number of journals including *Economic Policy*, *Journal of Urban Economics* and *Regional Science and Urban Economics*.

Thomas J. Prusa is Professor of Economics at Rutgers-The State University of New Jersey and is a Research Associate of the National Bureau of Economic Research. He has written and published extensively on the economics of dumping and antidumping policy. He is on the editorial boards of *Review of International Economics* and *Journal of International Economics*.

Stephen Redding is a Lecturer in the Economics Department of the London School of Economics, a Group Leader in the Globalization Programme of the Centre for Economic Performance, and a Research Affiliate in the International Trade Programme of the Centre for Economic Policy Research. He was recently awarded a Philip Leverhulme Prize Fellowship for his research on international trade and economic growth.

Henry Thompson is Professor of Economics at Auburn University. He has published numerous articles and a textbook, *International Economics*, and has presented many seminars. He is editor of the *International Economics and Finance Society* newsletter.

James R. Tybout is Professor of Economics at Pennsylvania State University, and was a professor at Georgetown University for many years. He is a Research Associate of the National Bureau of Economic Research and a co-editor of the *Journal of International Economics*. He is also an associate editor for the *Revista de Analysis Economico* and a member of the editorial board for the *Journal of Policy Reform*.

Anthony J. Venables is Professor of International Economics at the London School of Economics. He is also Director of the Globalization Programme at the Centre for Economic Performance, and co-director of the International Trade Programme at the Centre for Economic Policy Research.

David E. Weinstein is Carl S. Shoup Professor of the Japanese Economy in the Department of Economics at Columbia and the Associate Director of Research at the Center for Japanese Economy and Business. He is also a Senior Economist at the Federal Reserve Bank of New York and a Member of the Council on Foreign Relations.

Eden S. H. Yu is Head of the Department of Economics and Finance at the City University of Hong Kong. He has taught at the University of Oklahoma, Claremont McKenna College, Louisiana State University, and the Chinese University of Hong Kong. Dr Yu specializes in international trade and environmental economics.

Introduction

James Harrigan

International trade is perhaps the oldest sub-field of economics, dating back to Ricardo's demonstration of the law of comparative advantage. The beauty and surprise of Ricardo's model set a standard for theoretical elegance which continues to this day, through Viner, Samuelson, Meade, Bhagwati, Jones, Krugman, Helpman, Grossman, and many others. The achievements of the theorists make the absence of a long and deep tradition of empirical work all the more striking. Until recently, trade *theory* was virtually the whole of the economic analysis of international trade, a few counterexamples to the contrary (Leontief, Baldwin, and others) notwithstanding. Indeed, before its revision in 1990, the *Journal of Economic Literature* heading for international trade was "410 International Trade Theory," leaving no obvious place for theory-connected empirical research.

However, times have changed, and the prevailing intellectual winds have moved in an empirical direction. While great theory is still done (and remains to be done), international trade is more and more an empirical field, and this shift is reflected in this *Handbook*. Nine of the thirteen chapters are critical surveys of empirical research, while the chapters by E. Kwan Choi and Henry Thompson are theoretical essays motivated at least partly by developments in the empirical literature. The remaining two chapters are an elegant tour of factor proportions theory by Ron Jones, and a slog through the thickets of the traditional external economies literature by Jai-Young Choi and Eden Yu.

The new empirical literature in international trade can be dated to Leamer's classic 1984 book *Sources of International Comparative Advantage* (MIT Press). Leamer's book has had two lasting influences. The first is that it taught the importance of tying empirical research as closely as possible to specific models. The second is that it argued for the empirical relevance of factor proportions theory. The literature that was spawned most directly by *Sources* is surveyed in this *Handbook* by Harrigan and by Davis and Weinstein.

The testing and estimation of older models has been supplemented very recently by a small but growing literature that looks at models built on imperfect competition and increasing returns. Markusen and Maskus discuss work on multinationals, while Overman, Redding, and Venables survey the nascent empirical literature on economic geography. The chapter by Lipsey is focused on measurement and conceptual issues and is a valuable complement to the chapter by Markusen and Maskus. Tybout's chapter surveying studies using firm- and plant-level data is as much about methodology as it is about results, and a careful reader will likely come away with the view that industry data hides more than it reveals.

While testing trade theory has been a focus of the empirical literature, the theoretically rigorous empirical application of applied problems has arguably been more important. The best-known example of this has been the so-called "trade and wages" debate that has tried to sort out the links (if any) between globalization and wage inequality. In their chapter, Feenstra and Hanson make a persuasive case that there *is* an important link, but that the link comes less through the classic Stolper–Samuelson mechanism than through international outsourcing.

The trade and wages debate is of key policy concern, but trade policy in general is much less controversial among economists than it is in the broader public. Two chapters address some of the linkages between politics and trade policy: Blonigen and Prusa examine the determinants and effects of antidumping, while Gawande and Krishna cast a critical eye on the large political economy literature.

This *Handbook* is largely focused on the sub-sub-field of "empirical trade." While empirical trade dates back to Leontief and has its modern roots in the work of Leamer and others, it is no accident that it has flourished during Robert Feenstra's tenure as Director of the International Trade and Investment Program at the National Bureau of Economic Research. Feenstra's leadership of the ITI program, with the enthusiastic support of the NBER's President, Martin Feldstein, has been instrumental in the development of empirical trade, with many of the key authors being ITI affiliates and many of the best papers getting an early critical reception at ITI meetings. The editors of the *Handbook* are particularly grateful to Feenstra and Feldstein for turning the Spring 2001 Meeting of the ITI group over to a presentation and discussion of the nine empirical survey papers here.

Part I

Factor Proportions Theory

1

Trade Theory and Factor Intensities: An Interpretative Essay

Ronald W. Jones

CHAPTER OUTLINE

Ever since Heckscher's 1919 pioneering contribution to international trade theory, and especially since Samuelson's early papers in the 1940s (Samuelson, 1948, 1949; Stolper and Samuelson, 1941), the concept of *factor intensity* has played a key role in explanations both of trade patterns and the consequences of international trade for local income distribution. This chapter's purpose is to discuss the uses that have been made of this concept and its applicability to problems that are couched in higher dimensions. As well I would like to suggest that it has an important role to play even in "new" trade theory in which the strong link between commodity prices and costs of production may be removed by the existence of imperfectly competitive markets. In what follows I review uses to which the concept of factor intensity has been put.

1 THE SIMPLE 2 × 2 FRAMEWORK

Definitions of factor intensities are most simply provided in the case in which a pair of countries produces two commodities with the help of two distinct productive factors. Let labor and capital represent the two factors. Commodity 1 is deemed to be produced by relatively labor-intensive techniques if the ratio of labor to capital employed in its production exceeds that utilized by commodity 2. Assuming that technology exhibits constant returns to scale, this ratio is a non-increasing function of the ratio of the wage rate to capital rentals. For a country with given factor endowments, if the first commodity is labor intensive at one set of outputs, it must remain so for all feasible (and efficient) outputs in which factors are fully employed. However, even if the other country shares the same technology, the first commodity need not be labor intensive there; the factor-intensity ranking could be switched. We comment later on this phenomenon of *factor-intensity reversal.*

1.1 The Four Core Theorems

The various parts of Heckscher–Ohlin (HO) theory were brought together by Ethier (1974). In the 2×2 setting he conveniently referred to the four *core* propositions of this theory, stemming from the equilibrium conditions characterizing competitive markets. A pair of conditions links commodity outputs, x_1 and x_2, to the endowments of labor and capital, L and K *via* the technology matrix, A, and stipulates that the economy's demand for factors is equal to the available endowments. This presumes that there is enough flexibility in technology to allow this full employment of both factors:

$$a_{L1}x_1 + a_{L2}x_2 = L \tag{1.1}$$

$$a_{K1}x_1 + a_{K2}x_2 = K \tag{1.2}$$

A second pair of equilibrium conditions states that in a competitive equilibrium all profits are wiped out for commodities produced. That is, unit costs will equal prices:

$$a_{L1}w + a_{K1}r = p_1 \tag{1.3}$$

$$a_{L2}w + a_{K2}r = p_2 \tag{1.4}$$

The first core proposition is the Heckscher–Ohlin theorem, suggesting that relatively labor-abundant countries (with a higher labor to capital endowment ratio) will export labor-intensive commodities. The foundation for such a conclusion is the supply side of the model, since differences in tastes between countries, even those sharing the same technology, might offset systematic relative production differences reflective of factor endowment asymmetries. Is it the case that if both countries share the same technology, the country with the higher labor/capital endowment proportions will produce relatively more of the labor-intensive commodity when they both face the same free-trade commodity prices? Yes. If factor intensities are different between commodities, and both commodities are produced in each country, equations (1.3) and (1.4) state that factor prices are uniquely linked to commodity prices. (This relates to the second core proposition – the Factor Price Equalization theorem.) If commodity prices are fixed, the production pattern suggested by (1.1) and (1.2) is given by the *inverse* of the (technology) A-matrix; the relatively labor-abundant country will produce relatively more of the relatively labor-intensive commodity (x_1). The problem with identifying this result with the statement of the theorem (the *strong* form) is that tastes also affect the trade pattern. To get around this, a *weak* form of the theorem states that the country that has a relatively low autarky wage rate will export the labor-intensive commodity. This theorem makes use of the zero-profit conditions, equations (1.3) and (1.4), and does *not* require any matrix inversion, for it states that relatively low wage rates result in relatively low costs for the labor-intensive sector. The second core proposition, the Factor Price Equalization result, need not concern us here, other than to note that it requires (in the 2×2 case) that factor intensities between commodities indeed be different.

The third and fourth propositions (the Stolper–Samuelson theorem and the Rybczynski theorem) do not require that technologies be the same between countries. However, they do involve the properties of the inverse of the A-matrix. The Stolper–Samuelson theorem states that an increase in the relative price of the labor-intensive commodity serves unambiguously to increase the real wage, while the Rybczynski theorem (1955) states that an expansion of the labor endowment by itself (with no change in the capital supply) causes the capital-intensive activity to decline *if* commodity prices (and therefore factor rewards) remain the same. This latter proviso is necessary in order to keep the elements of the A-matrix unchanged.

Both of these latter two propositions involve more than a ranking of gainers and losers (among factor returns or outputs). As well they involve the *magnification* results that are more easily seen by considering small changes in prices and endowments and equilibrium adjustments in equations (1.1) to (1.4). Differentiating these two sets of equations, letting λ_{ij} indicate the fraction of the total supply of the ith factor required by the jth industry, and θ_{ij} the distributive share of the ith factor in the jth industry, with relative changes indicated by the hat notation ($\hat{x}$ is dx/x), yields equations (1.5) to (1.8);

$$\lambda_{L1}\hat{x}_1 + \lambda_{L2}\hat{x}_2 = \hat{L} + \delta_L(\hat{w} - \hat{r}) \tag{1.5}$$

$$\lambda_{K1}\hat{x}_1 + \lambda_{K2}\hat{x}_2 = \hat{K} + \delta_K(\hat{w} - \hat{r}) \tag{1.6}$$

$$\theta_{L1}\hat{w} + \theta_{K1}\hat{r} = \hat{p}_1 \tag{1.7}$$

$$\theta_{L2}\hat{w} + \theta_{K2}\hat{r} = \hat{p}_2 \tag{1.8}$$

where $\delta_L \equiv \lambda_{L1}\theta_{K1}\sigma_1 + \lambda_{L2}\theta_{K2}\sigma_2$; $\delta_K \equiv \lambda_{K1}\theta_{L1}\sigma_1 + \lambda_{K2}\theta_{L2}\sigma_2$. The σ's are the elasticities of substitution between labor and capital in the two sectors.

The first pair of full-employment equations states that the positive λ-weighted average of relative output changes is matched either by relative changes in factor endowments or by changes in factor prices that induce changes in input/output coefficients. The second pair does not need such a qualification, since the distributive share weighted average of the input/output coefficients in any industry vanishes as a second-order small when unit costs are being minimized.[1] Each equation states that the relative price change (equal to the relative unit cost change) is the appropriate weighted average of factor price changes.

The Stolper–Samuelson results can be obtained by subtracting equation (1.8) from equation (1.7) and solving for the change in the wage/rental ratio:

$$(\hat{w} - \hat{r}) = \{1/|\theta|\}(\hat{p}_1 - \hat{p}_2) \qquad (1.9)$$

The term, $|\theta|$, is the determinant of coefficients in equations (1.7) and (1.8), and is also equal to the difference in labor's distributive shares between industries, $(\theta_{L1} - \theta_{L2})$. It is straightforward to show that the sign of this determinant is indicative of the factor intensity ranking of the two industries, positive if the first industry is labor intensive. If so, an increase in the relative price of the labor-intensive sector must increase the wage/rental ratio. The magnification result follows since $|\theta|$ is a fraction. More directly, since each commodity price change is flanked by factor-price changes, an increase in the relative price of the first commodity must result in:

$$\hat{w} > \hat{p}_1 > \hat{p}_2 > \hat{r} \qquad (1.10)$$

A similar logic leads to the Rybczynski result. If commodity prices are held constant, so are factor prices (from (1.7) and (1.8)) and thus techniques, thereby simplifying equations (1.5) and (1.6). Subtracting equation (1.6) (thus simplified) from equation (1.5), letting $|\lambda|$ denote the determinant of factor allocation fractions or, what is the same thing, the difference between the fraction of the labor force used in the first industry and the fraction of the capital stock used there, $(\lambda_{L1} - \lambda_{K1})$,

$$(\hat{x}_1 - \hat{x}_2) = \{1/|\lambda|\}(\hat{L} - \hat{K}) \qquad (1.11)$$

An increase in the relative endowment of labor compared with capital raises by a magnified amount the relative output of the first commodity. In more detail, if the endowment of labor increases relative to that of capital, with commodity prices constant,

$$\hat{x}_1 > \hat{L} > \hat{K} > \hat{x}_2 \qquad (1.12)$$

The Rybczynski result refers to the fall in x_2's output if $\hat{K}$ is assumed to be zero.

1.2 The Extent of Differences in Factor Intensities: A Measure

Differences in the intensity with which factors are utilized in the two sectors are important for the core propositions of the Heckscher–Ohlin theory. The role played by the *ranking* of the intensities is clear from previous remarks. What is also important is the *extent* of the difference in factor intensities. But here there is a subtle remark worth making: factor intensity differences are important, but the required extent of changes in factor prices is larger the *smaller* is the difference in factor intensities. When the relative price of the labor-intensive commodity rises, an increase in the wage rate relative to capital rentals is what is required in order to

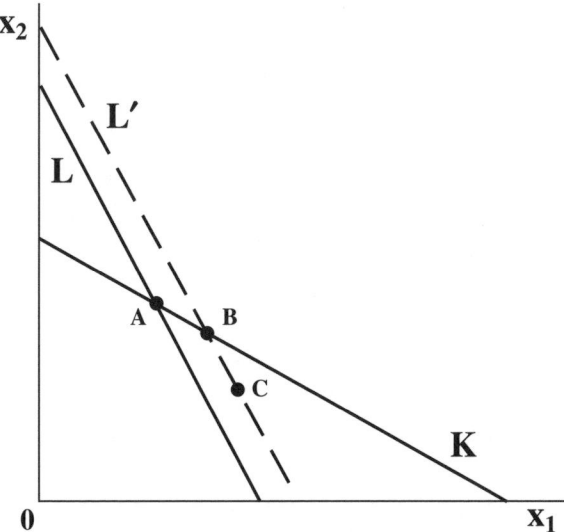

Figure 1.1 Endowments and outputs

raise the average cost of producing the labor-intensive commodity (relative to the capital-intensive commodity). Similarly, the necessary adjustment in outputs in response to a change in factor endowments is more severe the closer together are factor intensities. Figure 1.1 illustrates this point for an increase in the supply of labor with a given stock of capital and unchanged techniques (because commodity prices are being held constant as required to show the Rybczynski effect). For the given techniques the original labor and capital constraint lines intersect at A, where there is full employment of both factors. An increase in the supply of labor to the L'-line requires an output decline in capital-intensive x_2 and a magnified increase in labor-intensive x_1 (as in equation (1.12)) to point B. Now suppose the factor-intensity difference between commodities had been less pronounced – illustrated by a different capital-constraint line through point A but steeper, so that the increase in labor shifts outputs to point C instead of point B. The required output changes to accommodate a change in factor endowments would be more pronounced.

The $|\lambda|$ and $|\theta|$ determinants show the *ranking* of intensities by their sign and the *extent* of the difference in intensities by their size. There is a measure that serves to indicate the *size* of the difference in intensities, one that is always a positive fraction, and that is the product of the two determinants, $|\lambda|, |\theta|$. This is a measure that features prominently in the answer to the following question: if relative commodity prices change (by a small amount), by how much do relative outputs adjust? That is, what is the elasticity of relative outputs with respect to relative prices along the transformation schedule? Subtract equation (1.6) from equation (1.5) and solve for the relative change in outputs for given endowments:

$$(\hat{x}_1 - \hat{x}_2) = \{1/|\lambda|\}(\delta_L + \delta_K)(\hat{w} - \hat{r}) \tag{1.13}$$

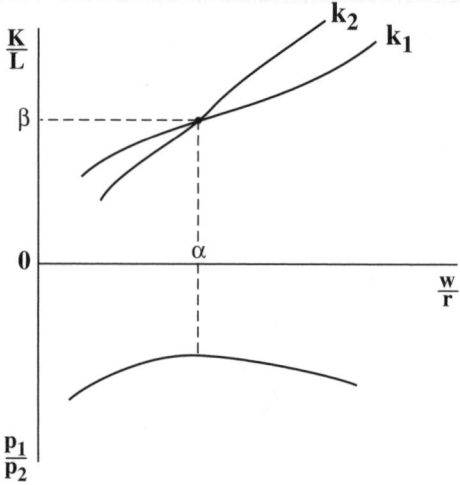

Figure 1.2   Factor-intensity reversal

From equation (1.9) the change in the factor price ratio is linked to the change in the commodity price ratio, so that substitution yields:

$$(\hat{x}_1 - \hat{x}_2) = \{1/|\lambda||\theta|\}(\delta_L + \delta_K)(\hat{p}_1 - \hat{p}_2) \qquad (1.14)$$

Furthermore, each of the δ's is linked to the elasticity of substitution between capital and labor in a particular industry. Suppose these two elasticities are the same, denoted just by σ. Then the expression for relative output changes shown by (1.14) can be simplified. Let the coefficient of $(\hat{p}_1 - \hat{p}_2)$ be defined as the elasticity of supply, σ_S, along the transformation schedule. Then it is easy to show that:

$$\sigma_S = \{(1 - |\lambda||\theta|)/|\lambda||\theta|\}\sigma \qquad (1.15)$$

The smaller is the product of the determinants (both positive if the first industry is labor intensive, and both negative otherwise) the greater must be the elasticity of supply. This product is thus a natural measure, lying between zero and unity, of the extent of the difference in factor intensities between sectors.

1.3   Factor-Intensity Reversals

Production functions can be characterized by constant returns to scale, identical between countries, and yet exhibit a different relative factor-intensity *ranking* between countries. The classic illustration is provided in figure 1.2, the so-called Harrod–Johnson diagram (Harrod, 1958; Johnson, 1957). The top quadrant relates the capital/labor intensity ratio to the wage/rental ratio for the common technology in the two countries. It illustrates a situation in which for low relative wages the first commodity is relatively capital-intensive, but for wage/rental ratios higher than α the ranking is reversed, with the first commodity becoming relatively labor intensive. If, in autarky, factor endowment proportions in the two countries lie on opposite sides of the critical β-ratio, the Heckscher–Ohlin theorem as a statement for trade patterns in both countries becomes logically invalid (Jones, 1956). Thus suppose that it is the home country that is capital abundant, with a wage/rent ratio higher than α, and suppose furthermore that it exports its capital-intensive commodity, x_2. That implies that the other country exports the first commodity, which, since its wage/rental ratio is lower than α, must be *its* capital-intensive commodity. That is, the labor-abundant country exports its capital-intensive good, violating the Heckscher–Ohlin theorem. In defense of the spirit of the Heckscher–Ohlin theorem, note that whatever the pattern of trade, the relatively capital-abundant home country must export a commodity that is produced by more capital-intensive techniques than is the commodity exported from abroad. This is little consolation, of course, to the Leontief procedure (1953) of comparing the manner in which the two commodities are produced within the same country in order to deduce the factor endowment ranking between countries.

The lower part of figure 1.2 illustrates the relationship between the commodity-price ratio and the wage/rental ratio. As shown, the relative cost of producing the first commodity would reach a minimum if the wage/rental ratio were given by α (in which case the transformation schedule would be linear). Thus the following theorem, in rough form, illustrates the connection between factor endowments and the trade pattern: the country whose endowment capital/labor ratio lies further away from critical β will have a comparative advantage in (and will be the exporter of) the commodity exhibiting the more flexible technology (the higher σ_j).

1.4 The Factor Bias in Technical Progress

The 2×2 framework has often been used to analyze the effect of technical progress on relative factor prices, especially in a context in which the two inputs are unskilled and skilled labor. One of the propositions often put forth by international trade theorists is a corollary of the Stolper–Samuelson theorem: if technical progress takes place in one sector of an economy facing a given set of commodity prices, the real wage rate of unskilled labor rises if and only if that sector is unskilled-labor inten-sive. The crucial aspect of this statement is what it leaves out – no qualification is made as to the *bias* in technical progress. It is purported to hold whether or not progress is unskilled-labor saving or labor using. The formal support for such a proposition is provided by the competitive profit equations of change, (1.7) and (1.8). Suppose progress takes place in the first sector, so that at *given* factor prices one or both of the input-output coefficients in equation (1.3) fall sufficiently that the distributive share average of such changes, $(\theta_{L1}\hat{a}_{L1} + \theta_{K1}\hat{a}_{K1})$, is negative. This is the Hicksian measure of technical progress, and in equation (1.7) the absolute value of this expression would appear on the right-hand side. If L refers to unskilled labor and K to skilled labor (human capital), with the first sector L-intensive, the real

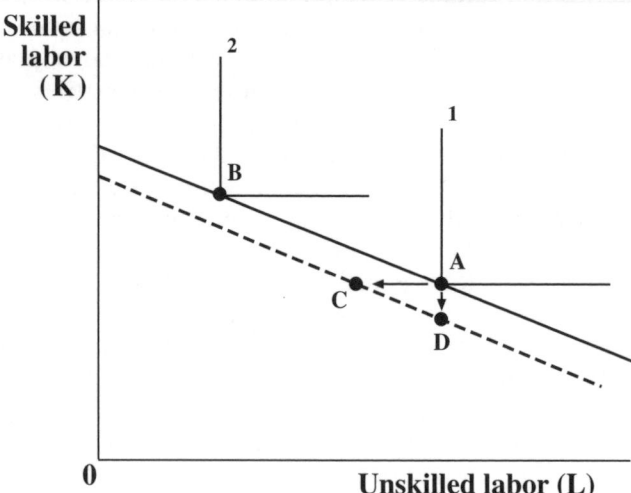

Figure 1.3 Biased technical progress

wage for the unskilled would unambiguously rise (and that for skilled workers would fall) regardless of the bias in such progress.

This result, which causes some dismay among labor economists (e.g., see the discussion in Collins, 1998), is very much a reflection both of the 2×2 dimensionality of the models and of an assumption that the extent of technical progress is small. By this is meant that the pattern of production is not affected. In section 2 we illustrate how, in a multi-commodity setting, progress in the capital-intensive sector might end up *improving* the position of unskilled labor. Here our objective is more modest: With finite technical progress, the *extent* of the factor-price change indeed depends upon whether progress is (Hicksian) unskilled-labor saving or labor using in its bias. The potential surprise lies in the nature of the connection. As I now illustrate, if technical progress takes place in the unskilled-labor intensive sector, the real wage for the unskilled will rise by *less* if such progress tends to require a higher ratio of unskilled labor (per unit of skilled labor) – i.e., if it is unskilled-labor using in its bias.

The argument follows that found in Findlay and Jones (2000). To simplify, suppose that there is no possibility of factor substitution in either sector. The initial situation is shown by points A and B for the two unit-value isoquants in figure 1.3. Points C and D indicate two alternative shifts in the corner-point A that represent the same Hicksian extent of technical progress (the dashed line is parallel to the initial line whose slope reveals the factor-price ratio). Point C represents pure Hicksian unskilled labor-saving progress and point D a pure skilled-labor-saving technical progress. The resulting effect on the relative wage rate for unskilled labor (L) would be revealed by the slope of the new factor-price line connecting point B either with point C or with point D. The unskilled real wage rate increases in either case, but even more so if progress *reduces* the demand for unskilled labor per unit

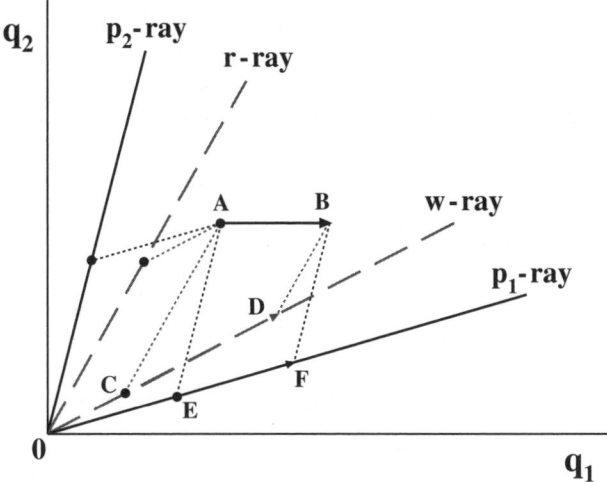

Figure 1.4 Joint production

of skilled labor (point C). The rationale for such a counter-intuitive result is that the move to C (instead of to D) narrows the extent of the factor-intensity difference between sectors (as measured earlier by $|\lambda|$ or $|\theta|$ or their product, $|\lambda| \, |\theta|$) and thus allows a greater magnification effect.

1.5   Joint Production

Two of the four core propositions depend heavily on an assumption about production that is standard in much of economic theory, *viz.* that production processes involve one or more inputs and yield a single output. Thus the strong asymmetries between output and endowment changes shown by the ranking in (1.12) and between commodity and factor price changes shown by (1.10) are supported by the assumption that there is no joint production. But these are not razor's edge types of results; a bit of jointness will not overturn the magnification effects.

Figure 1.4 illustrates a case in which the Stolper–Samuelson theorem holds despite the existence of joint production. (A similar use of this diagram was made by Chang, Ethier, and Kemp, 1980.) Shown along the axes are the prices of two different *activities*, each of which requires labor and capital as inputs, and yields outputs of commodities 1 and 2. On the one hand each price, q_i, represents the sum of labor costs and capital costs, much as in equations (1.3) and (1.4) with activity prices replacing the commodity prices, p_i. As well, the price of each activity is the sum of the value of commodity outputs from the unit level of the activity. In figure 1.4 the cone spanned by the wage ray and the rental ray is contained by the cone spanned by the two commodity price rays. If so, an increase in the price of the first activity with the price of the second activity held constant (the move from point A to point B), increases the price of the first commodity from 0E to 0F, and of the wage rate from 0C to 0D. The latter change is relatively larger, so that the real wage must rise as in Stolper–Samuelson, despite the presence of joint production. The key assumption is that the disparity in the composition of outputs in a comparison of the two activities is greater than the factor-intensity difference in inputs (further details are found in Jones, 2001).

As to the other pair of propositions in the core, the factor price equalization result is robust as long as the two activities are linearly independent,[2] and the Heckscher–Ohlin theorem can be restated in terms of the country location of *activities*. From such a pattern the actual trade routing of commodities could then be deduced from the output intensity of activities (as well as patterns of demand).

1.6 Factor-Market Distortions

A factor of production may be used in both sectors of the economy and yet receive a different remuneration in each. Harberger (1962) in his work on corporate income tax provided an early example. Johnson and Mieszkowski (1970) suggested that trade union activity also illustrated a case of factor-market distortion. In Jones (1971a) a general treatment was provided, one that came under heavy criticism from Neary (1978). Factor-market distortions open up the possibility that a ranking by distributive shares (the θ-matrix) could differ from the physical factor-intensity ranking provided by the ratios of factors used (or the λ-allocation ranking). For example, an industry that had a higher labor/capital ratio might pay its workers less than a unionized sector with a higher wage rate. Equations (1.5) and (1.6) suggest how the λ-ranking connects the output pattern to factor endowments, while equations (1.7) and (1.8) illustrate how the value distributive shares (the θs) connect factor returns to commodity prices. With factor-market distortions, the sign of the $|\lambda|$ determinant could become different from that of the $|\theta|$ determinant. This seems to open up the possibility that the increase in a commodity price might cause output in that sector to decline. If, say, the *first* commodity is labor intensive in a physical sense but capital intensive in a value sense, a rise in its price would lower the wage rate, encouraging more labor-intensive techniques to be adopted in each sector, and thus causing an increase in the output of the *second* commodity, which is capital intensive in a physical sense. Neary objected that such an inverse price–output supply relationship could be ruled out on stability grounds. Thus seeming paradoxical responses of outputs to changes in commodity prices would not be observed.

Later we discuss the specific-factors model. For example, two types of labor, unionized and non-unionized, might be considered as specific to each sector of a two-sector economy because the union can limit entry. But in this case the differences in wage rates are endogenous to the system, whereas the kinds of distortion to which the Neary objection holds are exogenous. Since labor has natural units, it would be possible to compare factor allocation coefficients as in the regular 2×2 model, but with different wage rates the $|\lambda|$ determinant and the share $|\theta|$ determinant could have different signs. Nonetheless, if the union-inspired wage discrepancy was to disappear, and over time wages adjust as the formerly unionized sector attracts labor, Jones and Neary (1979) argue that the adjustment process would be stable.

In the case in which there are potentially many commodities that a country could produce, but only two factors, there is little difficulty in ordering commodities by their factor intensities, assuming away, again, the problem of factor-intensity reversals. There are clear advantages that the multi-commodity case (still only two factors) has over the previous section's two-commodity framework. Perhaps the most important of these concerns the question of the degree of concentration allowed by, or forced by, the existence of free trade in world markets. In the limit a country may pull resources completely out of producing (n – 1) traded commodities. The two-commodity case severely limits the extent to which trade exhibits such concentration. A basic question then concerns *which* commodities are produced, and how are the differences in factor intensities and factor endowments connected to such a choice.

2.1 The Hicksian Composite Unit-Value Isoquant

The geometric construction known as the Hicksian composite unit-value isoquant is the device most often used to illustrate the multi-commodity case. Given a country's knowledge of technology and its factor endowments, exposure to world markets with known commodity prices suffices to determine the answer to questions about production patterns. If the country's technology does not match up with that available in other countries, there may be some commodities that this country could not efficiently produce in world markets regardless of its factor endowments; it may possess a Ricardian comparative disadvantage in such goods. For each of the other commodities consider the unit-value isoquant, combinations of labor and capital that produce a single dollar's worth of output at world prices. The *convex hull* of this set of isoquants represents the Hicksian composite, and the bold locus in figure 1.5 illustrates a three-commodity case. The intersection of the endowment ray with this composite yields the output bundle, which may consist of a single commodity or a pair. If world prices are unconnected with this country's technology, there will generally only be as many commodities that can be produced as there are factors, in this case two. For example if endowments are shown by the β-ray, only commodity 2 is produced. By contrast, with endowments given by the α-ray, the bundle of inputs at point G is the efficient way of earning $1 on world markets, and this involves producing around 30 cents worth of commodity 1 and 70 cents worth of the second commodity. The α-ray cuts the chord connecting technique A for producing the first good and technique B for producing the second at point G. Note that at these prices and endowments it is not only production of commodity 3 that is ruled out, also not viable are many *factor intensities* of producing the other two

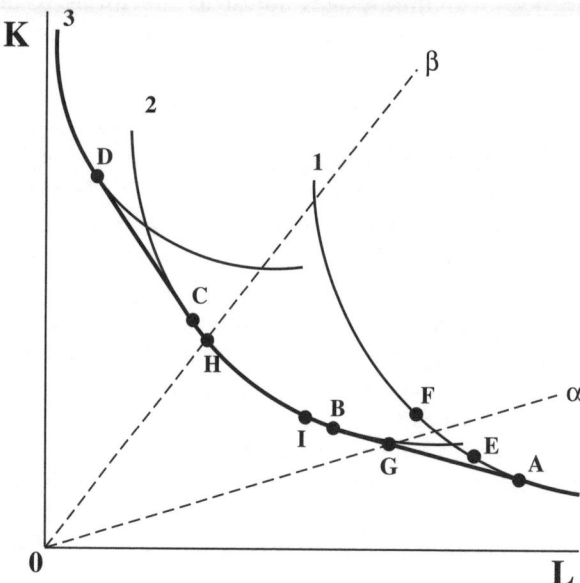

Figure 1.5 Hicksian composite unit value isoquant

commodities. Point F indicates a technique for producing the first commodity that would be ruled out by competition – indeed this technique is dominated by some of the techniques of producing commodity 2. But even point E is inefficient, not because there is another, better *single* way of earning $1, but because a combination of points A and B is superior.

In the case in which many commodities are represented in the Hicksian composite unit-value isoquant, what is the relationship between the *trade* pattern, factor endowments and factor intensities? An easier preliminary question concerns the *production* pattern. Each commodity represented in the composite has only a range of intensities that are viable. The endowment ray either selects a unique commodity with those exact factor proportions (e.g., point H for the β-ray), or, if two commodities are efficient, the two flanking techniques for the pair of commodities, e.g., techniques A (for the first commodity) and B (for the second) if the endowments lie along the α-ray. All commodities not produced will be imported if there is any local demand at world prices. Thus typically a country's imports will contain commodities that would, if produced at home, require more capital per unit of labor than contained in the endowment bundle as well as less capital per unit of labor than in endowments. As to exports, it will be the single good produced if there is only one such commodity, and either one or both of the commodities produced if the endowment ray cuts a flat. But relatively small variations in the endowment ray along a given flat could well alter the trading pattern as one of the commodities ceases to be exported and becomes imported instead. Perhaps the moral of the story is that in the multi-commodity case factor endowments are not clear

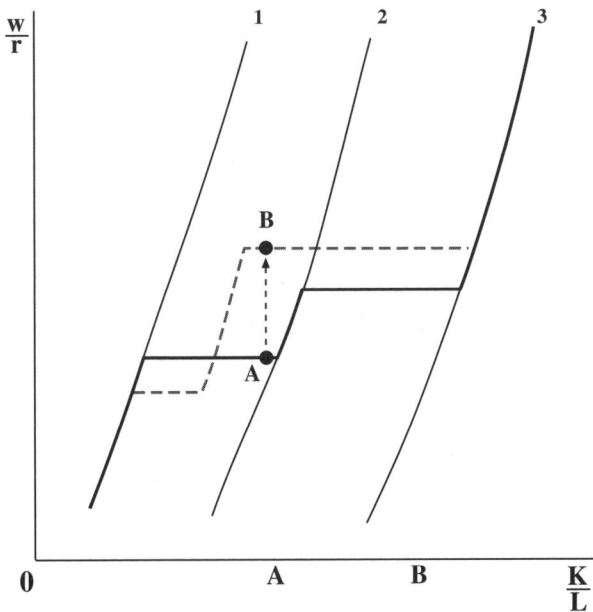

Figure 1.6 Technical change and factor prices

indicators of trade patterns, but they do serve to single out a production pattern involving one or two commodities produced using factor intensities *close* to the endowment ratio (Jones, Beladi and Marjit, 1999).

This setting is also useful in revealing likely alterations in production patterns for an open economy capable of growing in the sense of accumulating capital (relative to the size of its labor force). Such growth will certainly not be balanced. Instead, there would be a steady increase in the production of commodities with greater and greater capital/labor requirements coupled with declining production of the more labor-intensive items. Even smooth *aggregate* rates of growth would be accompanied by a strong asymmetry in *sectoral* performance at the micro level (Findlay and Jones, 2001).

2.2 Technical Progress of Finite Size

Previously we alluded to the possibility that the factor-saving bias in technical progress that is confined to the capital-intensive sector of an economy would have no effect on the result that the relative (and real) wage rate would fall if the change is small, but might reverse this outcome if the progress is of finite size (Findlay and Jones, 2000). Here we can illustrate this result in the three-commodity case, figure 1.6. The technology of producing the three commodities is reflected in the upward sloping schedules. For given initial world prices, the bold sections on each curve show ranges of factor endowment proportions in which complete specialization takes place. The two bold horizontal stretches illustrate ranges of factor endowments for which incomplete specialization to two different commodities is required to achieve full employment. Suppose the initial equilibrium reflects the endowment proportions and factor prices shown by point A. The dashed sections reflect technological progress of a finite extent in the second commodity (thus extending at both ends the range of factor endowments for which complete specialization in the second commodity would be achieved at the given world commodity prices). As illustrated, this change is biased in favor of requiring a heavier use of labor (or unskilled labor in the earlier interpretation) compared to capital (or skilled labor) at any given factor price ratio. Initially the country produces both commodities 1 and 2. Technical progress has taken place in the relatively more capital intensive of these two, but as a consequence the wage/rental rate has *increased* to the level shown by B. The pattern of production has been altered so that in the new equilibrium the country produces commodities 2 and 3 and in this pair commodity 2 is relatively labor intensive. With such a change in the production pattern the bias in technical progress comes into its own in affecting factor prices. Here it is the labor-using bias that results in an increase in the wage rate, a result in line with the partial-equilibrium reasoning often used by labor economists.

Jones and Kierzkowski (2001) argue that international *fragmentation* of a previously vertically-integrated production process is analogous to technical progress in that overall productivity can be increased by losing a fragment in which a country does not possess a comparative advantage. The point to emphasize here is that such fragmentation is not a marginal, infinitessimal event. By its very nature, fragmentation involves finite changes in the pattern of production.

3 THE MULTI-FACTOR CASE

Must the use of factor-intensity rankings be abandoned if more than two factors are used in production processes? No. A later part of this section addresses the general setting in which the economy produces many commodities, each requiring a unique composition of many inputs. But first I begin with the more simple three-factor case, and especially the most popular version, the specific-factors model.

3.1 The Specific-Factors Model in the 3 × 2 Setting

In this setting the factor proportions used in the two sectors are not directly comparable since each industry uses a (specific) factor not used in the other industry. This is a setting in which the use of distributive factor shares comes into its own. In the 2 × 2 case, if the first industry utilized a higher labor/capital ratio in production, it also exhibited a higher labor distributive share. If labor is the mobile factor in the specific-factors framework, a comparison once again can be made of its distributive share in the two sectors even though the other factor is different between sectors. The factor-intensity ranking would thus be freed up of the necessity of a focus on the *same pair* of factors.

Earlier, a comparison of the factor allocation fractions in an industry was also used to indicate a factor-intensity ranking. Applied directly here it would only state that each industry was intensive in the use of its specific factor. However, the λ-allocation fractions can be used to yield the same information about labor intensity as does the θ-distributive share ranking. Consider the ratio of labor's distributive share in the jth sector with the fraction of the labor force used there, θ_{Lj}/λ_{Lj}. Simple substitution reveals that this is equivalent to the ratio θ^L/θ_j, where θ^L refers to labor's share in the national income and θ_j refers to industry j's share of the national income. Alternatively phrased:

$$\theta_{Lj}/\theta^L = \lambda_{Lj}/\theta_j \tag{1.16}$$

As discussed more explicitly later, labor's share in the national income must be a weighted average of its share in every sector, and the share of the output of each industry in the national income must be a weighted average of the factor allocation fractions used in that industry. Therefore either expression in equation (1.16) could be taken as an index of the intensity with which labor is used in that sector.

Unlike the 2×2 case, factor intensities alone no longer determine factor prices from commodity prices. This is true in any setting in which factors outnumber commodities produced. Furthermore, even if commodity prices are held constant, any change in factor endowments requires output changes in order to equilibrate factor markets (as before), but such changes no longer depend only upon factor intensities. So what do factor intensities tell us even in this stripped-down specific factors context?

As developed in Jones (1971b or 2000), the most direct way to ascertain the role of factor intensities in the specific-factors model is to solve for changes in the return to the mobile factor. Let this be labor, with specific factor V_i in industry i. The full employment condition for labor is then as shown in equation (1.1). In addition, each output is constrained by the amount of the specific factor employed there: $a_{ii}x_i = V_i$. Differentiate each of these and substitute into the differentiated form of (1.1) to obtain (1.17):

$$\sum \lambda_{Li}(\hat{a}_{ii} - \hat{a}_{Li}) = -\{\hat{L} - \sum \lambda_{Li}\hat{V}_i\} \tag{1.17}$$

Changes in the factor intensities adopted in each industry can be related either to the change in the ratio of factor prices in that industry via the elasticity of factor substitution (as used previously in note 1) or to the change in the ratio of the wage rate (w_L) to the price of that industry's output via the elasticity of demand for labor in that industry (the elasticity of the marginal physical product of labor schedule). Taking the latter route,

$$(\hat{a}_{ii} - \hat{a}_{Li}) \equiv \gamma_{Li}(\hat{w}_L - \hat{p}_i) \tag{1.18}$$

This leads to the solution for the change in mobile labor's return with respect to changes in commodity prices and to changes in factor endowments:

$$\hat{w}_L = \sum \beta_j \hat{p}_j - [1/\gamma_L]\{\hat{L} - \sum \lambda_{Lj} \hat{V}_j\} \tag{1.19}$$

where $\beta_j \equiv \lambda_{Lj}\gamma_{Lj}/\gamma_L$ and $\gamma_L \equiv \Sigma \lambda_{Lj}\gamma_{Lj}$.

This solution confirms that the increase in either commodity price raises the return to mobile labor, but by a dampened relative amount. Clearly, both factor-demand elasticities and factor intensities enter into the determination of factor returns when commodity prices are altered. Rewriting each of the β-coefficients as the product of three terms helps to reveal the role of factor-intensity rankings. Thus:

$$\beta_j = \theta_j i_j s_j \tag{1.20}$$

where $i_j \equiv \lambda_{Lj}/\theta_j$ and $s_j \equiv \gamma_{Lj}/\gamma_L$.

The expressions s_j and i_j represent, respectively, the elasticity of demand for labor in sector j expressed relative to the economy-wide labor demand elasticity, and the labor intensity of sector j. As already argued, a sector is deemed to be labor intensive if and only if the fraction of the labor force it employs is greater than the fraction that sector's output represents of the national income. Therefore the extent of the wage rise when the price of a single sector increases depends on the importance of that industry, on the relative degree of substitutability between factors in that industry, and the labor intensity index of the industry (and is the product of these three characteristics).

Once the wage rate is determined, the competitive profit conditions can be utilized to solve for the change in rental rates for the two specific factors. In this 3×2 case,

$$\theta_{11}\hat{w}_1 + \theta_{L1}\hat{w}_L = \hat{p}_1 \tag{1.21}$$

$$\theta_{22}\hat{w}_2 + \theta_{L2}\hat{w}_L = \hat{p}_2 \tag{1.22}$$

In the 2×2 case competitive profit conditions are typically used to examine the effect of a change in relative commodity prices. In the specific-factors case a different use is often made of these two conditions. Suppose the relative price of goods remains unchanged. In particular, suppose commodity prices do not change but the return to the commonly used factor, labor, goes down. (For example, the labor supply might have increased.) What can be said about the returns (rentals) to the specific factors? Both returns rise, and the factor-intensity comparison now tells us which specific factor return rises relatively more. This will be the return to the first specific factor if and only if θ_{L1} exceeds θ_{L2}, that is, if and only if the first industry is labor intensive. If the wage rate had risen instead, the factor-intensity ranking would indicate which specific-factor return would change more, in this case in a downward direction.

How about endowment changes when commodity prices are kept constant? If the endowment of a specific factor increases, the output in which it is used goes up and the other output falls. (Note, however, that the output of the favored industry does not rise by proportionally as much as the endowment – no magnification effect here.) Suppose, instead, that the endowment of the mobile factor (labor) rises. Not surprisingly, both outputs expand. But which output rises relatively more? The answer does not depend only upon factor intensities, since the difference in the substitutability between labor and the specific factor from industry to industry is also important. However, suppose the elasticity of factor substitution is the same between sectors. Then the output of the first sector will rise by relatively more than that of the second if and only if the first sector is relatively labor intensive (Jones, 1971b). Factor-intensity rankings must share influence with characteristics of factor substitutability in the specific-factors model, but if the elasticity of substitution is similar between sectors, factor-intensity rankings once again dictate the behavior of output changes in response to alterations in factor endowments.

Suppose, now, that each sector uses a type of labor that has a unique level of skills. In particular, let the first industry use unskilled labor and capital as inputs, and the second industry use skilled labor and (the same kind of) capital. Off stage suppose there is an educational process whereby the unskilled can be converted to skilled. This is like a change in factor endowments. Assuming commodity prices are constant, what is the effect of such training on the wage rates of the two types of labor? The reduction in the supply of the unskilled serves to raise both wage rates (as the return to capital falls), but the increase in the pool of skilled labor would have the opposite effect – to raise the return to capital and lower both wage rates. What is the net effect? There are two aspects to this question. First, does the return to capital rise or fall? And second, if it rises, so that both wage rates fall, does the *wage premium* received by skilled workers increase or fall? The answer to the second query depends on the distributive-share version of the factor-intensity ranking. The answer to the first query, however, depends upon the physical capital/labor ratios in the two sectors. With both types of labor sharing a common physical unit of measurement, the λ-comparisons can be made, and the θ-comparison need not be the same. Thus if the sector employing skilled workers is physically the capital-intensive sector, the education process brings more labor to this sector, accompanied by a smaller supply of capital than is used in the second sector. The result is that the return to capital increases and both wage rates fall. However, if the skilled-wage premium is high enough, the second sector could be the labor-intensive sector measured by distributive shares. In such a case, the rise in the return to capital would lower the skilled wage rate by less than that for the unskilled. That is, the departure of some unskilled workers to join the ranks of the skilled could serve not only to lower the unskilled wage rate, but also to heighten the skill premium.[3] The discrepancy between the λ and θ rankings does not lead to the difficulties cited earlier since this is not a factor-market distortion.

3.2 The General 3 × 2 Model

The properties of the three-factor, two-commodity model in which all three factors are actively employed in each sector have been spelled out in Jones and Easton (1983). A new complication, absent in the specific-factors model, is the possibility of factor complementarity or of a strong asymmetry in the degree of factor substitutability. With all three factors mobile, factor i, previously the specific factor used in industry i, is now only the most intensively used factor there (i.e., an *extreme* factor). Once again we focus on the role of the factor-intensity ranking in connecting commodity price changes to factor returns, on the one hand, and endowment changes to outputs, on the other.

Suppose an economy with fixed endowments experiences an increase in the relative price of the first commodity. Could the same effect on factor prices as in the specific-factors model occur in this more general case? Yes, if there is sufficient symmetry among the various factor-substitution elasticities. But suppose the two "extreme" factors, V_1 and V_2, are especially good substitutes for each other, compared with the degree of substitutability of either extreme factor with labor. This implies that the factor returns, w_1 and w_2, cannot move very far apart. In such a case the burden of altering the relative cost of producing the two commodities (to match the given increase in the relative price of the first commodity) falls on a change in the wage rate. It is precisely at this point that the factor-intensity ranking becomes important. Although labor's distributive share lies somewhere in the middle of the share ranking (i.e., $\theta_{11} > \theta_{L1} > \theta_{21}$), more can be gleaned by a comparison of labor's distributive shares in the two industries. Thus if θ_{L1} exceeds θ_{L2}, the first sector is relatively labor intensive compared with the second and an increase in the wage rate will raise costs more in the first than in the second industry. The required factor-price changes, given that w_1 cannot alter much relative to w_2 because of the assumed relatively high degree of factor substitutability between the two extreme factors (in both sectors), are that the wage rate for labor rises relative to either commodity price change, and relative to changes in the other two returns. Although $\hat{w}_1$ will exceed $\hat{w}_2$, it might fall short of $\hat{p}_2$ (as must $\hat{w}_2$).

Without going into any detail, we might note that if both extreme factors are particularly good substitutes for each other, they come close to being a "composite" factor. In this case, let the first industry be labor intensive (as above) in the sense of having a larger labor share. Then an increase in the endowment of the first factor at constant commodity prices could serve to *reduce* the output of the first commodity because it is intensive in the factor (labor) that has *not* been increased. (Details are found in Jones and Easton, 1983. See also Thompson, 1987.)

3.3 Higher-Dimensional Cases

Before turning to a general statement of factor intensities, we consider briefly several other models where factors exceed commodities by one. First, consider the scenario in Jones and Dei (1983) and Jones (2000) concerning foreign investment. Assume that the home country, specialized completely in producing the first commodity at home, is able also to produce it in an enclave located abroad by utilizing the foreign labor force. Foreign labor is also used abroad to produce the second commodity, with the aid of a fixed amount of a specific factor. The specific factor used in the first industry (capital) is either used at home or shipped to the enclave. (The foreign country owns no capital of this type.) This is a 4×3 model: home labor and foreign labor, home type of capital and a foreign specific factor. Foreign labor can be used either to produce its own national commodity or sent to the enclave, while home capital also has two choices in producing a single commodity at home or in the enclave. (The three commodities are home output, output in the enclave, perhaps with different technology than used at home, and foreign national output.)

From an initial equilibrium in this setting, in which the rate of return to capital is equated between the home country and the enclave, suppose the price of the first commodity increases. Before any further international capital flows, the rate of return to capital goes up by the same relative amount at home as the price rise, but by a *magnified* amount abroad, because the enclave can attract foreign labor from the foreign hinterland. Hence more capital flows from home to the enclave. But what happens to the wage rate in each country? As capital leaves the home country the initial wage increase is dampened. Indeed, the wage rate might even fall. However, in the enclave the rise in price draws labor from the foreign national industry and thus causes the foreign wage to rise. It might rise even more than the home wage. What would be the necessary condition for this? With reference to equations (1.21) and (1.22) (with capital now the "mobile" factor), the paradoxical-sounding outcome in which foreign workers, producing their own national commodity (which has not risen in price), find their wages increasing by more than home workers (employed only in producing the good that has increased in price) must follow if home production is capital-intensive relative to that in the enclave.

Another example raises the number of factors and commodities by one. It pre-supposes that there are two countries, each producing both commodities, and the price of the first commodity increases throughout the world. (The number of commodities, four, treats each country's activities as separate from the other's.) The factor specific to the first commodity is assumed to be internationally mobile (such as oil rigs if oil is produced in the first industry). Thus this model is a juxtaposition of specific-factors models for each country, linked by the internationally mobile capital. Will the first specific factor move between countries? Yes, if the return prior to movement is different in the two countries, although in each the return will rise by a greater proportion than the commodity price. Suppose, now, that in the home country output of the first commodity represents a significantly larger fraction of the national income than it does abroad. In this event the wage increase at home can be expected to be larger than that abroad – note the role of θ_j in equation (1.20) – and, if technologies in the first industry are roughly comparable between countries, the return to the specific factor (prior to relocation) cannot rise by as much as in the foreign country. The consequence is a flow of the internationally-mobile factor specific to the industry that has gone up in price into the country that is the relatively *unimportant* producer.

In this 5×4 setting only one type of capital is internationally mobile. But suppose both types of capital can flow between countries although remaining specific to a certain kind of activity. This is the scenario investigated in the *neighborhood production structure* of Jones and Kierzkowski (1996). Thus let X-type and Y-type capital be sector specific, but internationally mobile, with labor trapped within the borders of each country. Suppose taste changes in the world cause an increase in the price of the X-type good produced in each country, with no change in the price of Y-type goods. The kind of reasoning associated with the specific-factors model might suggest a consequent magnified increase in the return to X-type capital, a dampened rise in the wage rate in each country, and a fall in the return to Y-type capital. This could be the outcome, but is not necessary. Even if in each country the

X-type good was capital-intensive compared with the Y-sector, the wage rate in both countries might increase by more than the price of X-type goods, and the return to X-type capital rise not by as much, or even fall. Certainly in this 4×4 setting factor intensities matter – indeed they are the *only* things that matter. However, it is the *intra-industry* comparison of capital's distributive share between countries that is crucial. For this bizarre-sounding result what is required is that one country have a higher intra-industry capital share *in both sectors,* and the share spread between countries in the favored X-industry exceed that in the other industry. Details are omitted here, but found in Jones and Kierzkowski (1996).

The specific-factors model in the 3×2 case generalizes very easily to the case in which there are n sectors, each employing a factor specific to that sector, and each sector as well making use of a mobile factor (e.g., labor) available to all sectors. This is a big advantage in empirical work, where the number of sectors the economy is deemed to have is arbitrary. Thus a single price rise will serve unambiguously to reward the factor used specifically in that sector, to reduce the return to all other specific factors, and to bring about a nominal increase in the return to the mobile factor, which is smaller, relatively, than the commodity price rise. Furthermore, the change in the reward to the mobile factor is given by an expression similar to that developed in equations (1.19) and (1.20). Suppose the mobile factor is labor (L). Now consider a price increase for a single commodity, j, in a country closed to trade. In general the price level change is $\Sigma \theta_i \hat{p}_i$. With only one price change this becomes $\theta_j \hat{p}_j$. If this commodity is "typical" in its degree of factor substitutability, so that s_j in equation (1.20) is unity, and assuming factor endowments do not change, $\hat{w}_L$ will exceed the change in the price level if and only if i_j exceeds unity. That is, for a closed economy the labor intensity of mobile labor indicates the direction of change in the return to the mobile factor in *real* terms in the sense of the price index (although not in terms of the single price rise).

Turning back to the more general 3×2 case, Ruffin (1981) noted the following property: suppose there is an endowment change at given commodity prices. Then the *sign*, although not the *size*, of the response of factor rewards depends *only* upon the factor-intensity ranking and not at all on the pattern of factor substitutabilities. This proves to be a result that generalizes to the case in which the number of factors exceeds the number of commodities by only one (Jones, 1985a). Formal solutions for factor price changes include characteristics of the degree to which factors are substitutable for each other since there are more factors than commodities. But their purpose is only to determine the size, not the direction, of factor movements. The key lies in the subset of competitive profit conditions, of the kind illustrated for the 2×2 case in equations (1.7) and (1.8). There are n of these in the general $(n + 1) \times n$ case, and they are completely free of substitutability characteristics because cost minimization sends the weighted average of changes in input-output coefficients in any industry to zero. In the more general case in which the number of factors exceeds the number of commodities by more than one, the sign of factor price changes subsequent to an endowment change depends both upon factor intensities and substitutabilities, but the competitive profit equations of change, involving only the intensity terms (through the distributive shares), still have an independent role to play. For example, suppose the price of a single commodity, j, increases. Take any two other industries, say i and m, and number the factors in descending order of the ratios of their factor intensities. Then it cannot be the case that every factor reward on one side of the ordering rises while all others fall (Jones, 1985a).

The importance of factor intensities in the multi-factor, multi-commodity case is especially revealing in the event that the number of factors exactly equals the number of produced commodities, and all activities are linearly independent. In such an event an alteration in commodity prices (not large enough to change the production pattern) results in a unique response of factor prices, independent of any (small) changes in factor endowments. And this response depends *only* upon factor-intensity rankings. Although the existence of open trading markets does not guarantee such a balance in numbers, it is generally true that a country need not produce more commodities than it has factors of production. In any event, this "even" case has attracted much attention in the literature. Are there restrictions on the array of factor intensities strong enough to ensure that the Stolper–Samuelson theorem survives? Strong skepticism was frequently expressed in earlier years, and of course much depends upon the particular way in which the theorem is expressed for higher-dimensional cases. The *strong* form of the theorem states that an increase in any commodity price is associated with a greater relative increase in the return to some factor "intensively" used in that sector and a fall in every other factor return. Kemp and Wegge (1969) provided what sounded like a quite restrictive condition on factor intensities to investigate this strong form of the theorem. They assumed that for any pair of distinct factors, s and r, and distinct industries, s and t, the distributive share matrix satisfies the condition:

$$\theta_{ss}/\theta_{rs} > \theta_{st}/\theta_{rt} \tag{1.23}$$

That is, each factor is paired with a particular industry such that its factor share there relative to any other factor's share in that industry exceeds the ratio of those two factor shares in any other industry. Kemp and Wegge proved that this condition was sufficient to establish the strong form of the Stolper–Samuelson theorem when there are three factors and three commodities, but supplied a counter-example for the 4×4 case. Although generally condition (1.23) is not sufficient, they did prove that it was necessary. Chipman (1969) examined the *weak* form of the Stolper–Samuelson theorem, stating that an increase in any commodity price would increase the real return to the associated intensive factor, although some other factor returns might rise as well. His restriction on intensities was weaker than in (1.23), requiring only that every θ_{ss} exceed the share of factor s in all other industries. This proves to be sufficient for the weak form in the 3×3 case, but not in higher dimensions.

Since that time stronger criteria for factor-intensity rankings were supplied for each version of the theorem – Jones, Marjit and Mitra (1993) for the strong version and Jones and Mitra (1999) for the weak version. In the strong version, for example, the extra conditions require that factor intensities (or ratios) for the unintensive factors used in an industry do not vary much from sector to sector. After all, the strong form requires all factors save one to lose when a price rises; this will follow if the ratio of the factor shares for the losers does not vary a great deal from industry to industry.

Even though sufficient conditions can thus be stated to prove strong or weak forms of the Stolper–Samuelson theorem (and, by reciprocity, the Rybczynski theorem) in the higher dimensional $n \times n$ case, the severity of these conditions might suggest that these propositions are best reserved for smaller-dimensional models. This would, in my view, represent a mistake because the essence of the Stolper–Samuelson theorem is that *any* factor of production can have its *real* return enhanced by the indirect means of altering some commodity prices (it may take more than one). All it takes to prove this is that there is no joint production (or not too much) and that there are at least as many commodities as factors of production (Jones, 1985b).

It is possible to give a factor-intensity ranking for an economy with any number of factors and any number of industries, making use of the factor-allocation λ-fractions and the distributive share θ-fractions so useful in the core 2×2 setting. First, we note that the share of any industry (j) in the national income, θ_j, is a weighted average of the allocation fractions used in that industry, with the weights provided by the share of each factor (i) in the national income, θ^i. Thus:

$$\sum_i \theta^i \lambda_{ij} = \theta_j \tag{1.24}$$

This implies that the weighted average of the (λ_{ij}/θ_j) is unity across factors. If one of these terms exceeds unity, we define industry j as being intensive in its use of factor i. This is an intensity comparison not between industry j's use of factor i with that of some other industry, but instead a comparison with the economy as a whole. Also, industry j can be considered to be intensive in its use of the ith factor compared with its use of the kth factor if (as in the 2×2 case) λ_{ij} exceeds λ_{kj}. A similar set of remarks applies to the θ-matrix of distributive factor shares. Thus a weighted average over industries of the share of the ith factor (with weights provided by industry shares of the national income) yields the share of the ith factor in the national income:

$$\sum_j \theta_j \theta_{ij} = \theta^i \tag{1.25}$$

Once again, this can be re-interpreted, in this case to state that the weighted average of the (θ_{ij}/θ^i) terms is unity across industries. Now recall equation (1.16). There are two equivalent ways to compare the intensity of industry j's use of factor i with the national average – the fraction of factor i allocated to the jth sector with the importance of the jth sector in the national income, on the one hand, and the distributive share of factor i in industry j compared with factor i's share of the national income on the other. For many purposes it is the bilateral comparison of the factor intensity in an industry with the national average that is required, and equation (1.16) indicates the two alternative routes that can be taken.[4]

This section concludes by pointing out two potential pit-falls in the use of factor intensities. The first refers to the example of distributive shares in the 3×2 case presented in Jones (1977): The three factors are labor (L), capital (K), and land (T), and the shares in each industry are: ($\theta_{L1}, \theta_{K1}, \theta_{T1}$) = (0.2, 0.1, 0.7) for the first industry and ($\theta_{L2}, \theta_{K2}, \theta_{T2}$) = (0.5, 0.3, 0.2) for the second industry. Since θ_{L1}/θ_{K1} does indeed exceed θ_{L2}/θ_{K2}, industry 1 employs a higher labor/capital ratio than industry 2. But suppose the wage rate rises by 10 percent and the rental on capital falls by 10 percent (with land rentals held constant). What happens to the ratio of costs in the two industries? In the first industry costs have risen by 1 percent while in the second industry costs have risen by double this amount, 2 percent. The direct difference between factor shares yields better information than does the ratio.

The second example is found in Minabe (1967), who cites the following distributive share θ-matrix and its inverse:

$$\begin{bmatrix} 10/26 & 8/26 & 8/26 \\ 8/20 & 10/20 & 2/20 \\ 8/20 & 2/20 & 10/20 \end{bmatrix}^{-1} = \begin{bmatrix} -39 & 20 & 20 \\ 26 & -90/8 & -110/8 \\ 26 & -110/8 & -90/8 \end{bmatrix}$$

Each diagonal entry is the largest in its row. However, the inverse of this share matrix has a strictly negative diagonal. That is, the increase of any commodity price causes the factor most intensively used there to suffer a fall in its reward. As discussed earlier, even stricter conditions are required to satisfy the Stolper–Samuelson theorem.

4   FURTHER REMARKS

Differences in the input composition with which commodities are produced have played a key role in the development of international trade theory. In more formal treatments, even of the core 2×2 version, a distinction is often made only of "commodity 1 vs. commodity 2". However, this framework has also been used to distinguish between two *classes* of commodities. Indeed, in the earlier contributions to growth theory (with some applications to trade theory), much attention was paid to the capital/labor-intensity ranking between consumption goods and capital goods. The specter of instability or lack of convergence to a long-run growth path was raised in the case in which capital goods were produced by capital-intensive techniques. If commodity prices did not adjust, the Rybczynski result from trade theory suggested that if capital were to grow more rapidly than labor, there would be magnified expansions of the capital goods produced, so that the gap between the capital stock and labor force would grow ever wider.

In trade theory a distinction is often made between those commodities that are traded *vs.* commodities that are not traded. A somewhat similar distinction can be made on the input side, between the class of inputs or productive factors that have international markets and those (such as labor) that have purely national markets. In the *middle products* approach of Sanyal and Jones (1982) this was a sharp distinction; all goods that were traded required a further input of local labor before appearing as final consumption goods. In this framework there is a natural tendency for non-tradeables (consumer goods) to be labor intensive compared to tradeables, since they add labor to tradeables. This invites the comparison with Wicksell's example wherein the final consumer good (wine) was naturally capital intensive because it added time to the capital stock (bottles in storage to be aged).

The entire literature that we have alluded to so far has typically been characterized by the assumption that markets are purely competitive. How does the concept of factor intensity fare when subjected to the kind of criticism emanating from "new trade theory" that markets are not perfectly competitive? After all, this has as a consequence that often commodity prices are no longer tied closely to costs – firms make profits. Therefore a detailed analysis of the composition of unit costs ceases to be that important.

Two comments on such a charge come to mind. First is the role of "shock absorber" played by profits over the course of the business cycle. In good times profits expand, thus moderating the increase in costs. In bad times profits contract or become losses, thus again serving to moderate downward pressure on unit costs. Thus compared with perfect competition, the induced effect on factor returns brought about by changes in commodity prices may be dampened if markets are imperfectly competitive. Second, consider the problem facing a multinational firm engaged in worldwide competition, albeit of an imperfectly competitive nature, when it has to decide on the country location of its productive activities. Even if such a firm makes profits, it is the cost comparisons between countries for various activities that become crucial, and with it a concern about differences in factor intensities between commodities and factor prices between countries.

Worth emphasizing as well is the treatment of factor intensities accorded by the early literature on monopolistic competition with increasing returns. Products were differentiated in the minds of consumers, but not in terms of production structures. Thus the factor intensity used in any (horizontally differentiated) variety was the same as in any other. Given this kind of assumption, it was difficult (of course) to link trade patterns for differentiated products to differences in factor endowments. Assuming that products were differentiated by quality instead opens up the possibility that higher quality varieties are produced by more capital-intensive techniques (Falvey and Kierzkowski, 1987), so that trade patterns can once again be linked to factor endowments.

Traditional trade theory has often focused on the impact of changes in commodity prices on the distribution of income. In technical terms this implies all the difficulties involved in finding regular patterns in the inverse of the matrix of input-output coefficients (assuming enough commodities are produced so that such a matrix is invertible). But such a process is not required in order to proceed from differences in wages and other factor prices to the consequences for unit costs. No matter how many commodities or factors are involved, a knowledge of distributive factor shares and factor allocation fractions yields information about the contribution of differences in factor prices to the array of costs of production. This highlights the importance of the concept of factor intensities to both "old" and "new" theories of international trade.

Notes

An earlier version of this chapter was published in *Review of International Economics* (2002).
1   The separate a_{ij} coefficients are solved from a pair of equations of change for each industry: Minimum costs entail $\Sigma_i \theta_{ij} \hat{a}_{ij} = 0$ and the definition of the elasticity of substitution

states that $\sigma_j \equiv (\hat{a}_{Kj} - \hat{a}_{Lj})/(\hat{w} - \hat{r})$. This yields the solutions: $\hat{a}_{Lj} = -\theta_{Kj}\sigma_j(\hat{w} - \hat{r})$ and $\hat{a}_{Kj} = \theta_{Lj}\sigma_j(\hat{w} - \hat{r})$ (see Jones, 1965).

2   For a disagreement on this statement see Samuelson (1992) and Jones (1992).

3   A more complete description of this kind of result, in which endowment changes lead to movements of skilled and unskilled wage rates in the same direction, is found in Jones and Marjit (2001).

4   Several results for general cases are available in the literature. Thus Ethier (1982) established a correlation result between the product of changes in factor prices and the technology matrix, on the one hand, and changes in commodity prices on the other. Dixit and Norman (1980) took a duality approach and suggested the second derivative of the revenue function (with respect to the price of commodity j and the endowment of factor i) as a more general definition of factor intensity. In cases of more factors than goods this mixes up intensity features with factor substitution elasticities. Neary (1985) introduced "as-if" input-output coefficients, but they may take on negative values in large-scale models that are aggregated.

References

Chang, Winston, Wilfred Ethier, and Murray Kemp 1980: The theorems of international trade with joint production. *Journal of International Economics*, 10, 377–94.

Chipman, John 1969: Factor price equalization and the Stolper–Samuelson theorem. *International Economic Review*, 10, 399–406.

Collins, Susan (ed.) 1998: *Imports, Exports and the American Worker*. Washington, DC: Brookings.

Dixit, Avinash and Victor Norman 1980: *Theory of International Trade*. Cambridge: Cambridge University Press.

Ethier, Wilfred 1974: Some of the theorems of international trade with many goods and factors. *Journal of International Economics*, 4, 199–206.

Ethier, Wilfred 1982: The general role of factor intensity in the theorems of international trade. *Economics Letters*, 10, 337–42.

Falvey, Rodney and Henryk Kierzkowski 1987: Product quality, intra-industry trade and (im)perfect competition. In H. Kierzkowski (ed.), *Protection and Competition in International Trade*, Oxford: Blackwell, 143–61.

Findlay, Ronald and Ronald Jones 2000: Factor bias and technical progress. *Economics Letters*, 68, 303–8.

Findlay, Ronald and Ronald Jones 2001: Economic development from an open economy perspective. In D. Lal and R. Snape (eds.), *Trade, Development and Political Economy*, New York: Palgrave, 159–73.

Harberger, Arnold C. 1962: The incidence of the corporation income tax. *Journal of Political Economy*, 70, 215–40.

Harrod, Roy F. 1958: Factor price relations under free trade. *Economic Journal*, 68, 245–55.

Heckscher, Eli 1919: The effect of foreign trade on the distribution of income. *Ekonomisk Tidskrift*, 497–512.

Johnson, Harry G. 1957: Factor endowments, international trade, and factor prices. *Manchester School of Economic and Social Studies*, 25, 270–83.

Johnson, Harry G. and Peter Mieszkowski 1970: The effects of unionization on the distribution of income: A general equilibrium approach. *Quarterly Journal of Economics*, 84, 539–61.

Jones, Ronald W. 1956: Factor proportions and the Heckscher–Ohlin theorem. *Review of Economic Studies*, 24, 1–10.

Jones, Ronald W. 1965: The structure of simple general equilibrium models. *Journal of Political Economy*, 73, 557–72.

Jones, Ronald W. 1971a: Distortions in factor markets and the general equilibrium model of production. *Journal of Political Economy*, 79, 437–59.

Jones, Ronald W. 1971b: A three-factor model in theory, trade and history. In J. Bhagwati, R. Jones, R. Mundell, and J. Vanek (eds.), *Trade, Balance of Payments and Growth*, Amsterdam: North-Holland.

Jones, Ronald W. 1977: Two-ness in trade theory: costs and benefits. *Special Papers in International Economics*, no. 12, Princeton University.

Jones, Ronald W. 1985a: A theorem on income distribution in a small, open economy. *Journal of International Economics*, 18, 171–6.

Jones, Ronald W. 1985b: Relative prices and real factor rewards: A re-interpretation. *Economics Letters*, 19, 47–9.

Jones, Ronald W. 1992: Jointness in production and factor-price equalization. *Review of International Economics*, 1, 10–18.

Jones, Ronald W. 2000: *Globalization and the Theory of Input Trade*, Cambridge, MA: MIT Press.

Jones, Ronald W. and Fumio Dei 1983: International trade and foreign investment: A simple model. *Economic Inquiry*, 21, 449–64.

Jones, Ronald W. and Stephen Easton 1983: Factor intensities and factor substitution in general equilibrium. *Journal of International Economics*, 15, 65–99.

Jones, Ronald W. and Henryk Kierzkowski 1997: Neighborhood production structures with an application to the theory of international trade. *Oxford Economic Papers*, 38, 59–76.

Jones, Ronald W. and Henryk Kierzkowski 2001: A framework for fragmentation. In S. Arndt and H. Kierzkowski (eds.), *Fragmentation: New Production Patterns in the World Economy*, Oxford: Oxford University Press, 17–34.

Jones, Ronald W. and Sugata Marjit 2001: Economic development, trade and wages. Unpublished manuscript.

Jones, Ronald W. and Tapan Mitra 1999: Factor shares and the Chipman condition. In J. Melvin, J. Moore, and R. Riezman (eds.), *Trade, Welfare and Econometrics: Essays in Honor of John S. Chipman*, London: Routledge.

Jones, Ronald W. and J. Peter Neary 1979: Temporal convergence and factor intensities. *Economics Letters*, 3, 311–14.

Jones, Ronald W., Hamid Beladi, and Sugata Marjit 1999: The three faces of factor intensities. *Journal of International Economics*, 48, 413–20.

Jones, Ronald W., Sugata Marjit, and Tapan Mitra 1993: The Stolper–Samuelson theorem: Links to dominant diagonals. In R. Becker, M. Boldrin, R. Jones, and W. Thomson (eds.), *General Equilibrium, Growth, and Trade II: The Legacy of Lionel McKenzie*, San Diego: Academic Press, 429–41.

Kemp, Murray C. and Leon Wegge 1969: On the relation between commodity prices and factor rewards. *International Economic Review*, 10, 407–13.

Leontief, Wassily 1953: Domestic production and foreign trade: The American capital position re-examined. *Proceedings of the American Philosophical Society*, 97, 332–49.

Minabe, Nobuo 1967: The Stolper–Samuelson theorem, the Rybczynski effect, and the Heckscher–Ohlin theory of trade pattern and factor price equalization: The case of the many-commodity, many-factor country. *The Canadian Journal of Economics and Political Science*, 33, 401–19.

Neary, J. Peter 1978: Dynamic stability and the theory of factor-market distortions. *American Economic Review*, 68, 671–82.

Neary, J. Peter 1985: Two-by-two international trade theory with many goods and factors. *Econometrica*, 53, 1233–47.

Ruffin, Roy 1981: Trade and factor movements with three factors and two goods. *Economics Letters*, 7, 177–82.

Rybczynski, T. M. 1955: Factor endowments and relative commodity prices. *Economica*, 22, 336–41.

Samuelson, Paul A. 1948: International trade and the equalisation of factor prices. *Economic Journal*, 58, 163–84.

Samuelson, Paul A. 1949: International factor-price equalisation once again. *Economic Journal*, 59, 181–97.

Samuelson, Paul A. 1992: Factor-price equalization by trade in joint and non-joint production. *Review of International Economics*, 1, 10–18.

Sanyal, Kalyan and Ronald W. Jones 1982: The theory of trade in middle products. *American Economic Review*, 72, 16–31.

Stolper, Wolfgang and Paul A. Samuelson 1941: Protection and real wages. *Review of Economic Studies*, 9, 58–73.

Thompson, Henry 1987: A review of advancements in the general equilibrium theory of production and trade. *Keio Economic Studies*, 24, 43–62.

2

Implications of Many Industries in the Heckscher–Ohlin Model

E. Kwan Choi

CHAPTER OUTLINE

This chapter examines the implications of many industries on the Heckscher–Ohlin (HO) model. Available empirical studies suggest that output prices are interdependent. When output prices are interdependent, the HO theorem obtained in the 2 × 2 case generally does not hold in the multi-commodity world. It is shown that mean Stolper–Samuelson elasticities as well as the mean Rybczynski effects would become negligible as the number of industries increases. Due to output indeterminacy, exports of a capital-abundant country need not be more capital intensive than imports. Leontief's two empirical studies on US trade patterns were invalid tests of the HO predictions that were derived from the 2 × 2 model. Thus, the so-called Leontief paradox may be commonly observed. The main results of the 2 × 2 HO model are peculiarities that have little relevance to the real world with many industries.

There is not much virtue in simplicity if a result that holds in a model of two countries, two commodities, and two factors does not generalize in any meaningful way to higher dimensions.

John Chipman (1987, p. 922)

1   INTRODUCTION

The two-factor, two-commodity Heckscher–Ohlin (HO) model contains four elegant propositions that have charmed many trade theorists. For instance, if the United States were a capital-abundant country, the HO theory predicts that it would export capital-intensive goods. Wassily W. Leontief (1953) conducted the first empirical test of the theory, using 1947 US trade data. Contrary to his expectation, however, Leontief discovered that US import-competing industries used 30 percent more capital per worker than export industries. This finding has come to be known as the Leontief paradox.

In all subsequent empirical studies, the number of industries has been much greater than the number of factors. For instance, Leontief's (1956) second test included 192 industries. Similarly, in Stern and Maskus (1981) and Trefler (1993), the number of industries was much greater than that of factors. Chipman (1987) noted that the elegance of a simple 2×2 HO model would lose much of its appeal if the results were not robust in the multi-commodity world.

The purpose of this chapter is to examine the implications of many industries on various propositions of the HO model. It is shown that once we depart from the simple 2×2 world, the extended HO model cannot predict the trade pattern using notions of factor abundance and intensities. Herman-Pillath (2000) expresses much of the frustration stemming from the indeterminacy of trade patterns. In the present chapter it is argued that the $n \times 2$ model does *not* predict that exports of a capital-abundant country will be capital intensive. The impacts of output prices on factor prices and the mean Rybczynski effects are shown to be negligible when there are many industries. Leontief's approach was not valid, because he expected the prediction of a 2×2 model to be borne out in his two empirical studies that included more than two industries.[1] Insofar as the number of goods is much greater than that of factors, the so-called Leontief paradox might be commonly observed.

2   INTERDEPENDENCE OF OUTPUT PRICES

At the outset it is important to note that while Leontief had intended to test the 2×2 HO model, in his first test he actually built a 38×2 model of US trade in 1947. Two stylized facts have emerged from this and other subsequent empirical studies on trade:

1   The number of outputs, n, is much greater than that of factors, m, used to produce the outputs.
2   Typically, a trading country produces k goods, $m < k < n$, and the k/m ratio is closer to n/m than to unity.

These stylized facts suggest that some of the essential results of the 2×2 HO theory may not hold in a higher-dimensional world or that the 2×2 model is insufficient to deal with empirical regularities in the data. The relationship between inputs and outputs is summarized by:

$$\mathbf{AY} = \mathbf{V} \tag{2.1}$$

where $\mathbf{A} = [a_{ij}]$ is an $m \times n$ matrix, $\mathbf{Y}$ is an $n \times 1$ output vector, and $\mathbf{V}$ an $m \times 1$ input vector. The trade vector is:

$$\mathbf{X} = \mathbf{Y} - \mathbf{C} \tag{2.2}$$

where $\mathbf{C}$ is an $n \times 1$ consumption vector and $\mathbf{X}$ an $n \times 1$ trade vector. The element x_j is positive (negative) if product j is exported (imported). Given the usual assumption of homothetic preferences, the consumption vector can be written as $\mathbf{C} = c\mathbf{I}$ where c is an $n \times 1$ vector of the average propensities to consume, and I is consumer income. Thus, the trade vector is:

$$\mathbf{X} = \mathbf{Y} - c\mathbf{I}$$

In order to predict which product a country will export, it is essential to know the output vector $\mathbf{Y}$. In the 2×2 case ($n = m = 2$), the system of equations in (2.1) has a unique solution, provided that $\mathbf{A}$ is nonsingular, i.e., its inverse exists. Hence, a given factor endowment uniquely determines the output vector, which then can be used, together with the consumption vector $c\mathbf{I}$, to determine the country's trade vector.

Consider the smallest uneven case, a 3×2 model, which is slightly more general than the 2×2 HO model, but is qualitatively similar to Leontief's first empirical 38×2 model. Predicting the output vector $\mathbf{Y}$ amounts to solving for three unknowns with two equations, one for each factor. Obviously, the output vector $\mathbf{Y}$ is not unique. Infinitely many different output vectors are consistent with a given factor endowment. In the 3×2 case, the output vector $\mathbf{Y}$ has one degree of freedom. If one output is fixed by government decree or if there is a constraint in the relationship between outputs, the output vector can be uniquely determined. As Leamer (1984, 1987) observed, in general the output vector will have $(n - m)$ degrees of freedom.[2]

Inputs may be classified into many different categories just as outputs are differentiated. For example, Trefler (1995) used nine categories of labor inputs. Depending on the type and length of education, workers and wages may be further differentiated. It may be argued that when the quality of labor is enhanced by education, the original unskilled labor is transformed into an intermediate input that embodies some human capital. The primary input, unskilled labor, remains the same. Thus, the number of primary inputs is still limited, relative to the ever-increasing variety of outputs produced.

In his first test of the HO theory using 1947 US trade data, Leontief (1953) included 50 sectors, and only 38 industries produced traded goods. Since Leontief assumed only two factors, capital and labor, the n/m ratio in the first test was 19. Using the US trade pattern in 1951, Leontief (1956) conducted a second test, in which he divided the US economy into 192 sectors. Since capital and labor were the only primary factors, the n/m ratio was 96 in that study.

Stern and Maskus (1981) constructed another HO model with three inputs (physical capital, human capital, and labor) for the period 1958 to 1976. They classified industries into three categories: the Ricardian goods, the HO goods, and the Product Cycle goods. Intuitively, in the production of Ricardian goods, natural resource components (e.g., weather, mineral deposits) are important. The HO goods are characterized by the use of standardized technology, whereas the Product Cycle goods are produced by constant product innovation. When they focused narrowly on the HO goods, the number of HO industries varied over the years, exceeding 120 industries during most of the period. Thus, in the Stern and Maskus study, the n/m ratio was about 40.

In a more recent study, Trefler (1993) converted trade data from the four-digit Standard Industrial Trade Classification (SITC) into 79 sectors and investigated trade flows of ten factors, including capital, cropland, pasture, and seven categories of labor. In this case, the n/m was close to eight. These empirical studies of US trade patterns indicate that the n/m ratio was much greater than one and exceeded ten in most instances.

We now consider the implications of a large n/m ratio on four components of the HO model: the Rybczynski theorem, the factor price equalization (FPE) result, the Heckscher–Ohlin theorem, and the Stolper–Samuelson theorem.

2.1 Long-run Indeterminacy of the Output Vector

The system of equations in (2.1) has $(n - m)$ degrees of freedom and for all practical purposes, a country's output vector is indeterminate. If the purpose of a model was to predict whether a sector will export its output, one would be disappointed because of output indeterminacy. Given the assumption of identical technologies, any industry can be induced to export its product. If an industry produces enough to export, then other industries must adjust their outputs accordingly. In fact, $(n - m)$ industries can choose their output levels arbitrarily. Then the outputs of the remaining m industries can be determined uniquely. However, it is not easy to predict how much an industry will actually produce and export because of the high degree of freedom that exists.[3]

Leamer (1987) offered one way to resolve this production indeterminacy. His model does not impose any constraints or relationships among commodity prices. Ethier (1984, p. 143) suggested that commodity prices are not drawn from an urn but are interconnected. However, for the sake of resolving this indeterminacy, first consider Leamer's approach and assume that commodity prices are arbitrarily chosen.

Since all industries are competitive, profit-maximizing efforts of competitive firms collectively maximize national income, $\mathbf{Py}$, subject to the resource constraints. Constant returns to scale imply that unit costs are independent of outputs, although the input-output coefficients are still functions of factor prices. The problem then is to choose the output vector $\mathbf{y}$ to maximize $I = \mathbf{Py}$ subject to: $\mathbf{Ay} = \mathbf{V}$, where $\mathbf{P}$ and $\mathbf{y}$

are $n \times 1$ vectors of exogenous prices and outputs, and $\mathbf{V}$ is an $m \times 1$ vector of fixed factor endowments.

The Lagrangian function associated with this problem is:

$$\mathcal{L} = \mathbf{Py} + \mathbf{W}(\mathbf{V} - \mathbf{Ay}) \tag{2.3}$$

where $\mathbf{W}$ is an $m \times 1$ vector of Lagrange multipliers, reflecting the shadow prices of the internationally immobile inputs. The solution to the problem yields optimal levels of output y and shadow prices $\mathbf{W}$. Specifically, Leamer (1987) shows that given an arbitrary price vector $\mathbf{P}$, optimal outputs are positive only for m industries and the outputs of the remaining sectors equal zero. However, in most empirical studies, the k/m ratio has been closer to n/m than to unity. For instance, in Leontief's first test, 35 industries were net exporters and three were net importers. This suggests that output prices are interlinked, as Ethier had suggested, and commodity prices move together, at least among the goods that are actually produced.

3   DIFFICULTY OF PREDICTING THE HECKSCHER–OHLIN TRADE PATTERN

In its simplest form, the Heckscher–Ohlin theorem states that in the 2×2 case, each country exports the commodity which intensively uses its abundant factor. Here are two notions that beg to be defined in the multi-commodity world: factor abundance and factor intensity. It is not difficult to generalize the abundance concept to a higher dimension. In the two-factor case, a country is abundant in capital if $K/L > K^*/L^*$. Let $I = wL + rK$ and $I^* = wL^* + rK^*$ denote home and foreign incomes, respectively, and let $\alpha = I/(I + I^*)$ denote the income share of the home country. Then a country may be said to be abundant in capital if:

$$\frac{K}{K + K^*} > \alpha, \tag{2.4}$$

which holds if and only if $K/L > K^*/L^*$. The abundance definition in (2.4) can be applied to any other factor, regardless of the number of factors or countries. For instance, a country is abundant in capital if its capital endowment share is greater than the consumption or income share, i.e., $K/K^w > \alpha$, where K^w is the world endowment of capital. With this definition, it is not possible for a country to be abundant or poor in all factors.

In the multi-commodity world there are at least two reasons why factor intensity definitions – however cleverly designed – cannot be used to predict with certainty which product will be exported. First, in the real world where $n > m$, the output vector is indeterminate and hence the trade vector cannot be predicted. Specifically, Leamer has shown that if output prices are independent of one another, only m goods will be produced. The contrapositive of Leamer's result is that *if more than m goods are actually produced, then output prices must be dependent on each other.*

Second, even when only m goods are produced, it is not clear how to predict which outputs will be exported using factor intensity definitions – unless the inverse of the input–output matrix is utilized. Also, the notion of factor intensity becomes ambiguous because the choice of numéraire is arbitrary. For instance, if N is a third factor representing natural resources, then $K_1/L_1 > K_2/L_2$ and $K_1/N_1 < K_2/N_2$ can hold simultaneously. Factor intensities can be defined between any pair of industries, and the number of pairwise comparisons increases much more rapidly than the number of goods. Such intensity definitions are of little use if they cannot be used to predict trade patterns. Alternative definitions of factor intensities may be devised and interpreted (Thompson, 1999), but none have been utilized to predict the trade pattern of a country as clearly as in the 2×2 case.

Theorists have focused on the even case ($n = m$), where the number of goods is equal to the number of factors. Suppose only m goods are produced. For those goods, the relationship between input and output vectors is written as $\mathbf{Ay} = \mathbf{V}$. If $\mathbf{A}$ is nonsingular, the output vector is written:

$$\mathbf{y} = \mathbf{A}^{-1}\mathbf{V} = \mathbf{BV} \tag{2.5}$$

where $\mathbf{B} = \mathbf{A}^{-1}$. The trade vector is simply $\mathbf{X} = \mathbf{A}^{-1}\mathbf{V} - \mathbf{C}$ and it can be predicted from the country's factor endowment vector $\mathbf{V}$. Obviously, in the 2×2 case, the effect of a change in factor endowment on the output vector can be predicted (the Rybczynski theorem) by linking outputs and factor intensities. However, no such intuitive predictions are possible for $m > 2$.[4]

Consider the output vector in (1.5). For instance, the output of industry 1 is written: $y_1 = \mathbf{b}_{1L}L + \mathbf{b}_{1K}K + \mathbf{b}_{1M}M + \mathbf{b}_{1N}N + \ldots$. Similarly, $y_2 = \mathbf{b}_{2L}L + \mathbf{b}_{2K}K + \mathbf{b}_{2M}M + \mathbf{b}_{2N}N + \ldots$, and so on. Let y^0 be the hypothetical output vector when the home country has an equal share α of the world endowment of each factor. For example, if a country has a 10 percent share of each factor, it would be in autarky. Now let the labor endowment increase above α so that the home country is abundant only in labor. Thus, from the initial situation y^0, only dL is positive and $dK = dM = dN = \ldots = 0$. In this case:

$$dy_1 = \mathbf{b}_{1L}dL,$$
$$dy_2 = \mathbf{b}_{2L}dL,$$
$$dy_3 = \mathbf{b}_{3L}dL,$$
$$dy_4 = \mathbf{b}_{4L}dL,$$

The Rybczynski result for a change in a factor endowment requires obtaining m cofactors as well as the determinant of the input-output matrix $\mathbf{A}$. In the 2×2 case, the sign of the determinant means a pairwise ranking of factor intensities of the two sectors. However, in the $m \times m$ case, pairwise rankings of m factor intensities cannot determine the sign of the determinant of the input-output matrix, nor the signs of any cofactors. In short, as the number of commodities increases beyond two, pairwise rankings of factor intensities cannot determine the signs of elements of $\mathbf{A}^{-1}$. This is one reason why the HO theorem cannot be generalized even to the $m \times m$ world using the standard factor intensity definitions.

3.1 How Outputs are Determined in the Short Run

If n exceeds m, the problem is more complicated. The HO model is based on the assumption that all product and factor markets are perfectly competitive. If all prices are equal to unit costs, the output vector will be indeterminate when there are more traded goods than factors. How then are the actual outputs determined in practice? Since the long-run output and factor employment in each sector are indeterminate, it is important to explain how the actual outputs might be determined.

It is useful to think of the HO model with two time frames. In the long run, all primary inputs are variables. In the short run, the actual output of a firm in a given industry is determined by the existing capital stock. If the output price deviates from its unit cost, firms can vary the quantities of the variable inputs in the short run. However, if all output prices are jointly determined and equal to unit production costs, then in the long run competitive firms in each industry earn zero profits, and no firms have any incentive either to enter or exit the market. This is consistent with the finding that the optimal size or output of a competitive firm is indeterminate when the production function is linearly homogeneous.

Instead of Leamer's problem, we now consider a short-run maximization problem. Since it is straightforward to generalize to the $n \times m$ case, it is sufficient to illustrate how the smallest of general uneven models, the 3×2 case, works. In the short run, capital input is fixed in each industry and the problem is to choose inputs, L_i, to maximize national income, subject to the variable input constraints. Thus, the short-run model becomes a specific factors model. Let $F^i(\bullet)$ denote the production function of good i. The Lagrangian function associated with this problem is:[5]

$$\mathcal{L} = p_1 F^1(L_1, K_1) + p_2 F^2(L_2, K_2) + p_3 F^3(L_3, K_3) + w[L - L_1 - L_2 - L_3]. \quad (2.6)$$

The first order conditions are:

$$p_i F^i_{Li}(L_i, K_i) - w = 0, \quad i = 1, 2, 3$$

The value of the marginal product of labor, $p_i F^i_{Li}$, can be added horizontally. The shadow price w is determined by the intersection of the aggregate value of the marginal product of labor and the vertical labor supply curve.[6] Once the shadow price is obtained, it can be treated as the wage by competitive firms or industries. Since capital inputs are fixed in the short run, labor demand functions are written as $L_i(K_i, p_i, w)$. The short-run supply function of good i is written as

$$y_i(K_i, p_i, w) = F^i[L_i(K_i, p_i, w), K_i].$$

However, long-run industry output is indeterminate and the long-run supply curve is horizontal,[7]

$$p_i = g_i(w, r) = a_{Li}(w, r)w + a_{Ki}(w, r)r.$$

Given an arbitrary capital allocation, $\underline{K} = (K_1, K_2, \ldots, K_n)$, there exists a unique solution to equation (2.6). Producers earn zero profits if prices are equal to unit production costs. Thus, in each industry, competitive firms have no incentive either to enter or exit the market. However, this does not mean that the output vector is unique in the long run. Another capital allocation $\underline{K}'$ will yield a different output vector, which also will be consistent with the given output prices.

4   THE MEAN STOLPER–SAMUELSON EFFECTS

In the 2×2 case, the Stolper–Samuelson theorem states that an increase in the price of a good increases the return to the factor used intensively in that industry and reduces the return to the other factor. Moreover, since the latter declines, the return to the intensive factor increases more than proportionately, a magnification effect. However, the amplified change in the return to the intensive factor may be a *peculiarity* that occurs in the even case where factor prices are determined uniquely.[8]

Leamer (1987) considered the $n \times 3$ case in which profit maximization results in the production of only three goods. In this case, the Stolper–Samuelson result may be obtained from a relevant 3×3 submatrix of **A**. If an increase in one price were to alter factor prices, realignment of most other output prices will necessarily follow. If this realignment of output prices is *precluded* artificially, the initial price change may be accompanied by quantity responses in many industries and the survival of only m industries, as indicated by Leamer's result. However, there is no a priori method to predict how output prices will be realigned.

We now argue that when n is large, a change in the price of one good has negligible effects on factor prices on average, i.e., factor prices are insensitive to a change in output price. This is not to deny the existence of a magnification effect. However, we show that the link between an output price and a factor price that exhibits the magnification effect is loose when n is much larger than m. The larger the number of industries, the smaller the impact of a change in a single output price on factor prices. This result holds in even models as well.

Even when output prices are interdependent, a tariff can be imposed arbitrarily on any imports. Will a change in the tariff on a product affect the returns to the primary factors? To examine its Stolper–Samuelson effect, first consider how factor prices are determined when n is large and there are two factors, K and L. An alternative formulation of Leamer's problem is to choose L_j and K_j to maximize $\Sigma_j P_j F^j(L_j, K_j)$ subject to $\Sigma_j L_j = L, \Sigma_j K_j = K$.

The long-run Lagrangian function associated with this problem is:

$$\mathcal{L} = \sum_{j=1}^{n} p_j F^j(L_j, K_j) + w[L - \sum L_j] + r[K - \sum K_j], \tag{2.7}$$

where w and r are the shadow price of labor and capital, respectively. Since industry outputs are indeterminate, supply curves are horizontal at prices equal to unit costs. If commodity prices were arbitrarily chosen, only two goods would be produced. However, output prices are assumed to be linked together so that prices are equal to unit costs in all industries. The first order conditions are:

$$P_j \frac{\partial F^j}{\partial L_j} - w = 0, \quad \text{for } y_j > 0,$$

$$P_j \frac{\partial F^j}{\partial K_j} - r = 0, \quad \text{for } y_j > 0.$$

How does a change in p_j – if it can be changed alone, for instance by a tariff – affect the factor markets when n is large? In this case, each industry's contribution to national income is small, and it behaves like a competitive firm or a price taker in factor markets. Since its labor demand accounts for only a small fraction of the aggregate labor demand, an increase in p_j shifts the aggregate labor demand only slightly to the right, resulting in a negligible change in the wage.

Recall that in his second test Leontief examined US trade patterns in 192 industries. In this situation, the labor share of an average industry is 1/192. Suppose a typical industry's output doubles. At given factor prices, doubling of output results in doubling of input requirements. However, this rise in labor demand in one industry increases, for example, the aggregate demand for labor by only 0.5 percent. Thus, doubling of input demands in one sector will have a negligible effect on the aggregate demand for each immobile factor. Accordingly, factor prices may not change as dramatically as in the 2×2 case.

Perfect competition implies that output price must be equal to unit cost in any industry that produces some output,

$$\mathbf{P} = \mathbf{A}'\mathbf{W}, \tag{2.8}$$

where $\mathbf{P}$ is an $n \times 1$ vector of output prices and $\mathbf{W}$ is an $m \times 1$ vector of factor prices. If output prices are independent of one another, only m goods are produced. If the submatrix corresponding to the prices of goods that are actually produced is invertible, (2.8) shows that output prices can be derived from input prices and vice versa, and the Stolper–Samuelson theorem can be obtained. However, equation (2.8) does not say whether output prices or input prices are dependent variables; it only links input and output prices. Thus, the causal relationship between input and output prices must be explained by other means.

When n is much larger than m, each industry becomes a price taker in factor markets, and hence factor prices dictate output prices. Of course, output prices may deviate from their unit costs in the short run, depending on demand and supply conditions. Industries that do not earn zero profits will be eliminated sooner or later. Thus, they cannot deviate from the unit costs for long. Long-run output prices are hardly affected by the demand side; they are primarily determined by the supply side. Changes in world demand for goods are accompanied by quantity adjustments, rather than long-run price adjustments. In other words, input prices dictate the output price levels when n is much larger than m. For instance, Federal Reserve chairman Alan Greenspan lowered the interest rates several times within a one-year period in 2001, and this was not in response to a rise in tariffs or prices in certain industries. This idea represents an important departure from the so-called

Stolper–Samuelson theorem, which is based on the notion that output prices affect input prices.

When there are two inputs K and L, the ith row of the system of equations in (2.8) for product j can be written as

$$P_j = a_{Lj}w + a_{Kj}r, \, j = 1, \ldots, n.$$

Since n is large, each industry behaves as a price taker in the factor markets, and factor prices are determined by the intersection of (domestic) aggregate demands and supplies of the factors. Once these factor prices (r and w) are determined, output prices are completely determined by (2.8), and in the long run industries cannot deviate from these equilibrium prices.

Although he was not interested in trade issues *per se*, Alfred Marshall (1961 [1890], p. 620) noted the relationship between output and factor prices in competitive markets:

> In the first place the undertaker's profits bear the first brunt of any change in the price of those things which are the product of his capital (including his business organiza-tion), of his labour and of the labour of his employees; and as a result fluctuations of his profits generally precede fluctuations of their wages, and are much more extensive. For, other things being equal, a comparatively small rise in the price for which he can sell his product is not unlikely to increase his profit manifold, or perhaps to substitute a profit for a loss . . . He will therefore be more able and more willing to pay the high wages; and wages will tend upwards. But experience shows that (whether they are gov-erned by sliding scales or not) they seldom rise as much in proportion as prices; and therefore they do not rise nearly as much in proportion as profits.

Thus, the zero profit condition in (2.8) suggests that when the n/m ratio is large, input prices become insensitive to changes in output prices. Changes in output prices will have little effect on factor prices. Domestic supply conditions of the primary inputs (and aggregate factor demands) determine the factor prices, which in turn dictate the output prices for all surviving industries. Thus, output prices are not free to deviate from the unit costs in the long run. However, they can be affected by policy variables such as tariffs. A tariff may cause a realignment of domestic output prices. If the new domestic price of a good is below the world price, the industry will be an exporter. If it is above the world price and there is free trade the indus-try will become extinct. Thus, a tariff in one industry may be accompanied by simultaneous tariffs or export taxes in other industries when the world prices are fixed.

4.1 Magnification Effect in the Even Case

In the presence of m factors, m output prices may be fixed arbitrarily and m input prices are then uniquely determined. For all n goods to be produced at zero profits $(n - m)$ output prices must be dependent on the other m output prices. We now con-sider the average effect on wages when one of the m independent prices, say p_1 is arbitrarily changed from p_1^0 to p_1' by a tariff while the other $(m - 1)$ output prices are held constant. Then $(p_1', p_2, \ldots, p_n)$ completely determine factor prices $(w_1, \ldots, w_m)$. The remaining $(n - m)$ output prices will have to change accordingly in order to maintain zero profits, and hence they need not be considered explicitly. If their prices do not change accordingly, their industries will not survive.

For instance, if p_1 is raised,

$$\hat{p}_1 = \theta_{11}\hat{w}_1 + \theta_{21}\hat{w}_2 + \ldots + \theta_{m1}\hat{w}_m > 0, \tag{2.9}$$

where the hat denotes a percentage change, i.e., $\hat{x} = dx/x$. Since $\hat{p}_1$ is a convex combination of percentage changes in factor prices, we obtain

$$\min[\hat{w}_1, \hat{w}_2, \ldots, \hat{w}_m] < \hat{p}_1 < \max[\hat{w}_1, \hat{w}_2, \ldots, \hat{w}_m]. \tag{2.10}$$

The second inequality in (2.10) is the *magnification effect* in the even case. If the other $(m - 1)$ independent prices are held constant, then

$$\hat{p}_2 = \theta_{12}\hat{w}_1 + \theta_{22}\hat{w}_2 + \ldots + \theta_{m2}\hat{w}_m = 0,$$

$$\ldots$$

$$\hat{p}_m = \theta_{1m}\hat{w}_1 + \theta_{2m}\hat{w}_2 + \ldots + \theta_{mm}\hat{w}_m = 0.$$

Since $\hat{p}_1 > 0$ and is a weighted average of percentage changes in factor prices, at least one factor price must rise. Since the other output prices are held constant, there is no other disturbance in the price equations that would further alter factor prices. In the three goods case, the two convex combinations of the percentage changes in factor price changes for $\hat{p}_2$ and $\hat{p}_3$ must add up to zero. Among $\hat{w}$, $\hat{r}$, and $\hat{s}$, one is already known to be positive. It follows that at least one of the other two must be negative. That is, if $\hat{w}$ is positive, then either $\hat{r}$ or $\hat{s}$ is negative.

This result also holds when one price changes while $(m - 1)$ output prices are held constant. Such a price change causes a realignment of all m factor prices. To see this, differentiate the Lagrangian function in (2.7) with respect to L,

$$\frac{\partial \mathcal{L}}{\partial L} = w. \tag{2.11}$$

Differentiating (2.11) with respect to p_i, we obtain the Stolper–Samuelson result,

$$\frac{\partial^2 \mathcal{L}}{\partial L \partial p_i} = \frac{\partial w}{\partial p_i} = \frac{\partial y_i}{\partial L}, \tag{2.12}$$

which shows the short-run reciprocity relation between the Stolper–Samuelson result and the Rybczynski theorem. Let

$$\varepsilon_{wi} \equiv \frac{\partial w}{\partial p_i} \frac{p_i}{w}$$

be the elasticity of wage with respect to p_i and let $\bar{\varepsilon}_w$ be the mean value of these Stolper–Samuelson elasticities on the wage:

$$\bar{\varepsilon}_w \equiv \frac{\dfrac{\partial w}{\partial p_1}\dfrac{p_1}{w} + \dfrac{\partial w}{\partial p_2}\dfrac{p_2}{w} \cdots + \dfrac{\partial w}{\partial p_n}\dfrac{p_n}{w}}{n} = \frac{\dfrac{\partial y_1}{\partial L}\dfrac{p_1}{w} + \dfrac{\partial y_2}{\partial L}\dfrac{p_2}{w} \cdots + \dfrac{\partial y_n}{\partial L}\dfrac{p_n}{w}}{n}.$$

Using the reciprocity relation in (2.12), the mean value of the Stolper–Samuelson elasticities can be written:

$$\bar{\varepsilon}_w = \frac{1}{n}. \tag{2.13}$$

Similarly,

$$\bar{\varepsilon}_r \equiv \frac{\dfrac{\partial r}{\partial p_1}\dfrac{p_1}{r} + \dfrac{\partial r}{\partial p_2}\dfrac{p_2}{r} \cdots + \dfrac{\partial r}{\partial p_n}\dfrac{p_n}{r}}{n} = \frac{\dfrac{\partial y_1}{\partial K}\dfrac{p_1}{r} + \dfrac{\partial y_2}{\partial K}\dfrac{p_2}{r} \cdots + \dfrac{\partial y_n}{\partial K}\dfrac{p_n}{r}}{n}.$$

Hence,

$$\bar{\varepsilon}_r = \frac{1}{n}. \tag{2.14}$$

Intuitively, if all output prices increase by 1 percent, the wage rate will increase by 1 percent. When the price of one good alone increases by 1 percent – for instance, due to a tariff – its determinate effect on the wage rate cannot be obtained unless the matrix is invertible. However, the mean value of the elasticities of the wage rate with respect to single output price changes is $1/n$ and the wage rate on average increases by $1/n$ percent.[9] Therefore, when the number of commodities is very large, the *average* effects of an increase in a single output price on factor prices become negligible.

Two important questions are whether it is possible to change a single output price while holding $(m-1)$ output prices constant, and whether this is likely to occur. In the even case, the Stolper–Samuelson theorem is based on the assumption that one price can be raised, while holding all other prices constant. However, in the uneven case where $n > m$, the stylized fact that most industries produce positive outputs suggests that all other prices cannot be held constant. If all industries produce positive outputs, a change in one price *necessarily* causes a change in at least $(n-m)$ output prices, and possibly more. But which output prices will change?

4.2 Magnification Effect in the Uneven Case

It is helpful to examine the 3×2 case at this juncture. Consider first the case where the price of the good with an extreme factor intensity rises while the price of the

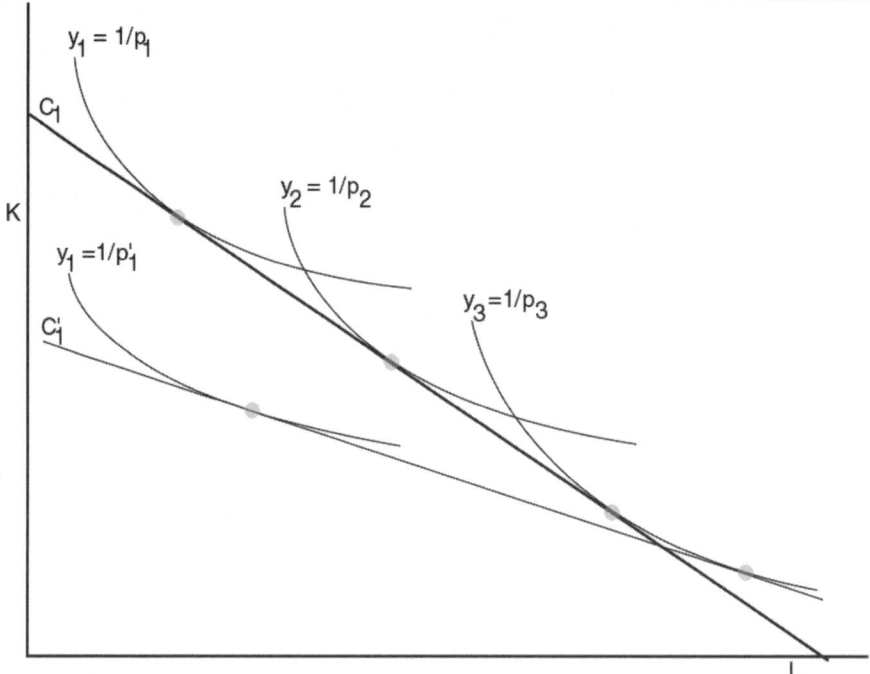

Figure 2.1 Price adjustment of the middle good

other extreme good is held constant, as shown in figure 2.1, where industry 1 is the most capital-intensive and industry 3 is least capital-intensive. As a result, the common isocost curve shifts downward from $C_1 = C_2 = C_3 = 1$ to C'_1. In this case, industries 1 and 3 can both survive but industry 2 cannot, because the cost associated with the new isocost curve $C'_2 = C'_1$ (C'_2 not drawn) is unity but the revenue is less than unity. Alternatively, the cost associated with the unit value isoquant $y_2 = 1/p_2$ is greater than unity. Thus, industry 2 must raise the price of the good in order to survive.

In figure 2.2, as p_1 increases, the unit value isoquant y_1 shifts downward while the unit value isoquant $y_2 = 1/p_2$ remains constant. In this case, a common isocost curve C_2 can be drawn (not drawn in figure 2.2), but since the isocost curve C'_3 is below C'_1, not all three industries can survive. Thus, either p_2 has to rise or p_3 has to fall, or both must occur. It follows that when the price of an extreme industry rises or falls, the price of an intermediate industry cannot remain constant without causing a further change in the price of the other extreme good.

Figure 2.3 examines the case where the price of an intermediate industry rises, shifting the unit value isoquant downward to y'_2. If p_1 is held constant, then p_3 must rise, resulting in a factor price ratio, $(w/r)^a$. On the other hand, if p_3 is held constant, then p_1 must rise and the resulting factor price ratio is $(w/r)^b$. It also is possible for both p_1 and p_3 to rise, so that all the three unit value isoquants lie on the same new isocost curve (not drawn).

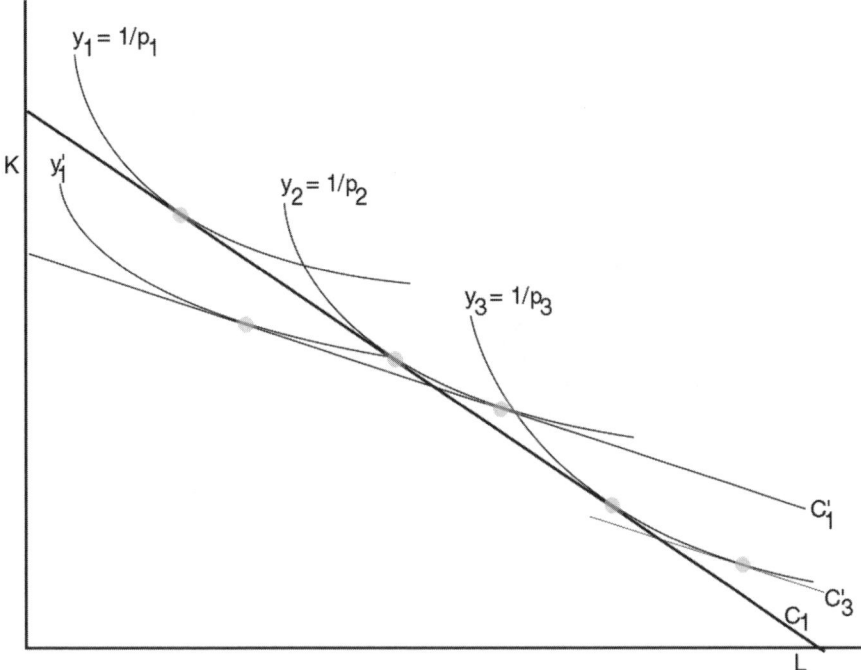

Figure 2.2 Adjustments of other prices

These diagrams do not show which prices will adjust in response to a change in the price of a good with extreme or middle factor intensity. They merely suggest various possibilities, which are based on the zero profit conditions, not on quantity considerations. The zero profit conditions do not indicate whether one industry is "more important" than others in the factor markets where the factor prices are determined. If industry 1's share of national income is very small relative to other industries, a change in its price will have a much smaller impact on the factor markets than other industries.

In the $n \times 2$ model, any pair of output prices completely determines the two factor prices (w, r). If the price of one good rises while another price is held constant, both factor prices change and all the other industries must change their prices to survive. When n is large, the industry whose price is held constant must be a major industry. The prices of all other industries must change accordingly. Otherwise, only two industries will survive and the rest will vanish. When n is not much larger than 2, it is quite possible and even plausible for an industry to survive without changing its price in response to a change in the price of another. However, when n is much greater than 2, an increase in the price of one industry initially necessitates its increased production, and all other industries collectively must shrink somehow, although every industry need not shrink. After the dust settles and factor prices are determined, the output vector again will be indeterminate.

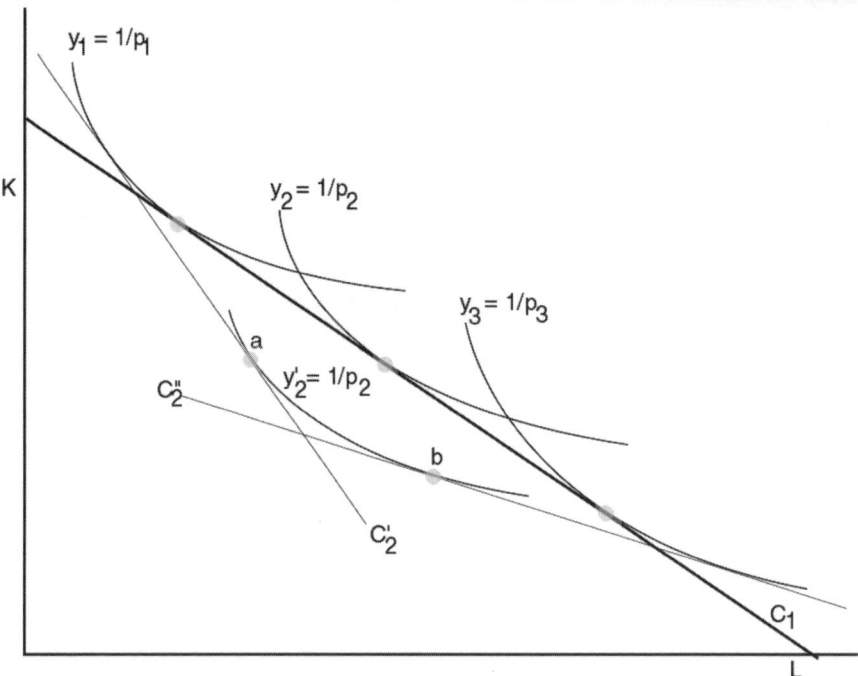

Figure 2.3   A change in the price of the middle good

In the 2×2 model, it is possible to shock the model by changing only one price while holding the other price constant and examine the ensuing changes in factor prices. In the 3×2 model, if the price of one good changes, at most the price of only one other good can be held constant; the prices of two other goods in general may change. Thus, asking the Stolper–Samuelson effect of an increase in p_1 is an *incomplete* question. The factor price pair (w, r) when p_2 is held constant will be different from another pair when p_3 is held constant, which still differs from a third pair when both p_2 and p_3 adjust somewhat. There *will* be a magnification effect, but which factor price will show the magnification effect depends on which price is held constant.

In the $n \times 2$ $(n > 2)$ model, if the price of one good changes, at most the price of only one other good (numéraire) can be held constant, but all other prices may change. Any pair of output prices completely determines the factor prices, and all other prices must adjust accordingly. In general, following the initial increase/decrease in a single price, one price may be held constant and all $(n - 1)$ other output prices may change. Likewise, in the $m \times n$ $(n > m)$ model, following an increase in the price of one good, at most $(m - 1)$ output prices can be held constant. These m output prices completely determine the m factor prices, and the remaining $(n - m)$ output prices must adjust accordingly.

If p_1 is raised, then regardless of the accompanying realignment of other output prices, we have:

$$\hat{p}_1 = \theta_{11}\hat{w}_1 + \theta_{21}\hat{w}_2 + \ldots + \theta_{m1}\hat{w}_m > 0. \tag{2.15}$$

Since $\hat{p}_1$ is a convex combination of percentage changes in factor prices, we still obtain:

$$\min[\hat{w}_1, \hat{w}_2, \ldots, \hat{w}_m] < \hat{p}_1 < \max[\hat{w}_1, \hat{w}_2, \ldots, \hat{w}_m]. \tag{2.16}$$

The second inequality shows the existence of a *magnification effect* in the uneven case, regardless of the realignment of other output prices. However, determining which factor price will show the magnification effect depends on the exact realignment of other output prices. For instance, for a given price configuration in which $(p_2, \ldots, p_m)$ is held constant, w_1 may show a magnification effect in response to an increase in p_1 while w_2 shows a magnification effect following an increase in p_1 with another price configuration in which $(p_3, \ldots, p_m, p_{m+1})$ is held constant.

Thus, "what will happen to factor prices when one price rises in an $n \times m$ world?" is an incomplete question. *It cannot be answered without knowing or assuming precisely how the other prices are to be realigned.* Moreover, if some output prices rise while others fall in response to an increase in p_1, any changes in the factor prices show the *combined* effect of these output price changes, not just the effect of an increase in p_1. As a result, the *magnification effect loses much of its application because it was based on the notion that a single price increase or decrease will raise some factor price more than proportionately.* Also, w_1 may show a magnification effect with respect to p_1, but not with respect to p_k whose price also rises with p_1.

Since there are n output prices, only $(n - 1)$ relative prices matter, and one price can always be held constant as the numéraire. If good 2 is used as the numéraire and p_2 is held constant,

$$\hat{p}_2 = \theta_{12}\hat{w}_1 + \theta_{22}\hat{w}_2 + \ldots + \theta_{m2}\hat{w}_m = 0. \tag{2.17}$$

Since a convex combination of percentage factor price changes is zero and one component is positive, equation (2.17) shows at least one other component is negative. Regardless of how other output prices are realigned, at least one factor price must decline. However, which factor price declines depends on how other output prices are realigned.

We now examine the *average* effect of a price change on factor prices while allowing other prices to be realigned. Since labeling of goods is arbitrary, we consider the effect of a change in the price of good 1, for instance, resulting from a tariff on it in the uneven $n \times m$ case. In response to this change, the prices of some goods, if not all, change accordingly. Thus, p_j can generally be written as $p_j(p_1)$. The Lagrangian function with interdependent output price is written:

$$\mathcal{L} = \sum_{j=1}^{n} p_j(p_1)y_j + w\left[L - \sum_{j=1}^{n} L_j\right] + r\left[K - \sum_{j=1}^{n} K_j\right], \tag{2.18}$$

where $p_1(p_1) \equiv p_1$ is an identity function and $p_k(p_1) = 1$ for some k whose price is held constant. The first order conditions are:

$$p_j(p_1)F_{Lj} - w = 0, \quad \text{if } y_j > 0. \tag{2.19}$$

Differentiating the Lagrangian function in (2.18) with respect to L and p_j gives

$$\frac{\partial L}{\partial L} = w, \tag{2.20}$$

$$\frac{\partial I}{\partial p_1} = \sum_{j \neq 1} p'_j(p_1) y_j + y_1, \tag{2.21}$$

$$\frac{\partial^2 L}{\partial L \partial p_1} = \frac{\partial w}{\partial p_1} = \frac{\partial (\partial I / \partial p_1)}{\partial L} = \frac{\partial \left(\sum_{j \neq 1} p'_j(p_1) y_j + y_1 \right)}{\partial L}. \tag{2.22}$$

Equation (2.22) shows that the *general* reciprocity relation holds in the $n \times m$ world. In the 2×2 case, it is clear that $p_2(p_1)$ is a constant function, and hence

$$\frac{\partial I}{\partial p_1} = y_1,$$

and

$$\frac{\partial w}{\partial p_1} = \frac{\partial y_1}{\partial L}, \quad \text{and} \quad \frac{\partial r}{\partial p_1} = \frac{\partial y_1}{\partial K},$$

which shows the reciprocity relations. In the $n \times n$ case, it follows that

$$\frac{\partial w_j}{\partial p_1} = \frac{\partial y_1}{\partial V_j},$$

where V_j and w_j are the supply and price of factor j, and similar expressions hold for other price changes as well.

From (2.22), the Stolper–Samuelson wage elasticity with respect to p_1 is written:

$$\varepsilon_{wi} = \frac{\partial w}{\partial p_1} \frac{p_1}{w} = \frac{\partial (\partial I / \partial p_1)}{\partial L} \frac{p_1}{w}. \tag{2.23}$$

Note that consumer income $I(p_1, p_2, \ldots, p_n)$ is homogeneous of degree one in all prices, which implies:

$$\frac{\partial I}{\partial p_1} p_1 + \frac{\partial I}{\partial p_2} p_2 \ldots + \frac{\partial I}{\partial p_n} p_n = I.$$

Thus, for the general uneven case, the mean value of the Stolper–Samuelson wage elasticities is written:

$$\bar{\varepsilon}_w = \frac{\partial\left(\dfrac{\partial I}{\partial p_1}p_1 + \dfrac{\partial I}{\partial p_2}p_2 \cdots + \dfrac{\partial I}{\partial p_n}p_n\right)}{\partial L}\frac{1}{wn} = \frac{\partial I}{\partial L}\frac{1}{wn} = \frac{1}{n}. \qquad (2.24)$$

Similarly, the mean value of the rental elasticities is:

$$\bar{\varepsilon}_r = \frac{\partial\left(\dfrac{\partial I}{\partial p_1}p_1 + \dfrac{\partial I}{\partial p_2}p_2 \cdots + \dfrac{\partial I}{\partial p_n}p_n\right)}{\partial K}\frac{1}{rn} = \frac{\partial I}{\partial L}\frac{1}{rn} = \frac{1}{n}. \qquad (2.25)$$

Thus, when n is large, the average effect of an increase in a single output price on factor prices becomes negligible, and this result holds in the general uneven case.

5   THE MEAN RYBCZYNSKI EFFECTS

In the 2×2 case, the Rybczynski theorem states that an increase in factor endowment increases the output of the good that uses that factor intensively and decreases the output of the other industry. Implicit is the assumption that before and after the change, the factor endowment belongs to the same cone of diversification so that factor growth does not affect factor prices. In the realistic case where n is much larger than m, the output vector is indeterminate, and hence, after a change in factor endowment the new output vector also is indeterminate. However, output indeterminacy does not imply that a small change in a factor endowment will cause a large response in the output vector.

How does the economy move from one equilibrium to another in response to a change in factor endowment when the output vector itself is indeterminate? Consider, for example, how the output vector will change in response to a change in the labor endowment. Because of constant returns to scale, an increase in factor endowment has no effect in the long run on factor prices within the cone of diversification. In the case of three industries, differentiating $F^i(L_i, K_i)$ with respect to L yields:

$$\frac{\partial y_1}{\partial L} = F_{K1}^1\frac{\partial K_1}{\partial L} + F_{L1}^1\frac{\partial L_1}{\partial L},$$

$$\frac{\partial y_2}{\partial L} = F_{K2}^2\frac{\partial K_2}{\partial L} + F_{L2}^2\frac{\partial L_2}{\partial L},$$

$$\frac{\partial y_3}{\partial L} = F_{K3}^3\frac{\partial K_3}{\partial L} + F_{L3}^3\frac{\partial L_3}{\partial L}. \qquad (2.26)$$

It is important to note that since output prices are held constant, an increase in the labor endowment does not affect the ratios of inputs used in each industry along its expansion path. An increment in the labor endowment must be used up in at least one industry. Suppose $\partial L_1/\partial L$ in (2.26) is positive. As long as factor prices stay constant, the ratio of these factors remains unchanged in each industry along the expansion path. In (2.26), $\partial L_1/\partial L$ is positive if and only if $\partial L_1/\partial L$ also is positive because both factors move together along an expansion path. Thus, an increase in labor endowment always increases the output of at least one sector. Moreover, $\partial K_1/\partial L > 0$, if and only if, $\partial K_2/\partial L$ or $\partial K_3/\partial L$ is negative. This implies that since in the long run all factors move together along each expansion path, industry 2 or 3 must shrink. Thus, *an increase in a factor endowment always causes at least one industry to expand and at least one other to shrink*. However, predicting which industry will expand or shrink amounts to predicting the signs of the determinant and cofactors of the input–output matrix. This cannot be accomplished by pairwise comparisons of the input–output coefficients, except in a low-dimensional case.

Instead of focusing on the physical quantities of output, it is more convenient to examine the effect of factor growth on the industry revenue. If output prices are fixed, revenue and output move in the same direction. Using (2.12), the effect of an increase in labor endowment on the industry revenue is written as:

$$\frac{\partial R_i}{\partial L} \equiv \frac{\partial p_i y_i}{\partial L} = w \frac{\partial L_i}{\partial L}. \tag{2.27}$$

The average value of L_i is:

$$\bar{L}_i = \frac{L}{n}.$$

Thus, the mean value of $\partial L_i/\partial L$ is:

$$\frac{\partial \bar{L}_i}{\partial L} = \frac{1}{n}.$$

Using (2.11), the mean revenue effect is written

$$\frac{\partial \bar{R}_i}{\partial L} = \frac{\dfrac{\partial L}{\partial L}}{n} = \frac{w}{n}. \tag{2.28}$$

Similarly,

$$\frac{\partial \bar{R}_i}{\partial K} = \frac{\dfrac{\partial L}{\partial K}}{n} = \frac{r}{n}. \tag{2.29}$$

Intuitively, if the labor force increases by one worker, national income increases by the wage. If the labor endowment increases by ΔL, national income increases by $w\Delta L$. The average industry gets only a small fraction $(1/n)$ of this increased income. On average, the industry revenue increases by $w\Delta L/n$. Thus, when n is large, it is not likely that a typical industry will display any magnification effect on its revenue.

6 FACTOR PRICE EQUALIZATION

The HO theory suggests that under certain conditions free trade of commodities will equalize the returns to internationally immobile factors. Immigration may be an indication that one country has a higher wage than another. The reasons cited for nonequalization of factor prices include factor intensity reversal and different production technologies as well as having more factors than products as in the specific factors model.

Samuelson (1949) wrote "Adding a third or further commodities does not alter our analysis much. If anything, it increases the likelihood of complete factor price equalization. For all that we require is that at least *two* commodities are simultaneously being produced in both countries and then our previous conclusions follow."

While Samuelson's conjectures are hardly true for other propositions, his statement on factor price equalization is insightful. From (2.8), if output prices are equal to unit costs, free trade of m goods completely equalizes m factor prices. As the number of commodities increases, holding the number of factors constant, the probability that m goods will be freely traded increases. Accordingly, the probability of factor price equalization increases as n increases.

In the 2×2 case, any fluctuation of an output price will cause a ripple in factor prices. However, when n is large (= 192) as in Leontief's second test, the probability that two goods will be freely traded in long-run equilibrium is much higher than in the 2×2 case. Equilibrium factor prices are derived from the zero profit conditions of two such markets. Long-run equilibrium prices of all other products, consistent with these factor prices, can then be derived and these industries will produce positive outputs. Other industries whose prices are not equal to unit costs derived in this manner are not in long-run equilibrium, and either entry or exit will occur. Thus, as the number of commodities increases, holding the number of factors constant, the international gap between factor prices is more likely to shrink given that there is some trade.

7 LEONTIEF WAS NOT RIGHT

Leontief aggregated industries into 50 sectors, but only 38 industries actually produced commodities that entered the international markets; the remaining sectors were either nontraded goods or accounting identities. In his model there were only two factors, labor and capital. He then estimated the capital and labor requirements to produce $1 million worth of typical exportable and importable goods in 1947. Capital per worker in the export sector was k_x = $14,300, and that in the import sector was k_m = $18,200. Thus, US imports were about 30 percent more capital-intensive than US exports in 1947.[10]

It was pointed out that 1947 was not a representative year suitable to test the HO theory. Many industries had not fully recovered from wartime damages, and postwar reconstruction was still under way. Leontief (1956) repeated the test for US trade in 1951. In this later study, he disaggregated the US production structure into

192 sectors and found that US import substitutes were still 6 percent more capital-intensive than US exports. Baldwin (1971) found that US import substitutes in 1962 were about 27 percent more capital-intensive than US exports. However, Stern and Maskus (1981) demonstrated that the paradox was reversed in 1972: the capital–labor ratio in US exports (about $18,700 per worker-year) was higher than in US import substitutes (about $17,300 per worker-year).

In his first test, Leontief used two factors of production, capital and labor. Of the 38 industries, 35 were net exporters, which indicates positive production in those industries. Leamer (1987, p. 986) investigated a three-factor (capital, labor, and land) model, reporting that in 1978 at the three-digit International Standard Industrial Classification level, every commodity group was produced by all 38 industries. These empirical results suggest that output prices are interdependent. For all of these outputs to be produced, output prices must have moved together to maintain the equality between prices and unit production costs.

Production of more than m goods implies that the prices are adjusted to the levels of unit costs. When this occurs, the output vector is indeterminate, and so is the trade vector. Thus, exports of a capital abundant country are not necessarily more capital intensive than their imports.

Was Leontief right when he compared the capital–labor ratios between the import and export sectors? When $n > m$, this extended HO model does *not* predict precisely that exports of a capital-abundant country will be capital intensive. Recall that in the 3×2 case, there is one degree of freedom in the output vector. Thus, for any given output of y_3, the remaining output vector can be uniquely determined. It is then possible to choose a sufficiently large volume of y_3 so that it is exported. Since the remaining two goods cannot both be exported, assume y_1 is exported and y_2 is imported. Then the capital–labor ratio of the export bundle is:

$$k_x = \frac{a_{K1}(y_1 - c_1) + a_{K3}(y_3 - c_2)}{a_{L1}(y_1 - c_1) + a_{L3}(y_3 - c_2)}, \tag{2.30}$$

and $k_m = a_{K2}/a_{L2}$, where c_i is consumption of good i.

We now show that when $n > m$, it is possible to increase the capital–labor ratio of the export bundle without affecting income or consumption. That is, k_x can be greater than or less than k_m. Since there is one degree of freedom, assume that y_3 is decreased. This causes movement from b to another point b′ in figure 2.4. Since industry 3 is the most labor-intensive, a decrease in its production has an effect similar to an increase in labor endowment to other industries. A new combination of the two products, y_1 and y_2, must yield a vector **Ob′**, resulting in a decrease in the production of the most capital-intensive good y_1 and an increase in the other good y_2 (not drawn), which is less capital intensive than y_1. This change in output mix, however, has no effect on income or consumption bundles. In equation (2.30) this change in the output mix results in a reduction of the export of the most capital-intensive good y_1 and an increase in the export of a less capital-intensive good y_2, thereby reducing the capital–labor ratio of the export bundle. Output indeterminacy results in indeterminacy of the capital–labor ratios of the export and import bundles, and there is no reason why the export bundle should be more

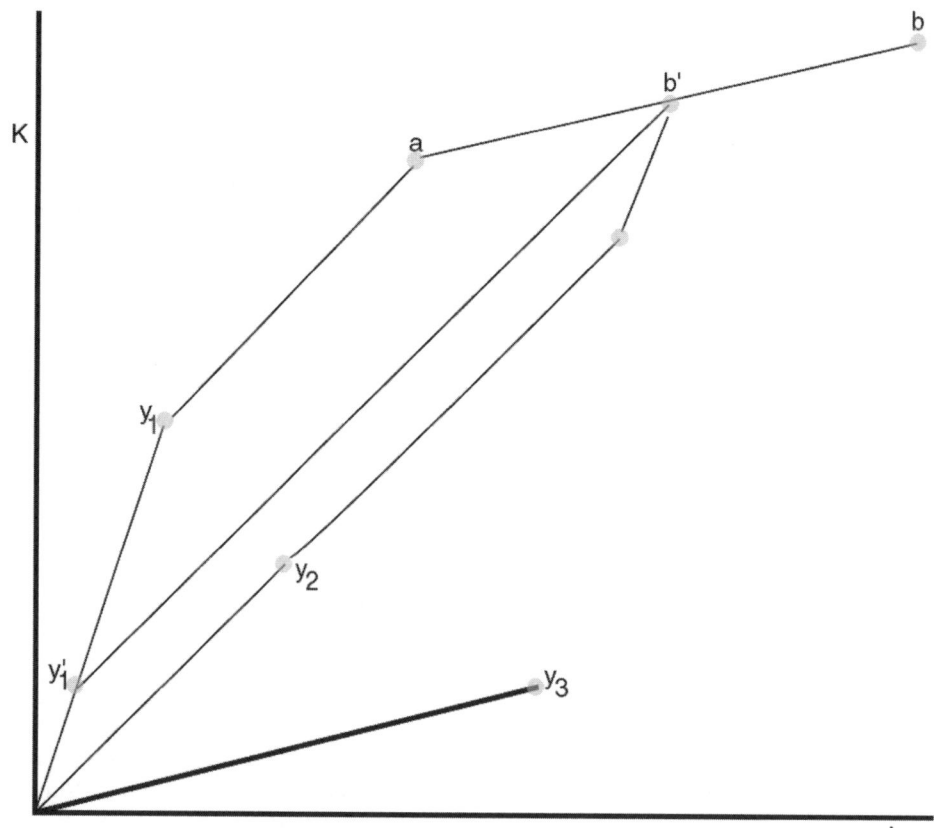

Figure 2.4 Why a Leontief paradox may occur

capital-intensive than the import bundle. Thus, a Leontief paradox is likely to be observed frequently in the multi-commodity world.

Trefler (1993) followed Leontief's (1953) hint that American workers may have been more productive than their foreign cohorts. He argued that if factor productivity or quality indices were incorporated, Leontief was right to claim that US exports were more labor-intensive than US imports in 1947. This analysis shows that the reverse result is equally likely to occur because, even in the absence of factor quality differences, the 38×2 model, or more generally, an $n \times 2$ model does not predict that exports of a capital-abundant country will be more capital-intensive than its imports. The Heckscher–Ohlin prediction in the 2×2 world simply does not carry over to the $n \times 2$ world. Thus, while Trefler used improved definitions of inputs, the test was to ascertain the validity of a nonexisting theorem. A similar analysis on Leontief's second test may reinforce or reverse Trefler's finding.

Thus, when there are two factors of production and n is large, there is no a priori theoretical basis to predict that the export sector of a capital-abundant country will be more capital-intensive than the import sector. This conjecture is well supported by the abundant occurrence of the Leontief paradox in empirical tests of the HO trade theory.

8 THE HECKSCHER–OHLIN–VANEK THEOREM

The HOV theorem explores the factor contents embodied in output trade. Specifically, the HOV theorem states that a capital-abundant country exports the services of capital input through commodity trade. Although the trade bundle is indeterminate, the factor contents embodied in the trade bundles are determinate. However, the exact factor contents of the trade bundle are unique only if the factor prices are equalized.

Let $\mathbf{V}^x = \mathbf{AX}$ and $\mathbf{V}^c = \mathbf{AC}$ denote the vector of factors embodied in the trade bundle and the consumption vector $\mathbf{C}$, respectively. If the jth element of $\mathbf{V}^x$ is positive (negative) it shows that product j is exported (imported). Premultiplying (2.2) by the input-output matrix $\mathbf{A}$ yields

$$\mathbf{V}^x = \mathbf{AY} - \mathbf{AC} = \mathbf{V} - \mathbf{V}^c = \mathbf{V} - a\mathbf{V}^w, \qquad (2.31)$$

where $\mathbf{V}^w$ is the world's factor endowment vector and α is the income share of the home country.[11] Thus, if a country is abundant in factor i ($\mathbf{V} > \alpha\mathbf{V}_i^w$) then $\mathbf{V}_i^x$ is positive. That is, a country exports the services of its abundant factor, despite the indeterminacy of the output and trade vectors. Thus, the HOV theorem survives in the $m \times n$ world. However, this result is predicated on factor price equalization.

When the physical definition of abundance is used, the home country is abundant in capital if $K/L > K^*/L^*$ or $K/K^* > L/L^*$ which holds if and only if

$$\frac{K}{K^*} > \frac{I}{I^*} = \frac{wL + rK}{wL^* + rK^*}. \qquad (2.32)$$

Let $\mathbf{Y}^w = \mathbf{Y} + \mathbf{Y}^*$ denote an $n \times 1$ vector of world outputs, and $\mathbf{C}^w = \mathbf{C} + \mathbf{C}^*$ an $n \times 1$ vector of the world consumption. The world as a whole must consume its outputs, and hence $\mathbf{Y}^w = \mathbf{C}^w$. Let $\alpha \equiv I/(I + I^*)$ be the home country's income share. Then the home country must consume α fraction of the world's output vector. It follows that the factor content of the home country's consumption bundle is:

$$\mathbf{V}^c = \alpha\mathbf{V}^w \qquad (2.33)$$

Then (2.32) is rewritten:

$$\frac{K}{K^*} > \frac{K_c}{K_c^*}. \qquad (2.34)$$

Thus, a capital-abundant country exports capital input through commodity trade.

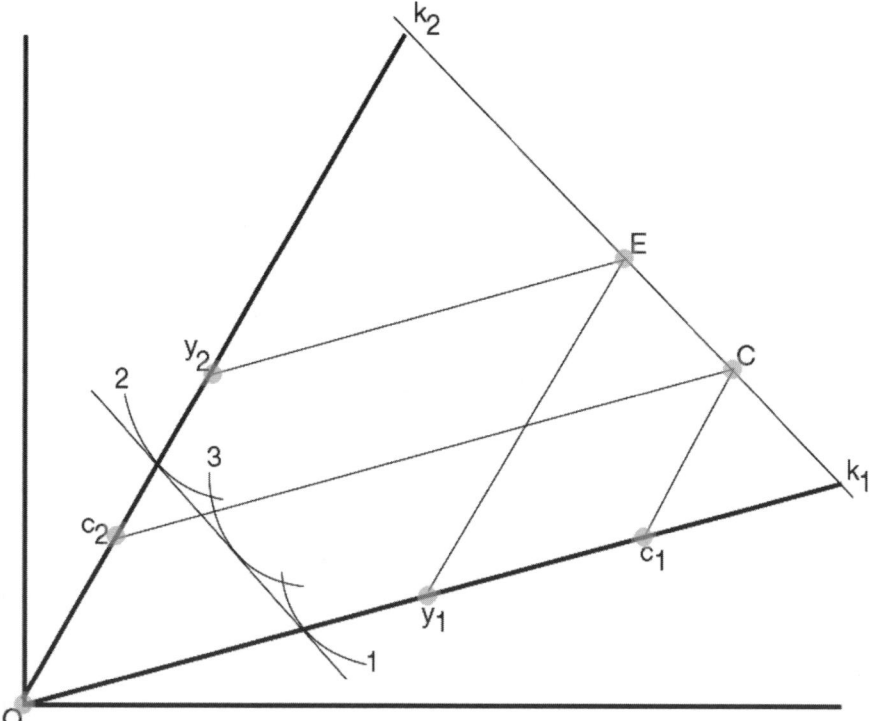

Figure 2.5 Indirect factor trade

In the absence of factor price equalization, capital abundance ($K/K^* > L/L^*$) does not imply

$$\frac{K}{K^*} > \frac{wL + rK}{w^*L^* + rK^*}. \qquad (2.35)$$

Moreover, equation (2.33) does not hold when factor prices are different between countries. Hence, the HOV theorem in (2.34) is not applicable when factor prices are not equalized.

Figure 2.5 illustrates the HOV theorem. Point E shows the given factor endowment $(\bar{L}, \bar{K})$. Ok_1 and Ok_2 are the expansion paths of industries 1 and 2 that are generated by a pair of unit value isoquants labeled 1 and 2 derived from output prices, p_1 and p_2. Points y_1 and y_2 show the factor allocations (L_1, K_1) and (L_2, K_2). If the country exports good 2, the amounts of factors embodied in consumption of good 2 are less than those at point y_2. That is, $(L_2^c, K_2^c) < (L_2, K_2)$. Since good 1 is exported, $(L_1^c, K_2^c) > (L_1, K_1)$. Trade of goods amounts to moving from the endowment point E to another point C on the isoincome line k_1k_2, along which national income $wL + rK = I$ remains constant. Note that the slope of the isoincome line is

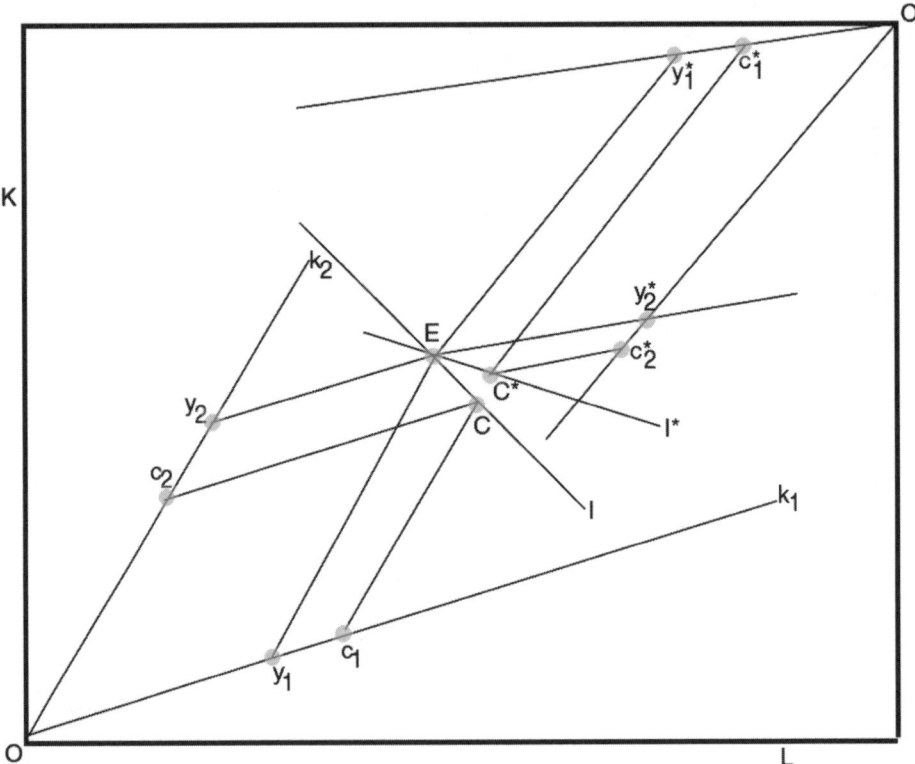

Figure 2.6 Factor content of trade without FPE

the domestic factor price ratio, w/r. Figure 2.5 illustrates that exports of the capital-intensive good amount to exports of capital and imports of labor services.

Adding more goods does not affect the result. Since all prices are equal to unit costs, the existence of industry 3 simply means that industry 1 or 2 or both must reduce production. However, the sum of all these vectors must add up to the endowment point E. Regardless of the composition of the consumption goods, if the factor content embodied in the consumption bundle C is to the right of E, the country is indirectly exporting capital and importing labor.

Figure 2.6 illustrates that the sum of factors exported by both countries need not be zero when factor prices are not equalized. Points c_1 and c_2 show the amounts of capital and labor inputs embodied in consumption of goods 1 and 2, respectively. Point C shows the factor content of the home country's consumption bundle. Given an isoincome line, the movement from E to C shows the quantities of factor trade. However, in the foreign country factor prices are different and trade in goods causes a movement from E to C*. Thus, the sum of any factor exported by both countries can be either positive or negative. This disparity occurs because the amounts of factors embodied in exports are based on domestic factor prices rather than world factor prices that do not exist when factor prices are not equalized.

This problem can become more acute when a factor intensity reversal occurs, because it is possible for both countries to claim to have exported the same factor indirectly through trade. This can be demonstrated even in the 2×2 case. Suppose the home country exports good 2, which is capital-intensive. Then the foreign country exports good 1, but since factor intensities are reversed, the foreign country also exports capital by exporting good 1. Thus, both countries may appear to be exporting capital and importing labor services via commodity trade.

While the HOV theorem is robust in the multi-commodity world, this result is disappointing because as Chipman (1987, p. 938) notes, it attempts to "replace the problem of explaining trade flows in actual commodities by that of explaining flows of abstract amounts of factors of production 'embodied' in the trade flows." The amounts of factors traded lose much of their significance when a factor intensity reversal occurs.

9   CONCLUDING REMARKS

In most empirical studies of the HO model the number of industries is much greater than that of factors. In this case, the output vector is indeterminate and exports of a capital-abundant country need not be capital intensive relative to its imports. It was erroneous to presume that US exports should be more capital-intensive than imports in 1947 even though the US is capital abundant.

When the number of industries increases, an increase in the price of one good will always have a magnification effect on some factor price, but which factor price will rise more than proportionately depends on which output prices are held constant. Moreover, as the number of outputs increases, the mean Stolper–Samuelson effect of output price changes on a given factor price becomes negligible. When the number of goods is much larger than that of factors, factor prices become much more stable than output prices. Many of the findings of the HO model are peculiarities that arise from the low dimensionality of the 2×2 world. Moreover, wage rates reflect labor productivity in competitive markets. The observed wage disparity among workers in various countries may reflect different labor productivities, rather than the magnification effects of tariff disparity between developing and developed economies.

Acknowledgment

I am indebted to Henry Thompson for his valuable comments. The usual caveats apply.

Notes

1 Casas and Choi (1984, 1985) demonstrate that a Leontief paradox could occur in the presence of a large trade imbalance. This is because in the presence of a large trade deficit (surplus) a country could import (export) some of the products that it would export (import) under balanced trade.

2 Jones and Scheinkman (1977) criticized the existing work and investigated the Rybczynski and Stolper–Samuelson propositions in the $n \times m$ world, where the number

of factors m exceeds the number of commodities n. The critical assumption in their model is that the number of factors is larger than that of commodities. Although this case is theoretically interesting, in most empirical studies n was much larger than m.

3 It is interesting to note Deardorff's (1994) result. Using the weak axiom of revealed preference, he shows a negative correlation between trade vector and differences between autarky and free trade prices. That is, if the free trade price is higher than the autarky price, the industry tends to export that product. The fact that the free trade price is higher than the autarky price does not imply that the industry will export the product, because all other prices are also determinants of supply (through the Stolper–Samuelson theorem) as well as of consumer demand.

4 Harkness (1978) focused on the even case ($n = m$) and suggested a hypothesis:

$$(\text{diag } Y)^{-1} E = \Theta \beta + \varepsilon,$$

where diag Y is an ($n \times n$) matrix with the elements of Y on the main diagonal. However, he provides no theoretical basis for supposing that regression coefficients on factor intensities will duplicate the factor abundance ranking. Leamer and Bowen (1981) even provided a counter-example.

5 If capital input were also a variable input, another constraint would be included in (2.6), and since all industries exhibit constant returns to scale, the output vector would be indeterminate if prices were equal to unit production costs.

6 A solution to the first order conditions yields labor demand functions $L_i(K_1, K_2, K_3, p_1, p_2, p_3)$ and the shadow price $w(K_1, K_2, K_3, p_1, p_2, p_3)$.

7 In the even case, although prices are equal to unit costs, industry outputs are uniquely determined by the Rybczynski result and industry supply curves are positively sloped. Indeterminacy makes industry supply curves horizontal in the uneven case.

8 Thompson (1999) reports that 11 magnification effects can occur in the two-good, three-factor model, compared to only one in the 2×2 model. However, this abundance of magnification may be due to the fact that factor prices depend not only on output prices but also on endowments.

9 Of course, if all prices rise by 1 percent, the wage rate will rise by the same proportion.

10 See Baldwin (1971) for a number of possible explanations for the Leontief paradox.

11 If trade is not balanced, α can be replaced by β, the consumption share of the country.

References

Baldwin, Robert 1971: Determinants of the commodity structure of US trade. *American Economic Review*, 61, 126–46.

Casas, François R. and E. Kwan Choi 1984: Trade imbalance and the Leontief paradox. *Manchester School*, 52, 391–401.

Casas, François R. and E. Kwan Choi 1985: The Leontief paradox: Continued or resolved? *Journal of Political Economy*, 93, 610–15.

Chipman, John 1987: International trade. In J. Eatwell, M. Milgate, and P. Newman (eds.), *The New Palgrave Dictionary of Economics*, Basingstoke: Macmillan, 922–55.

Deardorff, Alan V. 1994: Exploring the limits of comparative advantage. *Weltwirtschaftliches Archiv*, 130, 1–19.

Ethier, Wilfred J. 1984: Higher dimensional issues in trade theory. In Ronald W. Jones and Peter P. Kenen (eds.), *Handbook of International Economics*, vol. 1, Amsterdam: North-Holland, 131–84.

Harkness, J. P. 1978: Factor abundance and comparative advantage. *American Economic Review*, 68, 784–800.

Herman-Pilath, Carsten 2000: "Indeterminacy in international trade: Methodological reflections on the impact of non-economic determinants on the direction of trade and absolute advantage. *Aussenwirtschaft*, 55, 251–89.

Jones, Ronald W. and J. A. Scheinkman 1977: The relevance of the two-sector production model in trade theory. *Journal of Political Economy*, 85, 909–35.

Leamer, Edward E. 1984: *Sources of International Comparative Advantage*, Cambridge, MA: MIT Press.

Leamer, Edward E. 1987: Paths of development in the three-factor, n-good general equilibrium model. *Journal of Political Economy*, 95, 961–99.

Leamer, Edward E. and Harry P. Bowen 1981: Cross-section tests of the Heckscher–Ohlin theorem: Comment. *American Economic Review*, 71, 1040–3.

Leontief, Wassily W. 1953: Domestic production and foreign trade: The American capital position re-examined. *Proceedings of the American Philosophical Society*, 97, 332–49. Reprinted [1968] in R. E. Caves and H. G. Johnson (eds.), *American Economic Association, Readings in International Economics*, Homewood, IL: Richard D. Irwin, Inc.

Leontief, Wassily W. 1956: Factor proportions and the structure of American trade: Further theoretical and empirical analysis. *Review of Economics and Statistics*, 38, 386–407.

Marshall, Alfred 1961 [1890]: *Principles of Economics*, 9th (variorum) ed., with annotations by C. W. Guillebaud. London: Macmillan for the Royal Economic Society.

Samuelson, Paul 1949: International factor-price equalization once again. *Economic Journal*, 59, 181–97.

Stern, Robert M. and Keith E. Maskus 1981: Determinants of the structure of US foreign trade, 1958–76. *Journal of International Economics*, 11, 207–24.

Thompson, Henry 1987: A review of advancements in the general equilibrium theory of production and trade. *Keio Economic Studies*, 24, 43–62.

Thompson, Henry 1999: Definitions of factor abundance and the factor content of trade. *Open Economies Review*, 10, 385–93.

Trefler, Daniel 1993: International factor price differences: Leontief was right! *Journal of Political Economy*, 101, 961–87.

Trefler, Daniel 1995: The case of the missing trade and other mysteries. *American Economic Review*, 85, 1029–46.

3

Robustness of the Stolper–Samuelson Intensity Price Link

Henry Thompson

CHAPTER OUTLINE

The Stolper–Samuelson theorem isolates conditions under which factor intensity determines the qualitative factor price adjustments to price changes in general equilibrium. The present chapter examines the robustness of this "intensity price link" under relaxations of its sufficient conditions, with parametric specifications of the comparative static model based on neoclassical production, competitive pricing, and full employment.

1 ROBUSTNESS OF THE STOLPER–SAMUELSON INTENSITY PRICE LINK

The Stolper–Samuelson (1941) theorem isolates a set of conditions under which factor intensity is sufficient to determine the qualitative effects of price changes on factor prices. Its novel property is that factor substitution plays no role. A literature evolved pointing out that the theorem does not hold under other conditions, implicitly suggesting a limited scope. The present chapter points out, however, that the Stolper–Samuelson intensity price link is generally robust to parametric relaxations of its sufficient conditions. The scope of the theorem is widened as it is shown to hold under much wider initial conditions than suggested by the list of sufficient conditions. None of the sufficient conditions are necessary for the intensity price link.

The next section reviews the proof of the Stolper–Samuelson theorem. The following sections analyze the intensity price link assuming in turn international factor mobility, nontraded products, factor intensity reversals, elastic factor supply, unemployment, factor market distortions, noncompetitive pricing of outputs, increasing returns, and nonhomothetic production. The intensity price link may hold under any of these conditions and when it is relaxed it is only partly so. Increasing returns are analyzed with a general cost function revealing new patterns of factor price adjustments. A final section summarizes models with many factors and many products, including a high dimensional measure of factor intensity.

2 PROOFS OF THE INTENSITY PRICE LINK

Proofs of the Stolper–Samuelson theorem follow the work of Koo (1953), Jones (1956), Lancaster (1957), Bhagwati (1959), and Chipman (1966). Its sufficient assumptions include:

- two homogeneous traded products in a small open economy;
- two homogeneous factors, mobile nationally but immobile internationally;
- perfect competition in product and factor markets;
- perfectly inelastic factor supply;
- full employment; and
- linearly homogeneous production functions.

The following sections relax these assumptions using parametric modifications of the algebraic comparative static model. The linearly homogeneous assumption is relaxed with both variable returns and nonhomothetic production. There are other implicit underlying assumptions, including the absence of specific factors, joint production, intermediate products, depletable or renewable resources, and production of capital goods.

The starting point is a 2×2 production box, explaining in part the enduring pedagogical popularity of the theorem. Along the contract curve, suppose factor 1 is used intensively in product 1,

$$v_{11}/v_{21} > v_{12}/v_{22} \tag{3.1}$$

where v_{ij} is the input of factor i in the production of product j, $i,j = 1,2$. The contract curve does not cross the diagonal because with homothetic production if a point on the diagonal were on the contract curve all points would have to be. While there can be no factor intensity reversals due to price changes in the economy with linearly homogeneous production, with three factors there could be.

Each endogenous factor price w_i is equal across sectors in the economy and isoquants of the two sectors share a common tangency and the same relative factor price. Exogenous prices p_j for the two traded products determine output levels and corresponding relative factor prices along the contract curve. A higher relative price for product 1 would raise its output and the relative price w_1/w_2 of its intensive

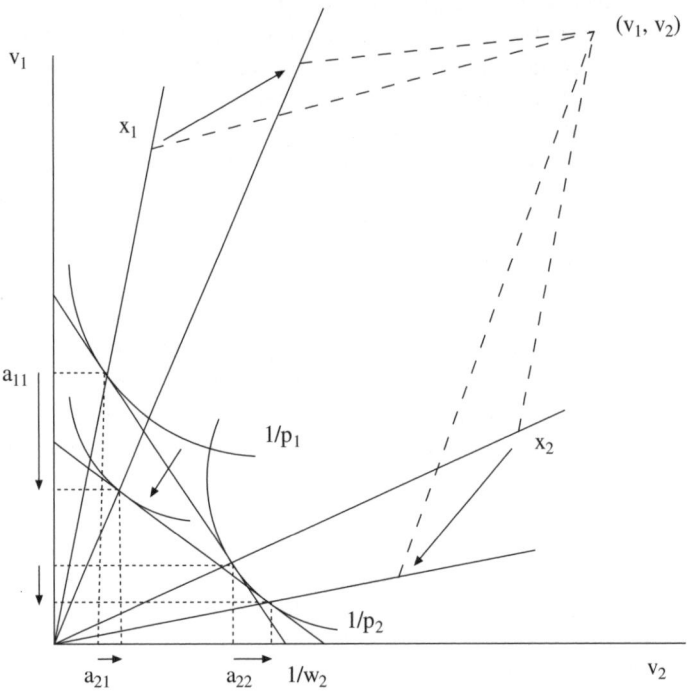

Figure 3.1 Stolper–Samuelson adjustment

factor. Input ratios v_{ij}/v_{2j} would fall in each sector as cost minimizing firms adjust to the new higher relative price of factor 1.

Figure 3.1 presents the corresponding 2×2 Lerner-Pearce production diagram. Unit value isoquants $x_j = 1/p_j$ represent the amount of each product worth one unit of numeraire. If dollars are the numeraire, it follows that $p_j = \$/\text{product}$ and $1/p_j = \text{product}/\$$. Neoclassical production functions imply concave isoquants with positions of unit value isoquants determined by exogenous prices p_j in the small open economy.

The unique unit isocost line $c_j = 1 = a_{1j}w_1 + a_{2j}w_2$ shows input combinations that cost \$1 and supports the unit isoquants due to cost minimization. Endpoints of the unit value isocost line are $1/w_i$. Firms minimize cost $c_j = \Sigma_i a_{ij}w_i$ where a_{ij} is the cost minimizing amount of factor i used in the production of a unit of product j. Competition ensures $p_j = c_j$, uniquely determining the endogenous w_i at the endpoints of the unit isocost line. The endogenous $a_{ij}(w)$ are functions of the vector of endogenous factor prices w. The factor intensity condition in (3.1) can be stated in terms of relative inputs,

$$a_{11}/a_{21} > a_{12}/a_{22} . \tag{3.2}$$

as reflected by the steeper expansion path for sector 1.

In Figure 3.1, a ceteris paribus increase in p_1 shifts that unit value isoquant toward the origin as one dollar's worth becomes less of the physical product. The isocost line rotates around isoquant 2, the price of intensive factor w_1 rising while w_2 falls. Production becomes more intensive in relatively cheaper factor 2 as a_{1j} falls and a_{2j} rises. In the matrix of $\delta w_i/\delta p_j \equiv w_{ij}$ results, there is a positive main diagonal with negative elements off the diagonal.

$$\begin{pmatrix} w_{11} & w_{21} \\ w_{12} & w_{22} \end{pmatrix} = \begin{pmatrix} + & - \\ - & + \end{pmatrix} \tag{3.3}$$

The algebraic general equilibrium model will be used to introduce parametric relaxations of the various assumptions. Chipman (1966) and Takayama (1982) present the foundations of full employment of factors and competitive pricing of products. Full employment for factor i is stated $v_i = \Sigma_j a_{ij} x_j$ where v_i is the endowment of factor i and x_j the output of product j. Differentiate to find $dv_i = \Sigma_j a_{ij} dx_j + \Sigma_j x_j da_{ij}$. With homothetic production, cost minimizing unit inputs a_{ij} are functions of factor prices alone and $da_{ij} = \Sigma_k(\delta a_{ij}/\delta w_k)dw_k$. It follows that $\Sigma_j x_j da_{ij} = \Sigma_k(\Sigma_j x_j \delta a_{ij}/\delta w_k)dw_k = \Sigma_k s_{ik}dw_k$ given the output weighted substitution term $s_{ik} \equiv \Sigma_j x_j \delta a_{ij}/\delta w_k$. Shephard's lemma states that cost minimizing inputs are partial derivatives of cost functions, $a_{ij} = \delta c_j/\delta w_i$ and it follows that $\delta a_{ij}/\delta w_k = \delta^2 c_j/\delta w_i \delta w_k$. Young's theorem on the symmetry of partial derivatives then implies $s_{ik} = s_{ki}$. For notation, $s \equiv s_{12} = s_{21}$. Own substitution terms s_{ii} are negative due to concavity of cost functions. Summing across weighted substitution terms, $\Sigma_i w_i s_{ik} = \Sigma_i w_i \Sigma_j x_j(\delta a_{ij}/\delta w_k) = \Sigma_j x_j \Sigma_i w_i(\delta a_{ij}/\delta w_k) = \Sigma_j x_j \Sigma_i w_i(\delta a_{kj}/\delta w_i) = 0$ by Euler's theorem. Without loss of generality, rescale factors so $w_i = 1$ and it follows that $s = -s_{11} = -s_{22} = s_{12} = s_{21}$. Full employment is stated in the first two equations of the comparative static system (3.4) below.

Competitive pricing for product j is stated $p_j = \Sigma_i a_{ij} w_i$. Differentiate to find $dp_j = \Sigma_i a_{ij} dw_i + \Sigma_i w_i da_{ij}$. Firms minimize cost, implying the slope of each unit value isoquant da_{1j}/da_{2j} equals the slope of the isocost line $-w_2/w_1$. The cost minimizing envelope $\Sigma_i w_i da_{ij} = 0$ follows, implying $dp_j = \Sigma_i a_{ij} dw_i$. Competitive pricing is stated in the second two equations of the 2×2 comparative static factor proportions model,

$$\begin{pmatrix} -s & s & a_{11} & a_{12} \\ s & -s & a_{21} & a_{22} \\ a_{11} & a_{21} & 0 & 0 \\ a_{12} & a_{22} & 0 & 0 \end{pmatrix} \begin{pmatrix} dw_1 \\ dw_2 \\ dx_1 \\ dx_2 \end{pmatrix} = \begin{pmatrix} dv_1 \\ dv_2 \\ dp_1 \\ dp_2 \end{pmatrix} = \begin{pmatrix} 0 \\ 0 \\ dp_1 \\ dp_2 \end{pmatrix} \tag{3.4}$$

Factor endowments are held constant, $dv_i = 0$. The factor intensity condition in (3.2) implies $a_{11}a_{22} - a_{12}a_{21} \equiv b > 0$. The positive determinant in (3.4) is $\Delta = b^2$. Factor price equalization occurs inside the production cone of McKenzie (1955) where $\delta w_i/\delta v_k = 0$.

The $\delta w_i/\delta p_j$ or w_{ij} terms are derived from cofactors in the lower left partition of the system matrix using Cramer's rule,

$$\begin{pmatrix} w_{11} & w_{21} \\ w_{12} & w_{22} \end{pmatrix} = \begin{pmatrix} a_{22}/b & -a_{12}/b \\ -a_{21}/b & a_{11}/b \end{pmatrix},$$ (3.5)

confirming the intensity price link in (3.3). Note that factor substitution has no effect on the w_{ij} terms. It is a surprise that factors might be perfect substitutes or not substitutes at all and the w_{ij} terms would be identical, a peculiar result that holds for "even" models with the same number of factors and products.

Jones (1965) develops the magnification effect that price changes are weighted averages of factor price changes. In the differentiated competitive pricing condition for product j, $dp_j = \Sigma_i a_{ij} dw_i$, divide both sides by p_j and multiply the left side by w_i/w_i to find $\Sigma_i \theta_{ij} \hat{w}_i = \hat{p}_j$, where $\hat{}$ represents percentage change and $\theta_{ij} = w_i a_{ij}/p_j$, a factor share. In even models, the intensity price link in elasticity form is determined by properties of the θ matrix in $\theta \hat{w} = \hat{p}$ since $\hat{w}/\hat{p} = \theta^{-1}$. Percentage price changes are weighted averages of factor price changes. In the 2×2 model, if $\hat{p}_1 > \hat{p}_2$ it must be that $\hat{w}_1 > \hat{p}_1 > \hat{p}_2 > \hat{w}_2$. If a single price increases, at least one factor price must rise more in percentage terms and the other factor price falls. For any nonzero vector of price changes, the real income of one factor must rise and the other must fall.

3   INTERNATIONAL MOBILITY OF FACTORS AND NONTRADED PRODUCTS

Adding internationally mobile factors of production or nontraded products may leave the intensity price link intact. As an example, consider the 3×2 model. The three factors capital, labor, and land provide the foundation for classical economics. Branson and Monoyios (1977) and Thompson (1997b) provide some motivation for trade models with separate skilled and unskilled labor. Batra and Casas (1976), Ruffin (1981), Takayama (1982), Suzuki (1983), Jones and Easton (1983), and Thompson (1985) develop theoretical properties of the 3×2 model. Factors can be unambiguously ranked according to factor intensity,

$$a_{11}/a_{12} > a_{21}/a_{22} > a_{31}/a_{32}.$$ (3.6)

Factor 1 is the extreme factor for product 1, factor 3 is extreme for product 2, and factor 2 is the middle factor. Thompson (1985) uncovers the possible sign patterns of w_{ij} terms, which depend on factor intensity as well as factor substitution. Isolating the two extreme factors, the possible sign patterns are

$$\begin{pmatrix} w_{11} & w_{31} \\ w_{12} & w_{32} \end{pmatrix} = \begin{matrix} + & - \\ - & + \end{matrix} \quad \begin{matrix} + & + \\ - & + \end{matrix} \quad \begin{matrix} + & + \\ - & - \end{matrix}$$
$$\qquad\qquad (a) \qquad\quad (b) \qquad\quad (c)$$ (3.7)

Sign pattern (3.7a) is the strong result, analogous to the 2×2 model. A higher price of product 1 unambiguously lowers the output of product 2 and demand for extreme factor 3 is expected to fall but in (3.7b) prices of both extreme factors rise. The expanding sector 1 can increase its input of factor 3, releasing complementary middle factor 2. In (3.7c), a higher price for product 2 also lowers the price of its extreme factor. Thompson (1986) isolates various conditions favoring factor price polarization, the separation of international factor prices with a move to free trade. The strong result in (3.7a) cannot be reversed completely as Thompson (1993) notes for the 3×2 magnification effect. Thompson (1995) uses sensitivity analysis in simulations of a 3×2 model of the US economy with skilled and unskilled labor and finds the intensity price link in (3.7a) due to the overwhelming influence of factor intensity.

Internationally mobile factors with factor prices exogenous at world levels can restore the intensity price link. If the middle factor in the 3×2 model is internationally mobile, there is the strong intensity price link in (3.7a). In the $r \times 2$ model when $r > 2$, the w_{ij} matrix has more than a single possible sign pattern and the intensity price link may break down. International mobility of $r - 2$ of the factors, however, would make factor prices exogenous and restore the intensity price link. In the $r \times 2$ model with $r - 2$ of the factors internationally mobile, there is an intensity price link for the internationally immobile factors.

With more products than factors in a small open economy, the comparative static system is overdetermined. Melvin (1968), Travis (1972), and Rader (1979) develop properties of the 2×3 and $2 \times n$ models, $n > 2$. Factor intensity can be unambiguously defined as a ranking of relative inputs across industries when there are two factors. When $n > r = 2$ in a small open economy, however, there are more than two arbitrarily placed unit value isoquants and for almost any set of world prices there is no unique supporting isocost line. Product prices may be assumed to adjust as in Choi (2003) but short of a solution algorithm little more can be said about the intensity price link.

Introducing nontraded products, however, endogenizes prices and can restore the intensity price link. Komiya (1967) and Rivera-Batiz (1982) develop models with nontraded products. In the $2 \times n$ model, if $n - 2$ of the products are nontraded there is a strong intensity price link for the traded products. In the 2×3 model with one nontraded product, Ethier (1972) examines conditions that lead to an intensity price link. Although demand conditions might relax the intensity price link, it is robust to "small" demand elasticities.

4   FACTOR INTENSITY REVERSALS AND THE INTENSITY PRICE LINK

Production cones are regions in factor space between expansion paths where all products can be produced with full employment of all factors. Expansion paths are linear with homothetic production. Production cones are generally not unique. Even in the 2×2 model, there are two production cones if the isoquants cross twice. Pearce (1951), James and Pearce (1951), and Harrod (1958) make the point that factor price equalization would not occur with free trade if endowments of the two trading countries lie in different production cones. The country abundant in a factor would maintain a lower relative price for that factor with free trade. The intensity price link would nevertheless hold inside each country because the opposite factor is used intensively in each country. If sector 1 uses factor 1 intensively in country 1 but uses factor 2 intensively in country 2, a higher price for product 1 would raise w_1 in country 1 and w_2 in country 2. The intensity price link holds in each country and free trade raises the price of cheap abundant factors.

"Internal" factor intensity reversals can occur in an economy with more than two factors because changing prices can potentially lead to factor intensity reversals inside the country. In the 3×2 model, a factor might be the extreme factor in one sector but could lose that ranking due to some vector of price changes. Wong (1990) shows that such internal factor intensity reversals are impossible with exponential production functions although they may not be ruled out for homothetic production functions. With nonhomothetic production functions, internal factor intensity reversals certainly may occur. While the observation of an internal factor intensity reversal is consistent with nonhomothetic production, it may only point to the presence of more than two factors. An internal factor intensity reversal does not violate the intensity price link as much as it requires a careful statement of the changes taking place in the economy.

5 ELASTIC FACTOR SUPPLY AND THE INTENSITY PRICE LINK

Factors supplies are assumed to be perfectly inelastic in the factor proportions model but there is ample evidence that quantity supplied increases with price in some labor and natural resource markets. Kemp and Jones (1962) examine the effects of elastic factor supply on offer curves. Upward sloping factor supply can be included directly in the algebraic comparative static model. Suppose the supply of factor 1 is a positive function of its own price, $v_1(w_1)$, where $dv_1/dw_1 \equiv v_{11} > 0$. In the comparative static model (3.4), the first equation becomes $(s_{11} - v_{11})dw_1 + s_{12}dw_2 + a_{11}dx_1 + a_{12}dx_2 = 0$ and the qualitative intensity price link could be affected by the elasticity of factor supply v_{11}.

Note, however, that substitution plays no role in the Stolper–Samuelson w_{ij} terms in (3.5) and that factor price equalization implies there would be no effect of the induced change in v_1 (w_1) on factor prices. Factor prices are insulated from induced factors supply changes if factor price equalization holds. In models without factor price equalization, factor prices would vary with an induced change in factor supply. The own effects of factor endowments on factor prices are negative, $\delta w_i/\delta v_i < 0$, implying factor demands slope downward in the general equilibrium. As an example, consider the 3×2 model and suppose $\delta w_1/\delta p_1$ would be positive in the absence of the induced effect on the supply of factor 1. An increase in w_1 induces an increase in v_1 dampening the increase in w_1. If v_{11} is large enough, the positive sign of $\delta w_1/\delta p_1$ is reversed suggesting elastic factor supply could alter the intensity price link. Nevertheless, factor intensity would remain a fundamental determinant of the w_{ij} sign pattern and would have to be overcome by a strong factor supply effect. The intensity price link would hold for a range of factor supply elasticities.

6   UNEMPLOYMENT AND THE INTENSITY PRICE LINK

Unemployment can arise for various reasons and there is a literature that bridges international and labor economics. The ultimate effect of introducing unemployment is that the wage does not fall to clear the labor market. In the general equilibrium model of Thompson (1989) with the unemployment rate varying endogenously and inversely with aggregate output, the intensity price link is unaffected.

In factor proportion models, unemployment occurs when the quantity of labor demanded falls short of the inelastic quantity supplied. Full employment of factor k can be stated $v_k = D_k(\mathbf{p}, \mathbf{v})$ where the quantity of labor demanded in the general equilibrium $D_k(\mathbf{p}, \mathbf{v})$ is a function of the vectors of exogenous variables $\mathbf{p}$ and $\mathbf{v}$. There is unemployment if $D_k(\mathbf{p}, \mathbf{v}) < v_k$ at the current wage. The general equilibrium effects of increased unemployment would be the same as a reduction in the labor endowment since the economy employs less labor.

In the 2×2 model, increased unemployment would affect outputs but because of factor price equalization factor prices and the intensity price link are not affected. The level of employment does not affect factor prices as long as employment remains inside the production cone, a principle in any model with factor price equalization. In models without factor price equalization, however, a change in the unemployment rate affects factor prices. An increased unemployment rate may involve a higher wage but some other factor prices would have to fall in the absence of factor price equalization, similar to the effects of a change in a factor endowment.

Thompson (1997) points out that the $\delta w_i / \delta v_k$ results are apparently nearly zero when they are not zero. This "near factor price equalization" suggests that changes in unemployment would generally have negligible impacts on factor prices and the intensity price link.

Turning briefly to a parameterized model, consider unemployment in the market for factor 1 with $\beta v_1 = \Sigma_j a_{1j} x_j$ where $\beta < 1$. If β is constant, the intensity price link in the comparative static w_{ij} terms is unaffected. The entire adjustment process in the factor markets is forced onto factor prices. To introduce flexibility, let β be a negative function of the factor price, $\beta(w_1)$ with $\beta' < 0$. The first equation in the comparative static system (3.4) becomes $(s_{11} - v_1\beta')dw_1 + s_{12}dw_2 + \Sigma_j a_{1j}dx_j = \beta dv_1 = 0$. The w_{ij} results in (3.5) are unaffected and the strong intensity price link holds. The w_{11} term is dampened by unemployment but if positive cannot switch signs. The higher w_1 due to an increase in p_1 lowers β, dampening the increase in w_1.

Unemployment has the potential to change the factor intensity of employed factors and alter interpretation of the intensity price link. Nevertheless, full employment is not a necessary condition for the factor intensity price link as the present parameterized model shows.

7   FACTOR MARKET DISTORTIONS AND THE INTENSITY PRICE LINK

The factor market distortions in the present section cause a factor price to be different across sectors. Taxes, unionization, minimum wages, location, and different working conditions can lead to such distortions. Johnson (1966), Johnson and Mieszkowski (1970), Jones (1971), Herberg and Kemp (1971), Magee (1971, 1973), and Bhagwati and Srinivasan (1971) introduce such distortions into the factor proportions model. The present section considers the robustness of the intensity price link in the presence of a parametric distortion in the intersector market for factor 1.

Let w_1^s be the price of factor 1 in sector s and suppose $\gamma w_1^1 = w_1^2$. If $\gamma = 1$ there is no factor market distortion. Consider the situation where $\gamma > 1$ and factor 1 receives a premium in sector 2. A change in w_1^2 would be written $dw_1^2 = \gamma dw_1^1 + w_1^1 d\gamma$. For simplicity, assume the premium is constant in the comparative statics, $d\gamma = 0$. A change in the price of product 2 is then $dp_2 = a_{12}dw_1^2 + a_{22}dw_2 = a_{12}\gamma dw_1^1 + a_{22}dw_2$. In sector 1, $dp_1 = a_{11}dw_1^1 + a_{21}dw_2$. Substitution terms have to be recalculated and are represented by s_d. The comparative static model with a factor price premium:

$$
\begin{pmatrix}
-s_d & s_d & a_{11} & a_{12} \\
s_d & -s_d & a_{21} & a_{22} \\
a_{11} & a_{21} & 0 & 0 \\
a_{12}\gamma & a_{22} & 0 & 0
\end{pmatrix}
\begin{pmatrix}
dw_1^1 \\ dw_2 \\ dx_1 \\ dx_2
\end{pmatrix}
=
\begin{pmatrix}
dv_1 \\ dv_2 \\ dp_1 \\ dp_2
\end{pmatrix}
=
\begin{pmatrix}
0 \\ 0 \\ dp_1 \\ dp_2
\end{pmatrix}
\tag{3.8}
$$

has determinant $\Delta_d = bb_\gamma$ where $b_\gamma \equiv (a_{11}a_{22} - \gamma a_{12}a_{21})$. In the undistorted model where $\gamma = 1$, the positive determinant is b^2 and the intensity price link in (3.5) emerges. If $\gamma > 1$, however, the signs of b_γ and Δ_d are ambiguous. The w_{ij} results are

$$
\begin{pmatrix}
w_{11}^1 & w_{21} \\
w_{12}^1 & w_{22}
\end{pmatrix}
=
\begin{pmatrix}
a_{22}/b_\gamma & -a_{12}\gamma/b_\gamma \\
-a_{21}/b_\gamma & a_{11}/b_\gamma
\end{pmatrix}
=
\begin{matrix} + & - \\ - & + \end{matrix}
\quad
\begin{matrix} - & + \\ + & - \end{matrix}
\tag{3.9}
$$

Related effects on the price of factor 1 in sector 2 are $w_{11}^2 \equiv \delta w_1^2/\delta p_1 = \gamma(\delta w_1^1/\delta p_1) = \gamma/b_\gamma$ and $w_{12}^2 \equiv \delta w_1^2/\delta p_2 = \gamma(\delta w_1^1/\delta p_2) = -\gamma^2/b_\gamma$. If $b_\gamma > 0$ the strong intensity price link holds but if $b_\gamma < 0$ it is reversed. If γ is large enough to make b_γ negative, factor intensity is effectively reversed making factor 1 intensive in sector 2 and reversing the intensity price link. These results would not necessarily change if γ were an endogenous function of other variables in the model. If γ starts at unit value and $b > 0$, letting γ increase will decrease b_γ, increasing the sizes of the w_{ij} terms. As b_γ approaches zero the model becomes unstable and the w_{ij} terms explode. When b_γ becomes negative the w_{ij} terms switch signs although there is instability in the neighborhood where $\gamma = a_{11}a_{22}/a_{12}a_{21}$. The important point for the present purpose is that the presence of a factor market distortion does not necessarily relax the intensity price link.

8 NONCOMPETITIVE PRICING AND THE INTENSITY PRICE LINK

Competitive pricing of products is another sufficient condition for the Stolper–Samuelson theorem. Models of production and trade for small open economies can be closed without a utility structure if competitive firms produce where cost equals the exogenous world price. Melvin and Warne (1973) examine monopoly pricing in the context of utility maximization. In models of monopolistic competition such as Krugman (1979) and Helpman (1981) demand is introduced and pricing remains competitive. Wong (1995, chapter 7) examines an international duopoly with products produced by single firms in each of two countries and finds the Stolper–Samuelson theorem may hold. Melvin and Warne (1973) make the same point when both sectors are international duopolists colluding to maximize joint profit. Kemp and Okawa (1998a, b) show the intensity price link is robust when oligopolists are a primary factor paid profit.

The present section introduces a wedge parameter between price and cost in a small open economy. Suppose there is a monopoly in sector 1 based on ownership of a natural resource or another legal entry restriction. Such a monopoly is a price taker in the international market but searches for the output that maximizes profit. Raising monopoly output increases cost in the general equilibrium by raising relative demand for its intensive factor, but revenue also increases. The monopoly has some monopsony power over the factor markets in the small open economy.

Competitive pricing implies a tangency between the unit value isoquant and the unit isocost line as in figure 3.1. If cost were less than price in sector 1 due to monopoly power, the unit isocost line would instead cut through the unit value isoquant. Given that the monopoly minimizes cost, the input ratio would be determined by the tangency of an isocost line with the c_1 isoquant that represents the amount of the product that costs one unit to produce at current factor prices. Product 1 is sold at a price higher than cost as pictured in figure 3.2. With restricted output, the relative price of factor 1 would be lower and the relative input of factor 1 higher than with competitive pricing.

Profit of the monopolist is $\pi_1 = (p_1 - c_1)x_1$. Maximizing π_1 with respect to c_1, $0 = \delta\pi_1/\delta c_1 = (p_1 - c_1)(\delta x_1/\delta c_1) - x_1$. As an alternative, the monopolist in Thompson (2002) maximizes profit with respect to output. The term $\delta x_1/\delta c_1$ in the general equilibrium is the same as $\delta x_1/\delta p_1 = c^2s/b^2$ from the competitive model in (3.4) where $c \equiv a_{12} + a_{22}$. When the monopoly restricts output, the cost reducing effect is similar to an exogenous decrease in p_1 in the competitive model (3.4). Substituting and solving for the optimal level of cost, $c_1{}^* = p_1 - (b^2x_1/c^2s)$ which implies $c_1{}^* < p_1$. A profit maximization is implied because $\delta^2\pi_1/\delta c_1{}^2 = (p_1 - c_1)(\delta^2x_1/\delta^2c_1) - \delta x_1/\delta c_1 - x_1 < 0$ given $\delta x_1/\delta c_1 = \delta x_1/\delta p_1 = c^2s/b^2$ and $\delta^2x_1/\delta^2p_1 = 0$. The relationship between p_1 and c_1 is summarized by $p_1 = \alpha c_1$, where $\alpha \geq 1$. If there is competitive pricing, $\alpha = 1$. Substituting the optimal $c_1{}^*$, $\alpha^* = p_1/(p_1 - (b^2x_1/c^2s)) = c^2sp_1/(c^2sp_1 - b^2x_1) > 1$.

The monopoly profit margin may be regulated to maintain cost at a constant proportion of price, $p_1 = \alpha c_1$ where $\alpha > 1$. The monopoly would restrict output to α^* but a regulator might set α above α^*. Profit would then be proportional to revenue,

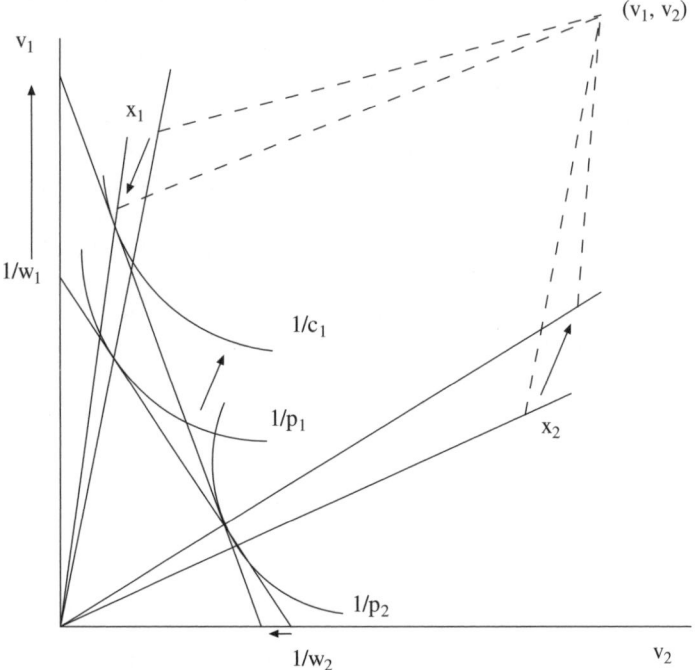

Figure 3.2   Monopoly output restriction

$\pi_1 = (1 - \alpha^{-1})p_1x_1 > 0$. With α constant, $dp_1 = \alpha dc_1 = \alpha\Sigma_i a_{i1}dw_i$ due to cost minimization along the monopoly unit cost isoquant, replacing the third equation in (3.4) and
the effects of a change in the price of the competitive product 2 are identical to the
competitive model (3.5). The factor price effects of a change in p_1 on the monopoly
comparative static system are $w_{11} = a_{22}/\alpha b$ and $w_{21} = -a_{12}/\alpha b$, smaller than with competitive pricing. Changes in the price of the monopoly product have dampened
Stolper–Samuelson effects relative to competitive pricing because of the corresponding proportional cost adjustment. The intensity price link, however, is robust
with respect to this monopoly power.

Suppose the profit margin varies with the level of output: $\alpha(x_1)$. The optimal α^*
increases with output, $\delta\alpha^*/\delta x_1 = b^2c^2sp_1/(c^2sp_1 - b^2x_1)^2 > 0$. A larger sector might have
increased political ability to persuade the regulator to set a higher α. The third equation in (3.4) becomes $\alpha\Sigma_i a_{i1}dw_i + \alpha'c_1dx_1 = dp_1$ where c_1 is the original cost in the
sector. The determinant of this model is $\Delta_f = c^2\alpha'c_1s + \alpha b^2 > 0$ where $c = a_{12} + a_{22}$ and
the w_{ij} results are:

$$
\begin{pmatrix} w_{11} & w_{21} \\ w_{12} & w_{22} \end{pmatrix} = \begin{pmatrix} a_{22}b/\Delta_f & -a_{12}b/\Delta_f \\ (\alpha'c_1cs - \alpha a_{21}b)/\Delta_f & (\alpha'c_1cs + \alpha a_{11}b)/\Delta_f \end{pmatrix} \quad \begin{matrix} + & - \\ - & + \\ (a) \end{matrix} \quad \begin{matrix} + & - \\ + & + \\ (b) \end{matrix} \quad (3.10)
$$

The strong intensity price link holds for the monopoly price but is potentially relaxed in part for the price of the competitive product. An increase in p_2 would lower x_1 implying a decline in α, loss of monopoly power, and a potential increase in w_1. If the derivative α' approaches zero, the strong intensity price link remains intact. While ambiguity arises in the w_{12} term, cost would have to rise substantially to make it positive as in (3.10b). Specifically, α' would have to be larger than $\alpha a_{21} b / c_1 cs$ to make w_{12} positive. Regardless, the intensity price link holds for the effects of the price of the noncompetitive product as well as the price of the competitive product on its intensive factor.

Consider an increase in p_2 holding p_1 constant. With $w_{22} > w_{12}$, percentage changes in prices and factor prices would be either $\hat{w}_2 > \hat{p}_2 > \hat{p}_1 = 0 > \hat{w}_1$ in (3.8a) or $\hat{w}_2 > \hat{p}_2 > \hat{w}_1 > \hat{p}_1 = 0$ in (3.8b). While w_1 may rise, the relative price of factor 1 would have to fall. The magnification effect would hold stated in terms of $\hat{c}_1$ instead of $\hat{p}_1$. The change in the real income of the owners of factor 1 becomes ambiguous while the real income of intensive factor 2 rises. If the owners of factor 1 consume little of good 1 their real income could rise if $\hat{w}_1 > 0$. Cost in sector 1 clearly rises with the increase in p_2 since $\delta c_1 / \delta p_2 = a_{11}(\delta w_1 / \delta p_2) + a_{21}(\delta w_2 / \delta p_2) = \alpha' c_1 cds / \Delta_f > 0$ where $d \equiv a_{11} + a_{21}$. The output of sector 1 falls as does profit with a higher price in the competitive sector. With falling output, the monopoly loses monopoly power.

The crucial point for the present section is that competitive pricing is not necessary for the intensity price link. While some behavioral mechanisms for noncompetitive pricing certainly relax the intensity price link, competitive pricing is not necessary. In the present model, the intensity price link is consistent with monopoly.

9   INCREASING RETURNS AND THE INTENSITY PRICE LINK

Increasing returns with economies of scale external to the firm in the terminology of Marshall (1930) may affect the intensity price link. Firms hire inputs as though their output decision has no effect on factor prices even though total output of all firms affects technology in this industrial structure. Inoue (1981) extends the Stolper–Samuelson theorem to include variable returns. Increasing returns can lead to a convex production frontier as shown by Chipman (1965), Jones (1968), Mayer (1974), and Panagariya (1983). Helpman and Krugman (1986, chapter 3) show that factor price equalization holds for some distributions of endowments across countries with increasing returns. Chipman (1970) develops a model with parametric external economies and Thompson and Ford (1997) examine the corresponding production frontiers, contract curves, relative price lines, and intensity price link.

The foundation of increasing returns is a production function of the form $\xi_1 = f(v; x_1)$ where ξ_1 is output of a typical firm in sector 1, v is its input vector, x_1 is output of the sector, and $\delta \xi_1 / \delta x_1 > 0$. In the literature on increasing returns, production functions are typically assumed to be separable in output, $\xi_1 = h(x_1) f(v)$ where $f(v)$ exhibits constant returns and $h' > 0$. Increasing returns occur, however, in a much wider class of production functions.

Variable returns can be generally specified with cost minimizing inputs a_{i1} functions of output as well as the vector $\mathbf{w}$ of factor prices, $a_{i1}(\mathbf{w}, x_1)$. A change in a_{i1}

would be written $da_{i1} = \Sigma_k(\delta a_{i1}/\delta w_k)dw_k + (\delta a_{i1}/\delta x_1)dx_1$. Increasing returns occur if $\delta a_{i1}/\delta x_1 < 0$ for every factor i. The isoquant map compresses as output increases, lowering unit inputs. Differentiate the competitive pricing condition to find $dp_1 = \Sigma_i a_{i1}dw_i + \Sigma_i w_i da_{i1}$ and expand the last term to $\Sigma_i w_i da_{i1} = \Sigma_i w_i(\Sigma_k(\delta a_{i1}/\delta w_k)dw_k + (\delta a_{i1}/\delta x_1)dx_1) = \Sigma_k(\Sigma_i w_i(\delta a_{i1}/\delta w_k)dw_k + \Sigma_i w_i(\delta a_{i1}/\delta x_1)dx_1)$. By Shephard's lemma, $a_{i1} = \delta c_1/\delta w_i$. Unit factor inputs are homogeneous of degree zero in factor prices since cost functions are homogeneous of degree one. Euler's theorem implies $\Sigma_i w_i(\delta a_{k1}/\delta w_i) = 0$ for each factor k. Shephard's lemma $\delta c_1/\delta w_i = a_{i1}$ and Young's theorem imply $\delta a_{i1}/\delta w_k = \delta a_{k1}/\delta w_i$. It follows that $\Sigma_i w_i(\delta a_{i1}/\delta w_k) = \Sigma_i w_i(\delta a_{k1}/\delta w_i) = \Sigma_i w_i \chi_i = 0$ where $\chi_i \equiv \delta a_{i1}/\delta x_1$. The competitive pricing condition then simplifies to $dp_1 = \Sigma_i a_{i1}dw_i + \Sigma_i w_i \chi_i = \Sigma_i a_{i1}dw_i + \Sigma_i \chi_i dx_1$.

The elasticity of the unit input with respect to output is $\sigma_i = \hat{a}_{i1}/\hat{x}_1 = (x_1/a_{ij})\chi_i$. With increasing returns, $\chi_i < 0$ and $\sigma_i < 0$. With homothetic production, as x_1 increases a_{11} and a_{21} fall proportionally. In other words, $\sigma_1 = \sigma_2 < 0$ with homothetic increasing returns. Note that $\delta(a_{11}/a_{21})/\delta x_1 = (a_{21}\chi_1 - a_{11}\chi_2)/a_{21}^2 = (a_{11}/a_{21})(\sigma_1 - \sigma_2) = 0$ implying $a_{21}\chi_1 - a_{11}\chi_2 = 0$ and $\chi_1/\chi_2 = a_{11}/a_{21}$. Further, $\sigma_i > -1$ since marginal products are positive, implying a negative slope for the production frontier. If $\sigma_i \geq -1$ and output increases, $0 < \hat{x}_1 \leq -\hat{a}_{i1}$. By definition $\hat{a}_{i1} = \hat{v}_{i1} - \hat{x}_1$ and $\hat{x}_1 - \hat{v}_{i1} \geq \hat{x}_1$ or $\hat{v}_{i1} \leq 0$, contradicting positive marginal productivity.

With nonhomothetic production, as x_1 increases the position of the new lower unit value isoquant would be biased toward an input axis. Suppose isoquants are biased toward factor 1 with expanding output. With factor prices constant, a_{11}/a_{21} rises with increased output, $\delta(a_{11}/a_{21})/\delta x_1 > 0$, and $-1 < \sigma_2 < \sigma_1 < 0$. Note also that $a_{21}\chi_1 - a_{11}\chi_2 > 0$ and $\chi_1/\chi_2 < a_{11}/a_{21}$. Figure 3.3 illustrates both homothetic and nonhomothetic increasing returns with shifts in unit isoquants to H and N due to an increase in output.

To complete the comparative static system, differentiate the full employment condition for factor i to find $dv_i = \Sigma_j (a_{ij}dx_j + x_j da_{ij})$. The second term becomes $\Sigma_j x_j da_{ij} = \Sigma_j x_j(\Sigma_k(\delta a_{ij}/\delta w_k)dw_k + \chi_i dx_1) = \Sigma_k s_{ik}dw_k + x_1\chi_i dx_1$. Note that $\delta a_{i2}/\delta x_1 = 0$. Without loss of generality rescale output so $x_1 = 1$ and the differentiated full employment condition simplifies to $dv_i = \Sigma_j a_{ij}dx_j + \Sigma_k s_{ik}dw_k + \chi_i dx_1$. Putting these conditions together, the comparative static system with increasing returns in sector 1 is:

$$
\begin{pmatrix}
-s & s & a_{11}+\chi_1 & a_{12} \\
s & -s & a_{21}+\chi_2 & a_{22} \\
a_{11} & a_{21} & \chi_1+\chi_2 & 0 \\
a_{12} & a_{22} & 0 & 0
\end{pmatrix}
\begin{pmatrix}
dw_1 \\
dw_2 \\
dx_1 \\
dx_2
\end{pmatrix}
=
\begin{pmatrix}
0 \\
0 \\
dp_1 \\
dp_2
\end{pmatrix},
\tag{3.11}
$$

with determinant $\Delta_i = b\beta - \mu c 2s$ where $b = a_{11}a_{22} - a_{12}a_{21} > 0$, $c = a_{12}+a_{22} > 0$, $\eta \equiv a_{12}\chi_2 - a_{22}\chi_1$, $\beta \equiv b - \eta$, and $\mu \equiv -(\chi_1 + \chi_2) > 0$. The sign of Δ_i is ambiguous but is negative if $\beta \leq 0$ and can only be positive if $\beta > 0$. Solving (3.11) for the w_{ij} terms

$$
\begin{pmatrix}
w_{11} & w_{21} \\
w_{12} & w_{22}
\end{pmatrix}
=
\begin{pmatrix}
a_{22}\beta/\Delta_i & -a_{12}\beta/\Delta_i \\
-(a_{21}\beta+\mu cs)/\Delta_i & (a_{11}\beta+\mu cs)/\Delta_i
\end{pmatrix}
\tag{3.12}
$$

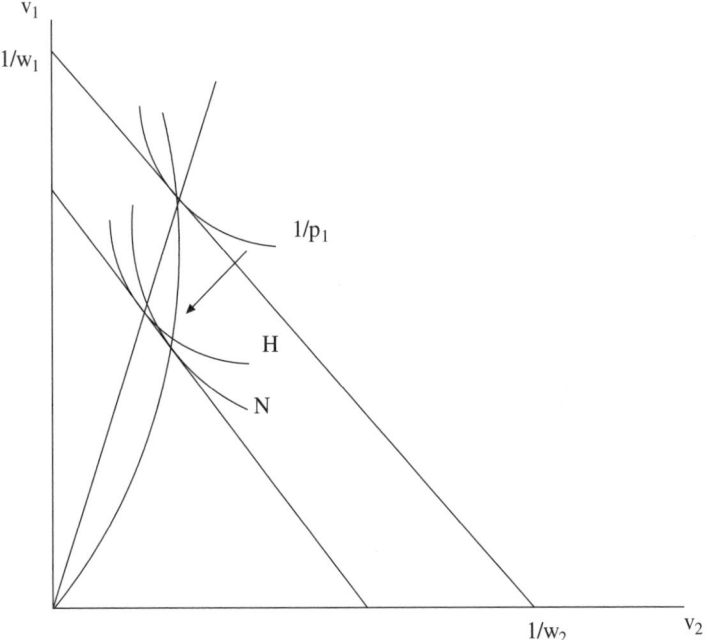

Figure 3.3 Homothetic and nonhomothetic production

The sign of β is critical. Note that a higher price for the product with increasing returns must have opposite effects on factor prices, a property that can be anticipated from the magnification effect. With constant returns in sector 2, $\hat{p}_2$ is a weighted average of $\hat{w}_1$ and $\hat{w}_2$. If $\hat{p}_1 \neq 0$ and $\hat{p}_2 = 0$, $\hat{w}_1$ and $\hat{w}_2$ must have opposite signs.

Before analyzing the w_{ij} matrix in more detail, consider the $x_{mj} \equiv \delta x_m/\delta p_j$ comparative static partial derivative production possibility matrix

$$\begin{pmatrix} x_{11} & x_{21} \\ x_{12} & x_{22} \end{pmatrix} = \begin{pmatrix} c^2 s/\Delta_i & -c(d-\mu)s/\Delta_i \\ -cds/\Delta_i & d(d-\mu)s/\Delta_i \end{pmatrix} \tag{3.13}$$

where $d = a_{11} + a_{21} > 0$. Each output must respond in opposite directions to a change in the price of either product since x_{j1} and x_{j2} have opposite signs. The term $d - \mu$ is positive: $d - \mu = (a_{11} + \chi_1) + (a_{21} + \chi_2)$ and $a_{j1} + \chi_j = a_{j1} + \delta a_{j1}/\delta x_1 > 0$ because an increase in x_1 cannot make a_{j1} negative. There are only two possible sign patterns for the x_{mj} matrix depending on the sign of Δ_i. If $\Delta_i > 0$, the x_{mj} matrix has the concave sign pattern with positive main diagonal elements (x_{11}, x_{22}) and negative elements (x_{12}, x_{21}) off the diagonal. If $\Delta_i < 0$, the signs are exactly reversed into a convex production frontier. A concave production frontier is associated with the strong intensity price link as developed by Kemp (1964). Markusen and Melvin (1981) and Wong

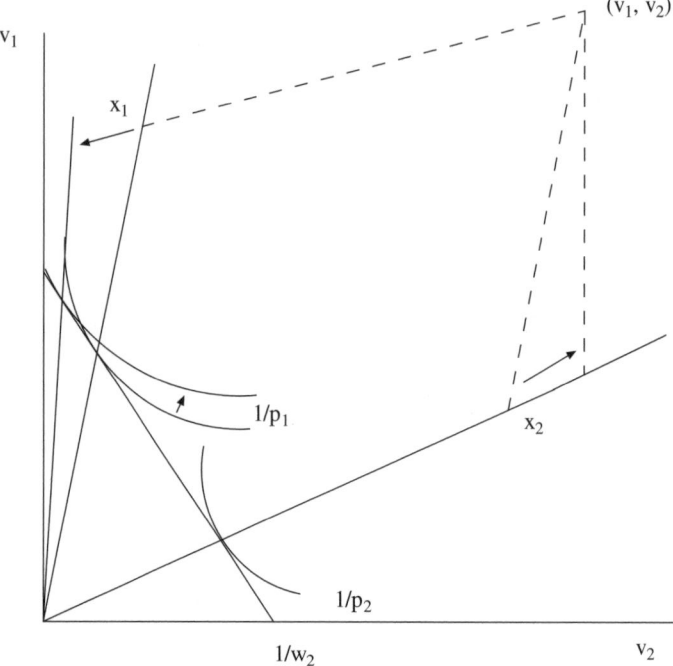

Figure 3.4 Convex PPF without factor price effects

(1995, chapter 5) show that with a separable production function a concave production frontier implies the intensity price link.

There are ambiguities in the signs of the determinant Δ_i and the w_{ij} matrix due
to β. If production is homothetic, $a_{11}/a_{21} = \chi_1/\chi_2$ and β expands to $b - \eta = a_{22}(a_{11} +
\chi_1) - a_{12}(a_{21} + \chi_2)$. Substitute $a_{11}\chi_2/a_{21}$ for χ_1 to find $\beta = b(1 + \chi_2/a_{21}) > b(1 - a_{21}/a_{21}) =
0$ since $\chi_2 > -a_{21}$. Homothetic production implies $\beta > 0$. With nonhomothetic pro-
duction, however, β may not be positive. In the special case when $\beta = 0$, $\Delta_i < 0$, the
production frontier is convex, and the w_{ij} matrix has the sign pattern

$$\begin{pmatrix} w_{11} & w_{21} \\ w_{12} & w_{22} \end{pmatrix} = \begin{matrix} 0 & 0 \\ + & + \end{matrix} \tag{3.14}$$

A higher price for the product with increasing returns has no effect on factor prices
while a higher price for the other product raises both factor prices as illustrated in
figure 3.4, an outcome that has not appeared in the literature. The unit value isoquant would shift toward the origin with the increase in p_1 but decreased output
causes it to shift out with a_{11}/a_{12} rising.

If $\Delta_i > 0$ it follows that $w_{12} < 0$ and $w_{22} > 0$. Note a positive Δ_i requires $\beta > 0$ which
implies $w_{12} < 0$ directly. Also $\Delta_i > 0$ implies $\beta > \mu c^2 s/b$. Substituting, $w_{22} > a_{11}\mu c^2 s/b -$

$\mu cs = \mu cs(a_{11}c - b)/b$. But $a_{11}c - b = b > 0$, implying $w_{22} > 0$. A positive Δ_i implies a concave production frontier and the strong intensity price link.

There are also other possible w_{ij} sign patterns. With homothetic production, if $\Delta_i > 0$ the production frontier is concave and the strong intensity price link occurs. If $\Delta_i < 0$ the production frontier is convex and there are two possible w_{ij} patterns,

$$\begin{pmatrix} w_{11} & w_{21} \\ w_{12} & w_{22} \end{pmatrix} = \begin{matrix} - & + \\ + & - \end{matrix} \quad \begin{matrix} - & + \\ + & + \end{matrix} \qquad (3.15)$$
$$\qquad\qquad\qquad (a) \qquad (b)$$

Pattern (3.15a) is the reversed intensity price link usually associated with a convex production frontier. In (3.15b) a higher price for the product with constant returns raises both factor prices, another possibility that has not appeared in the literature.

If production is nonhomothetic, additional situations arise when $\beta < 0$. First, the determinant Δ_i is negative and the production frontier is convex. The two possible w_{ij} patterns with nonhomothetic production are:

$$\begin{pmatrix} w_{11} & w_{21} \\ w_{12} & w_{22} \end{pmatrix} = \begin{matrix} + & - \\ - & + \end{matrix} \quad \begin{matrix} + & - \\ + & + \end{matrix} \qquad (3.16)$$
$$\qquad\qquad\qquad (a) \qquad (b)$$

The intensity price link occurs with a convex production frontier in (3.16a), a situation not found in the literature and pictured in figure 3.5. An increase in the price of the product with constant returns may raise both factor prices as in (3.16b). Neither of these outcomes can occur with separable production functions.

The bottom line is that factor intensity does not completely predict the intensity price link in the presence of increasing returns. A concave production frontier implies a strong intensity price link but when there is a convex production frontier exceptions including a complete reversal are possible. Factor intensity nevertheless sets the stage for increasing returns and with small output effects the intensity price link would remain intact.

The typical motivating story for increasing returns is specialization in the Adam Smith pin factory but such a situation is better modeled as an increase in the types of labor in a different production function. New capital machinery and equipment are better analyzed as a new production function. Proportional increases in the same types of inputs in a given production function should only be expected to lead to proportional output increases.

10 HIGH DIMENSIONAL EVEN MODELS AND THE INTENSITY PRICE LINK

High dimensional models have many factors and many products, and even models have the same number of each. Samuelson (1953), Minabe (1967), Diewart and Woodland (1977), Jones and Scheinkman (1977), Chang (1979), and Ethier

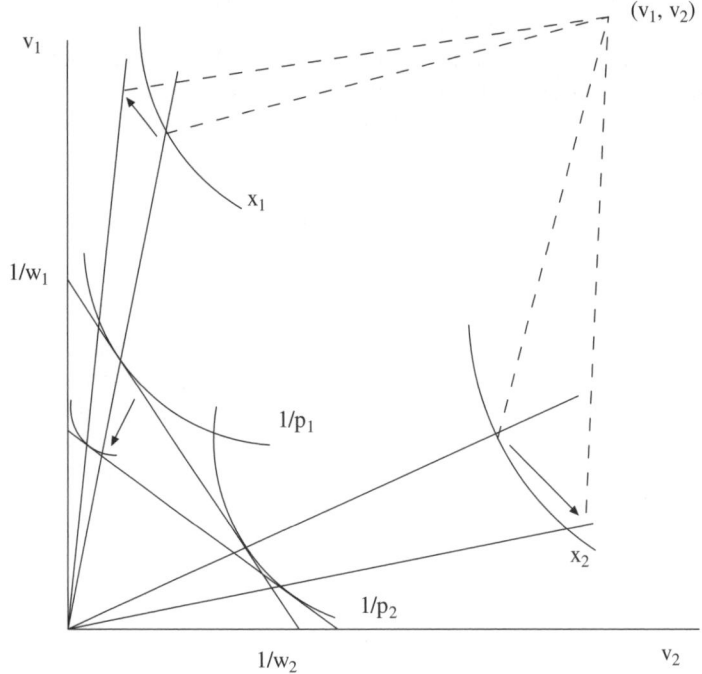

Figure 3.5 Stolper–Samuelson result with convex PPF

(1984a, b) develop properties of high dimensional even models. A strong intensity price link occurs if factors and products can each be aggregated into two groups, a point developed by Ethier (1982) and Neary (1985).

Chang (1979) shows that factor prices are homogeneous of degree one in prices given constant returns, since Euler's theorem implies $\Sigma_j p_j w_{ij} = w_i$. An implication is that for every factor i there must be at least one product m such that $w_{im} > 0$. Because factors are paid their marginal products and production is linearly homogeneous, Euler's theorem implies $\Sigma_i w_i v_{ij} = x_j$. A higher price for product n raises its output and there must be at least one factor k such that $w_{kn} > 0$. Jones and Scheinkman (1977) show that for every product n there must be at least one factor k such that $w_{kn} < 0$ if every factor is used in at least two sectors.

In even models, w_{ij} results can be derived from competitive pricing conditions alone without regard for factor substitution. Let $A(\mathbf{w})$ represent the full rank technology matrix of unit inputs a_{ij} with unique products. Competitive pricing implies cost equals price, $A(\mathbf{w})\mathbf{w} = \mathbf{p}$ in matrix notation. Totally differentiate and apply the cost minimization property $A'(\mathbf{w})\mathbf{w} = 0$ to find $A(\mathbf{w})d\mathbf{w} = d\mathbf{p}$ or $A(\mathbf{w})^{-1} = w_{ij}$. In even models, w_{ij} terms depend only on $A(\mathbf{w})^{-1}$. Converting to factor shares, $\theta\hat{\mathbf{w}} = \hat{\mathbf{p}}$ and $\hat{\mathbf{w}}/\hat{\mathbf{p}} = \theta^{-1}$.

Kemp and Wegge (1969), Inada (1971), Uekawa (1971), and Uekawa, Kemp, and Wegge (1973) examine properties of the θ matrix and the resulting $\hat{w}/\hat{p}$ elasticities.

The rows of θ sum to 1 and by implication the rows of θ^{-1} sum to 1. A θ^{-1} matrix with positive elements along the diagonal and negative elements off the diagonal is called a Leontief matrix. In the 2×2 model, the diagonal elements of θ^{-1} are the own $\hat{w}/\hat{p}$ terms linking each product with its intensive factor. The rows of θ^{-1} sum to 1 implying the diagonal elements of any Leontief matrix are greater than 1. This additional property makes every Leontief matrix a Minkowski matrix, called the strong Stolper–Samuelson property by Chipman (1969). In the 2×2 model, the magnification effect holds and θ^{-1} is a Minkowski matrix.

In high dimensional even models, θ^{-1} may not be a Minkowski matrix. The weak Stolper–Samuelson property refers to a θ^{-1} matrix with elements greater than 1 along the diagonal but nonnegative elements off the diagonal. Jones (1976) shows that for every unimportant factor k such that $\Sigma_j\theta_{kj} < 1$ there is a price p_m such that $\hat{w}_k/\hat{p}_m > 1$, and for every factor h there is sector m such that $\hat{w}_h/\hat{p}_m > 1$.

If factors and products can be renumbered so $\theta_{ii} - \theta_{ki} > 0$ where $k \neq i$, diagonal elements of θ^{-1} would all be greater than 1 as noted by Chipman (1969). For every product m there would be some factor k such that $\hat{w}_k/\hat{p}_m > 1$. Such renumbering, however, is not generally possible and even the weak Stolper–Samuelson property may not hold.

Much more unsettling for theory is the point that the numbers of factors and products is an empirical issue. Even two closely related products like natural gas and propane that might be aggregated into fuels should not be aggregated because their prices and quantities adjust independently. In practice, the most highly disaggregated data is overly aggregated. As an example for labor data, Clark, Hofler, and Thompson (1988) find that none of the eight skill groups in US manufacturing data can be aggregated.

A dilemma facing high dimensional models has been the lack of a general definition of factor intensity beyond situations with two factors or two goods. In the 3×3 model, for instance, the three pairs of factors can be ranked across each of the three pairs of sectors and a factor may be at the top of one ranking but the bottom of another. Thompson (1999) identifies special conditions under which there would be consistent factor intensity rankings in high dimensional models.

One option is to index factor intensity, perhaps to its average across products. With n products, let the mean input of factor i be $\mu_i \equiv \Sigma_j a_{ij}/n$ and the mean weighted input is $\alpha_{ij} \equiv a_{ij}/\mu_i$. There can be various possible w_{ij} patterns for any indexed intensity ranking, this definition may anticipate comparative static properties as discussed for factor abundance by Rassekh and Thompson (2002). As an example, consider the 9×3 model of the US economy in Thompson (1990) summarized in table 3.1. Factor shares θ_{ij} for capital and the eight skilled groups of labor in US Census data are the first entry of each column. A unit of output defined as one dollar's worth, $p_j = 1$, implying $\alpha_{ij} = \theta_{ij}/\mu_{\theta i}$ where $\mu_{\theta i} \equiv \Sigma_i\theta_{ij}/n$. Mean weighted factor shares equal mean weighted inputs α_{ij}, the second entry of each column in table 3.1.

The indexed factor intensities can be compared across rows for each factor and down columns for each product. Capital is intensive in agriculture, a sector that uses natural resource workers about three times as intensively as its next most intensive labor input, transport workers. Manufacturing has intensive inputs of operators, handlers, and craft workers. The service sector uses service, technical,

Table 3.1 An example of mean weighted factor intensity

	Agriculture			Manufacturing			Services		
	θ_{ij}	α_{ij}	w_{ij}	θ_{ij}	α_{ij}	w_{ij}	θ_{ij}	α_{ij}	w_{ij}
Capital	.576	1.65	0.32	.214	0.61	−0.45	.261	0.75	1.13
Professional	.059	0.37	−0.18	.148	0.93	−0.42	.269	1.69	1.60
Technical and sales	.003	0.28	−0.17	.115	0.96	−0.60	.211	1.76	1.78
Service	.003	0.18	−0.15	.008	0.47	−0.75	.041	2.41	1.90
Natural resource	.139	2.90	5.94	.002	0.04	0.16	.002	0.04	−5.11
Craft	.086	0.74	0.04	.167	1.44	1.31	.096	0.83	−0.36
Operators	.045	0.34	−0.17	.286	2.17	3.44	.067	0.51	−2.27
Transport	.030	0.94	0.01	.031	0.97	0.77	.036	1.13	0.22
Handlers	.008	0.44	0.25	.028	1.56	0.28	.018	1.00	0.47

professional, and transport workers most intensively, and professional workers more than four times as intensively as agriculture and almost twice as intensively as manufacturing.

The third entries in the columns of table 3.1 are the w_{ij} elasticities from the general equilibrium comparative static model. Substitution is estimated by factor share equations of translog production functions across states. Regarding sensitivity, these w_{ij} terms are very stable across Cobb–Douglas and a wide range of constant elasticity of substitution (CES) production functions in which factor "intensity" largely determines factor substitution elasticities.

The mean weighted factor intensity fairly well predicts the theoretical price adjustment pattern, essentially the intensity price link. There is a significant correlation of 0.786 between the mean weighted factor intensities and the comparative static price elasticities. Factor shares have an insignificant correlation of 0.311 with the w_{ij} elasticities. While it has no necessary theoretical connection with factor price adjustments, indexed factor intensity may prove useful. These sorts of links between relative inputs and w_i/p_j terms follow the spirit of the Stolper–Samuelson theorem.

11 CONCLUSION

While the theoretical literature on the Stolper–Samuelson theorem has emphasized various conditions under which it does not hold, its underlying importance remains intact. The essence of general equilibrium is the link between prices and factor prices. The property that factor intensity alone would determine these qualitative links is a coincidence of low dimensions and competition in the Stolper–Samuelson theorem. Nevertheless, factor intensity by some measure would generally influence general equilibrium price adjustments.

Studies are beginning to critically examine the empirical evidence regarding the intensity price link. Leamer and Levinsohn (1995) review the literature and Deardorff and Hakura (1994) develop a conceptual framework for addressing the theorem's empirical content. While Magee (1980) shows that congressional lobbying patterns do not appear to favor the theorem, it would be timely to extend the evidence to the more recent decades of increased international trade lobbying and government intervention. Leamer (1984) points out that direct application of the theorem is difficult because of colinearity in prices but recent advances in cointegration create some optimism about direct testing.

Lawrence and Slaughter (1993) argue that the changing prices due to trade in the US during the 1980s had little influence on wages, and Murphy and Welch (1992) are unable to isolate any effect of the level of trade on wages. In contrast, Batra and Slotje (1993) argue that increased trade has lowered US wages since the early 1970s. At any rate, prices and not the level of trade affect factor prices in factor proportions theory. Gaston and Trefler (1994) find that US tariffs have lowered manufacturing wages but the correlation with domestic prices would be critical. For the US, oil imports have little to do with factor intensity but the price of oil has been a driving force on relative prices. Bhagwati and Dehejia (1994) discount Stolper–Samuelson effects as accounting for any decline in unskilled wages in the US. Krugman and Lawrence (1994) uncover no evidence of substitution of relatively scarce unskilled labor for abundant skilled labor during the 1980s but present no evidence on relative prices or factor intensity.

Grossman (1987) finds weak links between industrial prices and US wages but recent research on wage convergence across OECD countries by Mokhtari and Rassekh (1989) and Rassekh (1993) and across many countries by Davis and Weinstein (2001) has restored some of the theorem's credibility. Rassekh and Thompson (1997) examine industrial adjustments across OECD countries between 1970 and 1985 controlling for exogenous conditions and find results consistent with the Stolper–Samuelson theorem. The different views of Leamer (2000), Krugman (2000), Deardorff (2000), and Panagariya (2000) on the theorem suggest various avenues for research.

Part of the appeal of the Stolper–Samuelson theorem is that factor intensity or other measures of relative factor inputs can be derived from primitive data without reliance on estimated production or cost functions. Thompson (1990, 1997) examines intensity price patterns in simulations of multifactor general equilibrium models and finds that relative factor shares dominate factor substitution in the comparative static price adjustments.

While the most difficult issue facing factor proportions theory remains developing models with many factors and many products, the present chapter shows that the Stolper–Samuelson intensity price link is robust to relaxing its sufficient conditions.

Acknowledgments

Thanks go to Kwan Choi, Ron Jones, Kaz Miyagiwa, Murray Kemp, Masayuki Okawa, Farhad Rassekh, and Roy Ruffin for comments and suggestions.

References

Batra, Raveendra and Francisco Casas 1976: A synthesis of the Heckscher–Ohlin and the neoclassical models of international trade. *Journal of International Economics*, 6, 21–38.

Batra, Raveendra and Daniel Slotje 1993: Trade policy and poverty in the United States: Theory and evidence. *Review of International Economics*, 1, 189–208.

Bhagwati, Jagdish 1959: Protection, real wages and real income. *Economic Journal*, 69, 733–48.

Bhagwati, Jagdish and Viveck Dehejia 1994: Freer trade and wages of the unskilled: Is Marx striking again? In Jagdish Bhagwati and Marvin Kosters (eds.), *Trade and Wages: Leveling Wages Down?*, Washington: AEI Press.

Bhagwati, Jagdish and T. N. Srinivasan 1971: The theory of wage differentials: Production response and factor price equalization. *Journal of International Economics*, 1, 19–35.

Branson, William and Nicolas Monoyios, 1977: Factor inputs in US trade. *Journal of International Economics*, 7, 11–131.

Chang, Winston 1979: Some theorems of trade and general equilibrium with many products and factors. *Econometrica*, 47, 709–26.

Chipman, John 1965: A survey of the theory of international trade: Part 2, The neo-classical theory. *Econometrica*, 33, 685–760.

Chipman, John 1966: A survey of the theory of international trade: Part 3, The modern theory. *Econometrica*, 34, 18–76.

Chipman, John 1969: Factor price equalization and the Stolper–Samuelson theorem. *International Economic Review*, 10, 339–406.

Chipman, John 1970: External economics of scale and competitive equilibrium. *Quarterly Journal of Economics*, 84, 347–85.

Choi, Kwan 2003: Implications of many industries in the Heckscher–Ohlin model. (This volume.)

Clark, Don, Richard Hofler, and Henry Thompson 1988: Separability of capital and labor in US manufacturing. *Economics Letters*, 26, 197–201.

Davis, Donald and David Weinstein 2001: An account of global factor trade. *American Economic Review*, 91, 1423–53.

Deardorff, Alan 2000: Factor prices and the factor content of trade: What's the use? *Journal of International Economics*, 50, 73–90.

Deardorff, Alan and Dalia Hakura 1994: Trade and wages: What are the questions? In Jagdish Bhagwati and Marvin Kosters (eds.), *Trade and Wages: Leveling Wages Down?*, Washington: AEI Press.

Diewart, Erwin and Alan Woodland 1977: Frank Knight's theorem in linear programming revisited. *Econometrica*, 45, 375–98.

Ethier, Wilfred 1972: Nontraded products and the Heckscher–Ohlin model. *International Economic Review*, 13, 132–46.

Ethier, Wilfred 1982: The general role of factor intensity in the theorems of international trade. *Economics Letters*, 10, 337–42.

Ethier, Wilfred 1984a: Some of the theorems of international trade with many products and factors. *Journal of International Economics*, 14, 199–206.

Ethier, Wilfred 1984b: Higher-dimensional issues in trade theory. In Ron Jones and Peter Kenen (eds.), *Handbook of International Economics*, Amsterdam: North-Holland.

Gaston, Noel and Daniel Trefler 1994: Protection, trade, and wages: Evidence from US manufacturing. *Industrial Labor Relations Review*, 47, 574–93.

Grossman, Gene 1987: Imports as a cause of injury: The case of the US steel industry. *Journal of Economic Integration*, 2, 1–23.

Harrod, R. 1958: Factor-price relations under free trade. *Economic Journal*, 68, 245–55.

Helpman, Elhanan 1981: International trade in the presence of product differentiating economies of scale and monopolistic competition: A Chamberlin–Heckscher–Ohlin approach. *Journal of International Economics*, 11, 305–40.

Helpman, Elhanan and Paul Krugman 1986: *Market Structure and Foreign Trade*, Cambridge, MA: The MIT Press.

Herberg, Horst and Murray Kemp 1971: Factor market distortions, the shape of the locus of competitive outputs and the relation between product prices and equilibrium outputs. In Jagdish Bhagwati, Ron Jones, Robert Mundell, and Jarosalov Vanek (eds.), *Trade, Balance of Payments and Growth: Essays in Honor of Charles P. Kindleberger*, Amsterdam: North Holland.

Inada, K. 1971: The production coefficient matrix and the Stolper–Samuelson condition. *Econometrica*, 39, 219–40.

Inoue, Tadashi 1981: A generalization of the Samuelson reciprocity relations, the Stolper–Samuelson theorem and the Rybczynski theorem under variable returns to scale. *Journal of International Economics*, 11, 79–98.

James, S. and Ivor Pearce 1951: The factor price equalization myth: Mathematical appendix. *Review of Economics Studies*, 19, 119–20.

Johnson, Harry 1966: Factor market distortions and the shape of the transformation curve. *Econometrica*, 34, 686–98.

Johnson, Harry and Peter Mieszkowski 1970: The effects of unionization on the distribution of income: A general equilibrium approach. *The Quarterly Journal of Economics*, 84, 539–61.

Jones, Ron 1956: Factor proportions and the Heckscher–Ohlin theorem. *Review of Economic Studies*, 24, 1–10.

Jones, Ron 1965: The structure of simple general equilibrium models. *Journal of Political Economy*, 73, 557–72.

Jones, Ron 1968: Variable returns to scale in general equilibrium theory. *International Economic Review*, 9, 261–72.

Jones, Ron 1971: Distortions in factor markets and the general equilibrium model of production. *Journal of Political Economy*, 79, 437–59.

Jones, Ron 1976: Twoness in trade theory: Costs and benefits. Frank Graham Lecture.

Jones, Ron and Stephen Easton 1983: Factor intensities and factor substitution in general equilibrium. *Journal of International Economics*, 13, 65–99.

Jones, Ron and José Scheinkman 1977: The relevance of the two-sector production model in trade theory. *Journal of Political Economy*, 85, 909–35.

Kemp, Murray 1964: *The Pure Theory of International Trade*. Englewood Cliffs: Prentice Hall.

Kemp, Murray and Ron Jones 1962: Variable labor supply and the theory of international trade. *Journal of Political Economy*: 70, 30–6.

Kemp, Murray and Masayuki Okawa 1998a: Market structure and factor price equalization. *Japanese Economic Review*, 49, 335–9.

Kemp, Murray and Masayuki Okawa 1998b: Variable returns to scale and factor price equalization. In K. J. Arrow, Y. K. Ng, and X. Yang (eds.), *Increasing Returns and Economic Analysis*, Basingstoke: Macmillan, 409–12.

Kemp, Murray and L. Wegge 1969: On the relation between commodity prices and factor rewards. *International Economic Review*, 10, 407–13.

Komiya, R. 1967: Non-traded products and the pure theory of international trade. *International Economic Review*, 8, 132–52.

Koo, Anthony 1953: Duty and non-duty imports and income distribution. *American Economic Review*, 43, 31–40.

Krugman, Paul 1979: Increasing returns, monopolistic competition and international trade. *Journal of International Economics*, 9, 469–79.

Krugman, Paul 2000: Technology, trade and factor prices. *Journal of International Economics*, 50, 51–71.

Krugman, Paul and Robert Lawrence 1994: Trade, jobs, and wages. *Scientific American*, 270, 22–7.

Lancaster, Kelvin 1957: The Heckscher–Ohlin trade model: A geometric treatment. *Economica*, 24, 19–39.

Lawrence, Robert and Matthew Slaughter 1993: International trade and American wages in the 1980s: Giant sucking sound or small hiccup? *Brookings Papers on Economic Activity*, 2, 115–80.

Leamer, Edward 1984: *Sources of Comparative Advantage*. Cambridge, MA: The MIT Press.

Leamer, Edward 2000: What's the use of factor contents? *Journal of International Economics*, 17–49.

Leamer, Edward and James Levinsohn 1995: International trade theory: The evidence. In Gene Gross and Kenneth Rugoff (eds.), *Handbook of International Economics*, vol. 3, Amsterdam: North Holland.

Magee, Stephen 1971: Factor market distortions, production, distribution and the pure theory of international trade. *Quarterly Journal of Economics*, 75, 623–43.

Magee, Stephen 1973: Factor market distortions, production, and trade: A survey. *Oxford Economic Papers*, 25, 1–43.

Magee, Stephen 1980: Three simple tests of the Stolper–Samuelson theorem. In Peter Oppenheimer (ed.), *Issues in International Economics*, London: Oriel Press.

Markusen, James and James Melvin 1981: Trade, factor prices and the gains from trade with increasing returns to scale. *Canadian Journal of Economics*, 14, 450–69.

Marshall, Alfred 1930: *Principles of Economics*, 8th edn. London: Macmillan.

Mayer, Wolfgang 1974 Variable returns to scale in general equilibrium: A comment. *International Economic Review*, 15, 225–35.

McKenzie, Lionel 1955: Equality of factor price in world trade. *Econometrica*, 23, 239–57.

Melvin, James 1968: Production and trade with two factors and three products. *American Economic Review*, 58, 1248–68.

Melvin, James and R. Warne 1973: Monopoly and the theory of international trade. *Journal of International Economics*, 3, 117–34.

Minabe, Nubuo 1967: The Stolper–Samuelson theorem, the Rybczynski effect, and the Heckscher–Ohlin theory of trade pattern and factor price equalization: The case of a many-commodity, many-factor country. *Canadian Journal of Economics and Political Science*, 33, 401–19.

Mokhtari, Manoucher and Farhad Rassekh 1989: The tendency towards factor price equalization among OECD countries. *The Review of Economics and Statistics*, 61, 636–42.

Murphy, Kevin and Finnis Welch 1992: The role of international trade in wage differentials. In Marvin Kosters (ed.), *Workers and Their Wages: Changing Patterns in the US*, Washington: AEI Press.

Neary, Peter 1985: Two-by-two international trade theory with many products and factors. *Econometrica*, 53, 1233–47.

Panagariya, Arvind 1983: Variable returns to scale and the Heckscher-Ohlin and factor-price-equalization theorems. *Weltwirtshaftliches Archiv*, 119, 259–79.

Panagariya, Arvind 2000: Evaluating the factor content approach to measuring the effect of trade on wage inequality. *Journal of International Economics*, 30, 91–116.

Pearce, Ivor 1951: The factor price equalization myth. *Review of Economic Studies*, 19, 111–19.

Rader, Trout 1979: Factor price equilibrium with more industries than factors. In Jerry Green and José Sheinkman (eds.), *General Equilibrium, Growth, and Trade*, New York: Academic Press.

Rassekh, Farhad 1993: International trade and the relative dispersion of industrial wages and production techniques in fourteen OECD countries, 1970–1985. *Open Economics Review*, 4, 325–44.

Rassekh, Farhad and Henry Thompson 1997: Adjustment in general equilibrium: Some industrial evidence. *Review of International Economics*, 5, 20–31.

Rassekh, Farhad and Henry Thompson 2002: Measuring factor abundance across many factors and many countries. *Open Economies Review*, 13, 237–49.

Rivera-Batiz, Francisco 1982: Nontraded products and the pure theory of international trade with equal numbers of products and factors. *International Economic Review*, 23, 401–9.

Ruffin, Roy 1981: Trade and factor movements with three factors and two products. *Economics Letters*, 7, 177–82.

Samuelson, Paul 1953: Prices of factors and products in general equilibrium. *Review of Economic Studies*, 21, 1–20.

Stolper, Wolfgang and Paul Samuelson 1941: Protection and real wages. *Review of Economic Studies*, 9, 58–73.

Suzuki, Kaksuhiko 1983: A synthesis of the Heckscher–Ohlin and neoclassical models of international trade: A comment. *Journal of International Economics*, 13, 141–4.

Takayama, Akira 1982: On theorems of general competitive equilibrium of production and trade: A survey of recent developments in the theory of international trade. *Keio Economic Studies*, 19, 1–38.

Thompson, Henry 1985: Complementarity in a simple general equilibrium production model. *Canadian Journal of Economics*, 28, 616–21.

Thompson, Henry 1986: Free trade and factor price polarization. *European Economic Review*, 30, 419–25.

Thompson, Henry 1989: Variable employment and income in general equilibrium. *Southern Economic Journal*, 55, 679–83.

Thompson, Henry 1990: Simulating a multifactor general equilibrium model of production and trade. *International Economic Journal*, 4, 21–34.

Thompson, Henry 1993: The magnification effect with three factors. *Keio Economic Studies*, 30, 57–64.

Thompson, Henry 1995: Factor intensity versus factor substitution in a specified general equilibrium model. *Journal of Economic Integration*, 10, 283–97.

Thompson, Henry 1997a: Free trade and income redistribution across labor groups: Comparative statics for the US economy. *International Review of Economics and Finance*, 6, 181–92.

Thompson, Henry 1997b: Free trade and income redistribution in a three factor model of the US economy. *Southern Economic Journal*, 64, April, 1074–83.

Thompson, Henry 1999: Definitions of factor abundance and the factor content of trade. *Open Economies Review*, 10, 385–93.

Thompson, Henry 2002: Price taking monopolies in small open economies. *Open Economies Review*, 13, 205–9.

Thompson, Henry and Jon Ford 1997: Global sensitivity of neoclassical and factor proportions models to production technology. *International Economic Journal*, 11, 61–74.

Travis, William 1972: Production, trade, and protection when there are many commodities and two factors. *American Economic Review*, 62, 87–106.

Uekawa, Yasuo 1971: Generalization of the Stolper–Samuelson theorem. *Econometrica*, 39, 197–217.

Uekawa, Yasuo, Murray Kemp, and L. Wegge 1973: P- and PN-matrices, Minkowski and Metzler-matrices, and generalization of the Stolper–Samuelson and Samuelson-Rybczynski theorems. *Journal of International Economics*, 3, 53–76.

Wong, Kar-Yiu 1990: Factor intensity reversal in a multi-factor, two-product economy. *Journal of Economic Theory*, 51, 434–42.

Wong, Kar-Yiu 1995: *International Trade in Products and Factor Mobility*, Cambridge, MA: The MIT Press.

4

Specialization and the Volume of Trade: Do the Data Obey the Laws?

James Harrigan

CHAPTER OUTLINE

The core subjects of trade theory are the pattern and volume of trade: which goods are traded by which countries, and how much of those goods are traded. The first part of the chapter discusses evidence on comparative advantage, with an emphasis on carefully connecting theory models to data analyses. The second part first considers the theoretical foundations of the gravity model, and then reviews the small number of papers that have tried to test, rather than simply use, the implications of gravity. Both parts of the chapter yield the same conclusion: we are still in the very early stages of empirically understanding specialization and the volume of trade, but the work that has been done can serve as a starting point for further research.

1 INTRODUCTION

The core subjects of trade theory are the pattern and volume of trade: which goods are traded by which countries, and how much of those goods are traded. Most of the rest of trade theory, such as the analysis of policy and the effects of trade on factor prices and welfare, is grounded in models that explain the pattern and/or volume of trade. As a consequence, it is impossible to assess the relevance of trade theory as a whole unless we understand the empirical performance of the core explanations for trade.

The oldest explanation for the pattern of trade, originally due to Ricardo, is comparative advantage. The law of comparative advantage is an unassailable intellectual cornerstone of economics, but until recently empirical research on it has been scant and only loosely connected to theory. In contrast, the law of gravity as applied to explaining the volume of trade has been the foundation for literally hundreds of applied studies, but the gravity model has had a comparatively shallow (if not shaky) theoretical foundation. The purpose of this chapter is to review and critique the last decade or so of empirical research on comparative advantage and gravity.

The first part of the chapter discusses evidence on comparative advantage, with an emphasis on carefully connecting theory models to data analyses. The second part first considers the theoretical foundations of the gravity model, and then reviews the small number of papers that have tried to test, rather than simply use, the implications of gravity. Both parts of the chapter yield the same conclusion: we are still in the very early stages of empirically understanding specialization and the volume of trade, but the work that has been done can serve as a starting point for further research.

2 TESTING THE GENERAL THEORY OF COMPARATIVE ADVANTAGE

Economists are proud of the theory of comparative advantage, seeing it as both beautiful and profound: beautiful because of its simplicity and elegance, profound because it is surprising and has deep implications for economic policy and our understanding of real economies.

But is the theory of comparative advantage actually useful for helping to understand the world? The most fundamental problem about comparative advantage is that it relates observables (trade flows and specialization patterns) to things which are by their nature almost always unobservable (autarky prices). For example, in Deardorff's (1980) definitive modern statement of the theory, the general theorem of comparative advantage for a single country is stated as "The value of net exports evaluated at autarky prices is non-positive" (Deardorff, 1980, p. 948). The assumptions required to prove this result are standard but minimalist: they include convex technology, perfect competition, and the existence of community indifference curves. Tariffs and transport costs are allowed, but not trade subsidies. Like all statements of the theory of comparative advantage, Deardorff's is a comparative general equilibrium result: allowing all goods and factor markets to clear simultaneously, it expresses a relationship that must hold between an endogenous variable in one equilibrium (autarky prices) and an endogenous variable in another equilibrium (net exports).[1]

If it were possible to test this theory there would be a lot at stake. The most interesting reasons why the prediction could fail include non-convex technology and/or imperfect competition, as well as perverse trade policies such as export subsidies. Alternatively, markets simply might not work the way we think they do. In short, failure or confirmation of the law of comparative advantage would be very interesting for theorists as well as policy-makers.

Perhaps surprisingly given the general invisibility of autarky prices, there are two recent papers that offer evidence on the relationship between autarky prices and trade flows. The first of these, in 1995, was Noussair et al.'s "An Experimental Investigation of the Patterns of International Trade." Noussair et al. ran laboratory experiments intended to satisfy the assumptions of comparative advantage theory. The experimental economy has two countries and two goods, with given linear production functions that differ across countries and identical preferences for all agents. The experimental subjects are undergraduates at Cal Tech and the University of Iowa. The autarky and free trade equilibria in this economy can be easily computed analytically, so the purpose of the experiment is to see how close the data is to the analytical equilibrium. Before considering the results, it is worth asking what can possibly be learned from this exercise. The authors themselves pose the question "Since the world's international economies are vastly more complicated than the economies created for this study, of what relevance are laboratory data?" (Noussair et al., 1995, p. 462). The authors do not satisfactorily answer this query. Their best attempt at an answer (p. 464) is:

> The preconditions for the operations of the principles [of comparative advantage] have been introduced by the experimenters. The experiments are able to provide some insights into how models . . . are able to organize the data, given that the situation is one in which the model can meaningfully be applied. The experiment cannot, however, answer the equally important questions about the relative likelihood that nature has created a situation for which the parametric and institutional features of the model are relevant.

Despite the poor writing, this passage illuminates what the contribution of the paper is. The paper is really about how markets work, about whether they can effectively exploit all the gains from trade that we know are there. It is hard to see how any experimental result could affect our view of the relevance of comparative advantage. The authors' results show that production, trade, and prices converge to the correct values, and they argue that the process of convergence is informative about how markets work. In particular, the paper has an extensive discussion of dynamics and the process of convergence to the full general equilibrium. This may be of interest to theorists but has little relevance for the applicability of the theory of comparative advantage.

In contrast to Noussair et al., Bernhofen and Brown (2001) provide actual historical evidence on the relationship between autarky prices and trade through an examination of Japan's opening to trade in the 1860s. This is a well-executed paper in several ways. First, the authors correctly apply Deardorff's (1980) general statement of the theory of comparative advantage. Second, they argue carefully and (to this non-expert) convincingly that Japan in the mid-nineteenth century met the requirements needed to apply the theory: Japan was completely closed to trade before 1854, and had fairly free trade (in particular, no export subsidies) by the late 1860s. They also recognize the biggest potential problem with applying the comparative advantage prediction to this episode: prices within Japan might have changed between 1854 and 1870 even in the absence of the opening to trade. The requirements for using 1854 prices in a test of comparative advantage are that economic growth was unrelated to trade, and that growth was not biased in favor of exportables.[2] They make a plausible historical case that these conditions held true. A short table confirms that the Deardorff condition is satisfied: Japan's trade was correctly predicted by her autarky prices.[3]

Bernhofen and Brown argue that, besides being closed to trade before 1854 and having no export subsidies after opening up, Japan's economy was fairly competitive before and after opening to trade. Does this mean that their results were fore-ordained? No. As Noussair et al. emphasize, just because the competitive and technological conditions of an economy satisfy the assumptions of the theory doesn't mean that the post-trade equilibrium will satisfy the law of comparative advantage – after all, humans and their institutions work in mysterious ways. Put differently, if the data had violated the law of comparative advantage, would it have shaken our faith in the theory? Yes: given the evidence that the authors provide about the structure of the Japanese economy in the mid-nineteenth century, Japan's trade should have been predicted by autarky prices, and if it hadn't we would have had to explain why. The fact that the post-trade general equilibrium behaved as expected is genuine news, and is evidence for the relevance of the theory of comparative advantage. The result is particularly interesting because it involves a large country that became one of the greatest trading nations ever.

In short, the standard view that the theory of comparative advantage has never been tested needs to be modified: with Bernhofen and Brown's contribution, we now have one paper that tests a very general version of comparative advantage, and comparative advantage passes. I think I can speak for many economists who have taught this theory with great fervor when I say "thank goodness."

3 TESTING CLASSICAL AND NEOCLASSICAL MODELS

Bernhofen and Brown (2001) is the exception to the rule: for all other contemporary and historical trading economies, we have no evidence on autarky prices. As a consequence, any application of comparative advantage theory must have an intermediate step between autarky prices and trade, one that relates autarky prices to observable features of economies. This means that empirical researchers must usually model production possibilities and preferences. In this section I discuss recent empirical work on these models, but first I will lay out a general model of comparative advantage that can be used to frame the discussion.

3.1 The Neoclassical Theory Of Production and Trade

Comparative advantage is a property of what I will call neoclassical trade models. These models all have at least two goods (so that there is a potential motive for trade), factors which are mobile between alternative uses, convex technology, and perfectly competitive markets for goods and factors. The equilibrium conditions for such economies include zero profit conditions for each sector:

$$p_g^c = a_g^c(\mathbf{w}^c)g = 1,\ldots,G, \mathbf{w}^c \in \mathbb{R}^F \tag{4.1}$$

where p_g^c is the producer price of good g in country c, and $a_g^c(\mathbf{w}^c)$ is the unit cost function for good g given the technology and factor prices $\mathbf{w}^c$ that prevail in country c. Constant returns to scale implies that the unit cost functions can be rewritten as

$$a_g^c(\mathbf{w}^c) = a_{1g}^c(\mathbf{w}^c) \cdot w_1^c + a_{2g}^c(\mathbf{w}^c) \cdot w_2^c + \ldots + a_{Fg}^c(\mathbf{w}^c) \cdot w_F^c \tag{4.2}$$

where each a_{fg}^c is the cost-minimizing amount of factor f used to produce one unit of good g, which depends on $\mathbf{w}^c$. Collecting all the zero profit conditions together we can compactly write the system as

$$\mathbf{p}^c = (A^c)'\mathbf{w}^c \quad \mathbf{p}^c \in \mathbb{R}^G \quad A^c \in \mathbb{R}^F \times \mathbb{R}^G \tag{4.3}$$

where the $F \times G$ matrix of cost-minimizing input coefficients A^c depends on $\mathbf{w}^c$. The other production side equilibrium conditions are that all factors v, which are in fixed aggregate supply, are fully employed. For a given factor f in country c, full employment is written as

$$v_f^c = a_{f1}^c x_1^c + a_{f2}^c x_2^c + \ldots + a_{fG}^c x_G^c \quad f = 1,\ldots,F \tag{4.4}$$

where x_g^c is output of good g, and the dependence of the a_{fg}^c on $\mathbf{w}$ is implicit. Collecting all F full-employment conditions together gives

$$\mathbf{v}^c = A^c \mathbf{x}^c \quad \mathbf{v}^c \in \mathbb{R}^F \tag{4.5}$$

The system given by (4.3) and (4.5) is $F + G$ equations in the $F + 2G$ unknown factor prices, output levels, and output prices.

Even at this level of generality, and before specifying G extra equations required to close the model, we can say something interesting about these economies. First, if there are at least as many goods as factors, $G \geq F$, then it is possible to solve the zero profit conditions in (4.3) for factor prices as a function solely of goods prices:[4]

$$\mathbf{w}^c = \mathbf{w}^c(\mathbf{p}^c) \tag{4.6}$$

This result, labeled "factor price insensitivity" or FPI by Leamer (1995), is remarkable: factor prices do not depend directly on factor supplies, and if country c is small (so that producer prices are determined in world markets that are unaffected by the output of country c), then factor prices are completely independent of domestic factor supplies.[5] Note also that FPI implies that the equilibrium technique matrix A^c will be independent of factor supplies if $G \geq F$, since unit costs depend only on factor prices.

We can also say some interesting things about the relationship between factor supplies and outputs. First, if there are *exactly* as many goods as factors, then A^c is both independent of factor supplies and square, which means it can be inverted. Premultiplying both sides of (4.5) by this inverse gives:

$$\mathbf{x}^c = (A^c)^{-1} \mathbf{v}^c \tag{4.7}$$

which is to say that industry outputs are a locally linear function of economy-wide factor supplies. With more goods than factors, $G > F$, A^c is not invertible: there are many output vectors which satisfy full employment, and which one will obtain in equilibrium will depend on goods market equilibrium conditions. If $G < F$, you might be tempted to think that you could take any G equations from (4.5) and solve for outputs without reference to the zero profit conditions (4.6); the error in that thinking is that with $G < F$ the equilibrium techniques are not independent of factor supplies. In the $G < F$ case, outputs are determinate, but they can't be solved for independently of the zero profit conditions.

Closing the model under autarky requires G goods-market equilibrium conditions, while with trade the G prices are given by global market clearing. With national income Y^c a function of producer prices and factor supplies,

$$Y^c(\mathbf{p}^c, \mathbf{v}^c) = \mathbf{w}^c(\mathbf{p}^c, \mathbf{v}^c) \cdot \mathbf{v}^c, \tag{4.8}$$

we can define the national indirect utility function $U^c(\tilde{\mathbf{p}}^c, Y^c)$, where $\tilde{\mathbf{p}}^c = \tilde{\mathbf{p}}^c(\tilde{\mathbf{p}}^c, \tau^c)$ is the vector of consumer prices as a function of producer prices and trade policy instruments τ^c.[6] With the normalization that the marginal utility of income is unity, Roy's identity gives the Marshallian demands $e_g^c(\tilde{\mathbf{p}}^c, Y^c)$ as the negative of the marginal indirect utilities:

$$\mathbf{e}^c(\tilde{\mathbf{p}}^c, Y^c) = -\nabla_p U^c(\tilde{\mathbf{p}}^c, Y^c), \quad \mathbf{e}^c \in \mathbb{R}^G \tag{4.9}$$

With the consumption and production sides of the model specified, it is trivial to write down the net export vector $\mathbf{t}^c$ as the difference between the two:

$$\mathbf{t}^c(\mathbf{p}^c, \tilde{\mathbf{p}}^c, \mathbf{v}^c) = \mathbf{x}^c(\mathbf{p}^c, \mathbf{v}^c) - \mathbf{e}^c(\tilde{\mathbf{p}}^c, Y^c(\mathbf{v}^c, \mathbf{p}^c)) \tag{4.10}$$

The fact that the determination of net exports can be separated into the determination of production and consumption is very far from being a trivial result, and does *not* generalize to most models with increasing returns and/or imperfect competition. Under most such models, output and consumption must be determined jointly (see Helpman and Krugman, 1985; and Fujita et al., 1999).

The development of the production model of equations (4.3) and (4.5) uses primal cost functions, and is useful for understanding the properties of the resulting equilibrium. But if all one is interested in is the equilibrium outputs and factor prices, then the model can be stated much more compactly using duality.[7] Under constant returns and perfect competition, national income is given by

$$Y^c = r^c(\mathbf{p}^c, \mathbf{v}^c) = \max_{x^c}\{\mathbf{p}^c \cdot \mathbf{x}^c \,|\, \mathbf{x}^c \in Y^c(\mathbf{v}^c)\} \qquad (4.11)$$

where $Y^c(\mathbf{v}^c)$ is the compact set of feasible net outputs. Equilibrium outputs and factor prices are then given by:

$$\mathbf{x}^c \in \nabla_p r^c(\mathbf{p}^c, \mathbf{v}^c) \qquad (4.12)$$

$$\mathbf{w}^c = \nabla_v r^c(\mathbf{p}^c, \mathbf{v}^c) \qquad (4.13)$$

Note that the gradient in (4.12) is a set, reflecting the indeterminacy in general of the output vector which will maximize national income. As indicated above, this indeterminacy disappears if $G \le F$ with no joint production, and we can differentiate the output vector with respect to factor supplies to get

$$\mathbf{x}^c = [\nabla^2_{pv} r^c(\mathbf{p}^c, \mathbf{v}^c)] \cdot \mathbf{v}^c = [R^c(\mathbf{p}^c, \mathbf{v}^c)] \cdot \mathbf{v}^c \qquad (4.14)$$

If $G = F$ and there is no joint production, then the square matrix $R^c = (A^c)^{-1}$, it is locally independent of factor supplies, and we just have a restatement of equation (4.7). The notation R^c is chosen to evoke the Rybczynski theorem, since the elements of R^c give the general equilibrium response of outputs to factor supplies.

What can be said in general about R^c? First, except in the case of $G = F = 2$ and no joint production, there is no necessary connection between a sector's factor intensity and its output response to a factor supply increase; for example, it is possible in general that the most capital intensive sector will shrink when capital becomes more abundant. A corollary is that it is impossible to generalize the Heckscher–Ohlin theorem beyond the 2×2 case: a country will not necessarily export goods that intensively use their abundant factors, even if every other condition of the theorem is satisfied.[8]

Second, for $G > F$, we cannot say anything about R^c because it doesn't exist due to the indeterminacy of output. This is alarming from an empirical point of view, but many theorists have argued that this case is irrelevant, since even tiny price changes will result in $G - F$ industries shutting down, leaving the economy with $G = F$.[9] This is a cute theoretical argument, but does not settle the case empirically.

Third, some important results are available for the general $G \le F$ case. A natural extension of the 2×2 production structure is to suppose that every sector uses at least two factors, and that there is no joint production. As Jones and Scheinkman (1977) show, with these assumptions and $G = F$, then when a factor supply rises, at least one industry will expand more rapidly than the factor, and at least one industry will contract. To state the result more colorfully, in this "even" case every factor is a friend to at least one industry and an enemy to another. In the uneven case of $G < F$ this result does not hold: an increase in a factor supply may cause all outputs to rise; a factor may be so good-natured that it is a friend to all and an enemy to none.[10] But the converse does not hold: for every industry, there is at least one factor whose accumulation will cause it to decline. That is, every industry has an enemy.

This is a rich set of important and testable empirical predictions. If every industry has an enemy, there are clear political economy implications: there will be political opponents to policies favoring the accumulation of some factors. The opposite can be said for factors that are friends to all: such factors are likely to face less opposition in the quest for favorable treatment. The effects of factor accumulation are also of interest to policymakers wishing to forecast the future sectoral composition of output. Empirically, there are several points to emphasize. First, the identification of friends and enemies cannot be accomplished just by looking at input cost shares. Second, the assumption of no joint production is crucial: with joint production the magnification results in even models do not hold, and the strong friends and enemies results can not be expected. Third, very little can be said if $G > F$: there may be no systematic relationship between relative factor supplies and the composition of output.

Most of the above discussion has concerned equilibrium in a single economy. Without putting further restrictions on how technology and tastes vary across countries, the model cannot say much about trade or international differences in outputs and factor prices. The generalized Heckscher–Ohlin approach (what I will call the factor-proportions model) to making cross-country predictions is to assume away *all* international differences in technology and preferences. Further assuming that preferences are homothetic (so that consumption shares do not depend on income), the equation (4.10) prediction for trade simplifies to

$$\mathbf{t}^c(\mathbf{p}^c, \tilde{\mathbf{p}}^c, \mathbf{v}^c) = \nabla_p r(\mathbf{p}^c, \mathbf{v}^c) - \tilde{\mathbf{e}}(\tilde{\mathbf{p}}^c) \cdot Y^c \qquad (4.15)$$

where $\tilde{\mathbf{e}} \in \mathbb{R}^G$ is a vector of consumption budget shares. In (4.15), the output and consumption functions are the same across countries (the c superscripts have disappeared from $r(\cdot)$ and $e(\cdot)$), and so could in principle be estimated with cross-country data. The prediction can be simplified further by assuming frictionless trade (so that $\mathbf{p}^c = \tilde{\mathbf{p}}^c = \mathbf{p}$), $G = F$, and that endowments are sufficiently close together so that all countries produce the same goods.[11] By equation (4.6), this means that factor prices and hence production techniques will be the same across countries. By equation (4.7), outputs will vary linearly with factor supplies. Considering (4.15) as a cross-section prediction at a point in time means that there is no variation in prices, so we can write the prediction for a country's trade as:

$$\mathbf{t}^c(\mathbf{v}^c, Y^c) = R \cdot \mathbf{v}^c - \tilde{\mathbf{e}} \cdot Y^c \qquad (4.16)$$

In words, trade depends only on relative factor supplies and country size.

This is an elegant prediction, and a version of it was investigated empirically in Edward Leamer's landmark 1984 book (Leamer, 1984). But the elegance of (4.16) comes at a high price in terms of empirically dubious assumptions, and much of the empirical work on the neoclassical trade model during the past decade has been aimed at relaxing some of these assumptions without giving up the ability to make cross-country inferences.

The assumption of identical homothetic preferences (IHP) used to derive (4.16) is implausible, and uninteresting in the sense that there is no real theory behind it.

Rather, the IHP assumption is just an analytical simplification used to translate the Rybczynski relationship (the mapping from endowments into outputs) into the Heckscher–Ohlin relationship (the mapping from endowments into net exports). An empirical rejection of IHP would rightly have no impact on our view of the underlying production model, although it could be interesting for other reasons.[12]

Another reason to be uninterested in IHP is that it treats all demand for traded goods as coming directly from the demand for final consumption goods. Intermediate products are readily introduced into the production model and have no implications for the production model results mentioned above, as long as we make the distinction between net and gross outputs. But allowing for trade in intermediate goods means that there will be no simple relationship between net exports and national income, even if IHP holds. Since a very large share of the volume of trade is intermediate goods, and essentially all imports require some domestic value added before they enter final consumption (see Rousslang and To, 1993), a more plausible simple model for trade would be that all trade is in intermediate goods, rather than none as assumed by the models that yield equations (4.10), (4.15), and (4.16).

3.2 When Worlds Collide: Data Meet the Neoclassical Model

Whatever assumptions are made about the demand for traded goods, no cross-country predictions can be made without taking a stand on how technology and prices vary across countries. The Leamer (1984) assumptions of identical technology, frictionless trade, and $G = F$ lead to a very simple prediction: for each industry at a point in time, output depends linearly on factor supplies:

$$x_g^c = \sum_{f=1}^{F} r_{fg} v_f^c \qquad (4.17)$$

This is the model estimated by Harrigan (1995). The empirical model in that paper considers ten large manufacturing sectors and four factor supplies: capital, skilled and unskilled labor, and land. For each industry, Harrigan analyzes a panel of 20 OECD countries and 16 years, using three different strategies for pooling over time: generalized least squares with and without fixed country effects, and a time-varying parameter model. Even the fixed-effects model has substantial residual autocorrelation, while the non-fixed-effects models all have first-order autoregressive parameters in excess of 0.9. This means that the parameters of the model are identified mainly from time series within-country variation – an unfortunate fact since the main interest is in explaining the cross-country distribution of production.

A striking result from Harrigan (1995) is that every industry was found to have at least one enemy, a factor whose abundance and/or accumulation leads to a decline in output (the enemy is usually skilled or unskilled labor, sometimes land). Capital is manufacturing's friend: it is estimated to have a positive effect on output for all ten industries in each specification. Despite the fact that Leamer (1984) used a cross-section of trade data, in contrast to a panel of output data, the inferences about comparative advantage are similar.

Although factor supplies are jointly statistically significant in each regression, the model does poorly in explaining the cross-sectional variation in the data, with large within-sample prediction errors. Harrigan identifies a number of potential explanations for this poor fit (including bad data, scale economies, and government policy) but does not mention other possibilities (such as indeterminacy in production, technology differences, different product mixes, or price differences caused by trade policy or transport costs). It seems fair to say that the factor proportions view of the world has mixed support from this paper: a poor overall fit, but fairly solid evidence of a systematic relationship between outputs and relative endowments.

Several papers have been at least partially motivated by the mixed results of Harrigan (1995). Bernstein and Weinstein (2002) focus on the question of output indeterminacy when $G > F$. They correctly note that this is an empirical question which has little to do with counting the numbers of goods and factors in any particular empirical exercise. They begin by noting that, with identical technology, frictionless trade, endowments which are not too far apart, and $G \geq F$, then the full employment conditions (4.5) will have the same A matrix for all c:

$$\mathbf{v}^c = A\mathbf{x}^c \tag{4.18}$$

They call this the Heckscher–Ohlin–Vanek or HOV model. If, in addition, G is exactly equal to F, then outputs are the same linear function R of endowments for all c, and as noted above $R = A^{-1}$. They express this implication as:

$$AR = \mathbf{I}_F \tag{4.19}$$

where $\mathbf{I}_F$ is the identity matrix of dimension F.

Using data from Japanese regions, they confirm that (4.18) holds, which indicates that techniques and factor prices are the same in all Japanese regions. This is not a trivial finding: it rules out increasing returns at the level of industries, and/or technological differences across regions. They also argue that it rules out $G < F$, but that is wrong: with intra-Japan mobility of factors, factor prices and techniques will be equalized regardless of the relative number of goods and factors. Despite the fact that (4.18) holds for Japanese regions, (4.19) fails miserably: outputs are not well-explained statistically by endowments alone, and the linear restrictions embodied in (4.19) are rejected. From this they conclude that $G > F$ and output indeterminacy is an empirically important fact about general equilibrium production.

They then apply (4.18) to international data, multiplying the Japanese A matrix by national output vectors $\mathbf{x}$ to get predicted national endowments $\mathbf{v}$:

$$\text{predicted } \mathbf{v}^c = A^{Japan}\mathbf{x}^c$$

These predicted endowments are not at all close to actual measured endowments, which leads them to reject the assumption that all countries produce the same goods using the same techniques. This result, while not new (see the chapter by Davis and

Weinstein in this volume for more evidence that techniques vary internationally), is nonetheless worth noting, since it suggests that economists should abandon the simple HOV model of international production.

Abandoning HOV is one thing, but replacing it with something else is another. One of the most appealing aspects of empirical work based on the even model pioneered by Leamer (1984) is that every parameter estimated has a clear structural interpretation. The challenge for researchers wishing to improve on this framework is to develop empirically implementable models that are equally closely tied to theory, but that relax the stringent assumptions used to derive equations like (4.16) and (4.17). In the factor content literature, this has been accomplished using restrictive models of international technology differences (Trefler, 1993, 1995) or two-factor models where factor price equalization fails (Davis and Weinstein, 2001).[13] These models may or may not be appropriate for studies of the factor content of trade, but they are too restrictive for studying comparative advantage, as they rule out all but very special types of cross-country technology differences. In searching for amendments to the factor proportions model, it is natural to consider general technology differences as a source of comparative advantage, not least because there is extensive evidence that, even among advanced economies, technology differences are large, ubiquitous, and non-transitory (see, among others, van Ark, 1993; van Ark and Pilat, 1993; Dollar et al., 1988; Dollar and Wolff, 1993; Harrigan, 1997b, 1999; Jorgenson and Kuroda 1990; and Jorgenson et al., 1987).

Harrigan (1997a) points out that using the dual, rather than the primal, representation of aggregate technology makes it possible to estimate more general models of specialization. Harrigan assumes that technological differences across countries are Hicks-neutral and industry specific. This can be incorporated into the revenue function approach in a very straightforward way:

$$r^c(\mathbf{p}^c, \mathbf{v}^c) = r(\theta^c \mathbf{p}^c, \mathbf{v}^c), \quad \theta^c = diag\{\theta_1^c, \ldots, \theta_G^c\} \tag{4.20}$$

where θ_g^c is a scalar productivity parameter which gives the level of technology in industry g of country c relative to productivity in a base country. This is a natural extension of the classical one-factor Ricardian model, and it has the virtue that the technology parameters are, in principle, measurable by applying the theory of total factor productivity (TFP) measurement. The usual derivative property applies to (4.20), so that outputs are given by the gradient of (4.20) with respect to prices:

$$\mathbf{x}^c = \nabla_p r(\theta^c \mathbf{p}^c, \mathbf{v}^c) \tag{4.21}$$

Note that if there are no cross-country differences in relative industry technology levels, that is $\theta_g^c = \theta^c \forall g$, then (by the homogeneity of the revenue function) technology differences become a scalar shift parameter, giving outputs as

$$\mathbf{x}^c(\mathbf{p}^c, \mathbf{v}^c) = \theta^c \mathbf{x}(\mathbf{p}^c, \mathbf{v}^c) \tag{4.22}$$

Equation (4.22) illustrates that technology differences that are neutral across sectors affect absolute, but not comparative, advantage.[14]

To implement the model given by (4.21), Harrigan (1997a) follows Kohli (1991) and assumes that the revenue function (4.20) can be adequately approximated by a translog functional form. This strategy leads to the following estimation equation:

$$s_{gt}^c = \sum_{k=1}^{G} a_{kg} \ln \theta_{gt}^c + \sum_{i=1}^{F} r_{if} \ln v_{ft}^c + \varepsilon_{gt}^c \qquad (4.23)$$

where s_{gt}^c is the share of good g value added in country c's GDP at time t, the a's and r's are parameters to be estimated, and ε_{gt}^c has a panel structure with fixed country and time effects to account for other unobservable influences on special-ization. There are a number of notable features of this specification. First, it allows Harrigan to simultaneously estimate the impact of Ricardian and Heckscher–Ohlin influences on specialization. Second, since the same technology parameters appear in each equation, it is possible to calculate cross-TFP effects on output shares, which is a key general equilibrium channel. Third, the estimated results do not directly tell us whether each sector has an enemy, in the sense of a factor that causes its output to decline in absolute terms, although the r's tell us which factors raise or lower a good's share of national income.[15] Fourth, because of the use of country fixed effects, all of the model's parameters are identified by within-country time series variation. Fifth, the specification of the model requires no assumption about any form of factor price equalization – this is one of the benefits of using a dual rather than primal approach.

Harrigan's results support the view that non-neutral technology differences are important for specialization. For most sectors, the own-TFP effects are positive, sta-tistically significant, and large. The largest effect is in the biggest sector, machinery. A 10 percent improvement in relative machinery TFP raises that sector's share of GDP by around 0.25 percentage points. As an example of the cross-TFP effects, technological progress in machinery comes at the expense of the chemicals and metals sectors, whose share of GDP declines. The inferences about factor supplies are roughly consistent with Harrigan (1995) and Leamer (1984): accumulation of producer durables and High-School educated workers generally lead to expanding manufacturing sectors, while growth in structures and highly educated workers are associated with declining manufacturing. These findings suggest a simple story: the service sector is intensive in non-residential construction (office buildings and retail stores) and college-educated workers (managers, professionals, educators), so that abundance in these factors draws other resources out of manufacturing and into the service sector. By contrast, the manufacturing sectors are intensive in producer durables and medium-educated workers, so that abundance in these factors draws resources out of services and into manufacturing sectors. While plausible, confir-mation of this explanation would require data on direct factor shares, which are not easily available in internationally comparable form.

Harrigan (1997a) fruitfully extends the literature on comparative advantage in one direction, by abandoning the Heckscher–Ohlin assumption that countries share the same technology. Another problematic feature of the standard factor propor-tions approach is the assumption that all countries produce the same goods and have the same factor prices. This "one cone" assumption is explicit in Leamer (1984), Harrigan (1995), and Bernstein and Weinstein (2002), as well as in most of the factor content literature (with the notable exception of Davis and Weinstein (1998)). Absolute factor price equalization is easy to reject by direct observation. It would be hard to explain mass migration from the South to the North if wages were the same everywhere. In the factor-content literature, the assumption of equal factor prices in levels is sometimes replaced with the weaker assumption that relative factor prices are equalized (see Trefler, 1995). Equal relative factor prices implies that, for a given sector across countries, input coefficients are constant and in particular do not vary with aggregate endowments (this is just a corollary of factor price insensitivity). This hypothesis can be tested by a simple non-structural cross-section regression pooled across goods g and countries c:

$$\frac{a^c_{Kg}}{a^c_{Lg}} = \beta_g + \beta \frac{K^c}{L^c} \qquad (4.24)$$

where the left-hand side is the capital–labor ratio in industry g in country c, which is regressed on an industry constant and country c's aggregate capital–labor ratio. Under the one-cone/FPI hypothesis, $\beta = 0$. There is ample evidence that this is not the case: Dollar et al. (1988, table 2.3) show that capital per worker in individual industries is highly correlated with capital per worker in aggregate manufacturing. More recently, Davis and Weinstein (1998, table 1) show the same thing, finding that techniques are strongly correlated with aggregate endowments.

A finding that $\beta > 0$ in equation (4.24) can be explained by a failure of factor price equalization (FPE). Retaining the Heckscher–Ohlin assumptions of frictionless trade, perfect competition, and identical technology across countries, FPE fails when countries have endowments which are too far apart, and as a result countries produce different goods, the so-called "multi-cone" equilibrium. The fact that we do not observe such specialization in the output statistics may simply be because different goods are lumped together into the same industrial classification. If this were true, then the sign of the Rybczynski effects of endowments on observed output aggregates would differ systematically across countries, and one-cone empirical models like Harrigan (1995) would be misspecified.

By using a dual approach, Harrigan (1997a) skirts this issue, but the general spirit of that paper is a one-cone model, since the translog approximation is assumed to be valid at all points in the sample. Schott (2000) tackles the multi-cone issue directly, and develops an empirical model where the set of produced goods and the associated Rybczynski effects depend on relative factor supplies. Schott's theoretical model is a standard one of two factors (capital and labor), many goods whose techniques of production are independent of factor prices, and many countries.[16] The equilibrium of this model has every country producing just two goods, one more and one less capital intensive than the country's aggregate endowment. Define

$$k_g = \frac{a_{Kg}}{a_{Lg}} \quad \text{and} \quad k^c = \frac{K^c}{L^c}$$

to be the fixed capital–labor ratio of good g and the capital–labor endowment of country c respectively, and number goods in order of increasing capital intensity, $k_1 < k_2 < \ldots < k_G$.

Then there are three possible linear relationships between the output of a good and a country's endowments:

$$
\begin{aligned}
x_g^c &= r_{1Kg}K^c - r_{1Lg}L^c && \text{if} \quad k^c \in [k_{g-1}, k_g) \\
x_g^c &= -r_{2Kg}K^c + r_{2Lg}L^c && \text{if} \quad k^c \in [k_g, k_{g+1}) \\
x_g^c &= 0 && \text{otherwise,}
\end{aligned}
\tag{4.25}
$$

where the r's are positive constants. In words, if a country's capital–labor ratio lies between k_{g-1} and k_g, then capital accumulation leads to an increase in the output of good g, and the opposite if k^c lies between k_g and k_{g+1}. If k^c does not lie between k_{g-1} and k_{g+1}, then country c will not produce any of good g at all; it will be producing the two goods closest to its aggregate capital–labor ratio instead.

Now imagine that a particular industrial classification includes two or more goods with quite different capital intensities (for example, textiles includes low-quality cotton cloth as well as high-tech synthetic fibers). With such aggregation of goods within a single classification, the Rybczynski effect of capital on output of the aggregate may switch sign more than once. At very low k^c the Rybczynski effect is positive, then it becomes negative as countries move out of the labor intensive good, then positive again as production of the capital-intensive good commences, etc. In this case trying to infer the effect of endowments on outputs by pooling across countries with very different endowments is a hopeless muddle: any estimated slopes will be a mix of effects of varying size and sign, and will have no structural interpretation.

Schott (2000) pursues two strategies for dealing with the complexities of multiple cones and multiple goods aggregated into a single category. The first is to take the existing output aggregates and estimate a piece-wise linear relationship between outputs and endowments. In this model, Schott simultaneously estimates the Rybczynski effects along with the capital–labor ratios at which the effects change. Schott uncovers four cones, which is to say that for each output aggregate, four Rybczynski effects are estimated at different points in the sample. This is an intricate empirical model and in the end is not too convincing, as the fitted and actual output levels are not at all close to each other, and the points at which the slopes change sign seem heavily influenced by a very small number of observations (see Schott, 2000, figure 3).

Schott's second empirical strategy is more promising. Rather than work with the usual output aggregates, he constructs three aggregates based on the capital intensity of each country–industry observation. Since (as $\beta > 0$ in equation (4.24) verifies) sectoral capital intensities are correlated with aggregate capital abundance, Schott's "Heckscher–Ohlin aggregates" group together products in different output categories that are produced by countries with similar capital abundance. For example, apparel produced in Guatemala is lumped together with electrical machinery produced in the Phillippines, while Swedish apparel is lumped together with transport equipment produced in Malaysia.

Using these three HO aggregates and estimating a version of equation (4.25), Schott finds what the multicone reasoning above suggests. The effect of capital accumulation on the least-capital-intensive aggregate is at first negative then zero, the effect is first positive and then negative for the middle aggregate, and is first zero and then positive for the third aggregate. In other words, he identifies two cones: in the first cone, countries produce the low- and middle-capital-intensive HO aggregates, and in the second cone countries produce the Middle and High capital intensive HO aggregates. There is some circularity in this procedure, since country capital abundance is in effect used to construct the HO aggregates, making it unsurprising (for example) that capital abundant countries specialize in the capital-intensive aggregate. Schott's results are also suspect because he uses total capital within manufacturing, rather than aggregate capital, to measure a country's overall capital–labor ratio; this means he is ignoring capital re-allocation between manufacturing and the rest of the economy. A broader criticism is that Schott's theoretical model is quite special and is taken perhaps too literally as a framework for data analysis. Leamer (1987), in contrast, also works with a multiple-cone model but regards the piece-wise linearity between outputs and endowments implied by the model to be too special to take seriously. Schott also completely ignores the issue of technology differences, which Harrigan (1997) showed to be important for specialization. Despite these caveats, Schott's study is important for two reasons: it provides some evidence that multiple cones are empirically important, and it forces us to think seriously about the heterogeneity lurking within measured aggregate outputs.

Harrigan and Zakrajšek (2000) consider the multiple-cone issue as well as several other open questions about specialization. As noted above, Harrigan (1997a) measures productivity differences using TFP indices (which, because of data availability, restricts the sample to OECD countries), and estimates a fixed-effects model of specialization that does not use any of the cross-country variation in the sample. Motivated by these limitations of Harrigan (1997a), Harrigan and Zakrajšek develop an empirical model that permits consistent estimation of the effects of factor endowments on specialization while allowing for unobservable technology differences. This allows them to analyze a larger number of countries (including a few from Latin America and East Asia), and to exploit the cross-section variation in the data. Their identifying assumption is that, except for country and time effects, any non-neutrality in technology differences is orthogonal to factor supplies. As in Harrigan (1997a), they adopt a dual-translog approach which allows them to avoid making any assumptions about factor price equalization, and which leads to an estimating equation which is a simplification of (4.23):

$$s_{gt}^c = \beta_g^c + \sum_{i=1}^{F} r_{if} \ln v_{ft}^c + \varepsilon_{gt}^c \qquad (4.26)$$

If the country effects β_g^c are also assumed to be orthogonal to factor supplies, then it is possible to use a random-effects estimator which combines the time-series and cross-country variation in the sample. They also report fixed effects estimates (which use only the time-series variation) and between estimates (which use only cross-country variation) of (4.26).

Unlike most other papers in this literature, Harrigan and Zakrajšek also consider alternative hypotheses. The statistical alternative they consider is simple, that specialization depends on aggregate productivity rather than on relative endowments:

$$s_{gt}^c = \beta_g^c + \beta_1 \ln \theta_t^c + \beta_2 [\ln \theta_t^c]^2 + \varepsilon_{gt}^c \qquad (4.27)$$

where θ_t^c is measured as real GDP per worker. This reduced form relationship can be loosely derived from a product cycle model, where new goods are first produced in rich countries and are later produced in poorer countries as technology is transferred. It can also capture multiple cone effects in a flexible way: models such as Schott's would predict an important role for the second-order term as countries move into and out of goods based on their overall per-capita income.

Harrigan and Zakrajšek find that estimating (4.26) gives a noisy but fairly consistent story about industrial specialization: human and physical capital abundance raise output in the heavy industrial sectors, while physical capital lowers output in food and apparel-textiles. The model has little success in explaining variation in output in the smaller, more resource-based sectors, probably because they have no measurements of resource abundance. Turning to the alternative model (4.27), results are roughly in line with what would have been expected from the factor proportions results: higher aggregate productivity is associated with lower output of food and higher output in the heavy industrial sectors (fabricated metals and the three machinery categories).

What about multiple cones? Following Schott's line of reasoning, this should show up in parameter instability across different regions of relative factor supply space. Harrigan and Zakrajšek used a number of formal and informal strategies to find evidence of such instability and found nothing. They did find some weak evidence of quadratic effects in equation (4.27), but the nonlinearity was only economically important for a single sector – food.

The bottom line from Harrigan and Zakrajšek (2000) is consistent with the message that has been developed in all of the papers reviewed in this section, as well as the factor content literature reviewed in this volume by Davis and Weinstein:

> Relative factor endowments have a large influence on specialization, in ways that are consistent with theory and stylized facts about the international economy. However, factor endowments leave much that is unexplained: there is a great degree of country-specific idiosyncrasy in specialization patterns, and there is also a great deal of noise.
> **(Harrigan and Zakrajšek, 2000, p. 23)**

3.3   What about Ricardo?

The papers discussed in the previous section all work with variants of multifactor models that have roots in the Heckscher–Ohlin tradition. This might seem odd to a reader familiar only with a much earlier literature on testing trade models, which concluded that Heckscher–Ohlin did very poorly (Leontief, 1954) while Ricardo did quite well (MacDougall, 1951, 1952). Empirical research on the static Ricardian model was quiescent for nearly three decades after Balassa's last word on the subject (Balassa, 1963). In the last few years, however, there have been a few papers on the Ricardian model, including the innovative work by Eaton and Kortum (2001) which is discussed in the context of the gravity equation below. Here I will discuss two recent papers that are very much in the spirit of MacDougall and Balassa.

Golub and Hsieh (2000) argue that a focus on labor productivity variation as the source of comparative advantage is appropriate because other factors of production (such as capital and raw materials) are internationally mobile. This is an oft-heard argument, which has at least two problems with it. First, it risks confusing free trade in financial assets with easy mobility of physical capital goods. What is relevant for comparative advantage is how easily productive factors are reallocated across alternative uses; the ownership of factors is relevant to the level of national income but not to the composition of national product. Despite the vast and rapid international flows of financial capital, I know of no evidence that suggests that physical capital is as easily reallocated internationally as it is intranationally. To make my point transparent, observe that structures are an important component of the capital stock which are immobile even within countries, never mind across borders, while ownership of structures can easily be transferred internationally. The same point can be made with reference to natural resource stocks: land cannot move, but its ownership can. The point is not to insist that physical capital and land *are* sources of comparative advantage, but to insist that it is an empirical question. Furthermore, the evidence reviewed in the preceding section suggests that non-labor endowments are relevant to specialization.

These objections notwithstanding, a case can be made that the Ricardian concept of output per worker may be what matters for comparative advantage. First, labor's share of manufacturing value added is quite high, meaning that labor productivity is closely linked to total factor productivity. Second, if differences in labor productivity reflect technological differences, then labor productivity will be a good predictor of specialization. This is the hypothesis that Golub and Hsieh investigate.

Golub and Hsieh do not derive their specification directly from a well-specified model, appealing instead to the earlier literature. This makes it impossible to interpret their results in a structural fashion, but the general idea is intuitive: if relative productivity in sector g in country c is higher than it is in the average sector in country c, then c specializes in g. An illustrative equation is:

$$\log \frac{X_{gb}}{X_{gc}} = \alpha_{bc} + \beta \log \frac{a_{gb}}{a_{gc}} + \varepsilon_{gbc} \quad g = 1, \ldots, G \tag{4.28}$$

where X_{gc} is a measure of export success in good g for country c, a_{gc} is output per worker in sector g in country c, ε_{gbc} is a residual, and α and β are parameters. The equation is pooled across goods g (and possibly across country pairs), and a positive value of β is taken as confirmation of the hypothesis that labor productivity determines comparative advantage.

The problem with specifications such as (4.28) is not just the usual one of a missing alternative hypothesis, which plagues most work on comparative advantage. Rather, the problem is that there is nothing inherently general equilibrium about the specification. Equation (4.28) simply says that productivity advantage in a sector is associated with export success in that sector, a prediction that arises from any number of partial-equilibrium supply and demand models (for example, a simple Cournot reciprocal dumping model predicts that export success will be negatively related to marginal cost). The critique is not that (4.28) is inconsistent with a Ricardian model, but that verification of $\beta > 0$ is not evidence in favor of Ricardo over any other explanation. A truly general equilibrium prediction of Ricardian models is that a productivity advantage in one sector can actually *hurt* export success in another sector, but Golub and Hsieh do not investigate this prediction.

The same critique applies to Choudhri and Schembri (2002), which looks at US–Canada trade. Choudhri and Schembri integrate product differentiation into the Ricardian model and derive their estimating equation carefully from theory, but the end result is something similar to (4.28), which relates export success in sector g to relative productivity in sector g. As with Golub and Hsieh (2000), they are silent on cross-productivity effects.

3.4 Conclusions and
Unfinished Business – Comparative Advantage

A decade of research on empirical models of comparative advantage has made some progress:

1 We now have our first confirmation of the theory of comparative advantage in its general, autarky price form (Bernhofen and Brown 2001).
2 Many papers have demonstrated that, at least for manufactured goods, relative factor supplies are an important influence on specialization (Bernstein and Weinstein, 2002; Harrigan, 1995, 1997a; Harrigan and Zakrajšek, 2000; and Schott, 2000).
3 Technological differences have been shown to be an important influence on specialization (Harrigan, 1997a).
4 The simple even factor-proportions model pioneered by Leamer (1984) is too simple: output indeterminacy (Bernstein and Weinstein, 2002), Ricardian effects (Harrigan, 1997), and multiple cones (Schott, 2000) are all empirically important.

All of the papers reviewed in this chapter have been guided by the view that a careful application of theory is important when investigating the theory of comparative advantage (perhaps this is partly in reaction to the prolonged, confused response of the profession to Leontief's alleged paradox).

It goes without saying that whatever progress has been made, we are a long way from fully understanding the determinants and empirical significance of comparative advantage. Some of the open questions are:

1 What is the role of transport costs, or distance more generally, in determining specialization?
2 How do non-comparative advantage influences on specialization, such as increasing returns, interact with technology and factor endowment differences to determine specialization?
3 How are trade flows determined? Is a simple model of preferences enough, or do we need to model income effects and/or the demand for intermediate goods?
4 What is the appropriate unit of analysis in thinking about comparative advantage? Should we be studying broad industries, or concentrating on firm or plant level models?
5 How can we measure and characterize the cross-sectional and time-series distribution of factor prices and goods prices?
6 Is there evidence for general equilibrium effects of sectoral productivity differences of the sort predicted by simple Ricardian models?

Some of these questions are addressed elsewhere in this volume, but empirical research on comparative advantage is still a young and underdeveloped field. There is plenty of opportunity for good empirical work to continue to sharpen our understanding of the relevance of our basic trade models.

4 THE GRAVITY EQUATION

James Anderson (1979, p. 106) began his 1979 article "A theoretical foundation for the gravity equation" by saying that: "Probably the most successful empirical trade device of the last twenty-five years is the gravity equation."

One could say the same thing today, as the gravity equation remains at the center of a great deal of applied research on international trade. Another thing that has not changed since 1979 is that there is great uncertainty about the foundations of the gravity model: what do we mean when we say that it "works," and why does it work? Recently there have been a few papers that try to empirically understand gravity, and a review of this recent research on the foundations of gravity is the focus of this section.

The gravity equation is so-named because it is a theory of trade volumes which is analogous to the physical theory of gravity: trade between a pair of countries depends positively on the product of economic size and negatively on distance, just as the force of gravity between two bodies increases with the product of their mass and decreases with distance. In its simplest form the gravity equation is

$$M_{cd} = k \frac{Y_c Y_d}{D_{cd}} \tag{4.29}$$

where M_{cd} denotes the value of imports by country c from country d, D_{cd} is the distance between the two countries, Y is a measure of economic size such as GDP, and

k is a constant. Introducing parameters that allow the elasticities of trade volumes with respect to size and distance to differ from one does not change the basic message. As it stands equation (4.29) is not an economic model, but it is nevertheless plausible. Transport and other trade costs are certainly correlated with distance, so distance will surely reduce trade. Equally obviously, trade between the United States and Japan will probably be larger than trade between Estonia and Portugal. Nevertheless, what is striking about equation (4.29) is that there is apparently no role for comparative advantage: neither relative endowments nor relative technology levels enter the equation. It is this apparent lack of connection to neoclassical trade theory that led to the widespread conclusion that the gravity equation had no theoretical foundation. A related observation is that neoclassical trade theory is generally not concerned with bilateral trade: in comparative advantage models, a country's trade is determined by its differences from the rest of the world, with no prediction about the pattern of bilateral trade.

Foundation or no, equation (4.29) fits the data remarkably well. Regressions (in logarithms) of bilateral aggregate trade volumes on the GDP of trading partners and the distance between them typically yield R^2s in the range of 0.65 to 0.95. What is important about these high R^2s is that they have led many researchers to use variants of the gravity equation as a benchmark for the volume of trade. This gravity-based benchmark is then used to evaluate economic policy issues such as the effects of protection (Harrigan, 1993), openness (Harrigan, 1996; Lawrence, 1987; Saxonhouse, 1989), the merits of proposed regional trade agreements (Frankel et al., 1997), and the effects of national borders (Anderson and van Wincoop, 2001; Evans, 2000; McCallum, 1995).

4.1   The Theory of Gravity

In fact, there are several theoretical foundations for the gravity model. One of the earliest is due to Anderson (1979), with other contributions from Bergstrand (1985, 1989). These models all have the feature that consumers regard goods as being differentiated by location of production, a modeling trick known as the "Armington assumption" (Armington, 1969). The standard specification for Armington preferences is a variant of the CES functional form:

$$U^c = \left[\sum_{d=1}^{C} \beta_d C_{cd}^{(\sigma-1)/\sigma} \right]^{\frac{\sigma}{\sigma-1}}, \sigma \in (1, \infty) \tag{4.30}$$

where c_{cd} is consumption by country c residents of goods produced in country d, and β_d and σ are parameters that are common across all countries. The key feature of these preferences is that goods are differentiated by country of origin only. Another feature of this function is that the marginal utility of consumption of goods from all countries d is always strictly positive, and infinite in the limit as consumption goes to zero. This implies that, whatever the price, country c will consume at least some of every good from every country.

Anderson's and Bergstrand's models, and most other explanations for the negative effect of distance on trade, assume that transport costs are of the "iceberg" form, where for every $t > 1$ units shipped from the exporter, only 1 unit arrives at the importer's location, the other $t - 1$ units having "melted" in transit. As long as exporters do not price discriminate across export markets, there will be a single fob price p_d for country d's exports, and the cif price in country c of imports from country d will be $p_d t_{cd}$. In empirical applications, t is usually assumed to be a monotonically increasing function of distance. This way of handling transport costs is ubiquitous not because it is realistic but because it is very handy. As Grossman (1998, pp. 30–1) notes, "few would consider the 'iceberg' formulation of shipping costs as anything more than a useful trick for models with constant demand elasticities, and possibly a good approximation to the technology for shipping tomatoes."

Hummels (1999) provides some evidence on the actual form of the relationship between transport costs and distance, while a number of authors (including Roberts and Tybout (1997) and Bernard and Jensen (2001)) have shown that there are important fixed costs to trade which are independent of distance.

These reservations about the iceberg assumption notwithstanding, it is crucial to deriving a closed-form gravity equation based on the preferences given by (4.30).[17] The basis of such derivations is the assumption that all goods are traded, so that national income is the sum of traded goods output, which in equilibrium is the sum of home and foreign demand for the unique good that the country produces. The demand function that arises from (4.30) is:

$$c_{cd} = \beta_d Y_c \frac{(p_d t_{cd})^{-\sigma}}{P_c^{1-\sigma}} \tag{4.31}$$

where the CES price index P_c is defined as:

$$P_c = \left[\sum_{b=1}^{C} \beta_b (p_b t_{cb})^{1-\sigma} \right]^{1/1-\sigma} \tag{4.32}$$

The goods market clearing conditions are:

$$Y_c = p_c \sum_{b=1}^{C} c_{bc} \tag{4.33}$$

These equations can be solved in a way that will generate the gravity equation. Choosing units so that all fob prices are equal to unity and letting $s_c = Y_c/Y_w$ be c's share of world income, it can be shown that:

$$s_c = \beta_c \sum_{b=1}^{C} s_b \left(\frac{t_{bc}}{P_b} \right)^{1-\sigma} \tag{4.34}$$

This equation states that country c's national income depends on two things: first, the popularity of the goods that it produces (the taste parameter β_c) and second, a GDP-weighted average of its distance from trading partners (assuming that distance and transport costs are positively related). The dependence of income on β_c is

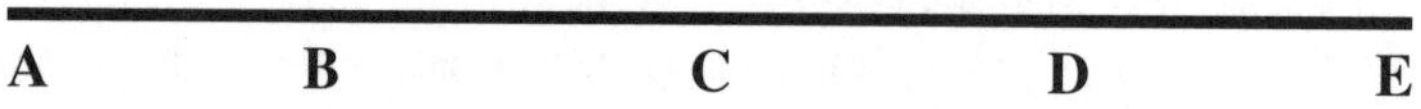

A   B   C   D   E

Figure 4.1 The relative distance effect

unattractive on economic grounds: is it really plausible that the US has a high GDP because consumers around the world have a taste for US goods? The negative effect of distance on income is much more believable, and is a common implication of economic geography models (see, for instance, the chapter in this volume by Overman et al.).

Solving the model (see Anderson and van Wincoop, 2001) for imports as a function of income and trade costs gives the gravity equation for imports by c from d:

$$M_{cd} = \frac{Y_c Y_d}{Y_W} \times t_{cd}^{1-\sigma} \times P_c^{\sigma-1} \times P_d^{\sigma-1} \tag{4.35}$$

where M_{cd} is the cif value of imports by c from d. The first and second terms are easy to understand: big countries import and export more than small countries, and trade costs reduce trade volumes with an elasticity of $(1 - \sigma)$. The third term is a substitution effect: if transport costs facing c are high on average so that P_c is large, then c will import more from d. The fourth term varies across exporting sources d and is increasing in a weighted average of d's transport costs: if d is on average a long way from its trading partners, it will have a low fob price, so c will import more. More succinctly, controlling for country size and bilateral distance, trade will be higher between country pairs that are far from the rest of the world than between country pairs that are close to the rest of the world.

The relative distance effect explains why the theoretically-derived gravity model of (4.35) differs from the simple gravity equation (4.29). To better understand this relative distance effect, consider a world of five equal-sized countries evenly spaced along a line as in figure 4.1.

Country B will import more from country A than it will from country C, despite the fact that B is an equal distance from both. This is because A is so far from everyone else that aggregate demand for its output will be low, resulting in an fob export price lower than C's fob export price. Therefore, B's cif import prices will be lower from A than from C.

The development of (4.35) makes heavy use of the CES and iceberg assumptions, but the point that relative as well as absolute distance matters for bilateral trade seems much more general. As a consequence, gravity equations that pool across bilateral pairs without controlling for relative distance are misspecified in a potentially important way. Structural estimation of (4.35) is difficult because of the non-linear functional form of the price index terms and the presence of the unknown parameters β (for an application which imposes all the structure of the model, see Anderson and van Wincoop (2001)). An intuitive if ad-hoc proxy for the inverse of the price term defined by (4.32) can be developed by taking $\sigma = 2$, replacing the unknown βs with income shares, and choosing units so that fob prices are unity to get a "centrality index:"

$$\Psi_c = \sum_{b=1}^{C} \frac{S_b}{t_{cb}} \tag{4.36}$$

According to (4.36), centrality is a GDP-weighted average of the inverse of trade costs. By the logic of the CES gravity model developed above, bilateral trade should be decreasing in the centrality of the two trading partners, since a central location means there are many alternative nearby sources of supply for the importer, and high demand and hence high fob prices for the exporter.

Different proxies have been used by several authors in the literature, including Helliwell (1997) and Wei (1996). Wei defines the "remoteness index" as a GDP-weighted average of distance:

$$R_c^{Wei} = \sum_{b=1}^{C} S_b t_{cb} \tag{4.37}$$

which is related in spirit to (4.32) but can not be derived from any simplification of the CES price index. Helliwell (1997) defines remoteness as:

$$R_c^{Hw} = \sum_{b=1}^{C} \frac{t_{cb}}{S_b} \tag{4.38}$$

which makes little sense, since distance from small countries matters more than distance from large countries in determining a country's remoteness.

This discussion makes the point that controlling for relative distance is crucial to estimating a well-specified gravity model, and that there are a number of reasonable ways to measure relative distance (although Helliwell's index is not one of them). However, if consistent estimation of the distance effect ($\sigma - 1$) is what is of interest, then researchers can impose the theory-required unit elasticities on income and run the following simple regression with country fixed effects:

$$\ln \frac{M_{cd}}{Y_c Y_d} = \delta_c + \delta_d - (\sigma - 1) \ln t_{cd} \tag{4.39}$$

where the δs are dummy variables that sweep out the influence of importer and exporter relative distance.

As a foundation for the gravity equation the Armington model just described relies on some convenient functional form assumptions (icebergs and CES) which can be criticized, but its biggest weakness is that there is no microfoundation for the production side of the model, if one can even say that there is a production side at all. It was left to the "new trade theory" of the 1980s to provide a solid theoretical grounding for the production side of the gravity equation. The monopolistic competition model (summarized elegantly in Helpman and Krugman (1985)) provides just such a model for the zero transport costs case. In the monopolistic competition model, a taste for variety interacts with firms who face increasing returns to scale in the production of varieties. With identical, homothetic CES preferences on the demand side and strong symmetry assumptions on the supply side, the equilibrium of the Helpman–Krugman model provides a rationalization for the Armington utility function (4.30), with the parameters β_c reinterpreted as proportional to the number of varieties produced in equilibrium in country c. One result is a strikingly simple model for bilateral trade:

$$M_g^{bc} = s_b x_g^c \tag{4.40}$$

where M_g^{bc} is country b's imports of good g from country c, s_b is b's share of world expenditure, and x_g^c is b's output of good g. Summing over all goods g gives the aggregate gravity model of equation (4.29) for $k = 1/Y^w$ and $D_{bc} = 1$. One appealing aspect of equation (4.40) is that it gives predictions on a sectoral basis, and so can be tested using sectoral data on production and trade.

Extending the monopolistic competition model to the case of positive trade costs is straightforward. If all goods are produced in monopolistically competitive sectors, then with CES preferences the equilibrium number of varieties per country is invariant to trade costs (see Krugman, 1980), and the model is isomorphic to the Armington model above. As a result, the gravity equation (4.35) follows immediately.

For the purposes of deriving a gravity equation, the key feature of the Armington and monopolistic competition models is that goods are differentiated by location of production, whether by assumption (Armington) or endogenously (monopolistic competition). Equivalently, countries are completely specialized in disjoint sets of goods. In contrast, Feenstra et al. (1998, 2001) consider whether it is possible to get a gravity-type relationship in a model of trade in homogeneous goods. Feenstra et al. consider a general equilibrium model of "reciprocal dumping," where Cournot–Nash oligopolists sell a homogeneous good in each others' markets à la Brander and Krugman (1983). The model is very simple, with two countries sharing the same technology and a single factor of production. To get analytical results they assume Cobb–Douglas preferences (implying unit elasticity of market demand) and no transport costs in the numeraire sector (guaranteeing factor price equalization). In footnote 2 of Feenstra et al. (2001) they assert that Feenstra et al. (1998) "derive and illustrate the gravity equation for the reciprocal dumping model," but that is not quite right. The 1998 paper shows, in a two-country world, that the sum of world exports is maximized when country size is equalized, a result that they call "the most important implication of the 'gravity' equation" (Feenstra et al., 1998, p. 9), but they do *not* show that bilateral imports or exports depend on the product of trading partner GDPs, which is the usual statement of the gravity equation (equation (4.29)). In fact, their reciprocal dumping model has some very un-gravity like implications: bilateral trade is increasing in country size only over a limited range, and two-way trade only occurs when countries are of similar size.

A model of trade in homogeneous goods that *does* generate a gravity-type relationship is developed in Eaton and Kortum (2002). Their framework is a multi-country perfectly competitive Ricardian model with a continuum of goods and iceberg transport costs, a complex set of assumptions that nonetheless yields intuitive and elegant implications. The foundation of their modeling strategy is the assumption that country c's productivity in g, $1/a_c(g)$, is a random variable drawn from the Frechet distribution function:

$$F_c(a) = \exp(-T_c a^{-\theta}) \tag{4.41}$$

where T_c has the interpretation of the absolute technology level in country c and $1/\theta$ is related to the dispersion of productivities across goods, and hence measures the potential for comparative advantage. Country c has wages w_c, so c's unit cost of producing good g is $w_c/a_c(g)$. With these costs, c supplies g to country d at a cost of:

$$p_{cdg} = \frac{w_c}{a_c(g)} \tau_{cd} \tag{4.42}$$

where $\tau_{cd} > 1$ is the iceberg transport factor between c and d. But d will not necessarily buy from c: it will only do so if c has the lowest cif price available in d. This will be more likely if c and d are close to each other, and if c is cost-competitive in a wide range of goods.

Prices in country d depend on technology and input costs in the rest of the world, and transport costs. The price index can be shown to be:

$$P_d = \sum_{c=1}^{C} T_c (w_c \tau_{cd})^{-\theta} \tag{4.43}$$

This price index is increasing in weighted distance: it is higher if you are a long way from countries with good technology (that is, high T_i's). For $\theta = 1$ it bears a family resemblance to the centrality index of equation (4.36), which confirms in a very different model the general point that relative distance matters for trade flows. A few more steps gives d's imports from c:

$$M_{dc} = Y_d \frac{T_c (w_c \tau_{cd})^{-\theta}}{\Phi_d} \tag{4.44}$$

This is starting to look a lot like a gravity equation, and in fact Eaton and Kortum show that it reduces to the frictionless gravity equation $M_{dc} = k Y_c Y_d$ when there are no transport costs. More generally, national income in c will depend on absolute advantage T_c and on c's location in the world, summarized by P_c, as well as the national endowment of labor. Therefore, just as in the Armington model of (4.35) above, bilateral trade in this Ricardian model depends on country size, distance, and relative distance. But the effect of distance here is very different from the Armington model: rather than reduce the volume of a given set of country c goods that are consumed, distance shrinks the set of goods that d chooses to buy from c. In the equilibrium of the model, many countries produce and export the same goods,

but they do not sell in the same markets: if a country imports a good it will generally do so from just one source. As such, Eaton and Kortum challenge the view that
complete specialization is a necessary condition for the gravity equation.

4.2 Why Does Gravity Work? Discriminating Among Alternative Explanations

We now have plenty of evidence for the aggregate gravity equation and plenty of
theoretical foundations for it. Is Deardorff (1998) correct that, with so many potential fathers, we can not determine the gravity equation's paternity? Deardorff's view
is supported by the results of Hummels and Levinsohn (1995), who found that
gravity worked just as well for poor countries as it did for rich countries.[18] They
argued that this was a surprise, since the production side of the monopolistic competition model (which they took to be the foundation of gravity) is likely to be
appropriate for rich, but not poor, countries. A number of recent papers argue that
Deardorff was too pessimistic, but empirically selecting among the potential explanations for gravity is still at a relatively early stage.

Most of the evidence that "gravity works" comes from aggregate data, where total
bilateral trade is regressed on GDP. This is despite the fact that the models developed to explain gravity often apply also at the sectoral level (see equation (4.40)).
Given this, it is surprising how little work has been done on examining disaggregated gravity equations, or on looking for instances where gravity fails. One
recent attempt to do so is Haveman and Hummels (2001), who examine a large
data set of bilateral trade flows at the 4-digit SITC level. The most striking result
in this paper is the number of bilateral zeros: most potential bilateral trades in a
given SITC code do not occur. In particular, when a country imports a good it
usually imports it from only one source, and when a country exports a good it usually
exports it to a limited number of countries. This pattern could be rationalized by a
model of product differentiation with non-CES preferences and/or fixed costs to
transporting goods (although no one has solved such a model), but it is certainly
at odds with the standard gravity model specification which assumes symmetric
CES preferences and iceberg transportation costs. A large number of zeros is
explicitly predicted by the Ricardian model of Eaton and Kortum (2002), which
is one of the few predictions about gravity from that model which differ from the
gravity predictions of complete specialization models. The Eaton–Kortum model
can also be expected to work just as well for poor countries that produce homogeneous goods as it does for rich countries, so the Hummels–Levinsohn critique of the
excessively good performance of gravity does not apply to the Eaton–Kortum
model.

Another paper that looks at disaggregated gravity predictions is Feenstra et al.
(2001). The authors present a series of simple models that generate gravity-like
equations, that is, where both importer and exporter GDP help to explain bilateral
trade. The theory models predict that where there is free entry there will be

Table 4.1 Gravity equation estimates for different types of goods

	Differentiated	Reference priced	Homogeneous
Exporter GDP	1.12	0.91	0.54
Importer GDP	0.72	0.74	0.81

Source: *Feenstra et al. (2001), table 2.*

home-market effects, that is, exports will be more than proportional to GDP. This implies that the effect of exporter GDP will be larger than the effect of importer GDP in a gravity equation. Conversely, when there are barriers to entry, there is a reverse home market effect, so the effect of exporter GDP will be smaller than the effect of importer GDP in a gravity equation. The empirical implication is that the GDP elasticities in a gravity equation should be different depending on whether or not there are entry barriers, and the empirical problem is that there are no internationally comparable barriers on sectoral entry barriers. They proceed under the hypothesis that different types of goods might have different types of entry barriers, which would imply different gravity equation coefficients for different types of goods. This is exactly what they find. Using a classification scheme due to Rauch (1999), they find large and precisely estimated differences in the GDP coefficients in the gravity equation across differentiated, "reference priced," and homogeneous goods. Some illustrative results, from 1990, are given in table 4.1.

The interpretation of these results is not straightforward, because of the limitations of the theory and because there is no direct evidence on entry barriers. Nonetheless, the results are striking and thought provoking, and suggest that further research on how gravity works for different types of trade flows will be fruitful.

Feenstra et al. disaggregate one side of the gravity equation, but not the other – their disaggregated imports are always explained by importer and exporter GDP. A different approach is based on equation (4.40) above, which states that sectoral trade flows depend on importer GDP (demand) and exporter sectoral output (supply). If (4.40) held true for all sectors, then the ratio of trade to output in sector g among a group of countries c is:

$$predicted \frac{M_g}{x_g} = \sum_{c=1}^{C} s_c \left(1 - \frac{x_{cg}}{x_g}\right) \qquad (4.45)$$

where M_g and x_g are the intra-group totals of trade and output of good g. Harrigan (1996) calculates that this predicted ratio is about 0.5 among the OECD countries in 1985, and shows that the actual ratio of trade to output is much less than 0.5 and varies by a factor of ten across manufacturing industries (see table 4.2).

Table 4.2 suggests some sector-specific explanations for trade volumes. The high volume of trade in leather shoes and transport equipment seems to fit the product differentiation story, while the low volume of trade in cement and publishing are

Table 4.2 The volume of trade relative to output within the OECD, 1985

Industry	Trade/output
Leather shoes	0.30
Transport equipment	0.26
Basic chemicals	0.24
Electrical machinery	0.18
Textiles	0.14
Basic iron and steel	0.12
Fabricated metals	0.07
Food	0.07
Cement	0.05
Printing and publishing	0.03

Source: *Harrigan (1996), table 1.*

probably due to transport costs (cement is heavy) and home-biased tastes (French people read few books published in English) respectively. Whatever the sector-specific explanations, the large cross-sector variation in trade relative to output suggests that empirical work on understanding the volume of trade should work with disaggregated data.

Harrigan (1994) was the first to look at equations like (4.40) in the context of trying to understand the performance of the gravity model, arguing that monopolistic competition predicts that the volume of trade will be higher in sectors characterized by scale economies. The specification in that paper is flawed since it fails to control for bilateral distance, but it is notable that Harrigan finds a fairly robust result that the volume of bilateral trade is higher in sectors with larger scale economy proxies.

Like Harrigan (1996), Lai and Trefler (1999) estimate sectoral gravity equations, but they are much more careful than Harrigan was to use all the structure given by the CES functional form assumption.[19] In addition to using the model for policy analysis, they focus on how well the model fits at a sectoral level. To control for distance and other time-invariant influences on bilateral trade, they use panel data with country-pair fixed effects. The fixed effects strategy has the usual advantages and disadvantages: it gives consistent estimates of the parameters of interest but discards the overwhelming majority of the variation in the data, which is in the cross-section of country pairs. They find that the correlation between fitted and actual trade volumes is highest for industries where (they claim) the monopolistic competition model is more appropriate, but they make no attempt to formally identify which industries "should" fit the model's predictions. In their figure 3, they show that all the hard work in dealing with the CES price term makes no difference to model fit: dropping the price term gives the same correlation as including it. They also confirm in their figure 3 that the fit is largely driven by the output terms on the right-hand side, that is, the gravity effect on the supply side. They refer to this as a data identity, but that is not correct. The presence of sectoral output in a disaggregated gravity equation reflects the assumption that products are differentiated. Their final conclusion is that the gravity model does not work nearly as well when it is scrutinized at a sectoral level. Among other anomalies, the volume of trade is less than predicted, the elasticity of trade with respect to partner production is not one, and the CES structure adds little to a more naive specification.

A paper that argues that we can use aggregate data to see why gravity works is Evenett and Keller (2002). Their approach is to derive the aggregate gravity model using several simple textbook trade models, and then see whether gravity works better in sub-samples of country pairs that are thought to better fit the presumptions of the different models. Unfortunately, their results are not informative about why gravity works for several reasons. Most importantly, they work with two-country frictionless models, which have no predictions for bilateral trade in a many-country world where trade costs matter. Second, they use intraindustry trade indices to stratify their sample, despite the demonstrations by Davis (1995, 1997) that the proportion of intraindustry trade has nothing to do with the causes of gross trade volumes.

4.3 Conclusions and Unfinished Business – Gravity

Despite being a staple of applied analysis because it "works well," the gravity model has been subject to surprisingly little empirical testing. Some of the facts that the papers reviewed in the previous section have uncovered can be summarized as follows:

1   There are many zero observations in disaggregated bilateral trade.
2   The volume of trade is much smaller than predicted by the frictionless gravity model.
3   Relative, as well as absolute, distance and trade costs matter for understanding bilateral trade in a multicountry world.
4   The elasticity of trade with respect to output differs from one and is not uniform across goods. These differences may be related to the type of good and/or market structure.
5   The CES model of preferences does not fit the data.
6   The ratio of trade to output varies by an order of magnitude across industries.
7   There is some evidence that the volume of trade is higher in sectors characterized by monopolistic competition and/or scale economies.

This list raises more questions than it answers. What explains the zeros? Why is the volume of trade to output so small, and why is there so much variation in it? What model of consumption might improve on CES? Is it really the case that the volume of trade is higher in industries with scale economies? No doubt the astute reader can think of other questions left unanswered, and perhaps ambitious readers will try to answer them.

5   General Conclusions

This chapter has surveyed a decade's worth of empirical research on how well the data obey the laws of comparative advantage and gravity. Detailed conclusions from the survey are summarized in sections 3.4 and 4.3.

Given the centrality of comparative advantage and gravity to applied international economics, it is surprising that there has not been more empirical research, and sobering if not frustrating that progress has been so slow. A clear message from this chapter is that, while we have learned something about how specialization and the volume of trade are determined, there are large gaps in our knowledge. The opportunities for future researchers to help fill these gaps are equally large.

Acknowledgments

This chapter has benefited from comments by other *Handbook* authors at the Spring 2001 NBER meeting of the ITI group. The views expressed in this chapter are those of the author and do not necessarily reflect the position of the Federal Reserve Bank of New York or the Federal Reserve System.

Notes

1   Stronger statements, such as "a country will export all goods which are cheaper in autarky, and import all other goods," are not possible except in restricted models.
2   A further condition which they do not mention is that tastes must have stayed the same.
3   The paper chooses a normalization for prices such that the magnitude by which the Deardorff condition is satisfied is uninformative. The authors tell me that the next version of the paper will express this magnitude relative to autarky GDP, giving a measure of the size of the gains from trade.
4   If $G > F$, then any F equations from (4.3) can be used to solve for the F factor prices; the other $G - F$ equations will be consistent by assumption.
5   For many decades until Leamer coined the term, the FPI result did not have its own name, and the result was often misleadingly referred to as "factor price equalization" or FPE. The terminology matters in this case, because true FPE – that is, the same factor prices in different countries – requires more assumptions (including frictionless trade and identical technology) than FPI, which is a property of any single economy. Succinctly, FPI is a necessary but not sufficient condition for FPE.
6   I am deliberately noncommittal here about how trade policy causes differences between consumer and producer prices. I also ignore the value of trade policy revenue (tariff revenue plus quota rents) in national income, and dismiss the possibility of aggregate trade imbalances, to keep the notation simple.
7   Woodland (1982) offers an especially clear and detailed development of the dual approach. For a more compact, if opaque, treatment see Dixit and Norman (1980).
8   Although the Heckscher–Ohlin theorem doesn't generalize, the result that countries will export the services of their abundant factors does generalize to higher dimensions. See the chapter by Davis and Weinstein for a discussion of the research on this so-called Heckscher–Ohlin–Vanek hypothesis.

9   The easiest way to understand this argument is to visualize the textbook two-good, one-factor Ricardian model. If relative prices equal relative labor productivities, both goods will be produced in indeterminate quantities, and increases in labor will have unpredictable effects on outputs. But if prices change even slightly, the economy will specialize completely in the good whose relative price has risen, and there will be a unique relationship between labor supply changes and output changes.

10 The simplest example comes from the textbook specific factors model: accumulation of the mobile factor causes both industries to expand.

11 Together these assumptions are sufficient for trade to reproduce an "integrated equilibrium" with determinate production. The integrated equilibrium is the allocation that would result in a world with no barriers to the movement of goods or factors. See Dixit and Norman (1980).

12 In a series of well-done papers, Markusen (1986), Hunter and Markusen (1988), and Hunter (1991) explore the role of non-homothetic preferences in explaining gross trade volumes.

13 See the chapter by Davis and Weinstein in this volume for details on these modeling strategies.

14 This is the model preferred by Trefler (1995) in his study of the factor content of trade.

15 It is straightforward to compute the effects on levels, rather than shares, of output, but Harrigan does not do this.

16 Schott's model in a more general form dates back at least to Deardorff (1979).

17 The derivation here follows Deardorff (1998) and Anderson and van Wincoop (2001).

18 See Debaere (2000) for a critique of Hummels and Levinsohn. Debaere argues that the Hummels and Levinsohn data are friendlier to the monopolistic competition model than they thought.

19 While Lai and Trefler claim that their paper casts light on the monopolistic competition model, in fact their model takes sectoral production as given, and should therefore be regarded as a general gravity equation in which the Armington and monopolistic competition models are isomorphic.

References

Anderson, James E. 1979: A theoretical foundation for the gravity equation. *American Economic Review*, 69, 1, 106–16.

Anderson, James E. and Eric van Wincoop 2001: Gravity with gravitas: A solution to the border puzzle. NBER working paper no. 8079.

Ark, B. van 1993: Comparative levels of manufacturing productivity in postwar Europe: Measurement and comparisons. *Oxford Bulletin of Economics and Statistics*, 52, 343–74.

Ark, B. van and D. Pilat 1993: Productivity levels in Germany, Japan, and the United States: Differences and causes. *Brookings Papers Microeconomics*, 2, 1–69.

Armington, P. S. 1969: A theory of demand for products distinguished by place of production. IMF staff papers, 16, 159–76.

Balassa, Bela 1963: An empirical demonstration of classical comparative cost theory. *Review of Economics and Statistics*, 4, 231–8.

Bergstrand, Jeffrey 1985: The gravity equation in international trade: Some microeconomic foundations and empirical evidence. *The Review of Economics and Statistics*, 67, 474–81.

Bergstrand, Jeffrey 1989: The generalized gravity equation, monopolistic competition, and the factor-proportions theory in international trade. *The Review of Economics and Statistics*, 71, 143–53.

Bernard, Andrew B. and J. Bradford Jensen 2001: Why some firms export. NBER working paper no. 8349.

Bernhofen, Daniel M. and John C. Brown 2000: A direct test of the theory of comparative advantage: The case of Japan. Clark University, manuscript.

Bernstein, Jeffrey R. and David E. Weinstein 2002: Do endowments predict the location of production? Evidence from national and international data. *Journal of International Economics*, 56, 1, 55–76.

Brander, James and Paul Krugman 1983: A "reciprocal dumping" model of international trade. *Journal of International Economics*, 15: 313–21.

Choudhri, Ehsan U. and Lawrence L. Schembri 2000: Productivity performance and international competitiveness: A new test of an old theory. Carleton University, manuscript.

Davis, Donald R. 1995: Intraindustry trade: a Heckscher–Ohlin–Ricardo approach. *Journal of International Economics*, 19, 3/4, 201–26.

Davis, Donald R. 1997: Critical evidence on comparative advantage? North–North trade in a multilateral world. *Journal of Political Economy*, 105, 5, 1051–60.

Davis, Donald R. and David E. Weinstein 2001: An account of global factor trade. *American Economic Review*, 91, 5, 1423–53.

Deardorff, Alan V. 1979: Weak links in the chain of comparative advantage. *Journal of International Economics*, 9, 2, 197–209.

Deardorff, Alan V. 1980: The general validity of the law of comparative advantage, *Journal of Political Economy*, 88, 941–57.

Deardorff, Alan V. 1998: Determinants of bilateral trade: Does gravity work in a neoclassical world? In Jeffrey A. Frankel (ed.), *The Regionalization of the World Economy*, Chicago: University of Chicago Press for the NBER, 7–22.

Debaere, Peter 2000: Testing "new" trade theory without testing for gravity: Reinterpreting the evidence. University of Texas, manuscript.

Dixit, Avinash and Victor Norman 1980: *The Theory of International Trade*. Cambridge: Cambridge University Press.

Dollar, D. and E. N. Wolff 1993: *Competitiveness, Convergence, and International Specialization*. Cambridge, MA: MIT Press.

Dollar, D., W. Baumol and E. N. Wolff 1988: The factor price equalization model and industry labor productivity: An empirical test across countries. In R. C. Feenstra (ed.), *Empirical Methods for International Trade*, Cambridge, MA: MIT Press.

Eaton, Jonathan, and Samuel Kortum 2002: Technology, Geography, and Trade. *Econometrica*, 70, 5.

Evans, Carolyn 2000: The economic significance of national border effects. International Research Department, Federal Reserve Bank of New York, manuscript.

Evenett, Simon J. and Wolfgang Keller 2002: On theories explaining the success of the gravity equation. *Journal of Political Economy*, 110, 2, 281–316.

Feenstra, Robert C., James A. Markusen, and Andrew K. Rose 1998: Understanding the home market effect and the gravity equation: The role of differentiating goods. NBER working paper no. 6804.

Feenstra, Robert C., James A. Markusen, and Andrew K. Rose 2001: Using the gravity equation to differentiate among alternative theories of trade. *Canadian Journal of Economics*, 34, 2, 430–47.

Frankel, Jeffrey A. with Ernesto Stein and Shang-jin Wei 1997: *Regional Trading Blocs in the World Economic System*. Washington DC: Institute for International Economics.

Fujita, Masahisa, Paul Krugman, and Anthony J. Venables 1999: *The Spatial Economy: Cities, Regions, and International Trade*. Cambridge, MA: MIT Press.

Golub, Stephen S. and Chang-Tai Hsieh 2000: Classical Ricardian theory of comparative advantage revisited. *Review of International Economics*, 8, 2, 221–34.

Grossman, Gene 1998: Comment on Deardorff. In Jeffrey A. Frankel (ed.) *The Regionalization of the World Economy*, Chicago: University of Chicago Press for the NBER, 29–31.

Harrigan, James 1993: OECD imports and trade barriers in 1983. *Journal of International Economics*, 35, 95–111.

Harrigan, James 1994: Scale economies and the volume of trade. *The Review of Economics and Statistics*, 76, 2, 321–8.

Harrigan, James 1995: Factor endowments and the international location of production: Econometric evidence for the OECD, 1970–1985. *Journal of International Economics*, 39, 1/2, 123–41.

Harrigan, James 1996: Openness to trade in manufactures in the OECD. *The Journal of International Economics*, 40, 23–39.

Harrigan, James 1997a: Technology, factor supplies and international specialization: Estimating the neoclassical model. *American Economic Review*, 87, 4, 475–94.

Harrigan, James 1997b: Cross-country comparisons of industry total factor productivity: Theory and evidence. Federal Reserve Bank of New York research paper no. 9734.

Harrigan, James 1999: Estimation of cross-country differences in industry production functions. *Journal of International Economics*, 47, 2, 267–93.

Harrigan, James and Egon Zakrajšek 2000: Factor supplies and specialization in the world economy 2000, NBER working paper no. 7848 (August) and Federal Reserve Bank of New York staff report no. 107.

Haveman, Jon and David Hummels 2001: Alternative hypotheses and the volume of trade: Evidence on the extent of specialization. Purdue University, manuscript.

Helliwell, John F. 1997: National borders, trade, and migration. NBER working paper no. 6027.

Helpman, Elhanan and Paul Krugman 1985: *Market Structure and Foreign Trade: Increasing Returns, Imperfect Competition, and the International Economy*. Cambridge, MA: MIT Press.

Hummels, David 1999: Toward a geography of trade costs. Purdue University, manuscript.

Hummels, David and James Levinsohn 1995: Monopolistic competition and international trade: Reconsidering the evidence. *Quarterly Journal of Economics*, 110, 3, 799–836.

Hunter, Linda 1991: The contribution of nonhomothetic preferences to trade. *Journal of International Economics*, 30, 345–58.

Hunter, Linda and James Markusen 1988: Per capita income as a basis for trade. In Robert C. Feenstra (ed.), *Empirical Methods for International Trade*, Cambridge, MA: MIT Press.

Jones, Ronald W. and José A. Scheinkman 1977: The relevance of the two-sector production model in trade theory. *Journal of Political Economy*, 85, 5, 909–35.

Jorgenson, D. W. and M. Kuroda 1990: Productivity and international competitiveness in Japan and the United States, 1960–1985. In C. R. Hulten (ed.), *Productivity Growth in Japan and the United States*, Chicago: University of Chicago Press.

Jorgenson, D. W., M. Kuroda, and M. Nishimizu 1987: Japan–U.S. industry-level productivity comparisons, 1960–1979. *Journal of the Japanese and International Economies*, 1, 1–30.

Kohli, Ulrich 1991: *Technology, Duality, and Foreign Trade*. Ann Arbor: University of Michigan Press.

Krugman, Paul 1980: Scale economies, product differentiation, and the pattern of trade. *American Economic Review*, 70, 950–9.

Lai, Huiwen and Daniel Trefler 1999: The gains from trade: Standard errors with the CES monopolistic competition model. University of Toronto: manuscript.

Lawrence, Robert Z. 1987: Does Japan import too little: Closed minds or markets? *Brookings Papers on Economic Activity*, 2, 517–54.

Leamer, Edward E. 1984: *Sources of International Comparative Advantage*, Cambridge, MA: MIT Press.

Leamer, Edward E. 1987: Paths of development in the three-factor, n-good general equilibrium model. *Journal of Political Economy*, 95, 961–99.

Leamer, Edward E. 1995: The Heckscher–Ohlin model in theory and practice. *Princeton Studies in International Finance*, 77.

Leontief, Wassily 1954: Domestic production and foreign trade: The American capital position re-examined. In Richard E. Caves and Harry G. Johnson (eds.) 1968, *Readings in International Economics*, London: Allen and Unwin, ch. 30.

MacDougall, G. D. A. 1951: British and American exports: A study suggested by the theory of comparative costs, Part I. *The Economic Journal*, 61, 697–724.

MacDougall, G. D. A. 1952: British and American exports: A study suggested by the theory of comparative costs, Part II. *The Economic Journal*, 62, 487–521.

Markusen, James 1986: Explaining the volume of trade: An eclectic approach. *American Economic Review*, 76, 1002–11.

McCallum, John 1995: National borders matter: Canada–US regional trade patterns. *American Economic Review*, 85, 615–23.

Noussair, Charles N., Charles R. Plott, and Raymong G. Riezman 1995: An experimental investigation of the patterns of international trade. *American Economic Review*, 85, 3, 462–91.

Rauch, James 1999: Networks versus markets in international trade. *Journal of International Economics*, 48, 7–37.

Roberts, Mark J. and James R. Tybout 1997: The decision to export in Colombia: An empirical model of entry with sunk costs. *American Economic Review*, 87, 4, 545–64.

Rousslang, Donald J., and Theodore To 1993: Domestic trade and transportation costs as barriers to international trade. *Canadian Journal of Economics*, 26, 1, 208–21.

Saxonhouse, Gary R. 1989: Differentiated products, economies of scale, and access to the Japanese market. In Robert C. Feenstra (ed.), *Trade Policies for International Competitiveness*, Chicago: University of Chicago Press for the NBER, 145–83.

Schott, Peter 2000: One size fits all? Heckscher–Ohlin specialization in global production. Yale University, manuscript.

Trefler, Daniel 1993: International factor price differences: Leontief was right! *Journal of Political Economy*, 101, 961–87.

Trefler, Daniel 1995: The case of the missing trade and other mysteries. *American Economic Review*, 85, 1029–46.

Wei, Shang-Jin 1996: Intra-national versus international trade: How stubborn are nations in global integration? NBER working paper no. 5531.

Woodland, Alan D. 1982: *International Trade and Resource Allocation*. Amsterdam: North Holland.

5

The Factor Content of Trade

Donald R. Davis and David E. Weinstein

CHAPTER OUTLINE

Study of the factor content of trade has become a laboratory to test our ideas about how the key elements of endowments, production, absorption, and trade fit together within a general equilibrium framework. Already a great deal of progress has been made in fitting these pieces together. Nevertheless, the existing research raises a great many questions that should help to focus empirical research in the coming years. Among the more pressing issues is a deeper consideration of the role of intermediates, the role of aggregation biases, and of differences in patterns of absorption. This work should provide a more substantial foundation for future policy work developed within a factor content framework.

1 INTRODUCTION

The concept of the factor content of trade originates with Vanek (1968). The original formulation is based on a simple model of international factor price equalization, or what is more precisely termed the "integrated equilibrium" (Helpman and Krugman (1985)). Under conditions of competition in goods and factor markets, free international arbitrage, common constant returns to scale technologies, and adequate restrictions on the distribution of world endowments, both goods and factor prices will be equalized internationally. Under these conditions, a good will embody fixed amounts of the services of the productive factors, independently of where it is produced. Trade then can be conceived of in two ways. The first is as the overt exchange of goods that traditional theory addresses. Vanek's contribution was to recognize that we could equally think of trade as the international exchange of the services of factors embodied in those goods. Vanek's formulation of the problem allowed an extension of the logic of the Heckscher–Ohlin theory to settings in which the pattern of trade may be indeterminate but in which the net factor content of trade may nonetheless be determinate. Expression of the theory in this form also highlights the deep logic of the Heckscher–Ohlin theory in its focus on the relative availability of factors. When we move beyond a fully integrated world economy, as we do at length below, we will have to take care in defining the factor content of trade appropriate to each setting.

A reasonable first question is why we should care about the factor content of trade. We think there are two good reasons. The first is that the study of the factor content of trade is a laboratory for general equilibrium. A first statement of general equilibrium is that the elements of the system should "hang together." In the case of international trade, the elements of interest are the technologies, productive endowments, outputs, and demands of all countries in the world. Study of the factor content of trade then becomes a first test of the reasonableness of our assumptions about how these elements interact. If our theories perform poorly in matching measured and predicted factor contents of trade, then this may point in directions in which our theories need to be modified for understanding the world. If our theories perform well, then this indicates that the relevant framework may be a reasonable representation of the world and so also a reasonable framework for policy studies.

Indeed, the second important reason for considering studies of the factor content of trade is precisely that they may one day prove helpful in addressing policy questions of the impact of openness on national income levels and distribution. There already is a substantial applied literature mapping measures of the factor content of trade into impacts on domestic relative wages for the US and other members of Organization for Economic Cooperation and Development (OECD). Likewise, there has developed a theoretical literature seeking to establish the conditions under which such a mapping makes sense. We believe that these literatures have been very important in clarifying the issues that need to be addressed in future work. However, we also believe that the results of the empirical studies must be treated with caution, since the theoretical frameworks in which such calculations have been shown to make sense bear little resemblance to the frameworks preferred in the studies of the factor content of trade. We conclude that a major area for future work is taking the empirical frameworks favored by the studies of factor content and working out within them the consequences of international integration on incomes and inequality.

The past 15 years have seen wide swings in trade economists' views of models of the factor content of trade. Early studies, such as Bowen, Leamer, and Sveikauskas (1987, hereafter BLS) and Maskus (1985), seemed very damning. It was not so easy to see that this represented only a phase in the development of the literature. More recent studies, such as Trefler (1995) performed the signal service of identifying anomalies in the data which further research could aim to understand. The most recent studies, such as Davis and Weinstein (2001a), have been much more positive for amended versions of the theory.

We do not at all want to suggest that all issues about the factor content of trade are settled. Future work needs to gather better and more extensive data sets, to consider more carefully the role of traded intermediates, cross-country differences in demand, the role of trade costs, and so on. But the progress made in the past 15 years surely holds promise that this will continue to be a fertile area for research.

2 THEORY

2.1 The Simple Heckscher–Ohlin–Vanek Model

We begin with the standard model of Heckscher–Ohlin–Vanek (HOV). Let there be G goods, each produced under perfect competition with constant returns to scale. Let there be F primary factors of production with factor markets competitive. Let technologies for all goods and quality of all factors be common for all countries of the world. Let there be at least as many goods as factors, i.e., $G \geq F$. Assume that trade between countries is free, so that goods' prices are equalized. Assume that the distribution of world endowments among countries satisfies the requirements to replicate the integrated equilibrium.[1] Then factor prices will be equalized (FPE), and for all countries $c \in C$, there is a common technology matrix:

$$\mathbf{B} = \mathbf{B}^c \tag{5.1}$$

Columns of this matrix represent input coefficients for a given good. Rows represent the input coefficients for a given factor across all goods.

For country c, let the output vector be given by $\mathbf{X}^c$ and the primary input vector be given by $\mathbf{V}^c$. Then under the maintained assumption that the technology matrix $\mathbf{B}$ is common to all countries, full employment of resources implies that:

$$\mathbf{B}\mathbf{X}^c = \mathbf{V}^c \tag{5.2}$$

Demand is assumed to be identical across countries and homothetic. Let $\mathbf{D}^c$ be country c's vector of final goods demand, $\mathbf{X}^W$ be the world output vector, and s^c be country c's share of world spending. Then, with free trade equalizing goods prices,

$$\mathbf{D}^c = s^c \mathbf{X}^W \tag{5.3}$$

Equation (5.3) provides a statement about demand for goods. By pre-multiplying by the common technology matrix $\mathbf{B}$, we can convert this to a statement about the factor content of consumption. First, we note that under the hypothesis of a common $\mathbf{B}$,

$$\mathbf{B}\mathbf{X}^W = \mathbf{V}^W \tag{5.4}$$

Then it follows that:

$$\mathbf{BD}^c = s^c \mathbf{V}^W \tag{5.5}$$

Finally, noting that the net trade vector is $\mathbf{T}^c = \mathbf{X}^c - \mathbf{D}^c$, we can difference equations (5.2) and (5.5) to arrive at the statement of the simple HOV model:

$$\mathbf{BT}^c = \mathbf{V}^c - s^c \mathbf{V}^W \tag{5.6}$$

For future reference, it is convenient to call $\mathbf{BT}^c$ the *measured* factor content of trade (MFCT) and $\mathbf{V}^c - s^c\mathbf{V}^W$ the *predicted* factor content of trade (PFCT). The first depends on trade flows weighted by a technology matrix. The latter is based on endowments relative to average endowments for a country of that size in the world.

It is straightforward to incorporate non-traded goods into the model with FPE.[2] Let $\mathbf{V}^{cN}$ be country c's devotion of primary factors to non-traded production. Then the residual endowments available for production of exportables are $\mathbf{V}^{cT} \equiv \mathbf{V}^c - \mathbf{V}^{cN}$. Similarly, for the world as a whole, the endowments devoted to production of tradables are $\mathbf{V}^{WT} = \Sigma_c \mathbf{V}^{cT}$. The predicted factor content of trade will then be the difference between the residual factors available for production of exportables and the factor content of consumption of tradables, or $\mathbf{BT}^c = \mathbf{V}^{cT} - s^c\mathbf{V}^{WT}$. However, with FPE and free trade, it is also true that $\mathbf{V}^{cN} = s^c\mathbf{V}^{WN}$. If we note this and add $\mathbf{V}^{cN} - s^c\mathbf{V}^{WN} = 0$ to the right-hand side of $\mathbf{BT}^c = \mathbf{V}^{cT} - s^c\mathbf{V}^{WT}$, we see that this returns us to equation (5.6). That is, so long as there is FPE, the presence of non-traded goods affects the predicted factor content of trade not at all, and empirical researchers are free to ignore them in spite of the fact that non-traded sectors are in practice very large. As we will see below, this changes importantly when FPE no longer holds.

2.2   Incorporating Intermediates into the HOV Model

When output of goods requires inputs both of primary factors and other goods as intermediates, we need to amend the foregoing. The matrix $\mathbf{B}$ should now be interpreted as the matrix of primary, or direct, factor inputs. In addition, there is an input–output matrix $\mathbf{A}$, with dimension $G \times G$. Each element in the input–output matrix is the unit input requirement of one good in the production of another good, where it is important to remember that industries may use their own output as an input. A row of the input–output matrix indicates the unit input requirement of a given good in the production of all other goods (e.g., how much steel is used in the production of a unit of trucks, planes, etc.). A column, then, indicates how a given good uses all other goods (e.g., how much steel, trucks, etc. are used in the production of a unit of planes). With the presence of intermediate usage, we have to distinguish between gross output, which we now call $\mathbf{X}^c$ and net output available for final demand, which we denote by $\mathbf{Y}^c$. Let $\mathbf{I}$ be the $G \times G$ identity matrix. Then the relation between net and gross output is given simply by:

$$\mathbf{Y}^c = (\mathbf{I} - \mathbf{A})X^c \tag{5.7}$$

Equations (5.2) and (5.4) continue to hold as factor market clearing conditions even in the presence of intermediates. Of course, only net output is available for final consumption, so (5.3) must be amended to:

$$\mathbf{D}^c = s^c \mathbf{Y}^W \tag{5.8}$$

Assuming $(\mathbf{I} - \mathbf{A})$ is invertible, we can define a new matrix of total, or direct plus indirect, factor inputs, given by:

$$\overline{\mathbf{B}} = \mathbf{B}(\mathbf{I} - \mathbf{A})^{-1} \tag{5.9}$$

With a little algebra, this allows for a statement of HOV in the presence of intermediates

$$\overline{\mathbf{B}} \mathbf{T}^c = \mathbf{V}^c - s^c \mathbf{V}^W \tag{5.10}$$

2.3   First Tests of the HOV Model

Equation (5.10) is based on observable variables, so can provide a test of the HOV model. A welcome feature for empirical implementation is that it can be implemented even if the researcher has data on only a subset of the primary factor inputs. Let $\overline{\mathbf{B}}^f$ be the fth row of the technology matrix, V^{fc} be country c's endowment of factor f, and V^{fW} be the corresponding sum for the world. Then we can imagine constructing matrices of HOV predictions with dimension $F \times C$ equal to the number of factors times the number of countries on each side of the equation. The typical elements of such matrices will be of the form:

$$\overline{\mathbf{B}}^f \mathbf{T}^c = \mathbf{V}^{fc} - s^c \mathbf{V}^{fW} \tag{5.11}$$

Various tests could be applied to this. Since corresponding elements of the matrices are supposed to be equal, one would at least like them to have the same sign. That is, one would like countries to be measured to export the services of factors that the theory identifies as abundant there. This may be called a sign test. An alternative is to note that corresponding columns and rows of the matrices are supposed to be equal, so one can test the weakened hypothesis that they will have a high rank correlation. For columns, this implies that, holding fixed a country, measured net exports by factor correspond to the abundance across these factors indicated by endowments relative to typical country endowments. For a row, this implies that, holding fixed the factor, measured net factor service exports across countries correspond to those predicted based on national and world endowments.

One strong requirement for implementing (5.10) is that it requires data on world factor endowments. This motivates an alternative that is frequently employed. Divide both sides of the equation by the income share and you get:

$$\frac{\overline{\mathbf{B}}\mathbf{T}^c}{s^c} = \frac{\mathbf{V}^c}{s^c} - \mathbf{V}^W \qquad (5.12)$$

Do this for two countries, c and c', take the difference and multiply through by the income share of the first, and you obtain:

$$\overline{\mathbf{B}}\left(\mathbf{T}^c - \frac{s^c}{s^{c'}}\mathbf{T}^{c'}\right) = \mathbf{V}^c - \frac{s^c}{s^{c'}}\mathbf{V}^{c'} \qquad (5.13)$$

As noted, this has the strong advantage in empirical implementation that one needs data only on the countries for which the bilateral comparisons are to be made. However, there is also a disadvantage. Suppose that the true model, instead of being (5.10) is instead:

$$\overline{\mathbf{B}}\mathbf{T}^c = \mathbf{V}^c - s^c\mathbf{V}^W + s^c\mathbf{\Lambda}^{c,c'} \qquad (5.14)$$

where the last term is any systematic deviation from HOV that is proportional to country size but otherwise common among the included countries.[3] If we apply the bilateral difference approach to (5.14), we again end up with (5.13). That is, the approach of (5.13) will not detect systematic and potentially large deviations from HOV that are of the form indicated by the last term in (5.14).

2.4 Adjusted Factor Price Equalization

The requirement in (5.1) that input requirements are identical everywhere is stringent, but can be relaxed. Suppose that across countries, there are differences in factor quality of a pure factor augmenting nature. In such a case, we need to distinguish between natural and efficiency units of factors. Suppose that there exists a common technology matrix $\overline{\mathbf{B}}$ and, for each factor and country, an adjustment scalar π^{fc} that satisfies:

$$\overline{\mathbf{B}}^{fc} = \pi^{fc}\overline{\mathbf{B}}^f \qquad (5.15)$$

Then we can say that the endowments of country c expressed in efficiency units are:

$$\mathbf{V}^{cE} = \frac{1}{\pi^{fc}}\mathbf{V}^c \qquad (5.16)$$

If all the other requirements of the HOV world are satisfied, this leads to a restatement of the factor content of trade in terms of efficiency units of factors:

$$\overline{\mathbf{B}}\mathbf{T}^c = \mathbf{V}^{cE} - s^c\sum_{c'}\mathbf{V}^{c'E} \qquad (5.17)$$

If country 0 is the base that defines $\overline{\mathbf{B}} \equiv \overline{\mathbf{B}}^0$, and if the return for factor f in country 0 is w^{f0}, then for any country c

$$w^{fc} = \frac{w^{f0}}{\pi^{fc}} \tag{5.18}$$

A special case of adjusted FPE is when for a fixed c, $\pi^{fc} = \pi^{fc}$ for all factors. This accommodates a world with scalar country differences in total factor productivity, which here will be interpreted just as common differences in factor quality.

2.5 Failure of Factor Price Equalization

Under a variety of conditions, factor prices may fail to equalize, even in efficiency terms. There are a variety of ways of dealing with this failure of FPE while continuing to work with predictions about factor contents of trade.

2.5.1 AN FPE CLUB

One approach is to ask how HOV should be modified if a subset of the world shares FPE, but not necessarily the whole world. Suppose that there is a set of regions, $r \in R$, that shares FPE even though this may not hold for countries $c \notin R$. Call R the FPE club. Then club members share a common technology matrix $\overline{\mathbf{B}}^R$. Hence for each $r \in R$ we continue to have

$$\mathbf{B}^R \mathbf{X}^r = \mathbf{V}^r \tag{5.19}$$

If trade continues to equalize goods prices and the other standard HOV demand assumptions hold, then:

$$\mathbf{D}^r = s^r \mathbf{Y}^W \tag{5.20}$$

We can always pre-multiply this by $\overline{\mathbf{B}}^R$, the difference being that absent world FPE, it is no longer the case that $\overline{\mathbf{B}}^R \mathbf{Y}^W$ will equal $\mathbf{V}^W$. Instead, the corresponding equation is that for members of the FPE club, and a common technology matrix $\overline{\mathbf{B}}^R$,

$$\overline{\mathbf{B}}^R \mathbf{T}^r = \mathbf{V}^r - s^r \overline{\mathbf{B}}^R \mathbf{Y}^W \tag{5.21}$$

This restriction can be examined for all members of the FPE club.

2.5.2 UNDERSTANDING THE BREAKDOWN OF FPE

A huge advantage of the last approach is that we can apply it to members of the FPE club without taking a stand on why FPE is breaking down. The big drawback of this approach is that we care why FPE breaks down. If FPE fails in a systematic way, then we can identify hypotheses that allow us to test an appropriately modified version of HOV.

If FPE breaks down, then this should show up in an examination of the technology matrices of the respective countries. Hence, a first approach is to return to equation (5.1) and check if there is a common $\mathbf{B} = \mathbf{B}^c$ for all c. FPE would imply that these technology matrices are equal. Unfortunately, a finding that they are not equal need not invalidate FPE if there are more goods than factors and our industrial categories, which define columns of the $\mathbf{B}$ matrix, are themselves composed of products of heterogeneous factor content.

To make this point clearly, it is best to depart from generality and think about a world of two factors, say of capital and labor. Let there be two countries, with the home country more capital abundant than the foreign. Suppose that there is a Dornbusch–Fischer–Samuelson (1980) continuum of goods with varying capital intensities. Assume as well that the distribution of world endowments is consistent with re-creating the integrated equilibrium. Then the HOV predictions will hold exactly, even though the pattern of trade in goods may not be fully determined because the number of goods exceeds the number of factors. Now assume that there are strictly positive costs of trade, although we can think of them as vanishingly small. In this case, the pattern of trade becomes determinate. The home country concentrates its exports among the most capital-intensive goods, and vice versa for the foreign country. Goods of intermediate factor intensity are non-traded. Formally, the exports of the countries are disjoint. If, however, our system of classifying goods into industries aggregates into the same industries goods of very different factor content produced in the two countries, then we will expect to find in the data that country capital abundance is correlated with industry capital intensity.[4] However, this would only be true for traded goods. With the vanishingly small trade costs doing little to disturb FPE, we should not find this correlation among non-traded goods. A second issue is that the average input coefficients that we calculate in the data are a weighted average of the goods that we actually export and our non-traded goods. In this simple framework, goods of intermediate factor intensity fall into the non-traded sector, so we tend to underestimate the true factor content of trade. Suppose that we could correct for this problem and define a technology matrix $\overline{\mathbf{B}}^{cDFS}$ that reflects the actual factor intensity of production of c's exports, E^c. Let the imports of c from a country c' be $\mathbf{M}^{cc'}$ (and for simplicity, let country c's demand for its own output be denoted $\mathbf{M}^{cc}$), then the appropriate HOV equation is:

$$\overline{\mathbf{B}}^{cDFS}\mathbf{Y}^c - \left[\overline{\mathbf{B}}^{cDFS}\mathbf{D}^{cc} + \sum_{c'} \overline{\mathbf{B}}^{c'DFS}\mathbf{M}^{cc'}\right] = \mathbf{V}^c - s^c\mathbf{V}^W \qquad (5.22)$$

The foregoing has allowed for differences in technology matrices for tradables by country, even though "approximate" FPE holds. The reason that the matrices differed for tradables, but not for non-tradables is that the former reflected heterogeneity of goods in an industry in spite of the approximate FPE, while this implied common input coefficients for the non-traded goods where homogeneity is more plausible.

An alternative that can be investigated is a breakdown of FPE, so that there is a systematic correlation between country capital abundance and industry input usage not only in tradables (where this now suggests specialization) but also in non-tradables (where this suggests factor substitution). Interestingly, the key to distinguishing this from the former case is to look for this systematic correlation in the input coefficients in the non-traded sector.

If this indicates a breakdown of FPE, there is yet another adjustment that needs to be made. Capital abundant countries with high wages will use more capital per worker in non-traded sectors, implying that standard measures of excess factor supplies overstate how much of the abundant factor is available for production of exportables, hence tend to predict too high a volume of factor trade. Since, in practice, non-traded sectors are large, these adjustments to the theoretical model may matter quite a lot. Let the appropriate matrix for country c in this case be $\mathbf{B}^{cH}$ (after Helpman, who suggested such an approach). Let a superscript T indicate traded output and an N indicate endowments dedicated to the production of non-traded goods. Then the appropriate measure for this amended HOV model is:

$$\overline{\mathbf{B}}^{cH}\mathbf{Y}^{cT} - \sum_{c'}\overline{\mathbf{B}}^{c'H}\mathbf{M}^{cc'} = [\mathbf{V}^c - s^c\mathbf{V}^W] - [\mathbf{V}^{cN} - s^c\mathbf{V}^{WN}] \qquad (5.23)$$

Here the measured factor flows of trade are measured using the *producer's* technology. The predicted factor flows are also adjusted for the fact that countries abundant in a factor tend to use that factor more intensively in non-traded production, so have less available for production of exportables than indicated in the standard HOV equation.

2.5.3 CROSS FLOWS OF FACTOR SERVICES IN A MANY-CONE WORLD

When endowment differences lead to a breakdown of FPE, then a set of equilibrium factor prices and the associated goods that can be competitively produced at these factor prices define a "cone" in factor space. Countries whose endowments lie within the same cone share FPE, while those that lie in different cones do not.

It is simplest to think about this in the case of two factors, say capital and labor. Consider a many-cone world. For simplicity, ignore non-traded goods, assume that each cone contains just one country and that the number of goods produced is sufficiently large that boundary goods produced by countries in different cones can be safely ignored. Consider the case of a country of intermediate capital abundance. Such a country will find that it trades both with countries that are more capital abundant than itself and also countries where the reverse is true. Importantly, the country should be a net *importer* of capital services from the countries more abundant than itself, and *simultaneously* a net *exporter* of capital services to those countries less abundant in capital. This suggests an important caution on any implicit welfare conclusions based on the magnitude of a country's total net factor trade services. The point is that even if the country is close to a zero net trader in the services of capital and labor when considering its trade with all countries, it could nonetheless be enjoying significant gains from factor service trade by being able to trade with countries both more and less capital abundant than itself. Let $C^+(c)$ denote the set of countries more capital abundant than c, and $C^-(c)$ the set of countries less capital abundant than c. Let $\mathbf{E}^{cc'}$ be exports from c to c' and $\mathbf{M}^{cc'}$ be imports to c from c'. Then, for example, the factor content of trade of c with those countries more capital abundant than itself is:

$$\bar{\mathbf{B}}^c \sum_{c' \in C^+(c)} \mathbf{E}^{cc'} - \sum_{c' \in C^+(c)} \bar{\mathbf{B}}^{c'} \mathbf{M}^{cc'} = \sum_{c' \in C^+(c)} s^{c'} \mathbf{V}^c - s^c \sum_{c' \in C^+(c)} \mathbf{V}^{c'} \qquad (5.24)$$

Naturally a similar condition could be written down for trade with those countries less abundant in capital than country c. Moreover, under the conditions stated, which imply full specialization in tradables, such factor content predictions can be written down bilaterally.

2.6 The Factor Content of Trade with Traded Intermediates

If intermediates are traded and all countries use identical techniques, the standard HOV equations can be implemented because goods will always embody the same amount of factors regardless of where they are produced. The mathematics becomes significantly more complicated in the case where FPE fails and intermediates are traded. The reason is that all exports and imports embody a combination of domestic and foreign factors. Hence, the factor content of any country's trade is going to depend on all of the input–output relationships and technological coefficients in all countries.

Surprisingly, Trefler (1996) claims to have modeled a world with traded intermediates without using any information about the requisite input–output matrices. The starting point of his work is the principle that HOV equations must *always* be of the form $\mathbf{V}^c - s^c \mathbf{V}^W = \mathbf{F}^c$, where the definition of $\mathbf{F}^c$ varies with the model. Note that the fixed point of this approach, $\mathbf{V}^c - s^c \mathbf{V}^W$, will only under restrictive circumstances be the predicted factor content of trade. That is, from the start, he abandons the idea of developing counterparts to predicted and measured factor contents of trade.

By using data identities, market clearing, and a stronger than usual assumption on demand – that *bilateral* consumption patterns are proportional to world income shares – Trefler (1996) derives a relation $\mathbf{V}^c - s^c \mathbf{V}^W = \mathbf{F}^c$. Since Trefler *defines* $\mathbf{V}^c - s^c \mathbf{V}^W$ to be the factor content of trade, it tautologically follows that $\mathbf{F}^c$ is likewise the factor content of trade, even though *neither term actually is the net exports of factors embodied in trade*. This is an important point that can be lost to the reader. Since Trefler is only interested in the aggregate restrictions on factor usage rather than tracking factor service flows, he is able to bypass using a complete set of input–output matrices. This enables him to show that $\mathbf{F}^c$ can be decomposed as follows:

$$\mathbf{V}^c - s^c \mathbf{V}^W = \mathbf{F}^c_{Cons} + \mathbf{F}^c_{Inter} + \sum_{c'} \mathbf{B}^{tc'} (\mathbf{D}^{cc'} - s^c \mathbf{D}^{Wc'}) \qquad (5.25)$$

where $\mathbf{B}^{tc'}$ is some transform of the standard technology matrix for country c'. The first two terms on the right-hand side might seem to be – but are *not* – the factor content of trade in final goods and intermediates respectively. As noted, while they might look like the factor content of intermediate and final goods trade, Trefler (1996) and close inspection makes clear this is not the case. The final term of $\mathbf{F}^c$ is a term that would equal zero if the strong assumption that *bilateral* consumption patterns are proportional to world income shares were exactly correct. What he has derived is a relationship between endowments, non-standard technology matrices, and trade, but it is hard to see what the economic meaning of these terms may be. This suggests that understanding how to incorporate traded intermediates into factor content studies remains an important area for future research.

2.6.1 COST RESTRICTIONS ON FACTOR CONTENT ABSENT FPE

An alternative approach to testing factor content predictions in the absence of FPE relies on the properties of cost minimization. Define the factor content of imports to c from c' as

$$\mathbf{M}_V^{cc'} \equiv \overline{\mathbf{B}}^{c'II} \mathbf{M}^{cc'} \tag{5.26}$$

Letting the vector of factor prices in c be denoted $\mathbf{w}^c$, Helpman (1984) shows that a restriction on costs implies that:

$$\left(\mathbf{w}^c - \mathbf{w}^{c'}\right)' \mathbf{M}_V^{cc'} \leq 0 \tag{5.27}$$

In simple terms, this restriction just says that if instead of importing the factor services we actually import, we had instead hired these same factors in our local market c at prices $\mathbf{w}^c$ to produce these goods ourselves, the cost would have been at least weakly greater than our import bill (equal to the cost of producing that import vector in the foreign country). Obviously, a correlative restriction to (5.27) can be placed on the costs of factor service imports to c'. We can also look at the difference between two such equations for c and c' to arrive at:

$$\left(\mathbf{w}^c - \mathbf{w}^{c'}\right)' \left(\mathbf{M}_V^{cc'} - \mathbf{M}_V^{c'c}\right) \geq 0 \tag{5.28}$$

On average, country c imports from c' the services of those factors that are relatively costlier in c than c'.

The restrictions in (5.27) and (5.28) can in principle be taken to data, since they involve observable post-trade factor prices and measurable factor service flows. However, there are two difficulties in implementing these. The first is that, in contrast to the other approaches to HOV derived above, it is crucial to have information about *all* factors of production. A second difficulty is that one must be able to measure with confidence the factor returns in each country, including the rental on capital.

3 DATA ISSUES

Empirical analysis requires the researcher to confront a spectrum of questions. What data is required to test the theory? When alternative measures are available, how do we choose among them? When alternative sources of data exist and they do not provide identically the same values, how do we choose among them? When some analytic elements must be constructed from more primitive data, how do we choose the method for such construction? Is there reason to believe that measurement error in the relevant data is large? Is there a way to minimize the impact of such measurement error on tests of the theory?

3.1 What is the Data?

The data required depend on the variant of the HOV theory to be tested and whether we also want to test some of the subsidiary hypotheses. Tests of HOV always require some measure of a technology matrix. Standard HOV theory requires a matrix of total (direct plus indirect) factor requirements. The next choice is how many technology matrices one wants to work with. Most of the literature has worked with a single technology matrix – typically that of the US, although occasionally also of Japan. When these papers (e.g., BLS, Trefler, 1993, 1995) have contemplated technological differences, these have been treated as parametric deviations from the US technology matrix. An alternative approach is to use distinct technology matrices for the countries in the study, as in Davis and Weinstein (2001a) or Hakura (2001).

Tests of HOV always require some measure of endowments. Standard HOV theory requires endowments of the entire world, although in practice researchers have worked with endowments for the largest set of countries they can obtain. When the tests are in the bilateral difference format of equation (5.13), endowments are only required for the countries considered. In standard tests of HOV, tests are factor by factor, so that omission of some factors from the test does not affect results for included factors. By contrast, tests of cost restrictions when FPE fails require data for all factors. An important question in practice is whether one wants to use coarse or fine definitions of the factors themselves. Alternative implementations of HOV have used two, three, up to as many as twelve factors of production. At times the choice is mandated by data availability or compatibility. At other times, there is a real choice. For example, do we want to characterize labor endowments by occupational category: managerial, production, service, sales, etc.? Or do we want to see it as stocks of high-skilled and low-skilled labor? The former has the advantage of providing a more detailed division of the labor types. However, the latter is probably closer to our idea of factors that can flow across occupational categories. Researchers also must address the issue of the compatibility of the data. Is a skilled worker in the US the same factor as a skilled worker in Cambodia? Are there quality differences? How shall we sum across countries to obtain some measure of world endowments?

The measurement of trade flows is relatively more straightforward. Standard HOV theory requires for each country only its net trade vector with the rest of the world. Some variants of HOV require that exports and imports be measured as gross flows, since they may have different factor content under what is nominally the same industry. Further refinements may require that this be refined to examine bilateral trade flows.

Implementations that examine the production side of HOV typically require some measure of output. Depending on the question at issue, this may require gross or net output.[5] The difference, of course, also requires an input–output matrix. Here there are choices about whether one computes this with absorption of domestic intermediates separated from those that are imported from various sources.

Standard HOV requires some measure of a country's share of world absorption. Often this is taken as the country's GDP share. Sometimes this is adjusted for trade imbalances, although these have typically had scant impact on the HOV results. The demand side of HOV also places restrictions on the pattern of absorption that can be examined more directly. Unfortunately, absorption is often not directly observed, and so inferences can only be made indirectly from factor service flow calculations.

Implementation of standard HOV does not require data on factor prices. However, some tests of HOV (e.g., Trefler, 1993) have relied on factor price data in a subsidiary manner to confirm the plausibility of parameters calculated from the data. When FPE fails, implementation of tests of cost restrictions relies importantly on high quality factor price data for *all* factors.

3.2 Data Quality and Compatibility

Trade is the difference between output and absorption. The factor content of trade is the difference between endowments (the factor content of production) and the factor content of absorption. From this perspective, trade in goods or factor services can be thought of as a residual that is frequently an order of magnitude smaller than output or absorption. This fact brings to the fore the issues of data quality and compatibility.

We have already talked about the data inputs required to test factor content theories. The researcher is then faced with the question of which data source to rely on for measures of the relevant variables. An unfortunate fact is that measures of the same variable for the same country and time period, but drawn from alternative sources, frequently differ – and the differences need not be small! There are many reasons for this, potentially including different definitions, different choices about which exchange rates are used to convert figures, different methodologies for constructing key variables, and so on.

Indeed, at times these problems may be sufficiently large that it might be impossible to observe relationships based on net factor flows even were the relationship to exist. A case in point is the study of BLS. BLS had stressed the importance of the fact that their tests use three independent sources of information on endowments, technology, and trade. To their credit, BLS report in their footnote 14 a check on measurement error in these data. If you pre-multiply the US gross output vector by the US technology vector, this should deliver as an identity the US endowments employed. Since BLS constructed the endowment data separately from the US technology matrix, this identity does not hold in their data, and frequently departs quite sharply from equivalence. For example, the imputed endowment of capital based on the technology matrix and the output levels exceeds the endowment of capital by more than 100 percent. Smaller, but substantial errors exist for other factors. Since one way of interpreting their tests is as a check of whether the entire world uses US technology, it should be more than a little troubling that in their data, even the US does not use US technology.

Such concerns lead us to believe that a great deal of attention must be paid to consistency in the construction of the data. National capital stocks cannot be constructed independently of the way that capital is constructed when the technology matrix is put together. Definitions for other variables likewise must be consistent. This also suggests the value of using one data source as an ultimate authority for a given project. When there are discrepancies between alternate sources, resolve them based on this authority and do re-scaling of supplementary data as needed. Naturally, this requires care in the selection of the highest quality database as the authority. But it at least allows the theory some chance to escape being swamped simply by inconsistent definitions of the same variables.

4 FACTOR CONTENT: WHAT ARE THE TESTS?

In the absence of a clear alternative framework relating endowments and trade, it is not possible to test HOV against a well-specified null hypothesis. As a result, researchers typically run horse races between various versions of the model, e.g., HOV with neutral technical shifts, home bias, etc. The statistical framework is typically Bayesian and simply asks which version of HOV is best supported by the data.

A major problem with such statistical tests of HOV is that one of the models must be deemed "best" even if it has little explanatory power. As a result, researchers also rely on goodness of fit criteria as a means of "testing" HOV. Typically researchers have focused on five such criteria. The first two measures are non-parametric. *Sign tests* ask whether the sign of MFCT is the same as that of PFCT. These tests identify what share of the data would lie in quadrants one and three if one plotted MFCT against PFCT. A strength of this test is that large outliers are unlikely to affect the results. The major weakness, of course, is that countries with small PFCT may have many sign errors without it indicating a major problem for the theory. Rank tests put a little more structure on the data by asking whether countries that are predicted to be large exporters (importers) of a factor are measured to do so. A problem in these tests arises when there are a large number of countries that have similar PFCTs.

A second major class of tests is the regression tests. Here three tests are standard. The first two arise from the slope and R^2 of a regression of MFCT on PFCT. In addition to the slope and R^2 tests, Trefler has utilized the missing (factor service) trade test (MT) which is defined as the variance of the MFCT, σ_M^2, divided by the variance of PFCT, σ_P^2.

How these tests are related is best understood by thinking about how each statistic is calculated. The formulas for the slope coefficient and R^2 in a linear regression are:

$$\hat{\alpha} = \frac{\sigma_{MP}}{\sigma_P^2} \quad \text{and} \quad R^2 = \frac{\sigma_{MP}^2}{\sigma_P^2 \sigma_M^2}$$

where $\hat{\alpha}$ is the slope coefficient of a regression of MFCT on PFCT. A little algebra shows that the three tests are related:

$$MT = \frac{\hat{\alpha}^2}{R^2}$$

In other words, any two tests are sufficient for identifying the outcome of the third.

4.1 First Generation Studies: A String of Empirical Rejections

The seminal empirical critique of Heckscher–Ohlin is due to Leontief (1953). Although this was not a test of the HOV theorem, the study clearly indicated that something was seriously amiss with how economists thought about trade. Leontief used data on input requirements and US trade to measure capital to labor ratios in US imports and exports separately. To universal surprise, widespread dismay, and scattered consternation, he showed that US imports were more capital intensive than US exports. This suggested that the US is relatively labor abundant – a result ever after known as the "Leontief paradox." Leamer (1980) showed, however, that Leontief applied a conceptually inappropriate test of the Heckscher–Ohlin hypothesis. When he re-examined the same data in a conceptually correct way, the paradox vanished. Nonetheless, this paradox refused to perish. Brecher and Choudhri (1982) pointed out that one (counterfactual) implication of Leamer's approach is that US expenditure per worker would have to be lower than for the world as a whole. Stern and Maskus (1981) applied Leamer's (1980) approach to US data for both 1958 and 1972, finding the Leontief paradox held in the former but not in the latter year. Extensive surveys of previous work on Heckscher–Ohlin can be found in Deardorff (1984) and Leamer and Levinsohn (1995).

The first real tests of HOV were conducted by Maskus (1985) and BLS (1987). The analytic foundation is given by equation (5.11). Their results severely undermined confidence in the robustness of the Heckscher–Ohlin framework. Maskus (1985) carried out both sign and rank tests on data for two time periods (1958 and 1972), and for three high quality factors (professional, unskilled labor, and capital). He reports results only for the US, perhaps because the Leontief paradox had focused on it. The sign test is correct for only one factor in 1958, but for all three in 1972. This might be seen to suggest that the Heckscher–Ohlin–Vanek relations fare well, at least in the latter period. However, the test lacks power. As Maskus notes, if we consider the alternative that the signs were determined randomly, we will have two or fewer sign failures out of six tries 34.4 percent of the time. Moreover, even if we limit ourselves to the 1972 data, under the same alternative, there will be no sign violations (as in his data) one in eight times. The results were, if anything, worse in the rank test. The direct measures of US factor abundance relative to the rest of the world were stable, with physical capital most abundant, professionals second, and unskilled labor least abundant. However, the trade-imputed measures of factor abundance in 1958 suggested the US was most abundant in unskilled labor, and least abundant in physical capital! The 1972 trade-imputed measure of factor abundance showed unskilled labor shifting dramatically to be least abundant, and reverses the relative abundance of physical capital and professionals. A repeat of the tests, restricted to OECD data, yielded no improvement. As Maskus noted, "paradoxical outcomes may be the rule rather than the exception."

BLS likewise report results widely viewed as undercutting Heckscher–Ohlin–Vanek. An important contribution was extending the test to a much broader set of countries (27) and factors (12). Thus, whereas the Maskus test was based on a matrix of only three cells for each time period, the BLS matrix had 324 entries. Because of the greater dimensionality of the matrix, it became possible to conduct sign and rank tests not only for a single country across factors (as in Maskus (1985)), but also for a single factor across countries. The sign test was correct more than half of the time for 11 of the 12 factors, but was correct over 70 percent of the time for only 4 in 12. The sign matches were correct more than half the time for 18 of 27 countries, but over 70 percent of the time for only 8 of the 27. Only 61 percent of the total sign matches were correct. They note that independence between the signs of corresponding entries can be rejected at the 95 percent level for only one factor in twelve, and for only four of the 27 countries. In effect, in determining which factors' services would on net be exported or imported, Heckscher–Ohlin did little better than a coin-flip.

The rank proposition fares no better. BLS report both rank correlations and the proportion of correct rankings when entries are compared two at a time. A zero correlation is rejected for only four of the 12 factors and eight of the 27 countries. Moreover, one factor and five countries have the wrong sign on the correlation. While the pairwise comparisons get over 50 percent correct rankings for 22 of the 27 countries, the same is true for only three of the 12 factors (all land variables). In sum, BLS note that the sign and rank propositions yield the Heckscher–Ohlin–Vanek model "relatively little support."

It is hard to overstate the impact that the Leontief and BLS studies had on the profession. Krugman and Obstfeld (1994, p. 78) summarized the thinking at the time in their textbook writing, "trade just does not run the direction that the Heckscher–Ohlin theory predicts." The problem was that there was no alternative. Ricardian and scale economies models were useful at explaining many problems, but it was hard to imagine that educational levels in the US had no impact on the US industrial mix. In large measure because we had to have some theory about these linkages, empirical researchers continued to search for ways of reconciling the theory with the data. In order to do this, they adopted two main approaches. The first was to see if simple amendments to the theory would yield new insights, and the second was to test the theory with better data.

The pessimism regarding Heckscher–Ohlin was partly relieved by Trefler (1993), only to be revived by Trefler (1995). One of his key insights was that it was not enough to simply say HOV fails without understanding why it fails. Trefler's two papers represent alternative approaches to resolving the problems identified by BLS. The former follows up on Leontief's suggestion that the failure of Heckscher–Ohlin may be due to factor-based differences in efficiency. Trefler chooses the efficiency factors so that the Heckscher–Ohlin–Vanek equations fit exactly. He then shows that the implied productivity differentials correlate nicely with evidence on cross-country differences in wages and rentals, suggesting a version of adjusted factor price equalization. Trefler (1995) returned to the simple Heckscher–Ohlin–Vanek framework. We had learned from Staiger (1988) that there were systematic ways in which factor content predictions missed the mark; Trefler went on to show us what those systematic problems were. In one exercise, he graphed the net factor trade residuals, $\varepsilon_T = \mathbf{B}(\mathbf{I} - \mathbf{A})^{-1}\mathbf{T} - (\mathbf{V} - \mathbf{s}\mathbf{V}^W)$, against the predicted net factor trade, $\mathbf{V} - \mathbf{s}\mathbf{V}^W$. Theory would predict that these should be centered around the line $\varepsilon_T = 0$. Instead they closely followed the line $\varepsilon_T = -(\mathbf{V} - \mathbf{s}\mathbf{V}^W)$, or equivalently, $\mathbf{MFCT} = \mathbf{B}(\mathbf{I} - \mathbf{A})^{-1}\mathbf{T} = 0$. This says that measured net factor trade is approximately zero, to which he applied the colorful moniker "the case of the missing trade."

An important insight into the work of Trefler was identified by Gabaix (1997). Gabaix tried to understand why the results looked so good in Trefler (1993) and so bad in Trefler (1995). What Gabaix realized was that these two sets of results were linked. In the first paper, Trefler calculated productivity parameters, π^{fc}, that solved the following problem:

$$F^{fc} = \pi^{fc}V^{fc} - s^c\sum_c \pi^{fc}V^{fc}$$

The second paper had demonstrated that the LHS of this equation was very close to zero. If we set it as exactly zero, then

$$0 = \pi^{fc}V^{fc} - s^c\sum_c \pi^{fc}V^{fc}$$

After a little algebra and remembering that s_c is the share of country c's GDP in the world, it is possible to show that

$$\frac{\pi^{fc}}{\pi^{fc'}} = \frac{Y^c/V^{fc}}{Y^{c'}/V^{fc'}}\left[\left(\frac{\tilde{V}^W - \tilde{V}^c}{\tilde{V}^W - \tilde{V}^{c'}}\right)\left\{\frac{(1-s^{c'})}{(1-s^c)}\right\}\right]$$

where Y^c is country c's GDP. If both c and c' are sufficiently small relative to the world, then the term in brackets on the right converges to unity. In that case, the calculated relative productivities are:

$$\frac{\pi^{fc}}{\pi^{fc'}} = \frac{Y^c/V^{fc}}{Y^{c'}/V^{fc'}}$$

In short, the productivity parameters would simply be GDP per factor. Hence, as long as wages are correlated with GDP per capita, it will not be surprising that the measured productivity parameters would be correlated with wages.

To drive home the point that missing trade was responsible for Trefler's 1993 results, Gabaix did an experiment in which he began with the hypothesis that the measured factor content of trade is minus the HOV prediction, i.e. –MFCT = PFCT.

Using this equation, he shows that the calibrated π^{fc} differ little from those of Trefler and relative π^{fc} correlate with relative wages nearly as well as in Trefler (1993). What this makes clear is that evidence that the calibrated relative π^{fc} correlate well with relative wages could not be used as evidence in favor of HOV.

These were not problems that Trefler could have foreseen when he wrote the original paper. However, it underscored Trefler's contention that understanding the mystery of the missing trade would be critical to understanding what was wrong with HOV. Indeed, once you understand that the MFCT is essentially zero, much of the HOV econometrics becomes quite simple.

Consider, for example, Trefler's preferred specification involving an Armington home bias. His estimating equation is:

$$F^{fc} = V^{fc} - s^c \left[(1 - \alpha_c^*) \frac{Y^W}{Y^c} V^{fc} + \alpha_c^* V^{fW} \right] + \mu^{fc}$$

If we make the assumption that trade balances are a small share of GNP and hence $s^c \approx Y^c/Y^W$, then this equation collapses to:

$$F^{fc} = \alpha_c^* (V^{fc} - s^c V^{fW}) + \mu^{fc}$$

or

$$\text{MFCT}^{fc} = \alpha_c^* \text{PFCT}^{fc} + \mu^{fc}$$

We already know from the first part of Trefler's paper that the LHS of this equation is close to zero so we may not be surprised to find evidence that α_c^* is much smaller than unity.

This may be evidence in favor of an Armington home bias, but it could be the result of any other process that results in little measured net factor trade. For example Conway (2001) argues that MFCT will be small if there is little factor mobility since trade will not move factors away from their autarky allocations. Using Trefler's data he estimates

$$F^{fc} = \frac{1}{1+\gamma^f} [V^{fc} - (\beta+1)s^c V^{fW}] + \varepsilon^{fc}$$

where γ^f and β are parameters to be estimated. He finds γ^f to be significantly greater than zero while β is indistinguishable from zero. In other words, for the case where β is zero, we can rewrite the specification as:

$$\text{MFCT}^{fc} = \alpha^f \text{PFCT}^{fc} + \mu^{fc}$$

Fundamentally, the difference between the two papers is in how they shrink PFCT to match MFCT – Trefler does it by country, and Conway by factor. In both cases $\hat{\alpha}$ will be significantly less than unity as long as MFCT is small.

The relationship between the various tests that we derived earlier gives us an insight into why these specifications succeed at eliminating the mystery of the missing trade. Recall that these authors declare victory over the missing trade when $\sigma_M^2 \sigma_{P'}^2 \geq 1$ where P' can now be defined as $\hat{\alpha}$ PFCT. Recalling our earlier discussion of regression tests, we know that this condition can be rewritten as $\sigma_M^2 (\hat{\alpha}^2 \sigma_P^2) \geq 1$ or MT/$\hat{\alpha}^2$, which just equals $1/R^2$. This implies that the missing trade statistic is bounded below by 1 and above by infinity in this type of specification. Hence any specification that can be written as $MFCT^{fc} = \alpha PFCT^{fc} + \mu^{fc}$ is guaranteed to deliver a missing trade statistic above one and so appear to solve the mystery of the missing trade. This "solution" is illusory and provides no information about the economics underlying missing trade. Oddly enough, as the fit deteriorates, missing trade will shift toward excess trade. This may help explain why in the preferred specification of Trefler (1995), the missing trade statistic is much larger than unity even though Gabaix finds that PFCT has almost no explanatory power.[6]

Is this all that is going on? First, we have already noted that such specifications are mathematically guaranteed to "solve" the mystery of the missing trade. The only remaining question is what they tell us about factor service flows. Gabaix (1997) noticed that tests of equation (5.6) can fail miserably even for preferred econometric specifications. In neither Trefler (1995) nor Conway (2001) do the authors take the estimated parameters and go back to the original puzzle to see if they successfully reconcile MFCT and PFCT. When Gabaix does this using Trefler's data, he finds that the amended model does little to reconcile predicted and measured factor trade.[7]

4.2 Putting the Pieces Together

As researchers puzzled over why HOV performed so badly, they began to ask which parts of the theory were causing the problems. As we have already noted, trade theory necessarily contains a theory of production and a theory of absorption. Davis, Weinstein, Bradford, and Shimpo (1997, hereafter DWBS) were the first to recognize that this naturally suggests that tests of HOV can be broken up into tests of production and absorption models. This enables one to test the theories directly on the relevant data rather than trying to infer parameters about demand and production from the factor content of trade.

Aware of many of the problems that had plagued testing of HOV on international data, DWBS developed a new approach to testing HOV. Several elements of that approach are worth noting. First, it examines the production and absorption sides separately. Prior HOV tests working with *trade* data could make inferences about the source of difficulties, but could not examine them directly. Second, we sought to bridge our own and prior work by starting with a strict HOV model and relaxing assumptions one at a time. This allowed us to identify which assumptions seemed to be crucial in driving the results. Third, we developed an approach that allowed us to make HOV predictions when only a subset of the world shared FPE. This draws on the analytics embodied in equation (5.21). In our case the relevant "FPE club" was a set of ten regions of Japan. Finally, we worked a data set in which identities held. The results, in contrast to prior work, were very positive for HOV.

The step-by-step approach in DWBS allowed us to see which elements of the theory were causing problems. We first considered the Heckscher–Ohlin theory of the pattern of production under the assumption that all countries in the world utilize the same input coefficients. Our results find little support for this version of Heckscher–Ohlin, confirming earlier studies. The results improve dramatically, though, under the more modest assumption that all Japanese regions share a common set of input coefficients. This indicated that although the theory was a powerful means of talking about production within an FPE club, it performed poorly as a description of international production patterns.

We then turned to the Heckscher–Ohlin theory of the pattern of consumption. We examined this first by considering Japanese regional absorption, which the theory suggests should be proportional to world net output. The Heckscher–Ohlin model of proportional absorption does surprisingly well under this assumption. Indeed while Trefler (1995) was forced to estimate home bias parameters from factor content data, we could examine the question on the actual consumption data. What we found was that the assumption that Japanese consumption differed from that in the rest of the world did no better than the standard prediction of homotheticity. In all, the Heckscher–Ohlin theory of consumption stands up remarkably well as a simple description of the data, at least for the regions of Japan.

We then assembled this information for a full test of the Heckscher–Ohlin theory of the net factor content of trade. Our earlier results showed that the theory could not account for the international pattern of production. Hence no point is served by looking at the implied net factor content of trade of the various countries, as positive results would have to be spurious. Instead, we focus on accounting for the net factor trade of the Japanese regions. Three approaches are developed. The first establishes a benchmark. It uses data on actual world factor endowments, implicitly assuming again that all countries use the same input coefficients. We show that the model performs poorly. In the next two cases, we examine this using the endowments imputed to the world, given their measured output, "as if" they had used the Japanese input coefficients. In the first of these, we assume that Japanese regional absorption is proportional to world net output. This model is a marked improvement over that based on measured world endowments.

In sum, DWBS found that the Heckscher–Ohlin model under the conventional restrictive assumptions is a poor predictor of the international pattern of production, hence of net factor trade. However, this changes markedly when applied to predictions for regions of Japan. Given the long string of empirical failures of Heckscher–Ohlin, it is surprisingly successful as a theory of the location of production and the pattern of consumption, hence the net factor content of trade of these regions.

DWBS was clearly only a stepping-stone in the understanding of how to implement HOV. While world trade and endowments were critical elements of the tests, there was a serious question why the international production model fared so poorly. Without answering that question, it would be impossible to understand how HOV worked internationally.

A paper closely related to the work of DWBS is that of Hakura (2001). Where DWBS focused on asking, if you assume that all countries use a common technology matrix, how badly does the model perform, Hakura approached the question from the opposite perspective. Taking direct measures of technology matrices for four OECD countries, she asked how much improvement we might attain if we got the technology side of the model to fit perfectly. Her answer – quite a lot! One can note some drawbacks of this approach. Because the technology matrices she works with fit as a matter of construction, her empirical exercises cannot "test" any of the hypotheses underlying the model of production. Rather, it must ask, when the production model fits as an identity, are the assumptions about international demand patterns sufficiently incorrect as to throw off the basic HOV predictions (in the bilateral difference form)? The answer is no. This left open the question of why technology matrices differ and in particular whether these differences can be systematically related to fundamental characteristics of the countries' trading system.

The starting point for Davis and Weinstein (2001a) was the realization that the existing literature had one major drawback. The hypothesized amendments concern technology and absorption. Yet, with the exception of Hakura, the empirical tests draw on only a single direct observation on technology (typically that of the US) and no observations whatsoever concerning absorption. Moreover, they aimed to understand whether these differences could be related to systematic differences among the included countries on the basis of theory.

The 1995 publication of the OECD's input–output database dramatically improved our ability to test trade theory. Prior to that, researchers had no access to large numbers of compatible IO tables. Its publication enabled us to construct technology matrices for ten rich OECD countries as well as for a composite rest of the world (ROW). The data cover both manufacturing and non-manufacturing with two factors of production, capital and labor.

An examination of the technology matrices allows testing of the nature of differences in techniques across countries. These differences in techniques correspond to a variety of economic hypotheses that can be related to observed characteristics of the countries. These allow us to make inferences not only about whether efficiency differences exist across countries but whether these efficiency differences are sufficient to capture the cross-country differences or whether one needs to take specific account of the failure of the world to replicate an integrated equilibrium. Using parameter estimates obtained from analyzing the technology matrices, one can then take the fitted technology matrices and apply them to the trade data to see which, if any, of the hypotheses may help to resolve the mystery of the missing trade.

Having gone this far purely from examining the technology matrices, one can take the further step of asking how much additional gain would come from a model that more accurately predicts the volume of trade than the frictionless model traditionally used. That is, how much of the missing net factor trade is due to the low volume of product trade? Here we estimate a gravity model and use the fitted values, in addition to our preferred model of production, to predict the factor content of trade.

Our estimation strongly rejects the traditional assumption of identical technologies, even for the ten rich OECD countries. Allowing for Hicks-neutral productivity differences greatly improves the fit of the production model, but surprisingly does very little to eliminate the mystery of the missing trade. A hypothesis that industry input usage is correlated with country factor abundance, which would not hold in conventional HOV models, is strongly confirmed in the data. If this held only in tradable sectors, then it would be possible that this correlation reflects only aggregation. But it holds about as strongly in non-tradable sectors as well, which indicates a breakdown in FPE and hence a departure from the integrated equilibrium. Once this departure from FPE is recognized, it is crucial to re-examine the treatment of non-traded goods within the predictions. In the conventional model in which all countries use the same techniques of production and preferences are identical and homothetic, the factor content of trade is invariant to the presence of non-traded goods. However this is not true when FPE breaks down. In this case, capital abundant countries use more capital per worker in non-traded sectors, which leaves the residual available for production of tradables diminished and so lowers the predicted factor content of trade. Allowing for the fact, very evident in the production data, that industry input usage is correlated with country capital abundance dramatically improves the performance of the model. The major previous research efforts had left measured factor trade as a minuscule proportion of predicted factor trade. In this last exercise, predicted factor trade is approximately 60 percent of predicted net factor trade. If one goes further to incorporate the fact that the volume of trade is smaller than predicted by the frictionless model, then measured factor trade rises to roughly 80 percent of that predicted.

In short, a few simple modifications provide a dramatically improved ability of the model to match the data. These modifications include cross-country Hicks-neutral efficiency differences; a breakdown of FPE with the consequence that industry input usage is correlated with country factor abundance; a recognition that the breakdown of FPE has important consequences for factor usage in non-tradables; and the fact that trade volumes are smaller than predicted by the frictionless model. Suitably modified, HOV works well.

4.3   An Integrated World or Not?

The preferred specification of Davis and Weinstein (2001a) is a multi-cone Heckscher–Ohlin model, so one in which the world fails to operate as an integrated equilibrium. In Davis and Weinstein (2001b), we show that thinking about the world in this explicitly non-integrated framework provides new insights about the nature of world trade. It yields strong restrictions that are counter-intuitive from the standpoint of an analysis based on the assumption of FPE, but that are nonetheless strongly endorsed by the data. *Inter alia*, the theoretical and empirical analysis allow us to gain a deeper understanding of the "mystery of the missing trade," the nature of intra-industry trade, and the role that net factor trade plays in the world at large, as well as specifically within the OECD.

The analytic model is based on Helpman (1984), and features many goods, factors, countries, and production cones. The principal results we derive are as follows. Using countries' actual technology matrices, we show that true net factor trade is much larger than that reported by previous studies. Moreover, the net factor trade looms quite large when scaled by resources employed in tradable sectors. In contrast to results from integrated equilibrium theory, our model predicts that the typical country will be a net exporter of the services of a factor to the set of countries less abundant in that factor, and a net importer of services of the *same* factor from the remaining countries. This prediction is strongly confirmed in the data.

We are able to decompose the true factor content of trade into the conventional measure plus three sources of error. We show that the traditional measure of the factor content of trade is much smaller than, and essentially uncorrelated with, the true measure of net factor trade. This is an important reason for the "mystery of the missing trade." It is important to realize, however, that this is a misnomer. What Trefler identified was missing *factor service* trade not necessarily missing trade *per se*. In other words, measured factor service trade could be small without trade volumes being small. One of the sources of error concerns intra-industry trade. While it has become a convention in the integrated equilibrium analytic literature to define intra-industry trade as the exchange of goods of similar factor content, this is not what the data reveal. We verify directly in the data that intra-industry trade between countries consists of the exchange of goods that differ systematically in their factor content, and that these differences reflect endowment differences. Indeed, the data show that for the typical country, approximately 40 percent of total *net* factor trade is accomplished via *intra*-industry exchange of commodities. For several rich countries, including the US, over two-thirds of the net factor trade is accomplished via intra-industry trade. Finally, our results demonstrate that trade *among* the rich countries of the OECD composes an important share of net factor trade for many of these countries.

5 FURTHER WORK

5.1 Incorporating Intermediates

Trefler and Zhu (2000) have criticized Davis and Weinstein (2001a) for the treatment of traded intermediates. Their paper builds on Trefler (1996) and seeks to implement the relationship described in equation (5.25). Trefler and Zhu (2000) use data on four countries (the US, Belgium, France, Germany and the Netherlands) and proceed in three stages. First, they demonstrate that the variance of $\mathbf{V}^c - s^c \mathbf{V}^W$ is large relative to the variance of the sum of the first two terms of $\mathbf{F}^c$ (i.e., $\mathbf{F}^c_{Cons} + \mathbf{F}^c_{Inter}$). Second, they show that assuming no trade in intermediates can, under some circumstances, improve the results. Finally, they show that even if they use the right level of intermediates trade and get the consumption side of the model right, the variance of $\mathbf{V}^c - s^c \mathbf{V}^W$ is substantially larger than the variance of $\mathbf{F}^c$.

It is very hard to know what to conclude from the exercise. The theory is based on Trefler (1996), and as we noted in the theoretical section, equation (5.25) has no economic implications beyond being an equation that *must* hold if some data identities, market clearing conditions, and a stronger than usual assumptions on demand also hold. Consider what this implies for the first test. When Trefler and Zhu (2000) constrain the term, $\sum_{c'} \mathbf{B}^{tc'}(\mathbf{D}^{cc'} - s^c \mathbf{D}^{Wc'})$, to be zero, it is not clear what it means to have one side of equation (5.25) with larger variance than the other since neither side has economic content. In particular, since the expression $\mathbf{F}^c_{Cons} + \mathbf{F}^c_{Inter}$ is *not* the net exports of factor services embodied in final and intermediates goods trade, what does it mean to say that the variance of $\mathbf{V}^c - s^c\mathbf{V}^W$ is bigger than that of $\mathbf{F}^c_{Cons} + \mathbf{F}^c_{Inter}$? This looks similar to a missing trade test *notationally*, but the meaning is completely different.

Things become more confusing when they try to incorporate traded intermediates. Their theory requires them to have information on the volume of final and intermediate goods exports and imports by country, but they lack the data. Hence their critique of Davis and Weinstein (2001a) is not based on *actual* flows of final and intermediate goods, but on what would happen if these flows were at some hypothetical level. So how do they calculate the level of final goods trade? They assume that the share of final goods in total trade equals the share of final demand divided by the sum of gross output and total imports. This makes little sense. Suppose the world is perfectly specialized and only final goods are produced. In this case, a country with a value of output (so total spending) equal to one dollar will consume one dollar's worth of final goods drawn from a variety of countries. The ratio of final absorption to the sum of output and imports will be less than unity even though there are no intermediates! By using this ratio as their indicator of the final goods share of trade, Trefler and Zhu systematically overstate the importance of traded intermediates. The reason why this matters is that by using the wrong levels of intermediates, equation (5.25) can fail even if the model is correct.

Finally, the last test of Trefler and Zhu is particularly puzzling. We have already argued that equation (5.25) must hold as an identity if some basic relationships are true. What they find is that $\mathbf{V}^c - s^c\mathbf{V}^W$ does not equal $\mathbf{F}^c$. How can this be? The relationship will only be violated if a full employment or market clearing condition fails or if their estimates of the level of final and intermediate goods trade are inaccurate. All of these constitute implementation or definitional problems and not real tests of the theory.

Hence the Trefler–Zhu exercise examines the relative variances of terms that have no real economic content and are equal only under highly restrictive circumstances. We don't think that much can be learned from the exercise. This notwithstanding, we do believe that the broader point of Trefler and Zhu (2000), that research ultimately needs to give a more complete account of the role of intermediates in factor service trade is correct. But we believe it needs to be done according to a theory designed to track measured and predicted factor contents as developed earlier.

5.2 Other Extensions

Feenstra and Hanson (2000) test the implication of Davis and Weinstein (2001a) that factor content of exports differs systematically from domestic production. They find strong evidence that it does. In particular, they find that the factor content of US trade rises in skill intensity as they use increasingly disaggregated data. Feenstra and Hanson go on to argue that this bias may help explain why Davis and Weinstein did not fully eliminate the missing trade phenomenon. While much work still needs to be done before this type of aggregation bias can be implemented into a full HOV model, we think that the results are important and encouraging.

Another area that cries out for more research is the demand side of the model. Clearly there is a lot less trade than one would expect in a frictionless but specialized world. This causes us to overestimate factor service flows. Understanding what is driving this puzzle seems to be a very important question for understanding HOV. Unfortunately, our models of absorption and trade in a world with frictions are still not well developed; however we feel that this is also an area that may be important to explore.

6 Conclusions

Study of the factor content of trade has become a laboratory to test our ideas about how the key elements of endowments, production, absorption, and trade fit together within a general equilibrium framework. Already a great deal of progress has been made in fitting these pieces together. Nevertheless, the existing research raises a great many questions that should help to focus empirical research in the coming years. Among the more pressing issues is a deeper consideration of the role of intermediates, the role of aggregation biases, and of differences in patterns of absorption. This work should provide a more substantial foundation for future policy work developed within a factor content framework.

Acknowledgment

The National Science Foundation provided support for the research reported in this chapter.

Notes

1   See Helpman and Krugman (1985).
2   For the conditions under which FPE will hold in the presence of non-traded goods, consult Helpman and Krugman (1985).
3   One of many possible examples is if the included countries share a demand structure that is identical to each other but systematically different from that of the rest of the world.
4   Note that this is very much at odds with the standard relation of Rybczynski, where capital abundance of a country affects output composition but not capital intensity by industry.
5   One should note that net output is conceptually quite distinct from value added. Net output of a good in a country equals its total output of that good less the output of that good used up as intermediates in that country. Note that it is possible for net output to be negative, for example when a country does not produce a good but does use imports as intermediates. Value added in an industry is the value of all output in an industry less the value of *all* intermediate inputs used to produce that output. Note that in a long-run equilibrium value added cannot be negative.

6   Similarly in Conway (2001), one derives estimates of the missing trade statistic of 50 or more in the preferred specifications.

7   It is also worth noting the role played by neutral technical differences. In Trefler (1995) the technical shift terms enter the analysis two ways: first as estimated parameters and second as data. When the technology parameters are estimated, the Schwarz criterion rejects them, but when the parameters are assumed to be proportional to per capita income, the Schwarz criterion accepts them. This result arises from the fact that the estimated parameters are similar to per capita income, and while the Schwarz criterion contains penalties for additional parameters it has no penalty for data transformations. Technically speaking, the results for the technology and consumption model cannot be compared with the other results of the paper because the underlying data are different.

References

Bowen, Harry P., Edward E. Leamer, and Leo Sveikauskas 1987: Multicountry, multifactor tests of the factor abundance theory. *American Economic Review*, 77, 791–809.

Brecher, Richard A. and Ehsan U. Choudhri 1982: The Leontief paradox, continued. *Journal of Political Economy*, 90, 820–3.

Conway, Patrick J. 2001: The mystery of the missing trade: Comment. *American Economic Review*, 92, 1, 394–404.

Davis, Donald R. and David E. Weinstein 1998: An account of global factor trade. NBER working paper no. 6785.

Davis, Donald R. and David E. Weinstein 2000: International trade as an "integrated equilibrium": New perspectives. *American Economic Review*, 90, 150–4.

Davis, Donald R. and David E. Weinstein 2001a: An account of global factor trade. *American Economic Review*, 91, 1423–54.

Davis, Donald R. and David E. Weinstein 2001b: Do factor endowments matter for North–North trade? NBER working paper no. 8516.

Davis, Donald R., David E. Weinstein, Scott Bradford, and Kazushige Shimpo 1997: Using international and Japanese regional data to determine when the factor abundance theory of trade works. *American Economic Review*, 87, 421–46.

Deardorff, Alan V. 1984: Testing trade theories and predicting trade flows. *Handbook of International Economics*. Amsterdam: New Holland, 467–517.

Dornbusch, Rudiger, Stanley Fischer, and Paul A. Samuelson 1977: Comparative advantage, trade, and payments in a Ricardian model with a continuum of goods. *American Economic Review*, 67, 823–39.

Feenstra, Robert C. and Gordon H. Hanson 2000: Aggregation bias in the factor content of trade: Evidence from U.S. manufacturing. *American Economic Review*, 90, 155–60.

Gabaix, Xavier 1997: The factor content of trade: A rejection of the Heckscher–Ohlin–Leontief hypothesis. Harvard University, mimeo.

Grimes, Donald R. and Penelope B. Prime 1993: A regional multifactor test of the Heckscher–Ohlin–Vanek theorem. University of Michigan and Kenesaw State College, mimeo.

Hakura, Dalia S. 2001: Why does HOV fail? The role of technological differences within the EC. *Journal of International Economics*, 54, 361–82.

Helpman, Elhanan 1984: The factor content of foreign trade. *Economic Journal*, 94, 84–94.

Helpman, Elhanan and Paul Krugman 1985: *Market Structure and Foreign Trade*. Cambridge, MA: MIT Press.

Horiba, Yutaka 1997: On the empirical content of the factor-contents theory of trade: A regional test. Osaka Economic Papers no. 47, 1–11.

Krugman, Paul R. and Maurice Obstfeld 1994: *International Economics: Theory and Policy*. Boston: Addison Wesley.

Leamer, Edward E. 1980: The Leontief paradox, reconsidered. *Journal of Political Economy*, 88, 495–503.

Leamer, Edward E. and James Levinsohn 1995: International trade theory: The evidence. *Handbook of International Economics*, 3, 1339–94.

Leontief, Wassily 1953: Domestic production and foreign trade: The American capital position re-examined. *Proceedings of the American Philosophical Society*, 97, 332–49.

Maskus, Keith E. 1985: A test of the Heckscher–Ohlin–Vanek theorem: The Leontief commonplace. *Journal of International Economics*, 19, 201–12.

Staiger, Robert W. 1988: A specification test of the Heckscher–Ohlin theory. *Journal of International Economics*, 25, 129–41.

Staiger, Robert W., Alan V. Deardorff, and Robert M. Stern 1987: An evaluation of factor endowments and protection as determinants of Japanese and American foreign trade. *Canadian Journal of Economics*, 20, 449–63.

Stern, Robert M. and Keith E. Maskus 1981: Determinants of the structure of U.S. foreign trade, 1958–76. *Journal of International Economics*, 11, 207–24.

Trefler, Daniel 1993: International factor price differences: Leontief was right! *Journal of Political Economy*, 101, 961–87.

Trefler, Daniel 1995: The case of the missing trade and other mysteries. *American Economic Review*, 85, 1029–46.

Trefler, Daniel 1996: The structure of factor content predictions. University of Toronto, mimeo.

Trefler, Daniel and Susan Chun Zhu 2000: Beyond the algebra of explanation: HOV for the technology age. *American Economic Review*, 90, 145–9.

Vanek, Jaroslav 1968: The factor proportions theory: The n-factor case. *Kyklos*, 21, 749–56.

6

Global Production Sharing and Rising Inequality: A Survey of Trade and Wages

Robert C. Feenstra and Gordon H. Hanson

CHAPTER OUTLINE

We argue that trade in intermediate inputs, or "global production sharing," is a potentially important explanation for the increase in the wage gap between skilled and unskilled workers in the US and elsewhere. Using a simple model of heterogeneous activities within an industry, we show that trade in inputs has much the same impact on labor demand as does skill-biased technical change: both of these will shift demand away from low-skilled activities, while raising relative demand for and wages of the higher skilled. Thus, distinguishing whether the change in wages is due to international trade, or technological change, is fundamentally an empirical rather than a theoretical question. We review three empirical methods that have been used to estimate the effects of trade in intermediate inputs and technological change on wages, and summarize the evidence for the US and other countries.

1 INTRODUCTION

One of the most widely discussed public policy issues in the US and many other industrial countries is the decline in the wages of less-skilled workers during the 1980s and 1990s, both in real terms and relative to the wages of more-skilled workers. What factors account for this change? One obvious explanation that comes to mind is increased competition from low-wage countries. Surprisingly, many economists researching this issue have come to the conclusion that trade is not the dominant – or even an important – explanation for the shift in wages. They have instead looked to the massive influx of computers into the workplace, and other forms of technological change, as the explanation.

In this survey, we present a contrary point of view, and argue that international trade is indeed an important explanation for the increase in the wage gap. Our argument rests on the idea that an increasing amount of international trade takes the form of trade in intermediate inputs. This is sometimes called "production sharing" by the companies involved, or simply "outsourcing."[1] Trade of this type affects labor demand in import-competing industries, but also affects labor demand in the industries using the inputs. For this reason, trade in intermediate inputs can have an impact on wages and employment that is much greater than for trade in final consumer goods. As we shall argue, trade in inputs has much the same impact on labor demand as does skill-biased technical change: *both* of these will shift demand away from low-skilled activities, while raising relative demand and wages of the higher skilled. Thus, distinguishing whether the change in wages is due to international trade, or technological change, is fundamentally an empirical rather than a theoretical question.

In the next section, we review the basic evidence that has been used to conclude that trade has not been a significant cause of US wage changes. We argue that this evidence still leaves room for trade to be important, especially trade in intermediate inputs. Empirically, a good deal of trade is in intermediate inputs, and the impact of this on wages and other factor prices is quite different from that obtained with just trade in final goods. This is shown in section 3, where we present a simple model of trade in intermediate inputs. In section 4 we discuss various methods of estimating this model, and summarize the evidence for the US and other countries. Conclusions and directions for further research are given in section 5.

2 CHANGES IN WAGES AND EMPLOYMENT

The basic facts concerning wage movements in the US are fairly well understood.[2] For full-time US workers between 1979 and 1995, the real wages of those with 12 years of education fell by 13.4 percent and the real wages of those with less than 12 years of education fell by 20.2 percent. During the same period, the real wages of workers with 16 or more years of education rose by 3.4 percent, so that the *wage gap* between less-skilled and more-skilled workers increased dramatically.[3] To illustrate these trends, we can use data from the US manufacturing sector for "nonproduction" and "production" workers. The former are often used as a proxy for more-skilled workers, and the latter as a proxy for less-skilled workers.[4] These trends are shown in figure 6.1, which graphs the relative annual earnings of nonproduction/production workers in US manufacturing, and figure 6.2, which graphs their relative annual employment.

In figure 6.1, we see that earnings of nonproduction relative to production workers in the US moved erratically during the 1960s and 1970s, but then increased substantially during the 1980s and 1990s. Turning to figure 6.2, we see that there has

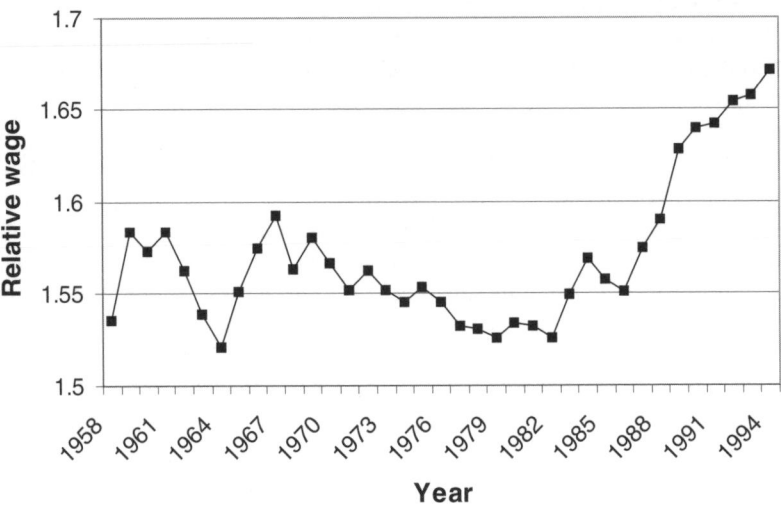

Figure 6.1   Relative wage of nonproduction/production workers, US manufacturing

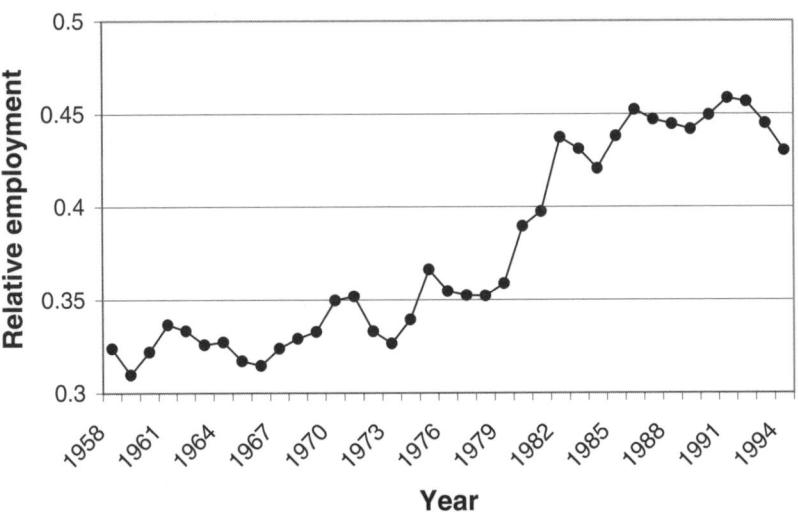

Figure 6.2   Relative employment of nonproduction/production workers, US manufacturing

been a steady increase in the ratio of nonproduction to production workers used in US manufacturing, with some leveling off recently. This increase in the supply of workers can account for the *reduction* in the relative wage of nonproduction workers from 1970 to the early 1980s, as shown in figure 6.1, but is at odds with the *increase* in the relative nonproduction wage after that (Katz and Murphy, 1992). The rising relative wage should have led to a shift in employment *away* from skilled workers, along a demand curve, but it has not. Thus, the only explanation consistent with the facts is that there has been an *outward shift* in the demand for more-skilled workers since the mid-1980s, leading to an increase in their relative employment and wages (Katz and Autor, 1999).

The same decline in the relative wages of blue-collar workers during the 1980s and into the 1990s can be found for Australia, Canada, Japan, Sweden, and the UK (Freeman and Katz, 1994; Katz and Autor, 1999),[5] and also for Hong Kong and Mexico (Cragg and Epelbaum, 1996; Hanson and Harrison, 1999; Hsieh and Woo, 1999). What factors account for these changes? Most widely cited are international competition from low-wage countries and skill-biased technological change due to the increased use of computers, with the latter considered as the most important.[6] There are at least three reasons why trade is thought to have played a rather minor role, and these are reviewed in the next sections.

2.1 The Magnitude of Trade

First, it is often noted that the magnitude of trade flows to and from the US, especially with developing countries, is too small to lead to the observed wage changes. Indeed, for many industrial countries, the ratio of trade to gross domestic product (GDP) in 1970 was no higher than it was just before World War I.[7] In the US, for example, the value of trade (an average of imports and exports) was 6.1 percent of GDP in 1913, but only 4.1 percent in 1970, rising to 8.8 percent in 1980. Other industrial countries have higher levels of trade, but many (including France, Germany, Italy, and Sweden) show the same time-pattern as in the US. A few other countries, such as Australia, Denmark, Japan, and the UK, still have not reached the trade/GDP ratio that they had in 1913. Krugman (1995, p. 331) uses these observations to conclude that: "it would be hard to argue that the sheer volume of trade is now at a level that marks a qualitative difference from previous experience."[8]

But the ratio of trade to GDP does not tell the whole story. All industrial countries have had increasing shares of their economies devoted to services rather than merchandise (i.e., manufacturing, mining, and agriculture). To make a better comparison of trade with overall production, we should measure merchandise goods in both the numerator and the denominator – i.e., compare merchandise trade to merchandise value-added. When this is done, there are still two countries for which this ratio was larger in 1913 than in 1990 (Japan and the UK) and one other for which this ratio changed little (Australia). But all other industrial countries have experienced *substantial growth* in trade relative to merchandise value-added between 1913 and 1990: this ratio has increased by about one-third for Denmark and Norway; by three-quarters for Canada; has doubled for France, Germany, Italy, and Sweden; and has nearly tripled for the US, rising from 13.2 percent in 1913 to 35.8 percent in 1990. We conclude that merchandise trade has indeed grown substantially relative to the production of these commodities in many advanced countries.

Has the composition of merchandise trade changed over time? Various evidence indicates that intermediate goods play an increasingly important role in trade. One approach is to look at "processing trade," which is defined by customs offices as the import of intermediate inputs for processing, and subsequent re-export of the final product. This activity has grown enormously in China, for example, for which Hong Kong often serves as an intermediary. For example, between 1988 and 1998, processing exports grew from $12.4 billion to $97.2 billion, or from about one-third to over one-half of total Chinese exports (Feenstra and Hanson, 2001, table 1). This outward processing serves newly industrialized countries in Asia, but also developed countries such as the US, Japan, and Europe. Between the industrialized countries, too, there has been an increase in processing trade. Görg (2000, table 1) reports on the increase in US processing trade with the European Union (EU) between 1988 and 1994. He finds that US processing imports into these countries (as a share of their total US imports) increased slightly from 17.7 percent to 19.8 percent, but this same ratio increased more significantly from 13.7 percent to 23.7 percent for the "periphery" countries of Greece, Ireland, Portugal and Spain.

In addition to processing trade, the *total* amount of imported intermediate inputs can be estimated by using the purchases of each type of input, and multiplying this by the economy-wide import share for that input. Summing this over all inputs used within each industry, we obtain estimated imported inputs, which can then be expressed relative to total intermediate input purchases. Feenstra and Hanson (1999) perform this calculation for US manufacturing industries, and find that imported inputs have increased from 6.5 percent of total intermediate purchases in 1972 to 8.5 percent in 1979, and 11.6 percent in 1990.

Campa and Goldberg (1997) make the same calculation for Canada, Japan, the UK, and the US, and their results are shown in table 6.1.[9] The US shows a doubling of the share of imported inputs between 1975 and 1995 for all manufacturing, though it is still at a low level compared to Canada and the UK, where over 20 percent of inputs were purchased from abroad in 1993. The UK, especially, shows a large absolute increase in foreign outsourcing. For individual industries, the chemical industry has a lower share of imported inputs than overall, whereas machinery (non-electric and electric) and transportation equipment have higher shares in these three countries. The machinery and transportation industries have especially rapid growth in imported inputs, with the shares doubling or even tripling between 1974 and 1993. The exception to these observations is Japan, where the share of imports in these heavy industries is lower than in overall manufacturing, and has generally been falling. With this single exception, the increased use of imported inputs is a characteristic feature of many industrial countries over the past two decades.

2.2 Changes in Import Prices

The second reason why some authors have argued that international trade is not a significant factor in explaining the movement in wages has to do with the behavior of import and export prices. In widely cited work, Lawrence and Slaughter (1993) have shown that the movement of prices across industries seems to contradict the movement of relative wages.[10] In order for international competition to be the cause of the fall in the relative wage of less-skilled workers, we should see that prices of

Table 6.1 Percentage share of imported to total intermediate inputs

Country	1974	1984	1993
All manufacturing industries			
Canada	15.9	14.4	20.2
Japan	8.2	7.3	4.1
United Kingdom	13.4	19.0	21.6
United States	4.1	6.2	8.2
Chemical and allied products			
Canada	9.0	8.8	15.1
Japan	5.2	4.8	2.6
United Kingdom	13.1	20.6	22.5
United States	3.0	4.5	6.3
Industrial machinery (non-electrical)			
Canada	17.7	21.9	26.6
Japan	2.1	1.9	1.8
United Kingdom	16.1	24.9	31.3
United States	4.1	7.2	11.0
Electrical equipment and machinery			
Canada	13.2	17.1	30.9
Japan	3.1	3.4	2.9
United Kingdom	14.9	23.6	34.6
United States	4.5	6.7	11.6
Transportation equipment			
Canada	29.1	37.0	49.7
Japan	1.8	2.4	2.8
United Kingdom	14.3	25.0	32.2
United States	6.4	10.7	15.7

US estimates are for 1975, 1985, and 1995.
Source: *Campa and Goldberg (1997, tables 1, 3, 5, and 7).*

the least-skill-intensive goods – such as apparel – have fallen relative to other goods. While relative prices for apparel goods fell in the 1970s, they were stable in the 1980s (Leamer, 1998). Prices for other less-skilled-intensive goods actually rose in the 1980s.

This can be seen from table 6.2, which is taken from the work of Lawrence and Slaughter (1993) and Lawrence (1994). For each country, the first row is a weighted average of the change in manufacturing prices over the 1980s, where the weights are the industry's share of total manufacturing employment of *nonproduction* workers. The second row is again the weighted average of the change in prices over the 1980s, but this time using the industry's share of employment of *production* workers. For US import prices, for example, we can see that when industries are weighted by their production workers, the average price increase is *higher* than when we weight by non-production workers. The same pattern can be seen by

Table 6.2   Employment weighted percentage changes in domestic and import prices

	Domestic price	**Import price**
United States (1980–89)		
All manufacturing industries		
Nonproduction labor weights	33.1	26.0
Production labor weights	32.3	28.1
Japan (1980–90)		
All manufacturing industries		
Nonproduction labor weights	−5.60	−18.23
Production labor weights	−3.90	−17.29
Without Office Machines		
Nonproduction labor weights	−7.09	−18.69
Production labor weights	−4.72	−17.50
Also without Petroleum Products		
Nonproduction labor weights	−6.98	−18.45
Production labor weights	−4.66	−17.39
Germany (1980–90)		
All manufacturing industries		
Non-manual labor weights	23.98	15.24
Manual labor weights	26.03	17.07
Without Office Machines		
Non-manual labor weights	24.79	15.38
Manual labor weights	26.21	17.11
Also without Petroleum Products		
Non-manual labor weights	24.97	15.70
Manual labor weights	26.28	17.24

The averages shown weight each industry's price change by that industry's share of total manufacturing employment or nonproduction and non-manual workers, or production and manual workers. Industries are defined at the 3-digit standard industrial classification (SIC) level for the US, and generally correspond to the 2-digit level for Japan and Germany.
Source: *Lawrence and Slaughter (1993, tables 3 and 4) and Lawrence (1994, table 4).*

comparing the rows for other industrial countries. This means that some of the industries that use the *most* production – or less-skilled – workers are those with the *highest* price increases. This finding led Lawrence and Slaughter (1993) to conclude that the price movements due to international competition could not explain the wage movements.

However, if we accept that industries are engaged in importing intermediate inputs, then this suggests a different way to look at the price data. Rather than comparing prices *across* different industries, depending on their skill-intensity, it now makes sense to compare import and domestic prices *within* each industry. The types of goods being imported within each industry (e.g., auto parts) are not the same as those being sold domestically (e.g., finished autos). Indeed, as US firms find imported inputs at increasingly lower prices – through outsourcing activities that

Table 6.3   Employment and wages of nonproduction workers, 1973–1979 and 1979–1987

Year	Change in employment			Change in wages		
	Between		**Within**	**Between**		**Within**
A. Industry Level Decomposition (%)						
1973–79	0.121		0.199	0.119		0.212
Total		0.320			0.381	
1979–87	0.184		0.362	0.309		0.410
Total		0.546			0.719	
B. Plant Level Decomposition (%)						
1973–79	0.101		0.170	0.140		0.134
Total		0.271			0.274	
1979–87	0.177		0.215	0.315		0.221
Total		0.392			0.536	

Numbers are percentage changes between years. Between *numbers represent shifts across 4-digit SIC industries in part A, and shifts across plants in part B.* Within *numbers represent changes within industries in part A, and within plants in part B. All calculations have been annualized.*
Source: *Part A from Berman et al. (1994), and part B from Bernard and Jensen (1997).*

they used to do at home – we would expect to see that US prices within each industry should be *rising* relative to import prices. In terms of table 6.2, we should be comparing the price changes across columns rather than across rows. We see that for the US during the 1980s it is indeed the case that domestic prices rose faster than import prices, and the same is true for Japan and Germany. These price movements are entirely consistent with a model of foreign outsourcing, whereby the US and other industrial countries are continually seeking lower-cost sources of supply. Based on this logic, there is no "contradiction" at all between the movement of prices and relative wages.

2.3   Employment Changes Within and Between Industries

The third piece of empirical evidence comes from decomposing the shifts in the relative employment of less-skilled workers into those occurring *within* industries, and those occurring *between* industries. According to this line of reasoning, international trade should have the effect of moving workers *between* sectors, as industries expand or contract in response to foreign competition. In contrast, new technology, such as the increased use of computers, would change the ratio of more-skilled to less-skilled workers employed *within* each sector. Some evidence on this *within versus between* industry distinction is contained in table 6.3, which is taken from Berman et al. (1994), and Bernard and Jensen (1997).

Part A of table 6.3 decomposes the change in the relative employment and relative wages of nonproduction workers into those that occurred within and between industries. We can see that in the period 1979 to 1987, the relative employment of nonproduction workers increased by slightly more than one-half of one percent per year (0.546 percent), with about two-thirds of that (0.362 percent) explained by *within* industry movements. On the wages side, the relative annual earnings of nonproduction workers increased by about seven-tenths of a percentage point per year (0.719 percent), with more than half of that change (0.410 percent) explained by *within* industry movements. The conclusion suggested by Berman et al. (1994) is that trade cannot be a dominant explanation for the wage and employment shifts, because the *between* industries movements are smaller than the *within* industry movements.

However, that conclusion raises the question of what is occurring *within* these industries, and whether that shift could itself be related to international trade. Bernard and Jensen (1997) have obtained some suggestive evidence on this point, by doing the same decomposition but using *plant-level* data rather than *industry-level* data. This is shown in part B of table 6.3. Looking again at the period 1979 to 1987, we can see that nearly one-half of the relative increase in the employment of nonproduction workers (0.392 percent) occurred due to shifts *between* plants (0.177 percent), and more than one-half of the increase in the relative wage of nonproduction workers (0.536 percent) is also explained by movements *between* manufacturing plants (0.315 percent). Furthermore, Bernard and Jensen have found that the plants experiencing the greatest increase in relative nonproduction employment and earnings are precisely those that are engaged in export activity.

The results of Bernard and Jensen provide *prima facie* evidence that trade has had an impact on factor demand and wages. In order to understand what these linkages are, we present in the next section a simple model of outsourcing, that builds upon the key insight of their empirical work: the heterogeneity of production activities within industries.

3 A SIMPLE MODEL OF OUTSOURCING

Of the many activities that take place within any industry, let us identify just three: the production of an unskilled-labor intensive input, denoted by y_1; the production of a skilled-labor intensive input, denoted by y_2, and the "bundling together" of these two goods into a finished product. The two intermediate inputs are produced at home and also traded internationally; by including such trade in intermediate inputs, our model therefore incorporates outsourcing or "production sharing." We shall simplify the analysis, however, by assuming that the production of these two inputs and the "bundling" activity are *always* performed at home; thus, we are ruling out corner solutions where one of these activities is done entirely abroad. In reality, corner solutions such as this are very common. For example, many US firms export intermediate inputs to the *maquiladora* plants in Mexico, where assembly of the inputs and other production activities take place there rather than in the US.[11] A model of production sharing that emphasizes the movement of entire activities across countries is developed by Feenstra and Hanson (1996). Our theoretical treatment in this survey is simplified by only examining the *marginal* movement of production across countries, as induced by changes in prices. Despite this simplification, we will be able to motivate much of the empirical work in this area.

We note that theoretical models of production sharing are only starting to take hold within international economics. In addition to Feenstra and Hanson (1996), examples include the papers gathered in Arndt and Kierzkowski (2001), as well as Kim and Mieszkowski (1995), Leamer (1996), Marjit and Acharyya (forthcoming), Xu (2000), and Yi (2000).[12] This concept is also used in economic sociology (Gereffi and Korzeniewicz, 1994), geography (Dicken et al., 2001; Yeung, 2001) and other social sciences, where production sharing is referred to by the more general name "commodity chains." A commodity chain consists of the sequence of activities involved in the manufacture of a product, from initial development through to production, marketing, and sales, especially as these activities cross international boundaries. In these disciplines, commodity chains are seen as an integral part of the development process for countries that are still industrializing, i.e., a country's position in the commodity chain will impact its standard of living. While we will be taking a less grand view, it will still be the case in our simplified model that production sharing has a substantial impact on wages.

We will suppose that the two inputs y_i, $i = 1, 2$, are each produced using unskilled labor (L_i), skilled labor (H_i), and capital (K_i), with concave and linearly homogeneous production functions,

$$y_i = f_i(L_i, H_i, K_i), \qquad i = 1, 2. \tag{6.1}$$

For example, the unskilled-labor intensive input y_1 might represent the activities done within a factory, while the skilled-labor intensive input y_2 might represent the research and development activities within the industry, as well as marketing and after-sales service. These are both needed to produce the final manufacturing product. But some of the activities done within the factory can instead be outsourced, i.e., imported from abroad; and conversely, the services associated with research, development and marketing can be exported to support production activities abroad. We therefore let $x_1 < 0$ denote the imports of input 1, and $x_2 > 0$ denote the exports of input 2. For convenience, we choose the exported intermediate input as the numeraire, so we will hold this price fixed (at unity), and let p denote the price of the imported input x_1.

The production of the final manufacturing good is given by $y_m = f_m(y_1 - x_1, y_2 - x_2)$, where this production function "bundles together" the amounts of goods 1 and 2 available, and is also concave and linearly homogeneous. We ignore any additional labor and capital inputs used in this bundling activity, so that the total factor usage in the manufacturing industry is,

$$L_1 + L_2 = L_m, \quad H_1 + H_2 = H_m, \quad K_1 + K_2 = K_m. \tag{6.2}$$

We can now solve for the optimal output in the industry, which includes the three activities. With perfect competition, the value of output from the final good, plus net trade, will be maximized subject to the resource constraints:

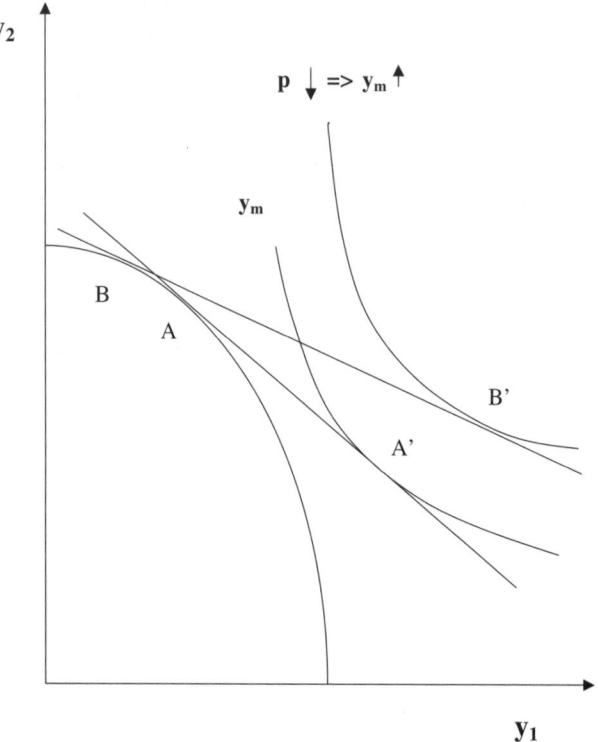

Figure 6.3 Production of industry output y_m

$$F_m(L_m, H_m, K_m, p_m, p) \equiv \max_{x_i, L_i, H_i, K_i} p_m f_m(y_1 - x_1, y_2 - x_2) + px_1 + x_2, \qquad (6.3)$$

subject to (6.1), (6.2), where p_m is the price of the final good, and p is the price of the imported intermediate input. Note that the optimization problem in (6.3) does *not* require that trade is balanced on an industry-by-industry basis, i.e. we do not require that $px_1 + x_2 = 0$. Of course, there will be some balance of trade constraint for the economy overall, but we ignore that here. The value of the industry production function in (6.3) can be thought of as value-added for the industry, i.e., nominal output including exports x_2 less the value of intermediate inputs px_1.

Problem (6.3) can be easily illustrated, as in figure 6.3, where we show the production possibility frontier between inputs 1 and 2, and several isoquants of the final good y_m. For the purpose of illustration we now add the extra condition that trade in the inputs is balanced ($px_1 + x_2 = 0$), so that the output of the final good is maximized on the isoquant that is tangent to the balanced trade line. At initial prices, for example, the industry produces inputs at A, and then trades to B. With a *drop* in the relative price of the imported input, the industry shifts production towards the skilled-labor intensive activity at A′, and then trades to B′, obtaining a higher output y_m. All this will look very familiar to most readers: the only special feature of figure 6.3 is that we think of these activities taking place *within* a single manufacturing industry. Let us define Y_m as the optimized value of (6.3), which measures value-added in industry m,

$$Y_m \equiv F_m(L_m, H_m, K_m, p_m, p) \tag{6.4}$$

Provided that the underlying production functions f_i, $i = 1,2,m$, are increasing and concave, then the function F_m will also be increasing and concave in (L_m, H_m, K_m). We can think of F_m as an "aggregate production function" for the industry.

The difficulty with using this "aggregate production function" for any empirical or theoretical work is that it implicitly holds fixed the level of labor and capital used in the industry, i.e. at those levels given by the constraints in (6.2). Instead, we would like to think of labor, and possibly capital too, as being optimally adjusted in response to changes in factor prices. To reflect this, we make use of the *cost function* that is dual to (6.4). First, we can define a *short-run cost function*, obtained when the level of capital and output are fixed:

$$C_m(w, q, K_m, Y_m, p, p_m) \equiv \min_{L_m, H_m} w L_m + q H_m, \quad \text{subject to (6.4),} \tag{6.5}$$

where w is the wage of unskilled labor and q is the wage of skilled labor. Alternatively, we can define a *long-run cost function*, obtained when labor and capital are both chosen optimally:

$$C_m(w, q, r, Y_m, p, p_m) \equiv \min_{L_m, H_m, K_m} w L_m + q H_m + r K_m, \quad \text{subject to (6.4).} \tag{6.6}$$

where r is the rental on capital.

Both of these cost functions have been used empirically, as we discuss in the following sections. Before turning to this material, however, it is well worth exploring a few theoretical properties. In particular, if we add the condition that marginal cost equals product prices, and then allow prices to change, what will be the impact on factor prices? In figure 6.3, for example, we showed how a fall in the relative price of imports p would raise final output y_m, but what is the corresponding impact on factor prices? In the remainder of this section we explore this question theoretically, making use of the long-run version of the cost function.

If both types of labor and capital are being optimally chosen for the industry overall, as in (6.6), then they must also be optimally chosen within each of the activities $i = 1,2$. So consistent with (6.6), we can also define the long-run cost functions for the disaggregate activities within the industry:

$$C_i(w, q, r, Y_i) \equiv \min_{L_i, H_i, K_i} w L_i + q H_i + r K_i, \quad \text{subject to (6.1), for } i = 1,2. \tag{6.7}$$

Since the activity production functions in (6.1) are assumed to be linearly homogeneous, then the activity-level cost functions in (6.7) will be homogeneous of degree one in Y_i. This implies they can be written as $C_i(w, q, r, Y_i) = Y_i c_i(w, q, r)$, where $c_i(w, q, r)$ is the *unit-cost* function (equal to marginal cost or average cost).

Then the zero-profit conditions for activities 1 and 2 can be written as:

$$p = c_1(w, q, r), \qquad 1 = c_2(w, q, r), \qquad (6.8)$$

These conditions must hold in order for the locally produced inputs y_i, $i = 1, 2$, to be competitive with those available from abroad, at the prices p and unity, respectively. Totally differentiating (6.8) using the familiar Jones' (1963) algebra, we can express the percentage change in factor prices $\hat{w}$, $\hat{q}$ and $\hat{r}$ as functions of the percentage change in the import price $\hat{p}$:

$$\hat{p} = \theta_{1L}\hat{w} + \theta_{1H}\hat{q} + \theta_{1K}\hat{r}, \qquad 0 = \theta_{2L}\hat{w} + \theta_{2H}\hat{q} + \theta_{2K}\hat{r}, \qquad (6.9)$$

where θ_{ij} is the cost-share of factor j in activity i, with $\Sigma_j\theta_{ij} = 1$. Treating the change in the import price $\hat{p}$ as exogenous, (6.9) gives *two* equations with which to determine *three* unknown factor prices changes – $\hat{w}$, $\hat{q}$ and $\hat{r}$. In general, these factor price changes will be difficult to pin down with only two equations. In terms of figure 6.3, when production shifts towards the skilled labor-intensive activity, from A to A', we do not know in general how factor prices are affected. But there are some simplifying assumptions we can make which allow us to determine these.

3.1   Case 1 – Equal Cost Shares of Capital

As in Feenstra and Hanson (1996), we can assume that capital has equal cost shares in the two industries, so that $\theta_{1K} = \theta_{2K}$. Using this, we take the difference between the two equations in (6.9) to obtain,

$$\hat{p} = (\theta_{1L} - \theta_{2L})\hat{w} + (\theta_{1H} - \theta_{2H})\hat{q} = (\theta_{1L} - \theta_{2L})(\hat{w} - \hat{q}), \qquad (6.10)$$

where the second equality follows since with equal cost shares of capital, the total cost shares of labor are also equal, so that $(\theta_{1L} + \theta_{1H}) = (\theta_{2L} + \theta_{2H}) \Rightarrow (\theta_{1L} - \theta_{2L}) = -(\theta_{1H} - \theta_{2H})$. With activity 1 assumed to be unskilled-labor intensive, we have that $(\theta_{1L} - \theta_{2L}) > 0$. Thus, (6.10) says that a *decrease* in the price of imported intermediate input, $\hat{p} < 0$, leads to a *decrease* in the relative wage of unskilled labor, $(\hat{w} - \hat{q}) = \hat{p}/(\theta_{1L} - \theta_{2L}) < 0$.

These results are illustrated in figure 6.4, where we graph the iso-curves of $p = c_1(w, q, r)$ and $1 = c_2(w, q, r)$. With the wages of unskilled and skilled labor labeled on the axis, we are implicitly holding fixed the rental on capital, r. Now suppose that there is a fall in the price p of activity 1, which is unskilled labor intensive. In figure 6.4, this will shift inwards the iso-cost line of that activity, and as shown, will lead to a *fall* in the relative wage of unskilled labor (from A to B). There will be some additional change in the rental on capital, but under our assumption of equal cost share of capital in the two industries, this will lead to an *equi-proportional* shift in the two iso-cost curves and therefore have no further effect on the relative wage. Thus, the drop in the price of the imported inputs leads to a fall in the relative wage (w/q) of unskilled labor.

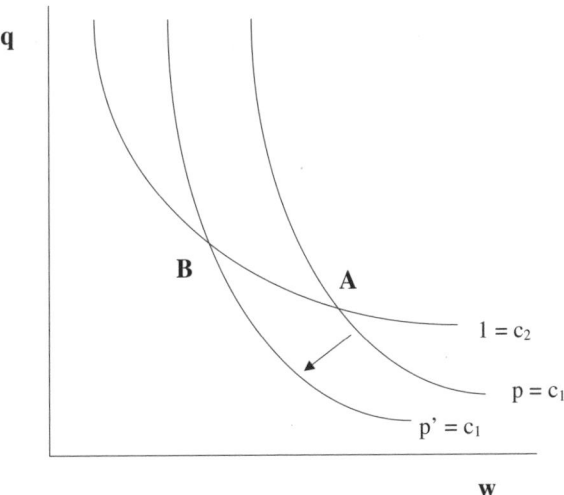

Figure 6.4 Change in wages due to fall in *p*

We can also ask what happens to the price of the final good p_m. Let $c_m(p, 1)$ denote the unit-cost function that is dual to $f_m(y_1, y_2)$, where recall that the price of activity 2 is unity. Then the price of the final good satisfies $p_m = c_m(p, 1)$, so that $\hat{p}_m = \theta_{m1}\hat{p}$, where θ_{m1} is the cost-share of input 1 in the final product. Thus, with a fall in the price of imported inputs, $\hat{p} < 0$, the price of the final good also falls but by *less*, $\hat{p} < \hat{p}_m < 0$. Stated differently, the price of the final good relative to imported inputs *rises*, $\hat{p}_m - \hat{p} > 0$. This in fact is what happened in the US and other industrial countries, as shown in table 6.2, where the change in domestic prices exceeds the change in import prices over 1980 to 1990. Our theoretical model therefore confirms that this price movement is consistent with the fall in the relative wage of unskilled labor.

3.2 Case 2 – The Unskilled-Labor Intensive Activity is also Capital Intensive

A second case, emphasized by Sachs and Shatz (1998), is where activity 1 uses more unskilled labor, $(\theta_{1L} - \theta_{2L}) > 0$, and also more capital, $(\theta_{1K} - \theta_{2K}) > 0$; think of factory production, for example. They suppose that the price of the imported input is *constant*, $\hat{p} = 0$, but that the rental price on capital *increases*, $\hat{r} > 0$, because capital is leaving the country. In figure 6.5, this will lead to an inward shift in both iso-cost curves, but since activity 1 uses more capital, a *larger* shift in that curve. Thus, the factor-price equilibrium will shift from A to B in figure 6.5, where the wage of unskilled labor has fallen. We are not sure whether the wage of skilled labor rises or falls, but in any case, we obtain a fall in the relative wage (w/q) of unskilled labor.[13] Intuitively, because activity 1 uses both unskilled labor and capital intensively, when capital leaves it is then unskilled labor that suffers. In this case, the cause of the change in wages is an outflow of capital from the country.[14]

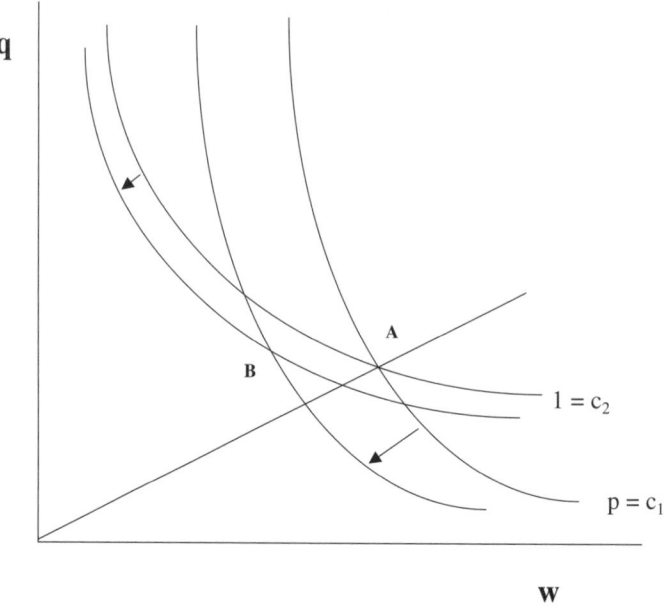

Figure 6.5 Change in wages due to rise in r

Notice that the change in relative wages occurs without any change in the price of the imported input or the final good. We might expect, though, that there will be some impact on the price of a nontraded good. Denoting the zero-profit condition for a nontraded good by $p_n = c_n(w, q)$, we can totally differentiate this expression to obtain:

$$\hat{p}_n = \theta_{nL}\hat{w} + \theta_{nH}\hat{q}, \tag{6.11}$$

where θ_{nj} is the cost-share of factor $j = L, K$. For simplicity, we assume the nontraded good uses no capital in production. In terms of figure 6.5, the nontraded good would have an additional iso-cost line (not drawn) that goes through both points A and B. The question we wish to determine is whether the change in factor prices from A to B implies an *increase* or a *decrease* in the price of the nontraded good.

To answer this, let us consider two extreme cases: where the nontraded good uses only unskilled labor, or only skilled labor. In the first case, the iso-cost line for the nontraded good would be vertical in figure 6.5, i.e., each level of the unskilled wage w would correspond to a unique value for costs $c_n(w)$. In that case, the movement of the factor-price equilibrium from A to B would require a shift in the iso-cost line of the nontraded good to the left, and a corresponding *fall* in the price of the nontraded good (exactly like the fall in unskilled wages). Alternatively, if the nontraded good uses only skilled labor, then its iso-cost line would be horizontal in figure 6.5, so that each level of the skilled wage q corresponds to a unique value for costs $c_n(q)$. In this case, we are *unsure* whether the movement of the equilibrium from A to B implies a rise or fall in the price of the nontraded good. If the iso-cost line of activity 1 shifts down sufficiently more (i.e., activity 1 is much more capital intensive than activity 2), then it is visually apparent that point B would imply a *higher* wage for skilled labor, and a *higher* price for the nontraded good if it uses enough of this factor. In fact, Sachs and Shatz (1998) argue for the US that nontraded goods are indeed skilled-labor intensive relative to manufacturing overall. In that case, the exit of capital, and increase in the relative wage of skilled labor, can be expected to lead to a *rise* in the price of the nontraded good. Conversely, if the nontraded good is more unskilled-labor intensive, then its price will *fall*.

The evidence for the US is that skilled-labor intensive nontradables experienced a *rise* in price during the 1980s, whereas unskilled-labor intensive nontradables experienced a *fall* in prices, consistent with these theoretical predictions. As we shall discuss at the end of the next section, Harrigan and Balaban (1999) and Harrigan (2000) find that these changes in nontradables prices are highly correlated with change in relative wages, but this leaves open the question of *causality*: are the prices of nontradables driving the relative wages or, as we have suggested here, are the relative wages driving the prices of nontradables? We have shown that the exit of capital in an open economy can quite plausibly have the effect of raising *both* the relative wage of skilled labor and the price of skill-intensive nontradables, and lowering *both* the relative wage of unskilled labor and the price of unskilled-intensive nontradables, which is consistent with evidence for the US during the 1980s.

4   RESULTS FROM EMPIRICAL STUDIES

Summarizing our argument so far, the decision of companies to purchase intermediate inputs from overseas will most certainly affect their employment at home, and can be expected to differentially affect skilled versus unskilled workers. With firms in industrial countries facing a higher relative wage for unskilled labor than that found abroad, the activities that are outsourced would be those that use a large amount of unskilled labor, such as assembly of components and other repetitive tasks. Moving these activities overseas will reduce the relative demand for unskilled labor in the industrial country, in much the same way as replacing these workers with automated production. *This means that outsourcing has a qualitatively similar effect on reducing the relative demand for unskilled labor within an industry as does skilled-biased technological change, such as the increased use of computers.* Thus, determining which of these is most important is an empirical question. We will examine three methods that have been used to estimate the effects of trade versus technological change on wages and employment.

4.1   Estimation of Demand for Skilled Labor

The first empirical method estimates industry production functions, such as (6.4), and attempts to determine which factors affect the relative demand for skilled labor. The starting point is to consider the short-run cost function that is dual to the industry production function, $C_m(w, q, K_m, Y_m, p, p_m)$, as derived in (6.5). Notice that we have included the price of imported inputs p in this cost function, as well as in the industry price p_m, since they also appear in the production function (6.4). More generally, *any structural variables that shift the production function and therefore affect costs* should be included as arguments. We will denote these variables by the vector $\mathbf{z}$; in addition to the price of imported inputs, this can include expenditures on computers and other new types of capital equipment. We therefore rewrite the cost function in (6.5) as $C_m(w, q, K_m, Y_m, \mathbf{z})$.

The next step is to choose a functional form for costs. A convenient choice is the translog cost function, which was introduced by Diewart (1974, p. 139) and initially used in the international trade literature by Kohli (1978, 1991). This function is written in a general notation as:

$$\ln C = \alpha_0 + \sum_{i=1}^{I} \alpha_i \ln w_i + \sum_{k=1}^{K} \beta_k \ln x_k + \frac{1}{2}\sum_{i=1}^{I}\sum_{j=1}^{I} \gamma_{ij} \ln w_i \ln w_j$$

$$+\frac{1}{2}\sum_{k=1}^{K}\sum_{\ell=1}^{K} \delta_{k\ell} \ln x_k \ln x_\ell + \sum_{i=1}^{I}\sum_{k=1}^{K} \phi_{ik} \ln w_i \ln x_k \qquad (6.12)$$

where w_i denotes the wages of the optimally chosen inputs $i = 1, \ldots, I$, and x_k denotes either the quantities of the *fixed* inputs or outputs $k = 1, \ldots, K$, or *any other shift parameters*. In terms of the cost function in (6.11), there are just two optimally chosen factors – skilled and unskilled labor – while capital and output are treated as fixed in the short run. In order to ensure that the cost function in (6.12) is linearly homogeneous in wages, we impose the requirements,[15]

$$\sum_{i=1}^{I} \alpha_i = 1 \text{ and } \sum_{i=1}^{I} \gamma_{ij} = \sum_{j=1}^{I} \gamma_{ij} = 0. \qquad (6.13)$$

The usefulness of the translog function comes from computing its first derivatives, $\partial \ln C / \partial \ln w_i = (\partial C / \partial w_i)(w_i/C)$. Because $\partial C / \partial w_i$ equals the demand for the chosen input i, it follows that $(\partial C / \partial w_i)(w_i/C)$ equals the *payments to factor i relative to total costs*, which we denote by the cost-shares s_i. Thus, differentiating (6.12) with respect to $\ln w_i$, we obtain,

$$s_i = \alpha_i + \sum_{j=1}^{I} \gamma_{ij} \ln w_j + \sum_{k=1}^{K} \phi_{ik} \ln x_k, i = 1, \ldots, I. \qquad (6.14)$$

Given annual data on factor cost shares, wages, and fixed inputs and outputs, this set of linear equations can be estimated over time for a given industry to obtain the coefficients γ_{ij} and ϕ_{ik}.[16] Alternatively, the equations can be estimated for a single year, or the change between two years, by pooling data across industries. In the latter case, we are assuming that the *same* cost function applies across the industries. Despite this strong assumption, the cross-industry approach is popular and we shall follow it here.

Returning now to the notation $C_m(w, q, K_m, Y_m, \mathbf{z})$, we have two chosen inputs – skilled and unskilled labor. Focusing on the share equation for skilled labor, it will depend on wages for both types of labor, as well capital, output, and all other structural variables, $\mathbf{z}$. When (6.14) is estimated by pooling data across industries, as in Berman et al. (1994) for example, it is felt the cross-industry variation in wages has little information: wages differ across industries principally due to quality-variation of workers, so we do not expect high-wage industries to economize on those (high-quality) workers. Accordingly, the wage terms are typically dropped from the right of (6.14) when pooling data across industries. This leaves just fixed capital, output, and other structural variables. Taking the difference between two years, the estimation equation for the wage-share of skilled labor (s_{Hm}) in industries $m = 1, \ldots, M$ becomes:

$$\Delta s_{Hm} = \phi_0 + \phi_K \Delta \ln K_m + \phi_Y \Delta \ln Y_m + \phi'_Z \Delta \mathbf{z}_m, \, m = 1, \ldots, M, \qquad (6.15)$$

where $\mathbf{z}_m$ denotes the vector of structural variables that shift costs, and ϕ_z is the corresponding vector of coefficients. In particular, when the wage-share of skilled labor is increasing, we are interested in determining how much of that increase is due to changes in capital, output, and the structural variables.

Estimates of (6.15) for 447 industries within the US manufacturing sector, over 1979 to 1990, are shown in table 6.4. The data are from the NBER Productivity Database (Bartelsman and Gray, 1996, which is available at http://www.nber.org/nberces/). In these regressions we use nonproduction labor as a proxy for skilled labor, so the dependent variable is the change in the share of nonproduction labor in total wages within each industry. Over all manufacturing industries, the nonproduction wage share increased from 35.4 percent to 42.4 percent between 1979 and 1990, for an annual growth of 0.4 percent per year.

The specifications in table 6.4 are similar to those in Autor et al. (1998), Berman et al. (1994), and Feenstra and Hanson (1999). They include as regressors: the shipments of each industry (as a proxy for value-added Y_m); the capital/shipments ratio (reflecting the capital input K_m relative to Y_m); foreign outsourcing, measured by imported intermediate inputs as a share of total materials purchases (this term is used instead of the *price* of imported inputs p, since the prices are not observable); the shares of computers and other high-tech capital in the total *capital stock*, and the share of expenditures on computers in *total investment* (both these variables can be viewed as components of the overall capital stock K_m). The share of computers and other high-tech capital in the total *capital stock* is constructed using either *ex post* rental prices, or *ex ante* rental prices.[17] In contrast, the share of computer spending in *investment* is obtained from the *Census of Manufactures*, which simply asked firms to report what percentage of new investment was devoted to computers. This variable has been used previously by Berman et al. (1994) and Autor et al. (1998). We feel that measuring computers as a share of the total *capital stock* is preferable. All variables are at the industry level and all, except the computer investment share, are measured as annual changes. All regressions are weighted by the industry share of the total manufacturing wage bill.

In column (1) of table 6.4, we report the mean values of the dependent and independent variables for 1979 to 1990, and, following this, the regression coefficients in columns (2) to (4). Each regression uses alternative measures of the computer and other high-technology shares. In all the regressions, we see that outsourcing has a

Table 6.4   Dependent variable – change in nonproduction wage share, 1979–1990

	(1) Mean	(2) Regression	(3) Regression	(4) Regression	(5) Contribution (%)
Δln(K/Y)	0.706	0.047	0.044	0.040	7.3–8.5
		(0.011)	(0.011)	(0.009)	
Δln(Y)	1.541	0.020	0.017	0.010	4.0–7.8
		(0.006)	(0.006)	(0.006)	
Outsourcing	0.223	0.197	0.221	0.135	14.6–24.0
		(0.096)	(0.100)	(0.088)	
Computer and other high-tech capital measured with ex post *rental prices:*					
Computer share	0.251	0.195			12.6
		(0.091)			
Other high-tech share	0.144	−0.065			–
		(0.137)			
Computer and other high-tech capital measured with ex ante *rental prices:*					
Computer share	0.070		0.431		7.8
			(0.167)		
Other high-tech share	0.166		0.005		0.2
			(0.071)		
Computers measured as share of investment:					
Computer share	6.561			0.018	30.5
				(0.007)	
High-tech share (*ex post* rental prices)	0.395			0.032 (0.052)	3.3
Constant		0.203	0.206	0.157	40.4–53.1
		(0.043)	(0.040)	(0.045)	
R^2		0.156	0.159	0.189	
N		447	447	447	

The mean of the dependent variable equals 0.389. Standard errors (in parentheses) are robust to heteroskedasticity and correlation in the errors within two-digit industries. The first column shows mean values of the dependent and independent variables for 1979–90. All regressions and means are computed over 447 four-digit standard industrial classification (SIC) industries and are weighted by the average industry share of the manufacturing wage bill. Δln(K/Y) is the average annual change in the log capital–shipments ratio and Δln(Y) is the average annual change in log real shipments. The outsourcing variables and the computer and high-technology shares are in annual changes.

positive impact on the nonproduction share of the wage bill, as does the computer share. By multiplying the regression coefficients by the mean values for the change in each variable, we obtain the contributions of each to the total change in the nonproduction wage share, shown in column (5). We see that outsourcing accounts for 15 to 24 percent of the shift towards nonproduction labor.[18]

The results for computers depend on the specification. Measuring computer services and other high-tech capital as a share of the capital stock, using *ex post* rental prices, we see they account for 13 percent of the shift towards nonproduction labor. Measuring these shares using *ex ante* rental prices, we see that computers and other high-tech capital explain only 8 percent of this shift. In both cases, the contribution of computers and other high-tech capital is *less than* the contribution of outsourcing. In contrast, when computers are measured by their share of investment (and the high-technology capital share is also included), we see that these variables account for 31 percent of the shift toward nonproduction labor, which *exceeds* the contribution of outsourcing. Thus, whether outsourcing is more or less important than computers depends of whether the latter are measured as a share of the capital stock, or as a share of investment. It is fair to conclude that both these variables are important explanations of the shift towards nonproduction labor, with their exact magnitudes depending on how they are measured.

In related work, Morrison Paul and Siegel (2001) find a negative correlation between the demand for less-educated labor and high-tech capital, R&D investment, imports (as a share of output), and service purchases (i.e., domestic outsourcing), and a positive correlation between the demand for more-educated labor and high-tech capital, R&D investment, and imports. Their estimated impact of high-tech capital and R&D investment on skill upgrading is greater than that for imports or domestic outsourcing of services.

From these results, it appears that foreign outsourcing from US manufacturing is associated with the increased relative demand for skilled labor, as predicted by the theory outlined in section 3. One important question is what form this outsourcing takes. It may occur through foreign direction investment (FDI), as multinationals move production of parts and components or product assembly abroad, or it may occur through a shift in contracting practices, in which firms replace domestic production of intermediate inputs with imports purchased from arms-length suppliers located abroad. The first case appears to be consistent with what has occurred in the US automobile and semiconductor industries, while the second case appears to be consistent with what has occurred in the US footwear and personal-computer industries.

Slaughter (2000b) finds that during the 1980s FDI was *not* an important channel for moving US jobs abroad or for skill upgrading at home. Between 1977 and 1989, employment in majority-owned affiliates of US multinational enterprises (MNEs) fell, as it did in the US parents of these plants. Similar to US manufacturing plants, affiliates of US MNEs spent the 1980s shifting employment towards nonproduction workers and raising the capital intensity of production. Slaughter estimates a specification similar to (6.15), in which he includes as regressors shipments, the capital/shipments ratio, and the ratio of economic activity in foreign affiliates of US MNEs to economic activity in US manufacturing plants. The last variable captures the extent to which US MNEs are transferring production abroad. For several measures of economic activity in foreign affiliates, there is a weak *negative* correlation between the change in the nonproduction wage share and the change in foreign production transfer by US MNEs. Combined with the results in Feenstra and Hanson (1999), these results suggest that FDI is not the means through which outsourcing has induced skill upgrading in US manufacturing.[19] In related work, Blonigen and Slaughter (1999) find that inward FDI in US manufacturing during the 1980s, such as the construction of Japanese auto plants and other facilities, also did not contribute to skill upgrading in US manufacturing industries.[20]

The US is by no means the only country that engages in outsourcing. Many European nations are outsourcing, as well as industrialized Asian countries including Japan, Hong Kong, Korea and Taiwan (Ng and Yeats, 1999). In one study for the UK, Anderton and Brenton (1997) measure outsourcing by imports from *low-wage* countries. They find that such imports can account for about 40 percent of the rise in the wage bill of skilled workers of 1970–83, and approximately one-third of their increase in relative employment.

Over the past several decades, Japan has steadily moved production activities abroad, investing in both low-income and high-income countries. For firms in the Japanese electronics industry, overseas employment now greatly exceeds employment in Japan. These production shifts have coincided with skill upgrading at home. Since the early 1970s Japanese manufacturing industries have had a steady increase in the relative employment and relative total compensation of more-educated workers. Applying a specification similar to (6.15) to data on Japanese manufacturing plants over the period 1965 to 1990, Head and Ries (2000) find a strong *positive* correlation between the change in a firm's nonproduction wage share and the change in a firm's share of employment in low-income countries. This suggests that as Japanese manufacturing firms move production to *low-wage* countries they raise the skill intensity and the demand for skilled labor at home. The correlation between the nonproduction wage share and the employment share in high-income countries, in contrast, is statistically insignificant in most cases.[21]

During the 1960s and 1970s, Hong Kong produced and exported labor-intensive manufactures, such as apparel, textiles, footwear, toys, and consumer electronics. Since China began to open its economy to foreign trade and investment in the late 1970s, Hong Kong has begun to specialize in business services related to trade and investment in China. Over the past two decades, many Hong Kong manufacturing firms have moved their production facilities to China, and to the neighboring province of Guandong in particular, which they manage from headquarters in Hong Kong (Sung, 1997). Hong Kong firms typically supply plants in China with raw materials and often ship the goods through Hong Kong for final processing before exporting them to a final destination. As Hong Kong has shifted production to China, manufacturing has become a less important part of the Hong Kong economy, declining from 24 percent of GDP in 1980 to 7 percent of GDP in 1996 (Enright et al., 1997).

Hsieh and Woo (1999) find that outsourcing from Hong Kong to China has been associated with an increase in the relative demand for skilled labor in Hong Kong. Between 1981 and 1996, both the relative wage and relative supply of more-educated workers rose in Hong Kong, which suggests that there was an increase in the relative demand for skilled labor. The extent of skill upgrading in Hong Kong manufacturing was dramatic. The share of nonproduction workers in Hong Kong manufacturing employment rose from 13.1 percent in 1976 to 47.0 percent in 1996. Outsourcing to China appears to be an important contributing factor to this employment shift. Using a regression similar to (6.15), Hsieh and Woo find a strong positive correlation between the nonproduction wage share and imports from China (expressed as the ratio of industry imports from China to either industry absorption or total materials purchases) for Hong Kong industries. Over the period 1976 to 1996, outsourcing to China can account for 45 to 60 percent of the increase in the nonproduction wage share in Hong Kong manufacturing.

Outsourcing may also raise the relative demand for skilled labor in the country to which production is transferred. In Feenstra and Hanson (1996), firms in the skill-abundant North use firms in the non-skill-abundant South to produce intermediate inputs. Assuming wages differ between nations, the North specializes in high-skill tasks and the South specializes in low-skill tasks. If Northern firms outsource production to the South, they will choose to move the least skill-intensive activities that they perform. By moving these activities to the South, the average skill intensity of production *rises* in the North. The same also happens in the South, since the South initially specializes in the lowest-skill tasks. Thus, outsourcing from the North to the South raises the relative demand and so the relative earnings of high-skilled workers in *both* countries, contributing to a global increase in wage inequality.

During the 1980s Mexico liberalized foreign investment and trade, and experienced an increase in the relative wage of skilled labor (Hanson and Harrison, 1999). In the period following reform, FDI in Mexico was concentrated in foreign assembly plants, known as *maquiladoras*, most of which are located in Mexican states along the US border. These assembly plants are created, in most cases, by US firms outsourcing unskilled-labor intensive production activities to Mexico. Feenstra and Hanson (1997) find that for the period 1975 to 1988 the shift in Mexican manufacturing towards foreign assembly plants can account for 45 percent of the observed increase in the country's nonproduction wage share.[22]

Outsourcing changes the relative wage by inducing an outward shift in the relative demand for skilled labor. An alternative view is that international trade changes factor prices by flattening labor demand curves, making them more elastic. Leamer (1998) presents an extreme version of this story, in which the transition of an economy from autarky to trade transforms an economy's labor demand curve from being downward sloping to being horizontal, at least over sections that correspond to diversified production. Extending this logic, Rodrik (1997) identifies several mechanisms through which greater economic integration between countries may make labor demand curves flatter. In one of the few attempts to test this hypothesis, Slaughter (2001) estimates the own-price elasticity of labor demand for production and nonproduction workers in two-digit US manufacturing industries over the period 1960 to 1991. Over the entire sample, demand became more elastic for production labor, but not for nonproduction labor. The sectors with the largest increase in elasticities were food and tobacco, apparel and textiles, wood and paper, and primary and fabricated metals, which include some of the least-skill intensive manufacturing industries. The demand for production labor became more elastic in industries with more outsourcing, more investment in computers, and more investment in high-tech capital overall. These results are robust to controls for industry fixed effects but not time fixed effects, suggesting that changes in labor-demand elasticities are dominated by a trend component.

4.2 Estimation of Zero-Profit Conditions

In the second empirical method, we drop the short-run framework that was used above, and instead suppose that capital can be adjusted along with skilled and unskilled labor. The industry cost function is then written as in (6.6), which is re-expressed as:

$$C_m(w_m, q_m, r_m, Y_m, p, p_m) \equiv \min_{L_m, H_m, K_m} w_m L_m + q_m H_m + r_m K_m, \quad \text{subject to (6.4).} \quad (6.16)$$

Notice that in (6.16) we have allowed the factor prices w_m, q_m, and r_m to *differ* across the industries $m = 1, \ldots, M$. This reflects the empirical fact that factor prices, and wages in particular, do differ across industries (Krueger and Summers, 1988); this will turn out to be important in what follows. As before, the relative price of imported inputs enters this cost function because it also appears in the production function (6.4); we will replace this by the vector $\mathbf{z}_m$, which includes other structural variables. Since the production function (6.4) is linearly homogeneous in inputs, then we can rewrite the cost function in (6.16) as:

$$C_m(w_m, q_m, r_m, Y_m, \mathbf{z}_m) = Y_m c_m(w_m, q_m, r_m, \mathbf{z}_m), \quad\quad (6.16')$$

where $c_m(w_m, q_m, r_m, \mathbf{z}_m)$ denotes the unit-cost function.

The zero-profit conditions in the industries are therefore expressed as:

$$p_m = c_m(w_m, q_m, r_m, \mathbf{z}_m), \quad\quad m = 1, \ldots, M. \quad\quad (6.17)$$

In our theoretical model of section 3, we examined how changes in product prices would affect factor prices. Now, however, the presence of the structural variables $\mathbf{z}_m$ mean that the changes in prices reflect more than just changes in factor prices. Indeed, taking the difference between these, we can define *total factor productivity* (TFP) in the industry as:

$$TFP_m \equiv (\theta_{mL}\hat{w}_m + \theta_{mH}\hat{q}_m + \theta_{mK}\hat{r}_m) - \hat{p}_m, \quad\quad (6.18)$$

where the cost-shares of the three factors sum to unity, $\theta_{mL} + \theta_{mH} + \theta_{mK} = 1$. Productivity improvements mean that factor prices can rise more than product prices (or conversely, that product prices can fall further). Note that (6.18) is the "dual" definition of productivity, and empirically it is very close to the "primal" definition, which is the growth in output minus a weighted average of the growth in inputs. In either case, we should think of changes in the structural variables $\mathbf{z}_m$ as the underlying cause of changes in productivity.[23]

Shuffling the terms in (6.18) slightly, and replacing the instantaneous change in prices with discrete changes like $\Delta \ln p_m$, we obtain the equation,

$$\Delta \ln p_m = -TFP_m + \theta_{mL}\Delta \ln w_m + \theta_{mH}\Delta \ln q_m + \theta_{mK}\Delta \ln r_m, m = 1, \ldots, M. \quad (6.19)$$

Table 6.5 Dependent variable – log change in industry price, 1979–1990

	(1)	(2)	(3)	(4)	(5)
Effective TFP				−1.00	−1.00
				(0.007)	(0.001)
TFP	−0.96	−0.75			
	(0.07)	(0.08)			
Production cost-share	3.06	2.43	3.61	4.68	4.70
	(1.22)	(1.16)	(1.89)	(0.02)	(0.01)
Nonproduction cost-share	2.30	4.09	6.20	5.48	5.44
	(1.43)	(1.72)	(4.04)	(0.02)	(0.03)
Capital cost-share	7.89	8.06	9.54	3.95	3.97
	(0.78)	(0.94)	(2.19)	(0.01)	(0.02)
Materials cost-share times	1.00*	1.00*	1.22	1.00*	1.00
change in materials price			(0.25)		(0.002)
Energy cost-share times	1.00*	1.00*	−0.93	1.00*	1.00
change in energy price			(0.92)		(0.006)
Constant	−0.71	−0.83	−1.93		0.01
	(0.30)	(0.29)	(0.92)		(0.005)
R²	0.896	0.806	0.429	0.999	0.999
N	447	446	446	447	447

Standard errors are in parentheses. All regressions omit three industries with missing data on materials purchases or prices (SIC 2067, 2794, 3483) and are weighted by the industry share of total manufacturing shipments, averaged over the first and last period.

In columns (1) to (3), and (5), the dependent variable is the log change in the gross industry price, and the factor cost shares sum to one across all factors. The materials cost share is multiplied by the log change in the materials price; the energy cost share is treated similarly. In column (4), the dependent variable is the log change in the industry value-added price and factor cost shares sum to one across primary factors. Column (1) uses primal TFP as a regressor; column (2) drops the computer industry (SIC 3573) from the sample; column (3) also drops TFP as a regressor; and column (5) uses effective TFP as a regressor, where effective TFP equals primal TFP minus the change in factor-price differentials.
* These coefficients are constrained at unity.
Source: *Feenstra and Hanson (1999).*

We consider estimating (6.19) as a linear regression across industries, where the *data* are the change in log prices, productivity, and the factor cost-shares, while the change in factor-prices are *estimated* as regression coefficients. That is, we estimate the *implied* change in factor-prices ω_L, ω_H, and ω_K from the regression:

$$\Delta \ln p_m = -TFP_m + \theta_{mL}\omega_L + \theta_{mH}\omega_H + \theta_{mK}\omega_K + \varepsilon_m, \quad m = 1, \ldots, M. \quad (6.20)$$

where ε_m is an error term, specified more fully below. We interpret the coefficients ω_L, ω_H, and ω_K as the change in factor prices that are *mandated by* the change in product prices, which is the dependent variable in (6.19). Baldwin and Hilton (1984) were among the first to estimate a price regression like (6.20). Recent applications include Baldwin and Cain (1997), Feenstra and Hanson (1999), Krueger (1997), Leamer (1998), Sachs and Shatz (1994), and Slaughter (2000b).

Estimates of (6.20) for 447 US manufacturing industries, over 1979 to 1990, are provided in table 6.5. The dependent variable is the log change in the industry output price over the period, divided by the number of sample years to obtain an annualized difference. We use the primal measure of TFP, expressed as an annualized difference. The other independent variables are the average cost-shares (over the first and last year for the period) for production labor, nonproduction labor, and capital; the materials cost share times the log change in materials prices; and the energy cost share times the log change in energy prices.

In columns (1) and (2), we constrain the coefficients on the materials share times the materials price and the energy share times the energy price to be unity, which transforms the dependent variable to be the log change in value-added prices. This approximates the specification in Leamer (1998). In column (1), the coefficients on the labor shares imply a *decrease* in the nonproduction–production wage gap, since the nonproduction–production relative wages is mandated to change by 2.30% – 3.06% = –0.76% per year, which is consistent with the results in Leamer (1998). In fact, the nonproduction–production wage gap *rose* by 0.74 percent per year (actual annual average changes in factor prices are shown in column (5) of table 6.5). In column (2), we follow Sachs and Shatz (1994) and drop the office-equipment industry (SIC 3573), which *reverses* the predicted change in wage inequality. Now, nonproduction wages are mandated to rise by 1.5 percent per year more than production wages. In column (3), we approximate Krueger's (1997) specification by dropping TFP as a regressor, while estimating coefficients on materials and energy. There is again a mandated rise in the nonproduction–production wage gap, but one that is much larger than the actual increase in relative wages.

The estimates in table 6.5 are troubling because they show that slight changes in the data, such as dropping the office-equipment industry, have a dramatic effect on the results. While it is true that office equipment is an outlier, the sensitivity of the results to the specification suggests that something more basic is going on. To address this, let us ask: why do the estimates of ω_L, ω_H, and ω_K from (6.20) differ at all from the *actual average* change in manufacturing wages (shown in column (5)), which we denote by $\overline{\Delta \ln w}$, $\overline{\Delta \ln q}$, and $\overline{\Delta \ln r}$? The overbar indicates that we are averaging the change in factor-prices over all manufacturing industries. By just comparing (6.19) and (6.20), it seems that there should be some close connection between the estimates ω_L, ω_H, and ω_K and these average actual factor price changes, but we need to uncover what this connection is.

To achieve this, let us make the transition from (6.19) to an estimating equation more carefully. First, notice that we can rewrite (6.19) as,

$$\Delta \ln p_m = -TFP_m + \theta_{mL} \overline{\Delta \ln w} + \theta_{mH} \overline{\Delta \ln q} + \theta_{mK} \overline{\Delta \ln r} + \varepsilon_m \qquad (6.19')$$

where,

$$\varepsilon_m \equiv \theta_{mL}\left(\overline{\Delta \ln w} - \Delta \ln w_m\right) + \theta_{mH}\left(\overline{\Delta \ln q} - \Delta \ln q_m\right) + \theta_{mK}\left(\overline{\Delta \ln r} - \Delta \ln r_m\right). \quad (6.20')$$

Thus, we replace the *industry* wage changes on the right of (6.19) by the *average* wage changes, and incorporate the difference between these two into an error term. In economic terms, ε_m reflects interindustry wage differentials – i.e., the difference between wages paid in each industry and the manufacturing average. It is well known that these wage differentials vary systematically across industries (with capital-intensive industries paying higher wages), and are fairly stable over time (Krueger and Summers, 1988).

We can estimate (6.19′) as the regression (6.20), where now we have been careful to derive the error term ε_m. But this derivation is enough to answer the question we posed above. The estimates of ω_L, ω_H, and ω_K obtained from (6.20) will be unbiased estimates of the *average actual* factor price-changes in (6.19′) if and only if the error term ε_m in (6.20′) is *uncorrelated* with the cost-shares θ_{mL}, θ_{mH}, θ_{mK}. This result follows directly from the properties of ordinary least-squares, whereby the independent variables need to be uncorrelated with the error term to obtain unbiased estimates. But this property is unlikely to be true in our data. Industries such as office equipment have both a high share of nonproduction labor (e.g., engineers), and probably the fastest growing industry wage differential, as these workers have had very rapid wage gains. This means that the error term ε_m is negative for office equipment, resulting in a negative correlation with the cost-share of nonproduction labor. Indeed, this negative correlation may explain why the *estimated* change in nonproduction wages is *lower* in column (1) than in column (2) of table 6.5 (and why both estimates are lower than the actual change in nonproduction wages in column (5)).

To correct this problem, we can simply include the error term ε_m as an additional regressor in the equation, reflecting the change in interindustry wage differentials. It is convenient to combine ε_m with TFP_m, obtaining a measure of "effective" TFP:

$$ETFP_m \equiv TFP_m - \varepsilon_m$$
$$= \left(\theta_{mL}\overline{\Delta \ln w} + \theta_{mH}\overline{\Delta \ln q} + \theta_{mK}\overline{\Delta \ln r}\right) - \Delta \ln p_m \qquad (6.21)$$

Thus, this measure of effective productivity shows how the *average manufacturing factor-price changes*, weighted using the cost-share in each industry, differ from the change in product price of that industry. Making use of (6.21), the regression in (6.20) is written once again as:

$$\Delta \ln p_m = -ETFP_m + \theta_{mL}\omega_L + \theta_{mH}\omega_H + \theta_{mK}\omega_K, \quad m = 1, \ldots, M. \qquad (6.22)$$

Now, there is no error term at all in this regression, so it ought to provide a perfect fit when estimated. This will not be true exactly in our data, since we are using the primal rather than the dual measure of *TFP* to construct effective *TFP* in (6.21). These priors are confirmed in columns (4) and (5) of table 6.5. In column (4), the dependent variable is the log change in value-added prices; in column (5) it is the log change in output prices, since we allow the coefficients on the materials and energy shares to differ from unity. In either specification, the coefficients on the labor and capital shares are extremely close to the actual average annual percentage changes in factor prices, which are 4.71 for production labor, 5.44 for nonproduction labor, and 3.95 for capital. Thus, when we properly estimate (6.20), we end up with an identity!

Summarizing our results so far, we started with the goal of estimating the zero-profit conditions, to obtain "mandated" changes in factor prices that are consistent with the change in product prices. A number of researchers have estimated an equation like (6.20), without much attention to the error term in this regression. When we carefully derive the error term, as in (6.20′), we then realize that it may well be correlated with the factor cost-shares, which are the independent variables. To correct for this we can include the error term as data, by incorporating it into "effective" total factor productivity, as in (6.22). But now we encounter another problem: this gives essentially a perfect fit, just reproducing the *actual* change in factor prices. That means the regression does not provide us with any new information at all! This is a discouraging finding, and calls into question the whole approach.

To make further progress, Feenstra and Hanson (1999) propose a two-step estimation procedure. In the first step, we combine the variables $\Delta \ln p_m + ETFP_m$ that appear in (6.22), and regress these on the structural variables z_m. Supposing that there are only two structural variables, $z_m = (z_{1m}, z_{2m})$, we therefore run the regression:

$$\Delta \ln p_m + ETFP_m = \eta_0 + \eta_1 \Delta z_{1m} + \eta_2 \Delta z_{2m}, \quad m = 1, \ldots, M. \tag{6.23}$$

We then take the estimated coefficients $\hat{\eta}_1$ and $\hat{\eta}_2$ and use these to construct the dependent variables for the second-step regressions:

$$\hat{\eta}_1 \Delta z_{1m} = \theta_{mL} \omega_{1L} + \theta_{mH} \omega_{1H} + \theta_{mK} \omega_{1K}, \tag{6.24a}$$

$$\hat{\eta}_2 \Delta z_{2m} = \theta_{mL} \omega_{2L} + \theta_{mH} \omega_{2H} + \theta_{mK} \omega_{2K}, \; m = 1, \ldots, M. \tag{6.24b}$$

That is, we use the estimated coefficients $\hat{\eta}_1$ and $\hat{\eta}_2$ times each structural variable as the dependent variables in (6.24), and regress these on the factor cost-shares. The coefficients obtained from the second-stage regression, ω_{1L}, ω_{1H}, ω_{1K} and ω_{2L}, ω_{2H}, ω_{2K}, are interpreted as *the portion of the total change in factor-prices that are explained by that structural variable*. In this way, we are taking the total change in factor-prices, and decomposing it into parts that are explained by each structural variable.

In the estimation of (6.23) for US manufacturing industries over the period 1979 to 1990, Feenstra and Hanson (1999) find positive and statistically significant correlations between TFP-adjusted value-added prices and foreign outsourcing, the computer share of the capital stock, and the computer share of investment (but not with the high-tech capital share). This is consistent with these structural variables having positive effects on productivity, as expected, *and* on value-added prices.[24] The latter effect arises from the non-neutral impact that the structural variables have on industry productivity – outsourcing and capital upgrading both induce shifts away from production labor and towards nonproduction labor – which then leads to changes in relative product prices (in particular, raising value-added prices for skill-intensive goods). Over the period 1979 to 1990, the structural variables account for 11 percent to 23 percent of the variation in TFP-adjusted value-added prices in US manufacturing.

The second stage of this technique is to decompose the change in TFP-adjusted value-added prices into portions attributable to each structural variable and then, following (6.24), regress these decomposed product-price changes on the factor-cost shares to obtain mandated changes in factor prices. The results suggest that both outsourcing and capital upgrading contributed to rising wage inequality in the 1980s. Over the 1979 to 1990 period, outsourcing accounts for 15 percent of the increase in the relative wage of nonproduction workers, and computers measured using *ex post* rental prices account for 35 percent of this increase; thus, computers are twice as important as outsourcing. When instead the computer share of the capital stock is measured using *ex ante* rental prices, then outsourcing explains about 25 percent while computers explain about 20 percent of the increase in the nonproduction/ production wage. Finally, when the computer share of the capital stock is replaced with the computer share of *investment*, then the contribution of outsourcing falls to about 10 percent, while the contribution of computers rises so much that it explains the *entire* increase in the relative wage. Thus, as in table 6.4 where we examined the change in the nonproduction labor *share*, when we now consider the factors influencing the *relative wage*, we find that both outsourcing and computer expenditure are important with their exact magnitudes depending on how these variables are measured.

Economic integration between countries may, of course, also contribute directly to changes in factor prices, as lower tariffs or transportation costs lead to changes in product prices which would then affect factor prices in standard Stolper–Samuelson (1941) fashion. In principle, one could uncover the impact of changing tariffs and transportation costs on product prices and productivity, following (6.23), and use these results to estimate their impact on factor prices, following (6.24). Haskel and Slaughter (2000) show that in the 1970s US manufacturing industries with higher tariffs and higher transportation costs tended to have lower relative employment of nonproduction workers, and that over the period 1974 to 1988, reductions in tariffs and transportation costs were larger in less skill-intensive industries. This is suggestive evidence that falling trade costs may have contributed to rising wage inequality. But other evidence is missing: changes in tariffs and transportation costs do poorly in explaining changes in product prices across US industries over the 1974 to 1988 period. Robertson (2000) finds stronger results for Mexico: over 1987 to 1993, when Mexico's skilled–unskilled wage gap rose, tariffs fell more in less skill-intensive industries, and over 1993 to 1998, when Mexico's skilled–unskilled wage gap fell, tariffs fell more in skill-intensive sectors.

The UK is another country that has experienced rising wage inequality of the same magnitude as the US. Haskel and Slaughter (2001) apply the two-stage estimation procedure of Feenstra and Hanson (1999) to data on UK manufacturing industries over the period 1960 to 1990, using as structural variables union density (the share of union workers in industry employment), industry concentration (share of sales by the five largest firms), innovations per industry, import prices, and computerization (share of firms in the industry using computers). They find that TFP growth is higher in industries with more innovations, lower initial union density, lower initial sales concentration, and larger reductions in import prices (but is unrelated with computerization). Product price changes are lower in industries with smaller changes in import prices. During the 1980s, when UK wage inequality rose, the structural variable that appears to have contributed most to the increase in the skilled–unskilled wage gap is industry innovation. The contribution of import prices is comparatively small. This contrasts with research (Anderton and Brenton, 1997) showing that rising imports over 1970 to 1983 is a significant determinant of the nonproduction labor *share* in the UK.

4.3 Estimation of Economy-wide GDP Function

The third empirical method we shall discuss takes the longest-run view of the economy, in which capital and all other factors fully adjust to their equilibrium levels across industries. Rather than focusing on each industry, we now look at the economy overall, and consider how gross domestic product (GDP) is produced from the total factor endowments, given the prices of domestic and traded goods. Letting (L_m, H_m, K_m) denote the factor demands within each industry $m = 1, \ldots, M$, the sum of these cannot exceed the endowments (L, H, K):

$$\sum_{m=1}^{M} L_m \le L, \quad \sum_{m=1}^{M} H_m \le H, \quad \text{and} \quad \sum_{m=1}^{M} K_m \le K. \tag{6.25}$$

Using the production functions in (6.3) for each industry, the GDP function for the economy is defined as:

$$G(L, H, K, \mathbf{P}) \equiv \max_{L_m, H_m, K_m} \sum_{m=1}^{M} F_m(L_m, H_m, K_m, p_m, p), \quad \text{subject to (6.25),} \tag{6.26}$$

where $\mathbf{P} = (p_1, \ldots, p_M, p)$ denotes the vector of all product prices p_m as well as the prices p of all imported intermediate imports. Let us say there are $N > M$ prices in total, so that $\mathbf{P} = (p_1, \ldots, p_N)$. Within the list of M industries, we are including both manufacturing and services, whether these products are traded or not.

In order to estimate (6.26) we need to choose a functional form, and as in our discussion of the cost function, a convenient choice is the translog function. This is written in a general notation as:

$$\ln G = \alpha_0 + \sum_{m=1}^{N} \alpha_m \ln p_m + \sum_{k=1}^{K} \beta_k \ln v_k + \frac{1}{2} \sum_{m=1}^{N} \sum_{n=1}^{N} \gamma_{mn} \ln p_m \ln p_n$$
$$+ \frac{1}{2} \sum_{k=1}^{K} \sum_{\ell=1}^{K} \delta_{k\ell} \ln v_k \ln v_\ell + \sum_{m=1}^{N} \sum_{k=1}^{K} \phi_{mk} \ln p_m \ln v_k \tag{6.27}$$

where p_m denotes the prices of the outputs and imported inputs, $m = 1, \ldots, N$, while v_k denotes the endowments of the factors of production, $k = 1, \ldots, K$. For the GDP function in (6.26), there are just three endowments – skilled and unskilled labor, and capital. In order to ensure that the GDP function is linearly homogeneous in prices, we impose the requirements:[25]

$$\sum_{n=1}^{N} \alpha_n = 1 \text{ and } \sum_{m=1}^{N} \gamma_{mn} = \sum_{n=1}^{N} \gamma_{mn} = 0. \tag{6.28}$$

As usual, we can differentiate the GDP function with respect to factor endowments to obtain factor prices, $\partial G/\partial v_k = w_k$. It follows that the derivative of the log of GDP with respect to the log of endowments, $\partial \ln G/\partial \ln v_k = w_k v_k/G$, equals the share of GDP paid to each factor, which we denote by s_k, $k = 1, \ldots, K$. Computing this for the GDP function in (6.27), we obtain:

$$s_k = \beta_k + \sum_{\ell=1}^{K} \delta_{k\ell} \ln v_\ell + \sum_{m=1}^{N} \phi_{mk} \ln p_m, \quad k = 1, \ldots, K. \tag{6.29}$$

In addition, differentiating the GDP function with respect to a product price yields output of that good (inclusive of exports), and differentiating with respect to an import price yields the negative of imports. Therefore, the derivative of the log of GDP with respect to the log of a price equals the share of GDP obtained from that output, which we denote by s_n, $n = 1, \ldots, N$. Note that for imported inputs, these shares are *negative*. Computing these from (6.27):

$$s_m = \alpha_m + \sum_{n=1}^{N} \gamma_{mn} \ln p_n + \sum_{k=1}^{K} \phi_{mk} \ln v_k, \quad m = 1, \ldots, N. \tag{6.30}$$

Thus, given annual data on product prices and quantities, along with factor prices and endowments, we can estimate (6.29) and (6.30) as a system of linear equations. This will allow us to determine the effect of product prices on factor shares – measured by ϕ_{mk}. Notice that these coefficients enter both the factor-share equations in (6.29), and the product-share equations in (6.30), so that estimating these simultaneously allows us to test the restriction that ϕ_{mk} estimated from (6.29) and (6.30) are equal. If this hypothesis is accepted, then the restriction can be imposed, and this allows the estimates of ϕ_{mk} to become more precise. An advantage of this system approach is that the number of years (say T) is multiplied by the number of equations, $(N - 1)$ for products plus $(K - 1)$ for factors, to obtain the total number of observations $T(N + K - 2)$.[26] Thus, even though the number of parameters being estimated is large, we can obtain reasonable estimates even if we only have annual data for one or two decades.

Estimates of the GDP function have been made by a number of authors for various countries, including the US. The reader is referred to Kohli (1991) for the most comprehensive treatment. For the purposes of this survey, we are interested in applications that distinguish skilled versus unskilled labor. Tombazos (1999) attempts to make this distinction by identifying *industries* that are intensive in skilled or unskilled labor, and then forming aggregate wages and employment indexes over each group of industries; these indexes are then used as a proxy for the price and quantity of skilled and unskilled labor. Imports are treated as an input into the production process, just as they are in the GDP function (6.26). Tombazos incorporates skilled labor, unskilled labor, capital and imports into the estimation of an aggregate cost function for the US, over 1967 to 1994, with a single aggregate output (including exports). His major conclusion is that a drop in the import price reduces the demand for unskilled labor, but *raises* the demand for skilled labor in the US. This is highly consistent with our theoretical model of section 3. According to Tombazos, an effect like this holds for the US economy in the aggregate. Missing from his analysis, though, is a discussion of *how much* import prices have fallen, and therefore, how much of the shift towards skilled labor can be explained by this channel of influence.

This shortcoming does not appear in the work of Harrigan and Balaban (1999) and Harrigan (2000). Harrigan and Balaban estimate the system of equations in (6.29) and (6.30) for the US over the period 1963 to 1991 using data on four factors (high-school dropouts, high-school graduates, college graduates, capital), and four sectors (skill-intensive traded goods, unskilled-intensive traded goods, skill-intensive nontraded goods, and unskilled-intensive nontraded goods). Thus, imports are not explicitly identified. In contrast, Harrigan (2000) has two categories of outputs (skill-intensive and unskilled-intensive final output), and seven factors including imports (oil imports, two other groups of imports, and the three types of labor and capital). It turns out that changes in the import prices have been quite small in comparison with other prices changes, especially in nontraded goods, so that changes in import prices *are not* an important explanation for changes in wages. We therefore focus below on the results of Harrigan and Balaban, which except for imports, are similar to those of Harrigan.

With the estimated coefficients from the share equations (6.29) and (6.30) in hand, Harrigan and Balaban calculate wage elasticities with respect to factor quantities and product prices. As expected, the own-quantity elasticity of each factor price is negative. Increasing the supply of capital raises wages for all workers, but these elasticities are increasing in education levels, such that a 10 percent increase in the capital stock would increase the college/high-school graduate relative wage by about 3.5 percent, and the college/high-school dropout relative wage by about 8 percent. The wage elasticities of *traded* goods prices are imprecisely estimated, while those for *nontraded* goods are somewhat surprising. Increases in prices of skill-intensive nontraded goods raises wages for college graduates and high-school dropouts, but lowers wages for high-school graduates, and increases in prices of unskilled-intensive nontraded goods has a large positive effect on high-school-graduate wages, a moderate positive effect on college wages, and a negative effect on high-school-dropout wages.

Putting the estimated wage elasticities together with observed changes in factor supplies and product prices, we can decompose the contribution of different variables to the observed change in factor prices. While capital accumulation contributed to an increase in the relative wage of college graduates, this effect was largely offset by increases in the supply of college graduates. The big changes during the latter part of the sample period were an *increase in the relative price of skill-intensive nontraded goods*, such as finance, insurance, and real estate. This had the largest impact on *raising* the college/high-school-graduate relative wage. Conversely, there was a *decrease in the relative price of unskilled-intensive nontraded goods*, such as wholesale and retail trade, which had the largest impact on *reducing* the relative wage of high-school dropouts. In short, the increase in the relative wage of skilled labor, in the 1980s and beyond, is highly correlated with the rise in the price of nontraded goods that use skilled labor, and similarly for unskilled labor where both the relative wage and price fell.

These correlations beg the questions of whether the change in nontraded prices caused the change in wages, or conversely. We provided a theoretical example in section 3 of a case where capital leaves the country, increasing the relative wage of skilled labor, and therefore raising the price of skill-intensive nontradables and lowering the price of unskilled-intensive nontradables. This story would be consistent with the estimates of Harrigan and Balaban. We cannot rule out, however, the idea that the nontradables prices are changing due to some other reason (e.g., rising incomes and demand leading to an increase in the price of skill-intensive nontradables), which is therefore the proximate cause of the change in wages. As Harrigan (2000, p.186) puts it: "To my knowledge, there are no scholarly studies of relative price determination in the United States that might shed light on the causes of the changes shown . . . and until we understand the cause of these price changes we cannot rule out an important role for import competition."

5 CONCLUSIONS

There is an emerging view in the literature on wage inequality in the US and other advanced countries that technological change matters for changes in the wage structure but international trade does not (Katz and Autor, 1999). The research we survey in this chapter fails to support this conclusion. While there is abundant evidence of skill-biased technological change, it also appears that international trade, in the form of foreign outsourcing, contributes to skill upgrading and increases in the skilled–unskilled wage gap.

The argument against trade is based, in part, on a misreading of the data. Stable trade to GDP ratios, an apparent increase in the relative price of skill-intensive goods, and employment shifts towards skilled workers that occur mainly within, rather than between, industries are all cited as evidence that trade cannot have contributed to rising wage inequality. This line of reasoning emphasizes trade in final goods and ignores the globalization of production and recent dramatic increases in trade in intermediate inputs. Much recent growth in trade has resulted from firms breaking industries apart by locating low-skill activities in low-wage countries and high-skill activities in high-wage countries. When trade takes this form, its impact on relative prices and factor allocation can be very different from that predicted by standard models of trade in final goods. Recent literature shows that trade to merchandise GDP ratios have risen sharply in recent years, with much of the growth in trade attributable to intermediate inputs, that changes in the relative prices of domestic versus imported goods are consistent with trade shifting out the relative demand for skilled labor, and that trade in intermediate inputs is consistent with skill upgrading being a within-industry phenomenon.

Beyond the *prima facie* case that trade raises wage inequality, there is evidence of a direct link. Using data on changes in industry behavior over time, we see that foreign outsourcing is associated with increases in the share of wages paid to skilled workers in the US, Japan, Hong Kong, and Mexico. In several of these cases, outsourcing can account for half or more of the observed skill upgrading. For the US, there is evidence that during the 1980s and 1990s outsourcing contributed to changes in industry productivity and product prices that in turn mandated increases in the relative wage of skilled labor.

Existing literature has just begun to scratch the surface of how the globalization of production changes industry structure and factor demand in advanced and emerging economies. There is, as yet, little research on foreign outsourcing in Eastern Europe, Southeast Asia (Cheng and Kierzkowski, 2001), or Central America and the Caribbean (Feenstra et al., 2000), though anecdotal evidence suggests that it is an important mechanism through which countries in these regions integrate themselves into the world economy. There are clearly rich opportunities for research in this area.

Global production sharing and trade in intermediate inputs matter more generally for how we apply trade models to data. In tests of the Heckscher–Ohlin model, it is standard to assume that exports are produced entirely by combining domestic factors of production with domestically-produced intermediate inputs. We now know that this assumption is wrong. Antweiler and Trefler (2002), Davis and Weinstein (2000) and Trefler and Zhu (2000) show that trade in intermediate inputs can help resolve the mystery of the missing trade (Trefler, 1995), in which the estimated factor content of trade is near zero, and that existing tests of trade theory may produce severely biased estimates of the factor content of trade if they fail to account for global production. While we can easily address this problem by adopting more general trade models in which trade occurs in both final and intermediate goods, the literature has yet to take this necessary step.

Notes

1   Alternatively referred to as outsourcing (Katz and Murphy, 1992, Feenstra and Hanson, 1996), de-localization (Leamer, 1998), fragmentation (Arndt and Kierzkowski, 2001; Deardorff, 2001; Jones, 2000), intra-product specialization (Arndt, 1997, 1998), intramediate trade (Antweiler and Trefler, 2002), vertical specialization (Hummels et al., 2001), and slicing the value chain (Krugman, 1995), this phenomenon refers to the geographic separation of activities involved in producing a good (or service) across two or more countries. The term "production sharing" was coined by management consultant Peter Drucker ("The Rise of Production Sharing," *The Wall Street Journal*, March 15, 1977), as we have adopted in our title.

2   For a detailed discussion, see Katz and Autor (1999), whose wage figures we report below.

3   Only the highly skilled have had large real-wage gains. For the 1979 to 1995 period, real wages for those with 18 or more years of education rose by 14.0 percent and for those with 16 to 17 years of education rose by only 1.0 percent.

4   The breakdown of workers according to whether or not they are engaged in production activity is made in the US *Annual Survey of Manufactures*, and is used as a proxy for the occupational-class or skill-level of workers. While there are problems with using the production–nonproduction classification as a proxy for skill, there is evidence that in practice the classification shows similar trends as using skill categories (Berman et al.,

1994; Berman et al., 1998; Sachs and Shatz, 1994). The increase in the nonproduction–production relative wage is only a small part of the total increase in wage inequality between more- and less-skilled workers that occurred during the 1980s. See Katz and Murphy (1992) and Katz and Autor (1999) for a discussion.

5   Rising wage inequality has been relatively modest in Australia, Canada, Japan, and Sweden. Among advanced countries, only the UK has had relative wage changes comparable to the US (Machin, 1996).

6   See the surveys by Feenstra (1998), Freeman (1995), Johnson and Stafford (1999), Richardson (1995), and Wood (1995), and the volumes by Bhagwati and Kosters (1994) and Collins (1998).

7   Data on the ratio of trade to GDP is provided in Feenstra (1998), who also computes the ratios of merchandise trade to merchandise value-added, as discussed below.

8   Krugman (1995, 2000) provide the *theoretical* argument for why a small share of trade in the US makes it unlikely that trade can account for the change in wages. For alternative views, see Deardorff (2000), Leamer (2000), and Panagariya (2000).

9   Imported intermediate inputs have also been computed for nine OECD countries by Hummels et al. (2001). They find that 30 percent of OECD exports are attributable to imported intermediate inputs used in their production.

10 See Slaughter (2000a) for a discussion of literature on relative-price changes.

11 For a discussion of the Mexican *maquiladora*, see Feenstra and Hanson (1997). The export of inputs from the US for assembly overseas also occurs in other countries under the US "offshore assembly" program: see Feenstra et al. (2000).

12 Other models that emphasize the movement of production activities across countries in a product-cycle framework, and the effect on wages, include Dinopoulos and Segerstrom (1999), Glass and Saggi (2001) and Zhu (2000a), with corresponding empirical work by Zhu (2000b). The reader is also referred to the collection of papers in the June 2001 issue of the *Journal of International Economics*, 54(1).

13 To verify this, use $\hat{p} = 0$ in (6.9) and then solve for $\hat{w}$ and $\hat{q}$ as: $\hat{w} = -\hat{r}\,(\theta_{2H}\theta_{1K} - \theta_{1H}\theta_{2K})/(\theta_{1L}\theta_{2H} - \theta_{1H}\theta_{2L})$, and $\hat{q} = \hat{r}(\theta_{2L}\theta_{1K} - \theta_{1L}\theta_{2K})/(\theta_{1L}\theta_{2H} - \theta_{1H}\theta_{2L})$. Combining these, we readily obtain $\hat{w} - \hat{q} = -\hat{r}(\theta_{1K} - \theta_{2K})/(\theta_{1L}\theta_{2H} - \theta_{1H}\theta_{2L})$, which is negative when $\hat{r} > 0$ under our assumptions that activity 1 is intensive in both unskilled labor and capital.

14 Sachs and Shatz (1998, pp. 220–21) emphasize that this capital outflow *need not* be foreign direct investment, in which a domestic firm takes ownership of capital abroad. Rather, the domestic capital could simply be sold to a foreign firm (which would not show up as foreign direct investment).

15 Without loss of generality, we also impose the symmetry restrictions $\gamma_{ij} = \gamma_{ji}$ and $\delta_{jk} = \delta_{kj}$.

16 Generally, the dependent variables in the system (6.14) sum to unity, which means that one of the equations can be derived from the others. Under these conditions, one of the equations is dropped before system (6.14) is estimated. In addition, the cross-equation symmetry restrictions $\gamma_{ij} = \gamma_{ji}$, and homogeneity restrictions $\Sigma_j \gamma_{ij} = 0$, should be tested, and imposed if accepted. Additional tests can be used to check that the estimated cost function is concave in wages.

17 Multiplying the *ex post* rental price of each capital asset in an industry times the stock of that asset, and summing over all types of capital, equals observed payments to capital (i.e. value of shipments less payments to labor and materials). The share of computers in the capital stock is measured by taking the computer stock times its rental price, divided by the sum over all assets of each asset stock times its rental price. The *ex ante* rental prices are constructed by omitting capital gains on each asset, and using a "safe" rate of return. See Feenstra and Hanson (1999) for further details on these rental prices and the computer and other high-tech shares.

18 Autor et al. (1998) obtain smaller estimates for the impact of outsourcing on the non-production wage share. This appears to be due to the fact that they also include as regressors industry measures of imports and exports, which are highly correlated with imported intermediate inputs.

19 This finding may be driven by the fact that through the 1980s US MNEs continued to concentrate their foreign operations in OECD countries, where their production activities are similar to those in US manufacturing plants. During the 1990s, this pattern began to change, as FDI by US MNEs shifted towards emerging economies. Future foreign production transfer by US MNEs may then be associated with skill upgrading in the US. See Blomstrom et al. (1997) and Lipsey (1999).

20 See also Brainard and Riker (1997) and Riker and Brainard (1997). Lipsey (1994) and Feliciano and Lipsey (1999) discuss employment and compensation practices of foreign MNEs in the US.

21 Head and Ries also find that when Japanese firms move production to low-income countries they raise input purchases from these countries, but when they move production to high-income countries they do not. One interpretation of these results is that when Japanese firms move production to low-wage countries they mainly outsource low-skill tasks, which raises skill intensity at home, but when they move production to high-wage countries they tend to replicate production activities done at home, which may lower employment in Japan but does not change skill intensity.

22 Their estimation equation is based on Feenstra and Hanson (1996), and differs somewhat from that in (6.15). In this specification, the level of foreign assembly activities is treated as an endogenous variable.

23 We convert (6.18) to a discrete-time formula by replacing the instantaneous changes by the change in log prices between two years. In that case, we need to be specific about the year in which the factor shares are measured. A preferred method is to use the *arithmetic average* of the factor cost-shares in the two years, and this formulation is called the Tornqvist index of productivity. Caves et al. (1982a, b) show that the Tornqvist index is a valid measure of Hicks-neutral or factor-biased productivity change – i.e., it is valid even when the shift parameters in the translog production or cost function have a non-neutral impact on factor demands.

24 Feenstra and Hanson (1999) verify that the structural variables affect both TFP and value-added prices directly. Were the structural variables to affect just TFP, they would affect value-added prices indirectly, through the pass-through of productivity changes to product-price changes. Feenstra and Hanson find that the structural variables affect value-added prices over and above their impact on productivity.

25 Without loss of generality, we also impose the symmetry restrictions $\gamma_{mn} = \gamma_{nm}$ and $\delta_{mk} = \delta_{km}$.

26 Because the shares sum to unity, one product-share and one factor-share equation must be dropped.

References

Anderton, Bob and Paul Brenton 1997: Outsourcing and low-skilled workers in the UK. London: National Institute of Economic and Social Research, mimeo.

Antweiler, Werner and Daniel Trefler 2002: Increasing returns and all that: A view from trade. *American Economic Review*, 92, 1, March, 93–119.

Arndt, Sven 1997: Globalization and the open economy. *North American Journal of Economics and Finance*, 8, 1, 71–9.

Arndt, Sven 1998: Globalization and the gains from trade. In K. Jaeger and K.-J. Koch (eds.), *Trade, Growth and Economic Policy in Open Economies*, New York: Springer-Verlag.

Arndt, Sven and Henryk Kierzkowski (eds.) 2001: *Fragmentation: New Production and Trade Patterns in the World Economy*, Oxford: Oxford University Press.

Autor, David, Lawrence F. Katz, and Alan B. Krueger 1998: Computing inequality: Have computers changed the labor market? *Quarterly Journal of Economics*, 113, 1169–213.

Baldwin, Robert E. and Glen G. Cain 1997: Shifts in U.S. relative wages: The role of trade, technology and factor endowments. NBER working paper no. 5934.

Baldwin, Robert E. and R. S. Hilton 1984: A technique for indicating comparative costs and predicting changes in trade ratios. *Review of Economics and Statistics*, 64, 105–10.

Bartelsman, Eric J. and Wayne Gray 1996: The NBER manufacturing productivity database. NBER technical working paper no. 205.

Berman, Eli, John Bound, and Zvi Griliches 1994: Changes in the demand for skilled labor within U.S. manufacturing: Evidence from the *Annual Survey of Manufactures*. *Quarterly Journal of Economics*, 104, 367–98.

Berman, Eli, John Bound, and Stephen Machin 1998: Implications of skill-biased technological change: International evidence. *Quarterly Journal of Economics*, 113, 1245–80.

Bernard, Andrew B. and J. Bradford Jensen 1997: Exporters, skill upgrading and the wage gap. *Journal of International Economics*, 42, 3–32.

Bhagwati, Jagdish and Marvin H. Kosters (eds.) 1994: *Trade and Wages: Leveling Wages Down?* Washington, DC: American Enterprise Institute.

Blomstrom, Magnus, Gunnar Fors, and Robert E. Lipsey 1997: Foreign direct investment and employment: Home country evidence in the United States and Sweden. NBER working paper no. 6205.

Blonigen, Bruce and Matthew J. Slaughter 1999: Foreign-affiliate activity and U.S. skill upgrading. NBER working paper no. 7040.

Bound, John and George Johnson 1992: Changes in the structure of wages in the 1980s: An evaluation of alternative explanations. *American Economic Review*, 82, 371–92.

Brainard, S. Lael and David A. Riker 1997: Are U.S. multinationals exporting U.S. jobs? NBER working paper no. 5958.

Campa, J. and L. Goldberg 1997: The evolving external orientation of manufacturing industries: Evidence from four countries. NBER working paper no. 5919; also in: The Federal Reserve Bank of New York, *Economic Policy Review*, July 1997.

Caves, D. W., Laurits R. Christensen, and W. Erwin Diewert 1982a: The economic theory of index numbers and the measurement of input, output and productivity. *Econometrica*, 50, 1393–414.

Caves, D. W., Laurits R. Christensen, and W. Erwin Diewert 1982b: Multilateral comparisons of output, input, and productivity using superlative index numbers. *Economic Journal*, 92, 73–86.

Cheng, Leonard and Henryk Kierzkowski (eds.) 2001: *Globalization of Trade and Production in South-East Asia*. New York: Kluwer Academic Press.

Collins, Susan M. (ed.) 1998: *Imports, Exports, and the American Worker*. Washington, DC: Brookings Institution Press.

Cragg, M. and M. Epelbaum 1996: Why has wage dispersion grown in Mexico? Is it the incidence of reforms or the growing demand for skills? *Journal of Development Economics*, 51, 99–116.

Davis, Donald R. and David E. Weinstein 2000: International trade as an "integrated equilibrium": New perspectives. *American Economic Review*, 90, 150–4.

Deardorff, Alan V. 2000: Factor prices and the factor content of trade revisited: What's the use? *Journal of International Economics*, 50, 73–90.

Dicken, Peter, Philip F. Kelley, Kris Olds and Henry Wai-Chung Yeung 2001: Chains and networks, territories and scales: Towards a relational framework for analyzing the global economy. *Global Networks*, 1, 99–123.

Diewart, W. Erwin 1974: Applications of duality theory. In M. Intriligator and D. Kendrick (eds.), *Frontiers of Quantitative Economics* vol. II, Amsterdam: North-Holland, 106–71.

Dinopoulos, Elias and Paul Segerstrom 1999: A Schumpeterian model of protection and real wages. *American Economic Review*, 89, 3, June, 450–72.

Enright, Michael J., Edith E. Scott, and David Dodwell 1997: *The Hong Kong Advantage*. Hong Kong: Oxford University Press.

Feenstra, Robert C. 1998: Integration and disintegration in the global economy. *Journal of Economic Perspectives*, 12, 31–50.

Feenstra, Robert C. and Gordon H. Hanson 1996: Foreign investment, outsourcing and relative wages. In R. C. Feenstra, G. M. Grossman and D. A. Irwin (eds.), *The Political Economy of Trade Policy: Papers in Honor of Jagdish Bhagwati*, Cambridge, MA: MIT Press, 89–127.

Feenstra, Robert C. and Gordon H. Hanson 1997: Foreign direct investment and relative wages: Evidence from Mexico's maquiladoras. *Journal of International Economics*, 42, 371–94.

Feenstra, Robert C. and Gordon H. Hanson 1999: Productivity measurement and the impact of trade and technology on wages: Estimates for the U.S., 1972–1990. *Quarterly Journal of Economics*, 114, August, 907–40.

Feenstra, Robert C. and Gordon H. Hanson 2001: Intermediaries in entrepôt trade: Hong Kong re-exports of Chinese goods. NBER working paper no. 8088.

Feenstra, Robert C., Gordon H. Hanson, and Deborah L. Swenson 2000: Offshore assembly from the United States: Production characteristics of the 9802 program. In Robert Feenstra (ed.), *The Impact of International Trade on Wages*. NBER and University of Chicago Press, 85–122.

Feliciano, Zadia and Robert E. Lipsey 1999: Foreign ownership and wages in the United States, 1987–1992. NBER working paper no. 6923.

Freeman, Richard and Lawrence Katz 1994: Rising wage inequality: The United States vs. other advanced countries. In Richard Freeman (ed.), *Working Under Different Rules*, New York: Russell Sage Foundation.

Freeman, Richard B. 1995: Are your wages set in Beijing? *Journal of Economic Perspectives*, 9, 15–32.

Gaston, Noel and Daniel Trefler 1995: Union wage sensitivity to trade and protection: Theory and evidence. *Journal of International Economics*, 47, 1–25.

Gereffi, Gary and Miguel Korzeniewicz (eds.) 1994: *Commodity Chains and Global Capitalism*. Westport, CT: Praeger.

Gibbons, Robert and Lawrence Katz 1992: Does unmeasured ability explain inter-industry wage differentials? *Review of Economic Studies*, 59, 515–35.

Glass, Amy Jocelyn and Kamal Saggi 2001: Innovation and wage effects of international outsourcing. *European Economic Review*, 45, 67–86.

Görg, Holger 2000: Fragmentation and trade: U.S. inward processing trade in the EU. *Weltwirtshcaftliches Archiv (Review of World Economics)*, 136, 403–22.

Hanson, Gordon and Harrison, Anne 1999: Trade, technology, and wage inequality. *Industrial and Labor Relations Review*, 52, 271–88.

Harrigan, James 2000: International trade and American wages in general equilibrium, 1967–1995. In Robert C. Feenstra (ed.), *The Impact of International Trade on Wages*, Chicago: University of Chicago Press, 171–93.

Harrigan, James and Rita A. Balaban 1999: U.S. wage effects in general equilibrium: The effects of prices, technology, and factor supplies, 1963–1991. NBER working paper no. 6981.

Haskel, Jonathan E. and Matthew J. Slaughter 2000: Have falling tariffs and transportation costs raised U.S. wage inequality? NBER working paper no. 7539.

Haskel, Jonathan E. and Matthew J. Slaughter 2001: Trade technology and U.K. wage inequality. *Economic Journal*, 110, 1–27.

Head, Keith and John Ries 2000: Offshore production and skill upgrading by Japanese manufacturing firms. *Journal of International Economics*, 58, 1, October, 81–106.

Hsieh, Chang-Tai and Keong T. Woo 1999: The impact of outsourcing to China on Hong Kong's labor market. Princeton University, mimeo.

Hummels, David, Jun Ishii, and Kei-Mu Yi 2001: The nature and growth of vertical specialization in world trade. *Journal of International Economics*, 54, 75–96.

Johnson, George and Frank Stafford 1999: The labor market implications of international trade. In Orley Ashenfelter and David Card (eds.), *Handbook of Labor Economics*, vol. 3B, Amsterdam: Elsevier Science, 2215–88.

Jones, Ronald 1963: The structure of simple general equilibrium models. *Journal of Political Economy*, 73, 557–72.

Jones, Ronald W. 2000: *Globalization and the Theory of Input Trade*. Ohlin Lectures vol. 8. Cambridge, MA; and London, UK: MIT Press.

Katz, Lawrence F. and David Autor 1999: Changes in the wage structure and earnings inequality. In Orley Ashenfelter and David Card (eds.), *Handbook of Labor Economics*, vol. 3A, Amsterdam: Elsevier Science, 1463–555.

Katz, Lawrence F. and Kevin M. Murphy 1992: Changes in relative wages, 1963–1987: Supply and demand factors. *Quarterly Journal of Economics*, 107, 35–78.

Kim, Dae Il and Peter Mieszkowski 1995: The effects of international trade and outsourcing on relative factor prices. Rice University, mimeo.

Kohli, Ulrich R. 1978: A gross national product function and the derived demand for imports and supply of exports. *Canadian Journal of Economics*, 11, 167–82.

Kohli, Ulrich R. 1991: *Technology, Duality and Foreign Trade*. London: Harvester Wheatsheaf.

Krueger, Alan B. 1997: Labor market shifts and the price puzzle revisited. NBER working paper no. 5924.

Krueger, Alan B. and Lawrence Summers 1988: Efficiency wages and the inter-industry wage structure. *Econometrica*, 56, 269–93.

Krugman, Paul 1995: Growing world trade: Causes and consequences. *Brooking Papers on Economic Activity*, 1, 327–62.

Krugman, Paul 2000: Technology, trade and factor prices. *Journal of International Economics*, 50, 51–72.

Lawrence, Robert Z. 1994: Trade, multinationals, and labor. NBER working paper no. 4836.

Lawrence, Robert Z. and Matthew Slaughter 1993: International trade and American wages in the 1980s: Giant sucking sound or small hiccup? *Brookings Papers on Economic Activity: Microeconomics*, 161–226.

Leamer, Edward E. 1996: The effects of trade in services, technology transfer and delocalisation on local and global income inequality. *Asia-Pacific Economic Review*, 2, 44–60.

Leamer, Edward E. 1998: In search of Stolper–Samuelson linkages between international trade and lower wages. In Susan M. Collins (ed.), *Imports, Exports, and the American Worker*, Washington, DC: Brookings Institution Press, 141–203.

Leamer, Edward E. 2000: What's the use of factor contents? *Journal of International Economics*, 50, 17–50.

Lipsey, Robert E. 1994: Foreign-owned firms and U.S. wages. NBER working paper no. 4927.

Lipsey, Robert E. 1999: Foreign production by U.S. firms and parent firm employment. NBER working paper no. 7357.

Machin, Stephen 1994: Changes in the relative demand for skills in the United Kingdom labor market. In Alison Booth and Denis Snower (eds.), *Acquiring Skills: Market Failures, Their Symptoms and Policy Response*, Cambridge: Cambridge University Press.

Machin, Stephen 1996: Wage inequality in the UK. *Oxford Review of Economic Policy*, 12, 47–64.

Marjit, Sugata and Rajat Acharyya forthcoming: *International Trade, Wage Inequality and the Developing Economy: A General Equilibrium Approach*, Heidelberg: Physica Verlag, Contribution to Economics Series.

Morrison, Paul, Catherine Siegel, and Donald Siegel 2001: The impacts of technology, trade and outsourcing on employment and labor compensation. *Scandinavian Journal of Economics*, 103, 2, June, 241–64.

Ng, Francis and Alexander Yeats 1999: Production sharing in East Asia: Who does what for whom and why? The World Bank, mimeo.

Panagariya, Arvind 2000: Evaluating the factor-content approach to measuring the effect of trade on wage inequality. *Journal of International Economics*, 50, 91–116.

Richardson, J. David 1995: Income inequality and trade: How to think, what to conclude. *Journal of Economic Perspectives*, 9, 33–56.

Riker, D. and S. Brainard 1997: U.S. multinationals and competition from low wage countries. NBER working paper no. 5959.

Robertson, Raymond 2000: Relative prices and wage inequality: Evidence from Mexico. Macalester College, mimeo.

Rodrik, D. 1997: *Has Globalization Gone Too Far?* Washington, DC: Institute for International Economics.

Sachs, Jeffrey D. and Howard J. Shatz 1994: Trade and jobs in U.S. manufacturing. *Brookings Papers on Economic Activity*, 1, 1–84.

Sachs, Jeffrey D. and Howard J. Shatz 1998: International trade and wage inequality: Some new results. In Susan M. Collins (ed.), *Imports, Exports, and the American Worker*, Washington, DC: Brookings Institution Press, 215–40.

Slaughter, Matthew J. 2000a: What are the results of product-price studies and what can we learn from their differences? In Robert C. Feenstra (ed.), *The Effects of International Trade on Wages*, Chicago: University of Chicago Press, 129–65.

Slaughter, Matthew J. 2000b: Production transfer within multinational enterprises and American wages. *Journal of International Economics*, 50, 449–72.

Slaughter, Matthew J. 2001: International trade and labor-demand elasticities. *Journal of International Economics*, 54, 27–56.

Stolper, Wolfgang and Paul A. Samuelson 1941: Protection and real wages. *Review of Economic Studies*, 9, 51–68.

Sung, Yun-Wing 1997: Hong Kong and the economic integration of the China Circle. In Barry Naughton (ed.), *The China Circle*. Washington, DC: Brookings Institution Press.

Tombazos, Christis G. 1999: The role of imports in expanding the demand gap between skilled and unskilled labor in the U.S. *Applied Economics*, 31, 509–16.

Trefler, Daniel 1995: The case of missing trade and other mysteries. *American Economic Review*, 85, 1029–46.

Trefler, Daniel and Susan Chun Zhu 2000: Beyond the algebra of eExplanation: HOV for the technology age. *American Economic Review*, 90, 145–9.

Wood, Adrian 1995: How trade hurt unskilled workers. *Journal of Economic Perspectives*, 9, 57–70.

Xu, Bin 2000: The relationship between outsourcing and wage inequality under sector-specific FDI barriers. University of Florida, mimeo.

Yeung, Henry Wai-chung 2001: Organizing regional production networks in Southeast Asia:

Implications for production fragmentation, trade and rules of origin. *Journal of Economic Geography*, 1, 3, 299–321.

Yi, Kei-Mu 2000: Can vertical specialization explain the growth of world trade? Federal Reserve Bank of New York staff report no. 96.

Zhu, Susan Chun 2001a: Trade, product cycles and inequality within and between countries. University of Toronto, mimeo.

Zhu, Susan Chun 2001b: Product cycles and skill upgrading: An empirical assessment. University of Toronto, mimeo.

7

External Economies in the International Trade Theory: A Survey

Jai-Young Choi and Eden S. H. Yu

CHAPTER OUTLINE

The chapter surveys the international trade literature on intraindustrial and interindustrial production externalities. It places particular emphasis upon the literature on variable returns to scale (VRS) developed along the Kemp (1955) line that the externalities are output-generated, and the economies of scale are external (internal) to individual firms (industry). The discussion touches upon the literature examining the implications of VRS for fundamental trade theorems, trade policies, economic growth, and welfare. The chapter extends the survey to writings on the Meade-type interindustrial production externalities.

1 INTRODUCTION

Increasing returns to scale (or economies of scale) in production are an indisputable phenomenon characterizing real world production, and, as such, they have long been recognized as a principal source of economic prosperity.[1] Nonetheless, they have never played a major role in the traditional theory of international trade (i.e., both the classical Ricardian theory and the neoclassical Heckscher–Ohlin theory). This may be attributable to the fact that, until the 1930s, the compatibility of increasing returns to scale (IRS) with perfectly competitive equilibrium was a matter of intense debate that did not yield a definite conclusion.[2]

Meanwhile, during the early postwar period, the traditional theory of international trade was subject to intense scrutiny. In particular, with the emergence of the Leontief paradox (1953, 1956), numerous attempts have been made to test the validity of the neoclassical Heckscher–Ohlin theory of comparative advantage. The results of these tests have been mostly inconclusive and often controversial, and this consequently has provoked mounting discontent with the traditional theory.[3] The discontent has been exacerbated by the emergence of two new patterns of world trade that are contradictory to the prediction implied by the traditional theory of international trade: increasing intraindustry trade among nations, and an increasing share of world trade among industrialized nations.[4] These developments have provided a catalyst for launching new inquiries into the causes and nature of international trade.

International economists are now divided into two broad groups adopting different lines of approach to the inquiry. One group seeks to salvage the traditional theory by either relaxing certain restrictive assumptions or by incorporating some important (but missing) factors into the conventional model of general equilibrium. The other group attempts to discard entirely the traditional theory by developing new alternative models to explain trade.[5] It is noteworthy that a significant body of the trade literature tackling the issue of IRS (or more broadly, variable returns to scale (VRS)) has emerged using both lines of approach. The VRS literature of the first line of approach usually adopts the celebrated proposition by Kemp (1955) that perfect competition can prevail under conditions of IRS if the economies of scale are external to individual firms and internal to industry, and the competitive output is efficient if the externalities are output-generated. The strength of this line of approach lies with its capability to retain the conventional general-equilibrium model of international trade. This model is undoubtedly an elegant and powerful intellectual construct that is capable of yielding many valuable insights into world trade. Nevertheless, it suffers from the drawback that the types of economies of scale compatible with perfect competition are limited, consequently restricting the scope of the model's applicability. The VRS literature of the second line of approach usually discards the traditional general-equilibrium model and adopts models of imperfect competition. The merit of this is the ease with which it can be reconciled with IRS (*vis-à-vis* the perfect-competition case of the former line). But it also has a weakness in that even today a general theory of imperfect competition has not been formulated, so studies generally resort to a collection of small models dealing with special cases.

The purpose of this chapter is to survey the literature on production externalities, with particular emphasis placed upon IRS, developed along the first line of approach discussed above. This seems to be important for several reasons. First, incorporating IRS (or more broadly variable returns to scale (VRS)) into the general-equilibrium model of perfect competition can reveal vital information on the role IRS plays in determining international trade relationships *vis-à-vis* the traditional case of constant returns to scale (CRS) – for example, the nature of the non-Pareto-optimum situation created by non-CRS, and its policy implications. Second, using this line of approach, the traditional theory of comparative advantage need not be discarded but can be considered in conjunction with the issue of returns to scale. Third, it has been found that several significant results based on this line of approach hold in certain models of imperfect competition.[6] Fourth, an increasing number of industries have been identified as operating under output-generated externalities that are external to the firm and internal to the industry. This type of externality, compatible with (or with the outcome of) perfect competition, has been observed in many technology-intensive (or some contestable) industries. Fifth, this line of approach can effectively explain certain trade phenomena that cannot be explained by traditional theory – for example, the two new trends of international trade (increasing intraindustry trade among nations, and increasing share of world trade among industrialized nations).

Section 2 discusses the nature of externalities and presents the three variations of a general-equilibrium model with VRS. They are derived mainly from the frameworks constructed by Kemp (1969) and Jones (1966, 1968). The discussion also touches upon the literature examining the production side of the VRS model, as well as several fundamental theorems of international trade including the Rybczynski and the Stolper–Samuelson theorems. Section 3 surveys the literature on the analysis of the implications of VRS (or intraindustrial externalities) for trade policies, economic growth, and welfare. Section 4 extends the survey to include writings on Meade-type interindustrial production externalities. Section 5 presents concluding remarks.

2   VRS MODELS AND THEIR BASIC PROPERTIES

2.1   Nature of Economies of Scale

Nonmarket interdependence among various economic agents is described as technological external economies and diseconomies. The technological externalities may be intraindustrial or interindustrial. Our main concern in this section is with the technological externalities of an intraindustrial nature that cause IRS or decreasing returns to scale (DRS) in the industry.

IRS (or DRS) are usually attributable to certain economies (or diseconomies) that are reflected in production costs. They may be internal or external to the firm. If the economies of scale are internal to the firm, perfect competition breaks down because one firm (or a small number of firms in certain cases) would eventually supply the whole industry output. To be specific, assuming the CRS industry production function, the production function of the firm can still exhibit increasing, constant, and decreasing returns to scale, as shown by the usual U-shaped long-run average cost curve. The phase of IRS in the firm's production function is due to internal economies arising from labor and managerial specialization and/or use of more efficient capital. These internal economies are typically followed by CRS and then DRS, owing to difficulties of controlling and coordinating a large firm's operation. Here, if the internal economies to the firm were to continue indefinitely (e.g., by the input-generated externalities), costs would fall with the scale of production, and hence firms that expanded first could undersell competing firms that had not expanded, eventually driving them out of the industry. In this case, perfect competition cannot prevail in the industry, and instead, some form of imperfect competition, such as monopolistic competition, oligopoly, or monopoly, must emerge. Economists have long recognized this fact, and thus the debates (on the compatibility of IRS with perfect competition) have been centered on the type of economies of scale that are external to the firm.

If the technological economies are external to individual firms, expansion of the industry's output shifts down the cost curves of all firms in the industry, although each firm's production function faces constant cost per unit of output – i.e., CRS. The cost curves of the firms may shift down, for example, owing to the technological externalities generated from learning-by-doing, diffusion of knowledge across the industry, sharing of improved infrastructure, improved quality of labor, effective supply of inputs, etc.[7] In this case, returns to scale are constant for individual firms of the industry but, by virtue of technological intraindustrial externalities, might be increasing for the industry as a whole. The origination or growth of this kind of industry may be autonomous or government-sponsored, and examples are numerous, such as the classical case of the watch industry in Switzerland (Chipman, 1965) and the geographical concentration of myriad (retail or wholesale) business establishments in garments, souvenirs, electronics, agricultural and fisheries, biotechnology, computers, and other information-technology industries. This type of technological externality, apparently compatible with perfect competition, provides the theoretical basis for the VRS literature that has developed with the approach of preserving the conventional theory.

2.2 General-Equilibrium Models of VRS

The VRS literature following this line of approach integrates VRS into a variety of general-equilibrium models. Among them, a VRS model of the neoclassical variety is most commonly employed by trade theorists for analytical purposes, mainly because the majority of traditional theories are built upon the neoclassical model.

2.2.1 THE NEOCLASSICAL VRS MODEL

The neoclassical VRS model is a straightforward extension of the neoclassical two-sector model of general equilibrium with CRS. The production side of the model consists of the following equations:

$$x_i = g_i(X_i)F_i(l_i, c_i), \quad i = 1,2 \tag{7.1}$$

$$x_i = g_i(X_i)F_i(L_i, K_i), \quad i = 1,2 \tag{7.2}$$

$$w = p_i g_i F_{li} = p_i g_i F_{Li} = p_i g_i [f_i - k_i f_i{}'(k_i)], \quad i = 1,2 \tag{7.3}$$

$$r = p_i g_i F_{ci} = p_i g_i F_{Ki} = p_i g_i f_i{}'(k_i), \quad i = 1,2 \tag{7.4}$$

$$L_1 + L_2 = L, \tag{7.5}$$

$$K_1 + K_2 = K. \tag{7.6}$$

Equations (7.1) and (7.2) are the production functions, where x_i is the output of the typical firm in industry i; c_i and l_i are capital and labor employed by it; X_i is the output of industry i, and K_i and L_i are its employment of capital and labor; g_i describes the role of externalities and is a positive function defined on $(0, \infty)$; and F_i is linearly homogeneous in its inputs. Equations (7.3) and (7.4) are profit-maximization conditions for factor employment, where F_{li} (F_{Li}) and F_{ci} (F_{Ki}) denote, respectively, the first partial derivative of F_i with respect to labor and capital of the firm (industry), a prime indicates the first partial derivative, and f_i, k_i, p_i, w, and r, respectively, stand for F_i/L_i, capital–labor ratio, price of the ith commodity, real wage, and real rental. Since the economies of scale are external to an individual firm and internal to the industry, each factor is paid the value of its marginal product to the individual firm, not the value of its marginal product to the industry. Equations (7.5) and (7.6) are the full-employment conditions of factors of production where L and K are fixed supplies of labor and capital, and they are perfectly mobile between the industries.

A crucial step in the use of this model is to identify the role of externalities for determining the returns to scale. This can be done by differentiating the industry production functions (7.2):

$$(1 - e_i)\mathrm{d}X_i = g_i(F_{Ki}dK_i + F_{Li}dL_i) \quad i = 1,2 \tag{7.7}$$

where $e_i = (\mathrm{d}g_i/\mathrm{d}X_i)\,(X_i/g_i)$ is the output elasticity of returns to scale of the ith industry, and the value of e_i determines the direction and degree of the returns to scale. Note that e_i is defined on $(-\infty, 1)$: $e_i > 0$ for an IRS industry, $e_i < 0$ for a DRS industry, and $e_i = 0$ for a CRS industry. Note that in the presence of external economies (diseconomies), private marginal product (g_iF_{ji}) of factor j ($j = K, L$) is smaller (greater) than its social marginal product, $g_iF_{ji}/(1 - e_i)$. In other words, private marginal cost exceeds (falls short of) social marginal cost.

2.2.2 STRUCTURAL MODELS OF VRS

Jones (1966) derived a structural model from the standard neoclassical model of general equilibrium to study some fundamental propositions in the theory of international trade. The structural model, which is better known as "equations of change," was later extended by Jones (1968) to the case of VRS, and the (extended) structural model of VRS was later utilized by many trade theorists including Herberg and Kemp (1969), Kemp (1969), and Mayer (1974). The Jones structural model of VRS, based on input–output coefficients (C_{ij}), consists of the following equations:

$$C_{L1}X_1 + C_{L2}X_2 = L \tag{7.8}$$

$$C_{K1}X_1 + C_{K2}X_2 = K \tag{7.9}$$

$$C_{L1}w + C_{K1}r = p_1 \tag{7.10}$$

$$C_{L2}w + C_{K2}r = p_2 \tag{7.11}$$

$$C_{ij} = C_{ij}(\omega, X_j) \quad i = L, K, \quad j = 1, 2 \tag{7.12}$$

Equations (7.8) and (7.9) are the full-employment conditions; (7.10) and (7.11) are the conditions for average-cost pricing; and (7.12) is the input–output coefficient of factor i ($i = L, K$) in industry j ($j = 1, 2$) which depends on the wage–rental ratio (ω) and the output of the industry.

The effect of the output-generated externalities on the input–output coefficients can be shown by differentiating (7.12):

$$\hat{C}_{ij} = \hat{A}_{ij} - R_{ij}\hat{X}_j \tag{7.13}$$

The circumflex denotes the relative change (or the rate of change) of the variable. $\hat{A}_{ij} = (1/C_{ij})(\partial C_{ij}/\partial\omega)d\omega$ is the change in input–output coefficient due to a change in the wage–rental ratio. $R_{ij} = -(X_j/C_{ij})(\partial C_{ij}/\partial X_j)$ is the change in C_{ij} due to a change in the output of the jth industry. Define

$$R_j = \theta_{Lj}R_{Lj} + \theta_{Kj}R_{Kj} \quad j = 1, 2 \tag{7.14}$$

where θ_{ij} is the share of the ith factor in the total value of the jth commodity ($i = L, K; j = 1, 2$). The industry production function $X_j = g_j(X_j)F_j(L_j, K_j)$ can be expressed as $X_j = G_j(L_j, K_j)$, where G_j is homothetic if F_j is linearly homogeneous. For homothetic production functions, $R_j = R_{Lj} = R_{Kj}$ ($j = 1, 2$).[8] Note that $R_j > 0$ for an IRS industry, $R_j < 0$ for a DRS industry, and $R_j = 0$ for a CRS industry.

Differentiating (7.8) to (7.11) and using the elasticity of factor substitution $\sigma_j = (\hat{A}_{Kj} - \hat{A}_{Lj})/(\hat{w} - \hat{r}) > 0$ ($j = 1, 2$) and unit cost-minimization condition $wC_{Lj}\hat{A}_{Lj} + rC_{Kj}\hat{A}_{Kj} = 0$ ($j = 1, 2$), we obtain a system of equations of change, providing a basis for VRS analysis.

Kemp (1969) then incorporated production functions into the Jones structural model; and later a modified structural model, which replaces cost functions in the Jones model with production functions, was utilized by several trade theorists, including Panagariya (1980, 1983, 1986), and Yabuuchi (1992). The modified structural model consists of the following equations in differentiated form:

$$(1 - e_i)\hat{X}_i = \theta_{Li}\hat{L}_i + \theta_{Ki}\hat{K}_i, \quad i = 1, 2 \tag{7.15}$$

$$\theta_{Li}\hat{w}_i + \theta_{Ki}\hat{r} = \hat{X}_i + \hat{p}_i - (\theta_{Li}\hat{L}_i + \theta_{Ki}\hat{K}_i), \quad i = 1, 2. \tag{7.16}$$

$$\lambda_{L1}\hat{L}_1 + \lambda_{L2}\hat{L}_2 = \hat{L}, \tag{7.17}$$

$$\lambda_{K1}\hat{K}_1 + \lambda_{K2}\hat{K}_2 = \hat{K}. \tag{7.18}$$

Note that this modified model uses production functions (7.15) instead of the cost functions in the Jones model. Also, the average-cost pricing condition, $wL_i + rK_i =$

p_iX_i, is used to obtain (7.16). Equations (7.17) and (7.18) are the full-employment conditions. These equations, coupled with the elasticity of factor substitution, $\acute{o}_i = (\hat{K}_i - \hat{L}_i)/(\hat{w} - \hat{r})$ for $i = 1, 2$, yield a system of equations of change representing the general equilibrium.

2.3 Production Possibilities Frontier (PPF) and Production Equilibrium

The introduction of VRS presents several problems to the production side of the general equilibrium; namely:

1 the PPF may not be concave to the origin;
2 production may not take place on the PPF;
3 at equilibrium, the marginal rate of transformation need not be equal to the commodity price ratio; and
4 multiple production equilibria may exist.

Jones (1968) and Herberg and Kemp (1969) have investigated the shape of the PPF under VRS. Jones (1968) has shown that the PPF exhibits locally the normal "bowed-out" shape if and only if the Rybczynski (1955) theorem is satisfied, and that sufficiently heavy IRS can make the PPF "bowed-in," but the "bowed-in" shape can occur if marginal and average factor intensities differ. Herberg and Kemp (1969) derived several important asymptotic properties of the PPF:

1 If a good is produced under conditions of DRS (IRS), then the locus of the PPF is concave (convex) to the origin in the neighborhood of zero output of the good regardless of the nature of scale returns in the other industry.
2 The locus of the PPF is uniformly concave (convex) to the origin if scale returns of each industry are nonincreasing (increasing) and have not too high positive (low negative) rates of change with increasing output.
3 In all other cases, the locus of the PPF may have strictly concave as well as strictly convex parts.

To understand the role of VRS for determining the shape of the PPF, we derive, from (7.7), the expression for the slope of the PPF:

$$dX_1/dX_2 = [(1-e_2)g_1(F_{K1}dK_1 + F_{L1}dL_1)]/[(1-e_1)g_2(F_{K2}dK_2 + F_{L2}dL_2)]. \quad (7.19)$$

Using $F_{L1}/F_{K1} = F_{L2}/F_{K2}$, (7.5) and (7.6), (7.19) can be re-expressed as:

$$dX_1/dX_2 = -[(1-e_2)g_1F_{K1}]/[(1-e_1)g_2F_{K2}]$$
$$= -[(1-e_2)g_1f_1'(k_1)]/[(1-e_1)g_2f_2'(k_2)]. \quad (7.20)$$

Equation (7.20) shows that the shape of the PPF is influenced by the two forces: returns to scale (e_1, e_2) and factor intensities (k_1, k_2). Under CRS, g_i is a constant and both e_1 and e_2 are zero, and hence only factor intensities affect the shape of the PPF. In particular, the PPF is linear if there is only one factor of production (e.g., the Ricardian case) or if the factor intensities of the two goods are constant. Under VRS, however, the PPF is not necessarily linear for either the one-factor case or the constant-factor-intensity case.

It is instructive to isolate the effect of returns to scale on the shape of the PPF from that of the factor intensities. So, we assume for a moment that both factor intensities are constant. Then $f'_1(k_1)/f'_2(k_2)$ in (7.20) becomes a positive constant, C. Suppose that g_i has a form $X_i^{a_i}$, so that $e_i = a_i$ for $i = 1, 2$. Then (7.20) can be re-expressed as:

$$dX_1/dX_2 = -C[(1-a_2)/(1-a_1)]X_1^{a_1}X_2^{-a_2}. \tag{7.21}$$

Differentiation of (7.21) with respect to X_2 yields:

$$d^2X_1/dX_2^2 = C[(1-a_2)/(1-a_1)]^2[(X_1^{(2a_1-1)}X_2^{-(a_2+1)})][a_2(1-a_1)X_1^{(1-a_1)}+Ca_1(1-a_2)X_2^{(1-2a_2)}]. \tag{7.22}$$

It is a simple matter to show that if industry 1 exhibits IRS and industry 2 exhibits DRS, $d^2X_1/dX_2^2 > (<) 0$ in the neighborhood of $X_1 = 0$ ($X_2 = 0$). Furthermore, there is only one inflection point at $d^2X_1/dX_2^2 = 0$. This result is consistent with the neighborhood properties shown by Herberg and Kemp (1969) and Panagariya (1981) (which was derived from a one-factor model). In the general case where both elasticities of returns to scale are variable, there may exist multiple inflection points, but the neighborhood properties remain unchanged.[9]

The effects of factor intensities on the shape of the PPF can be analyzed by using the Edgeworth box diagram and Savosnick's (1958) technique of deriving the PPF from a contract curve. Other things being constant, intersectoral factor intensity disparities tend to make the PPF "bowed-out" from the origin. In general, IRS tends to make the PPF "bowed-in" to the origin. Therefore, under IRS, the final shape of the PPF is determined by the relative strength of the two forces.

Our next task is to derive the necessary condition for production equilibrium. Kemp (1955, 1969) has shown that perfect competition and static increasing returns can be reconciled by introducing external economies; and, for competitive output to be efficient, it suffices that the externalities be output-generated.[10] By substituting (7.4) in (7.20), we obtain

$$dX_1/dX_2 = -[(1-e_2)(1-e_1)](p_2/p_1) \quad \text{or} \quad p_1(1-e_2)dX_1 + p_2(1-e_2)dX_2 = 0. \tag{7.23}$$

Equation (7.23) indicates that the marginal rate of transformation is not equal to the commodity price ratio unless the elasticities of returns to scale of the two industries are identical ($e_1 = e_2$), with CRS as its special case ($e_1 = e_2 = 0$). To be specific, the price line is flatter (steeper) than the slope of the PPF at the production equilibrium point if $e_1 > (<) e_2$.

The production equilibrium condition (7.23) can be generalized to multicommodity and multifactor cases such that[11]

$$\sum p_i(1-e_i)\mathrm{d}X_i = 0. \quad i = 1,2,\dots,n. \tag{7.24}$$

Notice that equations (7.20) and (7.21) indicate that, under VRS, multiple production equilibria may exist.

2.4 Major Production-Side Theorems Under VRS

VRS, embodied in the production process, can be a source of problems for the traditional theorems pertinent to the production-side of the economy. In the general-equilibrium analysis, the VRS issue is typically dealt with in the context of production distortion. Several studies have investigated the implications of VRS for major production-side trade theorems.

Minabe (1966) examined the Stolper–Samuelson theorem under the condition of VRS and argued that if the PPF is concave to the origin the theorem always holds. Batra (1968) challenged this conclusion by demonstrating that the theorem may cease to hold in the presence of variable returns, even when the PPF is concave to the origin. Jones (1968) investigated the structure of the two-sector production model by incorporating VRS into his neoclassical model of "equations of change." Allowing for nonhomothetic industry production functions, he showed that both the Rybczynski and the Stolper–Samuelson theorems based on the assumption of CRS do not readily carry over to the case of VRS, whereby the degree of economies of scale and the correspondence between average and marginal factor intensities play a crucial role.

The Jones analysis was expressed by Kemp (1969) in a condensed form by assuming that production functions are homothetic and economies of scale are the same in both industries. Nonetheless, Kemp's revised analysis could not restore the validity of the Rybczynski and Stolper–Samuelson theorems for the case of VRS. Herberg and Kemp (1969) showed that the output of a commodity responds positively (perversely) to an increase in its relative price if it displays DRS (IRS) in the neighborhood of its zero output, and that the response of output to a small price change cannot be inferred from the local curvature of the locus of the PPF, nor can the latter be inferred from the former.[12]

Mayer (1974) reconsidered the major trade theorems by utilizing dynamic stability analysis in which a Marshallian (Walrasian) adjustment process is assumed for commodity (factor) markets. He derived several significant results:

1   The Rybczynski and the Stolper–Samuelson theorems are valid in the presence of VRS if the system is stable and industry production functions are homothetic.
2   If the stability condition is satisfied but production functions are not homothetic, only the Rybczynski theorem carries over to the VRS case, whereas extension of the Stolper–Samuelson theorem requires that average and marginal factor intensities be the same.
3   Price–output response is positive in a stable system.

Following Mayer, Neary (1978) demonstrated that a perverse price–output response can not occur, even in the presence of distortion(s), if stability in factor movement is assumed. Panagariya (1980) showed that, in general, the validity of the Rybczynski or Stolper–Samuelson theorems is neither necessary nor sufficient for the PPF to be strictly concave to the origin, and that unlike the CRS case, VRS renders factor-returns a function of factor supplies.

In a two-factor, two-sector, two-country model with VRS, Laing (1961) and Kemp (1969) showed that, contrary to the standard CRS case, relative factor prices need not be equalized internationally. In a similar model, allowing for a different factor-endowment ratio, Panagariya (1983) demonstrated that the pattern of trade predicted by the standard Heckscher–Ohlin theorem may or may not hold in the presence of VRS.

Parai (1985) analyzed the effects of unionization on income distribution under VRS. He showed that, unlike the conventional results obtained by Johnson and Mieszkowski (1970) under the CRS assumption, with IRS it is possible for both union and nonunion workers to lose (gain) from unionization even when the unionized sector is relatively capital- (labor)-intensive, while under DRS, the conventional results hold.[13]

The effects of technical progress on sectoral outputs under VRS were examined by Choi and Yu (1987c). Assuming a stable system, they showed that, regardless of the direction and severity of the returns to scale, Hicks-neutral technical progress is ultra-biased in production (i.e., the output of the expanding industry is increased at the expense of the other industry at constant commodity prices). They also showed that the output effect of intensive-factor-saving technical progress is more ultra-biased (relative to neutral progress) regardless of returns to scale; and that intensive-factor-using technical progress may have any output effect.[14]

Ingene and Yu (1991) investigated the resource allocational implications of VRS in a two-region general-equilibrium model of production under uncertainty. They showed that standard results concerning changes in the goods–price ratio with CRS under uncertainty generalize to VRS, whereas standard results concerning changes in factor endowments readily extend from CRS to DRS but not to all permissible levels of IRS. Thus, such theorems as factor price equalization and Rybczynski do not generalize to all real-world levels of VRS.

3   TRADE POLICIES, ECONOMIC GROWTH, AND WELFARE UNDER VRS

This section reviews the literature on the implications of VRS for major theories of international trade, including gains from trade, protection (tariffs and quotas), trade integration, and economic growth. In the general-equilibrium analysis, VRS is customarily dealt in the framework of economic distortion and a "second-best world" argument.

Development of the theory of distortions owes much to several economists, including Bhagwati (1971a), Bhagwati and Ramaswami (1963), Cordon (1957), Haberler (1950), Johnson (1965), and Meade (1955).[15] Bhagwati (1971b) identified four major types of distortions. The case of an output-generated externality (VRS or Meade (1952)-type interindustrial externality) is the type 2 distortion characterized by DRT ≠ DRS = FRT, where DRT is the marginal rate of transformation in domestic production, DRS is the marginal rate of substitution in domestic consumption, and FRT is the marginal foreign rate of transformation. It is now known that distortions can render perverse effects on the economy and yield various novel results and policy prescriptions (*vis-à-vis* the normal case in the standard model without distortion). For example, a distortion can prevent the economy from attaining Pareto optimality, and the policy intervention to neutralize the distortions must be made based on the "specificity rule" (i.e., intervention must be directed to the exact source of the problem).

It seems appropriate here to mention that the aim of this survey is to introduce the various trade-theoretic results presented in the VRS literature. Owing to space constraints, the task of explaining how VRS is introduced in each case and what role VRS plays in shaping each result is not undertaken. It suffices to note that, in the presence of VRS, changes in exogenous variables (including policy variables) give rise to resource reallocational effects among industries of varying returns to scale in attaining the second-best economic efficiency, and in the process can lead to normal or novel results (*vis-à-vis* the results in the standard CRS model). Readers need to refer to the original articles for details.

Theory of gains from trade has a long chronicle dating back to Adam Smith. Embedded in his principle of absolute advantage is the idea of increased opportunities for *division of labor and specialization* provided by international trade. Smith's idea was refined by David Ricardo who advocated the principle of *comparative advantage*. This is the cornerstone of the classical and neoclassical theories of international trade. Taking the gains from trade based on comparative advantage for granted, modern (neoclassical) general-equilibrium theory developed by Heckscher and Ohlin describes *why* and *how* trade takes place. As discussed earlier, increasing returns have long been recognized as determinants of international trade, but only recently have they received attention and played an important role in both the classical and the neoclassical theories of international trade. The Kemp (1955) proof that IRS and perfect competition are compatible if the economies of scale are external to individual firms and internal to industry, and if they are output-generated, has inspired a number of trade theorists to scrutinize the role of VRS for gains from trade. From the complexities of the production possibility locus and the production equilibria under VRS (discussed in section 2), it is not difficult to infer that in the presence of VRS, the pattern of trade and the resulting economic effects are not simple matters to predict.

Kemp (1964) showed that in a two-commodity world (in which both industries experience identical IRS such that the PPF is convex to the origin and is tangent to the price line at the autarky equilibrium), the introduction of IRS in both industries can lead to multitudes of trading possibilities including specialization in either one of the two commodities. Using a similar framework, Melvin (1969b) demonstrated that IRS itself (apart from the comparative advantage resulting from the difference between autarky prices and international terms of trade) can be a basis for trade.

Panagariya (1981) analyzed, utilizing a one-factor and two-commodity model, the welfare implications and patterns of trade for the case with IRS in one industry and DRS in the other. In particular, he demonstrated that if a small open economy specializes completely in production, it will do so in the DRS commodity and not in the IRS commodity, and that if an internal production equilibrium exists, a welfare-maximizing small economy will never specialize completely in production even if the PPF exhibits IRS over a part of its range.

Kemp and Negishi (1970), using revealed preference arguments, proposed the sufficient conditions under which the opening of trade and improvement in the terms of trade are not harmful in the presence of variable returns to scale. Eaton and Panagariya (1979) reconsidered the same subject in the context of a Pareto welfare criterion.

The crucial implication of the generalized theory of distortions for trade policy under VRS is that, in the presence of VRS, the optimality of free trade breaks down and policy intervention may be required; but by the specificity rule, trade intervention – such as a tariff or import subsidy – is not the best policy to cure the nonoptimality of free trade (i.e., there is something else that can do better). Panagariya (1981) showed, in a VRS model of the classical type (i.e., two-commodity and one-factor model), that welfare maximization for a small country requires a permanent tax-subsidy scheme encouraging expansion of the IRS industry and contraction of the DRS industry.[16]

The Panagariya result was generalized by Choi and Yu (1984a) in the neoclassical model with VRS. They showed that the first best policy (optimum optimorum) in the presence of VRS is the production tax-cum-subsidy such that the output of the industry exhibiting greater (smaller) elasticity of returns to scale is pushed to the maximum (minimum). They further showed why, under VRS, the optimality of free trade breaks down; that a tariff need not lower welfare; that a tariff is necessarily inferior to an equivalent production subsidy, but it may be inferior or superior to an equivalent consumption tax; and that an optimum tariff exists for a small country, and it can be positive, zero, or negative depending on the relative magnitudes of the elasticities of industrial returns to scale.

Choi and Yu (1987b) analyzed the effects of a tariff on import demand, terms of trade, domestic prices, and welfare, and showed that the standard results as known for the standard CRS case do not carry over to the case of VRS in a straightforward manner. They derived the condition for the Metzler (1949) paradox and the optimum tariff formula under VRS, and argued that the "optimum optimorum" for a large country under VRS requires both a production tax or subsidy to correct the domestic (VRS) distortion, and a tariff to correct the international distortion.

Yabuuchi (1990) extended the studies on tariff-immiserization in the presence of internationally mobile sector-specific capital by including VRS. He showed that, unlike the Brecher and Diaz-Alejandro (1977) proposition, under certain conditions, tariff-induced capital inflow improves the host country's welfare even if the foreign capital receives the full (untaxed) value of its marginal product.

Chao et al. (1990) showed that, under VRS, a tightening of import quotas reduces (or increases) welfare for a small country. They derived a formula for computing the optimal domestic price ratio under a quota. Chao et al. (1993) extended the analysis to a large-country case, and concluded that many of the conventional results on quotas may not hold in the presence of strong VRS. In particular, they derived the conditions under which a quota can benefit the exporting country, the importing country, or both countries, and the conditions under which a quota generates opposite effects on the price ratio and welfare relative to the initial effects when the quota is introduced.

Kemp and Tawada (1986) considered the properties of the world production set under conditions of VRS, with some, but not all, factors and products internationally mobile. They set out sufficient conditions for the convexity (concavity) of the world production frontier in each of the several alternative patterns of international specialization, and demonstrated that the world production set has the same properties as the production set of a single closed economy.

Panagariya (1986) presented a two-country two-good model in which economies of scale form the basis of international trade. He demonstrated that the larger country exports the good characterized by IRS and imports the good subject to CRS, and that if international factor mobility is allowed, "cross hauling" of specific factors may be seen and such factor flows are likely to complement the global flow of goods.

Study of trade policy (in particular, tariffs) under VRS was stretched to the domain of economic integration. Customs unions have received the most attention in research. Lipsey (1960) saw the theory of customs unions as a branch of tariff theory that deals with the effect of geographically discriminatory changes in trade barriers.

Development of the theory of customs unions owes much to Viner (1950), who demonstrated that such unions may be welfare-reducing based on the now familiar concept of trade creation and diversion.[17] Viner's proposition was later elaborated by Batra (1973), Bhagwati (1971b), Gehrels (1956), Johnson (1974), Lipsey (1957, 1960), and Melvin (1969b). It is noteworthy that all these studies focus on the static effects of forming customs unions. Balassa (1961), Chacholiades (1978), Cordon (1972), Leibenstein (1966), and Scitovsky (1958) discussed important effects of customs unions (other than the static effects), including economies of scale and the dynamic effects such as technical change, increased competition, and changes in investment pattern.

Yu (1981, 1982) distinguished two types of trade creation and trade diversion according to the manner in which trade is being created or diverted. Choi and Yu (1984b) examined the cost-reduction effect of a customs union by integrating economies of scale (IRS) into the standard model of a customs union. They showed that, under VRS, the two types of trade creation may be welfare-decreasing and the two types of trade-diversion may be welfare-improving, whereby crucial factors determining the welfare change are the types of trade creation and diversion, and the rank between the industrial elasticities of returns to scale.

Yabuuchi (2000) investigated the effects of forming export processing zones on factor rewards, national income, and the intermediate-good-producing sector under VRS. He showed that the results obtained in the model under CRS are substantially modified if VRS is incorporated.

The inquiry into VRS was further extended to the transfer problem. The conventional theory of the transfer problem, which owes much to Samuelson (1952) and Mundell (1960), states that, assuming market stability, the welfare of the transfer-paying (transfer-receiving) country decreases (improves) regardless of the direction of shift in the terms of trade.

Bhagwati et al. (1983) established a proposition that a necessary, though not sufficient, condition for the paradoxes of immiserized recipient and enriched donor is the presence of a distortion in the system. Choi and Yu (1987a) examined the welfare effects of a unilateral transfer in the presence of VRS, and obtained the conditions for the strong paradox (i.e., the welfare of the paying (receiving) country improves (declines)) and for the weak paradox (both the transferer and the transferee gain or lose simultaneously).

The theory of economic growth is a major subject of international trade with a relatively long history. Section 2 reviewed the VRS literature dealing with basic properties of economic growth, such as the Rybczynski theorem and the effects of technical progress on outputs (the Findlay–Grubert (1959) theorem). Here, our survey is expanded to the literature on the welfare consequences of growth for an open economy under VRS. As with other studies of VRS, the analysis of economic growth is usually conducted in the context of distortion.

In his 1894 article, Edgeworth suggested the possibility that an expanding economy might be worse off after growth if a deterioration in the terms of trade outweighed the output gain as a result of growth. The theory of economic growth was later refined by the contributions of Hicks (1953), Bhagwati (1958), Johnson (1958), and Prebisch (1959), among many others. In his seminal work, Johnson (1967) demonstrated the possibility of immiserizing growth in a small-tariff-distorted economy in which the terms of trade are held constant. Bhagwati (1971) generalized Johnson's result such that immiserizing growth must involve some suboptimality (i.e., distortion).

The welfare analysis of economic growth under VRS was first produced by Eaton and Panagariya (1982). They derived sufficient conditions for growth, rising either from factor accumulation or technical progress, to improve the welfare of a small country characterized by VRS.

Choi and Yu (1985) analyzed the welfare effect of Hicks-neutral technical progress for a small as well as a large country in the presence of VRS. In a two-sector VRS model, they showed that, for a small country, technical progress improves welfare if it occurs in the industry in which external economies (diseconomies) are greater (smaller), but technical progress in the other industry need not improve welfare. Further, they derived the conditions under which technical progress worsens the terms of trade in the case of a large country, and analyzed the effects of technical progress in both countries on the terms of trade and welfare.

Chao and Yu (1991) showed that growth of a small open economy distorted by an import quota, in contrast to the case of tariffs, improves welfare when industries display identical VRS, and that growth can be immiserizing if the industry that experiences technical progress exhibits smaller returns to scale than the static industry.

Among the general-equilibrium models, the model that has received the most attention other than the Heckscher–Ohlin type is probably the Harris–Todaro model of unemployment. In their pioneering work of 1970, Harris and Todaro presented a simple general-equilibrium model of unemployment, which delineates persistent urban unemployment and a dual economic structure in developing countries. The model assumes that there are two sectors in the economy, a rural (agricultural) sector and an urban (manufacturing) sector. Unemployment resulting from an institutionally set minimum wage is a problem for the urban sector. The minimum wage in the urban sector results in wage differentials between rural and urban, and the wage differentials cause rural–urban migration that occurs until there is an equality between the actual rural wage and the expected urban wage. The Harris–Todaro paper stimulated a spate of contributions from trade theorists, including Lal (1973), Stiglitz (1974), Cordon and Findlay (1975), Khan (1980), Neary (1981), McCool (1982), and Das (1982).

Recently, Panagariya and Succar (1986) investigated the implications of economies of scale (IRS) for several fundamental theorems (e.g., the Rybczynski and Stolper–Samuelson theorems) in a two-commodity two-factor Harris–Todaro model allowing intersectoral capital mobility. It is noteworthy that their analysis is confined to the case in which IRS is present in one of the two sectors in the Harris–Todaro model – the urban (manufacturing) sector.

Beladi (1988) examined the welfare implications of free trade with those of export-promoting policies and import-replacing policies in the Harris–Todaro model with VRS. He showed that the export-promoting and the import-replacing policies can be superior or inferior to free trade, depending on the relative magnitudes of the elasticities of returns to scale of the two sectors. Yabuuchi (1992) reconsidered Beladi's analysis in the context of dynamic stability, and established the conditions under which the Beladi result holds.

Choi et al. (2003) analyzed the effect of technical progress on sectoral outputs and welfare under VRS in the Harris–Todaro model. They demonstrated that, in the dynamically stable system, Hicks-neutral technical progress has an "ultra-biased" effect on sectoral outputs. In contrast to the CRS Harris–Todaro model, technical progress can be immiserizing for a small country in the VRS Harris–Todaro model.[18]

Recently, Anwar (1999) has utilized a simple model of a closed economy with a public good under VRS and unemployment (caused by rigid wages). He showed that differences in the level of government spending on a public good alone can explain the pattern of trade and factor mobility between otherwise identical economies.

4   TRADE THEORIES UNDER INTERINDUSTRIAL AND INTRAINDUSTRIAL EXTERNALITIES

The discussion so far has been confined to the case of VRS (i.e., intraindustrial externalities), and hence has precluded all traditional externalities between industries (i.e., interindustrial externalities). These have received great attention in the evolution of welfare economics since Meade's (1952b) classic work in this area. Noteworthy is that, despite the recognition as a major element of welfare in the field of international trade, interindustrial externalities have received considerably less attention than the intraindustrial type. However, some efforts have recently been made to investigate the implications of interindustrial externalities for international trade.

Hazari (1978) investigated the implications of a Meade-type (unidirectional) production externality for various theories of international trade in a two-commodity two-factor model whereby interindustrial externalities are conferred by the first industry to the second. In such a model, he examined gains from trade, the Rybczynski theorem, and the relationships between terms of trade, and welfare, between technical progress and output levels, and between growth, terms of trade and welfare. He showed that the conventional theorems (derived in the absence of interindustrial externalities) do not generally carry over in the presence of interindustrial externalities, because the nature and the magnitudes of the interindustrial externalities play a crucial role in determining the final outcome.

Herberg et al. (1982) examined the topology of the set of production possibilities and the locus of competitive outputs, and the validity of several standard trade theorems allowing the incidence of externalities to lie in any industry and in all industries (i.e., both intraindustrial and interindustrial externalities). In particular, they have shown that the robustness of several trade theorems (i.e., the sign pattern of price–output responses, the Stolper–Samuelson and Rybczynski theorems) is lost in such a model. These theorems can be fully or partially restored only under rather restrictive conditions concerning the nature of the returns to scale and the interindustrial externalities.[19]

Chang (1981) has studied the further implications for trade theory of intraindustrial and interindustrial externalities. By appealing to the stability properties of the model, he obtained some new or weaker conditions concerning the nature of the returns to scale and the interindustrial externalities for the full or partial restoration of several trade theorems (e.g., the Stolper–Samuelson and Rybczynski theorems), and the relationships among price, outputs, factor rewards, and factor endowment.

Yu (1987) investigated the implications of allowing the externalities to lie in any industry and in all industries, for the terms of trade and welfare for a growing economy. In particular, he obtained several sufficient conditions for the growth to be immiserizing in terms of nature and ranking between output elasticities of interindustrial externalities as well as the effects of growth on the terms of trade of a large country.

Yu and Choi (1991) examined several aspects of the standard theory of tariffs – the effects of a change in the tariffs/terms of trade on import demand, as well as the effects of a tariff on the terms of trade and the domestic price ratio – in a framework allowing both intraindustry and interindustry externalities. In an identical framework, Choi and Yu (1992) derived the optimum tariff formula for a tariff-imposing country. They demonstrated that the optimum tariff of both a small and a large country depends on the relative magnitudes of the value-adjusted interindustrial externalities and of the output elasticities of intraindustrial externalities. Yu and Choi (1992) extended the analysis to the theory of customs unions. They showed that the ranking between the output elasticities of interindustrial externalities plays a crucial role in determining the welfare effect associated with trade creation and trade diversion; in particular, the mere presence of interindustry externalities without being accompanied by intraindustry externalities may be sufficient to generate paradoxical welfare effects in a customs union.

On the transfer problem, Kumar and Wang (1984) examined the welfare effects of a transfer for the donor country in the presence of unidirectional interindustrial externalities (conferred from the export sector onto the import sector), and derived conditions under which the transfer may raise the donor's welfare. Choi (1990) analyzed the welfare consequences of a transfer for the donor and the recipient countries in the presence of bidirectional interindustrial externalities. For the general case of bidirectional externalities, the welfare effects of a transfer depend on the direction of the transfer-induced shift in the terms of trade and the relative strengths of the value-adjusted interindustrial externalities in addition to the primary welfare effect of the transfer.

Utilizing the Harris–Todaro framework, Chao and Yu (1994) presented an analysis of the short-run and long-run welfare implications of policies for promoting urban growth for LDCs under production externalities. They showed that the effects of tariffs, urban wage subsidies, and urban production subsidies in the short run do not carry over to the long run; and that, along with agglomeration economies and intersectoral externality, the urban unemployment ratio plays a key role in determining social welfare.

5 CONCLUSIONS

Economies of scale in production have long been recognized as a crucial determinant of international trade, but they have been by and large ignored in the theoretical modeling owing to difficulties of incorporating them into the general equilibrium model. In the postwar period, however, the emergence of two new patterns of world trade – namely, increasing intraindustry trade among nations and increasing share of world trade among industrialized nations – led many economists to investigate the role of production externalities for international trade. Numerous articles on this topic have appeared.

This chapter has surveyed the trade literature on production externalities, with an emphasis placed upon VRS (or intraindustry externalities) literature developed along Kemp's (1955) line of approach. That is, perfect competition can prevail under the condition of IRS if the economies of scale are external to an individual firm and internal to the industry, and they are output-generated. Also included in this chapter, albeit moderate in coverage, is a survey of trade literature on externalities which exist between industries rather than within an industry.

In recent years, production externalities have been increasingly recognized as a determinant of international trade. In this regard, a question may arise as to the importance of production externalities relative to the traditional comparative advantage as such a determinant. This survey has led us to formulate the view that both are important as they can reinforce or mitigate against each other (depending on the structure of the economy). It is desirable that production externalities should not be considered separately from the traditional perspective of factor productivity or factor endowments, but rather in conjunction with the latter. For example, Kemp (1964) has shown that, under identical IRS in the two industries, trade may result in specialization, but the direction of specialization is uncertain. Husted and Melvin (1997, p. 145) suggest historical accident as a possible determinant for the direction of specialization, but this seems too much of a generalization. To resolve this issue, we may invoke comparative advantage based on factor endowment. For instance, we consider a country that initially exports a small quantity of a good owing to its comparative advantage in terms of a favorable factor endowment for the good. With IRS, costs begin to fall as the production of the good expands with export. The cost-reduction effect generates momentum, eventually leading to specialization in production of the good. Intraindustry as well as interindustry externalities are particularly relevant to the formulation of a strategic trade policy which seeks to create a comparative advantage different from those traditional ones based upon factor endowments and factor productivity. The policy has been adopted by an increasing number of countries to develop fields such as cyberports, telecommunication, biotechnology, genetic engineering, and other high-technology industries considered instrumental for future growth.

Hong Kong, as one of the freest economies in the world, is currently embarking upon government-sponsored projects to develop high value-added industries characterized by production externalities. At the theoretical level, externalities play a crucial role in the recent endogenous growth theory which explains growth in the long run via induced externalities offsetting any propensity to marginal returns to capital accumulation.

To conclude this survey, further research in the area of intraindustry and interindustry externalities are suggested, as follows. The role of IRS can be re-examined in a simple dynamic two-period model or an infinite-period framework, which allow for intertemporal substitution in production and/or consumption. The role of externalities can also be re-examined in a monetary economy in which money is introduced via the cash-in-advance constraint, as modeled by Palivos and Yip (1997) and Chao and Yu (1999).

Acknowledgments

We are indebted to Wolfgang Mayer for many insightful comments. Any remaining shortcomings are our own.

Notes

1 According to Chipman (1965), the recognition of increasing returns to scale (as a principal determinant of international trade) can be traced back to Adam Smith's (1776) discovery of the division of labor as the fundamental source of the wealth of nations.

2 Chipman (1965) argues that IRS tends to be ignored in theoretical models not so much on empirical grounds, as for the simple reason that the theoretical difficulties are considerable. For detailed discussions on the compatibility of IRS with perfectly competitive equilibrium, see Chipman (1965, 1970).

3 Early studies of the classical theory include the empirical tests of the theory by MacDougall (1951), Stern (1962), and Balassa (1963b). For a summary of the various

tests of the neoclassical (Heckscher–Ohlin) theory following Leontief (1953), see, for example, Appleyard and Field (1992, ch. 9) and Husted and Melvin (1997, ch. 5).

4   Note that the current trend of increasing intraindustry trade and an increasing share of world trade among industrialized nations appear contradictory to the predictions based on the classical and the neoclassical theories, in which one might expect more international trade to take place for commodities that are produced using different factor proportions, and between countries that are different in economic structure and factor endowment.

5   The first group usually retains but modifies the general-equilibrium framework by assuming a second-best situation created by all sorts of endogenous and policy-induced distortions such as wage differentials, factor immobility, unemployment, taxes or subsidies, or output-generated intra- or interindustry externalities. The alternative approach and theories suggested by the latter group include the imitation lag hypothesis (Hufbauer, 1966), the product cycle theory (Vernon, 1966), the Linder theory of demand (1961), and the model of imperfect competition and economies of scale by Krugman (1979) and Helpman and Krugman (1985). Ethier (1979) broadened the idea of IRS from a national market to the world market. He emphasized the IRS of the world market (owing to ease of communication, the predominance of international firms, and the integrated world economy), and suggested a basis for a theory of trade in intermediate goods between similar economies.

6   See, for example, Kemp (1964, ch. 8) and Krugman (1979, 1983).

7   The cost reduction may arise due to lower factor prices. This is known as "pecuniary external economies." If the cost reduction occurs owing to the monopolistic industry supplying factors of production, perfect competition must be ruled out. However, if the cost reduction arises owing to technological external economies in the supplying industry, the pecuniary economies are of a technological variety, and hence compatible with perfect competition. For pecuniary externalities, see Chacholiades (1978), Chipman (1965), and Kemp (1955).

8   For discussion on homothetic industry production functions under VRS, see Kemp (1969) and Mayer (1974).

9   For multiple inflection points under VRS, see Herberg and Kemp (1969).

10   Herberg and Kemp (1969) showed that, in the presence of external economies, production may take place inside a PPF. However, with output-generated economies, the production equilibrium of a competitive economy remains on the PPF. See also Meade (1952a).

11   For the production equilibrium for multicommodity and multifactor case, see Choi (1987).

12   In response to the criticism of their 1969 theory of joint production, Herberg and Kemp (1991) argued that the theory does not rely on the indispensability of any factor of production and is valid whether or not there are industry-specific factors.

13   Johnson and Mieszkowski (1970) analyzed the problem in the traditional two-sector framework with CRS. They demonstrated that, if the unionized sector is relatively capital-intensive, union labor must gain and nonunion labor may also gain; but if the unionized sector is relatively labor-intensive, nonunion workers must lose, while union workers may also lose.

14   For analysis on Hicks-neutral, intensive-factor-saving, or intensive-factor-using technical progress under CRS, see Findlay and Grubert (1959), Johnson (1962, ch. 4), and Batra (1973, ch. 6).

15   For a neat summary of domestic distortions, see Chacholiades (1978, ch. 20).

16   Marshall (1890) presented arguments for taxing industries subject to DRS and subsidizing industries subject to IRS. Meade (1952b) assumed that taxes and subsidies are

such as to remove the divergence between private and social costs. See Chipman (1965, pp. 746–8) and Chacholiades (1978, ch. 20).

17 Before Viner (1950), it was generally believed that a customs union represents movement towards free-trade allocation of resources and hence is beneficial for the welfare.

18 Beladi and Naqvi (1988) showed that, for a small country, economic growth (resulting from either factor growth or technical progress) cannot be immiserizing in the Harris–Todaro model with CRS.

19 Production functions allowing both intraindustry and interindustry externalities can be written as $X_i = g_i(X_1, X_2)F_i(K_i, L_i)$ for $i = 1,2$. Output elasticity of interindustry and intraindustry externalities (e_{ij}) may be expressed as $e_{ij} = (\partial g_i/\partial X_j)(X_j/g_i)$ for $i, j = 1,2$. Here $e_{ii} > (<) 0$ for IRS (DRS) industry. If $i \neq j$, e_{ij} reflects the interindustry externalities. To assure that outputs are positively responsive to inputs, it is assumed that e_{ii} is defined in $[-\infty, 1]$ and $(1 - e_{ii})(1 - e_{jj}) - e_{ij}e_{ji} > 0$ for $i \neq j$. Further, it is assumed that $\lim_{x_j} \to 0$ $e_{ij} = 0$.

References

Anwar, Sajid 1999: Government spending, trade and capital mobility in the presence of unemployment. *Indian Journal of Applied Economics*, 8, 195–205.

Appleyard, Dennis R. and Alfred J. Field 1992: *International Economics*. Homewood, IL: Richard D. Irwin.

Balassa, Bela 1961: *The Theory of Economic Integration*. Homewood, IL: Richard D. Irwin.

Balassa, Bela 1963: An empirical demonstration of classical comparative cost theory. *Review of Economics and Statistics*, 45, 231–8.

Batra, Raveendra N. 1968: Protection and real wages under conditions of variable returns to scale. *Oxford Economic Papers*, 20, 353–60.

Batra, Raveendra N. 1973: *Studies in the Pure Theory of International Trade*. New York: St Martin's Press.

Beladi, Hamid 1988: Variable returns to scale, urban unemployment and welfare. *Southern Economic Journal*, 55, 412–23.

Beladi, Hamid and Nadeem Naqvi 1988: Urban unemployment and non-immiserizing growth. *Journal of Development Economics*, 28, 365–76.

Bhagwati, Jagdish N. 1958: Immiserizing growth: A geometrical note. *Review of Economic Studies*, 25, 201–5.

Bhagwati, Jagdish N. 1971a: Trade diverting customs unions and welfare improvement: A clarification. *Economics Journal*, 81, 580–7.

Bhagwati, Jagdish N. 1971b: The generalized theory of distortions and welfare. In Jagdish N. Bhagwati et al. (eds.), *Trade, Balance of Payments, and Growth*, Amsterdam: North-Holland.

Bhagwati, Jagdish N. and V. K. Ramaswami 1963: Domestic distortions, tariffs, and the theory of optimum subsidy. *Journal of Political Economy*, 71, 44–50.

Bhagwati, Jagdish N., Richard A. Brecher, and Tatsuo Hatta 1983: The generalized theory of transfers and welfare: Bilateral transfers in a multilateral world, *American Economic Review*, 73, 606–18.

Brecher, Richard A. and C. F. Diaz-Alejandro 1977: Tariffs, foreign capital and immiserizing growth. *Journal of International Economics*, 7, 317–22.

Chacholiades, Miltiades 1978: *International Trade Theory and Policy*. New York: McGraw-Hill.

Chang, Winston W. 1981: Production externalities, variable returns to scale, and the theory of trade. *International Economic Review*, 22, 511–25.

Chao, Chi-Chur and Eden S. H. Yu 1991: Immiserizing growth for a quota-distorted small economy under variable returns to scale. *Canadian Journal of Economics*, 24, 686–92.

Chao, Chi-Chur and Eden S. H. Yu 1994: Urban growth, externality and welfare. *Regional Science and Urban Economics*, 24, 565–76.

Chao, Chi-Chur and Eden S. H. Yu 1999: Shadow prices and trade restrictions in a monetary economy. *Journal of Macroeconomics*, 21, 755–64.

Chao, Chi-Chur, Hong Hwang, and Eden S. H. Yu 1990: Welfare effects of quotas under variable returns to scale. *Southern Economic Journal*, 57, 160–6.

Chao, Chi-Chur, Hong Hwang, and Eden S. H. Yu 1993: Effects of quotas under variable returns to scale: The large country case. *Southern Economic Journal*, 59, 675–86.

Chipman, John S. 1965: A survey of the theory of international trade. 2: The neoclassical theory. *Econometrica*, 33, 685–760.

Chipman, John S. 1970: External economies of scale and competitive equilibrium. *Quarterly Journal of Economics*, 84, 347–85.

Choi, Jai-Young 1987: Nontraded goods, variable returns to scale and welfare. *Southern Economic Journal*, 33, 874–83.

Choi, Jai-Young 1990: Transfers, welfare and inter-industrial externalities. *International Economic Journal*, 4, 55–67.

Choi, Jai-Young and Eden S. H. Yu 1984a: Gains from trade under variable returns to scale. *Southern Economic Journal*, 50, 979–92.

Choi, Jai-Young and Eden S. H. Yu 1984b: Customs unions under increasing returns. *Economica*, 51, 195–203.

Choi, Jai-Young and Eden S. H. Yu 1985: Technical progress, terms of trade and welfare under variable returns to scale. *Economica*, 32, 365–77.

Choi, Jai-Young and Eden S. H. Yu 1987a: Immiserizing transfer under variable returns to scale. *Canadian Journal of Economics*, 20, 634–45.

Choi, Jai-Young and Eden S. H. Yu 1987b: Nominal and optimum tariffs under variable returns to scale. *Oxford Economic Papers*, 39, 785–98.

Choi, Jai-Young and Eden S. H. Yu 1987c: Technical progress and outputs under variable returns to scale. *Economica*, 54, 249–53.

Choi, Jai-Young and Eden S. H. Yu 1992: Optimum tariff and production externalities. *International Review of Economics and Finance*, 1, 195–202.

Choi, Jai-Young, Eden S. H. Yu, and Jang C. Jin 2003, forthcoming: Technical progress, urban unemployment and welfare under variable returns to scale. *International Review of Economics and Finance*.

Cordon, Warner M. 1957: Tariffs, subsidies, and terms of trade. *Economica*, 24, 235–42.

Cordon, Warner M. 1972: Economies of scale and customs union theory. *Journal of Political Economy*, 80, 465–75.

Cordon, Warner M. and Ronald Findlay 1975: Urban unemployment, intersectoral capital mobility and development policy. *Economica*, 62, 59–78.

Das, Satya P. 1982: Sector specific minimum wages, economic growth and some policy implications. *Journal of Development Economics*, 10, 127–31.

Eaton, Jonathan and Arvind Panagariya 1979: Gains from trade under variable returns to scale, commodity taxation, tariffs and factor market distortions. *Journal of International Economics*, 19, 481–501.

Eaton, Jonathan and Arvind Panagariya 1982: Growth and welfare in a small open economy. *Economica*, 49, 409–12.

Edgeworth, Francis Y. 1894: The theory of international values. *Economic Journal*, 4, 35–50.

Ethier, Wilfred J. 1979: Internationally decreasing costs and world trade. *Journal of International Economics*, 9, 1–24.

Findlay, Ronald and Harry Grubert 1959: Factor-intensities, technological progress and the terms of trade. *Oxford Economic Papers*, 11, 111–21.

Gehrels, Franz 1956: Customs unions from a single country view-point. *Review of Economic Studies*, 24, 61–4.

Haberler, Gottfried 1950: Some problems in the pure theory of international trade. *Economic Journal*, 60, 220–40.

Harris, John R. and Michael P. Todaro 1970: Migration, unemployment and development: A two sector analysis. *American Economic Review*, 60, 126–42.

Hazari, Bharat R. 1978: *The Pure Theory of International Trade and Distortions*. New York: John Wiley.

Herberg, Horst and Murray C. Kemp 1969: Some implications of variable returns to scale. *Canadian Journal of Economics and Political Science*, 2, 401–15.

Herberg, Horst and Murray C. Kemp 1991: Some implications of variable returns to scale: The case of industry-specific factors. *Canadian Journal of Economics*, 24, 703–9.

Herberg, Horst, Murray C. Kemp, and Makoto Tawada 1982: Further implications of variable returns to scale. *Journal of International Economics*, 13, 65–84.

Helpman, Elhanan and Paul R. Krugman 1985: *Market Structure and Foreign Trade*. Cambridge, MA: MIT Press.

Hicks, John R. 1953: An inaugural lecture. *Oxford Economic Papers*, 5, 117–35.

Hufbauer, Gary C. 1966: *Synthetic Materials and the Theory of International Trade*. Cambridge, MA: Harvard University Press.

Husted, Steven and Michael Melvin 1997: *International Economics*, 4th edn. New York: Addison-Wesley Longman.

Ingene, Charles A. and Eden S. H. Yu 1991: Variable returns to scale and regional resource allocation under uncertainty. *Journal of Regional Science*, 31, 445–63.

Johnson, Harry G. 1958: *International Trade and Economic Growth*. London: George Allen & Unwin.

Johnson, Harry G. 1962: *Money, Trade and Economic Growth*. Cambridge, MA: Harvard University Press.

Johnson, Harry G. 1965: Optimal trade intervention in the presence of distortions. In R. E. Baldwin et al. (eds.), *Trade, Growth and the Balance of Payments*, Chicago, IL: Rand-McNally.

Johnson, Harry G. 1967: The possibility of income losses from increased efficiency or factor accumulation in the presence of tariffs. *Economic Journal*, 77, 151–4.

Johnson, Harry G. 1974: Trade diverting customs unions: A comment. *Economic Journal*, 84, 618–21.

Johnson, Harry G. and Peter M. Mieszkowski 1970: The effects of unionization on the distribution of income: A general equilibrium approach. *Quarterly Journal of Economics*, 4, 539–61.

Jones, Ronald W. 1966: The structure of simple general equilibrium models. *Journal of Political Economy*, 73, 204–12.

Jones, Ronald W. 1968: Variable returns to scale in general equilibrium theory. *International Economic Review*, 9, 261–72.

Kemp, Murray C. 1955: The efficiency of competition as an allocator of resource: I. External economies of production. *Canadian Journal of Economics and Political Science*, 30–42.

Kemp, Murray C. 1964: *The Pure Theory of International Trade*. Englewood Cliffs, NJ: Prentice Hall.

Kemp, Murray C. 1969: *The Pure Theory of International Trade*, 2nd edn. Englewood Cliffs, NJ: Prentice Hall, ch.8.

Kemp, Murray C. and Takashi Negishi 1970: Variable returns to scale, commodity taxes, factor market distortions and their implications for trade gains. *Swedish Journal of Economics*, 72, 1–11.

Kemp, Murray C. and Makoto Tawada 1986: The world production frontier under variable returns to scale. *Journal of International Economics*, 21, 251–68.

Khan, M. Ali 1980: The Harris–Todaro hypothesis and the Heckscher–Ohlin–Samuelson trade model. *Journal of International Economics*, 10, 527–47.

Krugman, Paul R. 1979: Increasing returns, monopolistic competition, and international trade. *Journal of International Economics*, 9, 469–79.

Krugman, Paul R. 1983: New theories of trade among industrial countries. *American Economic Review, Papers and Proceedings*, 73, 343–7.

Kumar, Rajib and Leonald F. S. Wang 1984: Production externalities and the transfer problem. *Indian Economic Journal*, 31, 73–8.

Laing, N. F. 1961: Factor price equalization in international trade and returns to scale. *Economic Record*, 37, 339–51.

Lal, Deepak 1973: Disutility of effort, migration and the shadow wage rate. *Oxford Economic Papers*, 25, 112–26.

Leibenstein, Harry 1966: Allocative efficiency versus X-efficiency. *American Economic Review*, 56, 392–415.

Leontief, Wassily W. 1953: Domestic production and foreign trade: The American capital position reexamined. *Proceedings of the American Philosophical Society*, 97, 332–49.

Leontief, Wassily W. 1956: Factor proportions and the structure of American trade: Further theoretical and empirical analysis. *Review of Economics and Statistics*, 38, 386–407.

Linder, S. Burenstam 1961: *An Essay on Trade and Transformation*. New York: John Wiley.

Lipsey, Richard G. 1957: The theory of customs unions: Trade diversion and welfare. *Economica*, 25, 40–6.

Lipsey, Richard G. 1960: The theory of customs unions: A general survey. *Economic Journal*, 70, 496–513.

Marshall, Alfred 1890 [1920]: *Principles of Economics*, 8th edn. London: Macmillan.

MacDougall, G. D. A. 1951: British and American exports: A study suggested by the theory of comparative advantage. *Economic Journal*, 61, 697–724.

Mayer, Wolfgang 1974: Variable returns to scale in general equilibrium theory: Comment. *International Economic Review*, 15, 225–35.

McCool, Thomas 1982: Wage subsidies and distortionary taxes in a mobile capital Harris–Todaro model. *Economica*, 49, 69–80.

Meade, James E. 1952a: *A Geometry of International Trade*. London: George Allen & Unwin.

Meade, James E. 1952b: External economies and diseconomies in a competitive situation. *Economic Journal*, 62, 54–67.

Meade, James E. 1955: *The Theory of International Economic Policy. II: Trade and Welfare*. Oxford: Oxford University Press.

Melvin, James R. 1969a: Increasing returns to scale as a determinant of trade. *Canadian Journal of Economics*, 3, 389–402.

Melvin, James R. 1969b: Comments on the theory of customs unions. *Manchester School of Economic and Social Studies*, 36, 161–8.

Metzler, Lloyd A. 1949: Tariffs, international demand and domestic prices. *Journal of Political Economy*, 57, 345–51.

Minabe, Nobuo 1966: The Stolper–Samuelson theorem under conditions of variable returns to scale. *Oxford Economic Papers*, 18, 204–12.

Mundell, Robert A. 1960: The pure theory of international trade. *American Economic Review*, 50, 67–110.

Neary, J. Peter 1978: Factor market distortions. *American Economic Review*, 69, 671–82.

Neary, J. Peter 1981: On the Harris–Todaro model with intersectoral capital mobility. *Economica*, 48, 219–34.

Palivos, Theodore and Chong K. Yip 1997: The gains from trade for a monetary economy once again. *Canadian Journal of Economics*, 30, 208–23.

Panagariya, Arvind 1980: Variable returns to scale in general equilibrium theory once again. *Journal of International Economics*, 10, 499–526.

Panagariya, Arvind 1981: Variable returns to scale in production and patterns of specialization. *American Economic Review*, 71, 221–30.

Panagariya, Arvind 1983: Variable returns to scale and the Heckscher–Ohlin and factor-price-equalization theorems. *Weltwirtschaftliches Archiv*, 119, 259–80.

Panagariya, Arvind 1986: Increasing returns, dynamic stability, and international trade. *Journal of International Economics*, 20, 43–63.

Panagariya, Arvind and Patricia Succar 1986: The Harris–Todaro model and economies of scale. *Southern Economic Journal*, 52, 984–98.

Parai, Amak K. 1985: Unionization and distribution of income under variable returns to scale. *Economics Letters*, 19, 95–8.

Prebisch, Raul 1959: Commercial policy in underdeveloped countries. *American Economic Review, Proceedings*, 49, 251–73.

Rybczynski, T. M. 1955: Factor endowment and relative commodity prices. *Economica*, 22, 336–41.

Samuelson, Paul A. 1952: The transfer problem and transportation costs: The terms of trade when impediments are absent. *Economic Journal*, 62, 279–302.

Savosnick, K. M. 1958: The box diagram and the production possibilities curve. *Ekonomisk Tidskrift*, 60, 183–97.

Scitovsky, Tibor 1958: *Economic Theory and Western European Integration*. Stanford, CA: Stanford University Press.

Smith, Adam 1776 [1977] *An Inquiry into the Nature and Causes of the Wealth of Nations*. London: J. M. Dent.

Stern, Robert M. 1962: British and American productivity and comparative costs in international trade. *Oxford Economic Papers*, 14, 275–96.

Stiglitz, Joseph E. 1974: Alternative theories of wage determination and unemployment in LDCs. *Quarterly Journal of Economics*, 88, 194–227.

Vernon, Raymond 1966: International investment and international trade in the product cycle. *Quarterly Journal of Economics*, 80, 190–207.

Viner, Jacob, *The Customs Union Issue*, New York: Carnegie Endowment for International Peace (1950).

Yabuuchi, Shigemi 1990: Tariff-induced capital inflow and welfare under variable returns to scale. *Economics Letters*, 33, 87–93.

Yabuuchi, Shigemi 1992: Variable returns to scale, urban unemployment and welfare. *Southern Economic Journal*, 58, 1103–9.

Yabuuchi, Shigemi 2000: Export processing zones, backward linkages, and variable returns to scale. *Review of Development Economics*, 4, 268–78.

Yu, Eden S. H. 1981: Trade diversion, trade creation, and factor market imperfections. *Weltwiltschaftliches Archiv*, 117, 546–61.

Yu, Eden S. H. 1982: Unemployment and the theory of customs unions. *Economic Journal*, 92, 399–404.

Yu, Eden S. H. 1987: Inter-industrial externalities, technical progress and welfare. *Southern Economic Journal*, 54, 412–21.

Yu, Eden S. H. and Jai-Young Choi 1991: The theory of tariffs under variable returns to scale and inter-industrial externalities. *Southern Economic Journal*, 57, 760–71.

Yu, Eden S. H. and Jai-Young Choi 1992: Inter-industrial externalities and the theory of customs unions. *International Economic Journal*, 6, 17–26.

Part II

Trade Policy

8

The Political Economy
of Trade Policy:
Empirical Approaches

Kishore Gawande and Pravin Krishna

CHAPTER OUTLINE

In order to explain the prevalence and persistence of trade protection, a large body of work that departs from the notion of welfare maximizing governments and emphasizes instead political-economic determinants of policy has recently emerged. This survey chapter summarizes and analytically evaluates the empirical component of this literature. We discuss a broad set of empirical findings that provide a convincing confirmation of the presence and significance of political economy influences. We also discuss some puzzles and controversies that have emerged in recent work.

1 INTRODUCTION

If, by an overwhelming consensus among economists, trade should be free, then why is it that nearly everywhere we look, and however far back, trade is in chains? Why do nearly all governments, unenlightened or enlightened, despotic or democratic, choose such apparently inefficient protectionist policies? In recent decades, an impressive theoretical and empirical literature on the "political economy of trade policy" has attempted to answer this question. The primary explanation offered in this literature is that suboptimal policies are chosen because policies are not set by those who seek to maximize economic efficiency.[1] Rather, they are set in political contexts where the objectives of the policy-makers are different from that of aggregate welfare maximization. This study of "endogenous" trade policy determination, which takes into explicit account the political circumstances under which policy is set, forms the core of the literature on the political economy of trade policy whose empirical ambitions and accomplishments to date this chapter attempts to survey.[2]

The main objective of this chapter, then, is to summarize and analytically evaluate the evidence in favor of endogenous protection. Conveniently for us, the literature has evolved in quite systematic ways. The early empirical work, until at least the late 1980s, mostly involved the examination of correlations between trade policies and various political economy factors that had been conjectured to be relevant in determining trade policy. While helping to loosely identify the relative importance of various political economy variables in determining policy, this literature has sometimes been criticized for employing econometric specifications whose links with the theories that motivated them were often only very tenuous. With the subsequent development of detailed theoretical platforms with strong econometric amenability, however, the recent empirical literature has moved in a somewhat "structural" direction establishing a much tighter link with the theory than has been traditional in this field (and, for that matter, in many other branches of economics). We begin by describing the methods and results of the traditional literature. We then discuss the various theoretical frameworks that have been developed to describe endogenous trade policy determination and the empirical attempts to evaluate the predictions that emerge from these theories. As with any intellectual endeavor, every success and resolution has only served to raise additional questions and challenges. Indeed, there has been a healthy interaction between theory and empirical work in this area, with the new set of theoretical models generating challenges and opportunities for empirical work and with the new empirical analyses, in turn, posing challenges for future theoretical development. We discuss some puzzles that have emerged in the current literature and discuss possible avenues for future work that may help resolve them.

2   THE DETERMINANTS OF TRADE POLICY: THEORETICAL CONJECTURES

This section discusses the broad set of economic and political factors that were conjectured to be relevant for trade policy determination and that formed the basis for much of the early empirical work in this area. Several hypotheses (explicated at various degrees of theoretical rigor and often only informally) were offered in the literature to answer the central questions of why industries received trade protection and why some industries received more protection than others. Following Baldwin (1985), on whom the following discussion relies quite heavily, these could be classified as follows:

- The *Pressure Group* or *Interest Group* model: This framework emphasizes the incentives faced by capitalists to influence politicians to move policy in a direction that would favor them – for example, we would expect capitalists in import-competing sectors to lobby governments for barriers against imports. In important contributions, Olson (1965), Peltzman (1976), Pincus (1975), and Stigler (1971), discuss the differing abilities of various industries to overcome free-rider problems and get organized to lobby government effectively. Since a small number of firms in the industry and a high degree of geographic and seller concentration imply a greater likelihood of effective coordination, the theory suggests that the level of protection in an industry and (equivalently) the ability of industries to resist trade liberalization should be positively linked with these variables. Olson (1983) also argues that economic groups may be more likely to organize in a context of a changing economic environment that threatens income and employment levels. This suggests further that industry protection be negatively related to industry *growth rates* in output and employment and positively related to increases in import penetration ratios. The theoretical demonstration by Mussa (1974) and Neary (1978) of the redistributive impact of tariffs in the presence of specific factors of production provided a foundation for understanding lobbying by specific factors such as industry specific capital or labor.

- The *Adding Machine* model, due to Caves (1976), emphasizes the voting strength of an industry in determining the extent of trade protection it receives. Since, according to this theory, elected officials tend to favor industries with the largest number of voters, the level of protection should be positively linked with the number of employees in the industry.

- The *Status Quo* model, due to Corden (1974) and Lavergne (1983), hypothesizes that government officials have "conservative respect" for the status quo, based either on regard for existing property rights (even in the form of rents generated by protection) or on a cautious response to the uncertainty associated with changes in policy, and further that governments wish to avoid large adjustment costs. Taken together, these dispositions imply that present protection should depend upon past levels of protection, a positive relationship between changes in tariff levels and changes in import penetration, and a positive relationship between changes in tariff levels and the variables used to measure the ability of workers in an industry to adjust to tariff reductions or changes in import penetration such as the proportion of old, unskilled and rural workers (whose ability to find new jobs is presumed to be lower) in a sector.

- The *Social Justice* or *Equity* model, due to Ball (1967), Constantopoulos (1974), and Fieleke (1976), emphasizes the motives of governments, on social justice grounds, to reduce the degree of income inequality in the economy by raising the living standards of the lowest income groups. This suggests that protection level will be high and tariff cuts will be low in sectors that employ low-income, unskilled workers.

- The *Comparative Cost* hypothesis suggests that industries in which the ratio of exports to production is high and the import penetration ratio is low will receive lower protection since they are not likely to be perceived as needing protection by either government officials or the management or labor force of the industry.

- The *Foreign Policy* model emphasizes the bargaining ability and possibilities
of countries in their trade negotiations as important determinants of trade
policy outcomes. Thus, for example, it is suggested that since developing countries had generally been exempt from the requirement of reciprocity in
matching the tariff cuts offered by industrial countries in the early postwar
rounds of trade negotiations, duty levels in industrial countries will be higher
on the exportables of developing countries relative to the exportables of other
developed countries practicing reciprocity. As another example, it is suggested
that a country would be more willing to lower its trade barriers against a
partner country in which it has substantial direct investment (since the bargaining ability of the foreign country is improved by its ability to restrict the
flow of earnings back to the investing country or otherwise lower the returns
on the investments).

The theories listed above propose several variables as determinants of trade policy:
industry size, employment, concentration ratios, levels of imports, changes in the
level of imports, and so on. A "first generation" of the empirical literature attempted
to explore the relevance of these variables using simple quantitative techniques and
regression analysis. We describe these results in the following section.

3   First Generation Empirical Evidence

A primary contribution of the "first generation" of empirical work on endogenous
trade policy was its demonstration of associations between protection levels and a
variety of political and economic variables.[3] The robustness of these findings provided a quite convincing affirmation of the endogeneity of trade protection.
Researchers also attempted to make inferences about the relative validity of particular theories of endogenous policy – a less successful enterprise, as we will argue
in some detail here.

A representative set of results are presented in table 8.1. Columns 1 and 2 present
Baldwin's (1985) estimates of alternate regression models attempting to explain the
cross-sectional variation of industry tariffs in the US. The dependent variable in both
columns is the average tariff level for the industry in 1976. The results indicate that
industries with low wages and a high level of labor per unit of output tend to be
highly protected. This gives some support to the social justice model that we have
described in the previous section: the government, acting on grounds of equity, provides the greatest protection to the low-income groups. They may also be interpreted as supporting, to some extent, the status quo model: protection levels are
high because the government is unwilling to lower tariffs in industries with low-
income (presumably unskilled and immobile) workers where the costs of adjustment to changes in the protection level would be the harshest. The adding machine
model receives support as well: protection levels are positively related to industry
employment levels. Finally, the number of firms in the industry (an inverse measure
of firm concentration and the ability of industries to overcome the free-rider
problem in getting organized to lobby) is negatively related to the level of trade

protection as predicted by pressure group theory. The comparative cost variables – the degree of import penetration and the degree of export orientation – do not show up as being significantly associated with the level of tariffs (although they are significant in other specifications not reported here). The foreign tax credits variable, representing the extent of investment abroad and thus the foreign policy model, does not appear as statistically significant in any of the specifications.[4] The measures of fit seem relatively high: up to half the interindustry variation in tariffs appears to be accounted for in some specifications.

Columns 3 and 4 in table 8.1 present estimates from Baldwin's (1985) regression model explaining tariff *cuts*. The dependent variable is the reduction in US tariffs in the Tokyo round of GATT negotiations (and is entered in the regressions with a *negative* sign). For the results presented in column 4, only industries in which the initial tariff level was greater than 5 percent were included. The regression results again suggest that industries with lower tariff cuts were industries in which workers tended to be unskilled and low paid. These industries were also ones with large numbers of workers, high and rising import penetration ratios, and high initial levels of protection. Thus, the adding machine model and the status quo model both find some support in these results. As Baldwin (1985) notes, however, proponents of other models can claim some support from these results as well. While variables such as firm concentration ratios and the number of firms in the industry, which represent the pressure group model, are not significant, other variables, representing (possibly) an industry's incentive to organize, such as changes in import penetration ratios and changes in employment, are significant. Thus, the pressure group model finds weak support in these results as well.

The econometric methodology employed in estimating the models we have just described is susceptible to criticism along several dimensions, regressor endogeneity being perhaps the most obvious among them. And the general absence of rigorous sensitivity analyses makes it hard to attach a great deal of credibility to inferences about any particular variable. The first study to address the two problems of regressor endogeneity and sensitivity to specification is the study of nontariff barriers (NTBs) in the US by Trefler (1993).[5] The final column in table 8.1 presents Trefler's estimates of the determinants-of-NTB equation, where the extent of NTB protection is measured by the NTB coverage ratio, that is, the fraction of commodities within any industry that is subject to any type of NTB. It indicates that comparative advantage factors (as measured by the change in the import penetration ratio, and the exports-to-value-added ratio) matter immensely to the determination of NTBs. A likelihood ratio test (not included in the table) indicates that comparative advantage factors (import penetration, changes in the import penetration ratio and exports) are at least five times as important as business interest factors (as measured by degree of concentration, scale, and capital measures). Additionally, the joint estimation of import penetration and NTB equations leads to a much higher estimate of the import restrictiveness of US NTBs than was in evidence in earlier studies of protection. These results illustrate the value of positive analysis in normative contexts:[6] considerations according to Trefler's estimates, US NTBs as of 1983 succeeded in restricting imports by $50 billion (that is, the import volume would be larger by $50 billion in the absence of NTBs) – a much higher

Table 8.1 Cross-sectional studies of the determinants of trade protection

Variables	Tariffs		Tariff Cuts		NTBs
	Baldwin (85) (1)	Baldwin (85) (2)	Baldwin (85) (3)	Baldwin (85) (4)	Trefler (93) (5)
Concentration					
Seller concentration	0.0002		−0.65 (−3)		.53**
Seller number of firms	−.46 (−5)**	−.32 (−5)**		−.14 (−4)	−.22*
Scale (output/firm)					−1.83**
Buyer concentration					1.13**
Buyer number of firms					−.06**
Geog. concentration					0.11
Trade					
Import penetration ratio		−0.02			0.17
Change in import penetration ratio			0.26	0.03**	3.31**
ln (Import Penetration Ratio)			0.54 (−2)	−0.03**	
Exports/value added					−1.82**
Exports/shipment	0.34 (−1)				
Capital					
Capital stock			.62 (−5)		−.27**
Labor					
Wage	−0.16 (−1)**			−0.13***	
Unskilled payroll/Total payroll		.14*	.97***		
Production workers/value added		.03**			
Unionization					0.1
Employment	0.94 (−4)*			0.51 (−3)***	0.08
Tenure					−0.01
% Change in employment	0.84 (−2)			−0.11*	
% Engineers and scientists					1.63*
% White collar					0.4
% Skilled					−0.31
% Semi skilled					0.15
% Unskilled					0.9
% Unemployed					1.22**
Labor intensity	0.19 (−1)				
Other variables					
Industry growth					0.03
Foreign tax credit/assets		1.1	9.90**		
Change in [(VA-Wages)/K-Stock]			−0.02		

Table 8.1   Cont'd

Variables	Tariffs		Tariff Cuts		NTBs
	Baldwin (85) (1)	Baldwin (85) (2)	Baldwin (85) (3)	Baldwin (85) (4)	Trefler (93) (5)
VA/Shipments		0.05		−0.14	
Tariff level			−0.13		
NTB indicator	0.46 (−2)**	.61 (−2)*	.03*		
Constant	0.26	0.150 (−1)	−0.81	−0.11	
Adjusted R²	0.39	0.51	0.1	0.18	
N	292	292	292	292	322

The dependent variable in columns 1 and 2 is the tariff level prior to the Tokyo Round of the GATT. In columns 3 and 4, the dependent variable is the average rate of tariff reduction in the Tokyo Round and is entered into the equations as a negative number. In column 5, the dependent variable is the NTB coverage ratio in 1983. All scaling is based on units of measurement in the original papers. See Baldwin (1985) and Trefler (1993) for detailed variable definition.
* denotes significance at the 10% level
** denotes significance at the 5% level
*** denotes significance at the 1% level
The number in parentheses indicates the direction and number of digits the decimal point should be moved.

estimate than those provided by single equation estimates that ignore the endogeneity of tariffs. From this, Trefler calculates that the 1983 NTBs on imports of manufactures had an *ad valorem* tariff equivalent somewhere between 20 percent and 40 percent. Lee and Swagel (1997) estimate a similar simultaneous equation system using a broader 1989 data set of pooled NTB data across industries and countries. They too find evidence consistent with a broad set of political economy theories of the determinants of protection and relatively high estimates of the impact of protection on trade flows.[7]

Overall, the results we have described above demonstrate the collective extent to which theories of endogenous protection explain inter-industry variation in trade barriers. They also illustrate the need to take explicit account of the positive aspects of trade policy determination in studying normative issues such as the impact of trade barriers on trade flows. The empirical results provide a measure of support to each of the theories that we have listed above.

Which theory has the greatest explanatory power? Gawande (1998a) attempts to formally compare (non-nested) models of endogenous trade protection using Bayesian methodology.[8] Roughly speaking, this proceeds as follows: First, in a nested comparison similar to the classic likelihood ratio test, the likelihood of a "full model" which uses a full set of explanatory variables relative to a model without variables representing a particular economic model (say the adding machine model)

Table 8.2 Comparisons of political economy models

Models compared	*Ad Valorem* Tariffs		Bilateral Price-NTBs		Bilateral Quant-NTBs	
	US – Japan	US – EC	US – Japan	US – EC	US – Japan	US – EC
1 F:F – IG	$6.3 * 10^4$	$2.31 * 10^{25}$	366	4880	1540	245.3
2 F:F – AM	39.47		14.52	3520	99.14	581.4
3 F:F – SQ	$3.98 * 10^8$	$2.98 * 10^{42}$	9.12	131.6	21.12	
4 F:F – SC	2.03	2.14	1.38	33.2		
5 F:F – CC	111.3	$7.03 * 10^5$	918.4	384.7	1780	$2.86 * 10^8$
6 F: F – (IG & AM)	$7.89 * 10^5$	Same as 1	63.15	$1.35 * 10^6$	$2.35 * 10^4$	$1.25 * 10^6$
7 F:F – (SC & SJ)	$5.43 * 10^7$	$4.91 * 10^{42}$	15.18	1050	Same as 3	
8 F – SI: F – AM	$6.25 * 10^{-4}$		0.04	0.71	0.06	2.37
9 F – SQ: F – SJ	$5.11 * 10^{-8}$	$1.12 * 10^{-43}$	0.15	0.25		

F denotes Full model, IG = the Interest Group model: (PAC/VA, Output per firm, Seller concentration); AM = Adding Machine model: (Number employed, %Unionized, Number of states with production, Seller concentration); SQ = Status Quo model: (Import Penetration, Earnings, Post-Tokyo Round Tariff.); SC = Social Choice model: (Payroll/Value-Added, Industry Employment growth, %Unskilled); CC = Comparative Cost model: (Bilateral Import Penetration, Bilateral exports/Value added, %Scientists, %Managers). EC denotes France, Germany, Italy and the UK. Blank cells indicate that the models are not comparable since at least two representative variables have the wrong sign. See original paper for details.
Source: *Gawande (1998a) tables 5a and 5b.*

is computed. The likelihood of the full model relative to the full model minus variables representing a different theory (say, the interest group theory) is then computed. Dividing the first ratio by the second provides a non-nested comparison of the likelihood of the first model relative to the other (the adding machine model relative to the interest group model in the present example). The results using data on post-Tokyo Round ad valorem tariffs are presented in table 8.2. Consider, for instance, the number 6.31×10^4 in the first column of table 8.2. This indicates that the full model (F) is 6.31×10^4 times as likely with the variables representing the special interest model (IG) than without them. The number 39.47 below it indicates how likely the full model is relative to the full model minus the variables that represent the adding machine (AM) model. Dividing the first ratio by the second yields the non-nested comparison of the IG model versus the AM model, given in row 8 as 6.25×10^{-4}. This exercise yields some interesting results. As the results in table 8.2 indicate, in the determination of US tariffs, the status quo (SQ) model performs exceedingly well. Taken together, the social justice (SJ) model and the status quo model dominate the interest group and the adding machine models – a conclusion that Baldwin (1985) reaches as well in the study of US tariffs that we have described above.[9] With nontariff barriers, the dominance is reversed: the interest group and the adding machine models are prominent and, taken together, dominate the status quo and social justice models overwhelmingly.[10]

A major drawback in studies that attempt to discriminate between models, as recognized, for instance, by Gawande (1998a) and Baldwin (1985), is that they require a prior and, importantly, one-to-one determination of which variables represent particular theories. And, unfortunately, there are significant overlaps. Similar (or identical) variables are argued to be proxies for quite different behaviors in different models. Thus, for example, both the pressure group model and the status quo model suggest that the level of protection should be positively related to the import penetration ratio. In the former framework, increases in import penetration may increase the incentives for import-competing lobbies to be formed and to lobby for higher protection, and in the latter model the government itself responds to increased import competition by providing higher tariffs in order to maintain the income levels of individuals in the import-competing sector. Similarly, the proportion of unskilled workers is claimed as a relevant proxy for both the social justice and the status quo models. In the former theory, industries with unskilled workers are granted higher protection on redistributive grounds. In the latter, protection is argued to be higher since unskilled workers are less mobile and would suffer disproportionately from any attempts to lower protection to their industries. This promiscuous relation between variables and theories and the inability of the literature to identify variables that would separate models more sharply has precluded the precise determination of the relative validity of the different models.

In partial response to these challenges, and aided by the theoretical development of formal models of political economy with increasingly well-specified microfoundations, the literature has moved in a "structural" direction, linking empirical work and the underlying theory more tightly. In the following section, we discuss the evolution of the formal theories of trade policy determination, from the early work of Findlay and Wellisz (1982), Hillman (1982), Magee et al. (1989), and Mayer (1984) to the more recent models of Grossman and Helpman (1994, 1995a), and discuss alongside the growing body of empirical work that has attempted to test the predictions of these theories.

4   THE DETERMINANTS OF TRADE POLICY: THEORETICAL MODELS

Where theoretical frameworks delivering specific and empirically testable predictions as to trade policy outcomes are concerned, there are two main branches in the literature. The first branch represents the direct democracy or *median-voter* approach. The implicit assumption in this formulation is that trade policy is actually being directly voted upon or alternately that the government chooses policies in a manner that reflects majority opinion on the issue. The second and dominant branch represents the *interest group* theories that we have mentioned before, where trade policy is seen to be determined by the interaction between the government and organized lobby groups representing the economic interests of their members. We discuss both sets of models and the empirical attempts to test them.

4.1 Median-Voter Model

In a uni-dimensional policy context (i.e., with a single policy variable under discussion, say an import tariff on a particular good) where individual preferences over this policy are single-peaked,[11] it has been shown that the median voter's preferred policy choice (e.g., the level of the tariff) cannot be dominated in a majority voting context by any alternative. This is the well-known median-voter result of Black (1958). Mayer's (1984) model of endogenous protection derives the implications of this median-voter result for trade policy in the context of fully specified general equilibrium models of trade. In the two-sector, two-factor, Heckscher–Ohlin version of Mayer's model, equilibrium trade policies are predicted to be as follows: If the median voter's ownership of capital is lower than mean ownership (as is the case in about all countries), trade policy is biased in favor of labor (as opposed to capital).[12] This implies that equilibrium trade policies are predicted to be biased against trade in capital-rich countries and for trade in capital-poor countries (since, as implied by the Stopler–Samuelson theorem, trade restrictions increase returns to *scarce* factors in a Heckscher–Ohlin world). We should expect to see import barriers in capital-rich countries and import subsidies in capital poor countries. Since trade policies are almost everywhere biased against trade, this prediction of the Mayer model is almost directly refuted by the data – bad news for the median-voter model.

Dutt and Mitra (2001) have focused, however, on a related prediction of the Mayer model that relates not to the absolute level of the tariffs but to the variation in the level of tariffs (as related to the degree of income inequality) across countries: It is easily verified, using the same reasoning as above, that an increase in the gap between the median capital–labor ratio and the mean capital–labor ratio raises barriers in capital-abundant countries and lowers them in capital-scarce countries. To test this prediction, Dutt and Mitra (2001), using a variety of measures of trade restrictiveness and income inequality, estimate relationships of the following type:

$$TR_i = \alpha_0 + \alpha_1 * INEQ_i + \alpha_2 * INEQ_i * (K/L)_i + \alpha_3 * (K/L)_i + \varepsilon_i \qquad (8.1)$$

where i indexes countries, TR denotes trade restrictions, $INEQ_i$ denotes inequality in country i and $(K/L)_i$ denotes the capital–labor ratio in country i.

Note that,

$$\frac{\partial TR}{\partial INEQ_i} = \alpha_1 + \alpha_2 * (K/L)_i.$$

Given that an increase in inequality leads to more restrictive trade policies in capital-abundant countries and less restrictive trade policies in capital-scarce countries, the theoretical prediction is that $\alpha_1 < 0$ and $\alpha_2 > 0$. This is precisely what Dutt and Mitra (2001) find. Thus, their findings provide tentative support for the median-voter model of trade policy determination.

The Dutt–Mitra framework conducts its analysis at a high degree of aggregation – it does not address, to any extent, the cross-sectional variation in tariffs within a country. Theoretical predictions regarding the cross-sectional pattern of tariffs in a median-voter context have been obtained by Mayer (1984) and also by Helpman (1997) in an economic context (i.e., with demand and supply relationships) identical to that of Grossman and Helpman (1994) – which we describe in greater detail in section 4.2.[13] Tariffs in this framework are predicted to be:

$$\frac{t_i}{1+t_i} = (1-\gamma_i^m)\left(\frac{z_i}{e_i}\right), \quad i = 1,\dots,n. \tag{8.2}$$

where γ_i^m denotes the fraction of specific capital in sector i that is owned by the median voter (with the mean ownership normalized to one), z denotes the inverse of the import penetration ratio and e denotes the absolute import demand elasticity. It should be readily evident that testing this prediction requires information on the median voter's characteristics on a sectoral basis that would be hard, if not impossible, to obtain in most contexts. Consequently, there have been no attempts in the literature to test the cross-sectoral predictions of the median-voter framework.

The multi-sector tariff predictions in the median-voter model described above have been derived under the assumption that ownership of specific factors is thinly dispersed in the population. Often, this is not the case. Ownership of production-specific production factors tends to be concentrated in the hands of relatively few agents. As Helpman (1997) points out, considering the extreme example of highly concentrated ownership, when all of the specific factor is owned entirely by a negligible fraction of the population, is instructive. In this case, members of the minority group that owns the factor in an import sector would vote for an import tax, whereas the rest would vote for an import subsidy (since they consume this good and would prefer to see its price lowered). The majority-voting outcome should therefore be an import subsidy. If anything, however, the opposite is generally true, i.e., import tariffs are seen instead – an observation that poses difficulties for median-voter theory.[14] A possible resolution of this puzzle derives from the argument of Olson (1965) that it is sectors with concentrated ownership that manage to overcome the free-rider problem and effectively lobby government to protect their sector-specific incomes. This argument gains substantial expression in the pressure group or interest group theory of trade policy determination that we consider next.

4.2   Interest Group Models

The interest group model that currently occupies center stage in the literature is the framework of Grossman and Helpman (1994), henceforth GH. GH models a small economy endowed with labor and n specific factors. These specific factors in combination with labor (which is mobile across sectors) produce n non-numeraire goods using CRS technology. In addition, a numeraire good (freely traded internationally) is produced using labor and Ricardian technology. Consumption preferences are identical across individuals within this economy and the representative agent's utility function is assumed to take the following quasi-linear form:

$$U = c_0 + \sum_i u_i(c_i) \tag{8.3}$$

where c_0 denotes consumption of the numeraire good (good 0) and c_i denotes consumption of goods $i = 1, \ldots, n$.

In order to see the basis for the popularity of the GH model, at least from the standpoint of empirical application, it is perhaps instructive to see what is predicted as to tariff rates in economies of the type described above by the interest group models in the literature that preceded GH. We consider two well-known models, both important theoretical contributions in their own right: Findlay and Wellisz's (1982) model using what has come to be called the "tariff formation function" and Hillman's (1982) model postulating instead a "political support function."[15] Our discussion borrows liberally from Helpman's (1997) survey of this literature.

4.2.1 TARIFF FORMATION FUNCTION

Findlay and Wellisz's (1982) seminal model describes the tariff rate as the outcome of lobbying competition between opposing lobbies in a two-sector, specific factors, general equilibrium of trade. The government, which receives the lobbying funds, trades off lobbying spending by two self-interested lobbies, one for protection and one against, and is represented simply by a tariff formation function (which takes the lobbying expenditure levels by the two lobbies as its arguments). Using the same economic structure as in the GH model, as described above, with lobbies lobbying to raise the domestic price of goods they produce and to lower the domestic price of the other goods they consume, with lobbying expenditure levels determined as the noncooperative outcome of a game in which each side chooses its lobbying expenditure to maximize its net benefits, and with tariffs ultimately determined by a tariff formation function just as in Findlay and Wellisz (1982), Helpman (1997) derives the following prediction for trade policy:

$$\frac{t_i}{1+t_i} = \frac{(1-\alpha_i)(b_i - 1)}{\alpha_i b_i + (1-\alpha_i)}\left(\frac{z_i}{e_i}\right), \quad i = 1, \ldots, n. \tag{8.4}$$

In (8.4), α_i is the proportion of the population that owns sector-specific inputs in sector i, and b_i is the marginal rate of substitution in the government's tariff formation function between the level of protectionist lobbying spending and the level of anti-protectionist lobbying spending. While b_i is positive, only when it is greater than one does a marginal dollar of protectionist lobbying raise the tariff by more than it declines as a result of an extra anti-protectionist lobbying dollar. Hence the sector is protected only when $b_i > 1$. If the marginal lobbying dollars are equally effective ($b_i = 1$), there is free trade.

4.2.2 POLITICAL SUPPORT FUNCTION

Hillman (1982) views instead the choice of the tariff rate as the solution to an optimizing problem in which the government trades off political support from industry interests against the dissatisfaction of consumers. Specifically, Hillman postulates a reduced form political support function for sector i with two arguments. The first argument is the gain in profits from a trade policy that raises the domestic price (p_i) over the free trade price (p), and the second argument is the loss in consumer welfare due to the price increase. Political support is increasing in the first argument but decreasing in the second. Using the same economic structure as in GH, Helpman (1997) derives the following prediction from the Hillman model:

$$\frac{t_i}{1+t_i} = \frac{1}{\alpha_{pi}}\left(\frac{z_i}{e_i}\right), \quad i = 1, \ldots, n. \tag{8.5}$$

In (8.5), a_{pi} is the marginal rate of substitution in the government's political support function between aggregate welfare and profits of special interests in sector i, which varies across sectors. Sectors in which special interests are active (a_{pi} is finite) will receive positive protection.[16]

As can be seen from (8.4) and (8.5), the tariff predictions of Findlay-Wellisz and Hillman (1982) are not directly testable since they contain characteristics of the tariff formation function and the political support function – the relevant marginal rates of substitution – which vary across sectors and are not observable. These difficulties are theoretically "resolved" in the GH model, which postulates a *linear* government objective function that trades off lobbying contributions with overall welfare at a constant rate, and derives closed-form expressions for the cross-sectional pattern of tariffs that are directly empirically testable.[17] It is to this framework that we next turn.

4.2.3 POLITICAL CONTRIBUTIONS APPROACH

As we have described above, Grossman and Helpman (1994) consider a multi-sector specific factor economy in which individuals have the quasi-linear preferences given by (8.3). Some of these sectors are politically organized. Others are not. The politically organized sectors influence politicians through campaign contributions. Politicians, in turn, maximize a linear objective function with two distinct components: political contributions by lobbies and aggregate social welfare. The interaction between the politicians and the lobbies is assumed to take the form of a menu auction (due to Bernheim and Whinston (1986)) where each organized lobby presents the government with a contribution schedule specifying the promised contribution level for each possible domestic price vector implemented by the government. In the first stage, lobbies present their contribution schedules, taking the contribution schedules of other lobbies as a given, and anticipating a second stage in which the government decides tariffs through an optimization process, taking all the lobby contribution schedules as a given. Protection across sectors is measured as a vector of import and export taxes and subsidies on the n goods. The GH framework makes the following prediction regarding the cross-industry pattern of protection:

$$\frac{t_i}{1+t_i} = \frac{I_i - \alpha_L}{a + \alpha_L}\left(\frac{z_i}{e_i}\right), \quad i = 1, \ldots, n. \tag{8.6}$$

In (8.6), $t_i = (p_i - p)/p$ is the *ad valorem* tariff or subsidy on good i in equilibrium, where p_i is the domestic price of good i and p its world price. On the right-hand side of (8.6), I_i is an indicator variable that equals one if sector i is organized into a lobby and zero otherwise. The parameter α_L is the fraction of the population organized into lobbies. Since not all industries are necessarily organized, $\alpha_L \leq 1$. $a > 0$ is the constant weight that the government places on aggregate welfare relative to aggregate political contributions in its linear objective function. $z_i = y_i/m_i$ is the equilibrium ratio of domestic output to imports (exports if m_i is negative) and $e_i = -m_i'p_i/m_i$ is the elasticity of import demand (positive) or export supply (negative).

The influence exerted by organized interests in securing trade protection is easily seen in (8.6). If industry i is an import-competing producer and it is organized ($I_i > 0$), then it is able to "buy" protection and obtains a protective import tax ($t_i > 0$). If it is an import-competing producer but it is not organized ($I_i < 0$), it receives a penalizing import subsidy ($t_i < 0$) instead. If industry i is an exporter and is organized, it is able to "buy" an export subsidy ($t_i > 0$), but if it is unorganized, then its exports are taxed. Three additional factors are emphasized: first, industry's stakes from protection, as measured by the output-to-import ratio, z_i, determine the extent of protection the industry receives.[18] Second, protection depends inversely upon the elasticity of import demand – this follows from the familiar Ramsey pricing scheme, that the best way to tax goods while minimizing welfare loss is to tax goods with low (absolute) demand elasticities at a higher rate than goods with high demand elasticities. Finally, the extent of lobbying competition manifests itself in the tariff expression. If all sectors were organized and in competition, they would cancel each other out: with the population entirely organized, we have $I_i = 1$ for all i, implying that $\alpha_L = 1$ and $t_i = 0$ for all i.

(8.6) may be written in an empirically testable form as:

$$\frac{t_i}{1+t_i} = \frac{\alpha_L}{a + \alpha_L}\left(\frac{z_i}{e_i}\right) + \frac{1}{a + \alpha_L}\left(I * \frac{z_i}{e_i}\right), \quad i = 1, \ldots, n. \tag{8.7}$$

Then the predictions are (i) the coefficient on z_i/e_i is negative, (ii) the coefficient on $I_i \times (z_i/e_i)$ is positive, (iii) and since $\alpha_L \leq 1$, the sum of the coefficients must be non-negative. In addition to those qualitative predictions, a quantitative implication of (8.7) is that the coefficients on z_i/e_i and $I_i \times (z_i/e_i)$ may be used to infer the size of a – the weight that government places on aggregate welfare relative to the weight on aggregate political contributions.

The predictions of the Grossman and Helpman model were first tested in two papers, Goldberg and Maggi (1999) and Gawande and Bandyopadhyay (2000).[19] The protection measure in both studies is the NTB coverage ratio in the US.

Table 8.3   Grossman and Helpman (1994) model estimation results

Variable	Gawande and Bandyopadhyay (2000)	Goldberg and Maggi (1999)
$\dfrac{z}{\varepsilon}$	3.08**	−0.009**
	(2.02)	(2.33)
$I\dfrac{z}{\varepsilon}$	3.14**	0.011**
	(2.00)	(2.00)
N	242	107
R^2	0.23	

See original papers for details on estimation procedure and variable definition. Additionally, only an abridged version of Gawande and Bandyopadhyay's specification is presented here. See the original paper for the full specification.
*** denotes significance at the 5% level*
Gawande and Bandyopadhyay (2000), and Goldberg and Maggi (1999).

Estimation of (8.7) requires data on two variables that are not directly measurable: import-demand elasticities and domestic political organization. For import-demand elasticities, both studies use estimates reported by Shiells et al. (1986). Both also use data on corporate political contributions to assign the domestic political organization variable, I. The assignment of I itself is done differently in the two studies, however. Goldberg and Maggi (1999) use various threshold levels in campaign contributions to determine whether the domestic organization variable is to be assigned the value 1. On the other hand, noting that the data on campaign contributions are overall contributions and not just contributions for trade related matters, Gawande and Bandyopadhyay assign the domestic political organization variable in the following manner: they first examine, using simple OLS regressions, the correlations between campaign contributions and a number of right-hand-side variables including measures of imports. In the next step, the organization variable is assigned the value 1 for those industries for which the relationship between campaign spending and trade flows is positive. Gawande and Bandyopadhyay also explicitly account for intermediate goods. The main results from these two studies are presented in table 8.3.

Table 8.3 shows that, despite the differing methodologies used in assigning the domestic contribution variable, both authors find support for the theory in the data. Political organization is found to influence the interindustry difference in trade protection in the manner predicted by the theory. *Ceteris paribus*, tariffs are higher, on average, in industries represented by organized lobbies.

Two issues relating to the data used in the estimation of (8.7) are worth noting. First, consider the variable on the left-hand side of (8.7), the *ad valorem* rate of protection t_i. In a world in which only tariff barriers are used, obtaining measures of t_i would be a relatively simple task. However, in practice, the trade barriers used are a complicated combination of tariff and nontariff barriers. Indeed, trade protection has been heavily dominated in recent decades by the use of nontariff barriers. The tests of GH we have discussed so far have both relied upon NTB data, using the

NTB coverage ratio as a proxy for the protection rate. However, it is unlikely that NTB coverage ratios accurately represent the actual extent of protection. Thus, consider the extreme example of a sector in which most goods are protected, albeit by large nonbinding quotas. The coverage ratio measure would be very high. However, the fact that the quotas are nonbinding implies that, at least in a perfectly competitive context, the level of actual protection is zero. Thus, the coverage ratio greatly overstates the extent of protection in this case. Equally, in sectors in which only a small fraction of goods are protected, but with very restrictive quotas, we have the coverage ratio possibly under-representing the extent of protection. This points to a difficult and potentially insurmountable issue with testing the model. Using data on tariffs alone in a world with significant NTB protection leads to inaccurate measures of the level of protection. Using NTB coverage data leads to a measurement error of a different sort. And constructing tariff equivalents of all NTBs with any acceptable degree of precision is an extremely challenging task.[20]

A second and equally important data issue arises in the assignment of the political organization variable, I. As we have mentioned previously, existing studies have relied upon data on corporate campaign contributions to assign this variable, thereby raising (at least) two issues. First, the corporate campaign contributions data represent overall contributions by corporations, not merely contributions intended to sway trade policy. The only attempt to identify trade-related corporate contributions has been by Gawande and Bandyopadhyay (2000), who, as we have discussed previously, assign the organization variable on the basis of significant association of corporate contributions with trade flows. While this is a reasonable first step, it has the demerit of being altogether ad hoc. Clearly, an analytically sound approach is desired. Second, the focus on corporate contributions has resulted in the exclusion of an equally important source of political contributions, labor unions. Although data on political contributions by labor unions is available, the problem has been that most of the labor lobby groups are aggregate lobbies combining workers from several different industries. The estimation of the GH model with US data has industries disaggregated at the 3- or 4-digit SIC level instead. It would be useful to use data on union membership to disentangle the 4-digit composition of unions, a task that Gawande and Krishna (2001a) have recently undertaken.

What else do we learn from the estimation of (8.7)? A distinguishing feature of the GH framework – in contrast with most empirical work conducted in economics – is the very close match between the economic model and the equation actually estimated. This match enables inference on values of the structural parameters of the model – in this case, the values of the parameter a which measures the preference of the government for welfare relative to campaign contributions. Clearly, for the model to have significance, the weight that government places on campaign contributions ($1/a$) must be relatively high. The more the government veers towards welfare maximization (i.e., the higher is a), the less appealing is the entire political economy enterprise. The Maggi–Goldberg and Gawande–Bandyopadhyay results suggest, however, that the estimates of a are really rather large: ranging from 100 to 3,000. Although such a magnitude does not compel rejection of the model, which does not specify any priors on the value of a, it is enough to cast doubt on the value of viewing trade policy determination through this political economy lens.

Equally troubling is the magnitude of the political contributions in relation to the level of the trade barriers. Thus, for instance, in the period studied by Maggi–Goldberg and Gawande–Bandyopadhyay, overall political contributions (again, not just trade-related) were in the range of $30 million. This is quite a small number compared to the efficiency losses in trade distortions alone, not to speak of the increase in producer surplus from the tariffs – the relevant consideration for corporate contributors.[21] Political contributors seem to be getting a much larger payoff in terms of trade protection than is suggested by the theory. The extent of the departures of the theoretically predicted contribution levels from the actual contribution levels given the amount of protection that is actually observed is investigated in Gawande and Krishna (2001b).

Finally, a direct implication of (8.6), as we have noted above, is that industries with higher levels of output relative to their trade volumes, but with the same trade elasticities, are predicted to get greater amounts of protection. As Rodrik (1995) has pointed out, this serves to illustrate the basic puzzle in the literature of why trade policies are biased against trade rather than being in favor of it. If the idea of comparative advantage carries any force, specialization in exportables will imply that the exportable sector will be larger than the importable sector. Equation (8.6) implies, in turn, that, *ceteris paribus*, we should observe a bias towards export subsidies rather than import tariffs.[22] That we observe, in general, a bias in policy against trade rather than for it is, as Rodrik (1995) has forcefully argued, a problematic issue. While a few theoretical attempts have been made to resolve this, we know of no empirical papers on this topic in the literature to date.

Do variables omitted from the empirical specification (8.7) matter? Both Gawande and Bandyopadhyay (2000) and Goldberg and Maggi (1999) have estimated extended models by including on the right-hand side of (8.7) a large number of additional regressors. Happily for the GH model, the coefficient on domestic organization survives (i.e., it remains positive and significant in most specifications). However, the estimates from the extended models raise other issues for the GH model. Thus, an extended specification estimated by Gawande and Bandyopadhyay, which includes the industry concentration ratio on the right-hand side in addition to the domestic organization variable, finds the coefficient on the concentration ratio to be significant. Equally, Gawande, Krishna, and Robbins (2001), whose work we discuss in greater detail below, also find that concentration ratios matter for trade policy, *even after* domestic organization is included in the right-hand side in the estimation of (8.7). Since a primary contribution of the GH model is its detailed articulation of the interaction between organized domestic interests and the government and the implications of this for trade policy, the finding that the determinants of political organization (e.g., concentration ratios, as Olson (1965) has argued and as we have discussed above) have a bearing on trade policy in a manner that is beyond that predicted by GH suggests that the role of political organization in determining trade policy has not been fully accounted for by the theory.

An important aspect of trade policy determination that is altogether excluded from GH and from the empirical exercises is the role played by international trade negotiations: GH treats trade policy as if it were determined entirely by domestic political pressures. A theoretical extension of GH, based on the idea of Putnam

(1988), that allows for international negotiations has, however, been provided by Grossman and Helpman (1995a).[23] In their "trade talks" equilibrium, the world trade policy vector is determined by cooperative bargaining between two governments.[24] Organized lobbies in both countries anticipate this in making their political contributions to their governments. The model provides the following (potentially) testable implications regarding trade policy:

$$\tau_i^h - \tau_i^f = \left(-\frac{I_i^h - \alpha^h}{a^h + \alpha^h} \frac{X_i^h}{\pi_i M_i^{h0}} \right) - \left(-\frac{I_i^f - \alpha^f}{a^f + \alpha^f} \frac{X_i^f}{\pi_i M_i^{f0}} \right) \tag{8.8}$$

where, π_i denotes the world price of good i, τ_i^h denotes the domestic price of good i in the home country, τ_i^f denotes the domestic price of good i in the foreign country, X_i denotes output and M_i denotes volume of imports (or exports) of good i. Intuitively, with international negotiations over trade policies, special interests in the two countries in any given industry take opposing sides. Each would like the trade policy vector to be bent in a direction that favors it at the expense of the other. Thus, if industry i is organized in country X, but not in country Y, this industry is predicted to obtain positive protection in X and negative protection in Y. Empirical tests of this prediction obviously require data on cross-sectional variance in political influences abroad. Unfortunately, actual implementation of such tests has been inhibited, to date, by the apparent absence of any data sets on political contributions by organized interests in other countries.

Foreign lobbies operating in the US and their influence on US trade policy are investigated in a recent paper by Gawande, Krishna, and Robbins (2001). They observe first that the domestic presence of foreign lobbies could be welfare improving since foreign lobbies would lobby to lower tariffs, and proceed to investigate this idea empirically. The theoretical platform supporting their empirical exercise is an oligopolistic extension (with linear demand and constant marginal costs) of GH. Equilibrium domestic tariffs are predicted to be (approximately):

$$\frac{\tau_i}{P_i} = \left[\frac{2I_i^h}{(a+\alpha)} + \left(\frac{2a}{a+\alpha} \right) \right]\left(\frac{z_i}{e_i} \right) - \left[\frac{2I_i^f}{a+\alpha} \right] \cdot \left(\frac{z_i}{e_i} \right) \tag{8.9}$$

where I^h and I^f are dummy variables denoting domestic and foreign organization. The model therefore implies that sectors politically represented by organized domestic lobbies are, *ceteris paribus*, likely to receive more protection and that sectors in which there is foreign political presence are likely to receive less protection. Finally, sectors in which there is neither domestic political representation nor foreign political presence are predicted to receive positive protection (which should not be surprising given the imperfectly competitive nature of the product market). The predictions are tested by estimating the following equation:

$$\frac{t_i}{1+t_i} = \beta_1\left[\frac{z_i}{e_i} \right] + \beta_2\left[I^h \cdot \frac{z_i}{e_i} \right] + \beta_3\left[I_i^f \cdot \frac{z_i}{e_i} \right] \tag{8.10}$$

where t_i denotes the (effective) *ad valorem* import tax (i.e $\tau_i/(P_i - \tau_i)$) and where $\beta_1 = 2a/(a + \alpha)$, $\beta_2 = 2/(a + \alpha)$ and $\beta_3 = -2/(a + \alpha)$ (where, clearly, β_1 and β_2 are greater than zero and β_3 is less than zero).

Gawande, Krishna, and Robbins (2001) estimate (8.9), using a recently compiled data set on foreign lobbying presence in the US and find broad support for the theory. Domestic organization and foreign organization are found to influence tariffs in a manner predicted by the theory. Specifically, industries with organized foreign lobbies have lower trade protection on average than industries without such lobbies.

One of the primary contributions of GH is that it provides the theory of government–lobby interactions with strong micro-foundations. Nevertheless, GH takes the presence of some organized lobbies to be given, paying little attention to the motivations of lobbies to get organized in the first place. From the standpoint of estimating the impact of lobbying on trade policies (the estimation of GH's basic equation (8.6), for instance), this is not a major problem since all the right-hand-side variables, including the organization dummies I and I^*, are treated as being endogenous in the empirical implementation. However, without a theory of lobby formation and estimates of the relative importance of the factors that determine lobby formation we cannot answer interesting comparative statics questions such as what happens to tariffs as the parameter a changes in (8.6), or what happens to tariffs if foreign political influence is somehow legally eliminated in (8.8).[25]

Given the prominence of interest group theories of protection in the literature, surprisingly little empirical work on the actual mechanics for lobbying for protection has been done.[26] While there has been indirect evidence on pro- and anti-protectionist preferences of firms (see, for example, Magee (1980), and Pugel and Walter (1985)), there is little direct analysis of their trade-directed lobbying efforts. The difficulty here is that lobbying spending is directed at a variety of redistributive instruments, of which trade protection is but one. Lobbying data thus come as a bundle, and it is difficult to disentangle the purely trade-related component of lobbying data. This problem may be alleviated by considering a set of industries whose primary lobbying concern is trade protection, as do Lopez and Pagoulatos (1996) for the food processing and tobacco industries. But to do a full cross-sectional study for all of manufacturing requires more care, both in the measurement of lobbying as well as its econometric treatment.

Some progress on investigating the incentives for lobby formation and lobby behavior in the context of trade policy determination is made in a study by Gawande (1998b), who examines the theoretical predictions of the Magee et al. (1989) model of lobby organization.[27] Magee et al. (1989) formalize Olson's (1965) intuition about how the free-rider problem makes lobby organization more difficult and arrive at predictions regarding the relationship between industry lobby spending and industry benefits from protection and the relationship between contributions per firm and the extent of the free-rider problem within the industry. Using cross-industry data on political contributions by corporate lobbies, Gawande finds evidence in support of these hypotheses. Gawande and Bandyopadhyay (2000) also investigate the lobbying side of the GH (1994) model. The evidence affirms the main GH prediction that lobby spending varies according to the deadweight loss from protection.

A second hypothesis on the lobbying side of the model is that competition among lobbies induces them to spend according to the political strength of their rivals, where rivalry is measured in terms of lobbying competition from downstream lobbies. Gawande and Bandyopadhyay (2000) find that PAC spending rises with the share of an industry's output used by downstream industries as intermediate inputs and with the concentration of downstream users.

Thus far, our discussion has mostly focused on the extent to which we can explain departures from free trade by appealing to the conjecture that policy makers in making their decisions regarding trade policy place an additional value on particular groups in society (be they immobile low-income workers or corporate interests). Somewhat implicit in this argument then, is the idea that free trade is the optimal (i.e., aggregate welfare maximizing) policy choice for governments and the policy that would be chosen had not governments such skewed preferences. As a caveat, it is, therefore, worth noting that the theoretical proposition that aggregate welfare is maximized by free trade only holds under the assumptions of a small, decentralized, competitive economy. As is well known, the *theoretical* literature on trade policy has demonstrated that with any departure from these assumptions, trade restrictions may improve upon the country's free trade level of welfare – even if *trade* restrictions are nearly always dominated in this regard by alternative policy instruments, as Bhagwati (1971) has shown.[28] Thus, in a wide variety of contexts, such as when a country is "large" in the production or consumption of its tradables (and therefore has monopoly power in trade) or in the presence of market failures, such as externalities in production or consumption, imperfectly competitive product or factor markets or in environments involving uncertainty, trade interventions have been shown theoretically to improve national welfare.[29] The literature has also argued that the practical value of such arguments for trade policy intervention may be limited due to the presence of rent-seeking (as in Krueger (1974)) or directly unproductive profit seeking (DUP) activity (to use Bhagwati's (1982) terminology) that dissipates any gains or due to informational constraints that limit the government's ability to recognize the appropriate contexts for trade interventions when (and if) they exist. Nevertheless, it can at least be argued that, in principle, observed interventions in trade may be (partially) explained by governments acting in cognizance (or perception) of such factors as externalities or imperfectly competitive product markets as we have listed above.[30] With the exception of some case studies,[31] the *empirical* literature has, however, not examined these as explanatory factors, or attempted to separate their explanatory power from that of political economy factors in any *systematic* fashion. They remain essential topics for future research.

5 TOPICS

Our discussion so far has focused on cross-sectional studies of the determinants of trade barriers. While this has certainly dominated the research interests of scholars working in the field, the literature has also examined a number of other topics. These include historical analyses of the enactment of major trade laws, attempts to discriminate between canonical trade models such as the Heckscher–Ohlin model and the specific factors model on the basis of observations of sectoral and class cleavages in attitudes towards trade policy, time-series analyses of the aggregate patterns of tariffs, case studies of various forms of administered protection, and the political economy of preferential trade agreements. This is an enormous literature whose detailed description here is precluded on account of space limitations. We limit ourselves to presenting some highlights from recent work.

5.1 Historical Studies of Major Trade Policy Measures

Irwin and Kroszner (1996) study voting patterns in the US Senate over tariffs on specific goods in order to understand the factors influencing the passage of the infamous Smoot–Hawley Tariff Act of 1930. Contrary to some other studies, which emphasize the partisan nature of voting over Smoot–Hawley, they identify the significant influence of economic interests in Senators' constituencies on the voting pattern.

Irwin and Kroszner (1999) study the Reciprocal Trade Agreements Act (RTAA) of 1934 through which Congress delegated its authority over tariff making to the President, giving him the authority to undertake reciprocal tariff reduction agreements with foreign countries without congressional approval. As an example of institutional change, the enactment of the RTAA is most interesting since it was passed just four years after the US Congress passed the Smoot–Hawley tariff, and it marked the beginning of a trend towards trade liberalization. The RTAA was enacted in the context of substantial differences in opinion across parties on the matter of tariffs. It was only firmly established after Republicans, long-time supporters of high tariffs who originally vowed to repeal the RTAA, began to support this Democratic initiative. Was this an ideological shift? Or was this prompted by shifting economic interests? Irwin and Kroszner use a detailed examination of the congressional voting record on the RTAA to argue that it was increased sensitivity to exporter interests (which the institutional structure of the RTAA, by providing greater incentives for exporters to develop as an organized lobby group, itself may have had stimulated) rather than ideological shifts that was responsible for the Republican conversion.[32]

5.2 Sectoral and Class Cleavages in Attitudes Towards Trade Policy

The question of whether trade-related political behavior takes place mostly along sectoral (industry) lines or along class (factor-ownership) lines has attracted the attention of numerous economists and political scientists. Two canonical models of international trade – the two-sector, two-factor Heckscher–Ohlin model and the Ricardo–Viner or specific factors model – provide divergent predictions. The former, where full mobility of factors across sectors is assumed, predicts that the country's relatively abundant factor of production gains with trade liberalization and that the less abundant factor loses, thus implying that there will be a split along class lines on the issue of trade liberalization. The latter, where factors of production are assumed to be specific to sector, predicts that economic interests will be organized along sectoral lines instead.

An early empirical analysis to discriminate between these competing hypotheses was conducted by Magee (1980), who examines testimony before the House Ways and Means Committee on the Trade Reform Act of 1973 and finds substantial support for the specific factors model, that in the vast majority of industries, factors of production are aligned along sectoral lines. Additional support for the specific factors model is provided by the more recent work of Irwin (1996), who examines voting patterns in the British general election of 1923, an election that hinged on the issue of free trade, and finds the occupational structure of the electorate to be far more significant in explaining the election outcome than was class structure. Baldwin and Magee (2000), in their examination of voting patterns by US Representatives on major trade bills (e.g., on the North American Free Trade Agreement), find stronger evidence supporting the class cleavage predictions of the Heckscher–Ohlin model than have previous voting studies. Factor status variables (such as the proportion of less educated workers in a representative's district) appear to have significant impacts on voting behavior. They find less support for the specific factors model. Few of the variables indicating occupational structure (e.g., the proportion of employment in particular industries) had large impacts on congressional voting. However, the prior policy views of legislators, as measured by their ratings by interest groups, were found to be important determinants of representatives' voting decisions. It should be readily evident, however, that to the extent that the policy positions taken by the representatives are likely to take into account the occupational/class structure of their constituents, it is difficult to infer the validity of particular theories from these estimates (for instance, because sectoral pressures may reflect themselves strongly through the policy position variable in ways that are not fully captured by the variables representing the sectoral status of the district in the multivariate regressions).

5.3 Trends in Trade Policy and Time-Series Studies

The literature has discerned two distinct trends in trade policy over the past decades. First, trade restrictions have been falling over time – in some cases (mostly developing countries) rather dramatically.[33] Second, countries have shifted away from tariffs to somewhat more complex forms of nontariff protection (see also section 5.4).

Decreasing budgetary reliance on trade taxes (relative to income taxes) as countries grow richer and develop a broader income tax base over time and a general disillusionment with import-substitution and infant-industry arguments for protection (born of adverse experiences with these policies in many instances) have both been argued to explain the trend towards lower trade protection. These arguments do have merit. The proportion of tax revenue contributed by trade taxes is negatively correlated with national income levels (as Rodrik (1995) has shown). And the public expressions of unhappiness with the import-substitution and infant-industry arguments by policy makers in many countries that have embarked on major trade reforms have been quite well documented. We should note that neither of the explanations of trends in trade policy relies upon political economy arguments. To what extent ideological shifts regarding trade policy reflect underlying shifts in economic interests and to what extent they are exogenous is a question that has not received as much attention in the literature as it should.[34] If shifts in ideology are driven by factors outside the domain of political economy and distributional conflict, they pose new problems of explanation.

The trend towards NTBs lacks a convincing explanation. Some analysts have argued that NTB protection allows governments some discretion in policy after their hands have been tied down by successive rounds of multilateral negotiation over tariffs. As Rodrik (1995) has noted, this nevertheless begs the question of why countries bother with trade negotiations when they are aware that the agreements will be flouted by the use of discretionary NTBs. Very little systematic empirical work on the determinants of NTBs in preference to tariffs has been done to date.

While trade restrictions have trended downward overall, this has been argued to have been quite non-monotone in some instances. Thus, in the twentieth century, the US time series data on nominal tariff revenue as a proportion of import value, or the "ad valorem tariff rate," has been documented by Irwin (1998) to have taken the following pattern: From around .50 in 1900, it declined to .40 in 1910 and then .16 in 1920, in part due to the Underwood Tariff Act of 1913. With the Fordney–McCumber Tariff Act of 1922 it reversed direction and began to ascend, peaking at .60 with the Smoot–Hawley Tariff Act of 1930. Reversing direction again, it declined sharply to .12 in 1950, and then dropped slowly to reach about .04 in 1980, after the implementation of the tariffs agreed to at the Tokyo Round of the GATT.

A number of analysts have attempted to explain this cyclical behavior of aggregate tariffs.[35] Magee and Young base their empirical investigation of the tariff data on the Magee, Brock, and Young (1989) general equilibrium model of endogenous protection. The familiar two-sector, two-factor Heckscher–Ohlin model with economy-wide mobility of factors of production and lobbying according to class (i.e., with labor's interests opposing that of the owners of capital) provides the foundations for the analysis. In an attempt to capture the political structure of the US, they develop an election model with electoral competition between two competing political parties,[36] Republicans and Democrats, to explain the supply of protection. The Republican Party is assumed to favor capitalists and the Democratic Party labor. The probability of Republicans winning the Presidency is related positively to lobbying by capitalists and negatively to lobbying by labor. Magee and Young's unit of observation is a Presidential term, yielding them twenty-one observations. Of the eight variables used in the analysis, of particular interest is the labor–capital ratio, which has direct links with the theory. The theory implies that as capital increases relative to labor, the election technology chooses a Republican administration, with the result that the tariff falls. Magee and Young find evidence in favor of this effect.[37]

Lohmann and O'Halloran (1994) examine the impact of the power structure *within* the US government and the degree of conflict between different branches of power on trade policy (an approach that has its roots in Weingast and Moran (1983) and McCubbins and Schwartz (1984)), also finding aggregate tariffs to be linked to political economy variables. Using tariff rate data from 1949 to 1990, they model the change in tariffs in order to discriminate between three hypotheses: the pressure group hypothesis represented by economic variables, and two "power structure" hypotheses, namely, the presidential dominance hypothesis and the congressional dominance hypothesis. The latter hypotheses are represented by a variable that qualitatively measures three possibilities: divided government (when the administration and Congress are controlled by opposing parties), split partisan control (when the same party controls the administration and a single chamber of Congress), and unified partisan control (when one party controls the administration and both chambers of Congress). They find a statistically significant association between the tariff level and these variables. Among other interesting results, they find the President's trade policy-making authority to be far more constrained during a divided Congress than under a unified Congress, and US trade policy to be far more protectionist under a divided Congress than a unified Congress.

An alternative (and rather a-theoretical) approach is taken by Bohara and Kaempfer (1991), who run Granger tests in order to determine which factors cause variations in tariff data over time. They find that unemployment and inflation are responsible for movements in the tariff time series. Their study has also generated many similar analyses of European and Japanese data whose findings confirm that the Bohara–Kaempfer results are quite robust. Indeed, Lohmann and O'Halloran (1994) also find that tariffs respond to the business cycle and that changes in tariffs are negatively associated with changes in inflation. No one has yet, however, followed up on these empirical findings by developing formal theories of endogenous protection which feature unemployment or the business cycle. This remains a theoretical challenge for future research.

Irwin (1998) casts doubt on Bohara and Kaempfer's conclusions, showing that it is not shifts in any underlying political economy factors, but rather that most US import tariff rates have been specific, not *ad valorem*, that has made tariff rates appear to respond to inflation. The simple fact is that, *ceteris paribus*, if the average rate is computed as a percentage of import value, it would decline when import prices rose and would rise when import prices increased. The US average tariff rate and average import price data (Irwin (1998, figure 1)) clearly show this relationship over time. Irwin estimates that the elasticity of the average tariff rate with respect to average import price is of the order of –.60. Since import prices were increasing throughout the postwar period, Irwin's results imply that the multilateral cuts should not be unduly credited with reducing the average tariff rate – a large part of the decline is an artifact of the specific tariffs. Irwin's inquiry into the political economy of the average tariff after controlling for the import price effect takes the form of estimating the effect on the average tariff of each of eight tariff legislations from the Tariff Act of 1872 through the 1948 formation of the GATT. While each of these legislations are found to significantly affect the tariff, thereby directly confirming the presence of a political economy component to the average tariff, controlling for import prices makes their effects slighter.

5.4 Case Studies in Administered Protection

Administered protection generally refers to protection resulting as a *statutory* response to specified market circumstances or events, usually as determined by an administrative agency. Several such statutes are "permitted" by the GATT/WTO under specific circumstances, including antidumping (AD) duties and countervailing duties (CVDs).[38] As Blonigen and Prusa (2003) note, administered protection has emerged in recent years as the most widespread impediment to trade, and while most other instruments of trade protection have been brought under greater GATT/WTO discipline, administered protection actions (ADs in particular) have flourished.

In the US, the International Trade Commission (ITC) is charged with making AD and CVD determinations. Several recent studies have examined various aspects of ADs, CVDs, and the ITC process. Thus, for instance, Blonigen et al. (1999) have studied the welfare costs of ADs and CVDs, Staiger and Wolak (1994) have studied the protective impact of the ITC procedure (finding significant costs even when ADs are ultimately not granted). Finger et al. (1982) and Hansen and Prusa (1997) have investigated the susceptibility of the ITC to being captured by special interests. The findings of these latter authors as to the extent of the influence of special interests on ITC decisions is interesting since the ITC process is supposed to be a purely statutory one, i.e., one merely reflecting market circumstances. These and other contributions are discussed in greater detail in chapter 9 in this volume.[39]

While the ITC makes determinations in AD and CVD cases, almost all other cases (particularly, those falling under Section 301 of the 1974 Trade Act regarding unfair foreign trade practices or Special 301 cases on intellectual property rights), whether multilateral, bilateral, or regional, come under the purview of the office of the US Trade Representative. USTR cases may be unilaterally initiated against a country by the US or, as is more likely, brought to the USTR by private parties to achieve redress. Noland (1997), in his examination of the political economy of USTR attentions and actions, finds that during the 1984 to 1995 period USTR attention was related to the size of the partner country, and that the existence of bilateral trade imbalances suggests that more went into the formation of trade policy than merely responding to interest group pressure.

5.5 Trade and Foreign Direct Investment

Branstetter and Feenstra (1999) jointly examine trade and Foreign Direct Investment (FDI) in China, drawing on GH and Grossman and Helpman (1995a) to model the political process, where, they assume, the social benefits from trade and FDI liberalization are being traded off against the losses incurred by state-owned enterprises from such reforms.[40] They use province-level data on trade and FDI flows at the four-digit level to estimate the parameters of the government's objective function (similar to the one in GH) and find that the government places only half the weight on consumer welfare that it does on the welfare of state-owned enterprises.

Bhagwati's (1985) theory of quid pro quo FDI argues that FDI may be undertaken by foreign firms that export into the domestic market with the motive of creating jobs there and lowering the threat that their exports will be restricted by local politicians seeking to protect their constituents from foreign competition. A simple interpretation of this theory suggests that politicians should cast votes for free trade in exchange for greater FDI in their state or district. Blonigen and Figlio (1998) examine the effect of state-level FDI using data on Senate votes on trade issues from 1985 to 1994 and also study the effect of district-level changes in FDI on House trade protection votes in two high profile industries: automobiles and textiles/apparel. Their findings are somewhat ambiguous. They find that legislators are influenced by FDI, but in a dichotomous fashion. FDI makes protectionist lawmakers even more likely to vote for protection in the future, while it leads politicians that generally vote for free trade to be even less likely to vote for protection. These results are robust across both House and Senate votes.

5.6 Preferential Trade Agreements

Various aspects of the political economy of preferential trade agreements between countries (which often take the form of either free trade areas (FTAs), in which the parties to the agreement maintain independent trade policies against outside countries, or Custom Unions (CUs), in which parties to the agreement maintain a common trade policy against the outsiders) have been studied recently. Grossman and Helpman (1995b), Krishna (1998), Levy (1997), and Panagariya and Findlay (1996) have each analyzed theoretically the political and economic conditions under which such agreements are entered into by countries and the implications of such agreements for the conduct of their trade policy with countries outside the agreement.[41]

Empirical work testing the predictions of these models has, however, been quite limited.[42] A recent exception is the work of Gawande, Sanguinetti, and Bohara (2001), which examines the particular predictions of the Grossman and Helpman (1995b) framework regarding "industry exclusions" in preferential trade agreements.[43] Industry exclusions in Grossman and Helpman (1995b) are determined in a bargaining game between the member countries in which each country brings to the bargaining table a list of industries that it wants excluded. At the top of the lists are the most politically sensitive industries. If industry i is an import-competing producer then it will prefer to be excluded from the agreement (or to maintain the status quo), while if it is an exporter then it will want to be included due to the extra profits in the partner country that await it in the FTA. Industries high on the lists are likely to be excluded from the FTA, but which country gets the greater number of exclusions depends on their relative bargaining strengths. Gawande, Sanguinetti and Bohara (2001) and Olarreaga and Soloaga (1998) using data from the MERCOSUR trade agreement between Brazil, Argentina, Paraguay, and Uruguay, find evidence consistent with the predictions of the Grossman and Helpman (1995b) theory.

6 Conclusions

That politics plays an important role in shaping economic outcomes is an imme-
morial insight. We have intuited for perhaps just as long that a proper understanding of political influences in economic systems is crucial for estimating the impact
of our policy choices and for the design of our institutions. In this survey our attention was narrowly focused on empirical approaches in the study of the political
economy of policy interventions in trade. Specifically, the task that we set ourselves
was to chart the progress made in the literature in identifying and quantifying the
role played by various political factors in shaping trade policy. Researchers, combining a variety of data sources and methods, have provided a convincing confirmation of the presence and significance of political-economic influences.
However, where distinguishing among several alternative theoretical conjectures of
the determinants of trade policy is concerned, the literature has been less successful. Inference has generally been confounded by the insufficiently precise and often
promiscuous link between the theoretical conjectures and the political-economic
variables that have served as their proxies in empirical exercises. The recent development of formal theories of endogenous protection, which are characterized by
the unusual merit of directly testable predictions, has prompted a shift of the literature to a more "structural" direction – where the empirical specifications have tight
links with the underlying theory. As it stands, these theories themselves are narrowly
focused on a singular (albeit apparently important) determinant of policy – lobbying by organized interest groups. While the empirical analysis has provided a degree
of evidentiary support for the theories, it has also served to highlight a number of
internal inconsistencies and puzzles. As we have discussed, many important issues
remain unresolved. It is hoped that future theoretical development will, while main-
taining its econometric amenability, incorporate the insights of the both the theoretical and the earlier empirical literature regarding the broader set of influences
on protection, political-economic or otherwise, and that future empirical analysis
will provide a more comprehensive and unified account of the complex set of interactions that determine trade policy.

Acknowledgments

We wish to thank Rob Feenstra, Randy Kroszner, Steve Levitt, Devashish Mitra, Arvind
Panagariya, Sam Peltzman, George Stergios and seminar participants at the NBER ITI
Spring 2001 meetings for helpful suggestions and comments.

Notes

1 However, see section 4 for a discussion of contexts in which maximizing economic efficiency (theoretically speaking) entails departures from free trade.
2 Earlier surveys of the theoretical issues and contributions in this area include Hillman
   (1989, 1991), Helpman (1997), and Rodrik (1995). Surveys of the empirical literature,
   with which this survey overlaps in its discussion of early econometric contributions in

the area, include Baldwin (1985) and Magee (1994, 1997). A textbook treatment is provided by Vousden (1990).

3   The list of contributors to this literature is a long and illustrious one. It includes, among others, the following studies by political economists and political scientists: Baldwin (1985), Brock and Magee (1978), Caves (1976), Destler (1986), Keohane (1984), Marvel and Ray (1983), Milner and Yoffie (1989), Ray (1981), and Schattschneider (1935).

4   It must be noted that Helleiner's (1977) theory suggests, however, that it will be *countries* in which there is extensive US investment that are able to bargain for lower tariffs. This does not necessarily imply that the industries in which there is higher US investment abroad will have lower tariffs on imports. Thus, a cross-industry study of type conducted by Baldwin (1985) isn't, perhaps, the best context in which to test the foreign policy model.

5   It is additionally distinguished among empirical political economy studies of protection by its proper econometric treatment of endogeneity of imports in a model that *also* addresses censoring of the data.

6   For a recent *theoretical* analysis that illustrates the value of taking account of political economy factors in determining optimal policy, see Krishna and Mitra's (2000) paper on "reciprocated unilateralism," where unilateral trade liberalization by one country is shown to bring to it the benefit of endogenous reciprocity by its partner due to the induced change in the political economy equilibrium in the partner country by the initial (unilateral) liberalization.

7   Another interesting exercise on the restrictive impact of NTB protection was conducted by Harrigan (1993), who exploits the theoretical structure of the monopolistic competition model to derive expressions for bilateral trade flows, estimating them using data on bilateral trade flows and bilateral trade barriers. However, perhaps because he ignores the endogeneity problem, he finds NTBs to not be as restrictive. See also the cross-country study by Mansfield and Busch (1995).

8   It is worth noting that Gawande (1998a) analyzes *separately* "price NTBs" (such as antidumping duties and countervailing duties) and "quantity NTBs" (such as quotas and voluntary export restraints), thus allowing for these different types of instruments to have different effects (as predicted by a number of theories of trade under imperfect competition).

9   Viewing the interest group and adding machine models as models emphasizing the short-run self-interest motivations of various groups (including the government) and the status quo and social justice models as emphasizing social concerns, Baldwin (1985) has concluded that "models focusing exclusively on short-run and direct self-interest are insufficient for explaining the wide range of behavior patterns observable in the trade policy arena" and that "long-run self-interest" and "concern for welfare of other groups and the state" are also necessary to account for trade policy outcomes. However, the association of particular theories with short- or long-run self-interest (in Baldwin's terminology) is itself debatable. Thus, for example, a purely cynically motivated government with the short-run self-interest objective of winning re-election may be keen to do nothing to worsen the status quo.

10 The question of why models of NTB determination reach such different conclusions from theories of tariff protection regarding the merits of particular theories of endogenous protection is an interesting one. However, to our knowledge, it is a question that has not been pursued in the literature.

11 The determinants of *individual* preferences over trade policy have been studied recently by Scheve and Slaughter (2001), who find, using survey data, that preferences over trade

policy depend upon factor ownership (as postulated in median-voter models of trade policy) and asset holdings.

12 This should be easy to understand intuitively. As stated by the Stolper–Samuelson theorem, in the two-sector Heckscher–Ohlin model, a change in the tariff on the importable raises the return to one factor and lowers that to the other. If the median capital–labor ratio in the economy is low, the median voter will vote for a tariff policy that favors labor over capital.

13 It is perhaps worth noting that even in a multisector context, the voting process is still over a *single* variable – the tariff rate in any sector, *i*. The theoretical complexities inherent in multidimensional voting where various tariffs are voted upon simultaneously are well known and need not be repeated here (see, for example, Shepsle (1990)).

14 See, however, Mayer (1984) for an explanation of the power of concentrated owners that relies upon voting costs. It is argued there that if voters face some positive costs of participating in the voting process, individuals with small stakes in the voting process may choose not to vote because their net return from voting is negative. This makes it more likely that the majority of those that remain will vote for a tariff.

15 See also Bhagwati and Feenstra (1982).

16 Further, as in the GH model, which we discuss shortly, protection is higher the larger the sector in terms of output-to-imports ratio, and the smaller the sector's import demand elasticity.

17 It should be readily evident that the *linear* form of the government objective function here pins down the relevant marginal rates of substitution and thus avoids the difficulties associated with the empirical testing of the Findlay–Wellisz and Hillman models that we have just described.

18 A crude intuition may be provided as follows: The derivative of sector *i*'s profit function with respect to own price is x_i, while the lower the imports, the lower the social cost protection imposes on the public. Hence the greatest protection is afforded to industries with the highest value of $z = x/m$.

19 Recent work by Mitra et al. (2002) and McCalman (2002) have applied the GH model to, respectively, Turkey and Australia. Eicher and Osang (2002) perform a nonnested comparison of predictions from the GH model with predictions from other models of political economy.

20 Any attempt at measuring tariff equivalents is inhibited additionally by the non-equivalence between tariffs and non-tariff instruments in imperfectly competitive contexts (Bhagwati, 1965) and the problem that under different modes of imperfect competition, the same instrument may have quite different effects on the market outcome – as seen, for instance, by a comparison of the analysis of voluntary export restraints by Krishna (1989), who assumes Bertrand competition, with that of Harris (1985), who makes the Stackelberg assumption instead. Practitioners will nevertheless find useful suggestions regarding measurement methodology in Deardorff and Stern (1998a). See also Anderson (1998a, b) and Anderson and Neary (1996) for analytical discussions of theoretically rigorous measures of protection.

21 That the welfare losses from protection are large is demonstrated in studies of Hufbauer et al. (1986), and Tarr and Morkre (1984).

22 Rodrik argues this point in the context of a country with two non-numeraire sectors: a single import competing and a single exporting sector. He argues that, *under balanced trade*, the question of which industry gets more protection boils down to a question of which industry has the higher level of output. With comparative advantage, the exporting sector is argued to be larger and therefore larger export subsidies are predicted by

(8.6). However, Rodrik's argument regarding balanced trade and its implications for sectoral size and therefore trade policy in GH is slightly incorrect since it ignores, among other things, the role of the freely traded (by assumption) numeraire good in GH. The presence of this good to settle the balance of payments implies that the non-numeraire import-competing and exporting sectors bear no relation to each other in size. Indeed, both sectors could, in principle, be import-competing (or exporting) sectors. This should not take away from the significance or validity of the point that he forcefully makes as to the policy bias against trade, however.

23   It should be immediately obvious that allowing a role for international negotiations necessitates the abandonment of the "small country" assumption that underlies GH. A "small country's" trade policy does not impact world prices and there is no direct motivation for other countries to negotiate with it.

24   Non co-operative interactions between countries, have been the subject of the theoretical and empirical studies of Bayard and Elliott (1994), Chan (1988), Conybeare (1987), Copeland (1990), Gawande (1995), Johnson (1953), Milner and Yoffie (1989), Riezman (1982), and Tower (1975) among others.

25   An interesting theoretical contribution has been made by Mitra (1999), who endogenizes lobby formation in the GH framework. The decision to organize and form lobbies here is assumed to take place in a first stage, with the rest of the GH analytics following. Owners of specific factors in the various industries match the benefits from lobby formation to the total costs of being organized (which include any fixed costs of lobby formation itself and the contributions that the lobby ends up making to politicians), and get organized if the former dominate the latter in magnitude. This framework yields some interesting theoretical results relating to the impact on tariffs of changes in ownership distributions and changes in the government's preference for welfare relative to campaign contributions. The role played by the fixed costs of lobby formation is key, however, and being generally unobservable, makes empirical implementation rather difficult.

26   This is not a comment on the state of the art on the literature on lobbying at large, which is copious. Rather this is a comment on cross-industry studies of lobbying. To get a flavor for the issues and methods in the lobbying literature, see, for example, the surveys in Potters and Sloof (1996) and Morton and Cameron (1992), and studies on (i) Political Action Commitee (PAC) money and election outcomes by Levitt (1994), Magee (2002), and Stratmann (1992), and (ii) PAC money and Congressional voting by Baldwin and Magee (2000), Bronars and Lott (1997), Snyder (1992), and Stratmann (1998). Deardorff and Stern (1998b) provide studies on trade-related lobbying.

27   In this context see also the empirical study by Magee (2001) of the free-rider problem in lobby formation motivated by the model of Pecorino (1998) and the study by Gawande (1997).

28   A rich theoretical literature has developed on the issue of which policy instruments will actually be chosen in the context of particular institutional or political realities. See, for example, Feenstra and Lewis (1991), Mayer and Riezman (1990), Riezman and Wilson (1997), Rodrik (1986), and Rosendorff (1997).

29   See Bhagwati et al. (1998), Brander (1995), and Helpman and Krugman (1989) for comprehensive treatments of optimal trade policy in the presence of market failures and imperfect competition. See Eaton and Grossman (1985), Falvey and Lloyd (1991), Young and Anderson (1982), and Rodrik (1998) for discussions of trade policy in the presence of uncertainty.

30   Thus, for example, it is quite well recognized that the infant-industry argument for protection (whose logic usually relies upon a combination of dynamic learning-by-doing

externalities in production and credit constraints) was commonly used in developing countries to provide protective tariffs for their manufacturing sectors.

31 See, for instance, Baron (1997) and Busch (1999).

32 See Hisox (1999) for another study of the RTAA.

33 Thus, for example, in the 1980s and the early 1990s, Bolivia, Brazil, India, Mexico, Peru, and Turkey each implemented radical reforms of their trade policies, moving from highly protectionist environments to far more open ones. And second, countries have shifted away from tariffs to somewhat more complex forms of non-tariff protection (on which some more in section 5.4).

34 Irwin and Kroszner's (1999) study of the RTAA, which we have discussed above, does illustrate the complex interaction between economic interests, institutions, and ideology in shaping policy and provides a convincing candidate explanation for the downward movement in US tariffs. Nevertheless, to our knowledge, no similar shifts in institutional structure have been proposed to explain the dramatic changes in trade policy in the developing countries we have mentioned.

35 See O'Rourke and Williamson (1999) for a broad discussion of trade and immigration policy trends in the US in the twentieth century.

36 On the issue of electoral competition and special interest politics, see also Grossman and Helpman (1996).

37 Of course, since trade policy affects the incentives to accumulate capital, one expects the capital–labor ratio itself to be a function of trade policy in the long run, implying a more complex system than the one Magee and Young (1987) consider. This said, Magee and Young's work remains notable for its ambitious attempt to link theory to the data, as Leamer (1987) has noted.

38 More specifically, the GATT/WTO allows countries to levy ADs to protect their domestic industries against "dumping" by foreign firms (i.e., when foreign firms sell their product at "less than fair value" in the domestic market) and to levy CVDs if the exports of foreign firms are subsidized by their governments.

39 See also Krueger (1996) for a number of interesting case studies on particular industries.

40 For an alternate theoretical analysis of endogenous trade policy with FDI, see Konishi et al. (1999).

41 See also Cadot et al. (1999) and Richardson (1993) and the empirical study by Bohara et al. (2001). Bhagwati (1993) and Panagariya (2000) provide excellent surveys. Bhagwati et al. (1999) provide a comprehensive collection of papers on the topic.

42 There is a sizeable empirical literature estimating the economic impact of preferential trade agreements (including the recent work of Frankel et al. (1997) and Krishna (2003)), but this literature has ignored the issue of endogeneity of trade policy altogether.

43 Despite the fact that Article XXIV of the GATT mandates that trade be fully liberalized between signatories to a PTA, PTAs have almost always been accompanied by exclusions of some industries from the agreement. This was the case for the North American Free Trade Agreement (NAFTA) as well as for the European Union (EU). See Ozden and Parodi (2001) for a discussion of special industry clauses in MERCOSUR.

References

Anderson, James E. 1998a: Effective protection redux. *Journal of International Economics*, 44, 21–44.

Anderson, James E. 1998b: Trade restrictiveness benchmarks. *Economic Journal*, 108, 1111–25.

Anderson, James E. and J. Peter Neary 1996: A new approach to evaluating trade policy. *Review of Economic Studies*, 63, 107–25.

Baldwin, Robert E. 1985: *The Political Economy of US Import Policy*. Cambridge, MA: MIT Press.

Baldwin, Robert and Christopher Magee 2000: Is trade policy for sale? Congressional voting on recent Trade Bills. *Public Choice*, 105, 1, 79–101.

Ball D. S. 1967: United States effective tariffs and labor's share. *Journal of Political Economy*, 75, 183–7.

Baron, David P. 1997: Integrated strategy and international trade disputes: The Kodak–Fujifilm case. *Journal of Economics and Management Strategy*, 6, 291–346.

Bayard, Thomas O. and Kimberly A. Elliott 1984: *Reciprocity and Retaliation in US Trade Policy*. Washington, DC: Institute for International Economics.

Bernheim, B. Douglas and Michael D. Whinston 1986: Menu auctions, resource allocations and economic influence. *Quarterly Journal of Economics*, 101, 1–31.

Bhagwati, Jagdish 1965: On the equivalence between tariffs and quotas. In Caves et al. (eds.), *Trade Growth and the Balance of Payments*, Chicago: Rand McNally.

Bhagwati, Jagdish 1971: The generalized theory of distortions and welfare. In *Trade, Balance of Payments and Growth: Papers in International Economics in Honor of Charles Kindleberger*, Amsterdam: North Holland.

Bhagwati, Jagdish 1982: Directly-unproductive profit seeking (DUP) activities. *Journal of Political Economy*, 90, 988–1002.

Bhagwati, Jagdish 1985: Protectionism: Old wine in new bottles. *Journal of Policy Modeling*, 7, 23–34.

Bhagwati, Jagdish 1993: Regionalism and multilateralism: An overview. In DeMelo and Panagariya (eds.), *New Dimensions in Regional Integration*, Cambridge: Cambridge University Press.

Bhagwati, Jagdish and Robert Feenstra 1982: Tariff seeking and the efficient tariff. In J. Bhagwati (ed.), *Import Competition and Response*, Chicago: University of Chicago Press.

Bhagwati, Jagdish, Arvind Panagariya, and T. N. Srinivasan 1998: *Lectures on International Trade*. Cambridge, MA: MIT Press.

Bhagwati, Jagdish, Pravin Krishna, and Arvind Panagariya 1999: *Trade Blocs: Alternate Analyses of Preferential Trade Agreements*. Cambridge, MA: MIT Press.

Black, Duncan 1958: *The Theory of Committees and Elections*. Cambridge: Cambridge University Press.

Blonigen, Bruce A. and David N. Figlio 1998: Voting for protection: Does direct foreign investment influence legislator behavior? *American Economic Review*, 88, 1002–14.

Blonigen, Bruce A. and Thomas J. Prusa 2003: Antidumping. This volume.

Blonigen, Bruce A., Michael Gallaway, and Joseph Flynn 1999: Welfare costs of US antidumping and countervailing duty laws. *Journal of International Economics*, 49, 211–44.

Bohara, Alok K. and William H. Kaempfer 1991: A test of tariff endogeneity in the US. *American Economic Review*, 81, 952–60.

Bohara, Alok K., Kishore Gawande, and Pablo Sanguinetti 2001: Trade diversion and declining tariffs: Evidence from Mercosur. Manuscript.

Brander, James A. 1995: Strategic trade policy. In G. M. Grossman and K. Rogoff (eds.), *Handbook of International Economics*, vol. III, Amsterdam: North-Holland.

Branstetter, Lee and Robert Feenstra 1999: Trade and FDI in China. NBER working paper no. 7100.

Brock, William P. and Stephen P. Magee 1978: The economics of special interest politics: The case of tariffs. *American Economic Review*, 68, 246–50.

Bronars, Stephen and John Lott 1997: Do campaign donations alter how a politician votes?

Or, do donors support candidates who value the same things that they do? *Journal of Law and Economics*, 40, 317–50.

Busch, Marc L. 1999: *Trade Warriors*. Cambridge: Cambridge University Press.

Cadot, Oliver, Jaime de Melo, and Marcelo Olarreaga 1999: Regional integration and lobbying for tariffs against non-members. *International Economic Review*, 40, 635–57.

Caves, Richard E. 1976: Economic models of political choice: Canada's tariff structure. *Canadian Journal of Economics*, 9, 278–300.

Chan, Kenneth S. 1988: Trade negotiations in a Nash bargaining model. *Journal of International Economics*, 25, 353–63.

Constantopoulos, M. 1974: Labor protection in Western Europe. *European Economic Review*, 5, 313–18.

Conybeare, John A. C. 1987: *Trade Wars: The Theory and Practice of International Commercial Rivalry*. New York: Columbia University Press.

Copeland, Brian R. 1990: Strategic interaction among nations: Negotiable and non-negotiable trade barriers. *Canadian Journal of Economics*, 23, 84–108.

Corden, W. Max 1974: *Trade Policy and Welfare*. Oxford: Oxford University Press.

Deardorff Alan V. and Robert M. Stern 1998a: *Measurement of Nontariff Barrriers*. Ann Arbor: University of Michigan Press.

Deardorff Alan V. and Robert M. Stern (eds.) 1998b: *Constituent Interests and US Trade Policies*. Ann Arbor: University of Michigan Press.

Destler, I. M. 1986: *American Trade Politics: System Under Stress*. Washington, DC: Institute for International Economics.

Dutt, Pushan and Devashish Mitra 2001: Endogenous trade policy through majority voting: An empirical investigation. Manuscript.

Eaton, Jonathan and Gene M. Grossman 1985: Tariffs as insurance: Optimal commercial policy when domestic markets are incomplete. *Canadian Journal of Economics*, 18, 258–72.

Eicher, Theo and Thomas Osang 2002 (forthcoming): Protection for sale: An empirical investigation: Comment. *American Economic Review*.

Falvey, Rod E. and P. J. Lloyd 1991: Uncertainty and the choice of protective instrument. *Oxford Economic Papers*, 43, 463–78.

Feenstra, R. C. and T. R. Lewis 1991: Negotiated trade restrictions with private political pressure. *Quarterly Journal of Economics*, 106, 1287–307.

Fieleke, N. 1976: The tariff structure for manufacturing industries in the United States: A test of some traditional explanations. *Columbia Journal of World Business*, 11, 98–104.

Findlay, Ronald and Stanislaw Wellisz 1982: Endogenous tariffs and the political economy of trade restrictions and welfare. In Jagdish Bhagwati (ed.), *Import Competition and Response*, Chicago: University of Chicago.

Finger, J. M., H. Keith Hall, and Douglas R. Nelson 1982: The political economy of administered protection. *American Economic Review*, 72, 452–66.

Frankel, Jeffrey, Ernesto Stein, and S-J. Wei 1997: *Regional Trading Blocs in the World Economic System*. Washington, DC: Institute for International Economics.

Gawande, Kishore 1995: Are US nontariff barriers retaliatory? An application of extreme bounds analysis in the Tobit model. *Review of Economics and Statistics*, 77, 677–88.

Gawande, Kishore 1997: US nontariff barriers as privately provided public goods. *Journal of Public Economics*, 64, 61–81.

Gawande, Kishore 1998a: Comparing theories of endogenous protection: Bayesian comparison of Tobit models using Gibbs sampling output. *Review of Economics and Statistics*, 80, 128–40.

Gawande, Kishore 1998b: Stigler–Olson lobbying behavior and organization. *Journal of Economic Behavior and Organization*, 35, 477–99.

Gawande, Kishore and Usree Bandyopadhyay 2000: Is protection for sale? A test of the Grossman–Helpman theory of endogenous protection. *Review of Economics and Statistics*, 89, 139–52.

Gawande, Kishore and Pravin Krishna 2001a: Trade unions and US trade policy. Manuscript.

Gawande, Kishore and Pravin Krishna 2001b: Protection for sale: A re-examination. Manuscript.

Gawande, Kishore, Pravin Krishna, and Michael Robbins 2001: Foreign lobbies and US trade policy. Manuscript.

Gawande, Kishore, Pablo Sanguinetti, and Alok K. Bohara 2001: Exclusions for sale: Evidence on the Grossman–Helpman theory of free trade agreements. Manuscript.

Goldberg, Penelopi and Giovanni Maggi 1999: Protection for sale: An empirical investigation. *American Economic Review*, 89, 1135–55.

Grossman, Gene M. and Elhanan Helpman 1994: Protection for sale. *American Economic Review*, 84, 833–50.

Grossman, Gene M. and Elhanan Helpman 1995a: Trade wars and trade talks. *Journal of Political Economy*, 103, 675–708.

Grossman, Gene M. and Elhanan Helpman 1995b: The politics of free-trade agreements. *American Economic Review*, 85, 667–90.

Grossman, Gene M. and Elhanan Helpman 1996: Electoral competition and special interest politics. *Review of Economic Studies*, 63, 265–86.

Hansen, Wendy, L. and Thomas J. Prusa 1997: The economics and politics of trade policy: An empirical analysis of ITC decisions making. *Review of International Economics*, 5, 230–45.

Harrigan, James 1993: OECD imports and trade barriers in 1983. *Journal of International Economics*, 35, 91–112.

Harris, Richard 1985: Why voluntary export restraints are "Voluntary," *Canadian Journal of Economics*, 18, 799–809.

Helleiner, G. K. 1977: The political economy of Canada's tariff structure: An alternative model. *Canadian Journal of Economics*, 4, no.2, 318–26.

Helpman, Elhanan 1997: Politics and trade policy. In D. M. Kreps and K. F. Wallis (eds.), *Advances in Economics and Econometrics: Theory and Applications*, vol. II. Cambridge: Cambridge University Press.

Helpman, Elhanan and Paul Krugman 1989: *Trade Policy and Market Structure*. Cambridge, MA: MIT Press.

Hillman, Arye 1982: Declining industries and political support protectionist motives. *American Economic Review*, 72, 1180–7.

Hillman, Arye 1989: *The Political Economy of Protection*. New York, NY: Harwood Academic Publishers.

Hillman, Arye, 1991: Protection, politics and market structure. In E. Helpman and A. Razin (eds.), *International Trade and Trade Policy*, Cambridge, MA: MIT Press.

Hisox, Michael J. 1999: The magic bullet? The RTAA, institutional reform, and trade liberalization. *International Organization*, 53, 669–98.

Hufbauer, Gary C., Diane T. Berliner, and Kimberly A. Elliott, 1986: *Trade Protection in the US: 31 Case Studies*. Washington, DC: Institute for International Economics.

Irwin, Douglas A. 1996: Industry or class cleavages over trade policy? Evidence from the British general election of 1923. In R. C. Feenstra, G. M. Grossman, and D. A. Irwin (eds.), *The Political Economy of Trade Policy: Papers in Honor of Jagdish Bhagwati*. Cambridge, MA: MIT Press.

Irwin, Douglas A. 1998: Changes in US tariffs: The role of import prices and commercial policies. *American Economic Review*, 88, 1015–26.

Irwin, Douglas A. and Randall S. Kroszner 1996: Log rolling and economic interests in the passage of the Smoot–Hawley tariffs. *Carnegie-Rochester Conference Series in Public Policy*, 45, 173–200.

Irwin, Douglas A. and Randall S. Kroszner 1999: Interests, institutions and ideology in securing policy change: The Republican conversion to trade liberalization after Smoot–Hawley. *Journal of Law and Economics*, 42, 643–73.

Johnson, Harry G. 1953: Optimum tariffs and retaliation. *Review of Economic Studies*, 21, 142–53.

Keohane, Robert O. 1984. *After Hegemony: Cooperation and Discord in the World Political Economy*. Princeton, NJ: Princeton University Press.

Konishi, Hideo, Kamal Saggi, and Shlomo Weber 1999: Endogenous trade policy under foreign direct investment. *Journal of International Economics*, 49, 289–308.

Krishna, Kala 1989: Trade restrictions as facilitating practices. *Journal of International Economics*, 26, 251–70.

Krishna, Pravin 1998: Regionalism and multilateralism: A political economy approach. *Quarterly Journal of Economics*, 113, 227–51.

Krishna, Pravin 2003 (forthcoming): Are regional trading partners "Natural?" *Journal of Political Economy*.

Krishna, Pravin and Devashish Mitra 2000: Reciprocated unilateralism: A political economy approach. Brown University, manuscript.

Krueger, Anne 1974: The political economy of the rent-seeking society. *American Economic Review*, 64, 291–303.

Krueger, Anne (ed.) 1996: *The Political Economy of American Trade Policy*. Chicago: University of Chicago Press.

Lavergne, Real P. 1983: *The Political Economy of US Tariffs: An Empirical Analysis*. New York: Academic Press.

Leamer, Edward E. 1987: Comment [on the paper by Magee and Lee], in R. M. Stern (ed.), *US Trade Policies in a Changing World Economy*, Cambridge, MA: MIT Press.

Lee, Jong-Wha and Philip Swagel 1997: Trade barriers and trade flows across countries and industries. *Review of Economics and Statistics*, 79, 372–82.

Levitt, Stephen 1994: Using repeat challengers to estimate the effects of campaign spending on election outcomes in the US House. *Journal of Political Economy*, 102, 777–98.

Levy, Philip I. 1997: A political-economic analysis of free-trade agreements. *American Economic Review*, 87, 506–19.

Lohmann, Sussanne and Sharyn O'Halloran 1994: Divided government and US trade policy. *International Organization*, 48, 595–632.

Lopez, Rigoberto A. and Emilio Pagoulatos 1996: Trade protection and the role of campaign contributions in the US food and tobacco industries. *Economic Inquiry*, 34, 237–48.

Magee, Christopher, 2001: Endogenous trade policy and lobby formation: An application to the free-rider problem. *Journal of International Economics*, 57, 2, 449–71.

Magee, Christopher 2002 (forthcoming): Do political action committees give money to candidates for electoral or influence motives? *Public Choice*.

Magee, Stephen P. 1980: Three simple tests of the Stolper–Samuelson theorem. In P. Oppenheimer (ed.), *Issues in International Economics*, London: Oriel Press.

Magee, Stephen P. 1994: The political economy of trade policy. In D. Greenaway and A. Winters (eds.), *Surveys in International Trade*, Oxford: Blackwell.

Magee, Stephen P. 1997: Endogenous protection: The empirical evidence. In D. C. Mueller (ed.), Cambridge: Cambridge University Press.

Magee, Stephen P. and Leslie Young 1987: Endogenous protection in the United States, 1900–1984. In R. M. Stern (ed.), *US Trade Policies in a Changing World Economy*, Cambridge, MA: MIT Press.

Magee, Stephen P., William A. Brock, and Leslie Young 1989: *Black Hole Tariffs and Endogenous Policy Theory: Political Economy in General Equilibrium*. Cambridge: Cambridge University Press.

Mansfield, Edward D. and Marc L. Busch 1995: The political economy of nontariff barriers: A cross-national analysis. *International Organization*, 49, 723–49.

Marvel, Howard P. and Edward J. Ray 1983: The Kennedy Round: Evidence on the regulation of international trade in the United States. *American Economic Review*, 73, 190–7.

Mayer, Wolfgang 1984: Endogenous tariff formation. *American Economic Review*, 74, 970–85.

Mayer, Wolfgang and Raymond Riezman 1990: Voter preferences for trade policy instruments. *Economics and Politics*, 2, 3, 259–73.

McCalman, Phillip 2002 (forthcoming): Protection for sale and trade liberalization: An empirical investigation. *Review of International Economics*.

McCubbins, Matthew D. and Thomas Schwartz 1984: Congressional oversight overlooked: Police patrol versus fire alarms. *American Journal of Political Science*, 28, 165–79.

Milner, Helen and David Yoffie 1989: Between free trade and protectionism: Strategic trade policy and a theory of corporate preferences. *International Organization*, 43, 239–72.

Mitra, Devashish 1999: Endogenous lobby formation and endogenous protection: A long-run model of trade policy determination. *American Economic Review*, 89, 1116–34.

Mitra, Devashish, Dimitrios D. Thomakos, and Mehmet A. Ulubasoglu 2002: Protection for sale in a developing country: Democracy versus dictatorship. *Review of Economics and Statistics*, 84, 3, 497–508.

Morton, R. and Cameron, C. 1992: Elections and the theory of campaign contributions: A survey and critical analysis. *Economics and Politics*, 4, 79–108.

Mussa, Michael 1974: Tariffs and the distribution of income: The importance of factor specificity, substitutability and intensity in the short and long run. *Journal of Political Economy*, 1191–1203.

Neary, J. Peter 1978: Short-run capital specificity and the pure theory of international trade. *Economic Journal*, 88, 488–510.

Noland, Marcus 1997: Chasing phantoms: The political economy of the USTR. *International Organization*, 51, 365–87.

O'Rourke, Kevin H. and Jeffrey G. Williamson 1999: *Globalization and History: The Evolution of a Nineteenth Century Atlantic Economy*. Cambridge, MA: MIT Press.

Olarreaga, Marcelo and Isisdro Soloaga 1998: Endogenous tariff formation: The case of Mercosur. *World Bank Economic Review*, 12, 297–320.

Olson, Mancur 1965: *The Logic of Collective Action*. Cambridge, MA: Harvard University Press.

Olson, Mancur 1983: The political economy of comparative growth rates. In D. C. Mueller (ed.), *The Political Economy of Growth*, New Haven: Yale University Press.

Ozden, Caglar and Francisco Parodi 2001: Customs unions and foreign investment: Theory and evidence from MERCOSUR's auto industry. Manuscript.

Panagariya, Arvind 2000: Preferential trade liberalization: The traditional theory and new developments. *Journal of Economic Literature*, 38, 287–331.

Panagariya, Arvind and Ronald Findlay 1996: A political-economy analysis of free-trade areas and customs unions. In R. C. Feenstra, G. M. Grossman, and D. A. Irwin (eds.), *The Political Economy of Trade Policy: Papers in Honor of Jagdish Bhagwati*. Cambridge, MA: MIT Press.

Pecorino, Paul 1998: Is there a free-rider problem in lobbying? Endogenous lobbying, trigger strategies, and the number of firms. *American Economic Review*, 88, 652–60.

Peltzman, Sam 1976: Towards a more general theory of regulation. *Journal of Law and Economics*, 19, 211–48.

Pincus, J. J. 1975: Pressure groups and the pattern of tariffs. *Journal of Political Economy*, 83, 775–8.

Potters, J. and R. Sloof 1996: Interest groups: A survey of empirical models that try to assess their influence. *European Journal of Political Economy*, 12, 403–42.

Pugel, Thomas A. and Ingo Walter 1985: US corporate interests and the political economy of trade policy. *Review of Economics and Statistics*, 67, 465–73.

Putnam, Robert D. 1988: Diplomacy and domestic politics: The logic of two-level games. *International Organization*, 42, 427–60.

Ray, Edward J. 1981: The determinants of tariff and nontariff trade restrictions in the United States. *Journal of Political Economy*, 89, 105–21.

Richardson, Martin 1993: Endogenous protection and trade diversion. *Journal of International Economics*, 34, 309–24.

Riezman, Raymond 1982: Tariff retaliation from a strategic viewpoint. *Southern Economic Journal*, 48, 583–93.

Riezman, Raymond and John D. Wilson 1997: Political reform and trade policy. *Journal of International Economics*, 42, 67–90.

Rodrik, Dani 1986: Tariffs, subsidies, and welfare with endogenous policy, *Journal of International Economics*, 21, 285–96.

Rodrik, Dani 1995: Political economy of trade policy. In G. M. Groomsman and K. Rogoff (eds.), *Handbook of International Economics*, vol. III, Amsterdam: North-Holland.

Rodrik, Dani 1998: Do more open economies have bigger governments? *Journal of Political Economy*, 106, 997–1032.

Rosendorff, B. Peter 1997: Politics and the choice of instruments: Tariffs, subsidies, quotas and VERs. University of Southern California, manuscript.

Schattschneider, E. E. 1935: *Politics, Pressure, and the Tariff*. Englewood Cliffs, NJ: Prentice Hall.

Scheve, Kenneth F. and Matthew J. Slaughter 2001: What determines individual trade policy preferences? *Journal of International Economics*, 54, 2, 267–92.

Shepsle, Kenneth 1990: *Models of Multiparty Electoral Competition*. London: Harwood.

Shiells, Clint R., Robert F. Stern, and Alan V. Deardorff 1986: Estimates of the elasticities of substitution between imports and home goods for the United States. *Weltwirtschaftliches Archiv*, 122, 497–519.

Snyder, James 1992: Long-term investing in politicians; or, give early, give often. *Journal of Law and Economics*, 35, 15–43.

Staiger, Robert W. and Frank Wolak 1994: Measuring industry-specific protection: Antidumping in the United States. *Brookings Papers on Economic Activity: Microeconomics*, 51–118.

Stigler, George J. 1971: The theory of economic regulation. *Bell Journal of Economics and Management Science*, 2, 3–21.

Stratmann, Thomas 1992: Are contributors rational? Untangling strategies of political action committees. *Journal of Political Economy*, 100, 647–64.

Stratmann, Thomas 1998: The market for Congressional votes: Is timing of contributions everything? *Journal of Law and Economics*, 41, 85–113.

Tarr, D. G. and M. E. Morkre 1984: *Aggregate Costs to the United States of Tariffs and Quotas on Imports*. Washington, DC: Federal Trade Commission.

Tower, Edward 1975: The optimum quota and retaliation. *Review of Economic Studies*, 42, 623–30.

Trefler, Daniel 1993: Trade liberalization and the theory of endogenous protection: An econometric study of US import policy. *Journal of Political Economy*, 101, 138–60.

Vousden, Neil 1990: *The Economics of Trade Protection*. Cambridge: Cambridge University Press.

Weingast, Barry R. and Mark J. Moran 1983: Bureaucratic discretion or congressional control? Regulatory policy-making by the Federal Trade Commission. *Journal of Political Economy*, 91, 756–800.

Young, Leslie and James E. Anderson 1982: Risk aversion and optimal trade restrictions. *Review of Economic Studies*, 49, 291–306.

9

Antidumping

Bruce A. Blonigen and Thomas J. Prusa

CHAPTER OUTLINE

We review the growing literature on the effects of antidumping, a trade policy that has emerged as the most serious impediment to international trade. Over the past 25 years countries have increasingly turned to antidumping in order to offer protection to import-competing industries. Antidumping is a trade policy where the institutional process surrounding the investigation and determinations has significant impacts beyond the antidumping duty we observe, and where the filing decision, the legal determination, and the protective impact are all endogenous with firms' decisions in the market, leading to a wealth of potential strategic actions and distorted market outcomes. This theme underlies our discussion as we review the literature in three broad areas connected with different phases of the antidumping trade policy process: 1) pre-investigation; 2) investigation; and 3) post-investigation.

---

1 INTRODUCTION

Over the past 25 years antidumping (AD) has emerged as the most widespread impediment to trade. While most other instruments of trade protection, such as tariffs, quotas, voluntary export restraints, etc., have been brought under greater GATT/WTO discipline, AD actions have flourished. Consider, for instance, that since 1980 GATT/WTO members have filed more complaints under the AD statute than under *all* other trade laws combined, or that more AD duties are now levied in any one year worldwide than were levied in the entire period 1947 to 1970. Using a computable general equilibrium model, Gallaway et al. (1999) estimate that only the Multifiber Arrangement imposes larger welfare costs on the US economy than do AD actions and worldwide AD is likely the most costly form of protection.

If for no other reason, the widespread use of AD protection would make it an important research topic. As it turns out, however, AD is an important policy to study for many other reasons. While political-economy factors influence all forms of trade protection, no other trade instrument has AD's unique combination of political and economic manipulability, incentives, and intrigue. As we will detail below, AD protection is an excellent case study of almost all the standard micro-economic problems and concepts: from moral hazard, adverse selection, signaling, and contract theory to optimal tariff theory, comparative advantage, predatory pricing, and rent-seeking. This list does not even mention the political-economy issues generated by AD law: legislative delegation, bureaucratic oversight and discretion, log-rolling, and favoritism.

Moreover, the GATT/WTO AD code has undergone significant revisions every negotiating round. Individual countries, especially the US and EU, frequently amend their AD statutes, almost always to make AD protection easier to grant. Not only does AD law allow politicians to offer politically preferred industries protection without blatantly violating GATT/WTO principles, but they can also tinker with the rules to broaden the scope and availability of AD protection. As an example, the US has amended its AD rules at least a half dozen times over the past 25 years. Imports can now be deemed "unfair" even if foreign firms charge *higher* prices to their export market than they do at home and even if foreign firms earn healthy profits on each and every foreign sale. To politically powerful industries, losing a case is not a sign that the foreign competition is traded fairly; rather it is simply a sign that the law needs changing.

AD is a trade policy where the filing, the legal decision, and the protective impact is endogenous. A foreign industry can almost guarantee it will not be subject to AD duties if it charges sufficiently high prices in its export markets. On the other hand, a domestic industry might resist lowering its prices because doing so improves its chances of winning an AD case. In addition, the same industry might lay-off more workers than expected because doing so indicates injury.

Once the AD case has been filed, the decision to grant protection is subject to substantial discretion and, hence, can be influenced by the involved parties. Foreign parties can choose not to participate in the dumping margin phase of the investigation. This might be interpreted as an admission of guilt, but it can also signal their confidence in the facts (or perhaps the futility of resistance). Domestic parties can urge politicians to pressure the bureaucratic agencies by using the rhetoric of foreign unfairness to provide a vehicle for building a political case for protection.

Once an AD duty is in place, a foreign firm can often alter its pricing strategies to completely avoid paying the duty. That is, even though an AD duty is very similar to a tariff, the government may end up collecting no duties even though imports continue to enter the domestic market. Alternatively, a foreign firm can "jump" the AD duties and relocate its production to either the domestic market or to a third country that is not subject to the duties. In other words, AD can change the incentives to make foreign direct investments. If foreign firms differ in their ability to make such investments, then AD might particularly burden firms who cannot make such adjustments. Ironically, this means the foreign firms who are most able to "jump" the AD duty potentially have an incentive to encourage AD actions.

In this chapter we summarize the literature on AD and try to point out important research questions that remain unanswered. As our title indicates, this chapter is about antidumping, not dumping. There are two main reasons for our exclusive focus on AD actions. First, while there have a been a handful of important papers explaining why firms dump, the research focus has been overwhelmingly focused on the impact of AD. Second, given the substantial revisions to the GATT/WTO statutes over the past 25 years, the legal definition of "dumping" (and hence what actions can be sanctioned via antidumping actions) is almost completely divorced from any economic notion of dumping. Foreign firms who charge not only higher prices abroad than they do at home, but also higher prices than their domestic competitors, are still saddled with dumping margins of 50 percent and higher. AD no longer has anything to do with predatory pricing. Even more to the point, all but AD's staunchest supporters agree that AD has nothing to do with keeping trade "fair." AD has nothing to do with moral right or wrong, it is simply another tool to improve the competitive position of the complainant against other companies. As Stiglitz (1997) argues, there is essentially no connection between national welfare considerations and AD protection. It is simply a modern form of protection. As a result, there is little logical reason to necessarily connect the dumping literature with our review of the AD literature.

Finally, although the economic issues stemming from AD law are common to all GATT/WTO members, almost all research has focused on AD use in the US and EU. Thus, much of our discussion below suffers from this bias. We take special effort to try to clarify when we are making statements about GATT/WTO rules and when our discussion is limited to the US and EU experience.

The chapter is organized as follows. In the next section we review some of the trends in the use of AD. As we will discuss, AD was essentially an irrelevant, rarely used trade law until the mid-1970s. However, due to the fall in tariffs countries increasingly felt the need to offer protection to import-competing industries. Even though the GATT explicitly designed safeguard protection for these situations, AD has a number of advantages that have made it particularly popular. The remaining topics we organize by "time." In section 3 we review literature that has studied the impact of AD law *before* a case is even filed. We will explain how AD can facilitate collusion and can distort market prices even if cases are never filed. We will also explain how the trade impact of macroeconomic shocks, such as exchange rate movements and GNP fluctuations, are complicated by the presence of AD law. In section 4 we consider the AD investigation. We will explain what factors appear to be most important for the determination of injury and also what influences whether domestic and foreign parties participate in the investigation process. In section 5 we assess the market effect of AD protection. AD duties affect both the trade from subject countries and also the imports from non-subject countries. AD duties also encourage foreign firms to invest in protected domestic markets. We also discuss how the assessment of AD duties greatly complicates the pass-through behavior of sanctioned firms. Finally, in section 6 we summarize the state of the literature and highlight some open issues and puzzles that need to be addressed.

2 TRENDS IN THE USE OF ANTIDUMPING

While the first antidumping legislation dates to Canada's legislation in 1904, the modern history of AD begins with the 1947 GATT agreement. Largely at the insistence of the US, the original GATT agreement included provisions for the imposition of AD duties.[1] The 1947 GATT agreement defined dumping as the practice whereby the "products of one country are introduced into the commerce of another country at less than the normal value of the products," and permitted dumping duties only if such action caused "material injury" to a domestic industry.

Despite its long history, AD disputes were relatively few and far between until 1980. However, there is no exact accounting of worldwide AD activity before 1980. The main obstacle is that prior to 1980 the GATT did not require countries to report when they initiated AD actions. To our knowledge there is no source for pre-1980 filings (e.g., GATT Annual Reports or other similar documents). In fact, there is no guarantee that some early users have *any* record of their pre-1980 AD use.[2]

2.1 Pre-1980 AD Activity

Despite the lack of comprehensive data on pre-1980 AD activity, there is consensus on several key points. First, it appears that almost all AD activity was confined to six major users: The US, the EU, Australia, Canada, South Africa and New Zealand. Second, these major users filed at most two or three-dozen cases (total) per year. Third, the GATT rules for imposing AD duties were difficult to satisfy. For instance, the US did not levy duties in a single AD case during the entire decade of the 1950s. The pattern during the 1960s was about the same when only about 10 percent of US AD cases resulted in duties. The high standards meant that there was very little AD protection among all contracting parties. In 1958, when the contracting parties canvassed themselves about the use of AD, the resulting tally showed only 37 AD decrees in force across all GATT member countries, with 21 of these in South Africa (Finger, 1993). Simply put, until the mid-1970s it appears that in many years only a handful of cases were initiated worldwide, and in most years *no* investigations led to duties. The data we do have indicates that until the early 1970s less than 5 percent of AD cases resulted in duties.

Of course, it is now widely understood that an AD case can be "successful" even if it does not result in the imposition of duties. For instance, Prusa (1992) argues that withdrawn and terminated cases often involve voluntary export restraints. But the phenomenon of negotiated settlements was not common until the late 1970s. In addition, preliminary AD duties were not imposed until after the Tokyo Round, so the "investigation effect" emphasized by Staiger and Wolak (1994) is not likely to have been a serious issue in the earlier era.

All things considered, the small number of AD filings (exact number unknown), along with the high standards for awarding protection, meant that AD had very little trade impact until the mid- to late-1970s.

2.2 Post-1980 AD Activity

It is clear that the 1975 to 1979 period marked the end of AD's life in the back-water of trade policy. One of the things one must recognize when studying AD is that the law is constantly evolving. The type of behavior that is sanctionable changes over time.

The Tokyo Round, which concluded in 1979, contained numerous amendments to the AD statute. Of particular importance were two key provisions. First, the definition of "less than fair value" (LTFV) sales was broadened to capture not only price discrimination, but also sales below cost.[3] Cost-based allegations now account for between one-half and two-thirds of US AD cases (Clarida, 1996).[4] According to one noted legal expert, cost-based AD petitions have become "the dominant feature of US antidumping law" (Horlick, 1989, p. 136).[5] Second, while the Kennedy Round Code had required that the dumped imports be "demonstrably the principal cause of material injury" before duties could be imposed, in response to pressure from a number of the developed countries, the Tokyo Round Code revised this provision to render such a demonstration unnecessary.

These two amendments essentially changed the rules of the game. Almost as many cases were filed in the first three years following the Tokyo Round as during the entire decade of the 1970s. Overall, during the 1980s more than 1,600 cases were filed worldwide – a filing rate at least twice that of the 1970s.

From 1980 through 1985, four users (the US, the EU, Australia, and Canada) accounted for more than 99 percent of all filings (Finger, 1993). As the decade wore on, however, more and more cases began to be filed by "new" users. By the early 1990s new users accounted for almost one-quarter of AD cases and, by the mid-1990s, new users accounted for well over a half of AD complaints. Miranda et al. (1998) break down the patterns of using and affected countries over the past decade.

In terms of numbers, the EU and the US continue to file the most AD cases. However, Finger et al. (2000) argue that simply counting case filings is an inaccurate metric of AD use. In particular, they argue that the US and EU are the world's largest importers and, as a result, we should expect them to file more cases. As an alternative measure of the frequency of use of AD, they measure the number of cases per dollar of imports. Interestingly, by cases per dollar of imports, the US and EU have been among the least intense users over the 1995 to 1999 period.[6] Using this alternative metric, the most intense users of AD are developing countries (i.e., new users). For instance, Brazil's intensity of use is five times the US intensity, India's seven times, and South Africa and Argentina's 20 times the US figure. In fact, nearly all developed countries use AD more intensely than the US and EU.

The proclivity of AD use by developing countries has completely turned the table on the traditional proponents of AD, the US and EU. Traditional users are now more likely to defend themselves against AD allegations than they are to initiate actions. Over the past decade EU countries (as a group) have been the subject of more dumping complaints than any other country. The US increasingly finds itself subject to dumping charges as well, trailing only China and EU in alleged dumping activity.

Of course, we must reiterate that the increase in AD activity in no way means that there has been an increase in unfair trade or, in fact, that there has been any unfair trading at all. The ongoing tinkering with the AD statutes has weakened the law sufficiently that little real evidence of injurious dumping is required before duties are levied. As Patrick Low (1993, p. 86) stated "virtually any industry that considers itself adversely affected by foreign competition and presents a competently assembled petition, stands a good chance demonstrating . . . that it is under attack."

Researchers argue that the growing number of AD disputes is due to a combination of three factors: ongoing tariff liberalization, which simply leads to more trade and hence trade tensions; unsatisfactory safeguard provisions, which lead trade-injured industries to avoid using them; and increasingly weak AD standards (Finger et al., 2000; Hansen and Prusa, 1995; Miranda et al., 1998).

2.3 Comparison of AD Rules Across Countries

Each member state implements their national AD policies in accordance with the general guidelines specified by the GATT/WTO AD code. The WTO guidelines, however, are quite vague, and it is up to each country's implementing legislation to interpret the guidelines. Not surprisingly, there is substantial variation among AD statutes, with each country insisting that its procedures are the "fairest." The following discussion offers a short summary of some key similarities and differences among the countries and is based on the detailed discussions in Jackson and Vermulst (1989), Steele (1996) and, to a lesser extent, GAO (1991) and Messerlin and Reed (1995).

- All AD users delegate AD investigations to special bureaucratic units; the extent to which these units are isolated from political pressure and independent of Executive authority varies across member states. We note, however, that even in those countries where the investigative agency is independent, it appears that cases often hinge on political pressure. This issue is discussed in detail in section 4.
- Jurisdiction of the two key determinations is either bifurcated or unified. Countries like the US and Canada authorize one agency to handle dumping determination and another to handle the injury determination. The EU and Australia, on the other hand, have a single agency make both determinations. An argument in favor of the bifurcated approach is that the outcome is more likely objective since two mutually independent agencies must affirm the allegation. The unified approach, by contrast, minimizes resources and avoids conflicting judgments.[7] It is clear that either system will result in biased decision-making if the agencies are not independent of domestic industry pressure. This is an issue we discuss in detail in section 4.

- Transparency varies substantially across countries and seems to be a particular problem for new users. In particular, many new users do not provide explanation of their calculations and methods underlying their determinations.
- Confidential business information (e.g., firm-specific pricing and volume shipments, identity of purchasers) is almost always collected by the government agencies conducting the investigations; however, not all countries give interested parties access to this data. For instance, under EU and Australian law, only investigating authorities have access to all pertinent information; interested parties (e.g., the alleged dumper and its counsel) only get a summary description (Jackson and Vermulst, 1989). By contrast, under US and Canadian law, legal counsel (but not the parties themselves) have access to all confidential information.
- Price undertakings (i.e., agreements to revise prices in lieu of a formal judgment) are common in the EU and Australia, but less frequently used in the US and Canada.
- Most users begin collecting AD duties after a preliminary injury determination. In fact, until the Uruguay Round agreement mandated duties not be collected for at least 60 days, some new users collected AD duties within a few days after the petition was accepted. Using US industry-level data, Staiger and Wolak (1994) show that the value of preliminary relief may be sufficient to make filing a profitable strategy. That is, the fall in trade during the investigation period alone can substantially benefit the domestic industry, giving incentives for case filings even if a final affirmative decision is unlikely.
- Some countries, again most notably the US and Canada, mandate that the full AD duty be levied. Other countries, such as Australia and the EU, require that the AD duty be lower than the dumping margin if lesser duties would be sufficient to remove the injury caused by the dumping. The "full duty" rule means an affirmative dumping determination often leads to the complete cessation of imports from the subject countries.

3   PRE-INVESTIGATION ISSUES

3.1 AD Petition Filing

In practice, AD cases begin only when an interested domestic party (typically a domestic firm or industry group of firms) files a petition, so a natural research issue involves the determinants of who files for AD trade protection and when. The basic answer is the same as for any trade protection policy – it depends on the expected success of the petition, the expected benefit if successful, and the cost of the petition, including free-rider problems. However, the various features of AD law and its administration can often add a number of interesting details to this basic story. In addition, the volume of individual AD cases provides a relatively large sample of observations across time to examine these issues that may not be available for other forms of trade protection.

3.1.1 INDUSTRY-LEVEL DETERMINANTS OF AD PETITION FILINGS

A series of papers, including Blonigen (2000), Feinberg and Hirsch (1989), Finger (1981), Furusawa and Prusa (1996), Hansen (1990), Herander and Schwartz (1984), Krupp (1994), Lichtenberg and Tan (1994), and Sabry (2000), have estimated determinants of US AD filings by 3- or 4-digit SIC for a wide variety of time periods that fall between 1958 and 1992. All studies are single-equation, limited dependent variable specifications (such as probit, tobit, or Poisson) with the exception of Hansen (1990), which specifies a two-step nested logit model where the industry first decides whether to petition, and then the petition is either successful or not.[8] Despite these differences, there is general consistency in results across these numerous studies. Three types of observable variables seem to be the primary determinants of AD petition filings (at least, for the US): import penetration, domestic industry employment, and capital stock/intensity of the industry.

These findings accord well with the particular features of AD law and its administration in the US. In the US, the dumping and injury determinations are decided by two separate agencies, the US Department of Commerce (USDOC) and US International Trade Commission (USITC), respectively. The main hurdle is the injury test as the USITC rules affirmative in approximately 50 percent of the cases, while the USDOC almost always finds dumping. This implies that factors that affect the likelihood of a successful injury determination are most important, and import penetration and domestic industry employment (including changes in these variables) are observable variables used by the USITC for the injury determination.[9] Significant import penetration and employment are also likely to be proxying for the magnitude of benefits for a successful petition. Interestingly, domestic industry profitability and concentration do not seem to have much influence on petitions, though Feinberg and Hirsch (1989) find that more firms in an industry tend to lower the likelihood of petitions which supports the effects of free-rider problems.

A very recent focus in this area has been the additional consideration that domestic producers' export activity may also affect decisions to file AD petitions. Furusawa and Prusa (1996) consider a two-country model of reciprocal dumping where only one country has AD law. They find that firms in the AD country may not file AD petitions if market conditions are such that it leads to greater competition in the export market so that losses there more than offset the benefit of AD protection in their home market. Blonigen (2000) also considers a reciprocal dumping model, but allows both countries to have AD laws, so that retaliation is possible.[10] The model shows that if firms from both countries have sufficient exports to each others' market, a cooperative outcome is possible, where no AD petitions are filed. Using data on US AD filing activity from 1980 through 1992, the paper

finds larger export exposure dampens the incidence of US filings against some countries with AD activity over this period (Australia and New Zealand), but not others
(the EU and Canada).

Prusa and Skeath (2000) examine worldwide AD activity to determine ways in
which various countries' AD decisions are interdependent. They find that tit-for-tat,
or retaliatory, behavior is evident in these patterns. Finally Bown (2000) demonstrates the possible dampening effect that the WTO dispute settlement mechanism
may have on AD filings. These examinations of the interdependence of AD activity across countries are likely an important avenue of future research given the
recent proliferation of countries adopting AD laws and the difficulties the WTO is
facing in addressing this issue.

3.1.2 MACROECONOMIC EFFECTS ON AD PETITION FILINGS

Changes in macroeconomic variables, such as exchange rates and GDP, can affect
domestic and import variables used for determining government agencies' decisions
in AD cases across all industries in an economy. To what extent government agencies should or do discount industry outcomes in their AD decisions when these outcomes are probably due to these macroeconomic shocks is an open question.[11]
A few studies have examined the effect of macroeconomic variables on aggregate
AD filing activity. Feinberg (1989) examines the effect of exchange rate movements
on US AD filings across four import source countries (Brazil, Japan, Korea and
Mexico) for 24 quarters from 1982 through 1987. The paper finds that a US dollar
depreciation relative to the foreign currency leads to a significantly higher incidence
of AD petitions, particularly with respect to Japan. The explanation is that a US
dollar depreciation immediately lowers the price of the foreign firm's exports to the
US in the foreign firm's own currency, which is the price used by the USDOC to
determine dumping. Thus, if there is imperfect pass-through of exchange rates, or
foreign firms are slow in adjusting prices, the chances of finding dumping and the
magnitude of dumping rise.

Knetter and Prusa (2000) revisit this issue and come to substantially different
conclusions. They first develop a model that shows that exchange rates also affect
the injury determination and, in fact, this effect moves in the opposite direction from
the effect of exchange rates on the dumping calculation. A US dollar depreciation
decreases import penetration, *ceteris paribus*, making an injury determination less
likely. Thus, the effect of exchange rates on AD outcomes and, hence, petitions
should be ambiguous and depends on which decision, dumping or injury, is more
important. Knetter and Prusa (2000) test this with a substantially larger sample,
examining aggregate and bilateral AD filings for the US, Canada, EU, and Australia
from 1980 through 1998. In contrast to Feinberg (1989) they find overwhelming evidence that dollar *appreciations* lead to increased AD activity, which suggests that
the injury determination is more important to the success of a petition. Knetter and
Prusa (2000) also find that declines in real GDP also lead to increased AD activity,
which is consistent with Leidy (1997) who uses a much smaller sample of US aggregate filings.

3.2 Effects from Presence of AD Trade Protection

One of the most important insights of the AD literature is that the mere presence of AD law can affect the behavior of firms and, hence, market outcomes, even if no AD duty is ever imposed. Papers in this literature show that this phenomenon can lead to a wide variety of outcomes, some obviously unintended and even perverse to the likely objectives of AD protection. A crucial feature of AD law that creates these incentives for strategic behavior on the part of firms is the use of established criteria based on prior market outcomes to make AD case determinations. This allows relevant firms to act strategically to influence AD outcomes. In other words, AD trade protection is endogenous with the firms' market decisions. Given the issue of strategic behavior to influence subsequent outcomes, these papers rely on models of imperfect competition (often, oligopoly models) in games of at least two stages, where the focus is on firms' first-stage choices of a strategic variable, such as price, quantity, or quality.

3.2.1 NONCOOPERATIVE OUTCOMES

One of the first papers in this literature, Leidy and Hoekman (1990), examines the production decisions of a single exporting firm with some degree of market power that faces possible AD protection against its exports and random exchange rate shocks. A key issue in the paper, which will also be important for other papers discussed below, is how the AD authorities calculate the dumping margin. One method often used is the comparison between the prices set by an exporting firm, where the dumping margin is defined as the difference between the exporting firm's home price and its export price. Leidy and Hoekman (1990) call this "price-based AD law." A second alternative often used is a "cost-based" method where the dumping margin is the difference between a firm's (estimated) cost of production and its export price. Leidy and Hoekman (1990) show an important difference in the exporting firm's optimal behavior to avoid an AD duty when having to adjust prices due to an adverse exchange rate shock. Under price-based AD law the firm can re-equalize prices after an exchange rate shock by both decreasing supply to raise prices in its export market and increasing supply (or dumping) to lower prices in its own home market, whereas, under cost-based AD law, adjustment must come from the supply to the export market only. Thus, relief to domestic producers in the export market from AD protection may be largest when AD authorities use cost-based methods.

Ethier and Fischer (1987), Fischer (1992) and Reitzes (1993) broaden the focus on strategic behavior by examining oligopoly games involving both a foreign and domestic firm. These papers examine two-stage duopoly games (both in prices and quantities), where firms compete in the first stage and a government authority imposes trade protection based on market outcomes in the second stage. The focus in these papers is on the first stage, where the firms strategically alter behavior to influence the second-stage AD outcome. Like Leidy and Hoekman, one result is that the foreign firm tries to lessen the chance of trade protection, but an additional insight is that the domestic firm will act to make trade protection more likely.

Interestingly, and perhaps frustratingly, these incentive effects could lead to just about any combination of distorted market effects, depending on the characteristics of the strategic game being played by the firms.

For example, the actual market outcomes that occur based on these incentives differ significantly depending on whether the oligopoly game is in prices or quantities. Assuming a price-based method of determining the dumping margin, a domestic firm may increase output in a Cournot game to drive down the common price in the domestic market, while the foreign firm decreases its exports to the domestic market. This could actually improve welfare in the domestic market if the net effect is greater competition.[12] Under price competition, however, the foreign firm alone determines its export price which is the basis for the dumping margin calculation. Thus, foreign firms may have incentives to raise price and, if the goods are imperfect substitutes, the domestic firm may then raise prices as well, which would hurt domestic welfare. We stress the word "may" in the previous sentences because, as Fischer (1992) shows, even these results may be reversed for various games of price or quantities, depending on other market conditions. In addition, a wider variety of outcomes occur if one considers a game in prices with perfectly substitutable goods, as in Reitzes (1993), or if one examines these games when the dumping margin is calculated using a cost-based approach, as analyzed by Fischer (1992).

An important omission of these papers is consideration of the injury determination in AD cases. Firms are likely to have incentives to manipulate not only the dumping margin, but also the injury determination. In fact, given the evidence on the effect of exchange rates on AD filings discussed above, the injury determination may be more important. Prusa (1994) and Pauwels et al. (2001) examine this with respect to US and EU AD law, respectively. The additional insight from these papers is that the two considerations of dumping and injury may give the firms exactly opposite incentives to alter strategic variables. For example, while a domestic firm may want to increase output due to the dumping margin calculation in a game of quantities, they will have incentives to lower output to make an injury determination more likely.[13]

Given the ambiguous outcomes of possible market distortions by the presence of AD law, a number of papers have added important features to models based on relevant empirical information about the AD process that leads to more precise results. Kolev and Prusa (2002) explore market distortions of cost-based AD laws under the realistic assumption that AD authorities have incomplete information on foreign firms' costs. Because of this incomplete information problem, Kolev and Prusa develop a game theoretic model where efficient foreign firms pool with less efficient foreign firms and voluntarily restrain their exports (i.e., a VER). This then leads the AD authorities to impose AD duties that are undesirably low (from the standpoint of the domestic producers) for efficient foreign firms and too high for inefficient foreign firms.

The interaction between VERs and AD protection and its effect on incentives of firms and governments was first explored in a sequence of papers by James Anderson (1992, 1993). The literature above specifies the AD process in two stages. In the first stage, firms pick strategic variables that then impact the AD case outcome in a second stage. Based on the observation that many US AD investigations have led to VERs, Anderson adds an additional stage to this model of the AD process: The possibility of a negotiated VER after an AD case has been initiated. In practice, VERs are administered so that foreign firms receive the quota rents and these rents are based on the export shares of the foreign firms. These features lead to the possibility of a perverse market outcome called "domino dumping." In pursuit of quota rents from VERs based on export shares, foreign firms are encouraged by the trade protection policies to dump in order to start an AD investigation that will lead to a VER.[14] In a related paper, Rosendorff (1996) presents a model where AD investigations can provide a signal of a government's willingness to negotiate a VER with the foreign firms.

Blonigen and Ohno (1998) present another reason why the presence of AD law may actually encourage dumping on the part of foreign firms. They present an oligopoly model where foreign firms have different abilities to tariff jump AD protection in an export market. One possible outcome in the model is "protection-building trade" where a foreign firm dumps to elicit AD duties against all foreign firms in the industry,[15] and then tariff jumps into a market that is protected against exports from other foreign rivals that do not tariff jump. They present a few US AD case studies which are suggestive of protection-building trade behavior.

While all the papers in this section examine how price or quantity decisions may be affected by the presence of AD law, Vandenbussche and Wauthy (2001) consider how firms' product quality choices may be affected. They analyze a model of vertical product differentiation between a domestic and foreign firm, where firms first choose quality and then prices. They show that if a price undertaking is the anticipated outcome from application of the EU AD law, the foreign firm will be more aggressive in the quality game to have a higher quality than the domestic firm. The rationale is that price undertakings require the foreign firm to match the price of the domestic firm, which they will not be able to do and still compete in the market if they have the low quality product. Thus, AD law may reverse which firm "wins" the quality game and ultimately lead to lower welfare for the home country.

On a final note, given the nature of the issue, papers in this literature are almost exclusively theoretical. It is difficult to observe and measure how market outcomes are altered from the mere presence of AD law. One exception is an early paper by Herander and Schwartz (1984). The paper first estimates the probabilities of an AD filing and of an affirmative injury decision using data on US AD filings from 1976 through 1981. These probabilities are then specified as independent regressors in an equation explaining dumping margins over this period. The paper's hypothesis is that increased threats of AD duties (proxied by the two probabilities of case filing and injury determination) will lead foreign firms to alter their prices to avoid such an outcome and, hence, lower dumping margins. The paper finds mixed support for the hypothesis, which is probably due to a number of factors, including a limited time frame, insufficient methods to deal with endogeneity of the equations, and sample selection issues of focusing only on the pricing behavior of the firms that were involved in AD investigations. Nevertheless, the paper provides a useful insight into how empirical testing in this area may proceed in the future.

3.2.2 COOPERATIVE (COLLUSIVE) OUTCOMES

As Staiger and Wolak (1992) point out, a primary motivation for the origination of antidumping laws was to prevent foreign cartels from "dumping" their excess capacity into competitive markets and "unfairly" harming domestic producers. For example, Viner (1923) ascribes the 1916 US AD legislation as a reaction to the possibility of dumping by cartelized German steel producers. Staiger and Wolak (1992) examine a model where domestic competitive industry faces competition from a foreign monopolist, and the effect of AD law on market behavior. They show that dumping and, hence, AD activity is greater in periods of low foreign demand, which corresponds to this original rationale for AD laws. They also find that the foreign firm will choose lower capacity with the AD laws in place, which means lower exports even in periods where there is no AD activity.

In contrast to Staiger and Wolak (1992), who provide a formal model for why foreign cartels may dump and why AD laws may effectively reduce this dumping behavior, a number of theoretical papers show how AD law can create cartel behavior by facilitating collusion among domestic and foreign firms. Staiger and Wolak (1989) examine a market where the domestic and foreign firm are already tacitly colluding in an infinitely repeated game. The threat of AD acts as a mechanism to maintain the collusion, particularly when there are periods of low demand, which makes the tacit collusion more difficult to sustain.

In contrast, Prusa (1992) shows how AD law can lead to tacit collusion between domestic and foreign firms when collusion does not exist in the first place. Prusa (1992) makes two important observations about US AD cases. First, once domestic firms are involved in AD cases, they may be exempt from antitrust actions through a US legal principle called the *Noerr-Pennington* doctrine. This exemption opens the door for private (collusive) settlements between domestic and foreign firms once an AD case has been initiated. The second observation follows from the first: there are a lot of withdrawn AD petitions in the US. Between 1980 through 1985 about 38 percent of AD petitions were withdrawn; from 1980 to 1998 about 25 percent have been withdrawn. Prusa (1992) presents a bargaining model between a domestic and foreign firm competing in prices and shows that they will prefer settlements to AD duties and, hence, withdraw cases.

A shortcoming of Prusa's (1992) model is that it predicts there will always be a settlement. Panagariya and Gupta (1998), Gupta (1999) and Zanardi (2000) present models with additional considerations, such as incomplete information and negotiation costs, that predict that not all cases will be withdrawn. Zanardi (2000), which focuses on negotiation costs, also tests and finds evidence that domestic-side coordination costs and bargaining power affect the probability of withdrawal for US AD cases from 1980 through 1992 in ways that one would expect.

Finally, Veugelers and Vandenbussche (1999) examine the effect of AD law on a domestic cartel in the context of EU AD law. EU AD cases are about twice as likely to be resolved with price undertakings as US AD cases. They find that whether potential AD actions have a pro- or anti-competitive effect on the existing domestic cartel depends on cost asymmetries between the foreign and domestic firms and which agents in the domestic economy the AD authorities intend to help.

4 ISSUES RELATED TO THE INVESTIGATION

4.1 Analysis of Factors Determining Injury

According to GATT/WTO rules, there must be a determination of economic injury before AD duties can be levied. An ongoing research question is determining what factors drive the injury determination. Given the substantial data requirements to perform the analysis, the studies have focused entirely on EU and US decision-making.

Kaplan (1991) provides an excellent description of the USITC's decision-making process. Two key ideas emerge. First, agency discretion is paramount. Although Commissioners must look at statutorily defined factors, such as employment and the volume of imports, there is no precise formula for when material injury is by reason of dumped imports. Somewhat like the definition of pornography, they apparently know injury when they see it. Second, formal economic analysis is rarely done. "Trends analysis" is common, but this essentially means eyeballing charts and tables and confirming profits and employment are down. If imports have also increased, the causality connection is assumed. There appears to be no serious attempt to disentangle the injurious effects of dumped imports from other sources.[16]

Beginning with two seminal works, Finger et al.'s (1982) paper and Baldwin's (1985) book, a large literature has emerged testing the economic factors that determine injury. These two early studies deserve special recognition for framing the question and laying-out the institutional features and political economy dynamics of the administered protection process. All of the subsequent papers use the same general approach and estimate a decision function using binary regression techniques. In addition, given the substantial discretion the Commissioners have, most studies also test whether political pressure influences outcomes.

The research in this area can be distinguished by the disaggregation of the data, the number of cases included in the sample, and whether the Commissioner-specific votes are analyzed. On the one hand, studies such as Keith Anderson (1993), Baldwin and Steagall (1994), DeVault (1993), and Moore (1992) construct their samples using data from the case reports themselves. This means their data is very disaggregated, but they have a small number of observations, typically 50 to 60 separate cases. The drawback to this approach is that the USITC only provides data in the public reports when doing so will not release any confidential data and also when no participating firm objects. As a result, these papers have data on only about 20 percent of cases during the sample period under investigation. It also means that there is a potential sample selection problem, which results in the elimination of all cases concerning concentrated industries.

On the other hand, Baldwin (1985), Finger et al. (1982), Hansen and Prusa (1996, 1997), Tharakan (1991), Tharakan and Waelbroeck (1994a, b), and Prusa (1998) all use more aggregated data and are therefore able to construct much larger samples, typically 200 to 300 cases. The drawback to this approach, of course, is that the measures of economic injury are subject to measurement error due to the aggregation.

For instance, the import surge motivating the affirmative injury determination may only have occurred for a couple of products (i.e., tariff line items), while the data used are some combination of 4- or 5-digit aggregated imports along with 4-digit SIC industry statistics. Moreover, this set of papers always focuses on cases involving manufacturing industries.

Despite the differing philosophies in constructing the data, the papers reach many of the same conclusions. The results can be summarized as follows.

1   Economic factors do influence outcomes. The studies that use more disaggregated data find a stronger connection between economic trends and outcomes than those using more aggregated data. Nevertheless, it is clear that the larger the volume of imports and the larger the profit (or output) loss, the greater chance of an affirmative decision.

2   Examination of US data has found that USITC Commissioners significantly differ in their voting behavior (Baldwin and Steagall, 1994; Moore, 1992; DeVault, 1993). These papers make it clear that getting the "right" person on the Commission clearly changes outcomes. No formal study has been done, however, on relating the previous background of the Commissioners to their voting records. This would be a valuable contribution to the literature, especially in light of the ample anecdotal evidence that suggests candidates with a free trade bias are not nominated for the Commission.

3   Political pressure matters – a lot. While the studies vary in what proxies they construct to measure political pressure, all find non-statutory factors are significant. For instance, two key House and Senate subcommittees control the USITC's budget. Moore (1992), DeVault (1993), and Hansen and Prusa (1996, 1997) all find that industries with production facilities in the districts of oversight members fare better at the Commission.[17] To put relative impact into perspective, Hansen and Prusa's estimates imply that an additional oversight representative increases the probability of success by about 8 percent. Hansen and Prusa (1996, 1997) also find that PAC contributions to the oversight members also improve an industry's chances, which suggests that political pressure is generated not just by employment concerns, but also by reelection financing concerns. Anderson (1993) is the sole exception, as he finds no measurable impact from his political pressure variables. He does not find political pressure affecting the USITC decisions, but this is almost surely because his proxies of political pressure are poorly constructed.

4   Political pressure can also take the form of bias against certain trading partners. Moore (1992) and Hansen and Prusa (1996, 1997) find that US cases against Western European countries are biased toward rejecting. By contrast, cases against Japan and non-market economies are far more likely to result in duties. Non-market economies fare particularly poorly at the USITC, a finding due in part to the fact that rules for non-market economies are particularly protectionist.

5   The steel industry fares remarkably well. After controlling for industry size, employment, changes in profit, changes in trade volume, oversight representation, etc., study after study finds that US steel cases are about 30 percent

more likely to receive protection than non-steel cases. This could be due to the fact that the steel industry files so many cases and has learned what arguments work better, or perhaps steel firms simply hire better legal counsel. The finding is also surely due to the numerous provisions the steel industry has managed to get incorporated into the AD statutes that apply to essentially steel alone.[18]

6   The "bifurcated" injury approach has a significant impact on the outcomes (DeVault 1993). Bifurcated injury means the USITC first determines whether there is injury and then determines the role of imports. This approach has the undesirable attribute that AD protection is only offered to industries with *negative* profits. Industries simply earning lower, but not negative profits, are not given protection. In related papers, Hansen and Prusa (1993) find that industries receiving protection continue to significantly under-perform. This suggests that industries that receive protection are under-performing for reasons other than imports. Yet, USITC practice is to reward precisely these industries.

7   The same general lessons are revealed in EU cases: economics trends matter, country biases exist, and political pressure influences outcomes (Eymann and Schuknecht, 1996; Tharakan, 1991; Tharakan and Waelbroeck, 1994a, b). In fact, Tharakan and Waelbroeck (1994a, b) argue that the EU Commission is even more susceptible than the USITC to non-economic factors. They argue that this result follows from the EU's strict confidentiality rules where little information is revealed to parties. As a result, it is easier for political factors to influence the Commission's decisions since there is little formal accounting of the decision process. Eymann and Schuknecht (1996) argue, however, that over time the EU decisions have become somewhat less politically motivated while the US decisions have become somewhat more influenced by political pressure.

4.2   Cumulation and Increased Protection

As mentioned earlier, the rules governing AD law are constantly evolving. In 1984, the US amended the AD statute mandating that the USITC cumulate imports across countries when determining injury. Without cumulation, imports are evaluated on a country-by-country basis. When cumulation is applied, the USITC aggregates all like products from all countries under investigation and assesses the combined impact on the domestic industry. In work related to the papers discussed above, Hansen and Prusa (1996) quantify the impact of this change in the statute. Using AD determinations between 1980 and 1988, they are able to identify the effect of cumulation by comparing outcomes before cumulation (1980–4) and after cumulation (1985–8). In the pre-cumulation period there were cases that would have been cumulated had the amendment been in effect. They find that the amendment had a dramatic effect on the USITC. After controlling for all other factors, they find that cumulated cases are about 30 percent more likely to result in duties than non-cumulated cases. In other words, their findings suggest that upwards of 50 percent of USITC affirmative determinations from 1985 through 1988 would have been negative without cumulation.

That cumulation raises the probability of an affirmative injury finding is not surprising. What is surprising is that they find that the cumulation effect is super-additive. That is, holding the volume of imports constant, the USITC is more likely to vote affirmatively if cumulation is involved. In other words, under cumulation, the domestic industry has a greater chance of receiving protection by filing against two countries each with 20 percent of the import market than against a single country with a 40 percent import market share.

Tharakan et al. (1998) perform a similar "natural experiment" using EU data. They too find that cumulation increases the probability of levying duties and that it is super-additive. Moreover, they refine the Hansen and Prusa methodology and show that the super-additive finding is not simply due to having more countries involved in the investigation. Cumulation itself seems to have made the decision-makers more protective.

The reason for the super-additive effect is an open question. Hansen and Prusa speculate that the USITC took the amendment as a signal from Congress to be more protective. Panagariya and Gupta (2000) offer the first formal explanation of the finding and base their explanation on free-riding. Panagariya and Gupta assume that the probability of injury increases in the import market share under investigation and decreases in the legal defense expenditures. The legal defense, provided by one foreign firm, automatically becomes available to all foreign firms subject to the investigation. This leads every foreign firm to invest less on defense than would be the case in a cooperative solution. *Ceteris paribus*, the larger the number of foreign firms charged, the more serious the free-rider problem. If a single larger foreign firm is named, it internalizes all the benefits of defense expenditures, and hence spends more to acquit itself.

4.3 Methods for Determining Dumping

Most of the literature on US AD decisions has focused on the USITC's injury determination. One reason for this is that the USDOC almost always finds dumping. Over the past decade, for example, the USDOC has issued only three negative LTFV determinations (out of almost 400 determinations). Boltuck and Litan (1991) offer a comprehensive study of the USDOC's LTFV procedures. The Boltuck and Litan volume clearly indicates that both statutory rules and also agency-level discretionary decisions serve the purpose of producing very large margins.

Moreover, the USDOC not only finds dumping, they almost always find unbelievably large dumping margins. Any argument that AD law is designed to ensure "fair trade" looks ridiculous when confronted with the USDOC's margins. According to the statute, the dumping duties are designed to make the dumped imports "fairly traded" imports. Yet, the average dumping margin over the past decade is about 60 percent. The extraordinarily large margins are even more onerous in light of the US's refusal to adopt a "lesser duty" provision. Murray (1991) and Palmeter (1991) suggest that the entire dumping margin process is an exercise in futility for the foreign firms. For essentially all foreign firms, the question is only whether the margin will completely foreclose them from the US market.

Finally, the USDOC has increasingly more frequently relied on "facts available" methods.[19] In about one-third of its calculations, the foreign firms have either refused to provide information or the USDOC ignored information provided by foreign parties. Baldwin and Moore (1991) find that the use of "facts available" nearly doubles the average US dumping margin from around 35 percent to over 65 percent.

Lindsey (1999) conclusively documents how the fair trade rhetoric stressed by AD's supporters has little to do with its practice. In a meticulous study, Lindsey reviewed every USDOC decision over a four-year period. He finds that in 97 percent of its calculations the USDOC uses methods that allow it to construct or estimate the foreign firm's costs or market price. Of course, constructed value methods are precisely when the USDOC can be more arbitrary. As feared, the dumping margins increase as the USDOC moves further away from evaluating actual market transactions. For his sample, the average dumping margin is 95 percent when "facts available" are used.

4.4 Participating in the Investigation

AD law requires that the petition for relief must be on behalf of the entire domestic industry. In practice, this means that at least 50 percent of the domestic industry must not oppose the petition. However, domestic firms often oppose the petition. Although only a handful of petitions are rejected because of too much opposition, it seems a bit odd that domestic firms often do not support the petition. If reducing competition is possible, why not?

Cassing and To (2000) develop a model where informational asymmetries explain opposition. In their model, each firm's marginal cost is private information. By opposing the petition, low cost firms can signal their efficiency and gain at the expense of high cost domestic firms. For all domestic firms, the larger the imports, the greater are the benefits from protection. Combining the above two insights, Cassing and To show that if a firm opposes a petition when imports are large, it must be that it is quite efficient itself. They prove that the unique "refined" equilibrium involves low cost firms opposing the petition and high cost firms supporting the petition, assuming imports are sufficiently large.

Moore (2000) is also concerned with the decision to participate in the investigation. He studies why foreign firms often choose not to participate in the dumping margin calculation, and instead allow the case to proceed using "facts available," which always means very large tariffs. Moore argues that the foreign firm must trade-off the costs of participating in the USDOC investigation with the likelihood of receiving lower duties. He shows that even firms who are not dumping may nonetheless choose to not participate. In other words, not cooperating does not indicate guilt.

One concern with Moore's model is that he assumes that, if the foreign firm participates, the USDOC evaluates the firm's costs in a reasonable fashion. By this, we mean that the USDOC draws a realization of costs from the true distribution of costs. Given the papers by Murray (1991), Palmeter (1991) and Lindsey (1999), however, it is not clear that this assumption is consistent with USDOC methods. Nevertheless, this comment should not be taken as a serious criticism of Moore, but rather a call for more study of the issue of participation.

4.5 Designing Optimal AD Rules

A serious problem with AD investigations is that the investigating agencies do not observe the foreign firm's true costs and prices. This is the issue addressed in the Kolev and Prusa paper (2002) discussed above. Authorities also do not observe the domestic industry's true injury level. As a result, interested parties are likely to misrepresent the true information in the AD investigation. Kohler and Moore (1998, 2001) apply optimal contract theory to the problem and propose alternative AD rules to account for the parties' incentives to misrepresent their private information.

Kohler and Moore (1998) consider the problem of designing an AD policy when the government does not have complete information about injury to the domestic industry. They show that if the government can only offer per-unit compensation schemes, then it is not possible to induce the domestic industry to truthfully reveal its injury level. However, if the government can offer a two-part tariff, they show it is possible to get truthful revelation of injury. This is a nice result because the remedy allowed under WTO rules is a duty levied per unit of imports, precisely the type of remedy that Kohler and Moore argue encourages the domestic firm to lie about its injury. The practical problem with Kohler and Moore's scheme is that it requires a payment to the domestic industry even if no injury is found – a provision that would surely lead to even more filings.

Kohler and Moore (2001) take a more realistic tack by considering how an authority can audit information provided by the domestic firm to eliminate mis-representation of injury. They show that the appropriate penalty size along with an optimal probability of auditing leads to truthful announcements by the firm, minimizes auditing costs, and discourages frivolous petitions.

5 WELFARE EFFECTS AND MARKET OUTCOMES OF AD TRADE PROTECTION

As with any trade protection policy, an obvious issue for economists is the welfare effects and market outcomes of the trade protection policy. Consistent with the theme throughout this chapter, there are special issues connected with AD trade protection that affect the analysis of these issues. In particular, the investigation process surrounding AD protection, as well as the administration and procedures for recalculating AD duties after the case, affect welfare and market outcomes to the point that the observable AD duties may be almost secondary in importance to the investigation and administration processes.

5.1 Welfare Effects

Welfare consequences of a standard *ad valorem* tariff are well known, particularly for the case of perfectly competitive markets. Domestic producers gain, but this comes at the expense of consumers and creation of deadweight losses. For a small country, the losses outweigh the gains, whereas a tariff by a large country may depress import prices enough to lead to net gains. Since AD trade protection involves an *ad valorem* duty, this analysis is generally applicable. However, as with our earlier discussions of other papers on AD, features of AD law and administration can add important layers of complexity to any starting framework.

5.1.1 WELFARE EFFECTS FOR DOMESTIC PRODUCERS

A number of papers examining welfare effects of AD duties have focused on the benefits that accrue to domestic producers. Hartigan et al. (1989) use a capital market event study methodology to examine whether non-steel US AD petitions in the early half of the 1980s led to positive abnormal stock returns for the petitioning firms. The paper generally finds statistically significant effects on petitioner's stock returns from affirmative AD decisions, but curiously finds that it is cases where the USITC ruled there was a threat of injury behind this result, not cases where actual injury was found. Unfortunately, the paper does not translate these statistically significant abnormal returns into dollar figures, so it is impossible to know the magnitude of the benefits to domestic producers implied by their estimates. Mahdavi and Bhagwati (1994) and Hughes et al. (1997) use a similar approach to examine events surrounding the US trade dispute in semiconductors with Japan in the mid-1980s, including the AD cases that led to the Semiconductor Agreement. Neither study finds much impact from the AD investigation events, but significant positive abnormal returns for US firms from the Semiconductor Agreement.

Perhaps a more standard approach used by economists to estimate welfare effects is computable partial and general equilibrium models. DeVault (1996a), Kelly and Morkre (1998), Morkre and Kelly (1994), and Murray and Rousslang (1989) use computable partial equilibrium models to focus on the economic impact to the domestic industry implied by the dumping margin calculated for AD cases. The two papers by Kelly and Morkre examine all US AD and countervailing duty (CVD) cases from 1980 through 1988 for which they could obtain sufficient data from reports connected with the cases. They then examine each US AD (or CVD) case individually with a computable partial equilibrium model to assess the implied revenue loss to the US domestic industry due to the dumping margin, which is calculated by the USDOC. They find that the revenue decrease (or "injury") to the domestic industry in the large majority of cases is quite small even for parameter estimates that would give an upper-bound estimate of this injury.

A final approach to specifically examine effects of AD cases on domestic producers is by Nieberding (1999). This paper uses quarterly Compustat data on individual US petitioning firms for a select number of US AD cases to estimate changes in market power from AD outcomes. Nieberding's estimates find that US petitioning firms experienced statistically significant increases in market power from affirmative decisions in semiconductors and tapered roller bearings and significant declines from a negative decision in a hydraulic cement case.

5.1.2 OVERALL WELFARE EFFECTS

Since the calculated dumping margin becomes the *ad valorem* AD duty, a seemingly obvious implication of these partial equilibrium studies is that if dumping is not causing significant losses to the domestic industry, then the effects of the AD duty and, hence, overall welfare effects, are necessarily small. USITC (1995) and Gallaway et al. (1999) show that this implication is quite misleading. These two studies examine the aggregate welfare effects of all US AD and CVD orders in place as of 1993 using a computable general equilibrium model developed by economists at the USITC. A key insight that drastically affects the welfare analysis is that AD duties are not static over time. In a process known as an administrative review, the USDOC recalculates dumping margins as often as every year using the previous period pricing and/or cost data. As shown by DeVault (1996b), many foreign firms raise prices and then successfully lower dumping margins in administrative reviews to avoid the AD duty. Thus, by raising prices, foreign firms divert tariff revenue from the US government to their own revenue, not unlike switching from a domestic-held quota to a foreign-held quota. Gallaway et al. (1999) show in their model that the estimated welfare loss to the US economy from the *ad valorem* AD and CVD duties that one observes in 1993 is only $209 million annually. However, when one takes into account how much the AD duties fell over time from the administrative review process, the welfare loss ranges from $2–4 billion annually. This latter welfare estimate places AD and CVD trade protection as one of the costliest US trade protection programs.

Of course, these welfare estimates still may miss a number of very important considerations that affect welfare. First, given the discussion in section 3, there are likely substantial welfare effects occurring in markets for which we do not see any AD activity per se. Additional considerations below that are not included in these estimates include the effects of the investigation process itself, even for cases that do not lead to AD duties, and the possibility of subsequent tariff-jumping by foreign firms.

5.2 Other Specific Market Outcomes

5.2.1 IMPORT AND DOMESTIC OUTPUT OUTCOMES

While the administrative process connected with AD trade protection affects overall welfare estimates, a number of empirical papers have also found significant impacts of the AD investigation process on other market outcomes. Staiger and Wolak (1994) investigate the effect of not only AD duties, but also various AD investigation events, on imports and domestic production for US AD cases from 1980 through 1985. Perhaps the most sophisticated econometric model used in the AD literature to date, the authors build a structural econometric model that aggregates information on AD actions that occur across very narrow import product codes into more standard industry level classifications. They then use this model to jointly estimate equations explaining AD filing, imports, and domestic output across all US manufacturing industries. Use of indicator variables that count the number of various investigation events ongoing across import product codes in an industry at a given time allows the paper to estimate effects on these imports and domestic production during various phases of the investigation and for the variety of possible AD case outcomes.

The evidence in Staiger and Wolak (1994) suggests a wide variety of import and domestic production effects that depend on the outcome of the investigation events. In particular, they find substantial import and output effects from preliminary affirmative, final affirmative and suspended decisions. The imposition of AD duties reduces imports about $50 million (from an initial average base of $291 million), with almost similar gains in domestic output (average initial base of $2,167 million). Half of this change occurs at the preliminary affirmative decision and the other half at the final affirmative decision. A suspended case both reduces imports and increases domestic output by $25 million. Finally, the paper identifies two different filing strategies that imply substantially different effects on imports and domestic production during the investigation. An outcome filer is keenly interested in an affirmative final outcome and the trade-reducing impacts of the AD duty, whereas a process filer files in hopes that the petition itself will reduce imports. The paper finds most cases follow an outcome filer process where imports do not decline unless and until a preliminary affirmative decision is made.

Krupp and Pollard (1996) also examine the effect of AD investigation events, as well as the final outcome, on imports. Unlike Staiger and Wolak (1994), they solve data aggregation issues by focusing on specific chemical product codes subject to US AD investigations from 1976 through 1988 for which they can get necessary disaggregated US production data. They also split their data into import sources named in the investigation and non-named import sources and examine the impact of the AD investigation and outcomes on both import sources. This allows the analysis of what is termed trade diversion, where trade protection against one import source of a product may divert demand toward other import sources for the product rather than the domestic producers. In about half of the cases, the paper finds evidence that the investigation process itself dampens imports from named import sources, and that the investigation and affirmative outcomes lead to increased imports from non-named import sources (i.e., trade diversion).

The issue of trade diversion is an important one because of its implications for who actually benefits from trade protection, and it is prominent in AD cases where petitioners often specify only particular import sources.[20] Prusa (1997) gathers detailed product-level trade data for all US AD cases that received final determinations from 1980 through 1988 and examines whether trade diversion effects generalize beyond just the chemical product cases examined by Krupp and Pollard (1996). With this comprehensive set of products, Prusa (1997) finds very substantial trade diversion effects. For all AD cases (whether there is a final affirmative decision or not), Prusa finds that the value of imports from non-named countries goes up approximately 20 percent the first year after the case and over 40 percent after five years. The trade diversion effects are higher for cases where high AD duties are imposed, but still substantial for low-duty cases and rejected cases. Thus, the evidence suggests that the benefits to domestic petitioners may be significantly offset by trade diversion. In contrast, Vandenbussche, Konings, and Springael (1999) examine trade data on all products subject to European AD investigations from 1985 through 1990 and find no evidence of trade diversion. These different trade diversion effects may be due to institutional differences in the AD investigation process between the US and the EU, and should be the subject of future analysis.

5.3 Price Effects

An immediate effect of an AD duty is to raise the price paid by consumers in the protected market. However, if markets are imperfectly competitive, there is a number of interesting issues that influence how much prices rise and the responses of the other competitors in the market place.

5.3.1 PASS-THROUGH ISSUES

One of the first issues is the pass-through of the AD duty by the foreign firm onto consumer prices in the protected market. As with other issues discussed above, the administrative review process can have a substantial impact on pass-through of the AD duty. In the US, AD duties are assessed retrospectively. The initial AD duty is only an estimate, where the actual AD duty for a previous period is determined by recalculations during an administrative review and assessed *ex post*. This means that foreign firms may be able to avoid AD duties completely by appropriately altering their prices. Boltuck (1987) considers the case where the AD authorities calculate the dumping margin as the difference between the foreign firm's export price and its home price, and derives the market conditions that determine how much the foreign firm raises its export price and/or lowers its home price to decrease the AD duty.

Blonigen and Haynes (2002) develop and test two additional pass-through hypotheses. First, they show that because the USDOC uses the *ex factory* export price of the foreign firm (the price as the product leaves the factory), a firm wishing to eliminate an AD duty may have to allow up to 200 percent pass-through of the AD duty to the protected market consumers. Second, they show that the retrospective nature of the administrative review process structurally alters how firms allow exchange rate movements to pass-through to prices in the protected market. Using detailed product-level data on iron and steel products imported from Canada to the US before and after the 1992–3 US AD cases against these products, they find 160 percent pass-through of the AD duty onto US prices of Canadian steel and a substantial increase in exchange rate pass-through for these products after the case.

The pricing models in Boltuck (1987) and Blonigen and Haynes (2002) are static. Blonigen and Park (2001) develop a model of dynamic pricing for a foreign firm that faces potential AD duties with recalculations through administrative reviews. When antidumping enforcement is uncertain, firms with *ex ante* expectations that the probability of AD enforcement is low, or that the probability of a settlement/VER (instead of AD duties) is high, will decrease their dumping and AD duties over time in the administrative review process once they face AD duties. Using data on US AD duty changes over time from 1980 through 1991 they find evidence to support this hypothesis.

5.3.2 PRICING BEHAVIOR OF OTHER COMPETITORS

Given the number of theoretical papers suggesting that features of AD laws can facilitate collusive outcomes, there has been a paucity of empirical work to confirm this, particularly through exploration of price data. The one exception is Prusa (1997) which, as part of the analysis of trade diversion effects, examines unit values of products subject to US AD final determinations from 1980 through 1988 for both named and non-named sources. The paper finds that unit values of non-named import sources rise about two-thirds as much as the named import sources after an AD case, which may reflect the substitutability of products or, alternatively, may suggest some sort of collusive outcome.

5.4 Tariff-jumping FDI

We discussed earlier how trade diversion may occur in AD cases and lessen benefits to domestic producers. Another potential consequence of AD investigations and duties that may substantially lessen the benefits afforded the domestic industry is tariff-jumping by foreign firms. As shown by Haaland and Wooton (1998) and Vandenbussche, Veugelers, and Belderbos (1999), AD protection can induce foreign firms to locate in the protectionist country to avoid the tariff and actually make the domestic producers worse off from increased domestic competition.[21]

Empirical papers examining tariff-jumping of AD protection have mainly focused on the foreign direct investment (FDI) responses of Japanese firms using samples at different levels of disaggregation. The level of disaggregation is important because AD actions are often very narrowly targeted, which may make it difficult to identify its effects in more aggregate data. Barrell and Pain (1999) examine country-level Japanese FDI responses to AD activity in the US and the EU. Blonigen and Feenstra (1997) examine the interaction between trade policy measures (including AD protection) and Japanese FDI for the US from 1980 to 1988 using 4-digit SIC industry-level data. Belderbos (1997) and Belderbos and Sleuwaegen (1998), analyze tariff-jumping FDI of AD protection using a unique database of Japanese electronics firms and products. All these papers find significant tariff-jumping effects with respect to AD protection, and Blonigen and Feenstra (1997) even find that the threat of AD protection induces FDI.

One important policy issue with respect to tariff-jumping is the extent to which institutional differences in administration of the AD duties affect tariff-jumping incentives. In the EU, government officials often negotiate price arrangements between foreign and domestic firms, called "price undertakings," *in lieu* of AD duties. Vandenbussche, Veugelers, and Belderbos (1999) show that a strategic policymaker may prefer a price undertaking to an AD duty, in order to avoid tariff-jumping FDI. If this model is correct, one might expect there to be less tariff-jumping of EU AD duties than US AD duties, where there is no formal system for price undertakings.[22] Evidence in Belderbos (1997), however, finds that an affirmative AD decision raises the FDI probability from 19.6 percent to 71.8 percent in the EU, but only raises it from 19.7 percent to 35.95 percent in the US. Belderbos argues that this difference is due to the fact that it is difficult for firms to lower AD duties after the case in the EU, whereas this is relatively easier to do in the US with its retrospective administrative review process. Clearly, there is need for further research on this issue.

A final issue is whether the tariff-jumping responses found for Japanese firms characterize the responses of all firms. Blonigen (2002) analyzes tariff-jumping responses of all firms subject to AD duties in the US from 1980 through 1990 and finds substantially smaller tariff-jumping responses for this sample. The results suggest that tariff-jumping FDI is only a realistic option for multinational firms from industrialized countries, which comprise less than half the cases. This may be one reason why developing countries have been more concerned than industrialized countries about addressing AD protection in the WTO.

6   Conclusion and Issues for Future Research

Antidumping trade protection has a variety of unique features that set it apart from more traditional forms of trade policy. Virtually all trade economists realize that the effects of AD actions are not summarized by the AD duty one observes. However, the AD literature to date has taken this general observation and established a whole set of results that shows that what one sees with AD trade protection is far from what one gets.

This is seen first in the substantial literature that shows the mere presence of AD law, with its established rules for determining outcomes, alters incentives for market participants. Thus, a wide variety of potentially distorted market outcomes has been discovered. This includes such perverse results as domestic industries feigning injury, macroeconomic factors driving petition activity, foreign firms possibly dumping *more* than they otherwise would (through either domino dumping or protection-building trade reasons), and the facilitation of market collusion that is apparently exempt from antitrust laws.

Second, the literature has shown that AD law on paper is not necessarily the same as AD law in practice. Virtually every study of AD outcomes in the US and EU has shown that political factors influence outcomes. In addition, the practice of using estimated cost data and/or "facts available" to determine dumping margins has become institutionalized and led to larger AD duties. Perhaps most importantly, AD law on paper has evolved over time to make AD trade protection ever more likely and effective. This includes the GATT Tokyo Round changes in AD law to broaden the definition of dumping to include sales below cost and to no longer require that imports be "demonstrably the principle cause of material injury." It also includes the 1984 US legislation to allow cumulation for injury determinations and the EU legislation to strengthen anti-circumvention provisions.

Third, investigation events have been shown to have effects on imports and domestic production that rival the AD duty itself. On the other hand, the investigation and

AD duty can lead to other unintended market effects that can dilute the trade protection effectiveness, such as trade diversion and tariff-jumping FDI.

Fourth, and finally, the administration of AD duties *after* the cases has been shown by the literature to have substantial market and welfare effects that go beyond the observable AD duty. The literature has mainly focused on the retrospective administrative review process of the US, which has been shown to affect the pass-through of the AD duty and of exchange rates by the subject foreign firm. It has also been shown to lead to much more adverse welfare consequences for the US by allowing foreign firms to capture foreign rents at the expense of US tariff revenue.

6.1 Future Research Issues

There are some big issues and questions that remain for the AD literature and a whole set of new questions that loom given recent developments in worldwide AD activity. We start with remaining questions in the existing literature.

Despite the statistics in section 2 detailing the substantial and growing use of AD laws, one question is why there aren't more AD filings. The literature has found many positive effects for domestic producers, including the ability to facilitate collusive outcomes with foreign rivals while avoiding antitrust consideration. It has also shown how much AD laws are tilted in favor of affirmative findings. It seems strange that we don't see many more AD petitions. Of course, there are effects that have been uncovered that could substantially mitigate the benefits that domestic producers receive. Trade diversion is one of those effects. Yet, the US cumulation legislation should allow petitioners to more easily prevent trade diversion. Tariff-jumping is another effect that can mitigate benefits to the domestic producers, yet Blonigen (2002) finds that this is not a widespread phenomenon. Fear of retaliation is another possibility that has had little study. These explanations all assume that domestic firms are sufficiently aware of these laws to make informed choices about whether to file, which may be incorrect.

With the primary focus on domestic producers and market outcomes for the investigated product, there has been little study of effects for other agents affected by the AD law. Many, if not most, AD cases involve products that are important inputs into other sectors of the economy. Yet, with the exception of Feinberg and Kaplan (1993) and Hughes et al. (1997), there has been little study of the economic impacts to downstream sectors. Feinberg and Kaplan document how upstream AD protection spreads to downstream AD protection in US metal and chemical industries, presumably because the downstream sector became less competitive after its inputs became more costly. In contrast, Hughes et al. find that US downstream industries benefited from the US Semiconductor Agreement with Japan, presumably because of the positive externalities between these downstream industries and a strong domestic presence in the upstream industry. Clearly, there is room to investigate these issues further.

There are other agents that are affected by AD protection as well. US AD law requires that AD duties be collected from the US importers, not the foreign firms.

This must have impacts on the importing and distribution market that have so far been unexplored. Finally, there has been little study of market effects on foreign firms' home markets in the subject product once they are subject to AD duties, even though the literature has uncovered a number of theoretical possibilities in this regard.

While there has been preliminary work to compare the effects of differing features of AD laws and practice between the US and EU system (mainly by European researchers), more needs to be done in this area. The two most substantial differences examined so far are the prevalence of price undertakings in the EU, and the US retrospective administration of AD review and duty collection versus the EU's prospective system. Price undertakings should lead to greater occurrence of collusion, but no one has examined this, much less even formally tested for collusion for any market with AD activity in either country.[23] These differences may affect which industries file for AD relief in the two countries, yet, to our knowledge, there has been no study that has examined who files in the EU, much less how this may differ from the US. The US retrospective administrative review process has been shown to substantially affect market outcomes and welfare after the case, but much less is known about after-case market outcomes in the EU under a much different process.

A major reason why it is important to understand how these two systems yield different outcomes is because future WTO negotiations over AD laws will likely work toward further harmonization across countries. As the two major economies with active AD laws, the US and EU systems will be the basis for such a harmonization. However, without better information on the different economic impacts of these systems, economists will be less able to inform this upcoming process. And to this point, the evidence suggests that economists have been hardly heard by policymakers, as the evolution of the law has been to make it easier for domestic firms to gain AD trade protection. Future WTO negotiations are also likely to involve discussions on placing AD laws in the context of an overall competition policy. This is another issue that has had scant attention by economists to date.[24]

A final development that will require substantially more research attention is the growing proliferation of countries adopting and using AD laws. Researchers have just begun to document this proliferation (see Miranda et al., 1998, and Prusa, 2000) and preliminary work has only started to look at the interdependence of filings across countries (see Blonigen, 2000, and Prusa and Skeath, 2000). Will this proliferation in AD law adoption lead to greater AD activity and the possibility of a new round of tariff wars? Alternatively, will it possibly lead to less overall activity from some "cold war" outcome in the long run and/or push the traditional users of AD laws into abandoning their stout defense of the necessity of AD laws in the next WTO round?

In summary, AD trade protection laws and activity continue to evolve and will be one of the more important future issues for the WTO and the world community. There are many open research questions that remain with current AD laws and activity, and new questions arising given recent events. Economists have established important conclusions about AD law and activity that are often not heard or ignored by policymakers. In order to have a voice in policy, research in this area will need to not only evolve as quickly as the AD policy, but also anticipate the future issues in that policy's evolution.

Acknowledgments

We wish to thank Robert Baldwin, James Harrigan, Jesse Kreier, Andrew Szamosszegi, and Hylke Vandenbussche, as well as participants of the NBER International Trade and Investment Program Meetings, Spring 2001, for helpful comments. All remaining errors are our own.

Notes

1   The inclusion was not without controversy: the UK, for example, argued that the practice of dumping was not bad in itself and that the GATT should instead prohibit the imposition of AD duties. The UK's concern, shared by other participants, was that AD laws could compromise the overall objectives of the agreement to liberalize the international trading regime.

2   Clearly, a comprehensive study of pre-1980 use is an open area of research, and one that would shed a great deal of light on the spread of AD protection. However, given that the data sources are only available at country-level (if at all), it is a research project that could probably only be tackled as part of a large-scale research program (e.g., WTO or World Bank sponsored project). Baldwin (1998) provides some detail on US AD cases before 1980.

3   The rule codified recent practice in several of the signatory states, including Australia, Canada, and the US.

4   Different methods and definitions for evaluating US Department of Commerce methodology explain the different estimates. Note also that the EU, the other major user of AD, has similarly embraced cost-based methodology. Messerlin (1989) estimates that over 90 percent of EU cases against developing countries are based on constructed costs.

5   Lindsey (1999) provides strong evidence for Horlick's view: over the four-year period, 1995–8, only 4 of 141 LTFV calculations were based on a true price-to-price comparison.

6   This statement is conditional on being a user of AD protection. Countries such as Japan have initiated fewer than a half-dozen AD cases, despite having the law on the books.

7   For instance, with two separate agencies involved, one agency can define the competitive products narrowly in order to maximize the duty and the other agency can define the relevant competition broadly in order to maximize employment and profit loss.

8   The advantage of Hansen's (1990) econometric specification is that she can and does show that the second-stage outcome decision affects the first-stage petition regression in a statistically significant manner.

9   Interestingly, some studies (e.g., Blonigen, 2000, Furusawa and Prusa, 1996, and Sabry, 2000) find significant support that the level of import penetration positively affects petition activity, while other studies (e.g., Finger, 1981, Feinberg and Firsch, 1989, and Hansen, 1990) find evidence that *changes* in import penetration positively affect AD petition incidence. Finger (1981) is the only study that we have found that includes both the level and change in import penetration and the study finds that the level, and not the change, is a statistically significant determinant of AD petitions for the sample.

10   Anderson et al. (1995) likewise consider a reciprocal dumping model where both countries may adopt AD laws. They examine the game where countries have the strategic

choice over whether to adopt an AD law and find that an equilibrium where both countries adopt AD laws can lead to increased competition in both markets and actually benefit consumers.

11　A related case in this regard is the escape clause petition by US automakers in 1980, for which the USITC made an injury determination. A primary reason for the USITC negative decision was the determination that losses to US automakers during the time period in question were due to the oil shock and resulting recession, not due to Japanese imports.

12　Reitzes (1993) shows that this requires that the foreign firm's share of the domestic market needs to be sufficiently small.

13　Leidy (1994) summarizes most of this early work.

14　We note that the timing of the AD case and VER in James Anderson (1992, 1993) contrasts with that in Kolev and Prusa (2002). This is not necessarily inconsistent in that there is US evidence in these papers of the timing of the AD case and VER occurring in both possible sequences. In addition, a VER occurring before an AD case may not always be publicly announced or noticed.

15　Blonigen and Ohno (1998) detail how the administration of AD law often leads to AD duties across many related import sources, not just the primary dumping sources.

16　Pindyck and Rotemberg (1987) and Grossman (1986) develop methods for assessing whether imports have caused injury to a competing US industry. Both approaches suggest that the USITC is far too willing to attribute injury to imports. There is no evidence, however, that either paper has had any impact on actual USITC practice.

17　It should also be recognized that USITC Commissioners have often previously served on the staff of these subcommittees, which suggests that the budget may not be the only channel where that influence is felt.

18　The captive production provision is an example. Under this rule, any steel produced and then sent downstream for further processing (e.g., coating) is not considered produced. Thus, if the domestic steel mills want measured output in a given category to fall, they merely have to transfer product internally. In this case, imports could have nothing to do with a fall in measured output and everything to do with strategic product shifting. Once the AD order is in place, the mills are free to stop sending their product downstream.

19　This method was known as the "best information available" method prior to the Uruguay Round agreement.

20　This issue is obviously related to cumulation in the injury determination. Cumulation may make it easier to get affirmative decisions on a wider range of import sources to avoid trade diversion effects that would lessen the benefits to the domestic industry.

21　Of course, there are other welfare consequences as well. Increased domestic competition would benefit consumers and the foreign firms are presumably worse off because they had implicitly chosen to export rather than FDI before the AD duty. World welfare could be worse as well, despite the increased competition in an imperfectly competitive market, if the foreign firm's production costs rise with the relocation.

22　While the US does not have a formal mechanism for price undertakings as the EU, private price arrangements may occur and lead to withdrawals of cases, as shown in Prusa (1992). In addition, the US government has stepped in with other market arrangements, such as VERs, for high profile industries like steel and semiconductors.

23　In related work, Messerlin (1990) found that industries that received AD protection had a surprising propensity to be investigated for anticompetitive practices, a result that suggests AD protection promotes collusion.

24　Exceptions include Messerlin (1996), Prusa (1998) and Hartigan (2000).

References

Anderson, James E. 1992: Domino dumping I: Competitive exporters. *American Economic Review*, 82, 65–83.

Anderson, James E. 1993: Domino dumping II: Anti-dumping. *Journal of International Economics*, 35, 133–50.

Anderson, Keith B. 1993: Agency discretion or statutory direction: Decision making at the US International Trade Commission. *Journal of Law and Economics*, 36, 915–35.

Anderson, Simon P., Nicolas Schmitt, and Jacques-Francois Thisse 1995: Who benefits from antidumping legislation? *Journal of International Economics*, 38, 321–37.

Baldwin, Robert E. 1985: *The Political Economy of US Import Policy*. Cambridge: The MIT Press.

Baldwin, Robert E. 1998: Imposing multilateral discipline on administered protection. In Anne O. Krueger (ed.), *The WTO as an International Organization*, Chicago and London: University of Chicago Press, 297–327.

Baldwin, Robert E. and Michael O. Moore 1991: Political aspects of the administration of the trade remedy laws. In Richard Boltuck and Robert E. Litan (eds.), *Down in the Dumps: Administration of the Unfair Trade Laws*, Washington, DC: The Brookings Institute, 253–80.

Baldwin, Robert E. and Jeffrey W. Steagall 1994: An analysis of ITC decisions in antidumping, countervailing duty and safeguard cases. *Weltwirtschaftliches Archiv*, 130, 290–308.

Barrell, Ray and Nigel Pain 1999: Trade restraints and Japanese direct investment flows. *European Economic Review*, 43, 29–45.

Belderbos, Rene A. 1997: Antidumping and tariff jumping: Japanese firms' DFI in the European Union and the United States. *Weltwirtschaftliches Archiv*, 133, 419–57.

Belderbos, Rene A. and Sleuwaegen, Leo, 1998: Tariff jumping DFI and export substitution: Japanese electronics firms in Europe. *International Journal of Industrial Organization*, 16, 601–38.

Blonigen, Bruce A. 2000: US antidumping filings and the threat of retaliation. Unpublished manuscript.

Blonigen, Bruce A. 2002: Tariff-jumping antidumping duties. *Journal of International Economics*, 57, 1, 31–49.

Blonigen, Bruce A. and Robert C. Feenstra 1997: Protectionist threats and foreign direct investment. In Robert C. Feenstra (ed.), *The Effects of US Trade Protection and Promotion Policies*, Chicago: University of Chicago Press, 55–80.

Blonigen, Bruce A. and Stephen E. Haynes 2002: Antidumping investigations and the pass-through of exchange rates and antidumping duties. *American Economic Review*, 92, 4, 1044–61.

Blonigen, Bruce A. and Yuka Ohno 1988: Endogenous protection, foreign direct investment, and protection-building trade. *Journal of International Economics*, 46, 205–27.

Blonigen, Bruce A. and Jee-Hyeong Park 2001: Dynamic pricing in the presence of antidumping policy: Theory and evidence. NBER working paper no. 8477.

Boltuck, Richard D. 1987: An economic analysis of dumping. *Journal of World Trade Law*, 21, 45–54.

Boltuck, Richard D. and Robert E. Litan (eds.) 1991: *Down in the Dumps: Administration of the Unfair Trade Laws*. Washington, DC: The Brookings Institution.

Bown, Chad 2000: Antidumping against the backdrop of disputes in the GATT/WTO system. Unpublished manuscript.

Cassing, James and Ted To 2000: Antidumping and signaling. Unpublished manuscript.

Clarida, Richard H. 1996: Dumping in theory, in policy, and in practice. In Jagdish Bhagwati and Robert Hudec (eds.), *Fair Trade and Harmonization*, Cambridge: The MIT Press.

DeVault, James M. 1993: Economics and the International Trade Commission. *Southern Economic Journal*, 60, 463–78.

DeVault, James M. 1996a: The welfare effects of US antidumping duties. *Open Economies Review*, 7, 19–33.

DeVault, James M. 1996b: US antidumping administrative reviews. *International Trade Journal*, 10, 247–67.

Ethier, Wilfred J. and Ronald D. Fischer 1987: The new protectionism. *Journal of International Economic Integration*, 2, 1–11.

Eymann, Angelika and Ludger Schuknecht 1996: Antidumping policy in the European Community: Political discretion or technical determination? *Economics and Politics*, 8, 111–31.

Feinberg, Robert M. 1989: Exchange rates and unfair trade. *Review of Economics and Statistics*, 71, 704–7.

Feinberg, Robert M. and Barry T. Hirsch 1989: Industry rent seeking and the filing of "Unfair trade" complaints. *International Journal of Industrial Organization*, 7, 325–40.

Feinberg, Robert M. and Seth Kaplan 1993: Fishing downstream: The political economy of administered protection. *Canadian Journal of Economics*, 26, 150–8.

Finger, J. Michael 1981: The industry–country incidence of "less than fair value" cases in US import trade. *Quarterly Review of Economics and Business*, 21, Summer, 260–79.

Finger, J. Michael (ed.) 1993: *Antidumping: How It Works and Who Gets Hurt*. Ann Arbor, MI: University of Michigan Press.

Finger, J. Michael, H., Keith Hall, and Douglas R. Nelson 1982: The political economy of administered protection. *American Economic Review*, 72, 452–66.

Finger, J. Michael, Francis Ng, and Sonam Wangchuk 2000: Antidumping as safeguard policy. Unpublished manuscript.

Fischer, Ronald D. 1992: Endogenous probability of protection and firm behavior. *Journal of International Economics*, 32, 149–63.

Furusawa, Taiji and Thomas J. Prusa 1996: Antidumping enforcement in a reciprocal model of dumping: Theory and evidence. Unpublished manuscript.

Gallaway, Michael P., Bruce A. Blonigen, and Joseph E. Flynn 1999: Welfare costs of US antidumping and countervailing duty laws. *Journal of International Economics*, 49, 211–44.

General Accounting Office 1991: *Comparison of US and Foreign Antidumping Practices*. Washington, DC: General Accounting Office.

Grossman, Gene 1986: Imports as a cause of injury: The case of the US steel industry. *Journal of International Economics*, 20, 201–23.

Gupta, Poonam 1999: Why do firms pay antidumping duty? Unpublished manuscript.

Haaland, Jan I. and Ian Wooton 1998: Anti-dumping jumping: Reciprocal anti-dumping and industrial location. *Weltwirtschaftliches Archiv*, 134, 340–62.

Hansen, Wendy L. 1990: The International Trade Commission and the politics of protectionism. *American Political Science Review*, 84, 21–46.

Hansen, Wendy L. and Thomas J. Prusa 1993: Does administrative protection protect? A reexamination of the US Title VII and Escape Clause statutes. *Regulation*, 16, 35–43.

Hansen, Wendy L. and Thomas J. Prusa 1995: The road most taken: The rise of Title VII protection. *The World Economy*, 18, 295–313.

Hansen, Wendy L. and Thomas J. Prusa 1996: Cumulation and ITC decision making: The sum of the parts is greater than the whole. *Economic Inquiry*, 34, 746–69.

Hansen, Wendy L. and Thomas J. Prusa 1997: The economics and politics of trade policy: An empirical analysis of ITC decision making. *Review of International Economics*, 5, 230–45.

Hartigan, James C. 2000: An antidumping law can be procompetitive. *Pacific Economic Review*, 5, 5–14.

Hartigan, James C., Sreenivas Kamma, and Philip R. Perry 1989: The injury determination category and the value of relief from dumping. *Review of Economics and Statistics*, 71, 183–6.

Herander, Mark G. and J. Brad Schwartz 1984: An empirical test of the impact of the threat of US trade policy: The case of antidumping duties. *Southern Economic Journal*, 51, 59–79.

Horlick, Gary N. 1989: The United States antidumping system. In John H. Jackson and Edwin A. Vermulst (eds.), *Antidumping Law and Practice*, Ann Arbor, MI: The University of Michigan Press, 99–166.

Hughes, John S., Stefanie Lenway, and Judy Rayburn 1997: Stock price effects of US trade policy responses to Japanese trading practices in semi-conductors. *Canadian Journal of Economics*, 30, 922–42.

Jackson, John H. and Edwin A. Vermulst 1989: *Antidumping Law and Practice*. Ann Arbor, MI: University of Michigan Press.

Kaplan, Seth 1991: Injury and causation in USITC antidumping determinations: Five recent approaches. In P. K. M. Tharakan (ed.), *Policy Implications of Antidumping Measures*, Amsterdam, Oxford, Tokyo: North Holland, 143–73.

Kelly, Kenneth A. and Morris E. Morkre 1998: Do unfairly traded imports injure domestic industries? *Review of International Economics*, 6, 321–32.

Knetter, Michael M. and Thomas J. Prusa 2000: Macroeconomic factors and anti-dumping filings: Evidence from four countries. NBER working paper no. 8010.

Kohler, Philippe and Michael O. Moore 1998: Design of an antidumping rule with incomplete information about material injury. *Journal of Economic Integration*, 13, 62–88.

Kohler, Philippe and Michael O. Moore 2001: Injury-based protection with auditing under imperfect information. *Southern Economic Journal*, 68, 1, 42–59.

Kolev, Dobrin and Thomas J. Prusa 2002: Dumping and double crossing: The (in)effectiveness of cost-based trade policy under incomplete information. *International Economic Review*, 43, 3, 895–918.

Krupp, Corinne 1994: Antidumping cases in the US chemical industry: A panel data approach. *Journal of Industrial Economics*, 42, 299–311.

Krupp, Corinne and Patricia S. Pollard 1996: Market responses to antidumping laws: Some evidence from the US chemical industry. *Canadian Journal of Economics*, 29, 199–227.

Leidy, Michael P. 1994: Trade policy and indirect rent seeking: A synthesis of recent work. *Economics and Politics*, 6, 97–118.

Leidy, Michael P. 1997: Macroeconomic conditions and pressures for protection under antidumping and countervailing duty laws: Empirical evidence from the United States. *International Monetary Fund Staff Papers*, 44, 132–44.

Leidy, Michael P. and Bernard M. Hoekman 1990: Production effects of price- and cost-based anti-dumping laws under flexible exchange rates. *Canadian Journal of Economics*, 23, 873–95.

Lichtenberg, Frank and Hong Tan 1994: An industry-level analysis of import relief petitions filed by US manufacturers, 1958–1985. In Hong Tan and Haruo Shimada (eds.), *Troubled Industries in the United States and Japan*, New York: St Martin's Press, 161–88.

Lindsey, Brink 1999: The US antidumping law: Rhetoric versus reality. CATO Institute Center for Trade Policy Studies working paper no. 7.

Low, Patrick 1993: *Trading Free: The GATT and US Trade Policy*. New York: The Twentieth Century Fund Press.

Mahdavi, Mahnaz and Amala Bhagwati 1994: Stock market data and trade policy: Dumping and the semiconductor industry. *International Trade Journal*, 8, 207–21.

Messerlin, Patrick A. 1989: The EC antidumping regulations: A first economic appraisal, 1980–85. *Weltwirtschaftliches Archiv*, 125, 563–87.

Messerlin, Patrick A. 1990: Antidumping regulations or pro-cartel laws? The EC chemical cases. *World Economy*, 13, 465–92.

Messerlin, Patrick A. 1996: Competition policy and antidumping reform: An exercise in transition. In Jeffrey J. Schott (ed.), *The World Trading System: Challenges Ahead*, Washington, DC: Institute for International Economics, 219–46.

Messerlin, Patrick A. and Geoffrey Reed 1995: Antidumping Policies in the United States and the European Community, *Economic Journal*, 105, 1565–75.

Miranda, Jorge, Raul A. Torres, and Mario Ruiz 1998: The international use of antidumping: 1987–1997. *Journal of World Trade*, 32, 5–71.

Moore, Michael O. 1992: Rules or politics? An empirical analysis of ITC anti-dumping decisions. *Economic Inquiry*, 30, 449–66.

Moore, Michael O. 2000: Facts available dumping allegations: When will foreign firms cooperate in antidumping petitions? Unpublished manuscript.

Morkre, Morris E. and Kenneth H. Kelly 1994: Effects of unfair imports on domestic industries: US antidumping and countervailing duty cases, 1980–1988. Federal Trade Commission Bureau of Economics staff report.

Murray, Tracy 1991: The administration of the antidumping duty law by the Department of Commerce. In Richard Boltuck and Robert E. Litan (eds.), *Down in the Dumps: Administration of the Unfair Trade Laws*, Washington, DC: The Brookings Institute, 23–56.

Murray, Tracy and Donald J. Rousslang 1989: A method for estimating injury caused by unfair trade practices. *International Review of Law and Economics*, 9, 149–64.

Nieberding, James F. 1999: The effect of US antidumping law on firms' market power: An empirical test. *Review of Industrial Organization*, 14, 65–84.

Palmeter, David N. 1991: The antidumping law: A legal and administrative nontariff barrier. In Richard Boltuck and Robert E. Litan (eds.), *Down in the Dumps: Administration of the Unfair Trade Laws*, Washington, DC: The Brookings Institute, 64–89.

Panagariya, Arvind and Gupta, Poonam 1998: Anti-dumping duty versus price competition. *World Economy*, 21, 1003–19.

Panagariya, Arvind and Gupta, Poonam 2000: Injury investigations in anti-dumping and the super-additivity effect: A theoretical explanation. Unpublished manuscript.

Pauwels, Wilfred, Hylke Vandenbussche, and Marcel Weverbergh 2001: Strategic behaviour under European antidumping duties. *International Journal of the Economics of Business*, 8, 79–103.

Pindyck, Robert S. and Julio J. Rotemberg 1987: Are imports to blame? Attribution of injury under the 1974 Trade Act. *Journal of Law and Economics*, 30, 101–22.

Prusa, Thomas J. 1991: The selection of cases for ITC determination. In Robert E. Baldwin (ed.), *Empirical Studies of Commercial Policy*, Chicago and London: University of Chicago Press for National Bureau of Economic Research, 47–71.

Prusa, Thomas J. 1992: Why are so many antidumping petitions withdrawn? *Journal of International Economics*, 33, 1–20.

Prusa, Thomas J. 1994: Pricing behavior in the presence of antidumping law. *Journal of Economic Integration*, 9, 260–89.

Prusa, Thomas J. 1997: The trade effects of US antidumping actions. In Robert C. Feenstra (ed.), *The Effects of US Trade Protection and Promotion Policies*, Chicago: University of Chicago Press, 191–213.

Prusa, Thomas J. 1998: Cumulation and anti-dumping: A challenge to competition. *World Economy*, 21, 1021–33.

Prusa, Thomas J. 2001: On the spread and impact of anti-dumping. *Canadian Journal of Economics*, 34, 3, 591–611

Prusa, Thomas J. and Susan Skeath 2000: The international use of antidumping: Unfair trade or tit-for-tat? Unpublished manuscript.

Reitzes, James D. 1993: Antidumping policy. *International Economic Review*, 34, 745–63.

Rosendorff, Peter B. 1996: Voluntary export restraints, antidumping procedure, and domestic politics, *American Economic Review*, 86, 544–61.

Sabry, Faten 2000: An analysis of the decision to file, the dumping estimates, and the outcome of antidumping petitions. *International Trade Journal*, 14, 109–45.

Staiger, Robert W. and Frank A. Wolak 1989: Strategic use of antidumping law to enforce tacit international collusion. NBER working paper, no. 3016.

Staiger, Robert W. and Frank A. Wolak 1992: The effect of domestic antidumping law in the presence of foreign monopoly. *Journal of International Economics*, 32, 265–87.

Staiger, Robert W. and Frank A. Wolak 1994: Measuring industry specific protection: Antidumping in the United States. *Brookings Papers on Economic Activity: Microeconomics*, 51–118.

Steele, Keith (ed.) 1996: *Antidumping Under the WTO: A Comparative Review*. London: Kluwer.

Stiglitz, Joseph E. 1997: Dumping on free trade: The US import trade laws, *Southern Economic Journal*, 64, 402–24.

Tharakan, P. K. M. 1991: The political economy of anti-dumping undertakings in the European Communities. *European Economic Review*, 35, 1341–59.

Tharakan, P. K. M. and J. Waelbroeck 1994a: Determinants of anti-dumping and countervailing duty decisions in the European Communities. In Mathias Dewatripont and Victor Ginsburgh (eds.), *European Economic Integration: A Challenge in a Changing World*, Amsterdam, London, and Tokyo: North Holland, 181–99.

Tharakan, P. K. M. and J. Waelbroeck 1994b: Antidumping and countervailing duty decisions in the EC and in the US: An experiment in comparative political economy. *European Economic Review*, 38, 171–93.

Tharakan, P. K. M., David Greenaway, and Joe Tharakan 1998: Cumulation and injury determination of the European Community in antidumping cases. *Weltwirtschaftliches Archiv*, 134, 320–39.

US International Trade Commission 1995: The economy-wide effects of outstanding antidumping and countervailing duty orders. In US International Trade Commission, *The Economic Effects of Antidumping and Countervailing Duty Orders and Suspension Agreements*, Washington, DC: US International Trade Commission.

Vandendenbussche, Hylke, Jozef Konings, and Linda Springael 1999: Import diversion under European antidumping policy. NBER working paper no. 7340.

Vandendenbussche, Hylke, Reinhilde Veugelers, and Rene A. Belderbos 1999: Undertakings and antidumping jumping FDI in Europe. CEPR discussion paper 2320.

Vandendenbussche, Hylke and Xavier Wauthy 2001: Inflicting injury through product quality: How EU antidumping policy disadvantages European producers. *European Journal of Political Economy*, 17, 101–16.

Veugelers, Reinhilde and Hylke Vandenbussche 1999: European anti-dumping policy and the profitability of national and international collusion. *European Economic Review*, 47, 1–28.

Viner, Jacob 1923: *Dumping: A Problem in International Trade*. Chicago, IL: University of Chicago Press.

Zanardi, Maurizio 2000: Antidumping law as a collusive device. Boston College working paper no. 487.

Part III

Investment

10

Foreign Direct Investment and the Operations of Multinational Firms: Concepts, History, and Data

Robert E. Lipsey

Chapter Outline

The concept and measurement of foreign direct investment (FDI) have changed over time, and what is measured by balance of payments flows and stocks is quite different from what is implied by theories of direct investment. The industrial distribution of stocks of FDI, the most widely available measure, is only poorly related to the distribution of FDI production, and changes in stocks are poorly related to changes in production. FDI flows have grown in importance relative to other forms of international capital flows, and the resulting production has increased as a share of world output, but it was still only about 8 percent at the end of the twentieth century. The US began its role as a foreign direct investor in the late nineteenth century, while it was still a net importer of capital. It became the dominant supplier of direct investment to the rest of the world, accounting for about half of the world's stock in 1960. Since then, other countries have become major direct investors. The US share is now less than a quarter of the world total and the US has become a major recipient of FDI from other countries.

---

1 Introduction

The term "Foreign Direct Investment" (FDI) encompasses two related but different sets of topics or activities, explained by different theories and by different branches of economics. The first might be referred to as the international finance, or macro, view. The second might be referred to as the industrial organization, or micro, view.

The macro view sees FDI as a particular form of the flow of capital across national borders, from home countries to host countries, measured in balance-of-payments statistics. Those flows give rise to a particular form of stocks of capital in host countries, namely the value of home-country investment in entities, typically corporations, controlled by a home-country owner, or in which a home-country owner holds a certain share of voting rights. The variables of interest are the flow of financial capital, the value of the stock of capital that is accumulated by the investing firms, and the flows of income from the investments.

The micro view tries to explain the motivations for investment in controlled foreign operations, from the viewpoint of the investor. It also examines the consequences to the investor, and to home and host countries, of the operations of the multinationals or of the affiliates created by these investments, rather than the size of the flows or the value of the investment stocks or investment position. These consequences arise from their trade, employment, production, and their flows and stocks of intellectual capital, unmeasured by the capital flows and stocks in the balance of payments, although some proxies for the flow of intellectual capital are part of the current account. These motivations and consequences are intrinsically related to the investing firms' control of the affiliates and the ability of the multinationals to coordinate the activities of parents and affiliates.

The micro view is the older one, preceding interest in direct investment as a form of capital flow. It was reflected in concerns about the consequences of foreign control for the host economy, represented by book titles such as *The American Invaders* (1901), or *The American Invasion* (1902), two of the earliest titles listed by Wilkins (1970). It was also reflected in one of the earliest research studies of US direct investment, which attempted to explain the motivations behind firms' expansion into foreign countries (Southard, 1931).

2   CONCEPTS OF FOREIGN DIRECT INVESTMENT

2.1   What is a Foreign Direct Investment Entity?

Firms and individuals have many different possible ways of holding assets in foreign countries. Which of these are considered direct investment and which firms are considered multinational enterprises depends on the definition of a "foreign direct investment entity."

What constitutes a foreign direct investment entity has been defined differently for balance of payments purposes and for studies of firm behavior. It has also been defined in different ways by different countries and the definition has changed over time. The definition of foreign direct investment as a capital flow and a capital stock has changed correspondingly.

The dominant current definition of a direct investment entity, prescribed for balance-of-payments compilations by the International Monetary Fund (IMF)

(1993), and endorsed by the OECD (1996), avoids the notion of control by the investor in favor of a much vaguer concept. "Direct investment is the category of international investment that reflects the objective of a resident entity in one economy obtaining a lasting interest in an enterprise resident in another economy. (The resident entity is the direct investor and the enterprise is the direct investment enterprise.) The lasting interest implies the existence of a long-term relationship between the direct investor and the enterprise and a significant degree of influence by the investor on the management of the enterprise" (IMF, 1993, p. 86).

While the concept is vague, the recommended implementation is specific – "a direct investment enterprise is defined in this *Manual* as an incorporated or unincorporated enterprise in which a direct investor, who is resident in another economy, owns 10 percent or more of the ordinary shares or voting power (for an incorporated enterprise) or the equivalent (for an unincorporated enterprise)" (IMF, 1993, p. 86).

The IMF definition is governing for balance-of-payments compilations, but there is a different, but related, concept and a different official definition in the United Nations System of National Accounts, the rule book for compiling national income and product accounts, that retains the idea of control, and reflects the micro view more. In these accounts, which measure production, consumption, and investment, rather than the details of capital flows, there is a definition of "foreign-controlled resident corporations." Foreign-controlled enterprises include subsidiaries more than 50 percent owned by a foreign parent. "Associates" of which foreign ownership of equity is 10–50 percent, "may be included or excluded by individual countries according to their qualitative assessment of foreign control..." (Inter-Secretariat Working Group on National Accounts, 1993, pp. 340–1). Thus, from the viewpoint of a host country, and for analyzing production, trade, and employment, control remains the preferred concept.

In the US, the first official survey of outward direct investment, conducted by the US Department of Commerce for the end of 1929, sought to measure "the amount of capital involved in the extension of American enterprise into foreign countries..." (US Department of Commerce, 1930, p. 1). In that survey:

> Foreign "direct investments," as herein considered, include those commercial and industrial properties situated abroad and belonging to residents of the United States and its Territories, from which a return is normally expected. They are called "direct investments" to distinguish them from "portfolio investments" acquired through the purchase of foreign securities publicly offered and through the international securities movement; by definition, therefore, pure "interest capital" and capital that moves incidental to a migration of labor are, in large part, excluded. Investments of the "portfolio" type are included when they are a part of the holding of American commercial and industrial corporations. Pure "interest" capital is included when invested in American-controlled corporations operating abroad. (ibid., pp. 1–2)

The survey asked US companies for the value of "investments in lands, buildings, factories, public utilities, warehouses, shops, stocks of goods, wharves, marine equipment, and other property in foreign countries... that are owned in whole or in part by your company or by an affiliated or subsidiary corporation" (ibid., p. 51).

The next survey, for 1936, again emphasized the interest in "the international extensions of American business enterprise" (US Department of Commerce, 1938, p. 2). The control aspect of the definition was made more explicit, referring to:

> those foreign corporations or enterprises which are controlled by a person or small group of persons (corporate or natural) domiciled in the United States, or in which such person or group has an important voice. . . . The factor of control has been purposely emphasized in the definition, since it is considered to be the most significant basis for classifying investments. However, no hard and fast quantitative measurement of control has been devised. Minority interests have been included in these data in considerable number and volume. The reason, of course, is that the degree of control is not measured exactly by the percentage of common stock held. In no case has an investment holding of less than 10 percent been included in this category, and interests of less than 20 percent are few in number and small in value . . . (ibid., pp. 2–3)

It was later emphasized that using a 50 percent criterion "would be to miss its qualitative aspect . . . the quantitative basis fails to measure accurately the vital ties and connections between American and foreign corporations. The qualitative measure may also lead one into some errors because it is difficult to gage the force of character and leadership of the individuals associated with the enterprises . . ." (ibid., p. 45).

The outward survey for 1950 (US Department of Commerce, 1953) provided a more precise definition, covering four categories of FDI:

1   Foreign corporations, the voting securities of which were owned to the extent of 25 percent or more by persons or groups of affiliated persons, ordinarily resident in the United States.
2   Foreign corporations, the voting stock of which was publicly held within the United States to an aggregate of 50 percent or more, but distributed among stockholders, so that no investor, or group of affiliated investors, owned as much as 25 percent.
3   Sole proprietorships, partnerships, or real property (other than property held for the personal use of the owner) held abroad by residents of the United States.
4   Foreign branches of United States corporations.

By this time the Department had moved away from criteria requiring judgments as to degree of control toward those that could be implemented mechanically, perhaps because the number of firms involved had become too large for handicraft judgments. However, the idea behind the definition still stressed control and the thought that control was a determinant of behavior.

In recent years, the US Department of Commerce has followed what are now the IMF guidelines. The latest inward direct investment benchmark survey defines direct investment in those terms and uses the 10 percent criterion. In contrast to the 1950 rules, the survey publication states that "Direct investment refers to ownership by a single person, not to the combined ownership of all the persons in a country" (US Department of Commerce, 2001, p. M-4). However, "person" is fairly broadly defined, to encompass various types of organizations and even "associated groups." The latter are "two or more persons who exercise their voting privileges in a concerted manner – by the appearance of their actions, by agreement, or by an understanding – in order to influence the management of a business enterprise" (ibid.). Thus, a little leeway seems to be left for the collectors of data, beyond the 10 percent criterion, to interpret the idea of influence.

The abandonment of the idea of control is not the only respect in which the measures of direct investment depart from the theoretical models of the phenomenon. A single "direct investment enterprise" can be part of several different multinational firms, possibly from several countries. Duplication is avoided in investment flow and stock data by allocating the financial aggregates of an affiliate to the various owners according to the extent of their ownership. In this respect, the concerns of the producers of the balance of payments have come to outweigh those of the analysts of firm behavior.

Another respect in which this seems to be the case, again related to balance-of-payments definitions, is that the residence of a transactor, rather than of the ultimate owner, determines its nationality. Thus, a firm incorporated in the US that owns an affiliate or affiliates outside the country, is classified as a US parent company even if it is controlled by a foreign firm. For that reason, a US firm could be identified as both a US parent and a US affiliate of a foreign firm. In 1994, US parents "that were ultimately controlled by foreign parents accounted for . . . 11 percent of the assets and for 14 percent of the sales of all US parents" (US Department of Commerce, 1998a, p. M-7, n. 8). If nationality is a determinant of firm behavior or, probably more important, if status as a parent rather than an affiliate is a determinant of behavior, this treatment may blur the analysis of US parent activities and of the activities of foreign affiliates of US firms.

The ownership that defines the scope of a direct investment relationship includes indirect as well as direct ownership. Direct investment enterprises include branches of a parent investor, subsidiaries, defined as incorporated enterprises more than 50 percent owned by the direct investor, and associates, defined as incorporated enterprises owned 10–50 percent. A subsidiary or associate of a subsidiary is a direct investment enterprise of the parent, as is a subsidiary of an associate, even though the parent's interest could be below 10 percent. An associate of an associate is not part of the parent's direct investment enterprise, although it is part of the first tier associate's enterprise (IMF, 1995, pp. 150–1). The US requires direct and indirect ownership adding up to at least 10 percent (US Department of Commerce, 1998a, Form BE-10B(LF)).

One type of direct investment enterprise that creates problems with the interpretation of FDI data is what are called, in the *Balance of Payments Manual*, Special Purpose Entities, or SPEs. They include such categories as "holding company, base company, regional headquarters . . ." and have as their function "administration, management of foreign exchange risk, facilitation of financing of investments . . ." and their transactions are treated in the same way as those of other direct investment enterprises, with one exception: "for SPEs created with a sole purpose of serving in a financial intermediary capacity . . . transactions recorded under *direct investment* are limited to those associated with permanent debt and equity" (IMF,

1993, p. 87). Some implications of different treatments of SPEs are described later in the section on FDI flows.

Scholars studying multinational firms, rather than flows of capital, have set out more confined definitions. The early Harvard studies, under the direction of Raymond Vernon, confined their research to firms listed among the 500 largest US corporations among which "the U.S. parent system held equity interests in manufacturing enterprises located in 6 or more foreign countries, such equity interest in each case amounting to 25 percent or more of the total equity" (Vaupel and Curhan, 1969, p. 3). Mira Wilkins (1970, p. ix) defined "American multinational enterprise" as "the U.S. headquartered company that does business in two or more foreign countries," and a "genuine" multinational manufacturing corporation as one that "had direct investments in more than just sales abroad, that adapted to and respected foreign local traditions, and acted under foreign rules and regulations in the nations abroad where they operated."

Scholarly discomfort with the treatment of direct investment flows as capital flows goes back a long time. Kindleberger (1969, pp. 1–3), in his lectures on US multinationals, started out by saying that:

> Direct investment used to be thought of by economists as an international capital movement. . . . But economists trying to interpret direct investment as a capital movement were struck by several peculiar phenomena. In the first place, investors often failed to take money with them when they went abroad to take control of a company; instead they would borrow in the local market. Capital movement would take place gross . . . but not net. Or the investment would take place in kind, through the exchange of property-patents, technology, or machinery-against-equity claims, without the normal transfer of funds through the foreign exchange associated with capital movements. . . . Direct investment may thus be capital movement, but it is more than that.

The same idea, that there was something more, was expressed by John Dunning (1970, p. 4) at around the same time: "something other than money capital is (or may be) involved in international direct investment. This might simply be informal managerial or technical guidance; on the other hand it could incorporate the dissemination of valuable knowledge and/or entrepreneurship in the form of research and development, production technology, marketing skills, managerial expertise, and so on; none of which usually accompanies investment."

2.2 What is a Parent?

A multinational firm consists of a parent firm and the affiliates it owns or controls. Most of the home country surveys from which we know about FDI are surveys of affiliates. Very few countries make any effort to survey their parent firms, the main exceptions being the US, Sweden, and Japan. Surveys by host countries, usually taking the form of tagging foreign-owned establishments in their economic censuses, rarely ask anything about parent firms except their nationality. Again, the US is an exception in that a few other questions about parents are included in the inward surveys, including the name of the parent and its industry.

The term "parent" was used in the 1950 US outward survey to describe "the owners of a reportable interest . . ." in foreign-owned corporations and "collectively, individual holders of stock which in total constituted a reportable interest," which, for individual holders in that survey, was 50 percent (US Department of Commerce, 1953, p. 36). The individual holders' investments accounted for about 10 percent of the total. The other 90 percent was referred to as the value of investments by "reporters" (ibid., appendix table 10).

The 1966 US outward investment survey was much more explicit about the domestic side of the multinationals. It was the first to include a form specifically relating to the US firm involved, referring to it as the "reporter," rather than the parent firm. Information was collected on the reporter's industry, type of organization, assets, liabilities, net income, R&D expenditures, and natural resource exploration and development costs. The reporter was explicitly instructed to include in its answers data for "domestic subsidiaries or affiliates operating in the United States and usually part of the reporter's consolidation" (US Department of Commerce, 1975, p. 243). However, no information was requested for any firm of which the reporter was a subsidiary, a serious omission that was corrected in the 1977 survey.

The 1977 US outward survey elevated the role of the parent to something more like equality with that of affiliates, requiring a much fuller set of data and defining the parent more broadly and consistently from an economic point of view. Although the term "reporter" was still used in the forms, the instructions referred explicitly referred to the "U.S. Parent." The major change in definition was to require consolidation in the parent reports. It required an incorporated US parent to be "the U.S. parent corporation whose voting securities are not owned more than 50 percent by another U.S. corporation," and including "down each ownership chain from that U.S. corporation any U.S. corporation . . . whose voting securities are more than 50 percent owned by the U.S. corporation above it" (US Department of Commerce, 1981, pp. 3–4). The problem that the change in definition was intended to solve was that the reporters in earlier surveys were sometimes US corporations' holding company subsidiaries that had been created specifically to own foreign operations, but had no domestic operations of their own. Treating these as parents would give a distorted picture of the relationships between US parent and foreign affiliate operations. One result of the change was that the "parents" of 1977 and later years are not comparable to the "reporters" of 1966, and comparisons of "reporter" data for 1966 with "parent" data for later years are biased.

Parents, as defined in US data, are almost certainly not comparable to parents as reported in Japanese data. Consolidation of company accounts is less common in Japan than in the US, and there is no way to be sure that the reporting parents are not just fragments of much larger conglomerates. The Swedish surveys, which have been collected by a private research organization, do ask for consolidated reports by parent firms. Unlike the US outward investment surveys they exclude Swedish firms that are affiliates of foreign firms and also foreign investment undertaken by private individuals (Swedenborg, 1979, pp. 244–5).

2.3 What is an FDI Flow?

The definition of FDI flows has changed over time as the definition of FDI enterprises has changed. One such change for the US, for example, was the elimination from the US outward direct investment universe of foreign firms with large, but diffused, ownership by US citizens. That reclassification resulted in the reclassification of the investment flows to and from these firms as portfolio investment and the elimination of the retained earnings of these firms from the US accounts altogether. However, when the change in definition was adopted, in 1977, it was not carried back to earlier years, so that historical flow data reflect the earlier definition of FDI.

Direct investment capital flows are made up of "equity capital, reinvested earnings, and other capital associated with various intercompany debt transactions" (IMF, 1993, p. 87). The last category is the most troublesome, covering "the borrowing and lending of funds – including debt securities and suppliers' credits – between direct investors and subsidiaries, branches, and associates." The latter includes "Intercompany transactions between affiliated banks (depository institutions) and affiliated financial intermediaries (e.g., security dealers) – including SPEs with the sole purpose of serving as financial intermediaries . . ." However, the latter are now to be included in direct investment only if they are "associated with permanent debt (loan capital representing a permanent interest) and equity (share capital) investment or, in the case of branches, fixed assets. Deposits and other claims and liabilities related to usual banking transactions of depositary institutions and claims and liabilities of other financial intermediaries are classified, as appropriate, under *portfolio investment* or *other investment*" (IMF, 1993, p. 88). This last distinction was in recognition of the ambiguities that had developed in the division of investment between direct investment and other types.

In 1998, the Bureau of Economic Analysis (BEA) made a major change in the treatment of US affiliates that were primarily financial intermediaries, "established mainly to facilitate the foreign securities and financing businesses of their U.S. parents or to facilitate foreign borrowing by their U.S. parents . . ." The capital flows associated with these activities were "sizable and volatile." No lasting interest or desire to influence the management of an enterprise was involved in these transactions and it was decided that they should be treated as portfolio flows rather than direct investment flows. This treatment was described as in accord with the IMF guidelines mentioned above. It involved three groups of US affiliates "that had characteristics of financial intermediaries: (1) Financial affiliates located in the Netherlands Antilles, (2) financial affiliates whose U.S. parents are depository institutions, and (3) financial affiliates whose U.S. parents are securities dealers" (US Department of Commerce, 1998b, pp. 119–20).

The effect of the revised treatment was substantial. In 1997, for example, the net outflow of direct investment from the US was reduced by $11 billion, leaving a revised total of $119 billion after other adjustments. The inward flow was reduced by $54 billion, leaving a revised total of $108 billion. A similar change was made on the inward investment side, excluding intercompany debt positions with financial affiliates whose ultimate beneficial owners were depositary institutions or finance or insurance firms (Bach, 1998, p. 52).

A major effect of the change was on the reported volatility of FDI flows. These financial intermediary flows fluctuated far more widely than the remaining FDI flows, at least in 1994–7, the period for which the revisions were published. On the outward investment side, the changes in the financial intermediary flow ranged from a negative $2 billion to a positive $11 billion, while the revised total, excluding the financial intermediaries, varied from negative $75 billion to negative $122 billion, with no changes of direction. On the inward side, the financial intermediary flows, all negative, ranged from $–1 billion to $–54 billion, while the revised flows (inflows), excluding the intermediaries, all positive, increased in every year, from $46 to $108 billion (Bach, 1998, table 3).

Another way of describing the volatility of the financial intermediary flows is by comparing the average annual changes to the average annual flows. The average annual change in the outward flow for the financial intermediaries was over 100 percent of the average flow for the period, while the average change in the adjusted outflow was only 16 percent of the average adjusted outflow. On the inward side, the average change in the intermediaries' inflow was 120 percent of the average inflow while the average change in the inflows excluding the intermediaries was 24 percent of the average adjusted inflow. Thus, the financial intermediaries' flows were 5 to 6 times as volatile as the rest of the direct investment flows.

The question of how to treat financial intermediary subsidiaries was not a new one. The US outward investment total for many years showed a negative investment in the Netherlands Antilles that reached a peak of $–25 billion in 1984. That was 12 percent of the reported outward direct investment total, and over 40 percent of the reported investment in trade and services, excluding petroleum services (Lipsey, 1988, table 8.A.1). These large investments in the Netherlands Antilles were a result of the US withholding tax on interest paid by US firms on borrowing abroad. US parent firms set up affiliates in the Netherlands Antilles to borrow in European capital markets, free of the tax on interest payments, and relend the proceeds to their parents. In this way, a portfolio flow, mainly bond issues, was magically converted into a direct investment flow by passing through the affiliates. Since the direct investment flow was of parent firms borrowing from their affiliates, it became a negative element in the US outward investment position.

2.4 Do Investment Stocks Reflect the Economic Activity of Multinational Firms?

The only virtually universal measure of the activities of multinational firms outside their home countries is the amount of direct investment, or the "direct investment position," of a country, as calculated from direct investment stock data or cumulated flows of direct investment. These are the FDI data derived from balance of payments statistics. They do not purport to measure the size of multinational firms or their foreign affiliates, or their activities in their host countries. They measure only the value of the parent firms' financial stakes in their foreign affiliates. However, because of their wide coverage of countries, they are often used in analyses of the impacts of MNC activities on, for example, trade, or host country, home country, or parent employment or output.

Given this use of one concept of FDI to represent another, it would be useful to know how closely the investment position data are related to, for example, the economic activity of affiliates. One reason to expect that the relation might not be close is that the investment position data are based on the immediate sources and destinations of investment. In contrast, US surveys of the operations of US firms abroad and foreign firms in the US are based on the ultimate sources and final destinations of investment. An example of the difference is that, for example, of 234 affiliates in the US with ultimate beneficial owners (UBOs) that were Italian in 1987, 74 reported that their immediate parent was in a country other than Italy. Of 19 affiliates with South African UBOs, 17 reported other immediate parentage and of 123 affiliates of Saudi Arabian UBOs, 105 reported other parent locations (US Department of Commerce, 2001, p. M-12).

The same problem could affect the industry distribution of investment positions and affiliate activities. The investment position may report a holding company in an intermediate country as the source or destination of an investment that originated in an industrial firm or is intended for an industrial affiliate. The problem has become more serious over time because "U.S. parent companies have been funneling an increasing share of their direct investments abroad through holding companies. In 1982, foreign affiliates classified as holding companies accounted for only 9 percent of the U.S. direct investment position abroad, but by 2000, they accounted for 23 percent . . ." (Borga and Mataloni, 2001, p. 23).

Another problem with the reported stocks of FDI is that they are mostly cumulations of past direct investment flows and take no account of changes in currency values and asset values since the original investments were made. One exception to this is the FDI stock estimates for the US, which come in three variants, historical cost, current cost, and market value. They all take account of currency value changes and, as is explained later, the current cost estimates take account of price changes on fixed assets and the market value estimates take account of equity price changes.

An examination of the relation of FDI stock to FDI activity was performed for the US, the only country for which the comparison can be made by industry and location for a variety of activity measures (United Nations, 2000b, Annex D). It showed that in 1989, the distribution of the US outward FDI stock across host countries was strongly correlated with the distribution of affiliate sales. The distribution of the US inward FDI stock across countries of origin was similarly well correlated with the sales and employment of those countries' affiliates in the US. However, changes in the country distribution of US outward FDI were not closely related to changes in the location of sales and employment. The country distribution of changes in inward investment was weakly related to changes in the country distribution of employment ($r = .37$) and not related at all to changes in the country distribution of sales ($r = .015$). Thus it appeared that the country distributions of outward and inward investment stocks in one year were related to the country distributions of sales and employment, but changes in country distributions were poor indicators of changes in employment and sales.

Tests of the relation of the outward stock of FDI to measures of FDI activity for recent years are reported in appendix tables 10.A7 to 10.A10. If one wished to estimate the distribution of factor inputs or sales across both countries and industries from data on FDI stocks, the results would be quite inaccurate. Across 12 industry groups and 58 countries, less than 30 percent of the variation is explained, even for sales, 16 percent is explained for property, plant, and equipment (PP&E), and 10 percent for employment (appendix table 10.A8). Thus, while the distributions of aggregate FDI stocks, and stocks within broad industries, are fairly well related to the distributions of input and sales measures across countries, they are only weakly related to the distributions across even broad industry groups. For a finer level of industry detail, 63 industries and nine countries, only about 10 percent of the variation in sales is explained, and the relationship is even weaker for PP&E (4 percent) and employment (2 percent).

Absolute changes in aggregate and total manufacturing US outward direct investment stocks between 1982 and 1998 are quite closely related, across countries, to absolute changes in affiliate PPE and sales (appendix table 10.A9), but the relations are much weaker for relative changes in these variables. Again, if we examine the relationships across both countries and broad industry groups, or across country groups and detailed industries, they fall apart. None of the r^2s is above .30 and most are below .20 (appendix table 10.A10).

Thus, while the investment stocks tell us something about the country of location of FDI activity or changes in it, in the aggregate and within industries, they tell us very little about what kind of activity is taking place, or what they tell us is often wrong.

3 HISTORY

3.1 A Brief History of FDI and its Importance in International Capital Flows

FDI is sometimes thought of as originating with American firms, and some of its characteristics as we know it today developed mainly in American companies. However, Mira Wilkins (1970, p. 1) has called attention to its antecedents far back in history:

> in 2500 BC, Sumerian merchants found in their foreign commerce that they needed men stationed abroad to receive, to store, and to sell their goods . . . the East India Company, chartered in London in 1600, established branches overseas. . . . In the mid-seventeenth century, English, French, and Dutch mercantile families sent relatives to America and to the West Indies to represent their firms. So too, in time, American colonists found in their own foreign trade that it was desirable to have correspondents, agents, and, on occasion, branch houses in important trading centers to warehouse and to sell American exports . . .

Wilkins (1989, p. 6) describes the Virginia Company, chartered by King James I in 1606 to establish the first permanent English settlement at Jamestown, as "the first foreign direct investment in America . . ." By 1624 it was bankrupt. She identifies 1875 to 1914 as the period of "the rise of truly large-scale foreign investments in the private sector" (p. 609) including "more foreign direct investments than most subsequent commentaries have recognized" (p. 613). Wilkins (pp. 613–14) divides direct investments into two types:

> One involved investments that carried the potentials of control, but had a fragile, negligible, sometimes virtually nonexistent "home office" organization with little capacity beyond that of raising capital. These companies had no experience in operations at home to project abroad. . . . The second type of direct investment, akin to today's multinational enterprises, provided the extension into the United States of a company and its operating organizational talents – its own "package" of skills, experience, technology, management, and marketing experience.

In view of the current interest in multinationals and direct investment, it is striking that they play a minor role in descriptions of the period before 1913, the time of perhaps the largest total international investment flows in history, relative to output and fixed investment. Most writings about capital movements either did not mention direct investment at all (Iversen, 1936) or treated it as a minor form of international investment. Hobson (1914, p. 25) did describe "an enormous rise in the importance of the international company, in railways, mining, tramways, water, gas, electricity, banking, insurance, finance, land plantations . . ." and even manufacturing, "but there it is still somewhat rare." The consensus was probably well summarized by Arthur Bloomfield's appraisal that "portfolio investment was a far more important component of long-term capital movements before 1914 than direct investment" (1968, p. 3). He noted one exception, China, among developing country recipients of investment, and one, the US, among developed country investors. Another exception was apparently Japan as an investor, the counterpart of China as a recipient, as indicated in a number of sources cited in Wilkins (1986, pp. 3–4). Bloomfield (1968, pp. 3–4) suggested that before 1914, "the concept of direct investment (in its present-day sense) was not clearly distinguished from other (noncontrolling) equity investments in foreign private enterprises."

Svedberg (1978) challenged the idea that direct investment flows to developing countries were negligible before 1914. He claimed that it was an illusion stemming from the typical methods of estimating investment flows and stocks. These relied heavily on public flotations of securities and therefore missed many direct investments that did not pass through such exchanges. Svedberg estimated that some 44 to 60 percent of the $19 billion of accumulated investment in developing countries in 1913–14 was in the form of direct investment. Mira Wilkins (1989, p. xi), too, argued that "foreign direct investments . . . have often been shortchanged in the literature of U.S. economic history . . ."

For more recent years, the IMF has published comprehensive worldwide estimates of gross and net flows of direct investment since 1970, gross flows of portfolio and other investment since 1980, and net flows since 1970. Portfolio investment includes equity securities, debt securities in the form of bonds, and money market instruments, all excluding any of these included in direct investment or reserve assets. Financial derivatives, such as options, have been included in portfolio

Table 10.1 Percentage share of direct investment in total world capital outflow, 1970–1999

Excluding Hong Kong and Taiwan	
1970–74	5.8
1975–79	18.0
1980–84	11.6
1985–89	20.7
1990–94	25.4
Excluding Hong Kong but including Taiwan	
1990–94[a]	29.7
1995–99	29.6
1995	34.0
1996	28.7
1997	29.6
1998	29.5
1999	28.6
Including Hong Kong and Taiwan[b]	
1998	29.6
1999	29.3

[a] *Revised data.*
[b] *Total world capital flow does not include portfolio investment and other investment from Hong Kong.*
Source: *Lipsey (1999) and table 10.A1.*

investment, but not shown separately. The category of "Other investment" includes trade credit, loans, and financial leases. The data on gross direct investment flows indicate that direct investment has been an increasing part of total investment flows since the 1970s and early 1980s, when they were less than 15 percent. By the first half of the 1990s they accounted for 30 percent of total outflows and they stayed at that level in the second half of the decade (table 10.1). The largest source of gross direct investment flows since the 1980s has been Europe, followed by the US. Japan was the next major source until the 1990s, when it was overtaken and passed by Developing Asia (Lipsey, 1999, appendix table 6A.2 and appendix table 10.A2 of this chapter). A large part of European outflows has stayed within Europe; inflows into Europe were more than half of outflows in the 1970s and 1980s (Lipsey, 1999, appendix tables 6A.2 and 6A.3). That pattern persisted into the 1990s, with inflows two-thirds or more of outflows (appendix tables 10.A2 and 10.A3). The US, too, has been a major recipient of direct investment inflows, with the result that its former position as a major net provider of direct investment to other countries has almost disappeared. In the 1980s the US was a net recipient of direct investment from abroad, turned back to being a net supplier in the early 1990s, and again became a net recipient in the second half of the 1990s. Europe and Japan were more consistent, both being net suppliers, while Developing Asia and Latin America were steady net recipients (Lipsey, 1999, appendix table 6A.4 and appendix table 10.A4 of this chapter). Thus, a large part of the gross flows of direct investment are among the developed countries.

It is difficult to compare gross or net flows of direct investment with fixed capital expenditures for the world as a whole, but a comparison can be made for the OECD countries. Among 22 countries from 1970 through 1995, the average ratios of inward FDI flows to gross fixed capital formation were below 10 percent in 20 countries, and they were below 5 percent in most of the countries. When gross inflows in a five-year period were related to fixed capital formation in the subsequent five-year period, the coefficient was negative, although not statistically significant. It did not appear that FDI inflows were a major source of financing for capital formation in these countries. Gross outflows were negatively and significantly related to capital formation in the following period, but net flows were not related to capital formation at all (Lipsey, 2001). Thus there is some suggestion that outward direct investment competes with domestic plant and equipment expenditures for funds, as was found also for a group of US companies by Stevens and Lipsey (1992), but it is surprising that neither gross nor net inward FDI flows offset that competition.

Another way of judging the importance of FDI in the world economy is to ask how much of world production and employment are accounted for by the foreign operations that result from FDI, or "internationalized production." In the late 1950s, when a large part of the outward stock of FDI was owned by US firms, internationalized production might have represented about 2 percent of world output. By the late 1970s or early 1980s, after the period of rapid growth in US-owned production abroad, the share reached 5 percent. As US firms' operations abroad were reduced in the 1980s, those of other countries, particularly Germany and Japan, increased, but the pace of internationalization for the world as a whole was slower. In the 1990s, American firms resumed the growth of their overseas activities and the worldwide pace of internationalization rose again. By the late 1990s, about 8 percent of world production was internationalized (United Nations, 2000b).

These shares of output may not appear as large as one might expect from the volume of discussion of "globalization." One reason for a different impression is that direct investment and the resulting production are concentrated in two visible and closely watched sectors, manufacturing and petroleum. In the case of the US, for example, in the mid-1990s, these sectors accounted for about 18 percent of GDP, but for three-quarters of US-owned overseas production. US-owned affiliate production abroad was about 17 percent of home production in manufacturing, 100 percent in petroleum, but only 2 percent in all the other industries combined, which accounted for over 80 percent of total US output (Lipsey, 1998). Since the manufacturing and petroleum sectors are the source of most tradables, multinational firms account for a large proportion of international goods trade. In manufacturing, for example, exports by manufacturing affiliates of firms from the US, Japan, and Sweden, were about 10 percent of world manufactured exports in the mid-1990s. Since those three countries accounted for only about a third of the stock of outward FDI, if their affiliates' export propensities were not far from the average, the total internationalized share of manufactured exports might be somewhere around 30 percent.

In mining, of which petroleum is a large part, the output of foreign affiliates of US firms alone was almost a quarter of world output in 1977, but fell below 20 percent by 1990. The decline was much larger in developing countries, from 23 to 10 percent (Mataloni and Goldberg, 1994; United Nations, 1993), as several Middle Eastern countries nationalized what had formerly been US-owned properties.

The share of internationalized production in world manufacturing output is much higher than the share in total output. It was about 11.5 percent in 1977, when the share in total output was around 5 percent. By 1990 it was over 16 percent when the share in total output was less than half of that, and it has probably risen somewhat since then (Lipsey, 1998, pp. 12–13).

The share of world employment absorbed by internationalized production is far smaller than the share of production itself. It was probably not much above 1 percent in the late 1990s, as compared with 8 percent for production. The implication is obviously that output per worker was seven or eight times as high in internationalized production as in world production in general, the consequence of some combination of greater capital intensity and higher productivity (United Nations, 2000b).

3.2 The US as a Direct Investor and Recipient of Direct Investment

The US has been, since its earliest days as a foreign investor, exceptionally focused on direct investment. Frank Southard, in one of the first studies of US direct investment, commented about that early start: "it was the two decades just prior to the opening of the present century [the twentieth] that saw a startling development: the export of capital in significant amounts by American corporations for the establishment of European plants and sales organizations at a time when the United States was steadily importing capital" (1931, p. xiii). In 1897, the US, still predominantly a net recipient of capital from abroad, rather than a supplier of capital, held more than 90 percent of its outward investment in the form of direct investment (Lewis, 1938, p. 605). By 1914, that share had declined to three-quarters, but it was still far above the proportion in foreign investment in the US (ibid.), and in worldwide investment. World War I was the beginning of major US portfolio investment abroad, much of it in the form of loans to foreign governments that exceeded private financing. By the end of the war, in 1919, direct investment had been reduced to a little over a half of US private investment abroad, and to less than a quarter of total investment, including intergovernmental loans (ibid., p. 447). Both direct and portfolio investment grew rapidly during the 1920s, but that period differed from earlier ones in that portfolio investment accounted for a majority of the outward flow. By 1929, the value of US private portfolio investment abroad was greater than that of direct investment for the first time (ibid., pp. 450, 605).

The Great Depression of the 1930s reversed this movement toward the portfolio form that had taken place in the 1920s. Half of the foreign loans extended in the late 1920s went into default (Mintz, 1951, p. 6). US holdings of securities, even valued

Table 10.2 Percentage share of FDI in US private investment and inward FDI stock as percentage of outward, 1976–1999

Year	Share of direct investment						Inward as % of outward FDI stock		
	Outward			Inward					
	Market	Current	Book	Market	Current	Book	Market	Current	Book
1976	–	60.4	48.4	–	25.3	18.0	–	21.4	22.5
1977	–	60.0	47.1	–	27.7	19.3	–	22.5	23.7
1978	–	57.2	43.2	–	28.5	19.7	–	24.2	26.1
1979	–	57.5	43.1	–	28.6	19.7	–	26.3	29.0
1980	–	56.0	41.4	–	32.3	23.8	–	32.8	38.6
1981	–	50.6	36.4	–	34.2	25.5	–	40.4	47.6
1982	30.6	42.1	28.8	24.3	31.3	23.5	57.5	49.4	60.0
1983	29.7	35.3	24.6	22.6	27.0	20.7	55.9	54.5	64.6
1984	28.9	34.4	24.7	21.7	26.5	21.0	63.7	64.2	75.5
1985	35.3	34.4	25.2	21.9	24.0	19.1	56.9	66.6	77.4
1986	38.9	32.7	24.5	21.8	22.5	18.4	51.5	70.3	81.5
1987	39.2	34.3	26.3	22.2	23.2	19.2	53.6	70.0	80.7
1988	39.0	32.2	24.3	23.4	23.8	19.7	56.5	78.2	90.7
1989	39.7	30.5	23.2	26.0	23.5	19.5	64.2	84.6	96.6
1990	36.0	32.1	24.8	25.9	24.6	20.3	73.7	81.9	91.7
1991	37.1	31.4	25.0	28.7	24.3	20.1	80.9	82.9	89.6
1992	35.7	31.6	25.9	28.0	23.2	19.2	86.8	81.4	84.3
1993	36.6	28.9	24.1	28.2	23.3	19.3	74.8	82.0	82.8
1994	35.2	28.6	23.8	26.0	22.3	18.2	71.0	78.6	78.4
1995	36.2	27.8	23.3	27.8	20.6	17.0	76.9	76.8	76.6
1996	35.5	26.2	22.3	28.6	19.5	16.3	80.5	75.3	75.2
1997	35.2	24.4	21.0	29.8	17.6	15.1	92.2	78.0	79.2
1998	37.4	24.9	21.8	33.1	17.3	15.2	100.8	76.9	78.3
1999	37.6	23.5	20.7	36.0	18.4	16.5	107.1	84.5	87.1

Source: *Tables 10.A5 and 10.A6.*

at par rather than market, were reduced by almost 30 percent, or by almost 50 percent if defaulted bonds were valued at market prices. Short-term credits were also reduced almost by a half (Lewis, 1938, p. 454). By 1940 direct investment again accounted for more than a half of US private investment abroad, and that remained true through 1970 (US Bureau of the Census, 1975, series U26–U39). US government loans to foreign countries had expanded again during World War II and by 1950 the stock of such loans was almost twice the total private investment stock. Thus the restored dominance of direct investment in 1950 applied only to private investment.

By the late 1970s, the stock of direct investment, measured in the traditional way at book, or historical cost values, had fallen to between 40 and 50 percent of total private investment abroad, where other types of assets were measured at market values, where possible (table 10.2). There was some suspicion that historical cost valuation might seriously distort the valuation of direct investment, and in 1991, the BEA began to offer two alternative valuation methods (Landefeld and Lawson, 1991). One, referred to as "current-cost" valuation, attempted to apply inflation accounting to the asset side of the balance sheets of US-owned affiliates abroad and foreign-owned affiliates in the US. The tangible assets of affiliates were revalued, using a perpetual inventory calculation for plant and equipment and current price indexes for other forms of tangible capital. The "market valuation" method revalues, instead, the equity part of the parent's investment in affiliates, using broad stock price indexes for foreign countries and the US.

By the current cost valuation, the share of direct investment in US private investment abroad was still close to 60 percent in the late 1970s as compared with about 45 percent by the historical valuation (table 10.2). After that, the direct investment share fell, almost continuously, to about one quarter in 1997–9. Although the share fell in almost every year, most of the decline took place in the burst of portfolio and short-term lending that took place before and during the Latin American crisis of the early 1980s. Both the current-cost and historical valuations showed a direct investment share of 20 to 25 percent in US outward investment in the late 1990s, but the market value share, propelled by the rise in stock prices, produced a direct investment share of 35 to 40 percent (table 10.2). Some part of the reduction in the share of direct investment in the outward stock of private foreign investment stemmed from large upward revisions, by about 30 percent, in the estimates for purchases of foreign securities. The revisions stemmed mainly from two sources. One was a US Treasury benchmark survey of US portfolio investment abroad at yearend 1997, which indicated a 20 percent discrepancy between previous estimates and the survey results in the brief period since the previous survey in 1994. The other was an adjustment for US portfolio investment that took place in the course of foreign acquisitions of US firms, when the purchasing firms paid US stockholders with stock in the foreign acquirers (Bach, 2000, pp. 70–2).

Not only did the US have an exceptional share of its foreign investment in direct investment, but it also accounted for a large part of the world's stock of outward direct investment. In 1960, almost half of the world's outward stock of direct investment was owned by investors based in the US. No other country came close to that share; the next ranking holder was the UK, at 18 percent, followed by the Netherlands at 10 percent and France at 6 percent (United Nations, 1988, table 1.2). By 1999, the US share had fallen to less than a quarter. The UK, the Netherlands, and France remained important, the first two with reduced shares. Germany and Japan, with only 2 percent of the total between them in 1960, accounted for 15 percent in 1999. Even developing countries, which had been the homes for only 3 percent of the outward stock as late as 1980, owned 10 percent of it in 1999 (United Nations, 2000). Thus, the ability of firms to operate in foreign countries had become much more widely diffused among home countries over those 40 years.

Another indicator of that diffusion was the change in the direct investment balance of the US. In the late 1970s, US direct investment abroad was about four times the value of foreign direct investment in the US, both measured at current values. By 1997–9, foreign direct investment in the US had reached over three-quarters of the level of US direct investment abroad. The net US direct investment position, which had been a little over $200 billion in 1977–9, was only about $240 billion in 1997–9, when gross outward investment was five times as large.

4 Data on Foreign Direct Investment

There are two general types of data on foreign direct investment. One is the financial data from balance-of-payments accounting. These record inward and outward flows of direct investment and the resulting stocks. The stocks are the value of stocks of direct investment outside each home country owned by residents of that country and the value of stocks in each country that are owned by residents of other countries.

The second type of data is on the operations of FDI affiliates in their host countries and the operations of their parents in their home countries. Operations could include their sales, production, employment, wages, assets, expenditures for plant and equipment, and R&D expenditures. None of these characteristics are revealed by the financial data from the balance-of-payments. They are obtained from surveys of parent companies, in their home countries, or, in their host countries, from surveys of affiliates, often by identifying foreign-owned establishments in economic censuses.

4.1 Data on FDI Flows and Stocks

The only data on direct investment that cover virtually all countries are the balance-of-payments, or financial data. These are reported to the IMF and are published, for example, in IMF (2000a). The reports are separated into outward ("Abroad") and inward ("In Reporting Economy") flows, divided between reinvested earnings and other direct investment flows. Notes are provided explaining the sources of data for each country. In the past, many countries did not record reinvested earnings, but coverage has improved in recent years. The worldwide discrepancy between outward and inward direct investment flows, which should be zero if all flows were recorded fully and consistently by both sides, has been no higher than 8 percent in any year from 1993 to 1999, as contrasted with 40 or 50 percent for portfolio investment.

The *Balance of Payments Yearbooks* also call for the reporting of inward and outward stocks of direct investment, as part of their tabulations of the international investment position of each country. Most developed countries report their inward and outward stocks of FDI, but many developing countries do not. The IMF data, in summary form, are also available in *International Financial Statistics Yearbooks*, for example, IMF (2000b).

The quality of international data on FDI flows for measuring what is called for in balance-of-payments accounting was reviewed in IMF (1986) as part of the search for an explanation and cure for the enormous world balance of payments discrepancies. The world current account discrepancy did fall for a while, but it returned to well over negative $100 billion in 1999 (IMF, 2000a). The discrepancy for direct investment, which had been fairly small during most of the 1990s, jumped to

$64 billion in 1999, about 7.5 percent of the reported outflow. A deficiency of all the IMF compilations is that political considerations apparently dictate the omission of data for two important entities, Taiwan, and until 1998, Hong Kong. However, Taiwan does publish its data in the IMF format.

A source of inward and outward FDI flow and stock data that covers almost all countries is the UNCTAD World Investment Report (WIR), for example, United Nations (2000). These reports began with United Nations (1973, 1978, 1983, and 1988), and have been published annually since 1991. They provide annual data from 1990 to 1999 and at five-year intervals before that. There are also extensive notes on sources and listings of items omitted in various countries' reports. Annex B includes listings for each country covered indicating what items are omitted, sources of data, and major revisions. There are also tables of ratios of FDI flows to Gross Capital Formation and of FDI stocks to GDP. In contrast to the IMF reports, the WIR has consistently included information on FDI in and by Taiwan and Hong Kong.

A source of financial data on FDI that covers quite a few countries is the OECD *International Direct Investment Statistics Yearbook*, covering 28 countries in its latest edition (OECD, 2000), although not with complete data for all of them. It includes data on inflows and outflows and on inward and outward stocks, or the "direct investment position." A major advantage over the compilations of the IMF and UNCTAD is that there are data for most countries by broad industrial sectors and also by partner country, in a uniform format.

Data on direct investment flows and the international direct investment position of the US are published regularly in articles in the *Survey of Current Business* and have been summarized in a series of publications by the BEA. The period beginning in 1950 was covered, with substantial country detail, and a little industry information, especially starting in 1966, in US Department of Commerce (1982). Recent editions have included greater industry detail.

The traditional way of measuring inward and outward investment stocks at historical valuations came under increasing criticism in the 1980s. It did not take account of changes in prices and did not match the treatment of fixed capital in the US National Income and Product Accounts. As a result, the BEA, in 1991, began to publish its US investment position data in two alternative valuations, as mentioned earlier. One was a "current-cost" valuation, in which inflation accounting was applied to the assets of US affiliates abroad and foreign affiliates in the US. Affiliate tangible assets were revalued using a perpetual inventory calculation for plant and equipment and current price indexes for other types of tangible capital. The other method, described as "market valuation," revalues, instead, the liability side, in particular, the equity portion of the parent investment in affiliates. It uses broad equity price indexes for foreign countries to value the equity portion of US assets abroad and equity price indexes for the US to value the equity portion of foreign assets in the US.

As pointed out in the article announcing the new measures (Landefeld and Lawson, 1991), there are limitations to these measures, although not as great as those of the historical valuations. The new measures are the only ones now reported in the articles on the international investment position of the US. The inward investment measures at current cost are probably the most accurate of the four, two inward and two outward. The BEA produces price measures for US plant and equipment expenditures, and the only possibly major problem is that the composition of plant and equipment expenditures by foreign affiliates in the US is not known in detail and could differ from that of other firms in the US. The outward investment measure at current cost must make do with available foreign price indexes for capital goods. These do not exist for all the host countries, and even where they do, are not collected and calculated in comparable ways. The market value measures rely on the assumption that the market values of what are mainly privately-owned companies follow those of broad stock price indexes. The composition of these indexes may differ substantially with respect to industry, country, in the case of outward investment, and in other respects from the composition of the equities that are part of direct investment.

4.2 Data on FDI Operations

The balance-of-payments data suffer from two incurable problems. One is that, as described earlier, they trace only the immediate sources and destinations of investment, rather than the ultimate ones. A more serious one is that they contain no information on the economic activity of FDI affiliates and their parents. Thus they tell nothing about the characteristics of the parents, such as their industry, their size, employment, sales, assets, or technological activities. It is, therefore, difficult to use them to study the reasons for companies to invest in production abroad or the choices they make in such investing. The financial data also tell nothing about the economic activities of the affiliates. It is therefore difficult to use them to analyze the impacts of the affiliates' operations on their host countries or on the parents and their home countries. The only possible sources of information on the operations of parents are surveys carried out in their home countries. Information on the operations of affiliates can be collected from surveys of parent firms in their home countries or my surveys of affiliates in the host countries, done either specifically to examine foreign-owned operations or as part of economic censuses by tagging foreign-owned firms or establishments.

The most comprehensive data, by far, on FDI operations are those for the US. Annual data on the operations of both US nonbank affiliates abroad and foreign nonbank affiliates in the US are published in articles in the *Survey of Current Business*. More complete data, and particularly more US parent data, are available in reports published every year by the BEA. The most complete sets of information, include banking, appear in the BEA's benchmark surveys, which are usually conducted every five years. The latest inward survey is US Department of Commerce (2001), covering 1997, and the latest outward survey is US Department of Commerce (1998a).

Among the items included are balance sheets, income accounts, employment, exports (to affiliates and to others), imports, and R&D expenditures and employment. The benchmark surveys include more topics and more country and industry detail than the annual surveys.

The US also provides measures of the production, or gross product, of US parents and affiliates and of foreign affiliates in the US. That measure of FDI activity is preferable to sales or employment, partly because of its comparability with national accounts' concepts, such as GDP. For US affiliates abroad it is calculated for only majority-owned affiliates (MOFAs), because the survey form for other affiliates, which account for between 12 and 17 percent of total activity, depending on the measure used, lacks the required information (US Department of Commerce, 2000c, tables II.A-1 and III.A-1).

The estimates are built up by summation of factor costs and indirect taxes rather than by subtraction of intermediate inputs from gross output. They match the gross product measures in the National Income and Product Accounts (NIPAs) fairly well in concept. One difference is that depreciation is reported only at book value instead of the NIPAs' current value, using economic service lives and replacement cost valuation (Mataloni and Goldberg, 1994, p. 42). The effect is on the distinction between depreciation and profits within affiliates, rather than on total gross profit.

On the inward side, the BEA and the Census Bureau have matched reporting firm identifications to identify foreign-owned US establishments. They can thus provide US economic census establishment data divided between domestically-owned and foreign-owned establishments. These have been published for 1987 and 1992 for most US industries, in US Department of Commerce (1992) and (1997), and the linked data for 1997 are expected to be published in 2002. For years between 1987 and 1992, only manufacturing is covered, in a series of annual publications. The industry and geographical detail are extensive, but only a few items such as numbers of establishments, employment, and wages, are reported. An important distinction between these data and the BEA survey data is that the matched data are on an establishment basis, rather than an enterprise basis. A large enterprise often combines establishments belonging to several industries, possibly including both manufacturing and wholesale trade or manufacturing and mining, in the case of petroleum; the establishment data provide a more accurate account of the industry distribution of foreign-owned employment, sales, and other variables. A broader assessment of the quality of US data on FDI, dealing with concepts as well as arithmetic accuracy, is given in Stekler and Stevens (1991).

The OECD has begun to publish some data for inward investment operations in member countries, in, for example, OECD (1999). Response is not complete, but the publication attempts to cover numbers of foreign-owned enterprises and their production, turnover, value added, wages and salaries, R&D expenditures and employment, and trade.

Operations by Swedish firms abroad beginning in 1965 can be studied from surveys conducted at approximately five-year intervals by the Industriens Utredningsinstitut of Stockholm (now known as The Research Institute of Industrial Economics). Publications reporting on these surveys are listed in the references to Swedenborg (2001). The surveys included questions on employment, wages, fixed capital, trade, R&D expenditures, and other topics, mostly relating to foreign affiliates, but with some information about parents and about the relations between parents and affiliates.

The Swedish Central Bureau of Statistics (Statistics Sweden) has been publishing data, starting in 1990, on employment at home and abroad in Swedish-owned enterprise groups having subsidiaries abroad. The data are reported by detailed industry and by country, but not cross-classified, except to distinguish manufacturing from service industries (Sweden, Statistics Sweden, 2000a). A survey of R&D expenditures and R&D personnel inputs in Sweden and abroad in the 20 largest Swedish manufacturing groups and in foreign-owned enterprises in Sweden was conducted for 1997 (Sweden, Statistics Sweden, 2001).

A limited report on operations of foreign firms in Sweden was published annually by the Central Bureau of Statistics, starting with 1987. A much more extensive survey and analysis for 1970 appears in Samuelsson (1977). Beginning in 1994, the scope of reporting was expanded, although the survey remained voluntary. As in the outward survey, the main question is on employment, classified by industry and country of origin (Sweden, Statistics Sweden, 2000b). For 1997, a supplementary report included data on profits, liquidity, exports and export intensity, and value added (Sweden, Statistics Sweden, 2000c).

Information on the operations of both German firms abroad and foreign firms in Germany has been published in a series of reports by the Deutsche Bundesbank, at two-year intervals, such as in Deutsche Bundesbank (1999). The country and industry detail are extensive, but the list of variables is short, limited to numbers of firms, employment, annual turnover, and assets, with some breakdown by type of asset.

For Japan, the Ministry of International Trade and Industry (MITI, now METI), has published a series of annual and benchmark surveys of outward FDI since the 1970s. They contain a great deal of information on parent and affiliate operations, but suffer from low response, fluctuating over time and varying, within a survey, from question to question. The coverage and other quality aspects of these surveys have been discussed in Ramstetter (1996), and some of the individual MITI publications are listed there.

Recently, there have been efforts, supported by Japanese official agencies, to improve the quality of the MITI data. A paper by Fukao et al. (1999) estimated missing data from survey forms to produce better approximations to total employment and sales by Japanese affiliates and their distribution over host countries and industries.

The UK does not conduct regular surveys of its firms' outward FDI activities. A major one-time survey was conducted for the Reddaway (1967) and (1968) reports, but it was not repeated. Inward FDI activities can be followed by using economic census data, where foreign ownership is tagged.

France does not publish any readily available public data on the outward FDI activities of its firms. The French government has issued, since the 1970s, a series of reports on numbers of foreign-owned firms and their employment, wages, capital, and exports and, for each measure, the share in the French economy. The data are disaggregated by industry, country of origin, and location within France. The latest report, covering January 1, 1998, was summarized in France, SESSI (2000).

Canada is one of the world's major recipients of FDI and has a long history of collecting data on it, mainly on sales, exports, imports, and financial aspects. An early survey for 1964 and 1965 was published in Canada (1967). Employment, hours of work, and wages were added in some later surveys, such as Canada (1979), but the main source of data remains the reports under the Corporations and Labour Unions Returns Act, published by Statistics Canada in recent years. For the period of operation of the Foreign Investment Review Act, from 1974 to 1985, detailed data were published for individual firm applications to invest in Canada. These appeared in the annual reports of the review agency, the last of which was Canada (1985).

A collection of the available data on production at home and abroad by home country multinational firms and of production in many host countries by foreign-owned firms was assembled in Lipsey, Ramstetter, and Blomström (2000). Detailed source notes appeared in Lipsey, Blomström, and Ramstetter (1995). Among the host countries covered in Asia were China, India, Indonesia, Korea, Malaysia, Singapore, Taiwan, and Thailand, and in Latin America, Brazil, Mexico, and Uruguay. Developed host countries covered were Australia, Canada, Japan, Norway, the UK, and the US. A broader collection of indicators of multinational activity other than production is provided in United Nations (2001).

There have been several extensive surveys of the literature and research on multinational firms and FDI, fairly comprehensive at the time they were written. Two of the most extensive in coverage are Caves (1996) and Dunning (1992).

Acknowledgments

I am indebted to Ned Howenstine and Obie Whichard of the Bureau of Economic Analysis of the US Department of Commerce for comments and suggestions.

Appendix – Tables

Table 10.A1 World investment outflows, 1990–1999

Period	Direct investment[a]	Portfolio investment[b]	Other investment[b]	Total[c]
	(Millions of US dollars)			
1990	243,012	187,348	205,411	635,771
1991	198,259	333,194	164,231	695,684
1992	211,378	353,007	175,953	740,338
1993	245,564	535,832	177,941	959,337
1994	286,163	337,297	202,183	825,643
1990–1994 Average	236,875	349,336	185,144	771,355
1995	361,886	409,836	244,538	1,016,260
1996	396,785	651,301	267,472	1,315,558
1997	469,610	740,049	317,707	1,527,366
1998	680,768	1,016,928	565,727	2,263,423
1999	851,317	1,388,102	682,819	2,922,238
1995–1999 Average	552,073	841,243	415,653	1,808,969
1998	680,768	1,042,420[a]	575,997[a]	2,299,185[a]
1999	851,317	1,362,635[a]	694,629[a]	2,908,581[a]

[a] *Including Hong Kong.*
[b] *Excluding Hong Kong, except as noted.*
[c] *Excluding Hong Kong portfolio investment and other investment, except as noted.*
Source: *IMF (2000a) and earlier issues; United Nations (2000) and earlier issues; Republic of China (2000).*

Table 10.A2 Sources of direct investment outflows

Period	United States	Japan	Europe	Developing Asia	Latin America
	(Millions of US dollars)				
1990	29,951	48,050	139,955	17,000	1,067
1991	31,378	31,487	114,490	9,837	1,357
1992	48,730	17,390	113,020	18,415	1,913
1993	83,951	13,834	103,586	30,728	2,759
1994	80,167	18,089	134,564	35,444	3,475
1990–94 Average	54,835	25,770	121,123	22,285	2,114
1995	98,750	22,508	176,736	42,534	4,001
1996	91,883	23,442	208,355	48,147	3,194
1997	105,017	26,059	249,122	49,879	7,988
1998	146,053	24,625	435,645	30,490	8,499
1999	150,900	22,267	610,390[a]	38,884	8,236
1995–99 Average	118,521	23,780	336,050	41,987	6,384

[a] Excluding Norway.
Source: IMF (2000a) and earlier issues; United Nations (2000) and earlier issues; Republic of China (2000).

Table 10.A3 Destinations of direct investment inflows

Period	United States	Japan	Europe	Developing Asia	Latin America
	(Millions of US dollars)				
1990	47,918	1,760	104,310	21,479	7,666
1991	22,010	1,298	84,954	22,588	11,873
1992	20,975	2,760	88,646	28,416	14,308
1993	51,363	119	88,195	49,847	12,940
1994	46,121	912	85,972	65,134	27,457
1990–94 average	37,677	1,370	90,415	37,493	14,849
1995	57,776	39	138,554	70,256	28,802
1996	86,503	200	135,882	85,247	42,434
1997	106,035	3,200	164,505	91,677	63,026
1998	186,315	3,268	282,211	85,757	70,201
1999	275,535	12,308	396,612[a]	93,499	87,171
1995–99 average	142,433	3,803	223,553	85,287	58,327

[a] Excluding Norway.
Source: See table 10.A2.

Table 10.A4 Net inflows of direct investment

Period	United States	Japan	Europe	Developing Asia	Latin America
	(Millions of US dollars)[b]				
1990	17,967	−46,290	−35,645	4,479	6,599
1991	−9,368	−30,189	−29,536	12,751	10,516
1992	−27,755	−14,630	−24,374	10,001	12,395
1993	−32,588	−13,715	−15,391	19,119	10,181
1994	−34,046	−17,177	−48,592	29,690	23,982
1990–94 average	−17,158	−24,400	−30,708	15,208	12,735
1995	−40,974	−22,469	−38,182	27,722	24,801
1996	−5,380	−23,242	−72,473	37,100	39,240
1997	1,018	−22,859	−84,617	41,798	55,038
1998	40,262	−21,357	−153,434	55,267	61,702
1999	124,635	−9,959	−213,778[a]	54,615	78,935
1995–99 average	23,912	−19,977	−112,497	43,300	51,943

[a] *Excluding Norway.*
[b] *A positive sign connotes a net inflow and a negative sign a net outflow.*
Source: *Tables 10.A2 and 10.A3.*

Table 10.A5 US private investment abroad, 1976–1999

Year	Direct investment, valued at			Foreign securities	Other private claims	Total, with direct investment valued at		
	Market	Current	Book			Market	Current	Book
	(Millions of US dollars)							
1976	–	222,283	136,809	44,157	101,452	–	367,892	282,418
1977	–	246,078	145,990	49,439	114,818	–	410,335	310,247
1978	–	285,005	162,727	53,384	160,201	–	498,590	376,312
1979	–	336,301	187,858	56,769	191,520	–	584,590	436,147
1980	–	388,072	215,375	62,454	242,295	–	692,821	520,124
1981	–	407,804	228,348	62,142	336,260	–	806,206	626,750
1982	226,638	374,059	207,752	74,046	439,983	740,667	888,088	721,781
1983	274,342	355,643	212,150	84,723	565,834	924,899	1,006,200	862,707
1984	270,574	348,342	218,093	88,804	575,769	935,147	1,012,915	882,666
1985	386,352	371,036	238,369	119,403	589,235	1,094,990	1,079,674	947,007
1986	530,074	404,818	270,472	158,123	674,730	1,362,927	1,237,671	1,103,325
1987	590,246	478,062	326,253	188,589	726,825	1,505,660	1,393,476	1,241,667
1988	692,461	513,761	347,179	232,849	850,984	1,776,294	1,597,594	1,431,012
1989	832,460	553,093	381,781	314,294	948,124	2,094,878	1,815,511	1,644,199
1990	731,762	616,655	430,521	342,313	961,002	2,035,077	1,919,970	1,733,836
1991	827,537	643,364	467,844	455,750	946,697	2,229,984	2,045,811	1,870,291
1992	798,630	663,830	502,063	515,083	922,326	2,236,039	2,101,239	1,939,472
1993	1,027,547	723,526	564,283	853,528	928,267	2,809,342	2,505,321	2,346,078
1994	1,067,803	786,565	612,893	948,668	1,016,098	3,032,569	2,751,331	2,577,659
1995	1,307,155	885,506	699,015	1,169,636	1,135,716	3,612,507	3,190,858	3,004,367
1996	1,526,243	986,536	795,195	1,467,985	1,307,489	4,301,717	3,762,010	3,570,669
1997	1,778,189	1,058,735	871,316	1,751,183	1,526,993	5,056,365	4,336,911	4,149,492
1998	2,173,547	1,207,059	1,014,012	2,052,929	1,586,301	5,812,777	4,846,289	4,653,242
1999	2,615,532	1,331,187	1,132,622	2,583,386	1,753,811	6,952,729	5,668,384	5,469,819

Source: *Bargas (2000), and Scholl (2000).*

Table 10.A6 Foreign non-official assets in the United States, 1976–1999

Year	Direct investment, valued at			US securities	Other claims	Total, with direct investment valued at		
	Market	Current	Book			Market	Current	Book
(Millions of US Dollars)								
1976	–	47,528	30,770	61,941	78,218	–	187,687	170,929
1977	–	55,413	34,595	58,797	85,761	–	199,971	179,153
1978	–	68,976	42,471	62,464	110,307	–	241,747	215,242
1979	–	88,579	54,462	72,797	148,547	–	309,923	275,806
1980	–	127,105	83,046	90,227	175,574	–	392,906	348,847
1981	–	164,623	108,714	93,590	223,262	–	481,475	425,566
1982	130,428	184,842	124,677	118,746	286,785	535,959	590,373	530,208
1983	153,318	193,708	137,061	147,657	376,837	677,812	718,202	661,555
1984	172,377	223,538	164,583	190,598	430,391	793,366	844,527	785,572
1985	219,996	247,223	184,615	295,822	487,526	1,003,344	1,030,571	967,963
1986	272,966	284,701	220,414	405,881	573,797	1,252,644	1,264,379	1,200,092
1987	316,200	334,552	263,394	424,320	684,604	1,425,124	1,443,476	1,372,318
1988	391,530	401,766	314,754	493,169	791,164	1,675,863	1,686,099	1,599,087
1989	534,734	467,886	368,924	649,405	871,337	2,055,476	1,988,628	1,889,666
1990	539,601	505,346	394,911	613,096	932,590	2,085,287	2,051,032	1,940,597
1991	669,137	533,404	419,108	716,303	947,470	2,332,910	2,197,177	2,082,881
1992	693,177	540,270	423,131	797,186	988,175	2,478,538	2,325,631	2,208,492
1993	768,398	593,313	467,412	917,950	1,039,919	2,726,267	2,551,182	2,425,281
1994	757,853	617,982	480,667	975,379	1,181,927	2,915,159	2,775,288	2,637,973
1995	1,005,726	680,066	535,553	1,329,893	1,284,951	3,620,570	3,294,910	3,150,397
1996	1,229,118	743,214	598,021	1,702,023	1,361,821	4,292,962	3,807,058	3,661,865
1997	1,639,765	825,334	689,834	2,240,922	1,626,392	5,507,079	4,692,648	4,557,148
1998	2,190,990	928,645	793,748	2,742,169	1,682,354	6,615,513	5,353,168	5,218,271
1999	2,800,736	1,125,214	986,668	3,170,044	1,806,944	7,777,724	6,102,202	5,963,656

Source: *Bargas (2000), Scholl (1990 and 2000)*.

Table 10.A7 The relation of US affiliate activity to US outward FDI stock across countries

Regression	Sales 1998	Employment 1998 Adjusted R^2	PP&E 1994
All Industries	0.79	0.59	0.82
Petroleum	0.51	0.85	0.98
Manufacturing	0.91	0.85	0.88
Food	0.88	0.58	0.79
Chemicals	0.69	0.58	0.76
Metals	0.89	0.64	0.88
Nonelectrical machinery	0.93	0.89	0.84
Electrical machinery	0.70	0.51	0.72
Transportation equipment	0.46	0.69	0.78
Other Manufacturing	0.66	0.79	0.85
Wholesale	0.96	0.58	0.87
Finance (excl. Banking)	0.76	0.56	0.64
Services	0.91	0.78	0.70
Other industries	0.47	0.37	0.87

Source: *Outward FDI stock: US Department of Commerce (2000d); Affiliate Sales and Employment: US Department of Commerce (2000c); Affiliate PP&E: US Department of Commerce (1998a).*

Table 10.A8 The relation of US affiliate activity to the US outward FDI stock

Regression	Adj. R^2	No. of Obs.
63 Industry Groups in 9 Countries		
Sales (1998)	0.1020	304
Employment (1998)	0.0167	442
PP&E (1994)	0.0411	196
12 Industry Groups in 58 Countries		
Sales (1998)	0.2915	419
Employment (1998)	0.0980	579
PP&E (1994)	0.1551	339

Source: *See table 10.A7.*

Table 10.A9 The relation of changes in US affiliate activity to changes in US outward FDI stock

Regression	Absolute Changes		Relative Changes	
	Adj. R²	No. of Obs.	Adj. R²	No. of Obs.
Sales (1982–98)				
All Industries	0.7282	48	0.3910	48
Petroleum	−0.0617	18	0.1332	18
Manufacturing	0.8371	41	0.4741	41
Food	0.7925	17	−0.0593	13
Chemicals	0.5335	32	0.0897	31
Metals	0.7540	20	0.4941	17
Nonelectrical machinery	0.8944	31	0.5125	14
Electrical machinery	0.6513	26	0.1779	20
Transportation equipment	0.4088	19	0.0765	6
Other manufacturing	0.4869	7	0.0985	6
Wholesale	0.8013	26	0.7974	26
Finance (excl. Banking)	0.6707	19	0.1398	19
Services	0.9175	31	0.4073	30
Other Industries	0.0999	5	0.4838	4
PP&E (1982–94)				
All Industries	0.7166	49	0.1256	49
Petroleum	0.9610	12	0.1605	13
Manufacturing	0.8092	38	0.2032	37
Food	0.4990	22	0.9732	16
Food (w/o Turkey)			0.0408	15
Chemicals	0.6422	32	0.3400	30
Metals	0.4954	18	−0.0760	14
Nonelectric	0.6329	23	0.3290	12
Electric	0.6727	22	0.5593	15
Transportation	0.7494	18	0.8585	3
Other manufacturing	0.7709	11	0.8574	9
Wholesale	0.8765	22	0.8161	22
Finance (excl. Banking)	0.6383	15	0.0262	13
Services	0.5896	25	0.7521	23
Other Industries	0.7436	6	−0.2390	6
Employment (1982–98)				
All Industries	0.1335	52	0.2326	52
Petroleum	−0.0250	34	0.0066	33
Manufacturing	0.3219	49	0.5490	48
Food	0.0210	39	0.5408	32
Chemicals	0.0260	40	0.7148	39
Metals	−0.0211	29	0.2217	25
Nonelectric	−0.0051	40	−0.0500	22
Electric	−0.0208	33	−0.0161	26
Transportation	−0.0301	32	0.1265	15
Other manufacturing	0.3170	19	−0.0434	17
Wholesale	0.1381	35	0.3490	35
Finance (excl. Banking)	0.4273	32	0.1220	28
Services	0.7556	40	0.0202	39
Other Industries	−0.0013	17	−0.0633	16

Source: *Outward FDI stock: US Department of Commerce (2000d); Affiliate Sales and Employment: US Department of Commerce (1985; 2000c); Affiliate PP&E: US Department of Commerce (1985; 1998a).*

Table 10.A10   The relation of changes in US affiliate activity to changes in US outward FDI stock: 52 countries and 12 industry groups

Regression	Adj. R^2	No. of Obs.
Absolute Changes		
Sales (1982–98)	0.2705	251
PP&E (1982–94)	0.0605	227
Employment (1982–98)	0.0257	390
Relative Changes		
Sales (1982–98)	0.1212	204
PP&E (1982–94)	0.2788	176
Employment (1982–98)	0.1808	327

Source: *See table 10.A9.*

References

Bach, Christopher L. 1998: U.S. international transactions: Revised estimates for 1986–97. *Survey of Current Business*, 78, 7, 47–57.

Bach, Christopher L. 2000: U.S. international transactions: Revised estimates for 1982–99. *Survey of Current Business*, 80, 7, 70–7.

Bargas, Sylvia E. 2000: Direct investment positions for 1999: Country and industry detail. *Survey of Current Business*, 80, 7, 58–69.

Bloomfield, Arthur I. 1968: *Patterns of Fluctuations in International Investment Before 1914*. Princeton studies in international finance no. 21, Princeton, NJ: Princeton University, International Finance Section.

Borga, Maria and Raymond J. Mataloni, Jr. 2001: Direct investment position for 2000: Country and industry detail. *Survey of Current Business*, 81, 7, 16–29.

Canada 1967: *Foreign-Owned Subsidiaries in Canada*. Dominion Bureau of Statistics and Department of Trade and Commerce.

Canada 1978: *Compendium of Statistics on Foreign Investment*. Foreign Investment Review Agency.

Canada 1979: *Domestic and Foreign Control of Manufacturing, Mining, and Logging Establishments in Canada, 1974*. Statistics Canada.

Canada 1985: *Foreign Investment Review Act, Final Annual Report, 1984–85*, Investment Canada.

Caves, Richard E. 1996: *Multinational Enterprise and Economic Analysis*, 2nd edn. Cambridge Surveys of Economic Literature, Cambridge: Cambridge University Press.

Deutsche Bundesbank 1999: Kapitalverflechtung mit dem Ausland. Statistische sonderveröffentlichung 10, Frankfurt am Main.

Dunning, John H. 1970: *Studies in International Investment*. London: Allen & Unwin.

Dunning, John H. 1992: *Multinational Enterprises and the Global Economy*. Wokingham, UK: Addison-Wesley Publishing Co.

France, SESSI (Service des Statistiques Industrielle) 2000: Les entreprises étrangère dans l'industrie française: Une forte implantation. *Les 4 Pages des statistique industrielle*, no. 132, June.

Fukao, Kyoji, Tangjun Yuan, and Makoto Sakishita 1999: Estimating total overseas business activities of Japanese companies from extrapolations of panel data underlying the basic and annual surveys. In Japan, Institute for International Trade and Investment (ed.), *Analytical Research Based on Data from the Survey of Overseas Business Activities and Survey Research on Harmonizing Globalization Based on the 1997 Survey of Overseas Business Activities*, Tokyo: Institute for International Trade and Investment (in Japanese).

Hobson, C. K. 1914: *The Export of Capital*. London: Constable.

IMF (International Monetary Fund) 1986: *Final Report of the Working Party on the Statistical Discrepancy in World Current Account Balances*, December. Washington, DC: International Monetary Fund.

IMF (International Monetary Fund) 1993: *Balance of Payments Manual*, 5th edn. Washington, DC: International Monetary Fund.

IMF (International Monetary Fund) 1995: *Balance of Payments Compilation Guide*. Washington, DC: International Monetary Fund.

IMF (International Monetary Fund) 2000a: *Balance of Payments Statistics Yearbook*. Washington, DC: International Monetary Fund.

IMF (International Monetary Fund) 2000b: *International Financial Statistics Yearbook*. Washington, DC: International Monetary Fund.

Inter-Secretariat Working Group on National Accounts, 1993: *System of National Accounts: 1993*. Brussels/Luxembourg, New York, Paris, Washington, DC: Eurostat, IMF, OECD, United Nations, and World Bank.

Iversen, Carl 1936: *Aspect of the Theory of International Capital Movements*. Copenhagen: Levin and Munksgaard; London: Humphrey Milford; and Oxford: Oxford University Press.

Japan, Institute for International Trade and Investment (ed.) 1999: *Analytical Research Based on Data from the Survey of Overseas Business Activities and Survey Research on Harmonizing Globalization Based on the 1997 Survey of Overseas Business Activities*. Tokyo: Institute for International Trade and Investment.

Kindleberger, Charles P. 1969: *American Business Abroad: Six Lectures on Direct Investment*. New Haven and London: Yale University Press.

Landefeld, J. Steven and Ann M. Lawson 1991: Valuation of the U.S. net international investment position. *Survey of Current Business*, 71, 5, May.

Lewis, Cleona 1938: *America's Stake in International Investments*. Washington, DC: Brookings Institution.

Lipsey, Robert E. 1988: Changing patterns of international investment in and by the United States. In Martin Feldstein (ed.), *The United States in the World Economy*, Chicago: University of Chicago Press, 475–545.

Lipsey, Robert E. 1998: Internationalized production in developed and developing countries and in industry sectors. NBER working paper no. 6405, February.

Lipsey, Robert E. 1999: The role of FDI in international capital flows. In Martin Feldstein (ed.), *International Capital Flows*, Chicago: University of Chicago Press, 307–62.

Lipsey, Robert E. 2001: Interpreting developed countries' foreign direct investment. In Deutsche Bundesbank (ed.), *Investing Today for the World of Tomorrow*, Berlin: Springer-Verlag, 285–325.

Lipsey, Robert E., Magnus Blomström, and Eric D. Ramstetter 1995: Internationalized production in world output. NBER working paper no. 5385, Cambridge, MA: National Bureau of Economic Research, December.

Lipsey, Robert E., Magnus Blomström, and Eric D. Ramstetter 1998: Internationalized production in world output. In Robert E. Baldwin, Robert E. Lipsey, and David J. Richardson (eds.), *Geography and Ownership as Bases for Economic Accounting*,

NBER Studies in Income and Wealth, vol. 59, Chicago: University of Chicago Press, 83–138.

Lipsey, Robert E., Eric D. Ramstetter, and Magnus Blomström 2000: Outward FDI and parent exports and employment: Japan, the United States, and Sweden. *Global Economy Quarterly*, 1, 4.

Mataloni, Raymond J., Jr. and Lee Goldberg 1994: Gross product of U.S. multinational corporations, 1977–91. *Survey of Current Business*, 74, 2, February, 42–63.

Mintz, Ilse 1951: *Deterioration in the Quality of Foreign Bonds Issued in the United States, 1920–1930*. New York: National Bureau of Economic Research.

OECD (Organization for Economic Cooperation and Development) 1996: *OECD Benchmark Definition of Foreign Direct Investment*, 3rd edn. Paris: OECD.

OECD (Organization for Economic Cooperation and Development) 1998: *Activities of Foreign Affiliates in OECD Countries*. Paris: OECD.

OECD (Organization for Economic Cooperation and Development) 1999: *Measuring Globalisation: The Role of Multinationals in OECD Economies*, 1999 edn. Paris: OECD.

OECD (Organization for Economic Cooperation and Development) 2000: *International Direct Investment Statistics Yearbook, 1999*. Paris: OECD.

Ramstetter, Eric D. 1996: Estimating economic activity by Japanese transnational corporations: How to make sense of the data? *Transnational Corporations*, 5, 2, August, 107–43.

Reddaway, W. B., in collaboration with J. O. N. Perkins, S. J. Potter, and C. T. Taylor 1967: Effects of U.K. direct investment overseas: An interim report. Occasional paper 12, Department of Applied Economics, Cambridge University.

Reddaway, W. B., in collaboration with S. J. Potter and C. T. Taylor 1968: Effects of U.K. direct investment overseas: Final report. Occasional paper 15, Department of Applied Economics, Cambridge University.

Republic of China 2000: *Statistical Yearbook of the Republic of China, 2000*. Taiwan: Directorate General of Budget, Accounting, and Statistics, Executive Yuan, Republic of China.

Samuelsson, Hans-Fredrik 1977: *Utländska Direkta Investeringar I Sverige*. Stockholm: Industriens Utredningsinstitut.

Scholl, Russell B. 1990: International investment position: Component detail for 1989. *Survey of Current Business*, 70, 6, June, 54–65.

Scholl, Russell B. 2000: The international investment position of the United States at yearend 1999. *Survey of Current Business*, 80, 7, July, 46–56.

Southard, Frank A., Jr. 1931: *American Industry in Europe, Boston and New York*. Boston and New York: Houghton Mifflin Co.

Stekler, Lois E. and Guy V. G. Stevens, 1991: The adequacy of U.S. direct investment data. In Peter Hooper and David J. Richardson (eds.), *International Economic Transactions: Issues in Measurement and Empirical Research, Studies in Income and Wealth*, vol. 55. Chicago: University of Chicago Press.

Stevens, Guy V. G. and Robert E. Lipsey, 1992: Interactions between domestic and foreign investment. *Journal of International Money and Finance*, 11, 1, March, 40–62.

Svedberg, Peter 1978: The portfolio–direct investment composition of private foreign investment in 1914, revisited. *Economic Journal*, 88, 352, December, 763–77.

Sweden, Statistics Sweden 2000a: *Swedish Owned Enterprise Groups Having Subsidiaries Abroad 1997*. Stockholm and Örebro: Swedish National Board for Industrial and Technical Development (NUTEK) and Statistics Sweden.

Sweden, Statistics Sweden 2000b: *International Business: Foreign Owned Enterprises 1999*. Stockholm and Örebro: Swedish National Board for Industrial and Technical Development (NUTEK) and Statistics Sweden.

Sweden, Statistics Sweden 2000c: *Utlandsägda företag, Ekonomiska uppgifter 1997.* Stockholm and Örebro: Swedish National Board for Industrial and Technical Development (NUTEK) and Statistics Sweden.

Sweden, Statistics Sweden 2001: *Research and Development in International Enterprises 1997.* Östersund and Stockholm: Swedish Institute for Growth Policy Studies (ITPS) and Statistics Sweden.

Swedenborg, Birgitta 1979: *The Multinational Operations of Swedish Firms: An Analysis of Determinants and Effects.* Stockholm: The Industrial Institute for Economic and Social Research.

Swedenborg, Birgitta 2001: Determinants and effects of multinational growth: The Swedish case revisited. In Magnus Blomström and Linda Goldberg (eds.), *Topics in Empirical International Economics,* Chicago: University of Chicago Press.

Swedenborg, Birgitta, Göran Johansson-Grahn, and Mats Kinwall 1988: *Den Svenska Industrins Utlandsinvesteringar, 1960–1986.* Stockholm: Industriens Utredningsinstitut.

United Nations 1973: *Multinational Corporations in the World Economy.* New York: United Nations.

United Nations 1978: *Transnational Corporations in World Development: A Re-Examination.* New York: United Nations, Commission on Transnational Corporations.

United Nations 1983: *Transnational Corporations in World Development: Third Survey.* New York: United Nations, Center on Transnational Corporations.

United Nations 1988: *Transnational Corporations in World Development: Trends and Prospects.* New York: United Nations, Center on Transnational Corporations.

United Nations 1993: *MSPA Handbook of World Development Statistics.* New York: United Nations, Long-Term Socio-Economic Perspectives Branch, Macroeconomics and Social Policy Analysis Division, Department of Economic and Social Information and Policy Analysis.

United Nations 1998: *World Investment Report, 1998: Trends and Determinants.* New York and Geneva: United Nations Conference on Trade and Development.

United Nations 1999: *World Investment Report, 1999: Foreign Direct Investment and the Challenge of Development.* New York and Geneva: United Nations Conference on Trade and Development.

United Nations 2000: *World Investment Report, 2000; Cross-Border Mergers and Acquisitions and Development.* New York and Geneva: United Nations Conference on Trade and Development.

United Nations 2001: *Measures of the Transnationalization of Economic Activity.* New York and Geneva: United Nations Conference on Trade and Development.

US Bureau of the Census 1975: *Historical Statistics of the United States, Colonial Times to 1970.* Washington, DC: US Government Printing Office.

US Congress, House of Representatives 1978: *The Operations of Federal Agencies in Monitoring, Reporting On, and Analyzing Foreign Investments in the United States, Hearings before a Subcommittee of the Committee on Government Operations, 95th Congress, 2nd Session, September 19, 20, and 21, 1978.* Washington, DC: US Government Printing Office.

US Department of Commerce 1930: *American Direct Investments in Foreign Countries.* Trade information bulletin no. 731, Washington, DC: US Government Printing Office.

US Department of Commerce 1938: *American Direct Investments in Foreign Countries – 1936.* Bureau of Foreign and Domestic Commerce economic series, no.1, Washington, DC: US Government Printing Office.

US Department of Commerce 1953: *Direct Private Foreign Investments of the United States: Census of 1950, A Supplement to the Survey of Current Business.* Office of Business Economics, Washington, DC: US Government Printing Office.

US Department of Commerce 1975: *U.S. Direct Investment Abroad, 1966, Final Data*. Washington, DC: US Department of Commerce, Bureau of Economic Analysis.

US Department of Commerce 1981: *U.S. Direct Investment Abroad, 1977*. Washington, DC: US Department of Commerce, Bureau of Economic Analysis, April.

US Department of Commerce 1982: *Selected Data on U.S. Direct Investment Abroad, 1950–1976*. Washington, DC: Bureau of Economic Analysis, February.

US Department of Commerce 1985: *U.S. Direct Investment Abroad, 1982 Benchmark Survey Data*. Washington, DC: US Department of Commerce, Bureau of Economic Analysis, December.

US Department of Commerce 1986: *U.S. Direct Investment Abroad: Balance of Payments and Direct Investment Position Estimates, 1977–81*. Washington, DC: Bureau of Economic Analysis, November.

US Department of Commerce 1987: *Foreign Direct Investment in the United States: Establishment Data for 1987*. Washington, DC: Bureau of Economic Analysis and Bureau of the Census, June.

US Department of Commerce 1995: *U.S. Direct Investment Abroad: Balance of Payments and Direct Investment Position Estimates, 1982–88*. Washington, DC: Bureau of Economic Analysis, September.

US Department of Commerce 1997: *Foreign Direct Investment in the United States: Establishment Data for 1997*. Washington, DC: Bureau of Economic Analysis and Bureau of the Census, May.

US Department of Commerce 1998a: *U.S. Direct Investment Abroad: 1994 Benchmark Survey, Final Results*. Washington, DC: Bureau of Economic Analysis, May.

US Department of Commerce 1998b: U.S. direct investment abroad: Detail for historical cost position and related capital and income flows, 1997. *Survey of Current Business*, 78, 10, October, 117–56.

US Department of Commerce 2000a: Foreign direct investment in the United States: Detail for historical cost position and related capital and income flows, 1999. *Survey of Current Business*, 80, 9, September, 31–60.

US Department of Commerce 2000b: U.S. direct investment abroad: Detail for historical cost position and related capital and income flows, 1999. *Survey of Current Business*, 80, 9, September, 61–90.

US Department of Commerce 2000c: *U.S. Direct Investment Abroad: Operations of U.S. Parent Companies and Their Foreign Affiliates, 1998 Preliminary*. Washington, DC: Bureau of Economic Analysis.

US Department of Commerce 2000d: *U.S. Direct Investment Abroad: Balance of Payments & Direct Investment Position Estimates, 1982–1999*. Washington, DC: Bureau of Economic Analysis.

US Department of Commerce 2001: *Foreign Direct Investment in the United States: Final Results from the 1997 Benchmark Survey*. Washington, DC: Bureau of Economic Analysis.

Vaupel, James W., and Joan P. Curhan 1969: *The Making of Multinational Enterprise*. Boston: Harvard University, Graduate School of Business Administration, Division of Research.

Wilkins, Mira 1970: *The Emergence of Multinational Enterprise: American Business Abroad from the Colonial Era to 1914*. Cambridge, MA: Harvard University Press.

Wilkins, Mira 1986: Japanese multinational enterprise before 1914. *Business History Review*, 60, Summer, 199–231.

Wilkins, Mira 1989: *The History of Foreign Investment in the United States to 1914*. Harvard studies in business history, no. 41, Cambridge, MA and London: Harvard University Press.

11

General-Equilibrium Approaches to the Multinational Enterprise: A Review of Theory and Evidence

James R. Markusen and Keith E. Maskus

CHAPTER OUTLINE

From the early 1980s, theoretical analyses have incorporated the multi-national firm into the microeconomic, general-equilibrium theory of inter-national trade. Recent advances indicate how vertical and horizontal multinationals arise endogenously as determined by country characteristics, including relative size and relative endowment differences, and trade and investment costs. Results also characterize the relationship between foreign affiliate production and international trade in goods and services. In this chapter, we survey some of this recent work, and note the testable predictions generated in the theory. In the second part of the chapter, we examine empirical results that relate foreign affiliate production to country characteristics and trade/investment cost factors. We also review findings from analyses of the pattern of substitutability or complementarity between trade and foreign production.

1 INTRODUCTION

Both theoretical and empirical studies of the activities of multinational firms cover a wide range of topics. Often, the questions asked and analytical avenues taken draw from quite different sub-areas of economic theory. Some approaches are more the stuff of macroeconomics, some relate to general-equilibrium trade theory, and some more closely relate to the theory of the firm, the latter using the tools of game and information theories.

This chapter will concentrate on the general-equilibrium trade-theory view of the multinational firm, reviewing recent theoretical and empirical analysis. This in no way suggests that macroeconomic and theory-of-the-firm approaches to the multinational are unimportant or uninteresting. It is rather that the trade-theory approach reflects the expertise of the authors and it is quite enough for one chapter.

More specifically, we will begin with a theory review, noting how multinational firms have been added to the traditional competitive, constant-returns, model used by international trade economists for decades. We begin with early analyses that viewed the activities of multinationals as essentially a part of the theory of portfolio capital flows. This theory generated clear testable predictions, generally to the effect that multinational firms will be headquartered in capital-abundant countries and establish subsidiaries in capital-poor countries.

The next step in the evolution of the theory occurred early in the development of the industrial-organization approach to trade. This "new trade theory" incorporated elements of increasing returns to scale and imperfect competition into traditional general-equilibrium models. But soon there was a bifurcation of the sub-theory on multinationals into two branches. One could be called the "vertical" model in which firms geographically separate production by stages. This approach followed directly from the earlier work on direct investment as a branch of the theory of capital flows. The other could be referred to as the "horizontal" model in which a given firm produces roughly the same goods or services in multiple countries. These two alternatives have very different empirical implications, as we will note later.[1]

A third step in the development of the theory was to combine these two approaches into a richer framework that allows firms to choose among domestic, horizontal, and vertical strategies. Markusen (1997, 2002) has dubbed this the "knowledge-capital model," and tries to clarify the key unifying assumptions.

In the course of discussing the relevant models, we will note their testable implications. We will be particularly interested in their predictions regarding how the volume and pattern of affiliate production relate to country characteristics. These characteristics include markets sizes, differences in market sizes, differences in relative factor endowments, and trade and investment barriers. We will be interested further in testable implications relating to the relationship between affiliate activity and trade in goods.

Following the theoretical discussion, we turn to a review of empirical studies that address these questions. Empirical evidence suggests strong support for the horizontal approach, but little support for the vertical approach. The hybrid or "knowledge-capital" model gets good support, but in some cases the evidence does not allow it to be distinguished from the horizontal model.

2 DIRECT INVESTMENT AS A CAPITAL FLOW: A FACTOR-PROPORTIONS APPROACH

Early approaches to direct investment started with the basic workhorse model of international trade theory, the Heckscher–Ohlin (HO) model, or at least some sort of basic competitive factor-proportions model. There was no attempt to theoretically differentiate direct investment from portfolio investment. Factor-endowment differences between countries, combined with trade costs or specialization, meant that factor prices were not equalized internationally. Early papers, including MacDougall (1960) and Kemp (1962), often had a normative focus, addressing policy concerns about the appropriateness of restrictions to inward investment. Authors noted that a capital-scarce country could import capital up to the point where the return to capital was equalized internationally, and capture inframarginal gains on the inward investment in ways that improved welfare.

A more realistic approach was taken by Caves (1971), who used the Jones (1971) specific-factors model instead of a HO structure. Caves argued that direct investment is associated with firm-specific capital, and thus investment moved from an industry in the parent country to the same industry in the host country. The model was still a competitive, constant-returns approach in which firms are not really identified as distinct from industries, but Caves' paper was an important step in identifying something that differentiates direct investment from portfolio flows of homogeneous capital.

Although several papers had a normative focus as just suggested, these models have clear positive implications. Capital, whether of the homogeneous HO variety or the sector-specific variety, tends to flow from where it is abundant to where it is scarce. In particular, there is no motive for direct investment between identical countries.

3 REFINEMENTS OF THE FACTOR-PROPORTIONS APPROACH: THE VERTICAL MODEL OF THE MULTINATIONAL FIRM

The early 1980s saw the beginning of the industrial-organization approach to trade, which incorporated increasing returns to scale and imperfect competition into the general-equilibrium model of trade. In the latter, firms typically produced a single product in a single location. This is of course the pervasive assumption in the "strategic trade-policy" literature, which inevitably assumes single-plant, nationally-owned firms competing in world markets via exports.

An early model of multinationals was that of Helpman (1984), followed by Helpman (1985) and Helpman and Krugman (1985). We refer to these as "vertical" models, although some discussion of the terminology is needed. An alternative would be to use Brainard's (1993b) term and refer to these models as "factor-proportions explanations" for multinational activity. Helpman (1984) modeled a sector (X) as having two activities, a headquarters activity that produces blueprints, management, and the like, and a production activity. These two activities have different factor intensities, and they can be costlessly split apart geographically. The paper assumed zero trade costs, an assumption also made in Helpman (1985) and Helpman and Krugman (1985).

Helpman (1984) mentioned firm-level scale economies, which are vital to the theory of horizontal multinationals as we will see in the next section. But with the assumption of zero trade costs, this possibility plays no role. Within the factor-price-equalization (FPE) set, there is no advantage to multinationals and they do not arise. The focus of Helpman's paper was on points outside the FPE set, where firms have an incentive geographically to separate headquarters from plant. Specifically, multinationals are single-plant firms that geographically fragment the production process and arise only if countries differ sufficiently in their relative endowments of the two factors.

Helpman (1985) presented a significantly more complicated model and referred to multinationals as being both horizontally and vertically integrated. Here is where the terminology gets somewhat messy and it is our view that Helpman used the term "horizontal" in a non-standard way. In this model, enterprises are multi-product firms producing a range of differentiated final goods. Inside the FPE set, there is again no motive for multinational firms to exist. Outside this set, a firm may locate production of some varieties in one country and other varieties in another country. Each variety is sold in both countries, so intra-firm (cross-hauling) trade necessarily occurs along with multinational production. As in the case of earlier papers, multinational activity is therefore associated only with significant differences in relative endowments across countries.

Helpman (1985) thus used the term "horizontally integrated multinationals" to refer to firms producing a set of differentiated final goods, some at home and some abroad, with each variety being traded intra-firm. Many other authors, including some writing in the international business literature, use the term "horizontal" multinational to refer to firms that produce the same product or service in multiple countries and serve local markets by domestic production of that product rather than through trade. From this point of view, Helpman's definition does not fit very well into the horizontal approach, nor does it fit very well into the vertical approach as that term is often used. It does fit nicely into Brainard's terminology as a factor-proportions approach to the multinational and direct investment, in that differences in factor prices across countries are the motive for direct investment.

When we refer to the "vertical model" subsequently in this chapter, we will have in mind Helpman (1984) and Helpman and Krugman (1985) as primary examples. Specifically, vertical firms will refer to single-plant firms that fragment the production process into stages based on factor intensities and locate activities according to international differences in factor prices.

Regardless of the confusing terminology, the set of papers referred to in this section have clear testable implications. They predict that multinational activity will arise between countries that differ significantly in relative endowments and will not arise between very similar countries. We emphasize that this is as much due to the assumptions about zero trade costs as it is to the assumptions about technology. However, given the constellation of assumptions in these papers, their predictions do not differ substantially from those of the older literature, which posited a technical equivalence between direct investment and portfolio capital movements.

4   A HORIZONTAL OR "PROXIMITY-CONCENTRATION" APPROACH

Models that predict no role for multinational investment between similar countries are absolutely inconsistent with even the most casual glance at the data. But that is getting ahead of the story. An early model of an alternative approach to the multinational was the horizontal model of Markusen (1984). This model assumes the existence of firm-level scale economies as the driving force for direct investment. Two-plant firms have fixed costs that are less than double those of a single-plant firm, and therein lies the motive for multinational production. Multinationals are defined as firms that produce the same product in multiple plants, serving local markets by local production. Henceforth, this is what we will mean by a horizontal multinational, although such firms nevertheless do have some vertical element to them in that the services of firm-specific assets are produced in a headquarters location and supplied to a foreign plant.[2]

Extensions of this model are found in Horstmann and Markusen (1987, 1992) and Brainard (1993a), who referred to this approach as the "proximity-concentration" hypothesis. General-equilibrium extensions that make the model more comparable to the Helpman–Krugman vertical model are found in Markusen and Venables (1998, 2000), the latter also relying on the world Edgeworth box as a tool of analysis.

While the Markusen and Venables papers allow a comparison to Helpman–Krugman, the two approaches nevertheless generate very different predictions. Suppose we rule out vertical firms that have a headquarters in one country and a plant in the other country.[3] Perhaps there is an intrinsic connection between production and research so that one plant must be located together with the headquarters. Thus, firms are either "domestic" firms with a single plant and headquarters in one country or "horizontal" multinationals with a headquarters in one country and plants in both countries.

The horizontal model predicts that, given moderate to high trade costs and plant-level as well as firm-level scale economies, multinational activity will arise between similar countries. The intuition is best explained by considering what happens when two countries are asymmetric in either size or in relative endowments. Suppose first that the countries are of very different sizes. Horizontal multinationals will be at a disadvantage relative to domestic firms headquartered and producing in the large country. The multinational would have to install costly capacity in the small market, while the domestic firm would just incur trade costs on a relatively small amount of output exported to the small market. Suppose instead that the countries are of similar size but have very different relative endowments. Let skilled labor be the factor of production used intensively in the multinational sector in both fixed and in variable costs. Horizontal multinationals may now be at a disadvantage in that they have to incur a substantial portion of costs in a high-cost location. Domestic firms located in the skilled-labor-abundant country, on the other hand, incur all of their costs in the low-cost location.

5 AN INTEGRATED APPROACH: THE KNOWLEDGE-CAPITAL MODEL

Now allow firms to take on three different configurations. Single-plant firms with a headquarters and plant in the same location are referred to as domestic or type-*d* firms. Single-plant firms with a headquarters and plant in different countries are referred to as vertical or type-*v* firms. Two-plant firms with a headquarters in one country and a plant in the other country are referred to as horizontal or type-*h* firms. Three crucial assumptions about technology constitute what Markusen (1997, 2002) refers to as the knowledge-capital (KK) model.

1 *Fragmentation* – the location of knowledge-based assets may be fragmented from production. Any incremental cost of supplying services of the asset to a single foreign plant versus the cost to a single domestic plant is small.
2 *Skilled-labor intensity* – knowledge-based assets are skilled-labor intensive relative to final production.
3 *Jointness* – the services of knowledge-based assets are (at least partially) joint ("public") inputs into multiple production facilities. The added cost of a second plant is small compared to the cost of establishing a firm with a local plant.

The first two properties, fragmentation and skilled-labor intensity motivate vertical (type-*v*) multinationals that locate their single plant and headquarters in different countries depending on factor prices and market sizes. The third property, jointness, gives rise to horizontal (type-*h*) multinationals, which have plants producing the final good in multiple countries. Jointness is the key idea motivating the existence of firm-level scale economies.

It is important to note that properties (1) and (3) are not the same thing. A knowledge-based asset, such as a skilled engineer, may be easily transported to a foreign plant, but may be fully rival or non-joint in that his or her services cannot be supplied to two plants at the same time. Using alternative terminology, a firm may be able to geographically fragment production at low cost without having firm-level scale economies. Fragmentation is related to the concept of "technology transfer cost," or the ease of supplying services to a foreign plant. Fragmentation relates to supplying services to a foreign plant, regardless as to whether or not the firm has a domestic plant as well.

Jointness refers to the ability to use the engineer or other headquarters asset in multiple production locations without reducing the services provided in any single location. A blueprint is the classical example of a joint input. Jointness inherently refers to the costs of running two plants rather than one.

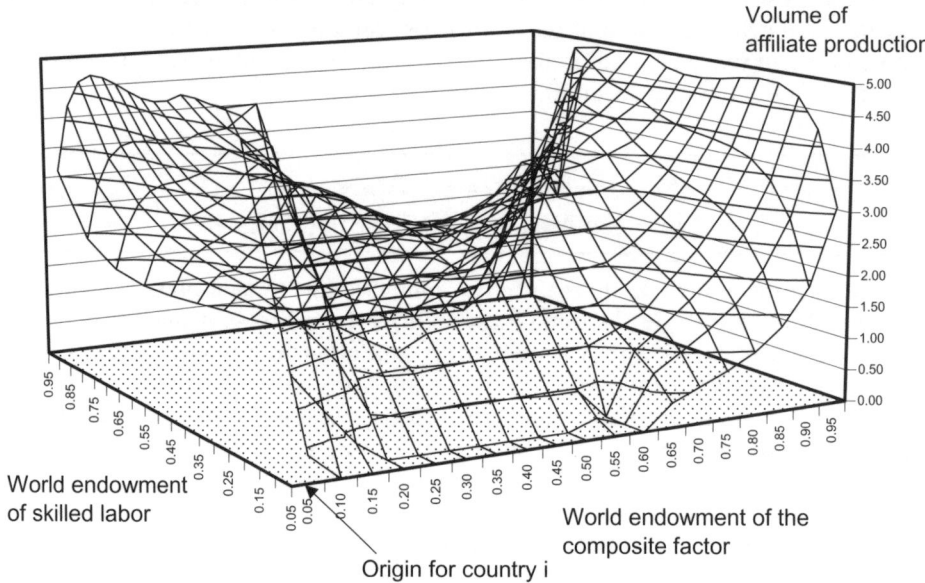

Figure 11.1 Volume of affiliate production, KK model

In the knowledge-capital model, both type-*h* and type-*v* multinationals can arise depending on country characteristics such as size, size differences, relative endowment differences, trade costs, and investment costs.

With this background, figures 11.1 to 11.3 present simulation results from Markusen (2002, ch. 8, ch. 12). The underlying model has two countries (i, j), two goods (Y, X), and two factors $(L$ – unskilled labor, S – skilled labor$)$. Y is produced with perfect competition and constant returns and is unskilled-labor intensive. X is a homogeneous good produced with increasing returns under Cournot competition. Markets are segmented. There are six possible firm types and there is free entry and exit into and out of firm types.

1   Type h_i – horizontal multinationals that maintain plants in both countries, headquarters is located in country i.
2   Type h_j – horizontal multinationals that maintain plants in both countries, headquarters is located in country j.
3   Type d_i – national firms that maintain a single plant and headquarters in country i. Type-d_i firms may or may not export to country j.
4   Type d_j – national firms that maintain a single plant and headquarters in country j. Type-d_j firms may or may not export to country i.
5   Type v_i – vertical multinationals that maintain a single plant in country j, headquarters in country i. Type-v_i firms may or may not export to country i.
6   Type v_j – vertical multinationals that maintain a single plant in country i, headquarters in country j. Type-v_j firms may or may not export to country j.

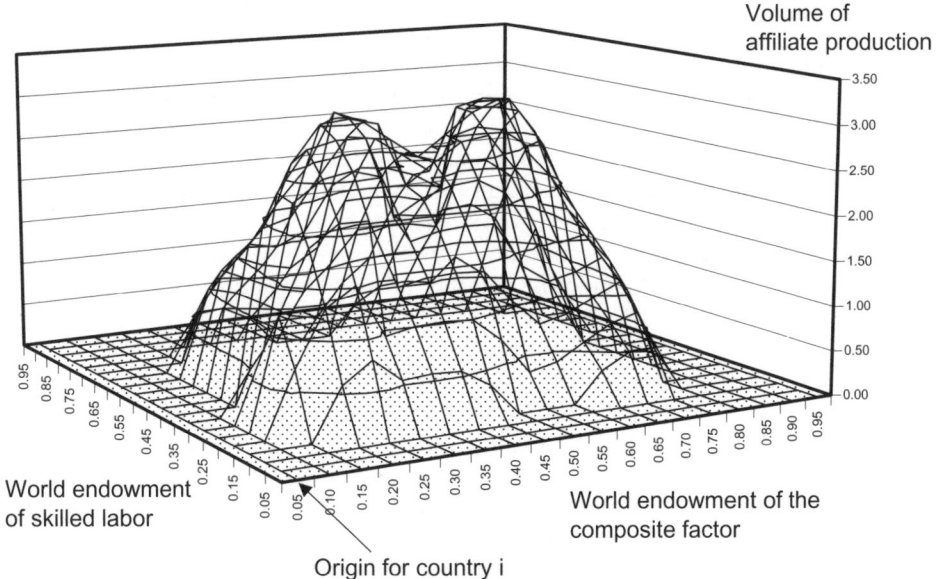

Figure 11.2 Volume of affiliate production, HOR model

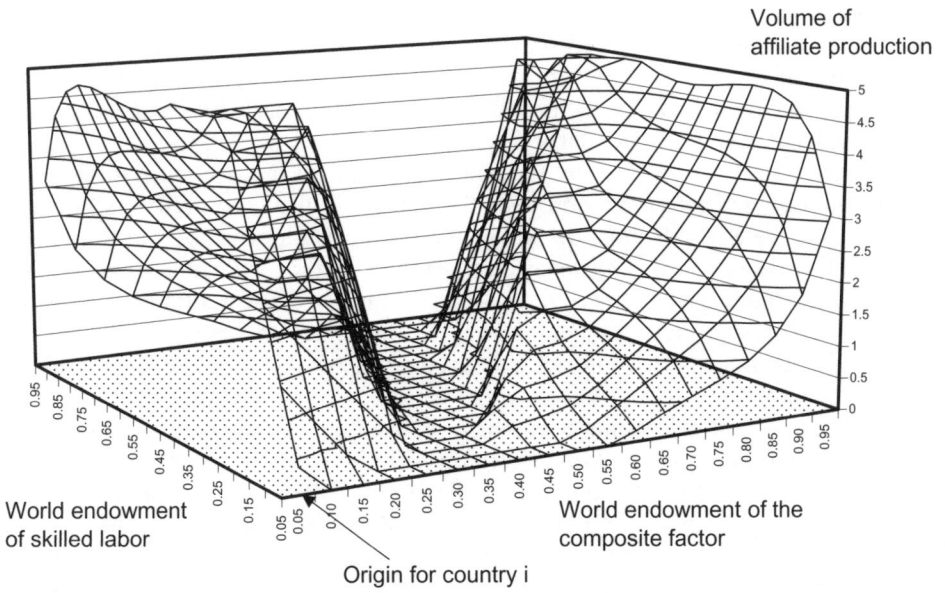

Figure 11.3 Volume of affiliate production, VER model

Factor-intensity assumptions are crucial to the results of the model. These are guided by what we believe are some empirically relevant assumptions. First, headquarters activities are more skilled-labor intensive than production plants (including both plant-specific fixed costs and marginal costs). This implies that an "integrated" type-d firm, with a headquarters and plant in the same location, is more skilled-labor intensive than a plant alone. Second, we assume that a plant alone (no headquarters) is more skilled-labor intensive than the composite Y sector. This is much less obvious, but some evidence suggests that this is probably true for developing countries: branch plants of foreign multinationals are more skilled-labor intensive than the economy as a whole. Assumptions on the skilled-labor intensity of activities are therefore:

$$[\text{headquarters only}] > [\text{integrated } X] > [\text{plant only}] > [Y]$$

A complete specification of this model is found in Markusen (2002). A numerical version of the model is solved over various parameter values, with the solution giving the types and numbers of firms active in equilibrium. However, available data do not provide figures on both numbers and types of firms, but rather the values of foreign affiliate production and sales. The simulation model can focus on these variables, and output is that shown in figures 11.1 to 11.3. These diagrams are world Edgeworth boxes, with the world endowment of skilled labor on one axis and the world endowment of the other composite factor (called unskilled labor) on the other axis. Country i is measured from the near or southwest (SW) corner, and country j's endowment from the far or northeast (NE) corner. The volume of affiliate production is measured on the vertical axis. This is defined as the value of the output of plants in country j of firms headquartered in country i; that is, the output of type-d_i and type-h_i firms in country j, and similarly for plants in country i of firms headquartered in country j.

Figure 11.1 shows results for the knowledge-capital model, with trade costs 20 percent of marginal production costs (20 percent is also used in figures 11.2 and 11.3). Along the SW–NE diagonal where the countries differ in size but not in relative endowments, there is an inverted U-shaped pattern, indicating that affiliate production is highest when the countries are the same size. The multinationals active here are type-h, two-plant horizontal firms. At the center of the box, each firm has symmetric plants in both countries, so exactly half of all world output is affiliate output.

The highest values of affiliate output in figure 11.1 occur when one country is both small and skilled-labor abundant. In this situation, most or even all of the firms are type-v firms headquartered in the small country, with a single plant in the large, skilled-labor-scarce country. The location of headquarters is chosen on the basis of factor prices, and the location of the plant is chosen both on the basis of factor prices and on the basis of market size. These motives reinforce one another for type-v firms when one country is small and skilled-labor abundant. Note that when all firms are type-v, then all world X output is, by definition, affiliate output. This explains the high affiliate production along the western and eastern edges of the Edgeworth box in figure 11.1.

Figure 11.2 presents results for a restricted version of the same model, which we will call the horizontal (HOR) model. There are two changes from the model used to generate figure 11.1. First, there is something inherent in the technology that makes fragmentation costs very high, such as the need for critical revision and feedback between the local plant and R&D personnel and managers. In particular, assume that the total fixed costs of a type-v firm are the same as for a type-h firm.[4] Second, the model is re-calibrated so that all X-sector activities (marginal costs, firm fixed costs, and plant fixed costs) use factors in the same proportion in figure 11.2. Thus there is not a factor-price motive for fragmenting activities.

Results in figure 11.2 show that affiliate activity is most important between countries that are similar in both size and in relative endowments. Earlier, we explained why differences in size or in relative endowments imply advantages for domestic firms headquartered in the large and/or skilled-labor-abundant country. At the center of the box, all firms are symmetric type-h firms, and so exactly half of all world X output is affiliate output. When one country is a bit smaller and more skilled-labor abundant, most of the headquarters of the type-h firms are located in the smaller, skilled-labor-abundant country while more of the production is located in the other country. Thus more than half of world output is affiliate output, which explains the twin peaks in figure 11.2. More generally, above the SW–NE diagonal most of the firms are headquartered in the skilled-labor-abundant country i. Thus, considering one-way activity (affiliates of country i firms producing in country j), outward investment is still positively related to a country's skilled-labor abundance.

The empirical implication of the HOR model is thus straightforward. Affiliate production should be most important among countries that are similar in both size and in relative endowments. But considering one-way activity, a country's outward affiliate activity will be positively related to the country's skilled-labor abundance.

Figure 11.3 presents results from a model that makes only one change from the KK model of figure 11.1. Figure 11.3 raises fixed costs for type-h firms until they are double the fixed costs for type-d firms so that there are no firm-level scale economies arising from jointness. All other features of the model are the same as in figure 11.1, including 20 percent trade costs. We will label the model of figure 11.3 the vertical (VER) model.[5]

Figure 11.3 is similar to figure 11.1 (and indeed identical at many points) when countries differ in relative endowments. But figure 11.3 has no multinationals active when countries are similar in relative endowments, in spite of the high trade costs. Indeed, there are no type-h firms active anywhere in the Edgeworth box of figure 11.3. In the central region of the box, type-d firms export at a price greater than marginal cost, and so have an advantage over type-h firms, which would have twice the fixed costs, but only local sales in each market.

The difference between figure 11.3 and figure 11.2 is striking, and they clearly have different predictions as to how affiliate production should be related to country characteristics. Figure 11.2, in which type-h firms arise but type-v firms are excluded by assumption, has multinationals arising between countries that are similar in size and in relative endowments. In figure 11.3, in which type-v firms arise but no type-h firms exist, multinationals arise between countries that differ in relative endowments and are particularly important when one country is both small and skilled-labor abundant.

6 TRADE VERSUS AFFILIATE PRODUCTION IN THE KNOWLEDGE-CAPITAL MODEL

It seems clear that affiliate production and trade in good X should be substitutes in the horizontal approach to the multinational, although the theoretical relationship can become more complicated when there are both intermediate and final goods produced within the firm. It also seems reasonable to conjecture that affiliate production and trade in X should be complements in the vertical approach. Specifically, if there is a foreign assembly plant that exports back to the parent country, the activity generates both affiliate production and trade. Empirically, both trade and affiliate production have clearly been rising throughout the world in recent years, but this may be merely a correlation based on fairly aggregate data, rather than a demonstration of complementarity.

In this section, we will look at how the knowledge-capital model generates predictions about the relationship between affiliate production and trade in X. Our first task is to define exactly what we mean by complements or substitutes. In more general microeconomics, we do this in terms of comparative-static experiments, such as asking how the demand for X is affected by a change in the price of Y. Here we will follow this methodology, and consider two experiments. First, we consider the effect of lower trade costs on the volume of affiliate production. Second, we consider the effects of liberalizing investment, beginning from a situation in which multinationals are banned, on trade in X. We do this once again over the world Edgeworth box since, as we will see, the results depend very much on country size and relative-endowment differences.

Figure 11.4 shows the effects of reducing trade costs from 20 percent to 1 percent on the volume of affiliate production. First, we see that the volume of affiliate production falls in a central SW–NE region where the countries are similar in relative endowments and not too different in size. This corresponds to the elimination of type-h firms: with zero trade costs and plant-level scale economies firms will not build branch plants. Above and below this central SW–NE region in figure 11.4 are regions in which the volume of affiliate production increases (gray shading). Consider the upper or more northwesterly of these two gray-shaded regions. With high trade costs, the region is generally type-h and type-d firms headquartered in the skilled-labor-abundant country (country i) or type-h firms only. Trade liberalization leads to the type-h firms being replaced by type-v firms headquartered in county i. We could think of this as "plant closures" in country i, with the lost output replaced with increased output in the country-j branch plants, that is then shipped back to country i. But the latter is counted as affiliate output while the lost output of the closed local plants is not. Thus the reorganization of X-sector output leads to an increase in total world affiliate output. Defining complements and substitutes as changes in affiliate production following trade liberalization, we can therefore say

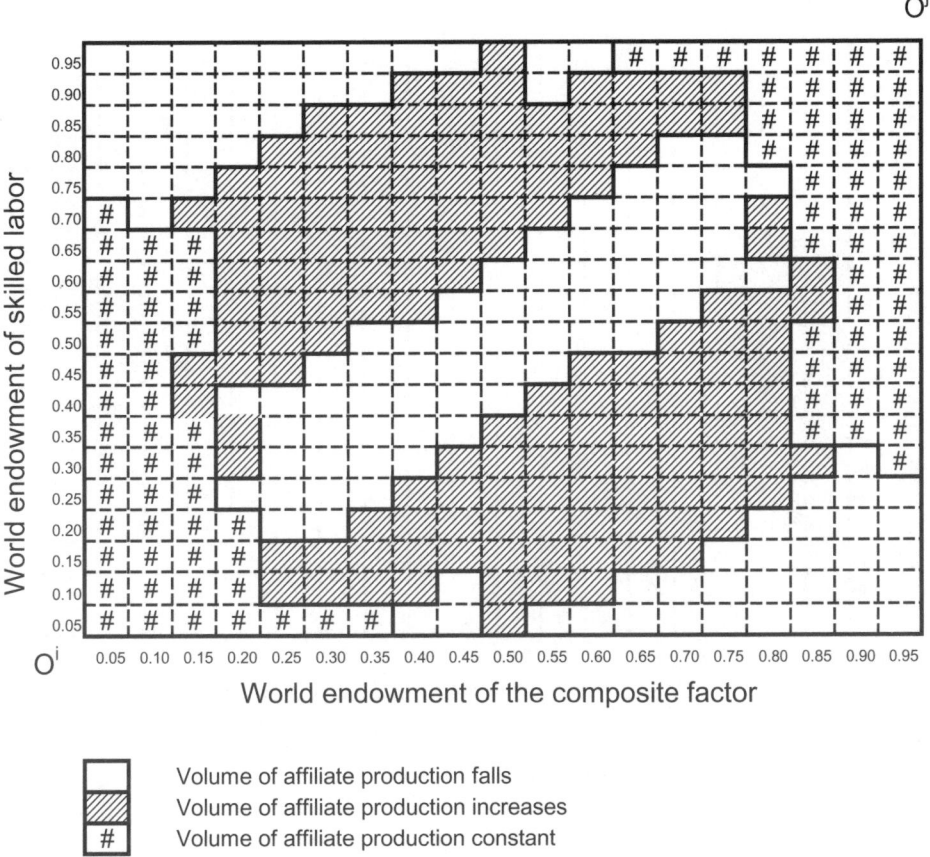

Figure 11.4 Change in the volume of affiliate production: trade costs reduce from 20% to 1%

rather loosely that affiliate production and trade are substitutes for very similar countries and complements for countries differing in relative endowments.

Figures 11.5 and 11.6 reverse the experiment, asking what happens to the volume of X trade when investment is liberalized, beginning with a situation in which multinationals (type-h and type-v firms) are banned. Figure 11.5 shows the results with high trade costs (20 percent) while figure 11.6 shows the result with low trade costs (1 percent). Consider the gray-shaded region on the "west" of figure 11.5. When multinationals are banned, there is a tension in determining "comparative advantage" and the location of X production. Country i has an advantage in that it is skilled-labor abundant, but country j has an advantage in that it is large. In this simulation, the tension is resolved in favor of country j, which exports X to country i (produced by local type-d firms). Investment liberalization switches some of these type-d firms to type-v firms headquartered in country i with a single plant

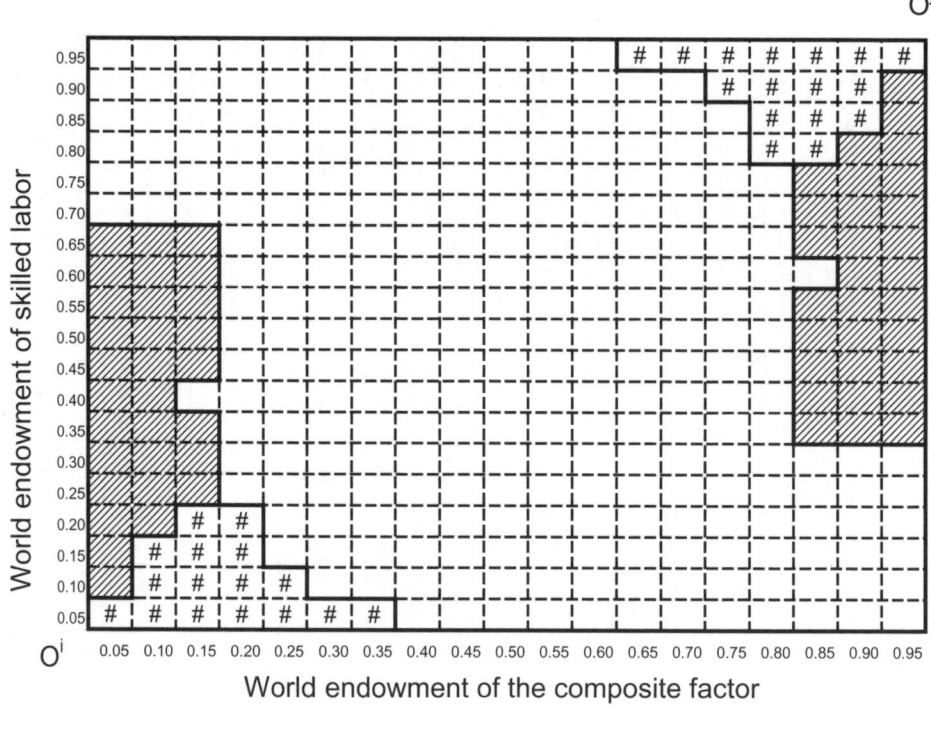

Figure 11.5 Change in the volume of trade following investment liberalization, high trade costs (20%)

in country j. This regime shift frees up scarce skilled labor in country j for actual production, which increases along with exports of X. In the central region of figure 11.5, the volume of X trade falls as type-h firms displace type-d firms.

In figure 11.6 where investment is liberalized in the presence of low trade costs, we have four regions in which the volume of trade increases. We could call these regions southwest, northeast, north-central and south-central. In the southwest and northeast regions, the explanation for the increased trade volume is the same as in the previous paragraph: type-v firms enter in the small, skilled-labor-abundant country, freeing up skilled labor in the large country for production and export.

In the north-central region of figure 11.6 the explanation is similar, but the cost savings are not sufficient to induce a regime shift with high trade costs (figure 11.5). In the north-central region of figure 11.6, domestic (type-d) firms headquartered in

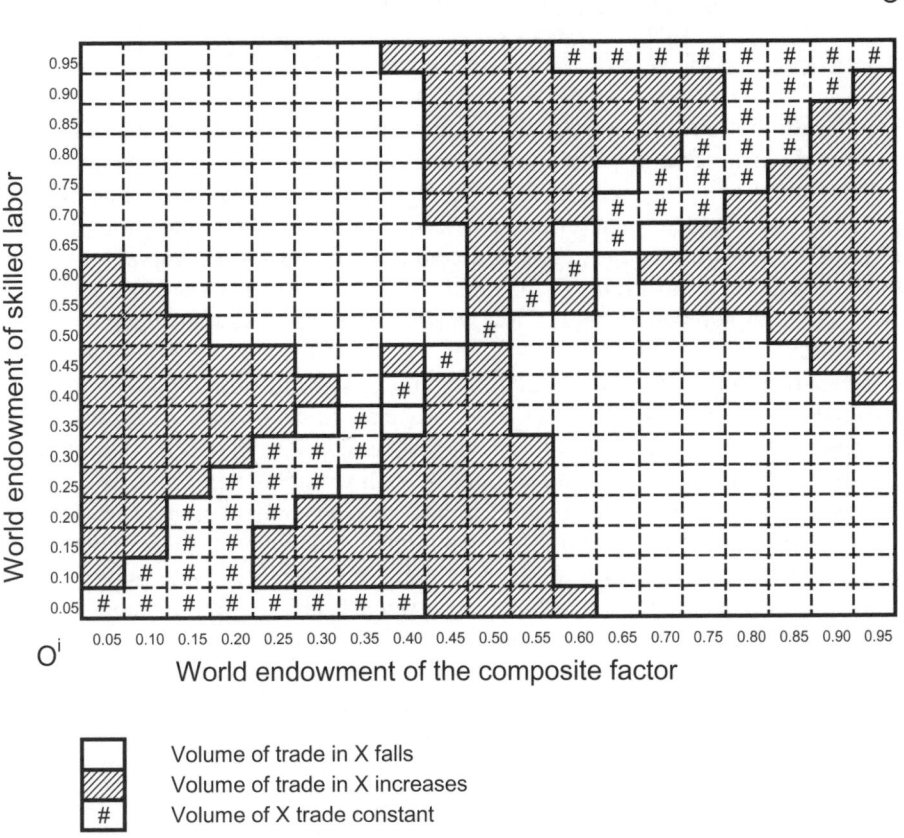

Figure 11.6 Change in the volume of trade following investment liberalization, low trade costs (1%)

the skilled-labor-scarce country j are displaced with vertical (type-v) firms head-quartered in the skilled-labor-abundant country i following liberalization. Again, this frees up skilled-labor for production in country j, and exports increase. We should note that trade volume here refers to *gross* (two-way) trade in X. In general, the increased volume of X exports from country j in the north-central part of figure 11.6 comes entirely at the expense of exports from i to j, and thus that the *net* volume of trade in X falls.

It is not easy to make any precise statements from the results shown in figures 11.4 to 11.6. It does appear that in some loose sense we can suggest that affiliate production and trade tend to be substitutes for similar countries. However, they tend to be complements for countries with widely differing relative factor endowments. For further discussion and evidence on these points, see also Ekholm (1998b) and Ekholm and Forslid (2001).

7 ECONOMETRIC STUDIES OF GENERAL-EQUILIBRIUM MODELS OF THE MULTINATIONAL ENTERPRISE

We reiterate that our intention in this chapter is to focus on papers that have analyzed the determinants of plant location and firm type within general-equilibrium models. Thus, despite the considerable interest that such studies bear, we do not consider analyses that focus on alternative determinants arising from other approaches to FDI. This literature is enormous and could command several survey papers on its own. Useful reviews of some of that analysis are in Maskus (1998a) and Markusen (1995). For completeness, however, it is worth mentioning a few such papers of particular note.

Alternative approaches essentially may be categorized broadly into four areas, though these are not independent. First, we may think of FDI as motivated by changes in macroeconomic conditions. In this conception, FDI is a component of aggregate economic activity that responds to such variables as market size, growth, unemployment, exchange rates, stability, and risk. Prominent papers in this area include Barrell and Pain (1996), Blonigen (1997), Cushman (1985), Goldberg and Kolstad (1995) and Wheeler and Mody (1992). The Blonigen paper is particularly interesting since it establishes a linkage between exchange rate changes and the value of firm-specific assets that motivate the industrial-organization approach to multinational activity.

A second area is the role of policy in attracting or repelling FDI, particularly as regards taxes on corporate activity. Blonigen and Davies (2000), Grubert and Mutti (1991), Maskus (1998b), and UNCTAD (1996) provide evidence that FDI flows are sensitive to international variations in taxes and incentives. However, Brainard (1997) found that host-country corporate taxes do not seem to repel affiliate activity and Markusen (1995) argues that the jury is still out on that issue. We note further the review by Jaffe et al. (1995) that cannot detect any systematic relation between environmental regulation and FDI. However, as we discuss below, restraints on trade and investment do have important effects on multinational activity. In an important recent paper, Feinberg and Keane (2001) demonstrate that mutual tariff cuts by the US and Canada induced a stronger export orientation on the part of Canadian affiliates of US parent firms. Those affiliates also increased their sales in Canada.

Third, several authors have detected empirical evidence that agglomeration effects importantly attract FDI flows at both the aggregate and sectoral levels. Wheeler and Mody (1992) and Woodward (1992) were early contributors to this literature, but the primary article is Head et al. (1995), which found considerable agglomeration on the part of Japanese firms in their location decisions in the US. If firms have preferences to locate near existing activity or near prior investments abroad by companies from their own countries or industries, the nature of dynamic competition depends on both flows of FDI and policies to influence them.

Fourth, some studies consider how firms invest abroad in order to exploit internalization advantages arising from proprietary knowledge or brand names. Such knowledge may be transferred abroad into productive use through FDI or licensing. It is evident from numerous studies that US-based multinationals are disproportionately high investors in R&D, both at home and in or for their foreign affiliates (Markusen, 1995). This result comes through powerfully in Brainard (1997), who also found that brand recognition, as proxied by advertising intensity of US multinationals, is a strong determinant of foreign affiliate sales. Additional studies have shown that multinational enterprises condition their choices between FDI and licensing on the strength of local patent rights in various markets (Ferrantino, 1993; Maskus, 1998a; Smith, 2001).

Finally, we note that there is an equally interesting literature about the effects that multinational activity may have on host and source countries. These papers consider such impacts as aggregate, sectoral, and factoral wage changes, productivity spillovers, and contributions to international trade. These questions are well beyond our scope.

7.1 FDI in Factor Endowment Models

We began our theoretical review by explaining that the traditional approach considered FDI to be a portfolio flow in response to relative international capital scarcities. Given the strong empirical interest in the factor content of trade (e.g., Davis and Weinstein, 1998; Trefler, 1995) it is remarkable that this proposition has attracted so little econometric study. In some degree, papers that place relative factor costs into FDI equations implicitly are looking for correlations between factor prices in segmented markets and investment flows. For example, Wheeler and Mody (1992) incorporate wage costs while Feinberg and Keane (2001) employ both wages and capital costs. However, the authors tend to think of absolute labor and capital costs (or relative measures between host and source) as repelling factors to firms rather than reflections of differential factor abundance.

To our knowledge, the idea that FDI flows are a response to varying factor endowments in a HO model with production specialization has not been formally tested in a well-specified general-equilibrium model. This is all the more remarkable given the importance of the issue in the globalization debate. Moreover, it is not difficult to see how one could go about this task, at least in principle, by modifying basic trade equations to reflect "effective scarcities" of factors in comparison to a situation with integrated factor markets. An interesting start in this regard is Ekholm (1998a) who placed implicit measures of headquarters services into a calculation of the factor content of trade. Perhaps the relative absence of such work simply suggests that economists do not believe that FDI exists for the purpose of equilibrating capital markets, an observation that is consistent with reports that FDI flows are more stable than portfolio flows in the presence of financial crises. Indeed, the existence of multinational firms is awkward for the perfectly competitive assumptions of the HO model. Nonetheless, we think that more work could usefully be done in this framework.[6]

An important paper that should be mentioned in this context is Eaton and Tamura (1994). The authors placed measures of relative factor endowments into gravity equations explaining US and Japanese exports, imports, and inward and outward FDI flows with approximately 100 countries between 1985 and 1990. Their essential interest was to discover whether the same features that explain international trade in a gravity framework are determinants of investment. In this context, they looked for complementarity between trade and FDI, an issue to which we turn next, rather than substitution as would be expected in a HO approach. Despite that predilection, their results suggested that Japanese firms engage in considerable FDI with countries that have low population densities (that is, they are scarce in labor relative to land), which suggests an attempt to compensate for land scarcity at home. In contrast, US investment flows are disproportionately high with countries that share high endowments of human capital. Overall, they found high correlations among countries in attracting both trade and FDI, suggesting that the balance of evidence favors complementarity. Unfortunately, interpretations of such correlations are clouded by the possibility that both trade and FDI may be increasing as a result of some third factor.

Lipsey (1999) provides interesting descriptive evidence on whether US and Japanese multinationals follow comparative advantage in their investments in developing countries of East Asia. He found that Japanese firms invested heavily in sectors of host-country comparative advantage, such as textiles and apparel and other manufacturing, though these affiliates initially were not heavily oriented toward export production. In contrast, US firms made early investments in electronics and computer-related machinery, which were sectors of American comparative advantage at the time, but focused that production on exports. Over time the Japanese affiliate production mix and exports converged toward the US pattern and became concentrated in electric machinery and transport equipment, both for domestic sales and exports. This evidence is intriguing, for it suggests that comparative advantage of both source and host countries may be involved in investment decisions. Again, more formal estimation in a structured framework would be beneficial.

7.2 Are Trade and Investment Complements or Substitutes?

As we discussed earlier, a fundamental question in general-equilibrium theory of the multinational firm is whether FDI substitutes for trade in goods or whether investment and trade move together as complements. Econometric models of substitution possibilities can, therefore, provide indirect evidence on the nature of multinational activity. In terms of the theories reviewed, substitution is the expected relationship under horizontal investment as firms economize on transport costs and trade barriers in servicing markets of similar size and endowments. The relationship would be complementary in vertical investments, particularly if vertical fragmentation results in the production of both intermediates and final goods within the firm.

There is again a large literature on the substitution versus complementarity effects of FDI and we consider only a few studies in detail. Early contributions were

Swedenborg (1979) and Lipsey and Weiss (1981, 1984), which found positive correlations between a country's exports and foreign affiliate sales, using aggregate, industry-level, and firm-level data. See also Blomstrom et al. (1988) for related evidence using firm-level data from the US and Sweden.

Lipsey (1991) found in a descriptive review of the sales, imports, and exports of foreign-owned manufacturing affiliates in the US that firms in different industries may behave differently. He found higher export shares of foreign-owned affiliates than for US parent firms in metals and chemicals, suggesting that foreign multinationals brought to the US both technological advantages and access to their source markets. In this regard, FDI and exports are complements for the host country in the sense that investment both reduces costs and raises export demand. However, the situation was different for non-electrical machinery and transport equipment, in which foreign-owned affiliates produced primarily for the US market, thereby substituting for imports from foreign parents.

In an important paper, Blomstrom et al. (1997) provided a statistical analysis of the substitution effects FDI may have on labor demand and employment in source countries. Using confidential firm-level data from US parents, they considered the effect of affiliate net sales (controlling for the level of parent sales) on parent employment. Interestingly, when they distinguished between foreign sales in developed countries and foreign sales in developing countries, they discovered a significantly negative impact of the latter on parent employment and no effect of the former. Thus, US parent firms do tend to substitute foreign production for home employment when they invest in developing nations and, according to their calculations, an increase in foreign sales by one million dollars reduces US employment by 12 to 18 workers. This effect does not hold in developed host nations, however.

Corresponding analysis of Swedish firms by the authors discovered a significant difference.[7] They found that the coefficient on host sales was positive and significant throughout the period 1970 to 1994, suggesting that foreign affiliate production raises the demand for Swedish labor. This result held also for sales in developing countries. Interestingly, the sales coefficient declined continuously over the period, which they attribute informally to a declining need for parent employment for purposes of monitoring and supervision of foreign affiliates. This result deserves further analysis. We note also that a number of econometric difficulties could be raised about the paper. There are likely to be substantial questions of endogeneity in a regression of parent employment on foreign sales, while it would be interesting to sort out the directions of causality. Moreover, their regression equations are remarkably parsimonious and the coefficients may suffer from omitted variable bias, rendering their comparative-static policy experiments questionable. For example, the equations are missing measures of trade costs, investment barriers, and foreign factor intensities. We note that such problems are common in this literature, contributing to the lack of clarity and consistency in results.

An improvement is the analysis by Brainard and Riker (1997) who took the question of substitution seriously by estimating a translog cost function for US-owned foreign affiliates in approximately 90 countries over 1983 to 1992.[8] For this purpose they used confidential firm-level data and assume strongly that firms share a single production function across host locations. This approach requires laborers in each country to be in perfectly elastic supply, so that wages are exogenous to the firm, though it permits differentiation of workers across sites. Thus, the authors computed labor–labor substitution across foreign (and parent) plants, establishing an explicit labor-market linkage. This could not be done in a completely flexible manner because of data limitations, so they assumed a short-run cost function with fixed capital. They further experimented by aggregating sites by geographical proximity to the US (Western versus Eastern hemispheres) and by level of development. The last assumption reflected the notion that developed and developing countries could differ in relative skill supplies and therefore offer different substitution possibilities. Given the nature of the data their translog specification was limited to cost shares, wages, firm-fixed effects, and year-fixed effects.

Their results suggested that labor substitution is high among locations at similar levels of economic development, especially in low-value added sectors in developing nations, though there is not much difference across locations. There is small net substitution with US parent employment. However, activities by affiliates at locations with different skill levels (proxied by level of development, or per-capita income differences) reveal complementarity. The authors interpreted these findings to mean that substitution is highest among workers at alternative low-wage locations but that production by affiliates in countries with differing skill levels displays a vertical and complementary division of labor. Thus, the most intensive competition resides between laborers in developing countries, while foreign investment only marginally reduces US parent employment.

In our view, these results are intriguing but not decisive. It is important to analyze the substitution question in a coherent framework, as the authors have done, which helps interpret the findings consistently. Nonetheless, the authors were constrained to make a number of simplifying assumptions and their findings say little about the extent of long-run substitution of labor across borders. Moreover, there was no discussion in the paper of how well the results satisfied required regularity conditions. More work along these lines would be beneficial.

Another interesting recent paper is Head and Ries (2001), who developed a simple theory in which FDI could result in substitution with exports in horizontal models but in complementarity due to demand effects and vertical integration raising intra-firm trade. They employed count data for 933 Japanese firms that engaged in FDI between 1966 and 1990. Their sample provided a natural experiment within which to see whether complementarity in FDI and parent-country exports stems from demand effects or vertical integration, because many of the firms are horizontal Keiretsu in the automobile and electronics sectors. They were also able to control simply for heterogeneity in firm productivity. They found that firms with higher manufacturing investments overseas tend to have higher exports, controlling for firm size, capital intensity, productivity, number of distribution investments, and fixed effects for firms and years. Thus, overall, Japanese FDI results in net complementarity. The authors calculated that a 10 percent rise in FDI abroad in distribution and manufacturing would increase Japanese exports by 1.5 percent and 1.2 percent, respectively.

Furthermore, a measure of vertical integration of Japanese firms had a positive interaction in the exports equation with overseas manufacturing investments, suggesting such integration expands trade within integrated firms. At the same time, the non-vertically integrated Keiretsu firms showed substitution between foreign production and exports. Thus, in inherently horizontal leading firms, foreign output tends to displace parent exports. Overall, therefore, their results strongly suggest that horizontal investment tends to substitute for home production and exports, while vertical investment provides a channel for expanding home exports through intra-firm trade in intermediates.

Blonigen (2001) extended this line of inquiry. He noted that a problem with prior studies was that aggregate, industry, or even firm-level data (for multi-product firms) could not sort out vertical linkages that expand demand for intermediates from competitive substitution effects. However, product-level data on trade and foreign production provide more scope for such discrimination, because products may be classified as differentiated consumer goods, which should be sensitive to export replacement in horizontal competition, and intermediates, which should experience rising exports as firms invest abroad in goods that use those intermediates. However, even intermediate inputs could suffer net substitution over time if final-goods producers shift intermediate production abroad as well. Blonigen explored these possibilities in two data sets, one involving Japanese exports of specific automobile parts to the US and one involving detailed categories of final consumer goods exported to the same market. All products were chosen so that there was Japanese-owned production in the US as well. The author hypothesized that there would be net complementarity between US production of Japanese-owned automobile factories and Japanese exports of automobile parts, but net substitution between those exports and US affiliate production of parts. There should also be net substitution in final consumer goods.

Blonigen developed a simple model of import demand, assuming perfect substitution between Japanese products and US-produced versions. Unfortunately, he was unable to model firm supply decisions, so questions remain about the meaning of the reduced-form coefficients. The author employed instruments for US employment (a proxy for sales) in the exports equations, expecting the coefficients to be negative if there were a relationship of substitution.

In Zellner iterative SUR equations for 10 automobile parts categories with the dependent variable being exports to the US of Japanese auto parts, Blonigen found negative but small coefficients for US automobile parts production in Japanese-owned affiliates but positive and large coefficients for Japanese-owned automobile production. These results strongly suggest that a primary source of complementarity between FDI and trade is induced increases in demand for intermediate inputs. Regarding consumer goods, nine of eleven categories registered negative relationships, seven of these being statistically significant, between US-based affiliate production and Japanese exports. Thus, substitution dominates for those products. Interestingly, substitution impacts appear to be large one-time changes rather than gradual movements over time.

Our reading of this literature suggests that it has moved from a frustrating degree of ambiguity in results and clarity in interpretation, stemming largely from weak statistical and econometric methods (albeit conditioned on limited data), to a much sharper picture in which complementarity stems primarily from increases in demand for intermediates in vertical relationships, and substitution emerges from trade displacement among final goods. We note that the complementarity story arises from studies of how foreign establishment of final-goods production facility rebounds into higher demand for intermediate goods. More formal studies of how these relationships emerge within vertically integrated firms would be useful, in order to assess whether these demand factors are two-way between affiliates and parents, as theory would suggest. Finer data definitions and close relationships to underlying theoretical models could improve this understanding even further. However, to place the basic inference into the context of our theoretical discussion, note that it suggests that models of vertical FDI in a single good (that is, with headquarters producing invisible services and the foreign plant producing the commodity according to factor costs) are not well supported by studies of substitution. More complicated models with intermediate production are supported, though they play little role in our earlier discussion. Substitution effects in horizontal models among similar products seem to dominate.[9]

7.3 Studies of the New General Equilibrium Models

We turn, finally, to econometric studies of general-equilibrium models of multinational firms as described in earlier sections of the chapter. Our focus will be on three questions. First, what are the fundamental national characteristics and industry characteristics that give rise to multinational activity? Second, are the data capable of discriminating between various theories in terms of their statistical relevance? Third, what are the determinants of intra-industry affiliate activity in relation to intra-industry trade?

An important study is Brainard (1997), who distinguished between the "proximity-concentration hypothesis" and the "factor-proportions hypothesis" regarding multinational firms. In the former, firms face a tradeoff between wishing to be near customers and suppliers and sacrificing scale economies from single-plant production. To the extent that plant-level increasing returns are small relative to firm-level increasing returns, horizontal FDI would be prominent, particularly among countries with similar per-capita incomes and high trade barriers. Equilibrium could involve two-way horizontal multinationals with no exports, pure national firms with no affiliate sales, or mixed solutions. This model is a variant of what we have termed the horizontal model.

The model Brainard took to the data captures these influences well. She noted the problems involved in endogeneity between affiliate sales and exports, so she focused on explaining shares of exports or affiliate sales in servicing particular markets. Thus, bilateral export shares (that is, parent-country exports divided by the sum of parent-country exports and affiliate sales) were modeled as linear in freight costs, bilateral tariffs, absolute differences in per-capita income (which she took to be a proxy for differences in factor endowments), corporate tax rates in the host, trade and investment costs in the host, and measures of plant scale economies and firm scale economies. She also worked with sales shares and, for inward data, import and sales shares. These models were applied to a cross-section in 1989 of 27 countries and 63 sectors with bilateral trade and affiliate sales with the US. Because not all cases involved both types of trade she employed both OLS and a two-stage Tobit procedure, including country and industry random and fixed effects.

The results provided strong support for the proximity-concentration hypothesis. In particular, differences in per-capita income raise the export share, suggesting that income similarities are stronger determinants of affiliate sales than exports. Trade restraints, measured by a suggestive index from the *World Competitiveness Report*, significantly increased the share of affiliate sales compared to exports, while an index of investment costs (from the same sources) reduced that ratio. Most significantly, sectors with high plant scale economies saw high export shares while sectors with high firm scale economies saw low export shares. These basic results were confirmed by regressions on levels in addition to inward shares in the US. Brainard interprets her findings as supportive of the horizontal model of FDI but contradictory to the factor-proportions hypothesis, which is consistent with her earlier empirical paper (Brainard, 1993b), which we review below. This is an important finding but she did not attempt a formal statistical discrimination between the two models.

An interesting attempt to implement the "convergence hypothesis" implicit in the horizontal model is Barrios et al. (2000). This hypothesis is that multinational activity should replace national firms and exports as countries get closer in relative size, relative endowments, and relative production costs. Employing a panel of bilateral affiliate employment levels for OECD countries over 1985 and 1996, they took as a dependent variable the MNE share of affiliate employment in total employment of host and source countries. Independent variables included the sum of parent and host GDP, absolute differences in GDP, absolute differences in skill endowments and capital endowments, the sum of R&D in both countries (an attempt to capture ownership advantages of the firm, or firm-level fixed costs), bilateral distance, and a common-language dummy. There are difficult econometric problems in their study, as they used a highly unbalanced panel and applied OLS without country fixed effects. We note also that their interpretation of the distance variable as capturing investment transactions costs is problematic given their failure to include a control for investment barriers. Given those caveats, their findings on the GDP variables and R&D support the horizontal FDI model. However, the endowment variables provide ambiguous results, with differences in capital endowments positively affecting the affiliate employment share.

Carr et al. (2001) adopt a broader approach in estimating the knowledge-capital model. Its innovation lies primarily in incorporating non-linear terms into the econometric explanation of affiliate sales in order to capture some complexities in the simulation model (see figure 11.1). Specifically, their basic estimation equation is:

$$
\begin{aligned}
RSALES = {} & B_0 + B_1 SUMGDP + B_2 GDPDIFSQ + B_3 SKDIFF \\
& + B_4 (GDPDIFF \times SKDIFF) + B_5 INVCJ + B_6 TCJ \\
& + B_7 (TCJ \times SKDIFSQ) + B_8 TCI + B_9 DIST + u
\end{aligned}
\tag{11.1}
$$

This specification relates the real volume of affiliate sales of either US-owned manufacturing affiliates abroad or foreign-owned manufacturing affiliates in the US to fundamental country characteristics. SUMGDP measures total bilateral market size and should positively affect sales. GDPDIFSQ is the square of the difference in country size, which should bear an inverted U-shape in relation to sales as relative sizes change, thereby predicting a negative coefficient. SKDIFF is the difference in relative skill endowments between host and source, with a positive anticipated coefficient reflecting the location of headquarters in skill-abundant nations and production in skill-scarce nations. The interaction between GDP sizes and skill differences should have a negative sign since the KK model strongly favors affiliate sales when the parent country is both small and skill-abundant. Variables capturing investment-cost barriers (INVCJ) and trade costs (TCJ) in the host country should have negative and positive signs, respectively, with the latter expectation based on the horizontal model. The interaction term between trade costs and squared differences in skill endowments captures the idea that trade costs may encourage horizontal investment but not vertical investment, while horizontal investment increases as endowments become more similar, suggesting a negative coefficient. Finally, trade costs (TCI) in the parent country should limit incentives for vertical FDI. They also included geographical distance (DIST) and argued that, while its sign would be ambiguous in theory, it would be negative to the extent that distance captures transactions costs in addition to those inherent in ICJ.

The authors estimated this model for a panel of 36 bilateral FDI partners with the US over the period 1986 to 1994, incorporating fixed effects for recipient countries. Both weighted least squares (to correct for heteroskedasticity in levels) and Tobit procedures (to account for zero observations in sales) were employed. Like Brainard and Riker (1997), they developed measures of trade costs and investment costs from the surveys published in the *World Competitiveness Report*. Such measures are certainly problematic given their subjective nature, however they may be defended as reasonable reflections of actual perceptions on the part of multinational enterprise managers. The authors did not consider any potential endogeneity in the survey indexes.

The results were remarkably supportive of the knowledge-capital model. Consider the Tobit results from their table 4 (n = 628, coefficients in bold are significant at the 95 percent level or higher):

$$RSALES = \mathbf{-53341} + \mathbf{16.6}(SUMGDP) - \mathbf{0.0009}(GDPDIFSQ) + \mathbf{29366}(SKDIFF)$$
$$- \mathbf{7.7}(GDPDIFF \times SKDIFF) - \mathbf{41.3}(INVCJ) + \mathbf{144}(TCJ)$$
$$- \mathbf{2273}(TCJ \times SKDIFSQ) - \mathbf{112.6}(TCI) - \mathbf{0.8}(DIST) \qquad (11.2)$$

All signs are as expected and only two coefficients fail to achieve significance. This result survived a number of specifications for robustness.

An important feature of these results is that they may be used to perform comparative-static experiments from changes in exogenous variables, accounting for non-linearities. These non-linear terms imply that the results are not necessarily the same for all country pairs (or, more precisely, in all regions of the Edgeworth box), leading to a rich menu of potential conclusions. We simply repeat their basic propositions here. First, regardless of the country pair, an increase in host-country trade costs generates a rise in affiliate production, strongly suggesting that substitution effects dominate in the data. Second, a balanced rise in host-country and parent-country trade costs tends to increase affiliate production when the non-US partner is a developed country but to reduce affiliate production when it is a developing country. In the former case, trade and FDI are substitutes but in the latter case they are complements, consistent with horizontal and vertical investment, respectively. Third, a convergence in size between bilateral country pairs, holding total GDP constant, increases affiliate production in both directions. Fourth, an increase in the partner country's skilled-labor abundance increases both US-owned affiliate sales and foreign-owned affiliate sales in the US, supporting the notion that endowment convergence favors horizontal investment. Finally, a joint increase in both host and source GDP levels raises affiliate production relative to GDP because affiliate activity is income-elastic. This result is consistent with the rising ratio of foreign affiliate production to GDP seen in many parts of the world.

A natural extension of this approach is to ask whether national characteristics have different impacts on local production and exports (Markusen and Maskus, 2001). Using the same data set as in Carr et al., they regressed local affiliate sales, affiliate exports, and the ratio of affiliate exports to local sales on the same variables (excluding the interaction between host trade costs and squared skill differences). They found that joint market size has a larger positive impact on local sales than exports and therefore an increase in combined GDP significantly reduces the ratio of affiliate exports to affiliate sales. Raising host-country GDP alone has the same effect. In contrast, differences in parent- versus host-country skill endowments have a larger effect on exports and increasing that difference substantially raises the ratio of exports to sales. Finally, the impacts of host-country investment costs and trade costs are considerably larger on affiliate sales than on exports. Investment costs have negative and significant coefficients in both equations. Trade costs have positive coefficients but only the sales impact is significant, which is intuitively sensible. Thus, the authors concluded that production for local sale is strongly attracted by trade protection while production for exports would be less interested in such protective locations. Further computations demonstrated that the elasticity of local sales with respect to an increase in host-country income is 1.6, which exceeds the export elasticity of 1.1. However, the negative elasticity of exports with respect to an increase in host-country skill abundance (a movement toward the US level) was larger in magnitude than that for affiliate sales. Thus, production for export sales is relatively more attracted to less skilled-labor abundant nations and production for affiliate sales is relatively more attracted by growth in market size.

From the theoretical analysis described in the first part of this chapter it is possible to specify the horizontal (HOR) and vertical (VER) models as nested versions of the knowledge-capital (KK) model. Accordingly, in a subsequent paper Markusen and Maskus (2002a) performed a statistical test to see which specification best fits their data set. For this purpose they defined two dummy variables, with D1 (= −1 or 0) selecting cases where the host country is skill abundant relative to the source and the other (D2 = 1 or 0) selecting the opposite cases. Taking KK to be the unrestricted model, affiliate sales volume should depend on the sum of GDP (SUMGDP), the squared difference in GDP (GDPDIFSQ), the second dummy interacted with the product of skill difference and GDP difference (D2 × SKDIFF × GDPDIFF), the second dummy interacted with the product of skill difference and the sum of GDP (D2 × SKDIFF × GDPDIFF), and the first dummy interacted with the same product (D1 × SKDIFF × GDPDIFF). As suggested by figure 11.2, HOR should not depend on D2 × (SKDIFF) × (GDPDIFF) and thus that variable was not included in its regressions. As suggested by figure 11.3, VER should not depend on SUMGDP and GDPDIFSQ and those coefficients were constrained to zero. Note from earlier work that these two variables have strong influences on affiliate activity, so this representation of VER was destined to be rejected. All three models permitted the inclusion of distance, host-country investment costs, and host-country and parent-country trade costs.

In the regressions, the interaction terms distinguishing KK from HOR were not significant in the former equations. Thus, the statistical tests could not discriminate between KK and HOR; essentially they are the same model. However, VER was rejected decisively at the 99 percent level of confidence. Thus, the data sample employed in this paper rejected VER in favor of the HOR specification. One weakness of the approach was that the fit of these models depends, in principle, on the location of data points within the Edgeworth box. Thus, one could argue that the data failed to include enough observations with significantly different factor endowments to support the VER model. We doubt this interpretation, however, both because 15 of the 26 countries in the sample were developing countries and because of the decisive nature of the rejection.

7.4 Intra-industry Affiliate Sales

A new empirical literature, based on these general-equilibrium considerations, is emerging on the determinants of intra-industry affiliate production. It is evident that in models supporting the existence of horizontal multinationals in both markets, intra-industry affiliate sales (IIAS) should be a variable of considerable interest.

Greenaway et al. (1998) developed a series of measures that may be used to account for IIAS and intra-industry FDI. A readily interpreted index was offered by Ekholm (2002) in a paper that was among the first to attempt an explanation of IIAS. Her index is:

$$IA_{jk} = 1 - \frac{\sum_i |A_{ijk} - A_{ikj}|}{\sum_i (A_{ijk} + A_{ikj})} \qquad (11.3)$$

where i = sector and j, k indicate host and partner countries. This index clearly was inspired by the Grubel–Lloyd index of intra-industry trade and runs from zero to one. Because of data constraints she used intra-industry affiliate employment to construct the index. Her interest was in seeing how well the Helpman–Krugman (1985) model of FDI in differentiated products fits data on bilateral affiliate activity of US and Swedish firms.

Employing a sample of 2-digit and 3-digit ISIC industries in 1990 for OECD partners, she regressed the log of this index on several national characteristics. First was the log of GDP in both host and parent, expecting positive signs. Second was the absolute difference in log GDP levels, expecting a negative sign because such activity should diminish with the degree of dissimilarity in size. Third were measures of differences in physical capital and human capital endowments. Dissimilarity in endowments should also diminish intra-industry activity, though she hypothesized that there would be a stronger effect from human capital differences. Controls were included for industry size and R&D intensity. Using logit estimation because of the limited range of IA, Ekholm achieved results consistent with her hypotheses. Country size differences negatively affect intra-industry affiliate employment, as do differences in physical and, especially, human capital. R&D intensity positively affects intra-industry activity, consistent with the internalization evidence we reviewed earlier.

An earlier investigation was Brainard (1993b), who specified Helpman and Krugman (1985) as the "factor proportions" hypothesis in which two-way FDI emerges in differentiated products. She calculated intra-industry sales (IIS) indexes to correspond with intra-industry trade (IIT) indexes for 27 bilateral US partners in the 1989 BEA Benchmark Survey, with 64 industries matched between bilateral exports and affiliate sales categories. IIS ranged from 0 for Argentina and Brazil to 0.4 for the UK, while IIT ranged from 0.08 for Venezuela to 0.66 for Mexico. These indexes were highly correlated. She first adopted Helpman's (1987) regression model, with the log of two-way gross affiliate sales and trade flows related to the log of GDP sum, the log of two-country GDP dispersion, freight factors, and industry effects. GDP was insignificant in the sales equation but highly significant in the trade equation, while GDP dispersion was strongly positive in both. Going on to an explanation of IIS and IIT, she found that IIS was weakly related to endowment differences, strongly affected by GDP dispersion, and unaffected by freight costs. IIT was also weakly influenced by endowments but was strongly negative in transport costs. These results were consistent with a monopolistic competition model in which trade and intra-industry affiliate activities are not much affected by factor proportions. Thus, she concluded that the data support what she elsewhere termed the proximity-concentration hypothesis.

A final paper worth mentioning is the most recent work by Markusen and Maskus (2002b). They ran simulations that provided predictions about how IIS and IIT (using Grubel–Lloyd definitions) would be affected by national characteristics. In their regressions, IIS fits the theory quite well, for the index gets larger as two countries become more similar in size and relative endowments. IIT regressions also support the theory, though weakly. Considering the ratio of IIS to IIT, their findings suggested that "balanced" affiliate activity is more strongly encouraged by higher incomes and country similarity than is intra-industry trade.

8 CONCLUDING REMARKS

In this review, we have taken a somewhat narrow approach to a broad literature on multinational firms and direct investment. But circumscribing our efforts to recent theoretical and empirical analyses that adopt a general-equilibrium trade-theoretic view of the multinational generates quite enough for one chapter.

Alternative theoretical approaches to the multinational are shown to generate different predictions as to how affiliate activity should be related to country, trade-cost, and investment-cost variables. These alternatives similarly suggest different relationships between affiliate production and trade. Overall, we believe that the empirical evidence gives strong support to the "horizontal" approach to the multi-national and little support to the "vertical" approach. It is similarities between countries rather than differences that generates the most multinational activity. The integrated "knowledge-capital" approach gets good support, but in some cases cannot be clearly distinguished from the horizontal model. On the question of whether or not trade and affiliate production are complements or substitutes, evidence is slowly emerging that affiliate production complements increased trade in intermediates but in general substitutes for trade in final goods. The latter result is another finding that fits well with the predictions of the horizontal model.

Notes

1 Unfortunately, these terms have been defined to mean somewhat different things by different authors. Furthermore, there is rarely a "pure" case of horizontal production in the sense that there is inevitably some vertical component to a firm. The services of firm-specific assets are supplied from parents to subsidiaries, even if the same final goods are produced in both parent and host countries. Further discussion is postponed until the next section.
2 We should emphasize again that Helpman (1984) mentioned firm-level scale economies but, due to the reliance on the FPE set and the assumption of zero trade costs, two-plant horizontal firms could not arise in equilibrium and they were not discussed in the paper. There are really two alternative assumptions, either of which will rule out two-plant horizontal firms. First, zero trade costs can be assumed as in Helpman (and there may or may not be firm-level scale economies). Second, it can be assumed that there are no firm-level scale economies (and there may or may not be positive trade costs).
3 Horizontal models including Markusen and Venables (1998, 2000) generally assume that fixed and variable costs have the same factor intensities, unlike the assumption used by Helpman. The former assumption largely, but not completely rules out incentives to vertically fragment a single-plant firm. (See Markusen, 2002, chapter 8.)
4 For example, suppose that firm-level fixed costs and the cost of a local plant are 10, but total fixed costs for a foreign plant are 6 regardless of whether or not there is a domestic plant. Then fixed costs are: type-d = 10, type-h = 16, type-v = 16. In such a situation, type-v firms will generally not arise, which is the result in figure 11.2.
5 The pattern of affiliate production looks very similar to figure 11.3 under the alternative assumption that there are firm-level scale economies, but zero trade costs. This alternative formulation is much closer to that of Helpman (1984) and Helpman and Krugman (1985), but generates essentially the same predictions as just noted.
6 Maskus and Webster (1995) provide one simplified attempt.
7 See also Lipsey et al. (2000), which demonstrated that foreign affiliate production of Japanese-owned firms is positively correlated with parent global exports and parent employment.

8 See also Slaughter (2000).
9 See also Egger (1999) and Denekamp and Ferrantino (1990) for evidence supporting his characterization.

References

Barrell, Ray and Nigel Pain 1996: An econometric analysis of U.S. foreign direct investment. *Review of Economics and Statistics*, 78, 200–7.

Barrios, Salvador, Holger Gorg, and Eric Strobl 2000: Multinational enterprises and new trade theory: Evidence for the convergence hypothesis. Centre for Research on Globalisation and Labour Markets, research paper 2000/19.

Blomstrom, Magnus, Gunnar Fors, and Robert E. Lipsey 1997: Foreign direct investment and employment: Home country experience in the United States and Sweden. *Economic Journal*, 107, 1787–97.

Blomstrom, Magnus, Robert E. Lipsey, and K. Kulchycky 1998: U.S. and Swedish direct investment and exports. In Robert E. Baldwin (ed.), *Trade Policy Issues and Empirical Analysis*, Chicago: University of Chicago Press, 259–97.

Blonigen, Bruce A. 1997: Firm-specific assets and the link between exchange rates and foreign direct investment. *American Economic Review*, 87, 447–65.

Blonigen, Bruce A. 2001: In search of substitution between foreign production and exports. *Journal of International Economics*, 53, 81–104.

Blonigen, Bruce A. and Ronald B. Davies 2000: The effect of bilateral tax treaties on US FDI activity. University of Oregon working paper.

Brainard, S. Lael 1993a: A simple theory of multinational corporations and trade with a trade-off between proximity and concentration. NBER working paper no. 4269.

Brainard, S. Lael 1993b: An empirical assessment of the factor proportions explanation of multinationals sales. NBER working paper no. 4580.

Brainard, S. Lael 1997: An empirical assessment of the proximity-concentration tradeoff between multinational sales and trade. *American Economic Review*, 87, 520–44.

Brainard, S. Lael and David A. Riker 1997: Are U.S. multinationals exporting U.S. jobs? NBER working paper no. 5958.

Carr, David L., James R. Markusen, and Keith E. Maskus 2001: Estimating the knowledge-capital model of the multinational enterprise. *American Economic Review*, 91, 693–708.

Caves, Richard E. 1971: International corporations: The industrial economics of foreign investment, *Economica*, 38, 1–27.

Cushman, David O. 1985: Real exchange rate risk, expectations, and the level of direct investment. *Review of Economics and Statistics*, 32, 297–308.

Davis, Donald R. and David E. Weinstein 1998: An account of global factor trade. Columbia University working paper.

Denekamp, Johannes and Michael J. Ferrantino 1990: Substitution and complementarity of U.S. exports and foreign affiliate sales in a demand-based gravity system. Unpublished manuscript, Southern Methodist University.

Eaton, Jonathan and Akiko Tamura 1994: Bilateralism and regionalism in Japanese and US trade and direct foreign investment. *Journal of the Japanese and International Economics*, 8, 478–510.

Egger, Peter 1999: European exports and outward foreign direct investment: A dynamic panel data approach. Unpublished manuscript, Austrian Institute of Economic Research.

Ekholm, Karolina 1998a: Headquarter services and revealed factor abundance. *Review of International Economics*, 6, 545–53.

Ekholm, Karolina 1998b: Proximity advantages, scale economies, and the location of production. In Pontus Braunerhjelm and Karolina Ekholm (eds.), *The Geography of Multinational Firms*, Boston: Kluwer Academic Publishers.

Ekholm, Karolina 2002: Factor endowments and intra-industry affiliate production. In Peter Lloyd, Herber Grubel, and Hyun-Hoon Lee (eds.), *The Frontiers of Intra-Industry Trade*, Melbourne: Macmillan, 220–36.

Ekholm, Karolina and Rikard Forslid 2001: Trade and location with horizontal and vertical multi-region firms. *Scandinavian Journal of Economics*, 103, 101–18.

Feinberg, Susan E. and Michael P. Keane 2001: U.S.–Canada trade liberalization and MNC production location. *Review of Economics and Statistics*, 83, 118–32.

Ferrantino, Michael J. 1993: The effects of intellectual property rights on international trade and investment. *Weltwirtschaftliches Archiv*, 129, 300–31.

Goldberg, Linda S. and C. D. Kolstad 1995: Foreign direct investment, exchange-rate variability and demand uncertainty. *International Economic Review*, 36, 855–73.

Greenaway, David, Peter Lloyd, and Chris Milner 1998: Intra-industry FDI and trade flows: New measures of globalisation of production. Centre for Research on Globalisation and Labour Markets research paper 98/5.

Grubert, Harry and John Mutti 1991: Taxes, tariffs and transfer pricing in multinational corporate decision making. *Review of Economics and Statistics*, 73, 285–93.

Head, Keith and John Ries 2001: Overseas investment and firm exports. *Review of International Economics*, 9, 108–22.

Head, Keith, John Ries, and Deborah Swenson 1995: Agglomeration benefits and location choice: Evidence from Japanese manufacturing investments in the United States. *Journal of International Economics*, 38, 223–47.

Helpman, Elhanan 1984: A simple theory of trade with multinational corporations. *Journal of Political Economy*, 92, 451–71.

Helpman, Elhanan 1985: Multinational corporations and trade structure. *Review of Economic Studies*, 52, 443–58.

Helpman, Elhanan 1987: Imperfect competition and international trade: Evidence from 14 industrial countries. *Journal of the Japanese and International Economies*, 1, 62–81.

Helpman, Elhanan and Paul Krugman 1985: *Market Structure and International Trade*. Cambridge, MA: MIT Press.

Horstmann, Ignatius J. and James R. Markusen 1987: Strategic investments and the development of multinationals. *International Economic Review*, 28, 109–21.

Horstmann, Ignatius and James R. Markusen 1992: Endogenous market structures in international trade. *Journal of International Economics*, 20, 225–47.

Jaffe, Adam B., Steven R. Peterson, Paul R. Portney, and Robert N. Stavins 1995: Environmental regulations and the competitiveness of U.S. manufacturing: What does the evidence tell us? *Journal of Economic Literature*, 33, 132–63.

Jones, Ronald W. 1971: A three-factor model in theory, trade, and history. In J. Bhagwati et al. (eds.), *Trade, Balance of Payments and Growth*, Amsterdam: North-Holland.

Kemp, Murray C. 1962: Foreign investment and the national advantage. *Economic Record*, 38, 56–62.

Lipsey, Robert E. 1991: Foreign direct investment in the United States and U.S. trade. *The Annals of the American Academy of Political and Social Science*, 516, 76–90.

Lipsey, Robert E. 1999: Affiliates of U.S. and Japanese multinationals in East Asian production and trade. NBER working paper no. 7292.

Lipsey, Robert E. and Merle Yahr Weiss 1981: Foreign production and exports in manufacturing industries. *Review of Economics and Statistics*, 63, 488–94.

Lipsey, Robert E. and Merle Yahr Weiss 1984: Foreign production and exports of individual firms. *Review of Economics and Statistics*, 66, 304–7.

Lipsey, Robert E., Eric Ramstetter and Magnus Blomstrom 2000: Outward FDI and parent exports and employment: Japan, the United States, and Sweden. NBER working paper no. 7623.

MacDougall, G. D. A. 1960: The benefits and costs of private investment from abroad: A theoretical approach. *Economic Record*, 36, 13–15.

Markusen, James R. 1984: Multinationals, multi-plant economies, and the gains from trade. *Journal of International Economics*, 16, 205–26.

Markusen, James R. 1995: The boundaries of multinational enterprises and the theory of international trade. *Journal of Economic Perspectives*, 9, 169–90.

Markusen, James R. 1997: Trade versus investment liberalization. NBER working paper no. 6231.

Markusen, James R. 2002, forthcoming: *Multinational Firms and the Theory of International Trade*. Cambridge, MA: MIT Press.

Markusen, James R. and Keith E. Maskus 2001: Multinational firms: Reconciling theory and evidence. In Magnus Blomstrom and Linda Goldberg (eds.), *Topics in Empirical International Economics: A Festschrift in Honor of Robert E. Lipsey*, Chicago: University of Chicago Press, 71–95.

Markusen, James R. and Keith E. Maskus 2002a: Discriminating among alternative theories of the multinational enterprise. *Review of International Economics*, 10, 4, 694–707.

Markusen, James R. and Keith E. Maskus 2002b: A unified approach to intra-industry trade and direct foreign investment. In Peter Lloyd, Herber Grubel and Hyun-Hoon Lee (eds.), *The Frontiers of Intra-Industry Trade*, Melbourne: Macmillan, 199–219.

Markusen, James R. and Anthony J. Venables 1998: Multinational firms and the new trade theory. *Journal of International Economics*, 46, 183–203.

Markusen, James R. and Anthony J. Venables 2000: The theory of endowment, intra-industry and multinational trade. *Journal of International Economics*, 52, 209–34.

Maskus, Keith E. 1998a: The role of intellectual property rights in encouraging foreign direct investment and technology transfer. *Duke Journal of Comparative and International Law*, 9, 109–61.

Maskus, Keith E. 1998b: The international regulation of intellectual property. *Weltwirtschaftliches Archiv*, 134, 186–208.

Maskus, Keith E. and Alan Webster 1995: Comparative advantage and the location of inward foreign direct investment: Evidence from the UK and South Korea. *The World Economy*, 18, 315–28.

Slaughter, Matthew J. 2000: Production transfer within multinational enterprises and American wages. *Journal of International Economics*, 50, 449–72.

Smith, Pamela J. 2001: How do foreign patent rights affect U.S. exports, affiliate sales, and licenses? *Journal of International Economics*, 55, 411–40.

Swedenborg, Birgitta 1979: *The Multinational Operations of Swedish Firms*. Stockholm: The Industrial Institute for Economic and Social Research.

Trefler, Daniel 1995: The case of the missing trade and other mysteries. *American Economic Review*, 85, 1029–46.

United Nations Conference on Trade and Development 1996: *Incentives and Foreign Direct Investment*. Geneva: UNCTAD.

Wheeler, David and Ashoka Mody 1992: International investment location decisions: The case of U.S. firms. *Journal of International Economics*, 33, 57–76.

Woodward, Douglas P. 1992: Locational determinants of Japanese manufacturing start-ups in the United States. *Southern Economic Journal*, 58, 690–708.

New Trade Theory

12

The Economic Geography of Trade, Production, and Income: A Survey of Empirics

Henry G. Overman, Stephen Redding, and Anthony J. Venables

CHAPTER OUTLINE

This chapter surveys the empirical literature on the economic geography of trade flows, factor prices, and the location of production. The discussion is structured around the empirical predictions of a canonical theoretical model. We review empirical evidence on the determinants of trade costs and the effects of these costs on trade flows. Geography is a major determinant of factor prices, and access to foreign markets alone is shown to explain some 35 percent of the cross-country variation in per capita income. The chapter documents empirical findings of home market (or magnification) effects, suggesting that imperfectly competitive industries are drawn more than proportionately to locations with good market access. Subnational evidence establishes the presence of industrial clustering, and we examine the roles played by product market linkages to customer and supplier firms, knowledge spillovers, and labor market externalities.

1   INTRODUCTION

Both first- and second-nature geography are major determinants of production structure, trade, and income. First-nature is the physical geography of coasts, mountains, and endowments of natural resources, and second-nature is the geography of distance between economic agents. Elements of first-nature are the subject matter of factor endowment-based trade theory, and our focus in this paper is largely – although not entirely – on second-nature. We shall ask: how does the spatial relationship between economic agents determine how they interact, what they do, and how well off they are?

How does geography shape interactions between economic agents? Distance directly increases transaction costs because of the transport costs of shipping goods, the time cost of shipping date sensitive products, the costs of contracting at a distance, and the costs of acquiring information about remote economies. The familiar gravity model indicates how rapidly distance reduces the volume of trade between countries.

Geography also shapes the activities undertaken in each country, as profits depend on proximity to linked activities. Thus, in addition to taking place where there are factor supplies, production will locate close to markets and to suppliers of intermediate goods. These obvious sounding statements immediately raise several questions. How are proximity to markets and to suppliers to be measured? To be operational we have to be able to make statements that one country has better market-access or better supplier-access than another.[1] And having measured these geographical characteristics of countries, which industries are most influenced by them? All activities would, other things being equal, locate in countries with good market-access and supplier-access, but in equilibrium other things are not equal. Prices of immobile factors adjust so that some activities locate in central countries and others go to more remote locations, but which activities go where? It depends on industry characteristics including the cost of transporting final output and the share of intermediate goods and services in costs. Also important is the extent to which it is possible for firms to divide production and operate in many locations. If production in all activities is perfectly divisible then economic geography effects are likely to be small.[2] But if firms have to make "either–or" choices and produce in only a subset of locations, then the effects will generally be larger. Thus, if there are industries with increasing returns at the plant level there will generally be "home market effects," leading these industries to be disproportionately represented in countries with good market-access.

Much of the interest of economic geography derives from the fact that the location of demand (determining market-access) and input supply (determining supplier-access) is not exogenous. From the theory standpoint this generates the possibility of "cumulative causation," agglomeration, and multiple equilibria; locations have one activity only because they have another, and vice versa. From the empirical standpoint it raises several questions. Is there evidence that industries are more agglomerated than would be suggested by the location of factor endowments or by chance? What sorts of industries – or what functional activities – tend to agglomerate? What are the sources of agglomeration: linkages to customer and supplier firms, technological externalities, or effects arising in factor markets? More fundamentally, how are the endogeneity issues associated with co-location of industries to be handled? And how should econometrics proceed if theory suggests that there is not a unique mapping from exogenous variables to endogenous ones?

As well as influencing trade flows and production structure, geography is also one of the determinants of how well-off people are. How disadvantaged are remote countries, and how much of the cross-country income distribution can be explained by geography? Spatial variations in goods prices will lead to spatial variation in factor prices, as predicted by the Stolper–Samuelson effects of traditional trade theory. Real returns to all factors may be low in remote locations, as the value added that firms can pay to immobile factors is squeezed by transport costs reducing export receipts and raising the costs of imported inputs. Where value added is only a small fraction of total costs it is possible that quite modest transport costs translate into large reductions in value added attributable to immobile factors.

The impact of geography on income levels may come not just through the mechanism of goods prices and transport costs, but also through spatial differences in institutions and in technology. For example, productivity may depend on the spatial density of economic activity, and technology transfer may depend on distance from technology producers. Empirical work has found such effects, although we argue that true productivity differences are very difficult to disentangle from price effects.

These three sets of issues – geography and trade flows, geography and income, and geography and the location of activity – are the subject matter of sections 3 to 5 of this review. The next section provides some of the theoretical structure that will be used at various stages.

2   A CANONICAL MODEL

In this section we outline some key elements of a canonical model that we draw on at various stages in the chapter. The oldest model in which the effects of economic geography on the structure of production and incomes is shown is that of von-Thunen (1826), and this can easily be set in an international context (see, e.g., Venables and Limao (1999)). The disadvantage of this model is that outlying regions trade with a single central location. To capture a full structure of bilateral trade flows in a tractable way we need a model that has product differentiation in at least some sectors, this possibly – although not necessarily – combined with monopolistic competition.

The model we use contains some number of countries (or more generally "locations") and a number of industries. Country specific variables are subscripted and industries represented by superscripts. Thus, x_{ij}^k is the quantity of an industry k good produced in country i and sold in country j. Underlying the demand side of the model is a price index (or expenditure function) for each industry that aggregates different varieties in the industry. This takes a CES form, is denoted G_j^k and defined by

$$G_j^k = \left[\sum_i n_i^k \left(p_i^k t_{ij}^k \right)^{1-\sigma^k} \right]^{1/(1-\sigma^k)} \tag{12.1}$$

In this equation n_i^k is the number of varieties of industry k products produced in country i, p_i^k their fob prices, and t_{ij}^k the iceberg cost factor on trading industry k

products from country i to country j. σ^k is the elasticity of substitution between varieties, and sectors in which $\sigma^k \to \infty$ produce homogeneous products.

If E_j^k is the total expenditure on industry k products in country j, then the sales of a single industry k product produced in country i and sold in j are given by

$$x_{ij}^k = (p_i^k)^{-\sigma^k}(t_{ij}^k)^{1-\sigma^k}E_j^k(G_j^k)^{\sigma^k-1} \tag{12.2}$$

The relationship is derived by using Shepard's lemma on the price index (see for example Dixit and Stiglitz, 1977). It contains information about bilateral trade flows between each pair of countries, i and j, and we use it for assessing the impact of geography on these flows. Adding over all markets and over all n_i^k varieties of industry k products produced in country i, we derive the following expression for the total value of industry k output produced by country i, y_i^k

$$y_i^k \equiv n_i^k p_i^k x_i^k = n_i^k (p_i^k)^{1-\sigma^k} \sum_j (t_{ij}^k)^{1-\sigma^k}E_j^k(G_j^k)^{\sigma^k-1} \tag{12.3}$$

where $x_i^k \equiv \sum_j x_{ij}^k$.

On the production side, prices are set proportional to marginal costs, according to:

$$p_i^k = \theta^k c^k(\mathbf{w}_i, \mathbf{G}_i) \tag{12.4}$$

where θ^k equals unity in perfectly competitive industries, and is greater than unity if firms mark up price over marginal cost. $c^k(\mathbf{w}_i, \mathbf{G}_i)$ is marginal cost, and is a function of prices of primary factors in country i, $\mathbf{w}_i$, and price indices of intermediates, $\mathbf{G}_i$.[3] If there is more than one primary factor or intermediate input these are vectors, so intermediate prices are given by the vector of industry price indices, $\mathbf{G}_i = G_i^1 \ldots G_i^k$.

Some sectors of the economy are perfectly competitive, and in these sectors the numbers of varieties produced in each country, n_i^k, are exogenously determined – an "Armington" assumption. Other sectors are monopolistically competitive, and the numbers are determined by zero profit conditions. Given that prices are proportional to marginal costs and assuming further that cost functions in these sectors have increasing returns and are homothetic, zero profits are made if firms' sales reach a given level, $\bar{x}^k$. Firms in monopolistically competitive industry k therefore make zero profits if their sales satisfy (using (12.4) in (12.2) with the definition of x_i^k),

$$[\theta^k c^k(\mathbf{w}_i, \mathbf{G}_i)]^{-\sigma^k} \sum_j (t_{ij}^k)^{1-\sigma^k}E_j^k(G_j^k)^{\sigma^k-1} = x_i^k = \bar{x}^k. \tag{12.5}$$

The other main relationships in the model are factor market clearing and the determination of expenditure. Factor market clearing is:

$$w_i L_i = \sum_k y_i^k \left(\frac{\partial c^k(\mathbf{w}_i, \mathbf{G}_i)}{\partial w_i} \cdot \frac{w_i}{c^k(\mathbf{w}_i, \mathbf{G}_i)} \right) \tag{12.6}$$

where s indexes factors of production, L_i^s denotes the endowment of factor s, and the expression is written in value form. The term in large brackets is the share of the primary factor in marginal costs (equal, with a homothetic cost function, to the share in average costs). Expenditure on each industry in each country is:

$$E_i^k = f_i^k + \sum_\ell y_i^\ell \left(\frac{\partial c^\ell(\mathbf{w}_i, \mathbf{G}_i)}{\partial G_i^k} \cdot \frac{G_i^k}{c^\ell(\mathbf{w}_i, \mathbf{G}_i)} \right) \quad (12.7)$$

where the first term, f_i^k, is final expenditure (itself depending on income and prices), and the second is derived demand, so the term in large brackets is the share of intermediates from industry k in industry l costs.

The sets of equations (12.1) to (12.7) characterize the international general equilibrium, and can be solved for quantities (x_{ij}^k, n_i^k, y_i^k) and for prices and expenditures $(p_i^k, \mathbf{w}_i^s, G_i^k, E_i^k)$. What are the properties of the model, and what hypotheses does it generate? We outline the answer here in very general terms, and are more specific in the following sections of the chapter.

The first broad property is that geography matters for factor prices and for the structure of production in each country. Geography enters the model through the trade costs, t_{ij}^k, which vary systematically with distance and other geographical forces, and also vary across industries. Trade costs are composed of a package of transport costs, time costs, and information costs – section 3 presents evidence on the size of these costs. Trade costs prevent goods price equalization from occurring, and hence also prevent factor price equalization. Since they vary across both locations and industries they provide a basis for comparative advantage.

The geographical structure of trade costs mean that some locations will be attractive to industry because of good market-access, and also because of good intermediate supplier-access. How does this show up in equilibrium? One manifestation will be through spatial variations in the prices of immobile factors, which will be bid up in regions with good market- and supplier-access. This will be the subject of section 4 of the paper. Another manifestation is in the structure of production. Some types of industry will be particularly drawn to these locations, and in section 5 we show how this can be combined with factor endowment theory to give hypotheses about industrial structure.

The fact that large markets are profitable locations and tend to have high factor prices creates a potential positive feedback, as large markets attract firms and mobile factors, so becoming still larger. As a consequence the model may have multiple equilibria, some unstable, and others manifesting agglomeration. For example, in Krugman (1991a, b) there are two sectors, one monopolistically competitive and the other perfectly competitive and freely traded. Production uses sector-specific factors (and no intermediate goods), the factor used in the monopolistically competitive industry being perfectly mobile between locations. Krugman shows how an increase in the amount of manufacturing in one location increases income and the size of the market and reduces the price index. If trade costs are low enough then this location attracts the mobile factor and leads to the agglomeration of all of manufacturing in one location. Krugman and Venables (1995) have the same two sectors and a single immobile factor. However, the presence of intermediate goods (manufacturing uses manufacturing as an input) creates agglomeration, as firms gain from being close to customer and supplier firms (see also Venables (1996, 1999)). Theoretical analysis of these models is synthesized in Fujita et al. (1999), but there is as yet little empirical investigation of clustering at the international level.[4] This survey reviews some subnational studies (section 5.3) that have attempted to identify agglomeration effects.

While the full model outlined above endogenizes all the main variables, the empirical studies we review below typically focus on a few key relationships, holding other variables exogenous. Thus, in section 3 we look at trade costs and examine trade flows based on equation (12.2), while holding all other variables exogenous. In section 4 we look at factor prices and incomes, and much of this is based on equation (12.5) with equation (12.1), which give values of factor prices and price indices, conditional on values of expenditure and numbers of firms in each location. Section 5 turns to equation (12.3), giving the structure of production of each location. We discuss measurement issues, descriptive studies, and attempts to econometrically estimate (12.3). A number of studies look at the relationship between expenditure and production, searching for home-market effects, and we review one study that endogenizes input prices and derived demands, estimating (12.3) with (12.1), (12.6) and (12.7).

3 TRADE COSTS AND TRADE VOLUMES

The dependence of trade volumes on geography is well known through the widespread use of gravity models. In this section we start by investigating the trade costs – the t_{ij}^k – that underlie the gravity relationship, and then turn to the relationship between trade and geography.

3.1 Trade Costs

Trade costs have many different elements, some observable (such as transport costs), while others, such as costs of acquiring information, are much more difficult to observe directly although inferences can be made from trade flows.

There are three main sources of data for transport costs between countries. The most readily available are the bilateral cif/fob ratios produced by the IMF by matching export data (reported by countries fob) and import data (reported cif). However, problems with this data include the fact that they are an aggregate over all commodities so they depend on the composition of trade, and that a high proportion of observations are imputed (see Hummels, 1999b for discussion). The second source is national customs data, made available by a few countries in a form that allows extraction of very detailed information. For example, the US Census Bureau make available data on US imports at the 10 digit level by exporter country, mode of transport, district of entry, and valued both inclusive and exclusive of freight and insurance charges (see Hummels, 1999a).

The third source is direct industry or shipping company information. These include indices of ocean shipping prices and air freight rates from trade journals (Hummels, 1999b), or direct quotes from shipping companies (e.g., Limao and Venables, 2001 who obtain quotes for shipping a standard container from Baltimore to various destinations).

We learn a number of things from studies of these data. First, there is a very wide dispersion of transport costs across commodities and across countries. Thus, for the US in 1994, freight expenditure was only 3.8 percent of the value of imports, but equivalent numbers for Brazil and Paraguay are 7.3 percent and 13.3 percent (Hummels, 1999a, from customs data). These values incorporate the fact that most trade is with countries that are close, and in goods with low transport costs. Looking at transport costs unweighted by trade volumes gives much higher numbers; thus, the median cif/fob ratio, across all country pairs for which data is available, is 1.28 (implying 28 percent transport and insurance costs). Looking across commodities, an unweighted average of freight rates is typically two to three times higher than the trade weighted average rate.

Estimates of the determinants of transport costs are given in Hummels (1999b) and Limao and Venables (2001). These studies find elasticities of transport costs with respect to distance of between 0.2 and 0.3. Limao and Venables find that sharing a common border substantially reduces transport costs, and overland distance is around seven times more expensive than sea distance. Being landlocked increases transport costs by approximately 50 percent. Infrastructure quality (as measured by a composite index of transport and communications networks) is important; for example, while the median cif/fob ratio is 1.28, this ratio's predicted value for a pair of countries with infrastructure quality at the 75th percentile rises to 1.40.

3.2 Trade Volumes

Equation (12.2) provides the basis for a gravity trade relationship.[5] It is usually estimated on aggregate data, so:

$$n_i p_i x_{ij} = n_i p_i^{1-\sigma} (t_{ij})^{1-\sigma} E_j (G_j)^{\sigma-1} \tag{12.2'}$$

(derived by dropping the industry specific superscript, and multiplying by the number of varieties produced in each country and their price). The left-hand side is simply the value of trade between country i and j; the main data source for this is the UN COMTRADE data base, made available by the NBER (Feenstra et al., 1997). The right-hand side contains exporter country information (numbers of varieties and their prices), importer country information (expenditure and the price index), and trade cost information, t_{ij}. The exporter and importer country information is typically proxied by income in each country. However, if the focus is on the geography of trade, then these terms can simply take the form of fixed effects for exporter and importer countries.[6]

Trade costs, t_{ij}, are typically assumed to be a function of a number of geographical variables, and perhaps also cultural or political variables. We look first at the geographical ones. Distance is the most important, and the elasticity of trade volumes with respect to distance is usually estimated to be in the interval −0.9 to −1.5.[7] Sharing a common border increases trade volumes, analogous to its effect on transport costs. Country characteristics that bear on trade costs include (see Limao and Venables) being an island, which increases trade volumes somewhat, and being landlocked, which reduces trade volumes by a massive 60 percent. Infrastructure also matters, with predicted trade volumes between two countries with infrastructure quality at the 75th percentile 28 percent lower than at the median.

Gravity estimates tell us that geography matters greatly for trade volumes, although it does not reveal whether this is through the impact of geography on trade costs, or the impact of trade costs on trade volumes. Several attempts have been made to make this separation, by combining information from estimates of trade costs and trade volumes. This can be done either by taking the ratio of the distance elasticity of trade to the distance elasticity of transport costs (Hummels, 1999a; Limao and Venables, 2001) or by using predicted values of t_{ij} derived from the estimated transport cost equation as an independent variable in a gravity model. The latter approach gives an elasticity of trade with respect to transport costs of approximately −3, and the former a range of around −2 to −5.[8]

We have so far concentrated on transport costs, and the role of geography in determining these. However, trade costs include a wider package of transactions costs, as well as policy measures. Hummels (2000) estimates the cost of time in transit. He uses data on some 25 million observations of shipments into the US (imports classified at the 10-digit commodity level by exporter country and district of entry to the US for 25 years), some by air and some by sea. Given data on the costs of each mode and the shipping times from different countries he is able to estimate the implicit value of time saved in shipping. The numbers are quite large. The cost of an extra day's travel is (from estimates on imports as a whole) around 0.3 percent of the value shipped. For manufacturing sectors, the number goes up to 0.5 percent. These costs are around 30 times larger than the interest charge on the value of the goods. They also carry the implication that transport costs have fallen much more through time than suggested by looking at shipping charges. The share of US imports going by air freight rose from zero to 30 percent between 1950 and 1998, and containerization approximately doubled the speed of ocean shipping. This gives a reduction in average shipping times of 26 days over 50 years, equivalent to a shipping cost reduction worth 12 to 13 percent of the value of goods traded.

Many studies have used a variety of further "between country" measures in the gravity estimation in order to try to capture the role of culture, history, and politics in influencing trade flows (see Frankel (1997) for a synthesis of some of this material). A recent example is the work of Rauch and Trindade (1999), who seek to explore the role of ethnic Chinese networks in promoting trade. Their gravity estimation includes dummies for sharing a common language, having shared colonial ties, and a variable that is the product of the share of ethnic Chinese in the populations of the importing and exporting countries. They find that colonial ties and Chinese networks have large significant effects in promoting trade (although the effects of language are mixed). Studies of this type remind us that while trade costs are important determinants of trade volumes, they are not just functions of physical geography.[9]

3.3 The Research Agenda

The studies above give some indication of the role of geography in determining transport costs and in choking off trade. There are several areas where much more work is needed.

Borders create very large trade barriers (Helliwell, 1996, McCallum, 1995, Wei, 1996), and work is needed to understand the difference between international and inter-regional trade. One aspect of this is to recognize that there are fixed (and perhaps sunk) costs, as well as marginal costs, to firms entering new markets. Understanding the nature of these costs is important as countries seek to promote "deep integration" to overcome international market segmentation, and also as these costs may pose important barriers to developing country export growth (Roberts and Tybout, 1997).

Research is also needed for a clearer understanding of the geography of information flows. Much trade involves a process of searching and matching between firms. Once a match has been made there may be monitoring and control issues (as downstream agents are concerned with the quality and delivery of supplies). These are areas where new technologies might possibly transform the geography of trade and production, but where very little is so far known.[10]

4 FACTOR PRICES AND INCOME

The fundamental determinants of the spatial variation of per capita income can be grouped into three broad headings. First, nature geography; the second, nature geography of access to markets, suppliers, and ideas; and third, the effects of social infrastructure, "the institutions and government policies that determine the economic environment within which individuals accumulate skills and firms accumulate capital and produce output" (Hall and Jones, 1999, p. 84). Each of these determinants affects income directly, as well as by changing the incentives to make investments and accumulate factors of production.

This is not the place to review the literature on social infrastructure and we simply note that attempts to quantify its role have drawn heavily on geographical variables as proxies.[11] For example, in Hall and Jones (1999), social infrastructure is modeled as a function of distance from the equator, a measure of openness to international trade, the fraction of the population speaking English, and the fraction of the population speaking a European language. They find that these four variables account for 41 percent of the cross-country variation in social infrastructure and 60 percent of the cross-country variation in income per capita.

The work of Sachs and his co-authors has focused largely on first-nature geography (Gallup and Sachs, 2000; Gallup et al., 1999; McArthur and Sachs, 2001; Sachs,

2000; and Sachs and Warner, 1999). Thus, Gallup et al. (1999) find that countries with a large percentage of their population close to the coast, low levels of malaria, large hydro-carbon endowments, and low levels of transport costs (as measured by IMF data on the cif/fob import price ratio) have higher levels of income per capita. These four variables alone explain nearly 70 percent of the variation in per capita income for a sample of 83 developed and developing countries.

Second-nature geography, or the location of economic agents relative to one another, affects per capita income through several different mechanisms. One is technology spillovers, which may diminish with the geographical distance between economic agents, as will be discussed further below. Another is countries' distance from the markets in which they sell output and from sources of supply of manu-factured goods, intermediate inputs, and capital equipment. Trade costs reduce export receipts and increase prices of these inputs, squeezing the value added attrib-utable to domestic factors of production.[12]

The idea that access to markets is important for factor incomes dates back at least to Harris (1954), who argued that the potential demand for goods and serv-ices produced in a location i depends upon the distance-weighted GDP (or, more generally, distance-weighted economic activity) in all locations:

$$MP_i = \sum_{j=1}^{R} GDP_j d_{ij}^{\gamma}, \qquad (12.8)$$

where MP_i is the "market potential" of country i, d_{ij} is the bilateral distance between locations i and j, and γ is a distance-weighting parameter, traditionally set at -1.

Much of the traditional geography focused on the implications of market poten-tial for the location of economic activity (see, for example, Clark et al., 1969; Dicken and Lloyd, 1977; and Keeble et al., 1982) with relatively little structural economet-ric estimation. Early econometric investigations of the role of market access in determining the cross-country distribution of income include Hummels (1995) and Leamer (1997). Hummels (1995) explores the role of three alternative measures of geographical location within the Solow and augmented Solow models. One is a measure of distance-weighted GDP in all other countries, constructed according to (12.8). The second two measures relate to a country's distance from the three main centers of world economic activity (the US, Japan, and Germany) and are respec-tively the sum and minimum of these three distances. In an equation for steady-state levels of per capita income, the geography measures are highly statistically significant, reduce the estimated magnitude of the coefficients on the Solow model variables, and improve the fit of the regression. Leamer (1997) examines the impor-tance of access to Western Europe markets for post-reform income per capita in Eastern Europe. He uses a measure of market-access based on equation (12.8), with the distance-weighting parameter γ derived from estimating a gravity equation. (Data on internal area is used to evaluate "own distance," d_{ii}.) The variation in access to Western markets within Eastern Europe suggests that these countries differ markedly in terms of their potential to achieve higher standards of living.

Although the focus is not on access to markets per se, Frankel and Romer (1999) explore the relationship between a measure of international openness (the ratio of trade to GDP) and levels of per capita income. One of the central problems in the literature concerned with openness and growth is the potential endogeneity of international openness. Therefore, Frankel and Romer (1999) use geography measures, including bilateral distance, area, land-locked status, and population, as instruments for bilateral trade flows. The predicted values for bilateral trade flows from this first-stage regression are then used to construct the ratio of total trade to GDP.[13] Evidence is found of a positive and statistically significant relationship between levels of per capita income and exogenous variation in the trade ratio due to the geography measures.

Redding and Venables (2000) use the structure of the Krugman and Venables (1995) model to obtain theory-consistent measures of both market-access and supplier-access.[14] From the theoretical discussion in section 2, a firm in a monopolistically competitive industry will make zero profits if it achieves a volume of sales equal to $\bar{x}$ in equation (12.5). The volume of sales achieved depends on prices, which are a constant mark-up over marginal cost. Equation (12.5) thus implicitly defines the maximum wage that a manufacturing firm in location i can afford to pay consistent with zero equilibrium profits. Dropping the superscript, and assuming that the marginal cost function is Cobb–Douglas in labor (with share β) and intermediate inputs (with share α) equation (12.5) is,

$$w_i^{\beta\sigma} = \left(\frac{\theta}{\bar{x}}\right) G_i^{-\alpha\sigma} \sum_j (t_{ij})^{1-\sigma} E_j (G_j)^{\sigma-1} \qquad (12.5')$$

The term in the summation is the *market-access* of country i,

$$MA_i \equiv \sum_j (t_{ij})^{1-\sigma} E_j (G_j)^{\sigma-1}, \qquad (12.9)$$

and is the theoretically founded analogue of market potential. It is comprised of expenditure in each market j, together with the price index (this measuring the amount of competition in the market, between which expenditure has to be shared), and adjusted according to transport costs from j to i. Terms in this expression are not directly observable, but can be derived from gravity estimation. We saw earlier how gravity models generate estimates of the between-country trade frictions, $(t_{ij})^{1-\sigma}$. The "own distance," t_{ii}, can be constructed using a number of alternative approaches, some of which exploit information on internal area. Country dummies are used to capture importer effects, $E_j(G_j)^{\sigma-1}$. Combining these yields an estimate of the market-access of country i.

If intermediate goods are used in production, $\alpha > 0$, then transport costs also reduce the wage payable via an increase in the price of intermediates. This is captured in the term $G_i^{-\alpha\sigma}$ in equation (12.5′). Using the definition of the price index (equation (12.1)) we define country j's *supplier access* analogously to market access as,

$$SA_j \equiv \sum_i n_i (p_i t_{ij})^{1-\sigma} = G_j^{1-\sigma} \qquad (12.10)$$

Once again, estimates of country dummies (now the exporter rather than the importer dummy) from the gravity model provide the information needed to construct the series.

Table 12.1 World market access, supplier access, and GDP per capita

ln(*GDP per capita*)	(1)	(2)	(3)	(4)
Observations	101	101	79	79
Year	1996	1996	1996	1996
α		0.5		
σ		10		
ln(FMA_i)	0.476	0.320	0.425	0.307
	[0.076]		[0.081]	[0.074]
ln(FSA_i)	–	0.178	–	–
		[0.039]		
R^2	0.346	0.360	0.248	0.152

Dependent variable is ln(GDP per capita). Independent variables are ln(Foreign Market Access), ln(FMA_i), and ln(Foreign Supplier Access), ln(FSA_i). ln(FMA_i) and ln(FSA_i) are generated from estimating the trade equation (equation (12.5)). Since these variables are generated from a prior regression bootstrapped standard errors are reported in square brackets (200 replications). The wage equation estimation sample in columns (1) and (2) is 101 countries. Column (3) estimates the model for the sample of 79 developing countries only. Column (4) estimates the model for 79 developing countries with a measure of ln(FMA_i) constructed only using data on OECD market capacities.
Source: *Redding and Venables (2000).*

Having used estimates from a gravity model to construct the market-access and supplier-access variables, these are then combined with cross-country data on per capita income to estimate (12.5') which, in logs, is

$$\ln w_i = \xi + \varphi_1 \ln SA_i + \varphi_2 \ln MA_i + u_i \tag{12.11}$$

where the parameters φ_1 and φ_2 are functions of underlying structural parameters of the model, $\varphi_1 \equiv \alpha/\beta \, (\sigma - 1)$, $\varphi_2 \equiv 1/\beta\sigma$. The stochastic error u_i includes cross-country variation in the price of other factors of production that enter manufacturing unit costs, technical differences, and other stochastic determinants of manufacturing wages.

Table 12.1 reports the results of estimating (12.11) using a cross-section of data on 101 developed and developing countries with GDP per capita as a proxy for manufacturing wages.[15] Because of the potential endogeneity of domestic market and supply capacity, only measures of *foreign* market and supplier access are considered (i.e., own effects are ignored, so summations in (12.9) and (12.10) are over $j \neq i$).[16] Column (1) presents the results using foreign market access alone. The estimated coefficient is positive and explains about 35 percent of the cross-country variation in income per capita. Column (2) includes information on supplier access as well. Separately identifying the coefficients on these two variables is difficult given their high degree of correlation. However, choosing values for α and σ implies a linear restriction on the estimated coefficients, $\varphi_1 = \varphi_2 \, \alpha\sigma/(\sigma - 1)$, and column (2) reports the results of estimating for values of $\alpha = 0.5$ and $\sigma = 10$, both of which are broadly consistent with independent empirical estimates. Including foreign supplier access reduces the magnitude of the estimated coefficient on foreign market access, but it remains highly statistically significant.

There are a number of concerns that one might have about these results. Is one really identifying an effect of economic geography, or just picking up that rich countries tend to be located next to rich countries, particularly within the OECD? Could the results not be explained by some third variable (e.g., unobserved technology differences), that is correlated with both income per capita and foreign market/supplier access? Redding and Venables undertake a number of robustness tests to address such concerns. These include augmenting the specification with a large number of control variables for factor endowments, physical geography, and social, political, and institutional considerations. For example, column (3) reports the results for non-OECD countries only, and column (4) presents results for non-OECD countries only, with their foreign market access calculated on the basis of their distance from OECD markets only: it asks, to what extent can variation in income per capita across developing countries be explained by access to OECD markets? In both cases, the effect of foreign market access is robust and highly statistically significant.

Wage gradients can be estimated on subnational as well as international data, and Hanson (1998a, 2000a) performs such an estimation using a panel of US counties. Ignoring intermediate goods, his specification is equation (12.5′) with $\alpha = 0$. In his basic specification this is estimated using county data on average earnings, and taking as independent variable the aggregate income of counties in a set of concentric circles at increasing distance around each observation, each distance weighted according to a factor $\exp(\beta_2 d_{ij})$, (where d_{ij} is distance, and this weighting factor corresponds to $(t_{ij})^{1-\sigma}$). The equation is estimated in first differences so that any time-invariant features of counties are swept out. Hanson finds a powerful wage gradient effect, with his measure of market access having a positive effect on earnings, and within this measure, distance (coefficient β_2) having a highly significant effect.

In the augmented version of his model Hanson addresses the endogeneity of the price index, G_j, by assuming that labor is perfectly mobile across counties (as in Krugman 1991a), so that real wages are equalized. Hypothesizing that housing is the only immobile factor (as in Helpman (1998)), and that it takes a fixed share $1 - \mu$ of income, real wages are $w_j/G_j^\mu P_j^{1-\mu}$ where P_j is the price of housing (so the denominator is the cost-of-living index in the jth county). The value of housing expenditure satisfies $P_j H_j = (1 - \mu)Y_j$ where H_j is the (exogenous) housing stock, so the equilibrium value of the price index is:

$$G_j^\mu = w_j \left(\frac{(1-\mu)Y_j}{H_j} \right)^{\mu-1} \tag{12.12}$$

Using this in (12.5), together with manufacturing expenditure $E_j = \mu Y_j$ gives the estimating equation,

Table 12.2 Market potential and wages across US counties

	(1)	(2)	(3)
Observations	3705	3705	3705
Time period	1970–80	1980–90	1980–90
σ	7.597	6.562	4.935
	(1.250)	(0.838)	(1.372)
μ	0.916	0.956	0.982
	(0.015)	(0.013)	(0.035)
τ	1.970	3.219	1.634
	(0.328)	(0.416)	(0.523)
Wage controls	no	no	yes
Adj. R^2	0.256	0.347	0.376
Log likelihood	−16698.1	−16576.9	−16479.9
Schwarz Criterion	−16714.0	−16592.9	−16575.5

Estimation is by non-linear least squares. Sample is all US counties in the continental US. The equation estimated is the time-difference of equation (12.13). All variables are scaled relative to weighted averages for the continental US. The dependent variable is the log change in average annual earnings from Regional Economic Information System (REIS), US BEA. Regional income is total personal income from REIS. The housing stock is measured by total housing units from the US Census of Population and Housing. The specification in column (3) includes controls for human capital, demographic characteristics, and exogenous amenities. Heteroskedasticity-consistent standard errors are in parentheses. The Schwartz Criterion is written as $\ln(L) - k*\ln(N)/2$, where k is the number of parameters.
Source: *Reported results are from Hanson (2000a).*

$$w_i = \xi + \sigma^{-1} \ln\left(\sum_j^R Y_j^{\frac{\sigma(\mu-1)+1}{\mu}} H_j^{\frac{(1-\mu)(\sigma-1)}{\mu}} w_j^{\frac{\sigma-1}{\mu}} e^{-\tau(\sigma-1)d_{ij}} \right) + u_i \qquad (12.13)$$

where transport costs are modeled as an exponential function of distance: $T_{ij} = e^{-\tau d_{ij}}$.

Columns (1) and (2) of table 12.2 present the results of estimating this specification using non-linear least squares for the periods 1970–80 and 1980–90. All variables are signed according to economic priors and are highly statistically significant. The inclusion of controls for the manufacturing price index, G_j, is found to improve the fit of the regression. The estimated values of the elasticity of substitution, σ, are broadly consistent with independent econometric estimates of this parameter, and are found to have fallen between the two sample periods. As implied by theory, the estimated expenditure share on tradable goods, μ, lies between 0 and 1, although a value above 0.9 is somewhat high. The estimated value of transport costs, τ, rises over time, and this may reflect a shift in production away from low-transport-cost manufactures to high-transport-cost services during the sample period. The estimated values of σ imply a markup factor of price over marginal cost that ranges between 1.15 and 1.25.[17,18]

The time-differenced specification controls for unobserved heterogeneity across counties in the level of manufacturing wages. However, it could be that wages have risen faster in counties with favorable exogenous amenities (e.g., weather or natural geography) or that have accumulated human capital (both through the private rate of return to human capital acquisition and through any externalities) and that these omitted variables are correlated with changes in market access. Since human capital accumulation may, in part, be determined by economic geography, it is not clear that one wants to exclude this component of the change in wages from the analysis. However, Hanson (2000a) shows that his results are robust to including a whole range of controls for levels of human capital, demographic composition of the working age population, and exogenous amenities.[19] Results including these controls are shown for the main estimation sample for the period 1980–90 in column (3).

The empirical results surveyed so far provide econometric evidence of wage gradients across geographical space (both across and within countries) consistent with the predictions of economic geography models.[20] *Ceteris paribus*, locations that are remote from markets and sources of supply of intermediate inputs are characterized by lower nominal wages. As always, there remain potential concerns relating to identification and simultaneity that could be resolved by observing a controlled or natural experiment that generates exogenous variation in market and supplier access. In the remainder of this subsection, we discuss a group of papers that have exploited trade liberalization in Mexico as precisely such an experiment.

In 1985 Mexico opened its economy to international trade, bringing to an end four decades of import-substitution industrialization. Hanson (1996, 1998b, c) finds that trade reform has contributed towards the breakup of the traditional manufacturing belt centered on Mexico City and the formation of new industrial centers in Northern Mexico.[21] For example, in the apparel industry Hanson (1996) finds that prior to trade liberalization, production was concentrated around Mexico City and largely oriented toward the Mexican market, with design and marketing concentrated in Mexico City and assembly in the neighboring states. With trade liberalization, there was a substantial relocation of manufacturing activity toward the US border, and the nature of manufacturing activity was also reoriented – away from domestic production towards offshore assembly for foreign (largely US) firms. There is evidence of a negative relationship between relative wages and distance from Mexico City prior to 1988, and of a statistically significant decline in the size of the estimated coefficient on distance from Mexico City between 1985 and 1988.[22] This provides support for the existence of a regional wage gradient centered on Mexico City prior to trade liberalization and of the partial breakdown of this regional wage gradient as production re-oriented towards the US.

Hanson (1997) analyzes the determinants of state relative to national manufacturing wages for a panel of two-digit Mexican manufacturing industries over the period 1965 to 1988. Nominal wages are found to be negatively correlated with both distance from Mexico City and distance from the Mexico–US border. A 10 percent increase in distance from Mexico City is associated with a 1.9 percent reduction in the relative state wage, while the same increase in distance from the Mexico–US border is associated with a 1.3 percent reduction.

4.1   Geography and Technology

Much of the discussion in this section has been concerned with distance from markets and sources of supply as an explanation for spatial variation in factor prices. Distance is important because of the transportation costs incurred on deliveries to markets and shipments of intermediate goods and capital equipment. An alternative explanation for variation in factor prices across space is the existence of technology differences, which may arise, for example, because knowledge spillovers diminish with geographical space between economic agents.[23] A number of papers have presented empirical evidence that knowledge spillovers are much greater within than between countries: see, for example, Branstetter (2001), Coe and Helpman (1995), Eaton and Kortum (1999a, b), Jaffe and Trajtenberg (1998), and Keller (2000, 2002). Much of the literature has been concerned with the extent to which international knowledge spillovers are trade-related (see, in particular, Coe and Helpman, 1995). Since, as discussed in section 3, distance plays a substantial role in explaining international trade flows, this suggests a potential role for geography in the diffusion of ideas. The role of international trade flows per se has been questioned by Keller (1998). Keller (2002) examines the direct relationship between distance and international knowledge spillovers. A 10 percent higher distance from a major technology-producing country such as the US is found to be associated with a 0.15 percent reduction in productivity.

5   THE LOCATION OF ACTIVITY

We now turn to the question of how geography determines the structure of production across locations. We organize the material into three subsections. The first deals with some measurement issues and descriptive studies. Is it possible to make statements along the lines of "the US is more regionally specialized than the EU," and what are the stylized facts concerning specialization and localization? The second and third sections seek to go behind the descriptives and ask what determines location. In 5.2 we look at studies on international data, and in 5.3 subnational studies. This subsection is also where we deal with the issues of clustering and agglomeration. Are industries more localized than would be suggested by alternative hypotheses, and if so, why?

5.1   Measurement Issues and Descriptive Studies

5.1.1   LOCALIZATION AND SPECIALIZATION

The researcher may wish to ask two distinct, but related, questions. One is how localized is a particular economic activity, and the other is how specialized is a particular geographical unit? This question can be addressed using different measures of activity, typically employment or production, and in the following discussion we refer to production. Denoting the production of industry k in location i as y_i^k, the localization of industry k can be addressed by looking at y_i^k relative to total production of that industry: $\ell_i^k = y_i^k/\Sigma_i y_i^k$. This measures the share of location i in the total production of industry k. Conversely, the specialization of a location can be studied by looking at y_i^k relative to the total production of that location, $s_i^k = y_i^k/\Sigma_k y_i^k$. This measures the share of industry k in region i's total production of all industries.

Recognizing that regions and industries differ in size we might want to normalize these two measures. If we normalize the first by the share of the location in overall activity and the second by the share of the industry in overall activity we end up with a measure which we call the *location quotient*,[24]

$$r_i^k = \frac{y_i^k/\sum_i y_i^k}{\sum_k y_i^k/\sum_i \sum_k y_i^k} = \frac{y_i^k/\sum_k y_i^k}{\sum_i y_i^k/\sum_k \sum_i y_i^k} \qquad (12.14)$$

These are two equivalent expressions or interpretations of the location quotient. The first is as a measure of the localization of industry k in i, relative to the localization of activity as a whole in i. The second is as a measure of location i's specialization in industry k relative to the share of the industry in total world output. It is important to be clear that economic geography models make statements about both localization and specialization. We shall refer to statements about the distribution of r_i^k across locations i for given industry k as statements about the localization of industry k, noting that k could be an aggregate of many or all sectors. And we shall refer to statements about the distribution of r_i^k across industries for a given location as describing the specialization of location i.

5.1.2 SUMMARY STATISTICS OF LOCALIZATION AND SPECIALIZATION

The matrix r_i^k contains the distributions of localization and specialization, and we typically want to be able to summarize these distributions in order to make statements such as "industry k has become more localized" or "location i is more specialized than location j." To do so requires calculation of a summary statistic of the distribution, and the problems of collapsing distributions down to a meaningful scalar representation is fraught with conceptual issues that have long occupied the literature on the distribution of personal income and wealth (see for example Cowell, 1995). In addition to these concerns, Duranton and Overman (2001) suggest five properties that, from a standpoint of economic geography, we would like such measures to satisfy:

1 they should be comparable across industries or locations;
2 they should take in to account the overall distribution of activity across different sectors (for specialization) and across different locations (for localization);
3 they should be able to distinguish between "lumpiness" in the unit of observation and geographical concentration;
4 they should be defined over the correct spatial units; and
5 they should allow the statistical significance of the measured specialization or localization to be assessed.

The measures discussed in the remainder of this section only satisfy properties 1 and 2. We consider indices that satisfy conditions 3 to 5 in section 5.3, as they have so far only been applied to subnational data.

Looking first at specialization, we seek a summary measure of the specialization of location i. Various measures of dispersion can be used, defined either on absolute production shares, s_i^k, or shares relative to industry size, r_i^k. For example, the Herfindahl index of absolute specialization, takes the form $h_i = \Sigma_k(s_i^k)^2$. For the bilateral comparison of the specialization of two different locations Krugman (1991b) computes the absolute value of the difference in production shares, $K_{ij} = \Sigma_k|s_i^k - s_i^k|$.

Analogous measures are used for localization. Various authors compute locational gini coefficients, $g^k = gini^k(r_i^k)$, referred to by Kim (1995) as "Hoover's coefficient of localization."[25] Haaland et al. (1999) argue that conditioning on the distribution of the location of activity as a whole is not consistent with the intuitive concept of agglomeration, and so they use an "absolute" gini coefficient, $ga^k = gini^k(\ell_i^k)$, calculated analogously.[26]

5.1.3 FINDINGS ON LOCALIZATION
AND SPECIALIZATION

In this section we review some of the main stylized facts that emerge from descriptive studies of the location of economic activity, before moving on in sections 5.2 and 5.3 to more formal work that seeks to disentangle the various forces determining location.

It is taken as self-evident by geographers that activity clusters. "In fact, the geographical concentration of economic activities, at a local or subnational level, is the norm not the exception . . . " (Dicken, 1998, p. 11). The most systematic evidence on overall agglomeration comes from the work of urban economists and historians on cities. In his classic book, Bairoch (1988) provides a wide range of data on the size of cities and the extent of urbanization. In 1300, Bairoch's estimates put the urban population at 41 million out of a total of approximately 460 million (an urbanization rate of roughly 9 percent). By 1900 this had risen to 260 million (an urbanization rate of 16 percent), while by 1990 the urbanization rate had risen to 37.6 percent, with roughly 1,670 million people living in urban areas. By 2025, he predicts a world level of urbanization of 57 percent. Not only does a high proportion of the world's population live in these cities, but there are also a large number of such agglomerations. In 1980, there were roughly 2,290,000 cities with more than 100 thousand inhabitants, and by 1995 15 cities had a population greater than 10 million. We also know how these patterns change during economic development. Studies of localization in developing countries confirm the hypothesis of Williamson (1965) that in growing from low-income levels countries go first through a period of regional divergence and concentration of development and industrialization in a restricted region of the country, followed by industrial deconcentration, growth of hinterland regions and a move towards regional convergence (see for example Henderson, 1988, and Henderson et al., 1999).

Particular types of economic activity are also massively localized. In 1995 the OECD countries produced 78 percent of the world's manufacturing output, despite containing only 15 percent of the world's population. A key feature of the process of economic development is the reallocation of resources from agriculture to manufacturing. Analysis of the spatial deconcentration of manufacturing production is therefore central to our understanding of economic development.

Turning to a finer sectoral level, there are a number of studies of the evolution of specialization and localization within countries or groups of countries. The US provides the longest available time series, and using this data Kim (1995) calculates specialization measures, K_{ij}, and the "coefficient of localization," g^k, and finds that changes from 1860 to 1987 have been non-monotonic. Industries became increasingly localized and states increasingly specialized up to 1930. From then state specialization fell substantially and is lower today than it was in 1860. On average, industries became less localized during this later period, but individual industries show large variations around this average trend.

In the EU, data is available over a much shorter period. However, there is evidence that, in contrast to the US, EU countries are becoming increasingly specialized as European integration proceeds. Amiti (1999) uses data on both employment and production for her study of a selection of EU countries; Midelfart-Knarvik, Overman, Redding, and Venables (2000) use data on gross output for the entire EU 12; while WIFO (1999) use value-added. The pattern of increasing specialization with respect to the EU average seems to be consistent from the mid-1980s onwards, although the changes are not particularly large. Midelfart-Knarvik et al. use K_{ij} to show that countries are also becoming less similar to one another, with 71 out of 91 bilateral comparisons revealing increasing dissimilarity. Industrial localization experiences (measured by g^k and ga^k) are diverse with some industries localizing and others dispersing. This is consistent with earlier work by Brulhart and Torstensson (1996) and Brulhart (1998).

A number of these papers push such descriptive exercises further by constructing measures of industry characteristics – for example the extent of increasing returns to scale and the resource intensity – and running regressions of localization coefficients on these industry characteristics (see, for example, Amiti (1999), Brulhart (1998), Brulhart and Torstensson (1996), Haaland et al. (1999), and Kim (1995, 1997)). Results are mixed, reflecting both the small number of observations, and the lack of any real theoretical foundation for the estimation. Some of the results are suggestive. For example, Kim (1995, p. 881) argues that his findings "support explanations based on production scale economies and the Heckscher–Ohlin framework but are inconsistent with explanations based on external economies." However the lack of theoretical foundations is an important limitation of these studies.

The measurement exercises reported above are clearly important in describing the data and trends in their evolution, but we need to go further to investigate the economic forces driving these variables. For example, evidence of increasing specialization in the EU does not, by itself, discriminate between comparative advantage and agglomeration as drivers of specialization. In the next two sections we look at studies that attempt to identify the mechanisms at work. In 5.2 we report the studies based on international data, and in 5.3 look at some of the (much larger number of) studies using subnational data.

5.2   International Studies

5.2.1   HOME-MARKET EFFECTS

We saw in section 2 that the number of firms (or varieties) in each location, n_i^k, might either be determined exogenously or, for monopolistically competitive industries, endogenously through a zero profit condition (equation (12.5)).[27] These two cases give rise to different predictions about the effect of demand (or market access) on production. More specifically, the presence of increasing returns to scale and transport costs in the monopolistically competitive case implies a "home market" or "magnification" effect, whereby an increase in demand for a good results in a more than proportionate increase in production of the good. Intuitively, increasing returns to scale imply that firms would like to concentrate production in a single location, while the existence of transport costs implies that, other things equal, this concentration will occur close to large markets.

The argument can be seen more formally by referring back to section 2. Suppose that all economies are identical, except that we now give country 1 a small increase in E_1^k. Suppose also that there are no intermediate goods and all factor prices stay constant. If n_i^k is fixed and industry k not monopolistically competitive, then we see from equation (12.3) that this increase in E_1^k will raise outputs in all countries, while increasing country 1's output less than proportionately. But if there is monopolistic competition, equation (12.5) must hold for all countries. It will do so if G_1^k falls so that $E_1^k(G_1^k)^{\sigma-1}$ remains constant, while all other price indices, $G_j^k, j \neq 1$, stay constant. From inspection of the price index (12.1), given $t_{ii} = 1$ and $t_{ij} > 1$ $(i \neq 1)$ this requires an increase in n_1^k and *fall* in all other $n_i^k, i \neq 1$. The falls in $n_i^k, i \neq 1$, must mean that country 1 output increases more than proportionately, if supply is to equal the new value of demand.[28]

Davis and Weinstein (1998, 1999) use this home-market effect as a basis for testing between models of imperfect competition/increasing returns to scale and perfect competition/constant returns to scale. It requires estimating the relationship between variations in expenditure and variations in output across countries and industries, and seeing whether there is a proportional response of more or less than unity. Davis and Weinstein (1998) consider a nested specification, where factor endowments are assumed to determine production at the more aggregate level (3 digit), while economic geography effects operate in disaggregated industries. Using data for 13 OECD countries, they first construct measures of "idiosyncratic demand" for each 4-digit industry based on demand in the country and its trading partners, distance weighted.[29] Estimating the effects of this demand variable on production in a pooled sample across countries and all 4-digit industries they find an elasticity of production with respect to demand of 1.6, indicating a strong home-market effect. Estimating a single coefficient across all industries is unsatisfactory, as we expect that industries have different market structures. Disaggregating and running separate regressions for each 3-digit industry (with the sample of countries and 4-digit subindustries), they find evidence of a home-market effect (coefficient greater than unity) in a majority of industries, the estimated coefficient being significantly greater than unity in four industries, and significantly less than unity in two.

These results are broadly similar to those obtained using a related specification on data for 29 sectors and 47 Japanese prefectures in 1985 (Davis and Weinstein, 1999). Statistically significant home-market effects are found in 8 out of 19 manufacturing sectors, including transportation equipment, iron and steel, electrical machinery, and chemicals. These effects are found to be quantitatively important – for the eight sectors with statistically significant home-market effects, a one standard deviation movement in idiosyncratic demand is found to move production, on average, by half a standard deviation.

Home-market effects have also been found by several other authors. Head and Ries (2001) look at the 1990 to 1995 US–Canada trade at the 3-digit level. Since they only have a single pair of countries they have to rely on cross-industry or time-series-variation in the data to identify the home-market effect, and only estimate a single effect for all industries (like Davis and Weinstein's pooled regression). They find a weak home-market effect in their industry cross-section (an elasticity of production with respect to local demand of 1.12), which becomes less than unity once the time series variation is employed. This is probably explained by the short time series – the home-market effect is essentially a long-run relationship driven by entry and exit of firms or varieties.

Feenstra et al. (2001) identify a home-market effect from estimating a gravity model separately for differentiated products, reference-priced exports, and homogeneous goods. The coefficient on income of the exporting country rises as they go from homogeneous to more differentiated products. For differentiated products the coefficient is slightly greater than unity and significantly greater than the coefficient on importer country income, indicating the presence of a home-market effect in these goods.

5.2.2 GEOGRAPHY AND COMPARATIVE ADVANTAGE

Whereas Davis and Weinstein separate out factor endowment effects (operating at an aggregate level) and geography effects (operating at a disaggregate level), Midelfart-Knarvik, Overman and Venables (2000) show how the effects can be combined. The basis of their approach is to estimate a linearized version of equation (12.3) on a panel of European countries and industries.

To implement this they assume first that all industries are perfectly competitive and that the numbers of varieties of each industry produced in each country are exogenously determined and proportional to the size of the industry and size of the country, thus $n_i^k = \Sigma_k y_i^k \Sigma_i y_i^k$. Using this together with (12.4) and (12.14) in (12.3) gives[30]

$$r_i^k \equiv \left(\theta c^k (w_{i'} G_i)\right)^{1-\sigma^k} \sum_j \left(t_{ij}^k\right)^{1-\sigma^k} E_j^k \left(G_j^k\right)^{\sigma^k-1} \tag{12.15}$$

Although the numbers of varieties are set exogenously, (12.15) indicates how both cost and demand factors determine the matrix of location quotients.

Linearization of the model gives, on the right-hand side, a sum of interactions between country characteristics and industry characteristics. Denoting the country

Table 12.3 Comparative advantage and geography: Dependent variable $\ln(r_i^k)$

	Variable Interactions: $\beta[j]$	1980–83	1985–88	1990–93	1994–97
$\beta[1]$	Agric. endowment * agricultural input intensity	0.078 (0.114)	0.140 (0.097)	0.166** (0.085)	0.158** (0.079)
$\beta[2]$	Skill endowment * skill intensity	1.503*** (0.439)	1.484*** (0.420)	1.479*** (0.463)	1.663*** (0.582)
$\beta[3]$	Researchers+scientists endowment * R&D intensity	0.584* (0.325)	0.741** (0.389)	1.108** (0.536)	1.624*** (0.581)
$\beta[4]$	Intermediate prices (supplier access) * intermediate goods intensity	0.570 (0.811)	0.754 (0.771)	0.799 (0.667)	1.096* (0.689)
$\beta[5]$	MA final demand – MA intermediate * share of output to industry	0.182*** (0.059)	0.171*** (0.052)	0.130*** (0.043)	0.083** (0.041)
$\beta[6]$	Elasticity of MA wrt transport intensity * transport intensity	−0.395 (0.315)	−0.270 (0.299)	−0.319 (0.290)	−0.382 (0.275)
	Adjusted R²	0.105	0.116	0.143	0.137
	Number of observations	456	456	456	456

*Standard errors reported in brackets; *** = significant at 1% level; ** = significant at 5% level; * = significant at 10%. All regressions are overall significant according to standard F-tests.*

characteristics $x_i[j]$ and industry characteristics $y^k[j]$, where j is an index running across the set of interactions, gives an estimating equation of the form,

$$\ln(r_i^k) = \zeta + \sum_j \beta[j](x_i[j] - \bar{x}[j])(y^k[j] - \bar{y}[j]) + \varepsilon_i^k. \tag{12.16}$$

The interpretation of this is seen by thinking of the interaction between, say, skilled labor abundance and skilled labor intensity. Countries which have skilled labor abundance greater than some reference level $x_i[j] > \bar{x}[j]$, will have high production in industries with skilled labor intensity above a reference level $y^k[j] > \bar{y}[j]$, and vice-versa – a Rybczynski effect. This multiplicative form of interaction holds for other pairs of country and industry characteristics. Expanding the products in (12.16) yields an equation in which the parameters to be estimated are $\beta[j]$, $\beta[j]\bar{x}[j]$, and $\beta[j]\bar{y}[j]$, and the estimates of $\beta[j]$ are given in table 12.3.

The first three are interactions of factor endowments with factor intensities. We see that all are significant by the end of the period, with the absolute magnitude of the scientist abundance/R&D intensity interaction having nearly trebled in size. The fourth interaction captures forward linkages, so interacts a measure of supplier access (proximity to other manufacturing sectors, as defined above) with the share of intermediates in production; the coefficient has the correct sign, although is barely significant. The fifth term measures backwards linkages. This is the relative importance of derived demand (measured as the difference between market access computed for final products and market access computed for intermediates) interacted with the share of each industry's output that is sold to industry. Backwards linkages are significant, although become less important over the period. Finally, to capture in a rigorous manner the possibility that high transport cost industries are drawn to central locations, the transport intensity of products is interacted with the elasticity of market access with respect to transport intensity. The estimated coefficient is insignificant and has the wrong sign.

Although this paper abstracts from monopolistic competition, it does show how geography can be combined with comparative advantage, and indicates the relative contributions of the two sets of forces.

5.3 Evidence from Subnational Studies

In this section we consider the lessons that we can learn from subnational empirical work. The literature here is much larger than the corresponding international literature, and addresses the issues of the existence and determinants of clustering. The reasons for the greater amount of empirical evidence would appear to be twofold. First, urban and regional economists have been interested in agglomeration economies for a longer period; second, comparable production data is more readily available for subnational units, particularly in the US. We organize our review in two sections. The first considers a number of papers that take a step back and test for the existence of localization against the alternative hypothesis of the random location of "lumpy" activity. The second section considers the determinants of specialization and localization at the subnational level.

5.3.1 LOCATION, LUMPINESS AND RANDOMNESS

In Section 5.1 we identified five properties that we think a good measure of localization or specialization should possess. The measures that we discussed earlier generally satisfied the first two of these properties (comparability and controlling for the distribution of aggregate activity). In this section we discuss the literature that proposes measures of localization that satisfy some of the remaining properties. That is: measures that control for industrial lumpiness (property 3); that consider the problem of spatial unit boundaries (property 4); and that assess the extent of localization against the null hypothesis of randomness (property 5).

Industries characterized by higher increasing returns to scale (larger plants) will *ceteris paribus* appear more spatially concentrated than industries characterized by low increasing returns (small plants), simply because they have relatively few plants. This observation is important if we want to compare the location of (say) aircraft manufacturing with that of textiles. After controlling for this, we might want to assess whether the patterns that we see are systematic or whether they could have occurred by chance. This emphasis on randomness is particularly appropriate in situations where departure from randomness (localization) is driven mainly by cumulative causation, because the multiple-equilibrium properties of these models tell us that localization will occur, but not where it will occur.

Ellison and Glaeser (1997) were the first to address these issues directly. They specify a stylized location model where industries may be localized because: (1) overall activity is agglomerated; (2) activity within the industry is concentrated in a few randomly located plants; and (3) activity within the industry is concentrated in non-randomly located plants. To separate out the third cause of localization from the first two, they proceed as follows. First, they define a measure of sectoral relative to overall localization, $G_{EG}^k = \Sigma_i(\ell_i^k - \ell_i)^2/(1 - \Sigma_i\ell_i^2)$ where using our earlier notation $\ell_i^k = y_i^k/\Sigma_i y_i^k$ is location i's share of industry k, and $\ell_i = \Sigma_k y_i^k/\Sigma_i\Sigma_k y_i^k$ is location i's share in overall activity. This measures the extent of localization for industry k over and above localization of activity as a whole. To allow for plant size, they first construct the standard Herfindahl index of *industrial* concentration for industry k, $H^k = \Sigma_j(z_j^k)^2$ where z_j^k is the share of *plant j* in total industry k output. They then use this to construct a measure, γ_{EG}^k, that controls for the localization that would arise just as a consequence of plant size and industrial concentration. The measure takes the form, $\gamma_{EG}^k = (G_{EG}^k - H^k)/(1 - H^k)$. They show that the expected value of this measure is zero if plants are randomly located, so positive values of γ_{EG}^k indicate "excess localization," relative to activity as a whole and relative to random location of the industry's plants.

Ellison and Glaeser calculate this measure for the location of employment in 459 industries across 50 states in 1987. They find that 446 of the 459 industries are more localized than we would expect to arise randomly. However, although localization is ubiquitous, many industries are only slightly localized, suggesting that previous literature may have over-emphasized the extent of localization. No clear classification of industries by extent of excess localization is possible – the characteristics of least and most localized industries are quite variable. Ellison and Glaeser calculate the index at a number of different spatial scales. The results suggest that departures from randomness are strongest at the county level, substantial between counties in the same state, but fairly weak at the regional level. They also calculate a related index of co-agglomeration. For both three- and two-digit industries, there is some evidence that subindustries within these categories co-agglomerate, although the extent of co-agglomeration varies substantially across industries. There is also some evidence of co-agglomeration among industries with strong upstream and downstream linkages.

Similar indices have been calculated by Maurel and Sedillot (1999) for France, and Devereux et al. (1999) for the UK. There are cross-country similarities in the most and least localized industries. For example, hosiery, jewellery, other carpets, and spirit distilling appear in the top 20 most concentrated industries in both the UK and US, while cutlery, woolen, and periodicals are among the top 20 most localized industries in France and the UK. One could argue that this is indicative of second-nature effects given the very different first-nature geographies of the three countries. Finally, Duranton and Overman (2001) suggest a further development of Ellison and Glaeser which allows for the fact the location decisions are made over a continuous rather than discrete space (property 4); and that also allows them to assess whether departures from randomness are statistically significant or not (property 5).

5.3.2 DETERMINANTS OF LOCALIZATION AND SPECIALIZATION

The results outlined above suggest that internal returns to scale play an important role in understanding the distribution of activity at the subnational level, and that there is localization in a large number of industries that cannot purely be explained by industrial concentration (plant size). In attempting to explain this excess localization, regional and urban economists seem far readier to admit that *both* comparative advantage and economic geography factors could matter for determining location. Possibly, this reflects the fact that the assumption of exogenous endowments of some factors (capital, skilled labor) is a much stronger one at the subnational level where mobility is substantially higher. We start by considering a small number of papers that attempt to assess the proportion of excess localization that can be explained by internal returns and the distribution of endowments. We then consider attempts to explain the residual excess localization.

Ellison and Glaeser (1999) consider how much localization can be explained by natural advantage by studying the shares of US states in different industries as a function of the interaction between industry and state characteristics. As discussed in section 5.2, Midelfart-Knarvik, Overman, and Venables (2000) show that such an interaction formulation can be derived as the solution to a fully specified trade model. Ellison and Glaeser (1999) use data on four-digit manufacturing for 1987. They have information on a range of state characteristics, including: electricity price; natural gas price; coal price; farmland; average manufacturing wage; percentage labor force with high skill; population density. The corresponding industry characteristics are: electricity use; natural gas use; coal use; agricultural input share; wages/value added; skilled labor intensity; percentage of output sold to consumers.

Their estimation takes the form of regressing state-industry employment shares (ℓ_i^k in our notation) on a non-linear function of state characteristics interacted with industry characteristics. They find that about 20 percent of the variation in these shares is explained by the characteristics, and suggest that this could increase to 50 percent with inclusion of more characteristics. There are problems with their approach, particularly in so far as it is not clear that some of the location characteristics are first-nature – this is particularly true of the wage, skill composition and population density measures. If they are not first-nature, they are surely endogenous and this problem is not corrected for. This makes both interpretation and evaluation of the results difficult. Even ignoring these problems, their results suggest that between 50 and 80 percent (at least) of localization at the state level is unexplained by natural advantages.

So, what explains the residual excess localization? Assuming that we have correctly conditioned for all other factors, the simple, but uninformative answer is "some sort of agglomeration economy." There are several related but separate strands to the empirical research on agglomeration economies. The first strand attempts to assess the importance of localization versus urbanization economies in explaining the location of activity. Localization economies occur when there is a positive externality on firm productivity from other firms in the same sector; urbanization when there is a positive externality on firm productivity from other firms in different sectors. Either type of externality could arise from Marshall's three agglomeration forces – knowledge spillovers, labor market externalities or input–output linkages. Research also considers whether or not these returns are static or dynamic and what characteristics of the local environment matter for determining the extent of these externalities. See Henderson (1999) for a recent discussion of the issues. Henderson (1988) is most closely associated with the finding that localization increases firm productivity, while Henderson et al. (1995) find that localization also increases growth. This contrasts with the results of Glaeser et al. (1992) who find that diversity raises growth. The issue remains unresolved and Combes (2001) identifies problems with the empirical approach in this literature.

A related literature has examined the effect of the scale or density of economic activity on productivity levels. Early studies of the effect of city population size on productivity include Sveikauskas (1975), Segal (1976), and Moomaw (1981). Ciccone and Hall (1996) use information on employment densities for US counties to construct an index of the density of economic activity at the state-level. According to their preferred instrumental variables' estimates, doubling the employment density in a county increases state labor productivity by 6 percent and total factor productivity (TFP) by 4 percent. Caballero and Lyons (1990, 1992) find substantially larger returns to scale for aggregate manufacturing in both the US and in Europe than for individual two-digit industries. One explanation is the existence of external economies of scale, although this interpretation has recently been questioned. Basu and Fernald (1997) find that estimates of returns to scale vary substantially according to whether one uses data on value-added or gross output, and argue that aggregation bias provides a more plausible explanation for these empirical findings.

Of more interest for us here, are the few papers that attempt to distinguish between the microeconomic mechanisms that might cause agglomeration economies. Dumais et al. (1997) use plant births and deaths to attempt to distinguish between the three possible sources. For selected years they have data on the population of manufacturing establishment in the US. Plants can be classified into 134 sectors located in one of 307 metropolitan areas and by US state. They find that, despite large plant turnover (73 percent of plants that existed in 1972 had closed by 1992) the extent of localization remains constant. To examine the determinants of localization, they construct three different measures. They use input–output tables to construct measures of supplier presence and product customer presence. To capture labor market agglomerations they construct a measure based on the risk of closure and a comparison of the plant's labor market mix to the average labor mix in the area. Finally, they construct a proxy for information flows using weights derived on co-ownership across multiple industries. With some caveats, their broad findings suggest that inputs help explain where existing firms locate new plants, while output matters more for plants created by new firms. Neither effect was very strong compared to the importance of labor mix (which was particularly important for new firms). Technology spillovers, although poorly proxied by their measure also seem to be important. Finally, input–output linkages seemed to be more important at the state level than the metropolitan level, consistent with assertions in some of the theoretical literature that these are generally useful for explaining large-scale agglomerations (Krugman, 1991b). Devereux et al. (1999, 2001) present some results along the same lines for the UK.

As we suggested, the technological proxy used by Dumais et al. is not a particularly good one. We do however have some additional evidence on the importance of *local* technological spillovers between firms. A series of papers starting with Jaffe et al. (1993) have compared the location of patent citations with the location of cited patents. For the US they find that the citation to domestic patents is more likely to be from domestic patents. They find a similar pattern at the state and particularly at the standard metropolitan statistical area level, even after conditioning for the localization of particular industries. This is the strongest evidence we have to date on the importance of local knowledge spillovers in determining location.

We have only been able to provide a very brief overview of a larger literature on the determinants of subnational localization. What lessons can students of international location take from this collection of subnational studies? First, and perhaps most importantly, nearly all the evidence that we have at a subnational level suggests that both endowments *and* geography matter in determining location. Second, the most informative descriptions of localization try to address all of the properties that we outline above. In addition, there is a clear feeling that these descriptive measures will be more informative if they can be closely related to theory. Finally, we may need to concentrate on developing micro- (firm-) level data rather than aggregate data if we wish to separate out the forces driving both subnational and international location decisions.

6 CONCLUDING COMMENTS

The evidence surveyed here strongly suggests the importance of geography in determining international economic interactions, in influencing cross-country income distribution, and in shaping the structure of production across space.

While the current state of knowledge establishes that geography matters, we know much less about exactly why it matters. Distance clearly chokes off economic interactions, but is it because of transport costs, time costs, fixed costs of entering new markets, informational barriers, or difficulties encountered in managing remote supply chains or production operations? Similarly, activity benefits from being agglomerated, but are the benefits from demand and supply linkages, from pools of labor-market skills, or from technical spillovers; and if the last of these, exactly how are they transmitted?

Answering these questions is crucially important as new technologies and further trade liberalizations continue to drive the process of globalization. What activities will relocate to developing countries, and what stay in established centers? What should be the trade and investment priorities of geographically disadvantaged regions? What are the implications of globalization for international inequality? Fortunately, both the analytical frameworks and the rich microeconomic data sets needed to address these questions are now becoming available, although much work remains to be done.

Acknowledgments

This work is supported by the UK ESRC funded Centre for Economic Performance at the London School of Economics. We are grateful to James Anderson, James Harrigan, James Markusen, and seminar participants at the NBER Spring Meetings, for helpful comments.

Notes

1 We use the term market-access to measure how well placed a location is with respect to markets, and supplier-access to measure how well placed it is with respect to suppliers.

2 The "folk theorem" of location theory says that, in the absence of increasing returns there will be "backyard capitalism," with production potentially locating wherever there is demand.

3 We make the usual assumption that the same price indices, G_i^k, hold for both consumers and intermediate users of good k in country i.

4 For recent reviews of the theoretical economic geography literature, see Neary (2001) and Ottaviano and Puga (1997). Hanson (2000b) surveys empirical work, concentrating largely on regional and urban research. For a review of the empirical trade literature that concentrates on the predictions of neoclassical theory, see Leamer and Levinsohn (1995).

5 See also Deardorff (1998).

6 These have the advantage of controlling for the extent of a country's barriers to trade with all of its partners – what Anderson and van Wincoop (2000) call "multilateral resistance."

7 See, for example, Feenstra et al. (2001), Frankel (1997), and Soloaga and Winters (1999). The difference in estimated coefficients arises, at least in part, because of the treatment of zeros. Tobit estimation typically yields larger coefficients.

8 This elasticity is on the transport cost factor, thus doubling transport costs from 20 percent to 40 percent reduces trade volumes to $(1.4/1.2)^{-3} = 0.63$ of their initial level.

9 See Anderson and Marcouiller (2002) for an analysis of the role of insecurity and risk of appropriation in determining trade patterns.

10 For further discussion of the impact of new technologies see Leamer and Storper (2000) and Venables (2001).

11 For a recent study of the effect of institutions on economic performance, which uses variation in settler mortality as an instrumental variable for the type of institutions adopted by European colonists, see Acemoglu et al. (2000). McArthur and Sachs (2001) emphasize the role of both institutions and physical geography.

12 For example, suppose that intermediates account for 50 percent of costs and transport costs are borne by the producing country. *Ad valorem* transport costs of 10 percent on both final output and intermediate goods have the effect of reducing domestic value-added by 30 percent (compared to a country facing zero transport costs); the reduction in value-added rises to 60 percent for transport costs of 20 percent and to 90 percent for transport costs of 30 percent. See Radelet and Sachs (1998) for further discussion of this point.

13 See Leamer (1988) for a related measure of international openness.

14 See also Fujita et al. (1999), chapter 14.

15   A similar pattern of results is observed using data on manufacturing wages per worker for a subset of countries.

16   The full results including own-country effects are given in Redding and Venables. The market-access measure including both foreign and domestic effects explains up to 75 percent of the cross-country income distribution.

17   These estimates imply a value of $\sigma/(\sigma - 1)$ greater than 1, and are thus consistent with increasing returns to scale. See Antweiler and Trefler (2000) for evidence of increasing returns to scale in a number of manufacturing industries from data on the net factor content of trade.

18   In Helpman (1998), the value of $\sigma(1 - \mu)$ is crucial for the determinants of agglomeration. All the parameter estimates in table 12.2 imply a value of $\sigma(1 - \mu) < 1$, so that an increase in transport costs increases the likelihood of agglomeration.

19   Roback (1982) and Kahn (1995) emphasize the relationship between local amenities and wages and land rents within cities. Rauch (1993) and Moretti (1998) provide empirical evidence of city-level human capital externalities, although Ciccone and Peri (2000) argue that these disappear when one controls for the potential complementarity between workers with different levels of human capital. Glaeser and Mare (1994) stress the role of human capital accumulation in explaining the urban wage premium.

20   See Dekle and Eaton (1999) for an analysis of wage and land rent gradients across Japanese prefectures. The wage and land rent data are used to estimate the effect of the agglomeration of economic activity on measured productivity. Relocating value-added 100 km away is found to reduce its impact on productivity by 9 percent in finance and 1 percent in manufacturing.

21   There is a literature concerned with the more specific question of the effects of export manufacturing in *maquiladoras* on employment and the relative wages of skilled and unskilled workers. See, for example, Feenstra and Hanson (1997).

22   To isolate regional wage differentials that are specific to the apparel industry, the data on wages in the apparel sector in each state relative to Mexico City are normalized by average manufacturing wages in each state relative to Mexico City. Similar estimation results are found using unnormalized wages. See Hanson (1996) for further discussion.

23   Even in the absence of underlying technology differences, measured aggregate Total Factor Productivity (TFP) may vary substantially across locations due to differences in the transport cost inclusive price of manufacturing inputs and output. Cross-country differences in measured productivity may partly reflect true underlying technology differences and partly reflect the considerations of access to markets and sources of supply emphasized above.

24   We are following Kim (1995), who followed Hoover (1936). Amiti (1999) points out the similarity to Balassa's (1965) measure of revealed comparative advantage.

25   The calculation of $gini^k(r_i^k)$ follows a method directly analogous to that used in the personal income distribution literature. First, rank regions by their location quotients in descending order. Second, evaluate the cumulative percentage of employment in industry k over the regions ($cemp^k$). Third, evaluate the cumulative percentage of employment in all industries over the regions ($cemp_i^k$). Graphing $cemp^k$ (y-axis) against $cemp_i^k$ (x-axis), we obtain a "localization curve." The area between the 45 degree line and the localization curve divided by the area under the 45 degree line is the locational gini.

26   See Amiti (1998) for discussion and comparison of some of these measures.

27   The exogenous case corresponding to an Armington model; the difference is immaterial as $\sigma \to \infty$ and all varieties are perfect substitutes.

28   For a complete derivation of the home-market effect, see Fujita et al. (1999), chapter 4.

See also the discussion in Krugman (1980), Krugman and Venables (1990), Davis (1999), and Krugman and Venables (2001). External economies of scale provide an alternative candidate explanation for home-market effects and are discussed in further detail below (see Markusen (1990) for an analysis of the microfoundations of external economies).

29 The exponent on distance, γ, is found by estimating a gravity model like equation (12.8).

30 r_i^k is the location quotient of equation (12.14) up to the normalization $\Sigma_k \Sigma_i y_i^k = 1$

References

Acemoglu D., S. Johnson, and J. Robinson 2000: The colonial origins of comparative development: An empirical investigation. NBER working paper no. 7771.

Amiti, M. 1998: New trade theories and industrial location in the EU: A survey of evidence. *Oxford Review of Economic Policy*, 14, 2, 45–53.

Amiti, M. 1999: Specialisation patterns in Europe. *Weltwirtschaftliches Archiv*, 134, 4, 573–93.

Anderson, J. and S. Marcouiller 2002: Insecurity and the pattern of trade: An empirical investigation. *Review of Economics and Statistics*, 84, 2, 342–52.

Anderson J. E. and E. Van Wincoop 2000: Gravity with gravitas: A solution to the border puzzle. Boston University, mimeo.

Antweiler, W. and D. Trefler 2000: Increasing returns and all that: A view from trade. NBER working paper no. 7941.

Audretsch, D. and M. Feldman 1996: R&D spillovers and the geography of innovation and production. *American Economic Review*, 86, 3, 630–40.

Bairoch, P. 1988: *Cities and Economic Development: From the Dawn of History to the Present*. Chicago: University of Chicago Press.

Balassa, B. 1965: Trade liberalisation and "Revealed comparative advantage." *The Manchester School of Economic and Social Sciences*, 33, 99–123. .

Basu, S. and J. Fernald 1997: Returns to scale in US production: Estimates and implications. *Journal of Political Economy*, 105, 2, 249–83.

Branstetter, L. 2001: Are knowledge spillovers international or intra-national in scope? Micro-econometric evidence from the US and Japan. *Journal of International Economics*, 53, 1, 53–79.

Brulhart, M. 1998: Economic geography, industry location, and trade: The evidence. *World Economy*, 21, 6, 775–801.

Brulhart, M. and J. Torstensson 1996: Regional integration, scale economies and industry location. CEPR discussion paper no. 1435.

Caballero, R. and R. Lyons 1990: Internal versus external economies in European industry. *European Economic Review*, 34, 4, 805–30.

Caballero, R. and R. Lyons 1992: External effects in US pro-cyclical productivity. *Journal of Monetary Economics*, 29, 2, 209–25.

Cairncross, F. 1997: *The Death of Distance*. Boston: Harvard Business School Press.

Ciccone, A. and R. Hall 1996: Productivity and the density of economic activity. *American Economic Review*, 86, 1, 54–70.

Ciccone, A. and G. Peri 2000: Human capital and externalities in cities. CEPR discussion paper no. 2599.

Clark, C., F. Wilson, and J. Bradley 1969: Industrial location and economic potential in Western Europe. *Regional Studies*, 3, 197–212.

Coe, D. and E. Helpman 1995: International R&D spillovers. *European Economic Review*, 39, 5, 859–87.

Combes, P. P. 2001: Marshall–Arrow–Romer externalities and city growth. Paris: CNRS–CERAS, mimeograph.

Cowell, F. 1995: *Measuring Inequality*, London School of Economics Handbooks in Economics Series, 2nd edn. Hemel Hempstead: Prentice-Hall.

Davis, D. R. 1999: The home market, trade, and industrial structure. *American Economic Review*, 88, 5, 1264–76.

Davis, D. and D. Weinstein 1998: Market access, economic geography, and comparative advantage: An empirical assessment. NBER working paper no. 6787.

Davis, D. and D. Weinstein 1999: Economic geography and regional production structure: An empirical investigation. *European Economic Review*, 43, 379–407.

Deardorff, A. 1998: Determinants of bilateral trade: Does gravity work in a neoclassical world? In J. Frankel (ed.), *The Regionalization of the World Economy*, Chicago: NBER & Chicago University Press, chapter 1.

Dekle, R. and J. Eaton 1999: Agglomeration and land rents: Evidence from the prefectures. *Journal of Urban Economics*, 46, 200–14.

Devereux, M., R. Griffith, and H. Simpson 1999: The geographic distribution of productive activity in the UK. Institute for Fiscal Studies working paper no. W99/26.

Devereux, M., R. Griffith and H. Simpson 2001: The geography of firm formation. London: Institute for Fiscal Studies, mimeo.

Dicken, P. 1998: *Global Shift: Transforming the World Economy*. London: Chapman.

Dicken, P. and P. Lloyd 1977: *Location in Space*. New York: Harper and Row.

Dixit, A. K. and J. E. Stiglitz 1977: Monopolistic competition and optimum product diversity. *American Economic Review*, 67, 297–308.

Dumais, G., G. Ellison, and E. Glaeser 1997: Geographic concentration as a dynamic process. NBER working paper no. 6270.

Duranton, G. and H. G. Overman 2001: *Localisation in UK Manufacturing Industries: Assessing Non-randomness Using Micro-geographic Data*. London: London School of Economics.

Eaton, J. and S. Kortum 1999a: International technology diffusion: Theory and measurement. *International Economic Review*, 40, 3, 537–70.

Eaton, J. and S. Kortum 1999b: *Technology, Geography, and Trade*. Boston University.

Ellison, G. and E. Glaeser 1997: Geographic concentration in US manufacturing industries: A dartboard approach. *Journal of Political Economy*, 105, 5, 889–927.

Ellison, G. and E. Glaeser 1999: The geographic concentration of industry: Does natural advantage explain agglomeration? *American Economic Review*, 89, 2, 311–16.

Feenstra, R. and G. Hanson 1997: Foreign direct investment and relative wages: Evidence from Mexico's maquiladoras. *Journal of International Economics*, 42, 371–94.

Feenstra, R., R. Lipsey, and H. Bowen 1997: World trade flows, 1970–1992, with production and tariff data. NBER working paper no. 5910.

Feenstra, R. C., J. A. Markusen, and A. K. Rose 2001: Understanding the home market effect and the gravity equation: The role of differentiated goods. *Canadian Journal of Economics*, 34, 2, 430–47.

Frankel, J. A. 1997: *Regional Trading Blocs in the World Economic System*. Washington, DC: Institute for International Economics.

Frankel, J. and D. Romer 1999: Does trade cause growth? *American Economic Review*, 89, 3, 379–99.

Fujita, M., P. Krugman, and A. J. Venables 1999: *The Spatial Economy: Cities, Regions and International Trade*. Cambridge, MA: MIT Press.

Gallup, J. and J. Sachs 2000: The economic burden of malaria. Harvard University, CID working paper no. 52.

Gallup, J. L. and J. Sachs (with A. D. Mellinger) 1999: Geography and economic development. In B. Pleskovic and J. E. Stiglitz (eds.), *Annual World Bank Conference on Development Economics, 1998*, Washington, DC: World Bank.

Glaeser, E. and D. Mare 1994: Cities and skills. NBER working paper no. 4728.

Glaeser, E., H. Kallal, J. Scheinkman, and A. Shleifer 1992: Growth in cities. *Journal of Political Economy*, 100, 1126–52.

Haaland, J., H. Kind, K. Midelfart-Knarvik, and J. Torstensson 1999: What determines the economic geography of Europe? CEPR discussion paper no. 2072.

Hall, R. and C. Jones 1999: Why do some countries produce so much more output per worker than others? *Quarterly Journal of Economics*, 114, 1, 83–116.

Hanson, G. 1996: Localization economies, vertical organization, and trade. *American Economic Review*, 86, 5, 1266–78.

Hanson, G. 1997: Increasing returns, trade, and the regional structure of wages. *Economic Journal*, 107, 113–33.

Hanson, G. 1998a: Market potential, increasing returns, and geographic concentration. NBER working paper no. 6429.

Hanson, G. 1998b: Regional adjustment to trade liberalisation. *Regional Science and Urban Economics*, 28, 4, 419–44.

Hanson, G. 1998c: North American economic integration and industry location. *Oxford Review of Economic Policy*, 14, 2, 30–44.

Hanson, G. 2000a: Market potential, increasing returns, and geographic concentration. University of Michigan, mimeo. (Revised version of NBER working paper no. 6249, February 1998.)

Hanson, G. 2000b: Scale economies and the geographic concentration of industry. NBER working paper no. 8013.

Harris, C. 1954: The market as a factor in the localization of industry in the United States. *Annals of the Association of American Geographers*, 44, 315–48.

Head, K. and J. Ries 2001: Increasing returns versus national product differentiation as an explanation for the pattern of US–Canada trade. *American Economic Review*, 91, 4, 858–76.

Helliwell, J. 1996: Do national borders matter for Quebec's trade? *Canadian Journal of Economics*, 29, 3, 507–22.

Helpman, E. 1998: The size of regions. In D. Pines, E. Sadka, and I. Zilcha (eds.), *Topics in Public Economics: Theoretical and Applied Analysis*, Cambridge: Cambridge University Press.

Henderson, J. V. 1988: *Urban Development: Theory, Fact and Illusion*. Oxford: Oxford University Press.

Henderson, J. V. 1999: Marshall's scale economies. NBER working paper no. 7358.

Henderson, J. V., A. Kuncoro, and M. Turner 1995: Industrial development and cities. *Journal of Political Economy*, 103, 1067–81.

Henderson, J. V., T. Lee, and J-Y Lee 1999: Externalities and industrial deconcentration under rapid growth. Brown University, mimeo.

Hoover, E. 1936: Spatial price discrimination. Reprinted 1995, in M. Greenhut and G. Norman (eds.), *The Economics of Location, vol. 2: Space and Value*, Cheltenham: Edward Elgar.

Hummels, D. 1995: Global income patterns: Does geography play a role? PhD thesis, University of Michigan, chapter 2.

Hummels, D. 1999a: Towards a geography of trade costs. Purdue University, mimeo.

Hummels, D. 1999b: Have international transport costs declined? Purdue University, mimeo.

Hummels, D. 2000: Time as a trade barrier. Purdue University, mimeo.

Jaffe, A. and M. Trajtenberg 1998: International knowledge flows: Evidence from patent citations. NBER working paper no. 6507.

Jaffe, A., M. Trajtenberg, and R. Henderson 1993: Geographic localisation of knowledge spillovers as evidenced by patent citations. *Quarterly Journal of Economics*, 63, 3, 577–98.

Kahn, M. 1995: A revealed preference approach to ranking city quality of life. *Journal of Urban Economics*, 38, 221–35.

Keeble, D., P. Owens, and C. Thompson 1982: Regional accessibility and economic potential in the European Community. *Regional Studies*, 16, 419–32.

Keller, W. 1998: Are international R&D spillovers trade-related? Analyzing spillovers among randomly matched trade partners. *European Economic Review*, 1469–81.

Keller, W. 2000: Do trade patterns and technology flows affect productivity growth? *World Bank Economic Review*, 17–47.

Keller, W. 2002: Geographic localization of international technology diffusion. *American Economic Review*, 92, 1, 120–42.

Kim, S. 1995: Expansion of markets and the geographic distribution of economic activities: The trends in US regional manufacturing structure, 1860–1987. *Quarterly Journal of Economics*, 110, 881–908.

Kim, S. 1997: Regions, resources, and economic geography: Sources of US regional comparative advantage, 1880–1987. NBER working paper no. 6322.

Knack, S. and P. Keefer 1997: Does social capital have an economic payoff? *Quarterly Journal of Economics*, 112, 1251–88.

Krugman, P. 1980: Scale economies, product differentiation, and the pattern of trade. *American Economic Review*, 70, 950–9.

Krugman, P. 1991a: Increasing returns and economic geography. *Journal of Political Economy*, 99, 3, 483–99.

Krugman, P. 1991b: *Geography and Trade*, Cambridge, MA: MIT Press.

Krugman, P. and A. J. Venables 1990: Integration and the competitiveness of the peripheral industry. In C. Bliss and J. Braga De Macedo (eds.), *Unity With Diversity in the European Economy: The Community's Southern Frontier*, Cambridge: Cambridge University Press.

Krugman, P. and A. J. Venables 1995: Globalization and the inequality of nations. *Quarterly Journal of Economics*, 110, 4, 857–80.

Krugman, P. and A. J. Venables 2001: *How Robust is the Home Market Effect?* London: LSE.

Leamer, E. 1988: Measures of openness. In R. Baldwin (ed.), *Trade Policy Issues and Empirical Analysis*, Chicago: University of Chicago Press, 147–200.

Leamer, E. 1997: Access to Western markets and Eastern effort. In S. Zecchini (ed.), *Lessons from the Economic Transition, Central and Eastern Europe in the 1990s*, Dordrecht: Kluwer Academic Publishers, 503–26.

Leamer, E. and J. Levinsohn 1995: International trade theory: The evidence. In G. Grossman and K. Rogoff (eds.), *Handbook of International Economics*, vol 3, Amsterdam: Elsevier Science.

Leamer, E. and M. Storper 2000: *The Economic Geography of the Internet Age*, UCLA.

Limao, N. and A. J. Venables 2001: Infrastructure, geographical disadvantage, transport costs and trade. *World Bank Economic Review*, 15, 3, 451–79.

McCallum, J. 1995: National borders matter: Canada–US regional trade patterns. *American Economic Review*, 85, 3, 615–23.

Markusen, J. 1990: Micro-foundations of external economies. *Canadian Journal of Economics*, August, 495–508.

Maurel, F. and B. Sedillot 1999: A measure of the geographic concentration in French manufacturing industries. *Regional Science and Urban Economics*, 29, 5, 575–604.

McArthur, J. and J. Sachs 2001: Institutions and geography: Comment on Acemoglu, Johnson, and Robinson 2000. NBER working paper no. 8114.

Midelfart-Knarvik, K., H. G. Overman, S. J. Redding and A. J. Venables 2000: The location of European industry. Economic papers no. 142, Brussels: European Commission, D-G for Economic and Financial Affairs.

Midelfart-Knarvik, K., H. G. Overman, and A. J. Venables 2000: Comparative advantage and economic geography. CEPR discussion paper no. 2618.

Moomaw, R. 1981: Productivity and city size: A critique of the evidence. *Quarterly Journal of Economics*, 96, 4, 675–88.

Moretti, E. 1998: Social returns to education and human capital externalities: Evidence from cities. Berkeley: University of California, Center for Labor Economics, working paper no. 9.

Neary, P. 2001: Of hype and hyperbolas: Introducing the new economic geography. *Journal of Economic Literature*, 39, June, 536–61.

Ottaviano, G. and Puga, D. 1997: Agglomeration in the global economy: A survey of the new economic geography. *World Economy*, 21, 6, 707–31.

Radelet, S. and J. Sachs 1998: Shipping costs, manufactured exports, and economic growth. Paper presented at the American Economic Association Meetings, Harvard University, mimeo.

Rauch, J. 1993: Productivity gains from geographical concentration of human capital: Evidence from cities. *Journal of Urban Economics*, 34, 380–400.

Rauch, J. E 1999: Networks versus markets in international trade. *Journal of International Economics*, 48, 1, 7–35.

Rauch, J. and V. Trindade 1999: Ethnic Chinese networks in international trade. NBER working paper no. 7189.

Redding, S. and A. J. Venables 2000: Economic geography and international inequality. CEPR discussion paper no. 2568.

Roback, J. 1982: Wages, rents, and the quality of life. *Journal of Political Economy*, 90, 1257–88.

Roberts, M. and J. Tybout 1997: The decision to export in Columbia: An empirical model of entry with sunk costs. *American Economic Review*, September, 545–64.

Sachs, J. 2000: Tropical underdevelopment. Harvard University, Center for International Development, September, mimeo.

Sachs, J. and A. Warner 1999: The big push, natural resource booms and growth. *Journal of Development Economics*, 59, 1, 43–76.

Segal, D. 1976: Are there returns to scale in city size? *Review of Economics and Statistics*, 58, 3, 339–50.

Soloaga, I. and A. Winters 1999: Regionalism in the nineties: What effect on trade? CEPR discussion paper no. 2183.

Sveikauskas, L. 1975: The productivity of cities. *Quarterly Journal of Economics*, 89, 3, 393–413.

Venables, A. J. 1996: Equilibrium locations of vertically linked industries. *International Economic Review*, 37, 341–59.

Venables, A. J. 1999: The international division of industries: Clustering and comparative advantage in a multi-industry model. *Scandinavian Journal of Economics*, 101, 4, 495–513.

Venables, A. J. 2001: Geography and international inequalities: The impact of new technologies. LSE, Centre for Economic Performance discussion paper.

Venables, A. and N. Limao 1999: Geographical disadvantage: A Heckscher–Ohlin–Von Thunen model of international specialisation. CEPR discussion paper no. 2305.

Von Thunen, J. H. 1826: *Der isolierte Staat in Beziehung auf landtschaft under nationalokonomie*, Hamburg. (English trans. by C. M. Wartenberg 1966, *Von Thunen's Isolated State*, Oxford: Pergamon Press.)

Wei, S. 1996: Intra-national versus international trade: How stubborn are nations in global integration? NBER working paper no. 5531.

WIFO 1999: Specialisation and (geographic) concentration of European manufacturing. Background paper for *The Competitiveness of European Industry: The 1999 Report*, EC Enterprise Directorate-General, working paper no. 1, Brussels.

Williamson, J.G. 1965: Regional inequality and the process of national development. *Economic Development and Cultural Change*, 13, 3–45.

13

Plant- and Firm-Level Evidence on "New" Trade Theories

James R. Tybout

CHAPTER OUTLINE

By relaxing the assumption of perfect competition, the "new" trade theory has generated a rich body of predictions concerning the effects of commercial policy on price–cost mark-ups, firm sizes, exports, productivity and profitability among domestic producers. This chapter critically assesses the plant- and firm-level evidence on these linkages. Several robust findings are identified. First, mark-ups generally fall with import competition. Second, import-competing firms cut back their production levels when foreign competition intensifies. Third, trade rationalizes production in the sense that markets for the most efficient plants are expanded, but large import-competing firms tend to simultaneously contract. Fourth, exposure to foreign competition often improves intra-plant efficiency. Fifth, firms that engage in international activities tend to be larger, more productive, and supply higher quality products. Finally, the short-run and long-run effects of commercial policy on exports and market structure depend upon initial conditions, sunk entry costs, and the extent of firm heterogeneity.

1 INTRODUCTION

Two decades ago, in an effort to become more relevant, trade economists began developing models with imperfectly competitive product markets. The result was a richer body of theory that describes how commercial policy might affect price–cost mark-ups, firm sizes, productivity, exports, and profitability among domestic producers. The literature also yielded formal representations of the channels through which commercial policy might influence growth. This chapter selectively surveys and interprets the firm- and plant-level evidence that has emerged on these theories.

Section 2 focuses on three static predictions of the "new" trade theory that have attracted attention from empiricists. First, protection can change firms' pricing behavior, thereby affecting the allocative efficiency of the economy and the distribution of real income. Second, when trade policies affect prices, they generally also change the set of active producers and/or their output levels. These adjustments induce productivity changes through scale effects and market share reallocations. Finally, changes in the intensity of foreign competition and/or in firms' opportunities to export can affect their technical efficiency.[1]

Section 3 continues to discuss firm-level responses to policy reforms in terms of pricing decisions, output levels, exports and productivity. However, rather than focus on comparative statics, the models and evidence in this section are explicitly dynamic. They allow for sunk entry costs, firm heterogeneity, and uncertainty. Thus they highlight the relation between responses, expectations and initial conditions. Finally, Section 4 briefly recaps what is known and what we would like to know, then mentions some directions for future research.

2 STATIC RESULTS: MARK-UPS, SCALE, AND PRODUCTIVITY

2.1 Pricing

2.1.1 THEORY

Except when collusive equilibria are considered, trade models with imperfect competition treat firms' pricing decisions as determined by static profit maximization. Accordingly, the ratio of output prices (p) to marginal costs (c) is typically a decreasing function of the elasticity of demand (η) that firms face:

$$\frac{p}{c} = \left(\frac{\eta}{\eta-1}\right). \tag{13.1}$$

It follows that when trade liberalization increases η, mark-ups should fall.

This kind of elasticity effect has been generated by a variety of modeling devices. For example, under the "Armington assumption" that foreign and domestic goods are imperfect substitutes, the demand elasticity for domestic goods rises as the relative price of foreign goods falls (e.g., Devarajan and Rodrik, 1991). Or, when protection takes the form of non-tariff barriers (NTBs), the removal of a quota can create heightened competitive pressures (Bhagwati, 1978). Finally, when liberalization makes more product varieties available (Krugman, 1979) and/or reduces the market share of domestic firms (Helpman and Krugman, 1985, pp. 85–112), these producers may perceive their demand elasticities to rise.

When collusive equilibria are modeled, trade liberalization can change the pay-off to defecting, change firms' ability to punish defectors, or make it more difficult to detect them (Prusa, 1992; Staiger and Wolak, 1989).[2] It is possible that coopera-tive behavior will become unsustainable and mark-ups will fall. Or, some have argued that collusive firms are likely to use the (exogenous) tariff-distorted price of imports as a reference price.[3] By construction, models that begin from this latter pricing rule predict that trade liberalization will depress the price of import-competing goods.

2.1.2 EVIDENCE

Several simple methodologies have been used to link mark-ups to import competi-tion. Prices and marginal costs are rarely observable, so each technique infers mark-ups indirectly. The most common approach is to use the price–cost margin (PCM) – that is, sales net of expenditures on labor and materials over sales. If one assumes that unit labor and material costs are flat with respect to output, and we interpret c as short-run marginal costs, this statistic is a monotonic transformation of the mark-up in equation (13.1):

$$PCM_{it} = \frac{p_{it}q_{it} - c_{it}q_{it}}{p_{it}q_{it}} = \frac{p_{it} - c_{it}}{p_{it}},$$

where q_{it} is the physical output of the ith firm in period t. The PCM is also current economic profits (π_{it}) over sales plus the competitive return on capital over revenues:

$$PCM_{it} = \frac{\pi_{it}}{p_{it}q_{it}} + \frac{(r_t + \delta)k_{it}}{p_{it}q_{it}},$$

where k_{it} is the capital stock, r is the market return on capital, and δ is the deprecia-tion rate.[4] By this logic, after controlling for the ratio of capital stocks to sales, vari-ables that measure the intensity of foreign competition should contribute nothing to the explanation of price cost margins in industries where free entry drives profits to zero. On the other hand, if economic profits are present ($\pi_{it} > 0$), these variables should correlate negatively with the PCM whenever trade liberalization increases demand elasticities or destroys collusive equilibria.

Most analyses of mark-ups based on the PCM begin from a simple regression like:

$$PCM_{it} = \beta_0 + \beta_1(k_{it}/p_{it}q_{it}) + \beta_2 I_{it} + \ldots + \varepsilon_{it} \tag{13.2}$$

where i may index either firms or industries, and I_{it} is a proxy for the intensity of import competition – either the import penetration rate, the effective protection rate, or a license coverage ratio. (Import competition can only be observed at the industry level, so when firm-level data are used, I_{it} takes the same value for all firms within each industry.) When industry-level, cross-sectional data are used, the typical finding is that "the ratio of imports to domestic consumption tends to be negatively correlated with the profitability of domestic sellers, especially when domestic concentration is high" (Schmalensee, 1989, p. 976).[5]

A handful of studies have implemented equation (13.2) with plant-level panel data, controlling for permanent cross-industry differences in technology with industry dummies, and controlling for efficiency-related variation in mark-ups by including plant-level market shares.[6] Results for Mexico (1985–90), Colombia (1977–85), Chile (1979–86), and Morocco (1984–9) all reveal the same basic pattern: "In *every* country studied, relatively high industry-wide exposure to foreign competition is associated with lower [price–cost] margins, and the effect is concentrated in larger plants" (Roberts and Tybout, 1996, p. 196, emphasis in original). This pattern seems robust with respect to measures of import competition. In the case of Mexico, where it was possible to explore alternative measures of protection, the pattern appears whether one uses import penetration rates, effective protection rates, or license coverage ratios (Grether, 1996).

The standard interpretation for these *PCM* findings is that large firms and/or concentrated industries enjoy the most market power, hence their prices are the most responsive to heightened foreign competition. But other explanations are also plausible. For example, it might be that "relatively efficient industries are more profitable, and thus better able to compete against potential imports (low import penetration)" (Roberts and Tybout, 1996, p. 195). Or, concentration might reflect large sunk entry costs instead of market power (e.g., Hopenhayn, 1992). Then, rather than squeezing monopoly profits, unanticipated foreign competition cuts into the revenues that firms had expected would cover their entry costs and makes them sorry, ex post, that they entered (e.g., Albuquerque and Rebelo, 2000). If this latter interpretation is correct, one should observe output contractions in high-sunk-cost industries and exit in the others when trade is liberalized. There is some evidence that this happens, as I shall argue shortly.

An alternative methodology for linking foreign competition and pricing begins from the standard Tornqvist growth decomposition. Suppose the ith firm produces output according to $q_{it} = A_{it}h(\mathbf{v}_{it})$, where $\mathbf{v}_{it} = (v_{it}^1, v_{it}^2 \ldots v_{it}^J)$ is the vector of J factor inputs it uses and A_{it} measures its productivity level at time t. Then, suppressing time subscripts, output growth can be decomposed into a weighted-average of growth rates in the factor inputs and a residual productivity growth term:

$$d\ln(q_i) = \sum_{j=1}^{J} \frac{\partial \ln(h)}{\partial \ln(v_i^j)} d\ln(v_i^j) + d\ln(A_i). \tag{13.3}$$

Hall (1988) notes that when product markets are imperfect, this expression can be combined with equation (13.1) and the cost-minimization conditions $c_i = w_j/(\partial q_i/\partial v_i^j)$, $\forall_j$, to link output growth, input growth, productivity growth and mark-ups:

$$d\ln(q_i) = \left(\frac{\eta}{\eta-1}\right) \sum_{j=1}^{J} \left(\frac{v_i^j w_j}{p_i q_i}\right) d\ln(v_{ij}) + d\ln(A_i). \tag{13.4}$$

Further, he argues that a regression of output growth on the share-weighted rate of input growth, treating $d\ln(A_i)$ as the mean productivity growth rate plus noise, should reveal the price-cost mark-up as the slope coefficient.

By allowing η to vary through time with trade reforms, one can test whether import competition affects mark-ups. Similarly, one can look for trade-related shifts in the mean rate of productivity growth. Several analysts have performed these exercises by fitting generalized versions of equation (13.4) to plant-level panel data.[7] Studying Turkey and Côte d'Ivoire, respectively, Levinsohn (1993) and Harrison (1994) conclude that certain protected sectors had significant mark-ups during the sample period, and that these mark-ups fell with trade liberalization or exchange rate appreciation. Krishna and Mitra (1998, p. 447) repeat the exercise using a panel of Indian firms and report "strong evidence of an increase in competition (as reflected in price-marginal cost mark-ups)" after the 1991 trade liberalization. Thus studies based on Hall's approach are consistent with studies based on the *PCM* – both methodologies suggest that heightened foreign competition forces down mark-ups among domestic firms.

However, Hall's approach is subject to several criticisms. First, profit-maximizing firms should adjust their factor demands in response to productivity shocks. Hence consistent estimators of the slope coefficient in (13.4) require instruments that are correlated with factor stock growth but not with transitory productivity growth. It is difficult to argue that any available instruments satisfy this criterion, so mark-up estimates are probably biased upward, and may exhibit spurious correlation with the trade regime (Abbott et al., 1989).

Second, the framework presumes that firms face no adjustment costs. If some or all of the factors are subject to such costs they will be paid less than their marginal revenue product during upswings (when factor inputs are growing rapidly) and more during downswings (when factor inputs are growing slowly or shrinking). This measurement error is counter-cyclic and productivity growth tends to be *pro*-cyclic, so the estimated mark-up may be understated. Further, if import competition depresses demand for domestic goods, it may appear to eliminate monopoly power when it merely creates under-utilization of capacity.

Third, inputs and outputs are typically poorly measured and year-to-year fluctuations in these variables are particularly noisy. For example, due to gestation lags and changes in capacity utilization, growth in capital stocks is quite different from growth in capital services.[8] Perhaps more importantly, growth rates in physical output are not really observed; what we observe is growth in nominal revenue deflated by a broad price index. If firms that expand rapidly also tend to drive their output prices down relatively rapidly, as one would expect in a differentiated product market, than true output growth is understated when input growth is rapid, and the mark-up estimate should be biased downward.[9] I will discuss these measurement problems further in section 2.3.

2.2 The Firm Size Distribution and Its Effects On Productivity

2.2.1 THEORY

The output changes that accompany price adjustments depend upon whether markets are segmented and whether entry or exit barriers inhibit adjustments in the number of producers. Head and Ries (1999) provide a useful synopsis of some alternative theories. In the absence of collusive behavior, unilateral trade liberalization either reduces firm size (when there are entry/exit barriers or markets are segmented) or leaves it unchanged (when entry and exit are free).[10] Alternatively, when firms collude to slightly undercut the tariff-inclusive price of imports, trade liberalization *cum* free entry and scale economies forces import-competing firms that remain in the market to operate on a larger scale.

As Head and Ries (1999) acknowledge, the invariance of firm size under free entry and no collusion is an artifact of the Dixit–Stiglitz demand system that is used in the models they consider. More generally, free entry is consistent with firm size adjustments whenever trade liberalization induces changes in the demand elasticities (η) that domestic firms perceive. In particular, when demand elasticities rise with liberalization, price–cost mark-ups are squeezed according to equation (13.1), and this should induce exit until the remaining firms can make up on volume what they lost on margin.

Business and labor groups care about policy-induced output adjustments because they are generally accompanied by job creation or destruction and by capital gains or losses. But trade economists have focused mainly on the ways the changes in the size distribution affect productivity. To summarize these effects, I shall adopt Tybout and Westbrook's (1995) decomposition of industry-wide productivity growth. As before, let output at the ith firm in year t be given by $q_{it} = A_{it}h(v_{it})$, but now write $h(v_{it}) = \gamma(g(v_{it}))$ where $g(v_{it})$ is a constant-returns homothetic function of the input vector, v_{it}, and $\gamma(\cdot)$ captures any scale economies. Also, let $S_{it} = g(v_{it}) / \sum_{k=1}^{n_t} g(v_{kt})$ be this firm's market share in terms of its input use and let $B_{it} = q_{it}/g(v_{it})$ be its productivity level. Then the rate of growth in industry-wide average productivity, $B_t = \sum_{i=1}^{n_t} B_{it}S_{it}$, can be decomposed as:

$$\frac{dB_t}{B_t} = \sum_{i=1}^{n_t}\left(\frac{dg_{it}}{g_{it}}\right)(\mu_{it}-1)\left(\frac{q_{it}}{q_t}\right) + \sum_{i=1}^{n_t} dS_{it}\left(\frac{B_{it}}{B_t}\right) + \sum_{i=1}^{n_t}\left(\frac{dA_{it}}{A_{it}}\right)\left(\frac{q_{it}}{q_t}\right) \quad (13.5)$$

where $\mu_{it} = d\ln(q_{it})/d\ln(g_{it})$ measures returns to scale at the ith plant in year t. The first right-hand-side term above quantifies efficiency gains due to scale economies at the margin, the second term quantifies gains due to market share reallocations toward relatively efficient producers, and the last term picks up residual intra-firm average efficiency changes that are unrelated to internal scale economies. I shall hereafter refer to these three quantities as *scale effects*, *market share effects* and *technical efficiency effects*.

In most trade models, all firms within an industry are characterized by a common technology and face identical demand conditions, so they expand or contract together in response to liberalization. Productivity gains or losses, when they are present, thus come exclusively from scale effects.[11] However, several models deal explicitly with intra-industry heterogeneity and show how size adjustments (including entry or exit) might affect productivity through the market share effects. For example, Bond (1986) shows how heterogeneous workers might endogenously allocate themselves between entrepreneurial positions and salaried employment. In his "normal" case, protection of the industrial sector increases firm heterogeneity and lowers average productivity by drawing low quality entrepreneurs into managerial roles.

Melitz (2000a) obtains a related set of results in a forward-looking model of steady state trade with firm heterogeneity and imperfect competition. Movement toward freer trade increases a country's imports and erodes each domestic firm's domestic sales and profits.[12] Firms at the lowest end of the productivity distribution contract or exit, while firms at the high end of the productivity distribution expand their exports more than they contract their domestic sales. Accordingly, aggregate productivity improves.

Still another version of the same basic idea can be found in Bernard et al. (2000), who use a static model to study the effects of liberalization on the size and productivity mix of producers. They show that when firms use Bertrand pricing rules to compete, trade liberalization expands the market shares of the most efficient firms by providing them with larger export markets, and it forces firms at the low-end of the productive efficiency spectrum to shut down as they face competition from abroad.

2.2.2   THE EVIDENCE, PART 1: SIZE DISTRIBUTIONS
AND TRADE

What do we know empirically about size distributions and trade? Many analysts have fit cross-sectional regressions that relate firm size measures to the intensity of import competition, controlling for a few other factors like domestic market size.[13] Whether the competition proxy is the import penetration rate or a measure of the industry-wide rate of protection, this literature finds that import competition reduces the average plant size, if it has an effect at all. Further, studies that include export shares in the explanatory variable set find that average plant sizes are relatively large in the export-oriented industries.

One limitation of this literature is that domestic output appears in the denominator of import penetration rates, so there may be spurious negative correlation between output per firm and this foreign competition proxy. A second problem is that causality may run from size to protection. Concentrated industries that are dominated by a few large producers may have an easier time coordinating lobbying efforts because they face less of a free-rider problem. Finally, most of these studies presume that firms in all industries will adjust to foreign competition in the same way. This runs contrary to theory, which tells us that industries with low entry barriers, like apparel, are likely to show relatively less size adjustment and more adjustment in the number of active firms.

Several more recent studies handle the first two criticisms by measuring exposure to foreign competition with policy variables like tariff rates and license coverage ratios; and by focusing on intra-industry *changes* in average firm size rather than cross-industry differences. Comparing industrial census data before and after Chile's trade liberalization, Tybout et al. (1991, p. 236) find that plants in "sectors with relatively large declines in protection have shown a greater tendency toward employment reductions."[14] Similarly, Tybout and Westbrook (1995) find that during

Mexico's unilateral trade liberalization of 1984–9, firms in the sectors that under-
went relatively large reductions in license coverage ratios tended to grow relatively
slowly, while firms grew quickly in sectors with rapid export growth.[15]

A subset of studies that deal with the first two criticisms also deal with the third
by allowing intra-industry changes in firm size to vary with entry costs (proxied by
industry-specific plant turnover rates). Perhaps the best is Head and Ries's (1999),
which uses the Canada–US Free Trade Agreement as a natural experiment. Their
regressions suggest that "Canadian tariff reductions lowered scale [in Canada] while
U.S. tariff reductions increased scale" (p. 309). Further, they confirm that entry
barriers affect the way that firms respond: industries with high turnover (low entry
costs) show relatively mild reductions in scale in the face of heightened import competition. Roberts and Tybout (1991) obtain similar findings by contrasting industry-
specific size distributions in Chile and Colombia and relating them to cross-country
industry-specific differences in effective protection.

2.2.3   THE EVIDENCE, PART 2: TRADE-INDUCED SIZE ADJUSTMENTS AND SCALE EFFICIENCY

In sum, the finding that foreign competition is associated with smaller firms in
import-competing industries seems robust. There is also some evidence that foreign
liberalization increases the size of exporting firms. We might reasonably ask, then,
how dramatically these trade-induced adjustments have affected scale efficiency.

Most of the studies that address this question are based on computable general
equilibrium (CGE) models, and they suggest that the scale-based efficiency gains
when trade is liberalized can range from 1 to 5 percent of GDP.[16] However, these
findings are suspect for two reasons. First, while CGE models often predict firm-size
expansion in *all* traded goods industries, the econometric evidence clearly suggests
that firms in import-competing sectors *contract* when import competition intensifies, at least in the short run. Second, even if exporter expansion were the dominant
effect of liberalization, it is unlikely that the gains in scale efficiency would amount
to much. Although CGE studies often presume returns to scale ranging from 1.10
to 1.25 at the margin, this is probably a gross overstatement of the extent of unex-
ploited scale economies. Exporting plants tend already to be the largest in their
industry (Aw et al., 1997; Bernard and Jensen, 1995, 1997; Bernard and Wagner, 1997;
Das et al., 2001). Thus they are not likely to exhibit much potential for further scale
economy exploitation. Similarly, since most of the production in *any* industry comes
from large plants, scale efficiency losses due to contraction in import-competing
sectors are also typically minor (Tybout and Westbrook, 1996).

As an alternative to CGE analysis, Tybout and Westbrook (1995) used panel
data on Mexican firms to estimate returns to scale (μ_{it}) as a function of size. Then
they combine these estimates with the firm-specific growth rates observed during
Mexico's unilateral trade liberalization of 1984–90 to implement equation (13.5).
Although the cumulative weighted-average growth rate in output was 53 percent
for the manufacturing sector, they find that the associated productivity growth
rate due to scale efficiency effects was only one-half of one percentage point.
This reflected the fact that large plants were operating in the flat portions of their

average cost schedule, and these plants accounted for the bulk of the output adjustments.

2.2.4   THE EVIDENCE, PART 3: MARKET SHARES AND
PRODUCTIVITY EFFECTS

Of course, scale effects are not necessary to link size adjustments and productivity growth. Trade-induced market share reallocations can affect industry-wide performance so long as firms are heterogeneous in terms of A_{it} (see equation 13.5). What do we know empirically about these effects?

A simple way to address this question is to view firms' sizes as reflecting their productivity.[17] Then, if liberalization causes large firms to expand while small firms contract or exit, the associated market share reallocations should improve efficiency. From this perspective, the very robust finding that larger firms are more likely to export suggests that access to foreign markets allows the most efficient firms to become larger, thus pulling up industry-wide productivity levels.

However, studies that associate *changes* in trade protection with changes in the intra-industry size distribution deliver mixed evidence. Head and Ries (1999) find that large Canadian firms grew the most dramatically with US tariff reductions, and they shrank the most dramatically in response to Canadian tariff reductions. Similarly, Roberts and Tybout (1991) find that shrinkage in response to import competition – proxied by import penetration rates or effective protection rates – was relatively dramatic among the large firms in Chile (1979–85) and Colombia (1977–87). But Dutz (1996) finds that as Morocco dismantled NTBs during the 1980s, *small* plants shrank relatively dramatically and their exit probabilities increased relative to others'. Also, Tybout et al. (1991) find that in Chile, reductions in effective protection between 1967 and 1979 were associated with balanced percentage reductions in employment across the entire size distribution.

These mixed findings could mean that the selection effects emphasized by Melitz (2000a) are not robust, or they could mean that size is a poor proxy for productivity, or both. To get at the latter issue, several studies measure share effects directly by constructing firm- or plant-specific B_{it} trajectories. Tybout (1991) simply uses revenue per worker as his productivity measure and measures share-based gains for Chile (1979–85), Colombia (1977–87) and Morocco (1984–7).[18] He finds that market share reallocations contribute to productivity growth among tradeable goods, but his data span periods of major macro shocks rather than major trade liberalization episodes so it is difficult to argue that the gains are trade-induced. Using the same Chilean data set Pavcnik (2000) measures total factor productivity much more carefully and also finds that the shifting of market shares toward more efficient plants was an important source of efficiency gain during the sample period. However, she does not investigate the link between market share reallocations and foreign competition. Similarly, Liu (1993), Liu and Tybout (1996), Tybout (1991), and Pavcnik (2000) all find that exiting plants were substantially less productive than surviving plants in Chile (and elsewhere), but none of these studies links this gap to import competition or exporting opportunities.[19]

Tybout and Westbrook (1995) have a better basis for inference in the unilateral Mexican liberalization of 1984–9. Using equation (13.5), as well as a similar decomposition based on cost functions, they find that this liberalization was associated with efficiency gains, and that some of these gains were due to market share reallocations. However, they do not find strong evidence that rationalization effects were concentrated in the tradeable goods industries. Similarly, studying the Canada–US FTA, Trefler (2001) finds little evidence that turnover-based productivity gains were concentrated in the industries subjected to the largest tariff reductions.[20]

In sum, market share reallocations (including entry and exit) do matter, but it is difficult to find empirical studies that convincingly link these processes to the trade regime.[21] This is not surprising, given that the effects of import competition on industrial evolution are inherently dynamic, and poorly captured by contemporaneous, reduced-form correlations. I will return briefly to this issue when I discuss transition dynamics in section 4.

2.3 Other Intra-firm Productivity Gains

Leaving aside productivity effects due to adjustments in the firm size distribution, there are many other linkages between commercial policy and efficiency gains. These are bundled together in the third right-hand-side (technical efficiency) term in equation (13.5). Some have to do with changes in the incentives to innovate or eliminate waste. For example, foreign competition or access to foreign markets may change the effort that a firm's managers put forth and/or the rate at which they improve their products and processes. However, a diverse body of theory suggests that the direction of change in efficiency hinges critically upon model specifics (Corden, 1974; Goh, 2000; Hart, 1983; Miyagawa and Ohno, 1995; Rodrik, 1992; Scharfstein, 1988; Voustden and Campbell, 1994).

Other effects on intra-firm productivity are more robust. As Ethier (1982) noted, intra-firm productivity gains may accompany trade liberalization if it expands the menu of intermediate inputs available to domestic firms. This allows each producer to match his or her input mix more precisely to the desired technology or product characteristics. Similar comments apply concerning access to capital goods, as de Long and Summers (1991) have stressed.

Trade may also act as a conduit for disembodied technology diffusion if firms learn about products by observing imported varieties, or by exporting to knowledgeable buyers who provide them with blueprints and give them technical assistance (e.g., Grossman and Helpman, 1991). Similar knowledge transfers may occur when domestic firms enter into joint ventures or sell equity to foreign multinationals, although these activities are less directly related to commercial policy.

Finally, domestic knowledge spillovers further confound the picture. If learning externalities are generated by experience producing a good, then changes in a country's product mix induced by commercial policy can change the rate at which domestic efficiency grows (e.g., Krugman, 1987; Young, 1991). Whether trade liberalization helps or hurts in this respect depends upon which productive processes generate the most positive externalities, and whether they expand or contract as protection is dismantled.

2.3.1   THE EVIDENCE, PART 1: PRODUCT VARIETY
AND PRODUCTIVITY

Very little firm-level empirical work has been done on the popular notion that increases in the menu of available inputs improve productivity. This lack of micro evidence reflects practical difficulties with identifying a firm's desired input mix, observing the actual input mix, and relating discrepancies between the two to measures of firm performance. It may also reflect a presumption that diversification of input bundles makes input use more heterogeneous at the industry level but not at the firm level.

Feenstra et al. (1992) provide the only exception I am aware of.[22] They argue that Korean conglomerates (*chaebols*) are vertically integrated, and thus when new intermediate producers join a conglomerate they effectively diversify the input menu for its final goods producers. Regressions confirm that, over a four year period, total factor productivity growth among final goods producers in 45 *chaebols* was positively correlated with the fraction of input expenditure going to new intra-*chaebol* intermediate goods suppliers.

This innovative study provides tantalizing evidence that input diversification contributes to productivity gains. However, data limitations prevent the authors from observing the connection between input variety and productivity as directly as one would like. Simultaneity bias is also an issue, since *chaebols* with high productivity growth are probably inclined to expand and incorporate new firms regardless of whether input diversification occurs.

2.3.2   THE EVIDENCE, PART 2: IMPORT
DISCIPLINE EFFECTS

It is much more common to relate firm-level productivity measures to proxies for the vigor of import competition. Most micro empirical studies that do so are based on first- or second-order approximations to the production function $q_{it} = A_{it}h(\mathbf{v}_{it})$, expressing the log of productivity, $\ln(A_{it})$, as a function of import competition proxies, I_{it}, and noise. In the first-order (Cobb–Douglas) case, this amounts to estimating:

$$\ln(q_i) = \sum_{j=1}^{J} \beta_t \ln(v_{ij}) + \gamma I_{it} + \varepsilon_{it} \tag{13.6}$$

Alternatively, the log of productivity can be thought of as a draw from a one-sided productivity distribution (e.g., $\alpha_{it} < 0$) plus an orthogonal transitory shock beyond the control of managers: $\ln(A_{it}) = \alpha_{it} + \varepsilon_{it}$.[23]

$$\ln(q_i) = \sum_{j=1}^{J} \beta_i \ln(v_{ij}) + \alpha_{it} + \varepsilon_{it} \tag{13.7}$$

Then, treating the distribution of α_{it} as dependent upon import competition, one can investigate whether mean productivity levels and/or productivity dispersion respond to trade liberalization.

Regardless of whether one uses equation (13.6) or equation (13.7), one cannot measure import competition at the firm level. Thus its effect is identified by cross-industry or temporal variation in I_{it}. The former type of identification is problematic because cross-industry regressions describe long run equilibria, and all industry characteristics – including import penetration rates, protection rates, and concentration – are endogenous in the long run (Schmalensee, 1989). Nonetheless, Caves and Barton (1990) use equation (13.7) to characterize the α_{it} distribution for each US manufacturing industry, and they use cross-industry variation in I_{it} to infer that "import competition (measured by imports' share of total supply) increases efficiency in industries whose domestic producers are concentrated" (p. 111).

Other studies use temporal variation in I_{it} to link import competition and productivity via equation (13.6) or (13.7). As I mention in Tybout (2000, p. 34), these studies "tend to find that trade liberalization is associated with rising average efficiency levels" (Harrison, 1996; Nishimizu and Page, 1982; Pavcnik, 2000; Trefler, 2001; Tybout et al., 1991; Tybout and Westbrook, 1995). Similarly, liberalization drives down measured productivity dispersion relatively more in import-competing industries (Haddad and Harrison, 1993; Pavcnik, 2000; Tybout et al., 1991).[24] Both sets of findings are consistent with the import discipline hypothesis, but they also could reflect the kind of selection effects described by Bond (1986), Melitz (2000a), and Bernard et al. (2000).

The implications of these studies are further clouded by methodological problems. Excepting Pavcnik (2000), they do not deal with the simultaneity bias that results from the dependence of factor inputs on productivity levels. Also, all of the studies use industry-wide price deflators to convert plant-specific revenues to plant-specific measures of physical output. But since products within each industry are heterogeneous, this procedure attributes relative price fluctuation to physical output fluctuation, and it thus confounds efficiency with monopoly power. Trade-induced reductions in measured "productivity" dispersion may be no more than the reductions in mark-ups among firms with market power that I discussed in section 2.1.

Finally, a general problem with this literature is that it tends to equate measured efficiency gains with welfare improvements. Thus when these gains are associated with trade liberalization, they are touted as a beneficial effect of foreign competition. But the costs of productivity gains are often embodied in overheads, license fees, training and other items that do not get measured in the input vector. Further, the benefits these expenditures generate are not fully reaped in the same periods in which they are incurred. I know of no study that attempts to measure the present value of firms' productivity-enhancing expenditures and compare them to the present value of the resulting productivity gains.

2.3.3 THE EVIDENCE, PART 3: TRADE AND TECHNOLOGY DIFFUSION

Does trade serve as a conduit for technology diffusion? Many studies have established that exporters tend to be bigger, more skill-intensive, and more productive than their domestically oriented counterparts (Aw and Hwang, 1995; Aw et al., 1997;

Bernard and Jensen, 1995, 1997; Bernard and Wagner, 1997; Chen and Tang, 1987; Handoussa et al., 1986). Further, the case study literature on exporters documents instances in which technologically sophisticated buyers transmit blueprints and proprietary knowledge to the exporting firms.[25] However, there is some doubt as to whether the cross-sectional correlation between performance and exporting mainly reflects causality from the latter to the former. Firms may self-select into export markets and/or be sought out by foreign buyers *because* they are high quality.

Several authors have attempted to resolve this issue by studying temporal *changes* in firms' performance and their relation to export market participation. These studies amount to Granger causality tests based on variants of the autoregressive specification:

$$\ln(A_{it}) = \beta_0 + \sum_{j=1}^{J} \beta_j \ln(A_{it-j}) + \sum_{j=1}^{J} \gamma_j y_{it-j} + \ldots + \varepsilon_{it}, \tag{13.8}$$

where y_{it} is a dummy variable that indicates whether the ith firm exports in period t. Causality tests in this context establish whether exporting experience in the past helps explain productivity in the present, once other determinants of current productivity (including previous productivity) are controlled for. Given that y_{it} responds to productivity shocks, the distributed lag $\sum_{j=1}^{J} \gamma_j y_{it-j}$ will be orthogonal to ε_{it} only when ε_{it} is serially uncorrelated, so it is key to use a generous lag length (J) for the term $\sum_{j=1}^{J} \beta_j \ln(A_{it-j})$.

Fitting a version of equation (13.8) to plant-level panel data from Colombia, Mexico and Morocco, Clerides et al. (1998) find very little evidence that past exporting experience improves performance. Bernard and Jensen (1999, p. 14) obtain similar results using US data: "Exporting does not Granger-cause productivity, but does Granger-cause employment, shipments and wages." On the other hand, Kraay (1997) finds that lagged y_{it} values help explain current productivity among Chinese firms; Bigsten et al. (1999) find evidence that exporting Granger-causes productivity among African firms, and Aw et al. (1997) obtain similar findings using census data from Taiwan and Korea.[26]

There are at least four problems with this literature. First, the contact between an exporting firm and its foreign client may occur well before export flows are actually observed in the data.[27] Second, as with the import discipline literature, there is a strong tendency to interpret productivity gains as good, but no effort to quantify the *costs* of these gains. Third, the measures of performance are quite crude, as discussed in connection with the import discipline literature. Fourth, almost all of these studies focus on single conduits for technology transfer. But international activities like exporting, importing intermediates, importing capital goods, and selling equity abroad are often complementary, so firms pursue them in bundles (Kraay et al., 2001). Studies that focus on one at a time may generate misleading conclusions regarding channels of international technology diffusion.

Kraay et al. (2001) tackle the third and fourth methodological problems using the same data sets that Clerides et al. (1998) used to study learning by exporting.

First, they document that international activities indeed come in bundles – exporting, importing intermediate goods, importing capital goods, and sales of equity to multinationals are clearly not independent activities.[28] Next, by using a nested logit representation of demand for the differentiated products, and by exploiting information on the market share of each product, they are able to separately measure product and process innovations at each firm.[29] Finally, they relate quality trajectories and average cost trajectories to firms' international activities, using generalized versions of equation (13.8). They find that activity histories don't usually help to predict future product quality or reduce average production costs, once the histories of these performance variables are controlled for. Nonetheless, Colombian firms that engage in at least some international activities – especially those that import their intermediate goods – tend to have higher product quality.[30] This finding suggests the kind of static efficiency effect that Ethier (1982) envisioned.

2.4 Summary

Measurement and methodological problems plague the literature I have reviewed in this section, but some findings seem robust. First, the evidence suggests that mark-ups fall with import competition. The most likely interpretation is that foreign competition increases the elasticity of demand that domestic firms face. However, it is not clear whether these trade-induced reductions in mark-ups reflect the elimination of market power or the creation of negative economic profits.

Second, contrary to the predictions of many simulation models, import-competing firms cut back their production levels when foreign competition intensifies. This is not consistent with the Helpman and Krugman (1985) monopolistic competition model, under which some domestic plants would exit and the remaining plants would either remain the same size (if their demand elasticities do not change) or expand (if their demand elasticities rise). Instead, it suggests that sunk entry or exit costs are important in most sectors.

Third, trade does seem to rationalize production in the sense that markets for the most efficient plants are expanded. Further, if we discount the methodological problems with measuring productivity, most studies suggest that exposure to foreign competition improves intra-plant efficiency. (At what cost, we don't know.) Finally, while firms that engage in international activities tend to be larger and more productive, it is not obvious whether the activities caused these characteristics or vice versa.

3 TRANSITION DYNAMICS

The theories I have mentioned thus far describe static or steady state equilibria, and the regressions that give them empirical content deal mostly with patterns of contemporaneous correlation. But some important issues are inherently dynamic. For example, when a developing country dismantles its trade barriers and devalues its currency, as the World Bank often recommends, the effect of the new regime on the

Central Bank's foreign currency reserves will depend upon the resulting changes in the export trajectory. Further, the political support for a given reform package will depend upon the associated changes in firms' market values and employment trajectories that business representatives and workers anticipate. All of the literature that I have reviewed thus far is silent on these high profile issues.

The dynamic effects of policy reforms are difficult to characterize because they reflect complex decisions on the part of firms. Faced with an uncertain future, some managers find themselves weighing the earnings effects of shutting down plants and/or firing workers against the associated severance costs and the option value of retaining plants or workers for possibly better days. Others must weigh the sunk costs of breaking into foreign markets, building new plants, and/or hiring workers against the net revenue streams that these activities might generate. Their decisions are further complicated by the need to anticipate the decisions of other managers producing competing products. Below I discuss a nascent literature that tackles the relation between commercial policy reforms and industrial responses in settings with these features.

3.1 Export Dynamics

3.1.1 THEORY

In the past 15 years, several theoretical contributions to the trade literature have incorporated sunk costs and uncertainty in dynamic models. Among the first to do so were the papers by Dixit (1989), Baldwin (1988) and Baldwin and Krugman (1989) on the role of sunk costs and expectations in driving exporters' behavior. Generalizing their specification in anticipation of discussion to follow, let us specify an export profit function for the ith firm that depends on the exchange rate (e_t), marginal production costs (c_{it}), a foreign demand shifter (x_{it}), and serially uncorrelated noise (ε_{it}): $\pi^f(e_t, c_{it}, x_t) + \varepsilon_{it}$.[31] Further, let us assume that firms without prior exporting experience must establish distribution channels, repackage their products, and learn bureaucratic procedures. Call the sum of these entry costs for new exporters Γ_S. Then, defining the indicator variable y_{it} to take a value of unity in periods when the ith firm exports and zero otherwise, the pay-off from being an exporter in year t may be written as:

$$u(e_t x_{it}, \varepsilon_{it}, y_{it}, y_{it-1}) = \begin{cases} \pi^f(e_t, x_{it}) + \varepsilon_{it} & \text{if } y_{it} = 1;\ y_{it-1} = 1 \\ \pi^f(e_t, x_{it}) - \Gamma_S + \varepsilon_{it} & \text{if } y_{it} = 1;\ y_{it-1} = 0 \\ 0 & \text{if } y_{it} = 0;\ y_{it-1} = 0 \end{cases}$$

Presuming that the vector (e_t, c_{it}, x_t) follows a first-order Markov process, risk-neutral managers do best to choose a sequence of decision rules, $y_{it} = g_t(e_t, c_{it}, x_{it}, \varepsilon_{it}, y_{it-1})$, that maximizes their expected profit stream from export market participation: $E_t = \sum_{j=t}^{\infty} u(e_j, c_{it}, x_{ij}, \varepsilon_{ij}, y_{ij}, y_{ij-1})\delta^j$. Equivalently, their patterns of export market participation should satisfy the following Bellman equation:

$$V(e_t, x_{it}, c_{it}, \varepsilon_{it}, y_{it-1})$$
$$= \max_{y_{it}} \{\pi^f(e_t, c_{it}, x_{it}) - (1 - y_{it-1})\Gamma_S + \varepsilon_{it} + \delta E_t V(e_{t+1}, c_{it+1}, x_{it+1}, \varepsilon_{it+1}, y_{it})\} \quad (13.9)$$

Here expectations are taken conditioned on (e_t, c_{it}, x_t) and the Markov process that governs this vector's evolution.

This framework implies that seemingly identical policies and macro conditions can lead to different levels of exports, depending upon how many firms have a history of export market participation: when firms have no exporting experience, they weigh the sunk costs of entry against the expected profit stream. But when most firms are already exporters, the aggregate response to export incentives reflects volume adjustments and has little to do with entry costs. Second, firms that begin exporting in response to a shock – say, a large devaluation – may not cease exporting when that shock is reversed. Third, expectations about future exchange rate trajectories and commercial policies may play a critical role in determining whether firms invest in becoming exporters today. Finally, export responsiveness to any shock or regime switch depends critically upon the amount of cross-firm heterogeneity in marginal costs and foreign demand, x_{it}. Many firms may be poised on the verge of exporting, or just a scattered few.

3.1.2 EVIDENCE

Several studies have explored the empirical relevance of the sunk-cost export model sketched above. Roberts and Tybout (1997) begin from the implication of (13.9) that firms will find it optimal to export whenever:

$$\pi^f(e_t, c_{it}, x_{it}) - (1 - y_{it-1})\Gamma_S + \varepsilon_{it}$$
$$+ \delta[E_t V(e_{t+1}, c_{it}, x_{it+1}, \varepsilon_{it+1}|y_{it} = 1) - E_t V(e_{t+1}, c_{it}, x_{it+1}, \varepsilon_{it+1}|y_{it} = 0)] > 0$$

The second bracketed term describes the option value of being an exporter in period t, that is, the expected current value of being able to export in period $t + 1$ without having to pay sunk entry costs. Accordingly, its magnitude depends upon expectations about the future operating profits one might generate by exporting. Combining terms that depend upon current values of the state variables, the ith firm will do best to export whenever:

$$f(e_t, c_{it}, x_{it}) + y_{it-1}\Gamma_S + \varepsilon_{it} > 0,$$

where:

$$f(e_t, c_{it}, x_{it}) = \pi^f(e_t, c_{it}, x_{it})$$
$$+ \delta[E_t V(e_{t+1}, c_{it+1}, x_{it+1}, \varepsilon_{it+1}|y_{it} = 1) - E_t V(e_{t+1}, c_{it+1}, x_{it+1}, \varepsilon_{it+1}|y_{it} = 0)]$$

Using a reduced form approximation to $f(\cdot)$, and assuming a particular distribution for the error term, ε_{it}, this equation implies a dynamic discrete choice model of export market participation. Bernard and Jensen (1999), Campas (1999), Roberts and Tybout (1997), and Sullivan (1997) have fit this model as a dynamic Probit or logit and tested whether sunk entry costs affect export market participation. This simply amounts to testing whether lagged exporting status affects current status, once the other sources of persistence in behavior have been controlled for: $(x_{it}, e_t, \varepsilon_{it})$. Critically, if other sources of persistence are *not* completely controlled for, this approach to inference mis-attributes serial correlation in exporting status to sunk costs. So it is important to treat ε_{it} as a serially correlated disturbance when estimating the equation.

The universal finding of these studies is that sunk costs are important. Even after serial correlation in ε_{it} is treated, the probability that a firm will export, given $(x_{it}, e_t, \varepsilon_{it})$, can be up to 0.70 higher if it exported last period. From this, researchers have typically concluded that export aggregates are subject to important hysteresis effects and that sunk costs matter.

More recently, Das et al. (2001) revisited the question of how sunk costs shape export responsiveness among Colombian chemical producers. Instead of using a reduced-form version of the decision rule, they fit a structural model that explicitly describes the profit function and the autoregressive processes that govern the vector $(x_{it}, c_{it}, e_t, \varepsilon_{it})$. Using their estimates, they then examine the option value of export market participation for each firm: $\delta[E_t V(e_{t+1}, x_{it+1}, \varepsilon_{it+1}|y_{it} = 1) - E_t V(e_{t+1}, x_{it+1}, \varepsilon_{it+1}|y_{it} = 0)$. This expression measures the importance of expectations about the future in shaping exporting decisions. They find that it is quantitatively important for small-scale exporters, whose foreign demand is relatively limited. However, the firms that supply the bulk of total exports earn operating profits that far exceed the option value term. Hence, hysteresis effects are important only for fringe players in the export markets, and *aggregate* exports are relatively insensitive to history or expectations. Put differently, if one is interested only in the aggregates, sunk entry costs and the subtleties they introduce may be ignorable for many industries.[32]

One robust finding concerning exporters is that they tend to sell very small fractions of their output abroad (Aw et al., 1997; Campas, 1999; Sullivan et al., 1995). In principle this could mean that foreign demand for each firm's product is very limited and inelastic, but this is not the way most people view foreign markets. A second explanation is that firms export just enough to exploit duty drawback schemes and purchase the imported intermediates or capital goods at duty-free prices. To my knowledge this hypothesis has not been pursued, although it would be easy to do so. A third hypothesis is that firms export partly to diversify their earnings stream, exploiting the imperfect correlation between foreign and domestic shocks. Small stable shares in foreign markets might be rational under these assumptions.

Maloney and Azevado (1995) develop a simple model of this diversification motive for exports and fit it to firm-level panel data from Mexico. They find, among other things, exchange rate volatility and the covariance between domestic and international demand shocks are significant determinants of export volumes. Hence, for example, when an over-valued exchange rate is allowed to float, the export response may be counter-intuitive.

In sum, the initiation of exports appears to invoke some sunk start-up costs. These costs matter a good deal for marginal exporters, but are unimportant relative to the operating profits that large exporters earn. Thus their effect on aggregate export responses to regime shifts or exchange rate shocks may not be large. Other determinants of export responsiveness that may be relevant include risk diversification considerations and domestic market demand shocks (when marginal costs aren't flat). There is some evidence that the former matters; the latter remains largely unexplored.

3.2 Industrial Evolution

3.2.1 THEORY

Theoretical models of industrial evolution demonstrate how the combination of sunk entry costs with imperfect foresight and cross-firm heterogeneity can lead to continual flux in the population of active firms (Ericson and Pakes, 1995; Hopenhayn, 1992; Jovanovic, 1982). They also describe the implications of this flux in terms of job turnover patterns and productivity growth. However, very little theoretical work has been done on the effects of commercial policy in an economy with these features.

Two exceptions merit note. The first is Melitz (2000a), who focuses on the relation between openness and the steady state distribution of firm types (see section 2). The other is Albuquerque and Rebelo (2000), who abstract from intra-industry heterogeneity to derive some analytical results about dynamic responses to trade liberalization. Only the latter paper deals with transition issues, so I shall focus on it here.

Albuquerque and Rebelo consider an open economy with homogeneous firms in each of two sectors. New firms must pay a sunk fee to initiate production, so incumbents may earn positive profits in steady state without inducing entry and multiple equilibria are possible. Further, responses to policy shocks depend upon the pre-reform equilibrium. When profits net of entry costs are zero in the exportable goods, and when profits *before* entry costs are zero in the import-competing sector, small reductions in the rate of protection should generate entry in the former and exit in the latter. Unanticipated reforms also induce inter-sectoral reallocations of variable factors in the period before entry and exit occur. Pre-announcing eliminates this short-run adjustment period. On the other hand, if the economy begins from an interior steady state and reforms are too mild to trigger entry or exit, the effects of policy reforms are limited to variable factor movements and capital gains or losses for the owners of incumbent firms.

The dichotomy between responses beginning from zero-profit *versus* interior profits is an artifact of the assumption that firms within each sector are homogeneous. Intra-industry heterogeneity will generally mean that operating profits are close to zero for the marginal incumbent, and profits net of entry costs will be close to zero for the marginal entrant. Nonetheless, the results I mentioned above suggest how responses to reforms should depend on the *density* of incumbents and potential entrants near the zero-profit margin.

3.2.2   THE EVIDENCE, PART 1: DESCRIPTIVE STUDIES

It is well established that, even within narrowly defined industries, plants are quite heterogeneous in terms of their size and measured productivity (see, for example, the references in section 2.2.2). Also, simultaneous plant entry and exit are the norm, as are market share reallocations and job creation/destruction among incumbent firms (e.g., Baldwin et al., 1998; Davis et al., 1996; Dunne et al., 1989; Roberts and Tybout 1996). These are the stylized facts that inspired the modern theory of industrial evolution and they are commonly cited as evidence of its relevance.

We know much less about the effects of commercial policy shocks on industrial evolution patterns, or how these effects depend upon the initial population of firms. A number of studies document patterns of contemporaneous correlation between openness, firm size distributions, and entry/exit or market-share-based efficiency gains (see section 2). There is also a small amount of evidence relating openness to patterns of job turnover (Levinsohn, 1999).[33] However, these studies tell us little about the dynamic responses to reforms when threshold costs and uncertainty make firms' adjustments forward-looking, gradual, and/or dependent upon initial conditions.

3.2.3   THE EVIDENCE, PART 2:
A STRUCTURAL MODEL

Lu and Tybout (2000) attempt to go beyond patterns of contemporaneous correlation and quantify these dynamic relationships. Drawing heavily on Ericson and Pakes (1995) and Pakes and McGuire (1994), they develop an empirical model with sunk costs, heterogeneity, and uncertainty. It portrays an import-competing industry populated by a finite number of potential entrepreneur/owners, including those already in the industry (*incumbents*) and those contemplating entry (*potential entrants*). Each incumbent is characterized by a unique product and a time-varying productivity index that summarizes both his product's appeal and his unit production costs. Imports are represented by a single foreign variety whose price responds to exchange rate shocks and commercial policy reforms, but not to domestic producers' behavior.

Entrepreneurs in this industry play a Markov-perfect dynamic game against one another. Each period, each entrepreneur attempts to maximize his discounted net profit stream, given the available information set. Potential entrants choose whether to enter the market, given their privately observed entry costs. Incumbents decide whether to remain in the market or exit, given the privately observed scrap value of their firms. The incumbents who remain active engage in Bertrand–Nash product market competition with one another, given the current price of the import-competing good and a simple logit demand system.

At the beginning of each period, all entrepreneurs learn the productivity level of each incumbent firm (*industry structure*), as well as the current realizations on the number of consumers and the real effective exchange rate (*market conditions*). If an incumbent firm remains in the industry, its productivity evolves from period to period according to a common knowledge exogenous Markov process, as do the exchange rate and the number of consumers. Firms solve for their optimal strategies and make their exit or entry decisions simultaneously. From period to period, the industry structure evolves with entry, exit, and random shocks to each firm's productivity.

Using Colombian panel data on the pulp and paper industry, Lu and Tybout (2000) estimate the demand parameters of their model. Combined with observed market shares these allow them to impute productivity trajectories for each producer, and to estimate the associated Markov processes. Finally, given these primitives, they calibrate the entry cost and exit cost distributions so that simulated plant turnover rates approximate the industry's actual figures.

Lu and Tybout's main computational experiment is to simulate responses to a change in the exchange rate process that gradually intensifies import competition. The impact effect of this regime switch is to squeeze price–cost mark-ups, just as the econometric evidence suggests. However, the new exchange rate regime also discourages entry (but not exit), so over time, the number of domestic producers gradually shrinks. With the menu of varieties falling, elasticities of demand for each variety fall too, allowing the remaining incumbents to restore their mark-ups and cover their operating costs. This transition path suggests that the robust margin squeeze effects and output contraction effects identified by contemporaneous correlation patterns may not be permanent (see sections 2.1 and 2.2 above).

Although consumers initially benefit from cheaper imported goods and cheaper domestic goods, they are ultimately left with fewer domestic varieties at prices close to pre-appreciation levels. Hence, in the scenario that Lu and Tybout analyze, the present value of consumer welfare actually falls with heightened import competition.[34] Producers suffer capital losses, of course, so they are worse off too.

Extra costs are also imposed on workers, who endure higher job destruction rates during the transition period. Indeed, the job turnover effects predicted by this model are implausibly high, suggesting that it should be generalized to include severance costs and/or screening costs, as in Hopenhayn and Rogerson's (1993) simulations. By the same token, the apparent importance of hiring and firing costs means that firms' expectations are critical and suggests that static calculations of the employment effects of trade policies can be very inaccurate.

Finally, this framework provides a conceptually rigorous way to address the question of how changes in the intensity of import competition affect the market-share-based efficiency changes that are described by the second term in equation (13.5). Lu and Tybout (2000) find that this type of efficiency gain is small for two reasons. First, most of the adjustment in varieties comes from less entry rather than more exit. Incumbent firms that are relatively inefficient don't increase the rate at which they jump out of the market because their entry costs are already sunk, their scrap values are small, and they perceive a possibility that conditions will improve in the future. Second, the firms that do enter or exit account for a relatively small fraction of total production. This is consistent with what we actually observe in the data, as discussed in section 2.2.

These simulations are subject to several criticisms. Most fundamentally, they are partial equilibrium and thus do not document the capital gains and growing number of product varieties in sectors that benefit from exchange rate appreciation. Second, they do not permit the number of imported varieties to adjust. If foreign firms face sunk entry costs when breaking into the domestic market, there will probably be some new ones that are induced to enter by the change in the exchange rate regime. Third, the model is highly stylized in many respects, including the demand system, the productivity growth process (which is presumed exogenous) and the distributions for entry costs and scrap values. Nonetheless, at a minimum the model demonstrates that conclusions based on contemporaneous patterns of correlation can be very misleading, and it brings together in a unified framework the phenomena that firms, workers, and consumers care about.

4   AN AGENDA

I shall close with a few observations on directions for future trade research using firm- or plant-level data. First, as the previous section suggests, I am personally enthusiastic about the new insights that we might gain from dynamic structural models that link trade regimes and industrial evolution. These models suffer from some serious limitations, but they integrate many pieces of the response story that were heretofore treated in disjoint literatures. They also provide a basis for counterfactual simulations in the presence of threshold costs, uncertainty and heterogeneous firms. As computers become more powerful and solution algorithms improve I am hopeful that econometrically estimated industrial evolution models can be made more realistic and used for applied policy work.

Second, despite the large volume of research on the link between trade and productivity, there are several senses in which this literature might be improved. One is to get away from pretending that firms in manufacturing industries produce homogeneous products, and to deal with pricing, output and productivity measurement in unified frameworks (e.g., Melitz, 2000b). Another is to tighten the link between theory and tests. Theory has emphasized the effects of enhanced input variety – including both capital and intermediate goods – and, more recently, efficiency gains due to geographic agglomeration. But we have very little direct micro evidence on the importance of either. These are relatively difficult topics to tackle, but creative empiricists should be able to make progress on both fronts.

Finally, although the relationship between trade and wages has attracted considerable attention, we have only limited evidence on the micro details of worker displacement, job-search processes and reemployment patterns that are triggered by changes in the trade regime. The census bureaus of several countries (including the US) have recently devoted some resources to matching household survey data with establishment survey data, so the characteristics of plants and workers can now be analyzed together and workers can be tracked as they change jobs. These matched data sets should provide a much better basis for inference on the employment effects of commercial policy reforms or changes in the exchange rate regime.

Acknowledgments

I am grateful to James Harrigan and participants in workshops at the NBER, the University of Toronto and the University of Texas-Austin for many useful comments.

Notes

1   I shall ignore the empirical literature on multinationals and foreign direct investment, which is treated in chapter 10.

2   In these models protection takes the form of institutional arrangements for anti-dumping measures.

3   See Head and Ries (1999) for discussion and references.

4   This measure presumes that intermediate input use and labor use are proportional to output, and the proportions are fixed across plants. See Schmalensee (1989) for further discussion of the limitations of *PCM* as a performance measure.

5   See also Lee (1991) and Roberts and Tybout (1996, pp. 188–99) for surveys of the literature on developing countries.

6   "Efficient plants should be larger and have higher profits, so a positive correlation is generally expected between market shares and price-cost margins, regardless of whether firms have market power . . ." (Roberts and Tybout, 1996, p. 196).

7   Generalizations have included allowing for non-constant returns to scale, and letting η and the mean productivity growth rate vary across firms. For example, see Harrison (1994).

8   Pakes and Griliches (1984) estimate that it may take several years for newly installed capital to reach full productivity.

9   Klette and Griliches (1996) and Melitz (2000b) discuss the consequences of this measurement problem for estimates of production function parameters.

10   The most common form of entry/exit barrier is sunk start-up costs. Firms will continue to operate so long as their expected earnings stream covers their expected future expenditures, even if *ex post*, they discover they cannot also recoup the sunk costs that they paid to enter (e.g., Albuquerque and Rebelo, 2000). Uncertainty about future market conditions is likely to increase the option value of remaining in operation, effectively compounding persistence in status. Firms that enjoyed excess profits before import competition intensified will also fail to exit.

11   I will not treat external returns to scale because these are nearly impossible to measure.

12   The cases he analyzes are: autarky versus free trade, more versus fewer countries in a customs union, and high versus low non-tariff barriers (at home and abroad).

13   These studies span a wide range of countries. See Baldwin and Gorecki (1986, table 7.1), Caves (1984), Muller and Owen (1985), Scherer et al. (1975), and Schwalbach (1988). Tybout (1993a, table 2a) provides further details on these studies.

14   This pattern is less apparent when size is measured with output or value-added, suggesting that efficiency gains occurred in the import-competing industries.

15   On the other hand, they find no significant cross-industry correlations between firm size and effective protection rates or import penetration rates.

16   See, for example, Brown et al. (1991), Harris (1984), Norman (1990), and Smith and Venables (1988). Tybout and Westbrook (1996) provide a more detailed discussion.

17   The size-productivity linkage is common in models with heterogeneous firms. See, for example, Bernard et al. (2000), Hopenhayn (1992), and Melitz (2000a).

18   His decomposition does not distinguish intra-plant productivity gains due to scale efficiency from other sources of intra-plant gains. Bernard et al. (2000) show that revenue per unit output is a monotonic function of true total factor productivity if firms compete Bertrand.

19   In any case, as Liu and Tybout (1996) point out, the impact of this differential on productivity growth was minor, given that they typically account for a very small fraction of output.

20 Trefler's (2001) intra-industry data are grouped by plant size, so he cannot rule out the possibility that the FTA generated productivity gains through reallocations *within* size classes or through entry and exit.

21 Bernard and Jensen (2000) link entry and exit patterns to trade indirectly by arguing that, with output prices pinned down by international arbitrage, Rybczynski effects should induce net entry in the sectors intense in the factors that are growing relatively rapidly. They confirm this conjecture using data from the US, first with cross-industry regressions at the national level, then with similar regressions at the regional level. They find that where human capital and physical capital have grown relative to unskilled labor, exit rates have been low among skill-intensive goods and high among low-skill goods.

22 While not at the firm level, Feenstra et al. (1999) do use detailed data on trade flows to link sectoral productivity to the diversity of final good and upstream exports.

23 Detailed discussions of this approach to productivity analysis may be found in the "stochastic frontier" literature (e.g., Greene, 1993).

24 There is also evidence that innovative activities are stimulated by import competition. See Blundell et al. (1999).

25 Much of this literature focuses on East Asia. Pack (2000) and Westphal (2002) provides recent surveys.

26 Both Kraay (1997) and Bigsten et al. (1999) are based on annual data with short lag lengths, J, and do not provide tests for serial correlation. Hence they may be picking up spurious correlation. Aw et al. (1997) compare censuses at five year intervals, so their study is likely to suffer from this problem.

27 For interesting discussions of the case study literature on pre-exporting contacts with buyers, see Pack (2000) and Westphal (2002).

28 Aw et al. (2001) document similar dynamic complementaries between worker training, R&D, and exporting using multinomial probit models.

29 One unappealing feature of their approach is that one must assume that the ratio of physical output to intermediate input use is constant across all producers in a given four digit industry and geographic region.

30 Given the way that Kraay et al. (2001) impute quality, this is almost a corollary to the finding that firms engaging in international activities have large domestic market shares.

31 Domestic product market conditions are kept out of the analysis by assuming flat marginal cost schedules with respect to output.

32 Using a reduced-form econometric model and descriptive statistics, Campas (1999) draws similar conclusions from Spanish data.

33 Levinsohn finds that job turnover patterns in Chile during the 1980s were not closely linked to commercial policy or exchange rate shocks. He does argue, however, that turnover rates were higher among tradeable goods than among non-tradeables. Thus, liberalization in economies like Chile's should reduce job security, and may meet resistance for the political economy reasons detailed by Fernandez and Rodrik (1991).

34 This result is partly an artifact of the demand system they use, which probably overstates the value consumers place on goods with small market shares.

References

Abbott, Thomas, Zvi Griliches, and Jerry Hausman 1989: Short-run movements in productivity: Market power versus capacity utilization. Harvard University, Department of Economics, working paper.

Albuquerque, Rui and Sergio Rebelo 2000: On the dynamics of trade reform. *Journal of International Economics*, 51, 21–48.

Aw, Bee-Yan and Amy Hwang 1995: Productivity and the export market: A firm-level analysis. *Journal of Development Economics*, 47, 313–32.

Aw, Bee-Yan, Xiaomin Chen, and Mark Roberts 1997: Firm-level evidence on productivity differentials and turnover in Taiwanese manufacturing. NBER working paper no. 6235.

Aw, Bee-Yan, Mark Roberts, and Tor Winston 2001: Investment in knowledge and the evolution of firm productivity in the Taiwanese electronics industry. Pennsylvania State University, Department of Economics, working paper.

Baldwin, John and Paul Gorecki 1986: *The Role of Scale in Canada–U.S. Productivity Differences in the Manufacturing Sector: 1970–79*. Toronto: University of Toronto Press.

Baldwin, John, Timothy Dunne, and John Haltiwanger 1988: A comparison of job creation and job destruction in Canada and the United States. *Review of Economics and Statistics*, 80, 347–56.

Baldwin, Richard 1988: Hysteresis and the beachhead effect. *American Economic Review*, 78, 773–85.

Baldwin, Richard and Paul Krugman 1989: Persistent trade effects of large exchange rate shocks. *Quarterly Journal of Economics*, 104, 635–54.

Bernard, Andrew and J. Bradford Jensen 1995: Exporters, Jobs and Wages in U.S. Manufacturing, 1976–87. *Brookings Papers on Economic Activity: Microeconomics*, Washington, DC: The Brookings Institution.

Bernard, Andrew and J. Bradford Jensen 1997: Why some firms export: Experience, entry costs, spillovers, and subsidies. Yale University.

Bernard, Andrew and J. Bradford Jensen 1999: Exceptional exporter performance: Cause, effect, or both? *Journal of International Economics*, 47, 1–26.

Bernard, Andrew and J. Bradford Jensen 2000: Who dies? International trade, market structure and plant closures. Dartmouth College, Tuck School of Business.

Bernard, Andrew and Joachim Wagner 1997: Exports and success in German manufacturing. *Weltwirtschaftliches Archiv*, 133, 134–57.

Bernard, Andrew, Jonathon Eaton, Samuel Kortum, and J. Bradford Jensen 2000: Plants and productivity in international trade. NBER working paper no. 7688.

Bhagwati, Jagdish 1978: *Foreign Trade Regimes and Economic Development: Anatomy and Consequences of Exchange Control Regimes*. Lexington: Ballinger for NBER.

Bigsten, Arne et al. 1999: Exports and firm-level efficiency in the African manufacturing sector. University of Montreal, School of Business.

Blundell, Richard, Rachel Griffith, and John van Reenen 1999: Market share, market value and innovation in a panel of British manufacturing firms. *Review of Economic Studies*, 66, 529–54.

Bond, Eric 1986: Entrepreneurial ability, income distribution and international trade. *Journal of International Economics*, 20, 343–56.

Brooks, Eileen L. 2001: Why don't firms export more? Manuscript, Harvard University.

Brown, Drucilla, Alan Deardorff, and Robert Stern 1991: A North American free trade agreement: Analytical issues and a computational assessment, University of Michigan: Department of Economics.

Campas, Jose 1991: Exchange rates and trade: How important is hysteresis in trade? New York University, Stern School of Business.

Caves, Richard 1984: Scale, openness and productivity in manufacturing. In Richard Caves and Lawrence Krause (eds.), *The Australian Economy: A View from the North*, Washington, DC: The Brookings Institution.

Caves, Richard and David Barton 1990: *Efficiency in U.S. Manufacturing Industries*. Cambridge, MA: MIT Press.

Chen, Tain-jy and De-piao Tang 1987: Comparing technical efficiency between import-substituting and export-oriented foreign firms in a developing country. *Journal of Development Economics*, 36, 277–89.

Clerides, Sofronis, Saul Lach, and James Tybout 1998: Is learning by exporting important? Micro dynamic evidence from Colombia, Mexico and Morocco. *Quarterly Journal of Economics*, 113, 903–47.

Corden, W. Max 1974: *Trade Policy and Economic Welfare*, Oxford: Clarendon Press.

Das, Sanghamitra, Mark Roberts, and James Tybout 2001: Micro-foundations of export dynamics. Pennsylvania State University, Department of Economics.

Davis, Steven, John Haltiwanger, and Scott Schuh 1996: *Job Creation and Destruction*, Cambridge, MA: MIT Press.

De Long, J. Bradford and Lawrence Summers 1991: Equipment investment and economic growth. *Quarterly Journal of Economics*, 56, 445–502.

Devarajan, Shanta and Dani Rodrik 1991: Pro-competitive effects of trade reforms: Results from a CGE model of Cameroon. *European Economic Review*, 35, 1157–84.

Dixit, Avinash 1989: Entry and exit decisions under uncertainty. *Journal of Political Economy*, 97, 620–38.

Dunne, Timothy, Mark Roberts, and Larry Samuelson 1989: Plant turnover and gross employment flows in the U.S. manufacturing sector. *Journal of Labor Economics*, 7, 48–71.

Dutz, Mark 1996: Oligopolistic firms' adjustment to quota liberalization: Theory and evidence. In Mark Roberts and James Tybout (eds.), *Industrial Evolution in Developing Countries*, New York: Oxford University Press.

Ericson, Richard and Ariel Pakes 1995: Markov-perfect industry dynamics: A framework for empirical work. *Review of Economic Studies*, 62, 53–82.

Ethier, Wilfred 1982: National and international returns to scale in the modern theory of international trade. *American Economic Review*, 72, 950–9.

Feenstra, Robert, Dorsati Madani, Tzu-Han Yang, and Chi-Yuan Liang 1999: Testing endogenous growth in South Korea and Taiwan. *Journal of Development Economics*, 60, 317–41.

Feenstra, Robert, James Markusen, and William Zeile 1992: Accounting for growth with new inputs: Theory and evidence. *American Economic Review: Papers and Proceedings*, 82, 415–21.

Fernandez, Raquel and Dani Rodrik 1991: Resistance to reform: Status quo bias in the presence of individual specific uncertainty. *American Economic Review*, 81, 1146–55.

Goh, Ai-Ting 2000: Opportunity cost, trade policies and the efficiency of firms. *Journal of Development Economics*, 62, 363–83.

Greene, William 1993: Frontier production functions. New York University, Stern School of Business, working paper no. EC-93-20.

Grether, Jean-Marie 1996: Mexico, 1985–90: Trade liberalization, market structure and manufacturing performance. In Mark Roberts and James Tybout (eds.), *Industrial Evolution in Developing Countries*, New York: Oxford University Press.

Grossman, Gene and Elhanan Helpman 1991: *Innovation and Growth in the Global Economy*. Cambridge, MA: MIT Press.

Haddad, Mona and Ann Harrison 1993: Are there positive spillovers from direct foreign investment? Evidence from panel data for Morocco. *Journal of Development Economics*, 42, 51–74.

Hall, Robert 1988: The relation between price and marginal cost in U.S. industry. *Journal of Political Economy*, 96, 921–47.

Handoussa, Heba, Mieko Nishimizu, and John Page 1986: Productivity change in Egyptian public sector industries after the "Opening," 1973–1979. *Journal of Development Economics*, 20, 53–73.

Harris, Richard 1984: Applied general equilibrium analysis of small open economies with scale economies and imperfect competition. *American Economic Review*, 74, 1016–32.

Harrison, Ann 1994: Productivity, imperfect competition and trade reform: Theory and evidence. *Journal of International Economics*, 36, 53–73.

Harrison, Ann 1996: Determinants and effects of foreign direct investment in Côte d'Ivoire, Morocco, and Venezuela. In Mark Roberts and James Tybout (eds.), *Industrial Evolution in Developing Countries*, New York: Oxford University Press.

Hart, Oliver 1983: The market mechanism as an incentive structure. *Bell Journal of Economics*, 14, 366–82.

Head, Keith and John Ries 1999: Rationalization effects of tariff reductions. *Journal of International Economics*, 47, 295–320.

Helpman, Elhanan and Paul Krugman 1985: *Market Structure and Foreign Trade: Increasing Returns, Imperfect Competition and the International Economy*. Cambridge, MA: MIT Press.

Hopenhayn, Hugo 1992: Entry, exit and firm dynamics in long run equilibrium. *Econometrica*, 60, 1127–50.

Hopenhayn, Hugo and Richard Rogerson 1993: Job turnover and policy evolution: A general equilbrium analysis, *Journal of Political Economy*, 101, 915–38.

Jovanovic, Boyan 1982: Selection and the evolution of industry. *Econometrica*, 50, 649–70.

Klette, Tor J. and Zvi Griliches 1996: The inconsistency of common scale estimators when output prices are unobserved and endogenous. *Journal of Applied Econometrics*, 11, 343–61.

Kraay, Aart 1997: Exports and economic performance: Evidence from a panel of Chinese enterprises. The World Bank, Development Economics Department.

Kraay, Aart, Isidro Soloaga, and James Tybout 2001: Product quality, productive efficiency, and international technology diffusion. Pennsylvania State University, Department of Economics.

Krishna, Pravin and Devashish Mitra 1998: Trade liberalization, market discipline, and productivity growth: New evidence from India. *Journal of Development Economics*, 46, 447–52.

Krugman, Paul 1979: Increasing returns, monopolistic competition and international trade. *Journal of International Economics*, 9, 469–79.

Krugman, Paul 1987: The narrow moving band, the Dutch disease, and the consequences of Mrs Thatcher: Notes on trade in the presence of scale economies. *Journal of Development Economics*, 27, 41–55.

Lee, Norman 1991: Market structure and trade in the developing countries. In Gerald K. Helleiner (ed.), *Trade Policy, Industrialization and Development: New Perspectives*, Oxford: Clarendon Press.

Levinsohn, James 1993: Testing the imports-as-market-discipline hypothesis. *Journal of International Economics*, 35, 1–12.

Levinsohn, James 1999: Employment responses to international liberalization in Chile. *Journal of International Economics*, 47, 321–44.

Liu, Lili 1993: Entry-exit, learning and productivity change: Evidence from Chile. *Journal of Development Economics*, 42, 217–42.

Liu, Lili and James Tybout 1996: Productivity growth in Colombia and Chile: Panel-based evidence on the role of entry, exit and learning. In Mark Roberts and James Tybout (eds.), *Industrial Evolution in Developing Countries*, New York: Oxford University Press.

Lu, Shihua and James Tybout 2000: Import competition and industrial evolution: A computational experiment. Pennsylvania State University, Department of Economics.

Maloney, William and Rodrigo Azevado 1995: Trade reform, uncertainty and export promotion: Mexico 1982–88. *Journal of Development Economics*, 48, 67–89.

Melitz, Marc 2000a: The impact of trade on intra-industry reallocations and aggregate productivity. Harvard University, Department of Economics.

Melitz, Marc 2000b: Estimating productivity in differentiated product industries. Harvard University, Department of Economics.

Miyagawa, Kaz and Yuko Ohno 1995: Closing the technology gap under protection. *American Economic Review*, 85, 755–70.

Muller, Jurgen and Nicholas Owen 1985: The effects of trade on plant size. In Joachim Schwalbach (ed.), *Industry, Structure and Performance*, Berlin: Edition Sigma.

Nishumizu, Mieko and John Page 1982: Total factor productivity growth, technological progress, and technical efficiency change: Dimensions of productivity change in Yugoslavia. *Economic Journal*, 92, 920–36.

Norman, Victor 1990: Assessing trade and welfare effects of trade liberalization. *European Economic Review*, 34, 725–51.

Pack, Howard 2000: Modes of technology transfer at the firm level. University of Pennsylvania, The Wharton School.

Pakes, Ariel and Zvi Griliches 1984: Estimated distributed lags in short panels with an application to the specification of depreciation patterns and capital stock constructs. *Review of Economic Studies*, 51, 243–62.

Pakes, Ariel and Paul McGuire 1994: Computing Markov-perfect Nash equilibria: Numerical implications of a dynamic differentiated product model. *RAND Journal of Economics*, 25, 555–89.

Pavcnik, Nina 2000: Trade liberalization, exit, and productivity improvements: Evidence from Chilean plants. Dartmouth College, Department of Economics.

Prusa, Thomas J. 1992: Why are so many antidumping petitions withdrawn? *Journal of International Economics*, 33, 1–20.

Roberts, Mark and James Tybout 1991: Size rationalization and trade exposure in developing countries. In Robert Baldwin (ed.), *Empirical Studies of Commercial Policy*, Chicago: University of Chicago Press for NBER.

Roberts, Mark and James Tybout (eds.) 1996: *Industrial Evolution in Developing Countries*, New York: Oxford University Press.

Roberts, Mark and James Tybout 1997: The decision to export in Colombia. *American Economic Review*, 87, 545–65.

Roberts, Mark, Theresa Sullivan, and James Tybout 2001: Micro-foundations of export booms. Manuscript, World Bank.

Rodrik, Dani 1992: Closing the technology gap: Does trade liberalization really help? In Gerald Helleiner (ed.), *Trade Policy, Industrialization and Development: New Perspectives*, Oxford: Clarendon Press.

Scharfstein, David 1988: Product market competition and managerial slack. *RAND Journal*, 19, 47–55.

Scherer, Frederic M. et al. 1975: *The Economics of Multi-Plant Operation: An International Comparison Study*, Cambridge, MA: Harvard University Press.

Schmalensee, Richard 1989: Inter-industry studies of structure and performance. In Richard Schmalensee and Robert Willig (eds.), *Handbook of Industrial Organization*, Amsterdam: North-Holland.

Schwalbach, Joachim 1988: Economies of scale and intra-community trade. In Commission of the European Communities, *Research on the "Cost" of Non-Europe: Basic Findings*, vol. 2, Brussels: Commission of the European Communities.

Smith, Alistair and Anthony Venables 1988: Completing the internal market in the European Community. *European Economic Review*, 32, 1501–25.

Staiger, Robert W. and Frank A. Wolak 1989: Strategic use of antidumping law to enforce tacit international collusion. NBER working paper no. 3016.

Sullivan, Theresa 1997: Estimating the manufactured export supply function for Morocco, PhD dissertation, Georgetown University.

Sullivan, Theresa, Mark Roberts, and James Tybout 1995: Micro foundations of export booms. Pennsylvania State University working paper.

Trefler, Daniel 2001: The long and short of the Canada–U.S. Free Trade Agreement. NBER working paper no. 8293.

Tybout, James 1991: Linking trade and productivity: New research directions. *World Bank Economic Review*, 6, 189–212.

Tybout, James 1993a: Internal returns to scale as a source of comparative advantage. Georgetown University working paper no. 93–101.

Tybout, James 1993b: Internal returns to scale as a source of comparative advantage: The evidence. *American Economic Review: Papers and Proceedings*, 83, 440–4.

Tybout, James 2000: Manufacturing firms in developing countries: How well do they do, and why? *Journal of Economic Literature*, 38, 11–44.

Tybout, James and M. Daniel Westbrook 1995: Trade liberalization and dimensions of efficiency change in Mexican manufacturing industries. *Journal of International Economics*, 39, 53–78.

Tybout, James and M. Daniel Westbrook 1996: Scale economies as a source of efficiency gains. In Mark Roberts and James Tybout (eds.), *Industrial Evolution in Developing Countries*, New York: Oxford University Press.

Tybout, James, Jaime de Melo, and Vittorio Corbo 1991: The effects of trade reforms on scale and technical efficiency: New evidence from Chile. *Journal of International Economics*, 31, 231–59.

Voustden, Neil and Neil Campbell 1994: The organizational cost of protection. *Journal of International Economics*, 37, 219–38.

Westphal, Larry 2002: Technology strategies for economic development in a fast-changing global economy. *Economics of Innovation and New Technology*, Aug–Oct, 11(4–5), 275–320.

Young, Alwyn 1991: Learning by doing and the dynamic effects of international trade. *Quarterly Journal of Economics*, 106, 369–405.

Index

Note: "n." after a page reference indicates the number of a note on that page.